BESS OF HARDWICK

ALSO BY MARY S. LOVELL

Straight on till Morning: The Biography of
Beryl Markham

The Sound of Wings: The Biography of Amelia Earhart

Cast No Shadow: The Spy Who Changed the
Course of World War II

A Scandalous Life: The Biography of Jane Digby

The Splendid Outcast: The African Short Stories
of Beryl Markham

A Rage to Live: A Biography of Richard and
Isabel Burton

The Mitford Girls: The Biography of
an Extraordinary Family

BESS OF HARDWICK

Empire Builder

MARY S. LOVELL

*'I assure you, there is no Lady in this land
that I better love and like.'*

Queen Elizabeth I about Bess of Hardwick

W. W. Norton & Company
New York   London

Originally published in Great Britain under the title
Bess of Hardwick: First Lady of Chatsworth, 1527–1608

Manufacturing by The Maple-Vail Book Manufacturing Group
Production manager: Amanda Morrison

Library of Congress Cataloging-in-Publication Data

Lovell, Mary S.
Bess of Hardwick : empire builder / Mary S. Lovell. — 1st American
ed.
p. cm.
Includes bibliographical references and index.
ISBN 0-393-06221-X (hardcover)
1. Shrewsbury, Elizabeth Hardwick Talbot, Countess of, 1527?–1608.
2. Countesses—Great Britain—Biography. 3. Great Britain—History
—Elizabeth, 1558–1603—Biography. 4. Women landowners—
Great Britain—Biography.   I. Title.
DA358.S4L68 2006
942.05'5092—dc22
[B]

2005030490

W. W. Norton & Company, Inc.
500 Fifth Avenue, New York, N.Y. 10110
www.wwnorton.com

W. W. Norton & Company Ltd.
Castle House, 75/76 Wells Street, London W1T 3QT

1 2 3 4 5 6 7 8 9 0

This book is dedicated to Deborah, Dowager Duchess of Devonshire with my grateful thanks. Debo, as she prefers to be known, loves and cares for modern-day Chatsworth as Bess did for the original, and she has followed my research into Bess's life with interest as well as much kind assistance.

CONTENTS

THE FAMILY TREE OF BESS

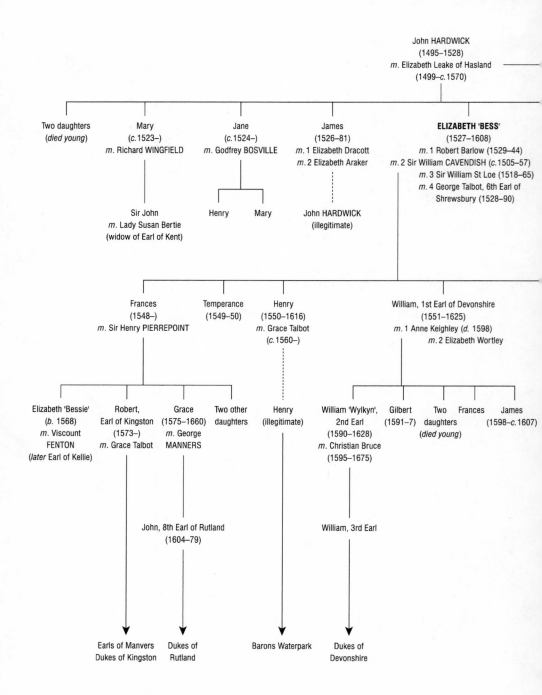

OF HARDWICK (1527–1608)

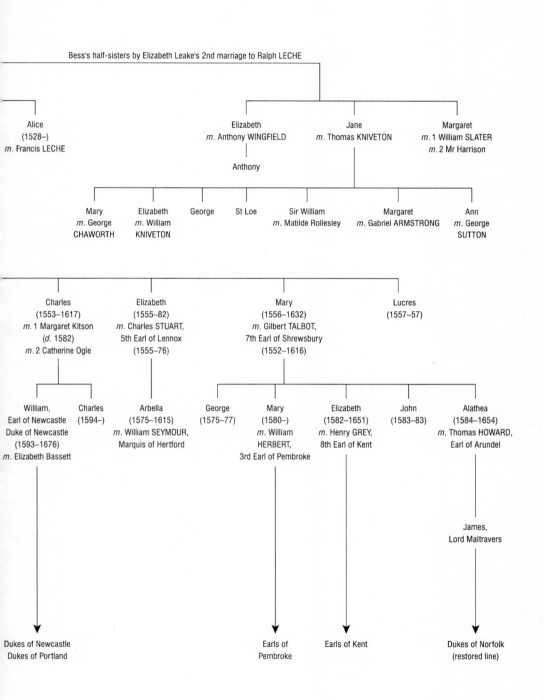

Bess's half-sisters by Elizabeth Leake's 2nd marriage to Ralph LECHE

Alice
(1528–)
m. Francis LECHE

Elizabeth
m. Anthony WINGFIELD

Jane
m. Thomas KNIVETON

Margaret
m. 1 William SLATER
m. 2 Mr Harrison

Anthony

Mary
m. George
CHAWORTH

Elizabeth
m. William
KNIVETON

George

St Loe

Sir William
m. Matilde Rollesley

Margaret
m. Gabriel ARMSTRONG

Ann
m. George
SUTTON

Charles
(1553–1617)
m. 1 Margaret Kitson
(*d.* 1582)
m. 2 Catherine Ogle

Elizabeth
(1555–82)
m. Charles STUART,
5th Earl of Lennox
(1555–76)

Mary
(1556–1632)
m. Gilbert TALBOT,
7th Earl of Shrewsbury
(1552–1616)

Lucres
(1557–57)

William,
Earl of Newcastle
Duke of Newcastle
(1593–1676)
m. Elizabeth Bassett

Charles
(1594–)

Arbella
(1575–1615)
m. William SEYMOUR,
Marquis of Hertford

George
(1575–77)

Mary
(1580–)
m. William
HERBERT,
3rd Earl of Pembroke

Elizabeth
(1582–1651)
m. Henry GREY,
8th Earl of Kent

John
(1583–83)

Alathea
(1584–1654)
m. Thomas HOWARD,
Earl of Arundel

James,
Lord Maltravers

Dukes of Newcastle
Dukes of Portland

Earls of
Pembroke

Earls of Kent

Dukes of Norfolk
(restored line)

INTRODUCTION

TO MOST PEOPLE WHO HAVE HEARD OF THE WOMAN WHO was born Elizabeth Hardwick in 1527, she is known simply as 'Bess of Hardwick' and forever coupled to the jingle, 'Hardwick Hall, more glass than wall'. This misquotation of a phrase said to have been coined by Robert Cecil referred to the innovative architecture of the new house Bess built for herself on her family property in Derbyshire. Anyone who has ever driven up the M1, north of the city of Nottingham, cannot fail to have seen the gaunt dark ruins of the old Hall at Hardwick dominating the skyline. Behind this structure lies another Hardwick Hall, a jewel of a building, and, amazingly, it remains intact, almost as Bess left it when she died in 1608.

Bess of Hardwick is remembered as a builder of great houses – Chatsworth, Hardwick, Oldcotes – and also as a dynast, for through her children she founded the Dukedoms of Devonshire, Portland and Newcastle, and the Barons Waterpark, and there is probably no aristocratic family in England, including the present monarchy, which does not contain her DNA. But there was far more to Bess than this.

She was born into a family of respectable gentry. They were landowners who lived in comparative comfort, but there was little money. Their land lay on the borders of Derbyshire and Nottinghamshire, remote from London by a journey of a week, and though good for raising sheep it was not especially valuable. In common with most girls of her class, her education was limited and Bess was not blessed with notable beauty. As the third daughter of five surviving children, her marriage settlement when she was married at the age of fifteen was respectable, but not significant. How, then, did this woman rise to become the Countess of Shrewsbury, and the most powerful woman in the land next to Queen Elizabeth I?

The simple answer would be that in her long life – she was over eighty when she died, which was considered an astonishing age in those days when few of her contemporaries reached three score and ten – she had four husbands, through whom she acquired her wealth. This received portrait of Bess was amusingly, though incorrectly, immortalised by Horace Walpole long after her death:

> *Four times the nuptial bed she warmed,*
> *And every time so well performed,*
> *That when death spoiled each husband's billing*
> *He left the widow every shilling.*

In an age when life was more precarious than it is now, Bess was far from being alone in having multiple spouses, yet no other non-royal woman of her times achieved a tenth as much as Bess did. And no other non-royal woman of her times comes down to us through history as a serious achiever. For that was what Bess was: an achiever. And she operated in an age when non-royal women had little education, virtually no legal rights, and were almost considered chattels of their husbands. How did she do it? I wanted to know.

In 1996 my literary agent and dear friend, the late Robert Ducas, suggested Bess of Hardwick as a subject for a biography. At that time I was deeply involved in other projects and I did no more than file the suggestion away with other 'possibles'. Five years later, Deborah, now the Dowager Duchess of Devonshire and widow of one of Bess's direct descendants, independently suggested to me that Bess was a very underrated personality.

Some basic exploratory research revealed that much of what had already been written about Bess concerned her life from middle age onwards, after she had married her fourth husband. I decided, when I first undertook to write this biography, to concentrate as far as possible on the early, unknown and unexplored parts of her life to discover how she developed into a formidably successful and frighteningly practical grand dame.

I first drew up a bibliography and followed this with a schedule of accepted academic research routes. One thing led to another, and after a while the known-about facts in published works began to give way to original material. At this stage satisfying chunks of new information began to appear. Major 'finds' are rare in historical research, and the work mostly consists of looking for pieces, as in a jigsaw, which will fit together with material already well known about, and explain some fact or facts in a new and more enlightened way. Serendipity often plays a major role, too. Browsing through a second-hand bookshop on a rare day off one might come across a book one did not know existed and an item in the index that points the way to a reference missed by previous researchers. Or someone met at a dinner party might steer one in a new direction. Both of these things happened to me while researching this book. But the most important piece of serendipity concerned my own family – or, to be strictly accurate, the family of my late husband.

Less was known about Bess's enigmatic third husband, Sir William St Loe, and their time together than almost any other period of her adult life. The surname St Loe is not a common one, yet when I read his name it was not unfamiliar to me. I could not think why this should be, but the name of his family home provided a clue: Sutton Court, in the village of Chew Magna, in the county of Somerset. My husband's maternal family has one of those old Tudor tombs in the ancient church of St Andrew at Chew Magna. The colourfully painted effigy of Francis Baber is set on a marble bier next to and slightly higher than that of his wife, Anne. There they have lain in quiet harmony through the centuries, clad in their Sunday-best robes, immaculately ruffed at neck and wrists, hands permanently joined in prayer, surrounded by family crests, pious words and symbolic carvings. Every decade or so our family holds a world reunion, and invariably this is held at Chew Magna with a service in the family chapel. I vaguely recalled that the name St Loe was somehow associated with this church, so, having already attacked the libraries and archives of the Bodleian in Oxford, the British Library in London, the Public Record Office at Kew, and the Folger Shakespeare Library in Washington, DC, I lowered my sights and looked in my own library at home, at the research my husband and a cousin had once made into his family history.

Immediately the name St Loe cropped up, because the two families – the Babers and the St Loes – were neighbouring landowners at Chew, and had intermarried on several occasions in the sixteenth and seventeenth centuries. My husband's family acquired Sutton Court from the St Loe family by marriage, lost it while supporting the wrong side in the Civil War, purchased it back from the Crown after the Restoration, and then lost it again through marriage into the Strachey family, who still own it. And, somewhat to my astonishment, without moving from my own home, I found among these books and papers more information on Sir William St Loe than had ever been previously published about him. I subsequently followed up this cache of information by researching the St Loe family in local and county archives in Wiltshire, Gloucestershire and Somerset to confirm what I had found. It is always immensely comforting when a new piece of information is verified by an unrelated source.

Apart from this wholly delightful and unexpected personal

bonus, the research into Bess's life has been a joy. The Tudor period has been an abiding interest of mine for as long as I can remember. But I can recall once, in the early days of my work, waking in the small hours, and wondering uneasily what I had taken on. After all, almost four hundred years had passed since Bess's death and there had already been several biographies written.

So what were the chances that I would find anything new, especially as I imagined that not much in the way of original documentation would have survived the ensuing four centuries? Apart from the great public libraries mentioned previously, the Duke and Duchess of Devonshire generously offered access to their extensive archives at Chatsworth, as did the Marquess of Bath at Longleat. And, to my surprise, far from a dearth of surviving documentation I found a positive glut. At first, whenever I found a relevant document – whether previously known or not known about – and wherever permitted, I photocopied the original to work on (to transcribe into modern English for ease of use while writing). When this was not possible I made a longhand or typed transcript. In the case of the great archive of printed matter contained in the Calendars of State Papers I photocopied the printed word. I then filed each of these documents in date order, in a series of lever-arch files. I was not too far into my researches before I had filled fourteen of these files dating from 1500 to 1610, and I realised that if I was not prepared to move to a larger house I had better be more circumspect in what I collected. It is no exaggeration to say that there are more surviving documents concerning Bess and her connections than there are about some modern-day subjects upon whom I have worked.

Every research project has its unique difficulties. In this case it was not the quantity of material available, but reading that material. The problems ranged from handwriting styles, inconsistent and archaic spelling, incomprehensible words, fading ink, crumbling parchments and, not least, the fact that some formal documents such as court hearings and inquisition post mortems were written in Latin. It was impractical, given the restrictions of publishing a commercial book and the cost of accommodation in cities such as London and Oxford, to sit in libraries and archives spending a day or more per document when there were hundreds to be read. So wherever possible I worked on photocopies at home. These were pored over with the aid of a very strong light and the largest magnifying glass I could lay hands on.

Because of the sheer number of documents, this involved a significant amount of eye strain, and even so some proved impossible fully to decipher. And when this occurred I decided to seek some professional assistance for at least the more difficult documents, and especially for those written in Latin, the contents of which, with dimly recollected shreds of school Latin, I could only guess at.

I asked the Public Record Office staff, at Kew, if they knew of an expert in the early modern period, based in Gloucestershire. They suggested a freelancer, Christine Leighton, who worked for them transcribing sixteenth-century documents. If I could pay her usual hourly fee, they thought she would be prepared to help. I wrote to Christine and she telephoned me. She said that she was interested in my proposition, but that she no longer lived at the address I had written to for she had just moved to live with her recently widowed father. 'Where are you living now?' I asked. 'Across the road from you,' she replied. Her father was my neighbour, and owned a cottage directly opposite my house. Indeed, I could see her front door from my study window. If this is not serendipity at work, it is difficult to know what else to call it.

There was another problem in research: the spelling of names was phonetic in Tudor documents, and hence erratic. For example the name St Loe was spelled in different documents (and sometimes even in the same document) as: St Lowe, St Loo, Sentlow, Sentloo, Seyntlowe, Sentloe, Santlo, Senteloo, Sayntlo, Sanctlo and St Cloo, with a number of other variations. For Hardwick I also had to check for: Hardwycke, Herdvyk, Herdwyke, Hardweeke etc., and the surname Frecheville was sometimes Fressheville, Fretteswell, Fretchvylle or Frytteville. This made searching through archive indexes a tedious business, since I had about thirty primary names on my search list.

Very few personalities in history, outside royal circles, have had blow-by-blow details of their marital problems preserved in the collection of State papers. But that is what happened to Bess and her fourth husband, the Earl of Shrewsbury. It was like the clash of two titans, involving the Court and many senior government ministers such as Lord Burghley, Francis Walsingham and the Earl of Leicester. Queen Elizabeth herself found it necessary to intervene on occasion, once ordering the protagonists to behave themselves for the sake of appearances at least. They rarely spoke directly to each other, so, fortunately for us, their differences survive in a series of explosive letters.

Very early in my research it became obvious that many previous biographers (mostly male) portrayed Bess as a hard and scheming woman who managed to get her hands on the fortunes of four weak or gullible, but always rich husbands with the sole aim of creating a mega-rich dynasty of her own. This is only partly correct. Bess was ambitious, certainly, and she was hugely successful. We know how, in our own times, people who make such fortunes enrich themselves and their families and those close to them, but they also make enemies of others who are not swept along on the tide of that fortune. Inevitably, Bess made some powerful adversaries, and the emotional opinions of these enemies have coloured her reputation down the centuries.

My research, however, reveals her as a highly energetic woman who used her abilities and native intelligence to rise above a relatively indifferent start in life and to overcome vicissitudes that would have daunted a lesser personality. Through a natural charm, rather than beauty, she attracted four personable husbands: three of whom were strong and powerful men, each one richer than his predecessor. Two of them, at least, were romantically in love with her when they married, and Bess returned their affection in full. Towards the end of her long life, widowed and in control of her own fortune, Bess had become – second only to the Queen – the richest and therefore the most powerful woman in the country. But she was also liked and respected, and as a widow in the last two decades of her life she was able to significantly increase her fortune, when, clearly, there was no masculine influence at work. In fact it would be fair to say that she succeeded even more spectacularly without the restraining hand of a man.

The best-known portrait of Bess is one painted when she was about sixty, and is a powerful image of a shrewd, intelligent woman. The original of this is lost. There is a copy at Hardwick Hall, her home until her death, which is thought to be taken from the original by Rowland Lockey. And there is another copy, owned by the National Portrait Gallery,* which has far more detail, and more expression. In this version there is a slight upward twitch in the corners of the mouth, making the subject look wryly amused and a little less forbidding. At her left temple there is an enlarged vein, and her ropes of magnificent pearls are graduated in colour, whereas in the Hardwick version the pearls are all cream.

In both examples, however, this portrait has had the effect of making people think of Bess in terms of the powerful woman she became in later life. There is no hint here of a laughing, dancing young Bess who captivated four highly eligible men, three of whom moved in Court circles, close to the monarchy, and the last of whom bore the resounding title of Earl Marshal of England.

I hope that in this book I have been successful in illuminating the experiences of this younger Bess. What I can say for certain is that we know more about Bess of Hardwick than we know about any other non-royal woman of the Tudor age. Hers is a truly remarkable story.

---

*Currently on semi-permanent loan to Montacute House.

CHAPTER I

MERRIE ENGLAND

(1520–40)

LITTLE BESS HARDWICK NEVER KNEW HER FATHER. HE DIED
at the age of thirty-three, when Bess was still a babe in arms.[1]

Bess was a fighter from the start, for whether born into a palace
or a cottage, life for any sixteenth-century child was uncertain.
Almost half of all babies died within twelve months of birth,[2] and
for those who survived that critical first year – tightly bound and
swaddled for the first six months to ensure straight limbs – plagues
and occasional epidemics were a constant danger as they grew.
Childhood was rarely entirely carefree. Girls in particular, dressed
in restrictive clothing that was a miniature replica of their mothers',
were taught never to be idle, and such education as there was for a
girl, non-existent among the poorer classes, had but one aim:
preparing her to be a good wife, homemaker and mother. This was
the ordained lot of the daughter born to John and Elizabeth
Hardwick sometime between June and November in the year 1527,
at the small manor farmhouse in Hardwick, Derbyshire.[3]

At the time of Bess's birth, thirty-six-year-old King Henry VIII
and his wife Queen Catherine of Aragon were on the throne. The
royal couple had been married for eighteen years, and between

1510 and 1520 the Queen had given birth to six babies, four of them boys. Two further pregnancies had ended before full term. But from this incessant round of conception and birth only one infant had survived: the Princess Mary, born in 1516. Everyone knew how much the king longed for – needed – a son, but the only son who lived beyond a month was the one he fathered by one of the Queen's ladies-in-waiting, Elizabeth Blount, in 1525.[*] The Queen was now past her child-bearing years and in that summer and autumn of 1527, although the people of England were not yet aware of it, the King had begun seeking ways to have his marriage legally annulled. He was infatuated with yet another lady-in-waiting, Anne Boleyn, who was young enough to give him sons. Such things were outside the lives of the Hardwick family, and yet they would be swept up, as was everyone, high-born or low, in the changes that would come about as a result of the King's secret passion.

Initially, the Hardwick baby, christened Elizabeth after her mother, grandmother and great-grandmother, but always known as Bess, would have been a disappointment to her parents. The Hardwicks already had four daughters,[†] but had only one son, James, born in April 1526, so they needed a second boy to secure the future of the family estate. However, we know from her later history and correspondence that Elizabeth Hardwick was a good, sensible mother, who loved and cared for all her children. She soon recovered from having another girl, and she was still young; there was time enough to have boys.[‡]

The Hardwicks lived on the property from which John

---

[*]The King openly acknowledged the boy and created him Duke of Richmond and Somerset.

[†]John Hardwick's will in January 1528 refers to five daughters, and this did not include Alice, who was born after her father's death. Of the five daughters mentioned we know only of Mary, Jane and 'Bess'. It appears therefore that there were two daughters, older than Bess, who did not survive into adulthood, but who died sometime after 1528.

[‡]Elizabeth was to have four more children, one by John Hardwick and three by her second husband: all were girls.

Hardwick's forebears had taken their name. Of no particular importance in the world, their half-timbered home, typical of its time, with barnyards, stables and a dovecot yard,[4] stood four-square on a rocky hilltop, giving it some prominence on the local skyline at least. The Hardwick family had lived on this land for at least two centuries by 1527,[5] by which time they farmed 450 acres in Derbyshire, and received rents on a further 100 acres in Lincolnshire,[6] The Hall and some lands were held 'in fealty' to Sir John Savage for an annual peppercorn rent of 'twelve pence, one pound of cumin, one pound of pepper and one clove a year'.[7] Further lands were leased from the Savages.

John Hardwick's lineage can be traced back to King Edward I of England and his Queen, Eleanor of Castile,* but by 1527 the Hardwick family had no pretensions to greatness, they were simply gentlemen farmers, respectable and locally respected, and with a few useful, if distant, good family connections. In the parlance of a later century they were country squires, or minor gentry, and in 1520 things must have been going well for the newly married twenty-five-year-old John Hardwick. He began to build, converting the original medieval farmhouse into a manor house.[8]

There are only a few surviving documents relating to Bess Hardwick's childhood, but it is possible to speculate about the world she lived in, and what were, inevitably, her childhood experiences. Following custom, Bess would have been baptised on the very first Sunday or Holy Day following her birth, having been carried to the local church of St John the Baptist at nearby Ault Hucknall by her godparents: two women and one man for a girl child. After being 'crossed' with sacred oil on the shoulders and chest, and the sign of the cross made in her right hand, she would have been dipped three times in holy water and then, having been named and received into the Church, the baby was considered safe from the devil and all his works.

*See Appendix 5.

Elizabeth Hardwick did not attend this ceremony because custom decreed that a new mother must have a month's lying-in. It was two weeks before she was even allowed to sit up after giving birth. And when the month was up she could not resume conjugal relations, or go visiting, until after she was 'churched'. So while baby Bess was being baptised, Elizabeth waited in bed at home, dressed for receiving, the house decorated with fresh strewing herbs and, since it was summer or early autumn, fresh flowers. A christening feast was prepared for those who had attended the service. Even in the poorest homes money was somehow found for this celebration, and in the home of a gentleman, as John Hardwick was, such a public occasion would normally call for food and drink to be liberally dispensed: 'all things fine against the christening day', contemporary fashion decreed. 'Sugar, biscuits, comfits and caraways, marmalade and marchpane, must fill the pockets of dainty dames'.[9]

On arrival at the parents' house the principal guests and godparents went first to the lying-in chamber to congratulate and honour the mother, gifts and blessings were bestowed upon the child, and then all the women – family, friends and neighbours – would crowd into the lying-in chamber to gossip and enjoy the occasion. This custom was called 'a Gossiping', and in a popular catchphrase of the day a person was said to be 'as drunk as women at a gossiping'.

It was strongly believed that sexual intercourse was damaging to breast-milk and therefore to the suckling child, so a breastfeeding mother would normally abstain from sex for some months at least. James Hardwick was born in June 1526, Bess twelve to fifteen months later in the summer or autumn of 1527, and their mother was already pregnant again in January 1528.[10] From this childbearing history it is reasonably safe to assume that Elizabeth employed wet nurses to suckle her babies. So many women were constantly pregnant and infant mortality so high it was not difficult, for those who could afford it, to find a woman glad of the additional income she could earn by wet-nursing. Usually a wet nurse would have been the wife of a tenant or some other local person that the mother could trust.

These are extrapolations of what we can safely assume would have happened to little Bess. What we know for sure about that first year of her life is that her father died before she was seven months old. He was ill for about three weeks in January 1528, and whatever ailed him was serious enough for him to make provisions for his family and direct his own funeral arrangements. At his own request he was buried 'in the Arch betwixt the chancel and the new aisle' in the church of Ault Hucknall,[11] No gravestone survives, but some fragments remain of what was once a painted-glass memorial window, commissioned by Elizabeth to commemorate John Hardwick's life and honourable stature in the community.[12] These were later incorporated into a nineteenth-century window, but the Hardwick coat of arms, and the words '*bono*' and '*Joh . . . is*' are all that is left of the original inscription, '*Orate pro bono statu Johannis Hardwyk generosi et uxoris ejus*'.* To the parson, John Hardwick left 'my best beast' to pay for his 'mortuary', and for funeral expenses such as candles, bread and ale 'on the day'. To Sir John Savage, effectively his liege lord, he bequeathed 'my young white gelding, unbroken'. Apart from these and a few small offerings to the mother church, all John Hardwick's thoughts were for his wife and children.[13]

Elizabeth Hardwick was twenty-eight years old when her husband died. She was a gentlewoman, the daughter of Thomas Leake of Hasland, which was only a few hours' ride away from Hardwick Hall.†[14] Furthermore, John Hardwick's younger brother Roger lived at Hardwick and seems to have acted as some sort of farm manager,[15] so, saving Elizabeth's natural grief at the loss of her husband, with family from both sides living close at hand, being left with so many small dependants should not, in itself, have been an insurmountable problem. With high prevailing mortality rates few men or women took for granted that they would live out the

---

*'Pray for the soul of John Hardwick, gentleman, and his wife'.
†The Leakes were lords of the manor of Wymeswold and Sutton Scarsdale.

biblical span of three score years and ten.[16] Widowhood was a constant possibility for both sexes, as was subsequent remarriage. The Hardwick farm was a well-established one, and had clearly been successful enough to allow John Hardwick to consider a fairly ambitious new building programme seven years earlier. What was against Elizabeth Hardwick's survival was the law of the land, which could make her under-age son a ward and appropriate her husband's lands and income for the Crown exchequer.

Soon after the New Year in 1528, when John Hardwick realised he was likely to die, his son and heir James was only eighteen months old. John had been in a similar situation himself, for his father had died in 1507 when John was only twelve. He and his brother had escaped being made wards of court because prior to his death his father had cleverly set up a form of Trust. That is, he made over his lands and property to friendly trustees or 'feoffees', including Sir John Savage, who obligingly returned the lands to John when he reached his majority. On 6 January 1528, John Hardwick attempted to do the same thing by 'giving' the estate to his brother Roger and seven feoffees for a term of twenty years.[17] When he made his will on 9 January, three weeks before he died,[18] John referred to this gift, but no deed had been drawn up so it was probably an ad hoc arrangement, cobbled together by a very sick man with his anxious friends and relatives,* gathered round his bedside all wanting to help.

All landowners were subject to an Inquisition Post Mortem, that is, an investigation, held some months following a death, concerning any properties the deceased person owned or had owned by courtesy of the Crown during their lifetime. An escheator was assigned to ascertain how the lands and properties had been acquired by the deceased, whether any others had an interest in them (widows' dower rights and jointures were

---

*Two of the seven feoffees were his wife's father and brother.

MERRIE ENGLAND

respected), and sundry information such as the name and age of the heir. It was a method of keeping track of all landholdings and properties.

John Hardwick's Inquisition Post Mortem, held on 2 October 1528, some nine months after his death, reveals that his plan to place Hardwick in trust for his son was at first successful. The escheator accepted the statements provided by the witnesses, and no query was raised in respect of the gift to the feoffees. But many months later in an exchequer office in London, a sharp-eyed clerk noticed something untoward in the Inquisition report.

By this time another child, Alice, had been born to Elizabeth, who must have had her hands full with so many small children to care for; three of them were under three and one of these was only a few weeks old. It is probable that her other four children were equally narrowly spaced in age. Initially, life at Hardwick would have gone on much as before, being managed by Roger Hardwick and his fellow executors.

By November 1529, almost two years after John Hardwick's death, and more than a year since the Inquisition Post Mortem, Elizabeth and the feoffees must have believed the estate was secure against the Office of Wards. But when Bess was just over two years old the matter was reopened.

Henry VIII by the Grace of God, King of England and France, defender of the faith and Lord of Ireland to his beloved and faithful John Gyfford, and his beloved John Vernon esquire, and Anthony Babbington esquire, greetings.

Know that we have assigned you . . . to enquire by the oath of worthy and true men of Derby . . . by whom the truth of the matter can be better known, what lands and tenements John Hardwycke of Hardwyke Hall, deceased, . . . held both in demesne and in service, in the county aforesaid, on the day which the same John died. And how much of others, and by what service, and how much those lands are valued . . . and on what day the said John died and who is the next heir and what age. We command that [on] a certain day and place which you will have provided,* to this diligently make inquisition . . . and [the answers] being clearly and openly made, we order you to send these without delay to us in the Chancery under your seals . . .'[19]

John Vernon of Haddon Hall and Anthony Babington were neighbours and friends, so doubtless Elizabeth Hardwick soon learned about this frightening new development. The triumvirate of commissioners appears to have stalled for a surprisingly long time considering that the King's seal was on the assignment, and matters were further complicated when Roger Hardwick died unmarried, in the spring of 1530, just two years after his brother's death. The inquiry was finally held on 8 September of that year, and concentrated on the nature of the so-called gift. Testifying before the court, some neighbours, 'four gentlemen and nine yeomen',† swore under oath: 'that for a long time before the aforesaid John Hardwycke died a certain Roger Hardwycke was seized in his demesne of one messuage called Hardwycke Hall together with its lands including others at Estwheytt, Heth, and Owlecotes. And that when he [Roger] died he left everything to his nephew James Hardwick.[20]

Despite this gallant lie the commissioners found that John Hardwick's property had legally passed directly to his son, and not to his brother Roger or the seven feoffees. They overturned the findings of the original inquisition, and the Hardwick estate,

---

*Throughout this book square brackets are used to contain text that I have inserted when a) I could not read a word or words in an original document, and have guessed at the lacunae, or b) when I judged an insertion necessary to make grammatical sense.
†Yeoman: the equivalent of the medieval 'freeman': the holder of a small farm or estate, either owned or as a tenant. In 1550 Sir Thomas Smith defined a yeoman as 'a man well at ease, and having honestlie to live, and yet not a gentleman'.

including responsibility for the welfare, education and ultimate marriage of young James, was taken into the control of the Office of Wards.* Elizabeth Hardwick was entitled to petition wealthy friends or relatives to purchase the wardship, but as it subsequently went to an outsider, it appears that she could not persuade anyone to do so.

The Hardwicks could claim distant kinship with a number of rich aristocratic families, which included that of the Duke of Suffolk.† Through their cousins the Wingfields, they were also distantly related to Thomas Grey, Marquess of Dorset, and yet another branch connected them to the Earls of Derby. These august contacts were either not applied to, or ignored the plea for help, or perhaps in the end Elizabeth was not given enough time to contact them.

Prenuptial agreements called Marriage Jointures were common, but it is not known what arrangements had been made for Elizabeth, or what she had brought to her marriage by way of dowry, which would have remained her own property after her husband's death. But Elizabeth had, by inalienable right, her widow's dower: that is, one-third of all income accruing from the estate. In his will John Hardwick specifically stated that he left Hardwick Hall and its lands and woods 'to the said Elizabeth my wife to have, hold and occupy to her own use . . . during the term of her life'.

Despite this, one-third of Hardwick and its demesne lands was retained by the Crown and rented back to Elizabeth, who thus had control of two-thirds of the Hardwick lands. The remainder was sold in wardship to John Bugby, the clerk assigned by the Chancery to record the inquisition before Messrs Gyfford, Vernon and Babington. While engaged on his assignment Bugby evidently recognised a good profitable opportunity, and he had none of the

---

*See Appendix 2 for an explanation about the wardship system.
†Charles Brandon, Duke of Suffolk, was the second husband of Princess Mary Tudor. She was Henry VIII's younger sister and had previously been the wife of King Louis XII of France.

finer feelings of the neighbouring gentlemen. He was one of Henry VIII's 'new men', one of many in that reign who recognised profitable commercial advantages within the law. He was not necessarily a villain or a cruel man; simply an opportunist. When the decision was made to sell the eighteen-year wardship of James Hardwick (reckoned to generate £5 a year in income) for the sum of £20, he applied immediately.[21]

With her income severely reduced, life for Elizabeth Hardwick and her young family became difficult. Not only would someone have to be paid to run what remained of the estate, but rent had to be paid for the lands leased back from the Crown. Elizabeth may also have been able to rent back the lands in the wardship, for what would a clerk be wanting with land other than to make money by it? But the fact remains that what had been a prosperous farm when John Hardwick was alive and working it himself with his brother's help would have barely provided Elizabeth and her seven children with even a basic living after his death.

No doubt her family, the Leakes, helped where they could, but less than three years after John's death Elizabeth did what most widows and widowers of the day did in similar circumstances. She looked for another partner to share her burden. A woman with so many small children, and a farm encumbered until young James reached his majority, was not an especially good catch. Nevertheless, she was a personable, educated woman of good local family.[22] Her second husband was Ralph Leche. The Leche family lived at Chatsworth, an estate some twenty miles from Hardwick, and they were part of the same social circle as the Hardwicks. Indeed Elizabeth's baby, Alice Hardwick, born about seven months after her father's death, would ultimately marry into the Leche family. From letters, account books and documents of the period we know that the gentry of the area called on each other frequently.[23] So the Hardwicks would have been on visiting terms with Derbyshire families of equal rank which included the Vernons, Babingtons, and Leches, the Folijambes of Barlborough, the

Frechevilles of Stavely, and the Knivetons (who were also cousins) of Mercaston.

Ralph Leche was a younger son; he owned a few odd pieces of land and some leases, but he had no significant property of his own.[24] The marriage was likely to have been as much a convenient arrangement as a love match. The Leakes must have been very concerned about their widowed daughter and fatherless grandchildren, and the Leche family anxious to better the lot of a younger son. While it would be eighteen years before the Hardwick estate was free of the Office of Wards and returned to young James, the manor house and Elizabeth's dower, at least, were sacrosanct during her lifetime.

After the marriage Ralph Leche took on the management of the encumbered Hardwick lands. Elizabeth was a fecund wife and was to have three further daughters by her second husband, Elizabeth, Jane and Margaret Leche, half-sisters to Bess and her siblings. As an adult Bess was very fond of all these girls, especially Jane, who was some five years her junior. So it would appear that Bess's childhood, spent growing up with her half-sisters, was a reasonably happy one. A house full of children is rarely miserable unless the adults are unhappy, and there is absolutely no evidence pointing to that at Hardwick Hall. Furthermore, since she was only two years old when her mother remarried, it is likely that Bess regarded Ralph Leche as her father.

Hardwick's hilltop situation is an extremely pleasant one for at least three-quarters of the year. The Hardwick and Leche children would have enjoyed good fresh air with plenty of space to run and play. Many of the games that children of the first half of the sixteenth century played, with home-made toys made by older members of the family and servants, or bought from pedlars, are familiar to us still: hoops (from old barrels) and sticks, the bat and ball, spinning tops and whips, skittles, bows and arrows, shuttlecock and battledore. Girls had stiff little dolls and toy animals such as lambs; boys had model ships, whittled from wood or moulded in tin, hobby horses and slingshots. They played hide-and-seek and leapfrog and chanted nursery rhymes. At the bottom of the steep hill was a millstream to swim in, on hot summer days. One can imagine Bess playing with her siblings: a slight, blue-eyed, pale-skinned child, her long, red, naturally curling hair worn loose under a 'neat' round cap of the sort she later prescribed for her own children.[25]

Even as a small child Bess would have dressed as her mother did, in a gown (or overdress) worn over a kirtle, worn over a chemise. A plain washable apron covered the gown for everyday domestic tasks. The gown would be lined with linen for summer, in warm kersey for winter, all made by the women and servants of the household. Knitted hose reached above the knee and were tied with garters, and shoes were slipper-like, bought from pedlars, or perhaps during a rare visit to Derby or Nottingham. For feast days and celebrations, Bess, like her mother, would have had a 'best' gown, perhaps banded with satin or velvet ribbon, probably handed down from one of her elder sisters. As she grew older this best gown would have been worn with a more decorative headdress for special occasions.

Though their financial circumstances were straitened, living in the country as they did Bess's family would have enjoyed a good basic diet. Derbyshire was then, and remains, sheep country; there was mutton from the farm, and occasionally beef and pork. There was game such as hare, rabbit and wood pigeon. There would always be pigeons from the dovecote, hens too old to lay, and capons fattened for the table. The millstream provided fresh fish, and to supplement the protein there would be whatever root vegetables, pulses and brassicas grew in the garden (no potatoes then, of course), and wheat and barley products, as well as honey from the hives. The day began with a breakfast consisting of bread and home-brewed ale for adults, and bread and milk for children. A light ale was generally drunk in preference to water at all times, because water supplies could rarely be totally relied upon to be untainted, especially in summer months.

The Tudor garden needed to be productive; there were shops in the towns and cities but in rural Derbyshire self-sufficiency was the order of the day. A herb garden was a necessity, since herbs were widely used in all aspects of cooking, medicine and sundry house-wifely tasks. All homes of any substance also grew fruit trees, apples of a variety dating back to the Roman occupation over a millennium earlier for cooking and eating, and crab apples for jellies and jams. Cherries, pears and figs for dessert were common. A good housewife prided herself on her pantry preserves of fruit and vegetable produce, stored against the iron-hard winters when there was little fresh food to be had. But no Tudor house worth mentioning was without a small flower garden, planted with forget-me-nots and gillyflowers, primroses and cowslips, pansies and roses, sops-in-wine and lavender, woodbine and love-lies-bleeding. These eased the heart and scented the home.

At the age of five (at just about the time that the unpopular new Queen, Anne Boleyn, gave birth to a daughter, the Princess Elizabeth), Bess would have been obliged to join her elder sisters in lessons at her mother's knee. Good manners and deportment were expected of a girl growing up in the house of a gentleman, even one in reduced circumstances, but these were absorbed rather than formally taught. There were often older unmarried women of the family – grandmothers, unmarried sisters and widowed aunts – living in Tudor homes who were involved in such day-to-day instruction. Bad or disobedient behaviour merited corporal punishment.[26]

Bess's handwriting as an adult, like her mother's, lacks the sophisticated flourishes of trained secretaries and clerks but it is the more readable for that, and it improved throughout her adult life, indicating a degree of self-education. Her spelling is idiomatic, but no worse than that of her peers; better than most, in fact, and her writing style is articulate and flowing. She always managed to express herself clearly, both in business matters and in personal correspondence. The handwriting of her brother James, who would have had, one assumes, a superior education with a private tutor, is far less fluent.

Standard lessons in the Tudor schoolroom for boys and girls consisted of reading and writing with the help of a hornbook,* arithmetic, rhetoric, deportment and religious studies. Children in gentle households may have been offered music and the chance to learn to play an instrument. The ability to play a lute, the virginals or harp was a definite social asset and anyone – male or female – with the least pretensions to culture needed to play an instrument. The only form of regular entertainment that existed was the home-made variety, with family and guests playing or taking part in singing after dinner. If they hoped to go on to university, older boys would expect to learn geometry, astronomy and logic from a hired tutor. In any gentleman's home in Tudor times, the education of a daughter was primarily aimed to prepare her for service in a noble household or at least with a family of higher social standing than her own, with the ultimate aim of making a good marriage. It is probable that Bess learned to play the virginals (an early form of spinet), since she always had one of these keyboard instruments in her homes as an adult, and she made sure her daughters and grand-daughters learned to play as well.

We do not know precisely what Hardwick looked like when Bess was growing up, only that it had been improved and extended by her father prior to her birth. But we do know how the houses of gentlemen of the period were furnished. Indoor walls were covered in a white limewash, and were invariably hung with tapestries or arras, a practical as well as decorative solution in large unheated houses. Sometimes beautiful works of art, these items were likely to have been made by the women of the household, and were handed

---

*A teaching aid: a paper containing the alphabet and the Lord's Prayer was mounted on a wooden paddle, and protected with a thin translucent sheet of horn. Hornbooks were used universally in primary education throughout the Tudor period.

down as treasured heirlooms. The subjects were usually biblical, though the figures were often clothed in contemporary dress and thus one might find Ruth and Naomi dressed in farthingales, or the baby Jesus lying in a cradle with Henry Tudor's coat of arms carved upon it. Bess was taught this sort of needlework from her earliest years, and we know that she must have heeded her instructor, for she was to become a needlewoman of more than average ability.[27]

Bess's mother had servants,* though we do not know how many, or what they did. But in any household below that of rich aristocrats, all the women of the house, including girls, would help with the indoor chores of baking, washing and cleaning, dusting and polishing, spinning, weaving and sewing. Outdoors a housewife was generally also responsible for poultry-keeping, bee-keeping (for honey and beeswax), looking after the dovecote, and the herb garden. All these housewifery tasks would have been part of the education of Bess and her sisters, but as they were the daughters of a gentleman, the obligation would not have been abused.

This local background to Bess's childhood needs to be viewed against national changes, which, although mainly affecting the great and the good, had repercussions throughout the land and at all levels of society. Bess was still a toddler in 1529 when the King effectively began what ultimately became the reformation of the Church in England, yet as an adult she would find herself very much part of the world of those most concerned with these great changes. She must have grown up hearing constant gossip about the King, his plundering of the monasteries, his womanising, his second marriage to Queen Anne Boleyn, the birth of the Princess Elizabeth, and the change in status of the Princess Mary to 'the Lady Mary'.

---

*Bess mentions one of her mother's servants in her household accounts, 'Harry, my mother's man[servant]'. These accounts are discussed in a later chapter.

Bess was nine when 'the old Queen', Catherine of Aragon, died – from a broken heart, many said. This was swiftly followed by the scarcely believable news of the trial and execution of Queen Anne Boleyn, and then, almost before her body was interred – indeed before many people in the provinces had even learned of her death – the King married yet again, to Jane Seymour, and the Princess Elizabeth was demoted to being called 'the Lady Elizabeth'. At least Queen Jane was a virtuous lady, and she quickly gave birth to a prince. Finally, the King had the son he wanted. Now perhaps he would settle down. But within weeks the poor Queen died of puerperal fever, the fear and dread of every woman of child-bearing age.

By the time Bess was eleven years old, the English countryside was in turmoil as the Dissolution of the Monasteries reached its height. Huge tracts of land were sold off to rich landowners. People had always grumbled about and humorously denigrated the lavish excesses and arrogance of the inhabitants of certain religious houses who preached one sort of life and lived another. Of particular irritation was the selling of indulgences to sinners. Even so, these monks and clergymen were the representatives of the Church, and, as such, surely of God? If respect for the King, the Church and one's betters was the warp of Tudor society, then fear and superstition was the weft. Many said the King, and per-haps the people of England too, would be punished for such a flagrant overturning of the Church. Perhaps they would be excommunicated – then they would burn in hellfire for eternity. Perhaps they would be visited by a plague in retribution. What was it all for?

How much did all this matter to Bess the child? We know that as an adult she grew up always with a watchful eye to political expediency. The Hardwick and Leche families evidently obeyed the edicts of the King and worshipped according to the new instruc-tions, for Bess and her family would become ardent adherents of the reformed religion. (They were not, at this time, called

'Protestants', which was a foreign word imported from Germany,[*] and not in everyday use in sixteenth-century England.[28] However, for the sake of clarity, the term 'Protestant' as we now understand it is used throughout this book.)

Initially the changes would have made a surprisingly small difference to provincial worshippers. Henry did not wish to overturn the actual method of worship, only to acquire the vast riches of the Church and establish himself as the head of the Church in his own realm. In a modest country church the differences would have been scarcely noticeable in the first instance, but in 1539 – only three years after William Tyndale had been martyred for writing the translation – Henry ordered that a copy of the English Bible be placed in every parish church. Now, at last, the people of England who could read could understand for themselves what the Bible actually said, instead of relying upon the interpretation of a priest.

But how could this eleven-year-old country girl have possibly guessed that within a decade she would become one of the main beneficiaries of the downfall of the old Church, and furthermore that it would set her out on a life which would eventually make her the second most powerful woman in the land?

[*]As, for example, foreign words such as 'glasnost' have been imported into twentieth-century everyday language.

CHAPTER 2

CHILD BRIDE, CHILD WIDOW

1540–7

BESS WAS ABOUT TWELVE WHEN SHE WAS SENT AWAY FROM home. The practice of sending gently born children from the age of ten upwards into service at the homes of richer families was well established throughout the Tudor period. Though their parents more often than not paid a premium for their board, the children acted as pages, gentlemen ushers and junior ladies-in-waiting, performing such light duties as running errands, sewing, writing letters, attending at a lady's toilette, wardrobe duties, entertaining young children of the household, and generally making themselves useful and pleasant company. In return they received their keep, and sometimes a small amount of pocket money.

This service must not be confused with servitude in the modern sense of the word; they were not servants per se. In superior establishments young people learned to dance, and take part in hunting and hawking. As they grew older they acted as companions of the family in all the amusements and sports that the house had to offer. They were always treated with the respect of their birthright, and formed part of the household. This is reflected in contemporary literature; for example in Shakespeare's plays a lord will address his gentleman servants as 'gentle sirs', and requests things of them rather than issuing orders. Lifelong trust and friendships often resulted from such relationships.

The system also taught young people, if it had not already been dinned into them, what was acceptable behaviour outside their own family, how to behave when no allowances would be made for familial attachment, how to get on with strangers, how to please a superior, how to manage servants, and how to make social contacts. Tudor society still operated on almost feudal, patriarchal lines, with the principle of service i.e. knight service, as a central tenet.[1] The children of untitled gentry served in the houses of knights, those of a knight could enter the service of an earl, and the offspring of an earl might wait upon a duke or a prince. What young people gained from this was, in fact, an informal apprenticeship in the art of the courtier.

Parents attempted to place their children with the most influential connections they had. Such relationships were all-important when a well-placed friend or cousin could sway a court judgement, assist in a money-making scheme, make an important introduction at Court, seek a favour, find a position at Court for a son or promote a daughter's favourable marriage. And kinship, no matter how distant, was generally respected over almost all other considerations. A family with no great material possessions but with a good network of powerful connections was considered as important as a rich family without. Rich parents would happily marry their children into a poor but well-connected family in order to gain access to such a network.

Bess was sent to the Zouche family of Codnor Castle in Derbyshire. Lady Zouche (formerly Anne Gainsford) was a distant cousin of the Hardwicks and the Leakes, and prior to her marriage had been a lady-in-waiting to two Queens, Anne Boleyn and Jane Seymour, so Bess's 'training' in such a household would have been of a superior type. Her service with the Zouche family took her from

the wilds of Derbyshire to London: a journey which took up to a
week on horseback, and an exciting experience for a country
child. Perhaps Elizabeth Leche gave Bess the same parting advice
as her contemporary, Lady Lisle, gave to her daughter in similar
circumstances: 'Serve God, and please my Lord and Lady, and so
doing I think the cost of you well employed and . . . keep you a
good maiden.'[2]

The facts about Bess's time with the Zouche family, which led to
her childhood marriage, have come down to us in the form of oral
history, captured and written down by the antiquarian Nathaniel
Johnson in 1692 when he was researching and writing a seven-
volume biography of the Earls of Shrewsbury at Chatsworth. Since
this was only eighty-four years after Bess's death, a matter of two or
three generations, it is likely to contain elements of truth, but as
with the game of Chinese Whispers, it is difficult to know just how
much. Johnson writes that he was told the story by 'two old men'
who were locals at Chatsworth. It is reasonable to assume that they
learned it from their parents, for whom gossip about the lady of the
manor would have been the breath of life. This is what they told
him:

> Bess's marriage was accomplished by her being at London,
> attending the Lady Zouch at such time as Mr Barlow lay sick
> there of a Chronical Distemper. In which time this young
> gentlewoman making him many visits upon account of their
> neighbourhood in the country, and out of kindness to him, being
> very solicitous to afford him all the help she was able to do in
> his sickness, ordering his diet and attendance, being then young
> and very handsome, he fell in love with her, of whose great
> affections to her she made such advantage, that for lack of issue
> by her, he settled a large inheritance in lands upon herself and
> her heirs, which by his death a short time after, she fully
> enjoyed.[3]

Parts of this story are demonstrably true. Bess's marriage to young Robert Barlow of Barlow (sometimes spelled Barley)* who was the son of a neighbour in Derbyshire, and Robert's death within a relatively short time of their marriage, are historical facts. Whether Bess cared for Robert while he was ill is not known, but it is quite possible. Helping to nurse a sick member of the household is exactly the sort of duty that would be required of a young gentlewoman in waiting service. But the 'large inheritance' that Robert is said to have settled on her, was, sadly for Bess, an exaggeration.

For the purposes of helping her biography along in this short period of her life where there is limited supportive evidence, let us assume that the old story that was passed on is correct, and that Bess and Robert became attached while she was nursing him through an illness. They had to meet somehow, and it is as good a supposition as any other. Bess was two years older than Robert. We know from surviving documentation that when they married in the spring of 1543, Bess was fifteen and Robert was thirteen, so they were probably fourteen and twelve when they met at the Zouche residence. Because of the difference in age we can suppose that Bess was already a member of the Zouche household when Robert joined it. Robert's family home at Barlow was only twenty miles distant from Hardwick. The two families were even related: Bess's great-grandfather had married a Margaret Barlow of Barlow as his second wife, and his parents were Roger de Hardwyke and Nicola Barlow of Barlow. In Tudor days this was sufficient cause for Bess and Robert to call each other 'cousin'.

The two families were known to each other, at the very least. So what could be more natural than for Robert's mother, knowing that Bess was already serving in the Zouche household, to ask Elizabeth

---

*Barlow of Barlow was also sometimes written Barley of Barley in contemporary documents. Both spellings, Barlow and Barley, were used indiscriminately by clerks about the same family. Except when quoting from original documents, I have used Barlow throughout to avoid confusion. Similarly Zouch/Zouche, Babbington/Babington, Foljambe/Folijambe, Stow/Stowe etc.

Leche to ensure that her daughter might 'look out for' her young
kinsman when he went up to London? And what could be more
natural than that two children from the same country neighbourhood, perhaps one or both of them homesick and living among
strangers, should become good friends?

What is certain is that Robert and Bess were married. Although
no record of the marriage exists in surviving church registers, there
are a number of legal documents at the Public Record Office at
Kew in which the fact is recorded. In a surviving record of a court
case brought by Bess in 1546, she explained to the court how three
years earlier, 'Arthur Barley', Robert's father, had contacted her
parents, Ralph and Elizabeth Leche, to promote a marriage
between his son Robert and Bess, 'in consideration of divers great
sums of money paid . . . to the said Arthur for the same. In the performance of which bargain the said Robert Barley was lawfully
married and espoused unto your said Oratrice* . . . your said
Oratrice being then of tender years.'† Frustratingly, because the ink
has entirely faded on parts of this ancient document, it is not possible to see the precise date of the marriage.[4] However, we know
from another document that Robert's marriage took place 'within
the life of his father',[5] and we also know from Arthur Barlow's
Inquisition Post Mortem that he died on 28 May 1543, at which
date his son, Robert, was 'thirteen years and ten months old'.

Why should Arthur have been so keen to hurriedly marry off his
thirteen-year-old son and heir to Bess, who had few prospects as
the third of four surviving daughters? And what were these great
sums of money paid to him by Bess's parents?

Arthur Barlow was doing pretty much what John Hardwick had
attempted to do when he realised he was dying: that is, to shield his
family from punitive legislation. It is too great a coincidence that
Arthur died so soon after making the proposition to Elizabeth and

---

*Oratrice: petitioner.
†Tender years: generally understood to mean under sixteen.

Ralph Leche in 1543, so it is a reasonable assumption that Arthur Barlow was already a sick man when he suggested that his son should marry Bess Hardwick. If he were to die while Robert was still a minor, not only could the property and lands at Barlow be taken over by the Office of Wards during Robert's minority, but Robert's appointed guardian could ensure a marriage that benefited the guardian rather than Robert. While Bess had no financial prospects, it appears that the children may have formed an attachment of sorts, and it was a case of 'the devil one knew'. That it was not a simple love match may be assumed by the fact that a sum of money, regarded as significant by Bess at least, was required by Arthur to seal the bargain.

This sum, referred to by Bess as 'divers great sums' when she gave evidence, would certainly have included her dowry, left to her under her father's will.

> . . . I will that each of my five daughters have 40 marks of good and lawful money of England to their marriage when they be of age and it to be guarded and taken up of the profits of all my said lands and tenements and woods with all other profits aforesaid. And if my said lands and tenements will more extend then I will that the whole overplus be equally parted amongst them . . . Also I will that if Elizabeth my said wife be with child now, at the making of this my present will, the child . . . to have likewise another 40 marks when it is of lawful age. Moreover, I will that if my said children die, as God forbear, within age and time of marriage then that part be equally divided and parted amongst my other children then being [alive]. Also I will that every of my said daughters shall take the advertisement and counsel of my executors . . .[6]

Since his wife was pregnant at the time of his death, John Hardwick's will provided 240 marks (six times forty) to be shared equally between his six daughters when they married. A mark was two-thirds of a pound sterling.[7] As it turned out, only four daughters survived to marry, so Bess's dowry was one-quarter of 240 marks: that is 60 marks, or £40 of good English money, worth about £2,000 today.* As part of the agreement Ralph Leche also wrote off some money he was owed by Arthur Barlow which had been the subject of a law suit between the two men in the previous year, when judgement was awarded to Leche.[8]

The marriage took place in the spring of 1543, probably in May shortly before Arthur died. On his father's death the entire estate including 'lands, tenements, and premises, descended unto the said Robert Barley as son and heir'. It was not until December 1543, after the Inquisition Post Mortem, that Robert was able to 'seize' his estates, in other words to take legal possession. As soon as this happened the Office of Wards moved in to 'manage' the estates during Robert's minority.† But at least Robert could not be forced to make an unsatisfactory match, and on this occasion a sympathetic family member was found to buy the wardship. He was Godfrey Bosville (aka Boswell) who was betrothed to Jane Hardwick, the second eldest of Bess's sisters. We know little about Mr Bosville, except that he is referred to as 'a gentleman', that he lived in Gunthwaite, Yorkshire, and that he and Jane subsequently married and had two children, Henry and Mary. It seems likely that Jane had met her future husband while she was in service, as Bess had met Robert. Godfrey Bosville paid £66 for the wardship, an investment from which he was destined to get little financial return.

---

*Historians argue ad infinitum about currency conversion, quoting complicated tables of property values versus what a sum of money might buy in terms of staple items in the mid-sixteenth century and what those staples would cost today. I have used the formula provided by Robin Morris, Emeritus Professor of Economics at Birkbeck College, cited by Andrew Holden in his biography *William Shakespeare* (Little, Brown, 2001), p.15. Morris advises the researcher simply to 'multiply by 50'. However, *The Economic History Resource* web site gives the 'purchasing power' today of £40 in 1545 as £13,012 (a multiplication factor of approximately 325). See www.eh.net.
†See Appendix 2.

History does not tell us where Bess and Robert lived after their marriage. Although it was not uncommon for betrothals and marriages of under-age children* to be contracted for dynastic purposes, the consummation of these marriages was discouraged before the age of fifteen at least, and more often sixteen for the health of the bride and any children she might bear. Often the newly-wed children returned to their own homes and life went on much as before until they became old enough to set up house together. Bess and Robert may have gone to live with Robert's widowed mother, but it is more likely that they remained within the Zouche household, as before, continuing their training as young courtiers.[9] Her marriage would have given Bess stature and a new measure of respect and independence. For example, as a married woman she was entitled to attend the lying-in of a new mother, as well as gossipings and churchings, occasions from which single women were excluded.[10]

Eighteen months after his father's death, Robert became ill. Perhaps he was not strong, as the two old men suggested. Anyway, on Christmas Eve 1544, he died. What a sad Christmas that must have been for the Barlow and Leche families. For sixteen-year-old Bess, widowed and very likely still a maid, it was a special tragedy. Bess's family always understood that the marriage was never consummated; information said to have been passed down from Bess herself. The wife of her great-grandson wrote, sixty years after Bess's death (i.e. within living memory), that Robert had 'died before they were bedded together, they both being very young'.[11] By then Bess had in fact reached the 'age of consent' and was a marriageable woman; it was Robert, two years her junior, who was too young, and perhaps too fragile, to be bedded. If Bess had indeed loved her young husband in a romantic sense then this would have been a very

---

*Under-age children: there was no legally prescribed age for the consummation of marriage. Usually this would be agreed upon by the respective parents when the couple reached about fifteen or sixteen.

painful time for her. But even if she was not 'in love' with Robert, it is likely that with their shared experiences there was a close friendship that would have been hard for her to lose.

The sympathetic Bosville wardship terminated upon Robert's death. Mr Bosville lost his investment, the estate bounced back within the scope of the Office of Wards and the wardship was up for sale again. In the absence of children from Robert's eighteen-month marriage to Bess, the heir to the estate was Robert's younger brother. Twelve-year-old George Barlow, unmarried and malleable, was a seriously attractive prospect to an investor and he became the ward of local landowner Sir Peter Frecheville. What the late Arthur Barlow had most feared, eventually happened: young George was ultimately married to Sir Peter's daughter Jane, and the Barlow family effectively lost control of their lands and properties.

After the death of her husband at Christmas in 1544, Bess was indisputably entitled, under a law of ancient derivation, to a widow's dower. This meant she could claim one-third of the income in rents and revenues from her late husband's estate. Elizabeth Leche would have learned from her unfortunate experiences with the Office of Wards, and was almost certainly the initiator of Bess's fight to obtain her rights. Soon after Robert's death Bess applied to the Barlow family and Sir Peter for some income from the estate. This was refused and in the following year Bess resorted to the courts to obtain justice. As the case proceeded, it is possible to chart through Bess's responses and decisions a growing confidence, and a determination to obtain what was rightfully hers.

She explained to the court that she was financially straitened. She could not look to her mother for assistance because her stepfather, Ralph Leche, had recently been committed to debtor's prison in Derby,[12] 'condemned in great sums of money'. As a result, Bess stated, her mother was 'very poor and not able to relieve herself . . . much less your said poor Oratrice'.[13]

Bess's eldest sister, Mary, had by this time married Richard Wingfield and moved to Crowfield in Suffolk. Her other elder sister, Jane, had married the amiable Mr Bosville and gone to live in Yorkshire. This left their mother, Elizabeth Leche, with Alice, the fifteen-year-old remaining daughter from her first marriage, and the three younger daughters by her second marriage to feed and care for, as well as seventeen-year-old James. Even in these circumstances it seems unlikely that Elizabeth would have refused to have Bess at Hardwick, and this is almost certainly what happened for a period at least, though Ralph Leche's spell in debtor's prison must have caused difficulties. It was not until some months after Bess's court hearing that Leche managed to discharge all his debts by selling off some leases and lands.

In the meantime, Bess gave evidence that she had applied to her brother-in-law, the twelve-year-old George Barlow, through his guardian Sir Peter Frecheville, 'who hath the custody of the body of George . . . to assign unto her the said dower, which they unjustly, and against all the laws of equity, refused to do'. Sir Peter, she stated, had 'untruly pleaded' a minor legal impediment concerned with the marriage of a minor (probably non-consummation), in order to 'delay and fatigue' the legal process and frustrate Bess's claim. Frecheville's defence was that part of the rents claimed by Bess were never owned by the Barlow estate, but were only leased.[14] His stalling device worked; it would take Bess several years and a number of court appearances[15] to get her legal entitlement from the estate.

In the autumn of the year after Robert's death, 1545, Sir Peter Frecheville offered Bess 'a small recompense . . . at his pleasure' if she would accept a yearly sum and waive her dower rights. In October 1546 she stated that she had been forced by financial necessity, and advised by her legal counsel, to accept this offer. But when she did so, 'with misgivings', the arrangement was overturned by the intervention of Sir John Chaworth, Robert Barlow's maternal uncle, who objected. That same month Bess was awarded her one-third dower rights, although the amount was about 10 per cent short of what she claimed was her entitlement. She would continue her fight, eventually winning her case, and also being awarded compensation equivalent to half a year's rents, for 'suffering the said most apparent wrongs and injuries since the death of her husband, without the succour or comfort of the said lands'.[16]

By that award, Bess became the life tenant 'of the third part of the manor of Barley with 80 messuages [dwelling houses], 7 cottages, 880 acres of land, 260 acres of meadows, 550 acres of pasture, 320 acres of woods, 400 acres of furze and heath, and £8.10.0d rent with appurtenances for sundry properties in the villages of Barley, Barley Lees, Dronfield and Holmfield.'[17] One can see why Peter Frecheville had fought Bess's claim so vigorously. Just as Hardwick was damaged by the need to pay rent for lands to the ward holder and the Crown, the Barlow estate was similarly affected by the need to pay one-third of its revenues to a very youthful widow for the term of her life.

Bess's dower did not constitute a fortune, as per the old story; Derbyshire rents were low by comparison with more accessible parts of the country. But it provided Bess with about £30 a year (about £1500 in today's currency),* a very respectable income for a seventeen-year-old single woman with no dependants. While she was fighting her case and until she obtained a favourable judgement, however, her options were limited. Having issued a writ against George Barlow and his guardian, she might not have been welcome at what she regarded as her marital home, although as she was to remain fond of the Barlow family throughout her life, there was evidently no lasting enmity involved. She could have returned to Lady Zouche, though the periods of service that young people served were not always intended to be long-term arrangements for others wanted any vacated place.

There is no historical evidence to prove what Bess did next, but in the light of future events it is most probable that sometime in 1545, in the year following Robert Barlow's death, Bess became a

*But see earlier remarks on monetary calculations.

waiting gentlewoman in the household of Lady Frances, wife of Henry Grey, Marquess of Dorset, at Bradgate Park in Leicestershire. The Greys were kinsmen of the Zouches and also, distantly, of the Hardwicks; all part of the network in other words.

Before her marriage to her cousin, Lady Frances was The Lady Frances Brandon,* with the status, if not the title, of a princess of the blood. She was the daughter of the marriage between Princess Mary[†], the King's younger and favourite sister, and Charles Brandon, Duke of Suffolk.[18]

In joining this august household, Bess, although only a poor and very distant kinswoman, was introduced into the top strata of Tudor society, but her earlier training in the Zouche household would have enabled her to serve with confidence. Bradgate, the country seat of the Grey family, had been built by Charles Brandon some years earlier, on property owned by the Brandon family for centuries, a few miles to the north-west of Leicester. It was set in a great deer park, and consisted of a palatial red-brick manor house which boasted turrets and a fine gatehouse.

The famous love match between Princess Mary and Charles Brandon is well known, and the marriage between their daughter, Lady Frances, and Henry Grey is, likewise, believed to have been founded on mutual love, as well as political expediency. It should have been a happy home for Henry Grey was by nature self-indulgent and generous. He loved books but he also enjoyed gambling (at which he lost more often than he won). His chief

---

*The use of the word 'the' in 'The Lady Frances' denoted her royal status.
[†]The eighteen-year-old Princess Mary was already in love with Brandon when Henry VIII arranged her marriage to the ailing fifty-two-year-old King Louis XII of France. She agreed to the marriage on condition that any subsequent marriage would be to a man of her own choice. She took no chances that Henry might renege on this promise. When her husband died, she summoned Brandon to France where they were hastily married in secret. Henry forgave them, and later named what was arguably his greatest warship the *Mary Rose* after his sister.

delight, however, was hunting, a pursuit he appears to have engaged in four or five days each week.

But Lady Frances had grown into a selfish and tyrannical woman who appears to have felt that fate had cheated her in some way. Her mother, after all, had once been a queen of France. Her uncle was King of England, and her aunt Margaret was Queen of Scotland. Discounting the claim of two Scottish claimants,[19] following the death of her brother she stood fourth in line to the throne, immediately after Henry VIII's own children, two of whom (her first cousins, Mary and Elizabeth) had been declared illegitimate. In order of precedence, Lady Frances was listed immediately after the King's daughters in all State documents and Court reports, such as at the reception for the arrival in England of Anne of Cleves in 1539, where the most senior ladies ordered to be present were: 'My Lady Mary, my Lady Elizabeth's grace, the Lady Frances . . .'[20]

When Lady Frances married in May 1533, the King had been the guest of honour at the lavish celebrations which cost the equivalent of half a million pounds in today's money.[21] It was to be the last appearance in public of the King's sister, Princess Mary, mother of the bride; she died soon afterwards.* So Lady Frances felt the weight of her lineage, and appears to have held the opinion that there ought to have been a greater role for her in history than that of a country gentlewoman.

Her first child had been a boy and the delighted parents planned to achieve their ambitions of great power and riches through the marriage of this hapless baby to either Princess Mary or Princess Elizabeth, who were his cousins. The child rewarded them by dying. Lady Frances then gave birth to three daughters, Jane,

---

*On the death of Princess Mary, Charles Brandon married his young ward, Katherine Willoughby. Katherine had been betrothed to Brandon's son, Henry Earl of Lincoln, so the marriage provoked a considerable scandal at Court, not least because of the youth of the bride. The jilted bridegroom, Henry, Lord Lincoln, died in 1534.

Katherine and Mary, to whom their parents made it abundantly clear that they were a major disappointment.

Lady Frances shared her husband's love of hunting, despite the fact that she also shared Henry VIII's genes and became very over-weight (her portraits show that she even resembled Henry facially). But the physical outlet of hunting did not, apparently, lessen her frustration. History relates that she became increasingly forceful, scheming, and cruel to her lower servants, and especially to her daughters. Bess, however, was something of a favourite of hers and this suggests that Bess possessed some special personal charm. Equally it might indicate an ability to fawn on a superior, though it must be said that there is little evidence of such a trait elsewhere in Bess's life. At some point during her service Lady Frances gave Bess a piece of jewellery, probably a ring, set with an agate. Bess treas-ured this item all her life.[22]

The eldest of the three daughters of the house, Lady Jane Grey, born in 1537, was nine years old when Bess joined the household. She was an extremely bright child, which was as well since her parents fully intended her to marry her cousin, the academic boy king-to-be, Edward. Her younger sister Katherine, aged seven, was a pretty feather-brain, and the new baby, Mary, born at about the time that Bess would have joined the Grey household, had a deformity of the spine. All three girls grew up experiencing little parental affection, with the rod applied frequently and often violently should they offend in the slightest way. Lady Frances literally 'boxed' Jane's ears for minor misdemeanours such as lateness.

The Grey sisters were to become close friends of Bess as they grew older, which suggests she made a good place for herself at Bradgate. Life in this extravagantly run home, with the best foods, fine wines and expensive clothes, with frequent hunting parties, important visitors and the favour of Lady Frances, would have been pleasurable. We know that Bess loved extravagant furnishings and good clothes and it was probably at Bradgate that she devel-oped her tastes in decor and furnishing. Despite a natural prudence in financial matters, Bess knew how to spend to achieve luxury, but she always made sure she got good value for her money.

No image survives of Bess as a very young woman but we know from the effigy on her tomb that she was about five foot four inches, and from the earliest portrait, painted when she was about thirty years old, that she was slender, with slim, well-shaped hands, and that she had an upright carriage. She had flame-coloured curling hair, blue eyes, and though she was not a great beauty she had attractive, regular features and an alert, intelligent expression.[23] No letters survive from this early period, but those written by Bess just a few years later suggest that she was a quiet, smart and capable young woman, eager to learn and get on in life, somewhat serious, but not lacking a gentle sense of humour. We know from her activities until she was almost eighty, that she was indefatigable, possessing enviable levels of energy.

Among the gentlemen members of the household was one Henry Cavendish, another distant kinsman to the Greys and he, in turn, was cousin to, or perhaps a nephew of, Sir William Cavendish who was a rising 'new man' at Henry's Court.[24] Was this the link which led to Bess meeting Sir William, to whom she became betrothed in 1547? It is certainly possible. However, it could equally have been simply because Henry Grey wished to entertain a man who could be politically useful to him. In the years that followed, William Cavendish was a member of Grey's inner circle and a gambling friend.

From this point onwards the need for supposition about Bess's life lessens, for sufficient material exists upon which to base a wholly supported biographical study. Previous biographers have speculated that it was at this very early period in her life that Bess made a conscious decision to marry William Cavendish in order to 'build a dynasty'. Young women in Bess's day were taught, and were inclined by social mores, to be submissive, and as yet Bess could have had no idea whether she was fertile, or could bear healthy children. It therefore seems highly unlikely that a teenager with such a limited education as Bess had received so far would have been capable of the necessary self-analysis to have reached such a well thought-out and fully developed ambition. However, it was an age when lineage was all-important. Bess may have grown up within an impoverished household, but her roots went back to an English monarch and it is inconceivable that this was not spoken of by her elders. It would have been a cause for intense pride, and perhaps the knowledge also helped to shape Bess's destiny, providing her with a desire to return her family to better things than she had known.

That Bess adopted a deliberate policy of dynastic design later in life is not in contention. But at nineteen, as she was when she met Sir William, it is more likely that she hoped for love, or at the very least a protector/provider, a father-figure who would shield her from the financial insecurity she had known for most of her young life.

William Cavendish was more than twice her age, forty to Bess's nineteen years, and already corpulent. There is no suggestion that it was in any sense an arranged marriage: rather it was a matter that Bess decided for herself, perhaps with some advice from Lady Frances. Sir William was a clever and serious man but not, from a study of his only known portrait, the sort of man to capture the heart of a girl unless she was indeed seeking a father-figure. He had been sworn on to the Privy Council and knighted by the King at Easter in the previous year, so marriage to him meant a significant social advancement for Bess. It would give her a title, it would bring her into contact with members of the Court as an equal, and she would be chatelaine of Sir William's two fine houses. She would also become the stepmother of his three daughters.

It was a great deal for a nineteen-year-old to take on.

CHAPTER 3

LADY CAVENDISH

1547

BESS WOULD HAVE BEEN VERY HARD-HEARTED INDEED HAD
she not felt some sympathy for the two elder Grey girls who were
aged nine and seven respectively when she joined the household.
They were surrounded by wealth and the symbols of status – their
mother insisted that they dressed and were treated as princesses of
the blood – yet they were emotionally impoverished, even for
Tudor children. From the age of four or five their daily regime
began at 6 a.m. winter and summer, and after a breakfast of bread,
meat and ale, they were taken to request a daily blessing from their
parents.* Then began for Jane and Katherine a day of unremitting
schoolwork. In the mornings, in addition to basic subjects such as
writing and deportment, they were taught classical languages:
Latin, Greek, and, in Jane's case at her own request, Hebrew. In
the afternoons they studied music (Jane played several instruments) and modern languages: French, Spanish, and Italian, and
read the Bible or the classics. In the evening they either practised

---

*Bess carried this tradition on with her own children, and even as grown adults, when
writing to her they invariably asked for 'your daily blessing'.

dancing or were expected to take up needlework until they went to bed at 9 p.m.[1]

For Jane, instead of the weight of schoolwork being a punishment it was a pleasure. She sopped up knowledge, and when her parents took her hunting as a rare treat, she was bored with the sport and irritated to be away from her books. Naturally this did not commend her to her hunting-mad parents. But, accustomed to cuffs, sarcasm and criticism from them, Jane discovered at a very early age that she could always escape from the difficulties of her life into intellectual study. She once told one of her schoolmasters, the famous Roger Ascham, about her treatment at the hands of her father and mother who, no matter how hard she tried,

> whether I speak, keep silence, sit, stand or go, eat, drink, be merry or sad, be it sewing, playing or dancing or doing anything else, I am so sharply taunted, so cruelly threatened . . . sometimes with pinches, nips and bobs, and other ways I will not name . . . that I think myself in hell till [the] time come that I must go to Mr Aylmer* [her full-time tutor], who teaches me so gently, so pleasantly . . . that I think the time nothing whilst I am with him . . .[2]

Having grown up among a large family of sisters and half-sisters, Bess would have related easily to the little Grey girls. It is likely that she attempted to alleviate their unhappiness in some way, for a long-term friendship developed between Bess and both girls. When Katherine suffered a major personal crisis as an adult, it was Bess to whom she would turn for help. But this is running ahead of the story.

In January 1547 King Henry VIII died; he was fifty-five, prematurely aged and raddled, and had reigned for thirty-eight years.

---

*John Aylmer coined the phrase, 'God is an Englishman'.

His extravagances had left the country bankrupt, and there was no universal mourning at his death. Deep mourning was observed by the Grey household, however. As the oldest male family member connected by blood (through his wife Lady Frances), Henry Grey was the Chief Mourner at the State funeral. He was also created Lord High Constable of England for three days in February 1547 to enable him to superintend the coronation of Edward VI. He was made a Knight of the Garter at the same time. It would have been unusual, given her position in the household as a waiting gentlewoman, if Bess had not been included in the party to assist Lady Frances when the household moved to their London home, Dorset House, to attend these important and historic occasions.

In fact Bess fitted so well into the Dorsets' ménage that when she married Sir William Cavendish later the same year, the wedding was held at Bradgate Park instead of at her own family home. Sir William kept a notebook in which he journalised important family events,[3] and in it he wrote:

> Memorandum. That I was married to Elizabeth Hardwick, my third wife, in Leicestershire at Bradgate, my Lord Marquesses house, the 20th of August in the first year of King Edward the 6, at 2 of the clock after midnight; the dominical letter B.*

Having retained his position as Treasurer of the King's Chamber under the new king and, even more importantly perhaps, under the Lord Protector, Sir William Cavendish was a welcome visitor in most houses. Anyone with direct daily access to the King and the Protector was liable to be regarded as a valuable connection, and the relationship cultivated against a time when such a friendship might prove useful. Bess was connected to the Greys by kinship, and it seems was

---

*The Dominical letter was any of the letters A–G used in Church calendars to indicate the date, between 1 and 7 January, of the first Sunday in the year. See *OED*.

a popular member of the household. These combined facts must have persuaded Lord and Lady Grey to host the wedding celebrations for Bess and Sir William at Bradgate. The time of the ceremony appears curious, but no obvious explanation presents itself; perhaps the priest was delayed by urgent business; perhaps the ceremony was performed after the wedding feast. Anyway, we know for sure that on this mid-August night in 1547, nineteen-year-old Bess became Lady Cavendish.

Who was Sir William Cavendish, and if, in marrying him, Bess saw a significant improvement in her position, why should such a successful and ambitious man choose Bess?

He was born in about 1505 a younger son of Thomas Cavendish of Cavendish in Suffolk, who was secretary to the Treasurer of the King's Exchequer under Henry VII, and Clerk of the Pipe – a senior position in the Exchequer – during the reign of Henry VIII. Thomas Cavendish was thus a man with Court contacts.[4] William's mother, Alice, died in 1515, leaving three sons: George,[5] aged fifteen, who was at Cambridge, William, then aged about ten, and Thomas, who was a few years younger.[6] Within a year their father married his second wife, Agnes, and the family moved from Cavendish in Suffolk (just south of Bury St Edmunds) to St Albans, where a daughter, Mary, was born.[7]

No evidence exists to show that William Cavendish attended Cambridge as his brother George did, but he was clearly well educated. By 1522 George was married to a niece of Sir Thomas More, had several children, and was in the service of Cardinal Wolsey (also a Suffolk man). William was then seventeen, and it is generally accepted that he followed his elder brother into the Cardinal's service, as a gentleman usher.

Thomas Cavendish died in 1524, leaving a considerable property in Kent to his widow Agnes, and, predictably, the major part of his estates to his eldest son George. He made provision for a dowry of £40 for his daughter Mary, and to his two younger sons, William and Thomas, he left some land in Suffolk and a half share each in whatever was left from the sale of the property in Kent after the death of their stepmother.[8] William obviously had to make his own way in the world, and he does not show up again in surviving documents until 1530, by which time, at the age of twenty-five, he was already established in the service of Thomas Cromwell.

After Wolsey's fall from grace, Thomas Cromwell virtually picked up where his former master left off, taking over many of Wolsey's servants, including William Cavendish,[9] and within a remarkably short time he became, effectively, a vice regent to the King. In 1532 Cromwell became Master of the King's Jewels and Clerk of the Hanaper, and between 1533 and 1536 he became, in turn, Chancellor of the Exchequer, Principal Secretary of State, Vicar General, Master of the Rolls and, finally, Lord Privy Seal. He would go on to become Baron Cromwell, Knight of the Garter and finally Earl of Essex. Some historians suggest that, during the mid 1530s, it was Cromwell, rather than the King, who was actually running the country. Whatever the answer, young William Cavendish rode securely along in the turbulent wake of his exceptional if not very likeable master.

Cromwell had gained Henry VIII's respect and confidence in a few short years by the simple expediency of making himself indispensable. He gave the King what the King wanted: answers to his most pressing concerns. He came up with a workable solution to annul the King's marriage to Catherine of Aragon. He also proposed that monasteries throughout the kingdom should be dissolved and their assets confiscated by the State (the Dissolution, as it has become known). He set up the Court of Augmentations to administer the transfer of ecclesiastical assets to the Crown, and developed a revenue policy to deal efficiently with the spoils. Later, he devised the commission for special investigation into 'all things treasonable' which led to the execution of Anne Boleyn and ultimately to the King's remarriage and the birth of a son.

Cromwell recognised in William Cavendish a servant with a quick brain, the ability to spot an opportunity, and a vaulting

ambition not dissimilar to his own. Cavendish had the same serious, heavy-set appearance as Cromwell, and even dressed in a
similar manner, with the furred black gown and secretarial cap. He
was already working for Cromwell prior to Wolsey's death in 1530,
for earlier that year he accepted the surrender of the priory and
convent at Sheen from the hands of the Prior on Cromwell's
behalf.[10] And in 1531 Cavendish visited, audited and accepted the
assets of several other religious houses.

The Abbey of St Albans was the wealthiest in the country[11] and
although he was Abbot for ten years, it is thought that, like his
predecessor, Wolsey,* Cromwell never visited it. In 1532 William
Cavendish was instructed to assess and audit the possessions of this
establishment in what was called 'a visitation'. He may have been
offered the job simply because his family dwelt in the town and he
knew the area. The holdings of the Abbey were vast, and included
lands in other counties beyond Hertfordshire, as well as many sub-
ordinate religious houses, cells and hospitals. Cavendish computed
its annual income at £2102. 7s. 1¾d.[12] and the neat audit of assets,
together with his efficient and unemotional demeanour, suggested
to Cromwell that in Cavendish he had a man with the right
attitude.

The small but beautifully situated Manor of Northaw was a
mere part of the great riches of the Abbey of St Albans. In 1534 the
copyhold (leasehold) of this property was offered to William
Cavendish on extremely favourable terms by the Abbot of St
Albans as a favour to Cromwell.[13] Probably William suggested to
the incumbent that it would be interpreted thus by Cromwell, who
was renowned for 'looking after' his best servants. Cromwell was,
indeed, happy to allow the transaction, though how much the
monk ultimately benefited by the obvious bribe is unknown. No
doubt it encouraged William to deal more sympathetically with

---

*Cardinal Wolsey was Abbot of St Albans from 1522 to 30 but never visited the
Abbey.

the Abbey than he might otherwise have done. By this time William had been married to his first wife Margaret Bostock[14] for two years, and in January that year Margaret gave birth to their first child. They named her Elizabeth, after the baby princess, daughter of Queen Anne. In the following year another daughter, Katheryne, was born, and William and Margaret Cavendish obtained the freehold of the manor and lands of Northaw by an outright grant.

William's career really took off in 1536 when the Court of Augmentations* was created in April of that year. A month later, on 12 May, he was appointed one of ten auditors at a salary of £20 a year, plus 'the profits of the office'.[15] These 'profits' far exceeded William's annual salary, which he referred to as 'a poor living', and made the job worthwhile; indeed, they founded William's fortune. In the dismantling of the great properties, estates and swathes of lands owned by religious houses, the prime properties went, of course, to the Crown and these were sold on to 'the gentry of each shire'.† But smaller parcels, too insignificant or isolated to be hugely worthwhile to the exchequer, were available for purchase, rent or lease at modest sums to members of the Augmentation Commission with an eye for a bargain. The fortunes of many great English families were founded during the Reformation and Dissolution, and the family of William Cavendish was one of them.

Initially, his appointment covered the counties of Bedfordshire, Berkshire, Buckinghamshire, Kent, Oxfordshire, Surrey and Sussex, and it was his job to rove about this area, often in the company of Commissioner Dr Thomas Leigh, evaluating and assessing the value of religious establishments then persuading them to 'submit wholly to the King's mercy' before taking their 'voluntary surrender'.[16] William Cavendish was not a brutal man, nor was he unscrupulous or unusually corrupt; despite received opinion,

*So called because it augmented the income of the office of the exchequer.
†Cromwell advised Henry VIII to sell the properties to 'the gentry of the shires' because this would make it difficult for the Church ever to recover them. This early

few of the commissioners working under Thomas Cromwell were any of these things.[17] William was methodical and efficient in the course of his duty, and a loyal civil servant to both Cromwell and the King. But he was also a man whose job placed him in a position to better himself and his family by acquisition of bargain pieces of land. Cromwell appears to have accepted, unquestioned, the valuations put on these properties which buyers such as William had themselves audited and assessed. It was a perquisite of the job.

Littered throughout surviving State papers is the evidence of William's remarkable industry and his importance in Cromwell's work. In 1536 he appears in a list of New Year 'remembrances' handwritten by Cromwell: '. . . send for Candisshe [Cavendish] to make a book of all the lands and revenues not yet given, which were part of Christchurch lands . . .'[18] He is also listed on 19 February 1536 as the senior auditor on the 4th circuit of the Court of Augmentations.* In June that year Cavendish wrote to Cromwell: 'We have been at the priory of Little Marlowe and have dissolved it. My lady takes this discharge like a wise woman and has made delivery of everything, of which we send you an inventory. She trusts entirely to you for a reasonable pension.' William recommends this course of action, but suggests that alternatively the Abbess might be transferred to another suitable establishment.[19]

On 5 September 1536, writing from Northaw, William has his eye on a London property as well. He asks Cromwell to assign him to the auditorship of 'St Johns', which included a small house that would make him a suitable pied-à-terre. Though the fee for the work involved was small, he wrote, 'it would be high advancement' for he would have 'meat and drink' for himself and his two servants, one of whom was John Bestenay, clerk,[20] 'with their

_____

date, before the Court of Augmentations was officially created, shows that Cromwell was already at work dissolving religious houses before the Act was passed.
*The 4th circuit covered Bedfordshire, Berkshire, Buckinghamshire, Kent, Oxfordshire, Surrey and Sussex.

liveries and chamber', during their constant journeys to and from London. Paying for the accommodation of himself and his servants while making up his books and reporting to Cromwell's office, he explained, took up a great part of his salary.[21] In the event he did not get the house at St John's. Cromwell actually wrote twice on William's behalf, but the position had already been offered to someone else and William eventually rented a small house in Newgate Street, a little to the north of St Paul's.[22] At the height of the Dissolution in 1537, William Cavendish was covering huge distances and dissolving religious houses at the rate of up to ten a month.

As an example of his diligence, in one two-week period during October 1538, William Cavendish visited, audited, and took the surrenders of the following monasteries in Shropshire: Merivale (15th), Brewood and Lylleshall (16th–17th); 'near Stafford': St-Thomas, and Delacres (18th–21st); in Derby: Darley Dale and Repton (24th–26th); in Leicester: Grace Dieu (28th); and he took yet more, day on day, in early November, as he travelled southwards towards London, through Northamptonshire and Cambridgeshire.

There was a hiccup in William's career when it was discovered that he and Dr Leigh had accepted some gifts of valuable plate from the Abbot of Merivale who thereby hoped for sympathetic treatment. Also, during that trip William had added some unsubstantiated disbursements totalling £34. 16s. 8d, which, 'written in his own hand without the knowledge of his clerks', did not place the best interpretation on his motives. But the two men apologised humbly for the 'misunderstanding' and their explanations were accepted. Probably Cromwell realised that the threat of losing their positions was enough to terrify these valuable servants into more scrupulous behaviour in future.[23]

In October 1538 William and Margaret Cavendish were granted lands in Cheshunt, Hertfordshire, Thetford in Norfolk, and Tallington in Lincolnshire.[24] And in 1539 'in consideration of his services',[25] William was allowed to purchase Northaw outright, together with the manors and lands of Cuffley and Childewyke in Hertfordshire (formerly belonging to the manor of St Albans), as well as 'the late priory of Cardigan in south Wales with its appurtenances, and the rectories and churches of Cardigan'.[26] Not bad for a civil servant on a salary of £20 a year, and this was just the start of his upward climb.

By this time three more children, John, Mary and Ann, had been born to the couple, but in June 1540, when Margaret Cavendish died, only three of their five children were still living, Katheryne, Mary and Ann. It was a period of great trauma for William Cavendish, since Cromwell, like Wolsey before him, had displeased the King over the matter of a queen. In this case it was Anne of Cleves, whom Cromwell had favoured and urged upon the King. Unfortunately for Cromwell the King so disliked his new consort on sight that instead of bedding her, he proclaimed her his sister. Cromwell was condemned under a bill of attainder and beheaded on Tower Hill in July 1540.

Things could easily have gone badly for William in the reorganisation immediately following Cromwell's death, for he was known to be Cromwell's man. So when he was ordered to Ireland a few weeks later, as part of a three-man team of commissioners (with Thomas Welsh and John Mynne),[27] he was probably considerably relieved.

His new mission was to survey and value lands which had fallen to the English during the Fitzgerald Rebellion, and also to examine the accounts of the King's Army in Ireland, which were the responsibility of the Vice-Treasurer in Ireland, William Brabazon. There had been many complaints concerning the ordinance, victualling and wages of the soldiers. It was, in fact, a mess, and Brabazon stood accused of incompetence if not outright corruption. William remained in Ireland for thirteen months (long beyond the original intention and long after his two fellow commissioners had returned home), and there, among the other senior officers in the company of Sir Anthony St Leger, Deputy of Ireland, he was introduced to Sir John St Loe of Somerset, who was shortly to be made the new Marshal. The St Loes were an old warrior family who had served with distinction in Ireland for over a decade. Besides Sir John, also serving in Ireland at that time were Sir John's younger brother William, Seneschal of Wexford, and Sir John's twenty-two-year-old son and heir, 'young William', who would play a significant part in Bess's story. Both Cavendish and St Loe appear in Cromwell's handwritten 'remembrances', sometimes in the same document, and as St Loe was a major figure in the King's Army in Ireland, Cavendish would have had a particular interest in his opinions, as well as his accounts.

William Cavendish's period in Ireland was wholly successful. There was general satisfaction from the Privy Council at his reports and suggestions, and even before he left to return home St Leger wrote to the King to highly commend him:

> Mr. Cavendish took great pains in your said service, as well with continual pains about the said accounts and surveys, as in taking very painful journeys about the same . . . to Limerick and those parts, where I think none of your Highness's English commissioners came these many years, and in such weather of snow and frost that I never rode in the like. And I note him to be such a man as little feareth the displeasure of any man in your Highness's service, wherefore I account him to be the meter man for this land.[28]

In the summer of 1542, William married his second wife, a widow, Elizabeth Parris (formerly Conningsby, née Parker),[29] at the church of Blackfriars in London.

In 1544, when Henry VIII left England for France (carried to war on a litter), William Cavendish was ordered to Boulogne as part of the royal entourage. A few days before he was due to embark, the order was countermanded and he was instructed to

remain at his post in London. Having expended the huge sum of
£200* on 'equipment appropriate to his position', which had
already been shipped ahead of him to Boulogne, William was more
than a little upset, correctly fearing that he had seen the last of his
property.[30] However, it meant he was on hand to support his pregnant wife. Elizabeth gave birth to a daughter, Susan, in October
1544, followed by a son John a year later, but both perished as
infants.

By this time, William was over forty: an age when a man is apt
to take stock of his life. He had played a leading role in the work
of the Court of Augmentations and he was undeniably successful.
The lands 'surrendered' by the monasteries that were sold off
'with reckless abandon'[31] by Cromwell contributed some
£800,000 to the exchequer. William Cavendish's part in this had
not passed unnoticed, nor did his unceasing diligence on the
King's behalf in the years following Cromwell's demise. In the
early months of 1546 when the Court of Augmentations was
winding down, he was offered the post of Treasurer to the King's
Chamber.

At face value no man would hesitate to accept the honour of
working in the King's presence, which held the possibility of
winning royal favour, but the offer came with a price tag. The King
wanted £1000 for the office,[32] a sum sufficient to purchase a large
country estate and still leave some change. On the assumption
that once installed he would invariably be the recipient of many
lucrative perquisites such as the ability to sell favours, even more
so than in the Augmentations Office, William borrowed the
money, was appointed Treasurer, and was also sworn on to the
Privy Council. Soon after his appointment there was a complaint
by members of the Privy Council that he was late presenting his
monthly report.[33] This coincided with the death of his wife

---

*This was almost ten times William's annual salary.

Elizabeth after giving birth to an unnamed stillborn baby girl, so perhaps his explanation was accepted for there was no retribution. Soon afterwards, on Easter Sunday 1546, William Cavendish was knighted by the King.

As he undoubtedly anticipated, his elevation to the King's immediate presence made Sir William Cavendish a man worth knowing; a man who could bestow favours. Not only was he responsible for accounting for the personal expenditure of the King, and also for managing certain household expenses of the heir to the throne, Prince Edward, but he also looked after certain expenses concerning the Lady Mary, the Lady Elizabeth and the Lady Anne of Cleves. Received by the best families in the land, he had become a man of considerable substance: lord of several manors in Hertfordshire, leaseholder of a fine London house and owner of a useful portfolio of lands and properties that stretched across the country from South Wales to Suffolk. But coming on top of his second widowhood, all his achievements may have served to make him question what his life's work was for. He had no son to inherit his acquired wealth. Of the eight children Sir William had fathered, he was left with only three survivors, all girls, and one of these, Mary, was in some way physically or mentally abnormal.

In the following January, when Henry VIII died and nine-year-old Edward VI ascended the throne, Sir William was reconfirmed in his position as Treasurer of the King's Chamber at a salary of £25 a quarter,[34] and indeed there is evidence that he was something of a favourite of the boy. Perhaps his own experiences at a similar age, with his father away at Court and his mother's death, made William more than usually sympathetic among the courtiers. It was at this point that Sir William proposed to Bess. Like his previous wife, his new fiancée was a widow, though a very young one; indeed she had yet to reach her twentieth birthday and was very probably still a virgin.

Bess was at the height of her attractiveness, and she had no dependants from her brief previous marriage to cause any step-sibling jealousies or needing to be provided for. She had good breeding, as good as, if not better than, Sir William's, and she was highly intelligent and personable. She possessed a modest income of her own, and she came of a healthy and fecund stock. She could demonstrate valuable connections such as the Greys, and, not least, she had that enchanting asset of youth. But did love play any part in this arrangement? Alas we can only speculate, for the only known surviving letter between Sir William and Bess is from a much later date. It concerns a small matter of business, and has a businesslike tone not dissimilar to that in letters he wrote to Cromwell and the Privy Council. But when she wrote about Sir William's death in a journal, Bess referred to him as 'my most dear and well beloved husband'.

Following their wedding at Bradgate in Leicestershire, Sir William and the new Lady Cavendish set out for Northaw in Hertfordshire, via London.[35] The couple would have travelled on horseback, Bess riding side-saddle on a palfrey[*] with her feet on a footboard. They would have broken their journey at wayside inns, travelling, as their station required, with a small retinue of servants, one of whom would ride ahead each day to bespeak clean beds, hot food and adequate stabling for the horses.

London was not, of course, a new sight to Bess, but it was always an exciting place. She had lived there during her time with the Zouches, and almost certainly spent time there during her service with the Greys as well. London was a comparatively small place in 1550, with only 12,000 inhabitants, but it was still the largest urban conglomeration in England.[36] Enclosed within the old walls, its skyline was dominated by the battlements of royal palaces, the massive bulk of St Paul's, and the spires and towers of numerous ancient parish churches. With the exception of

[*]Palfrey: a light horse, originally of French breeding, with a placid nature that made them safe for women to ride.

a few broad main thoroughfares, such as the Strand and the Chepe (Cheapside), the streets were narrow and noisome, running between medieval houses whose overhanging half-timbered upper storeys almost touched each other. There was no paving in these alleys and they lay thick with dust in dry weather, hock-deep in mud in the wet, and the central gutters ran with effluent, but London was a place full of life, colour and noise. Pedestrians jostled with animals being driven to market, and pack animals and carts bringing fresh supplies from the surrounding countryside, or transporting them from the wharfs of the Thames.

Fresh food was plentiful, and produce was brought in daily from the surrounding countryside, which could be reached within ten minutes on horseback in all directions. Shops run by tradesmen tended to group together, hence the streets called Fish Row, Butchers Row and Bakers Row and so on, but there were also hordes of hawkers and country people crying out their own call to advertise their pies and bread, flowers, spices, fruit, herbs, vegetables, and all manner of commodities, often displayed on hand-carried trays. Water supplies were dispensed to householders through conduits or fountains, such as the great open conduit in the Chepe, but wealthier citizens had water delivered to their homes by water carriers who were licensed and controlled by the mayor and aldermen.

Newgate, where Sir William's rented London house was situated, was close to the old medieval cathedral of St Paul's and also to Newgate Prison, 'a major venue for booksellers, barbers, beggars and cutpurses'.[37] To the east of his house lay the great Tower of London. To the west were the Inns of Court and the country's third university,[38] and beyond that was Westminster and Whitehall, the Court, Parliament, and the great houses of noblemen and wealthy citizens.

The Thames was a short walk to the south, spanned by the only bridge, London Bridge, which was regarded by at least one contemporary writer as 'among the miracles of the world, if men respect the building and foundation laid artificially . . . over an ebbing and flowing water upon 21 piles of stone, with 20 arches'.[39] These arches were sixty feet high to allow the passage of barges, and the structure itself was almost top-heavy with shops and tenements up to four storeys high; in places the buildings nearly touched each other over the narrow roadway. The drawbridge on the southern end, at Southwark, was always decorated with the severed heads of executed prisoners, in an attempt by the authorities *pour encourager les autres*.

If one did not wish to cross by the bridge, there were numerous boatmen to ferry a passenger across to Lambeth, or up and down the river to the palaces of Whitehall, Greenwich, Nonesuch or Hampton Court. It was a busy thoroughfare with every kind of waterborne traffic, from gloriously gilded State barges to humble private vessels, public wherries which acted as an early form of taxi service (the fare from the Tower to Blackfriars was not inexpensive – four pence).[40] There were merchant and naval ships of all sizes, fishing boats and swans. And when the great ocean-going galleons docked they brought with them the riches of faraway places: wines from France, spices and silks from the Mediterranean, the Adriatic and the Orient. They sailed laden with cargoes of best English wool. A housewife of Bess's rank would be routinely contacted by a ship's agent, asking her to let him know if she desired 'anything from the carrack . . . ? There are calicoes, sleved silks,* jams, spices, damasks and ebony wood . . .'[41] Raw sewage ran into the Thames through the drains of Moorditch and the Fleet ditch, but the daily ebb and flow of the great river was well able to cope with the effluent from 12,000 citizens. Indeed, fishermen made a good livelihood from daily hauls of salmon, trout, barbels, perch, flounders and shrimps, indicating that the water was in excellent health.

---

*Slea- or sleaved silk: a process using different thicknesses of thread to weave a pattern in the cloth.

The meadows along the Thames, and the fields bordering the city to the north and west, were full of wild flowers in the spring and summer months, but in the overcrowded and filthy neighbourhoods of the poor, disease flourished and when plague struck it engulfed the inhabitants like a tidal wave. House fires were a constant danger among the tightly packed wooden-framed houses where cooking was done over open fires. Beggars were everywhere, and crime was commonplace.

This was the London in which Bess began her life as Lady Cavendish, and soon after her marriage she was presented at Court. Here she would have had an unusual advantage, for if the young King chose to speak to her she would have been able to discuss his favourite cousin, Jane Grey, of whom he was especially fond, though not (so his journal tells us) as a potential wife. But the main task of the new Lady Cavendish was to run her husband's houses, rule their servants stoutly, care for his children, entertain his guests, and to bear children of her own – preferably sons – but not necessarily in that order.

When the couple finally reached Northaw, near St Albans, it was probably the first time Bess had seen it, and may also have been the first time she had met her stepchildren, the eldest of whom, aged twelve, was only seven years younger than Bess herself. So the first hurdle that the new Lady Cavendish faced was to establish herself at the head of the household, where she was no doubt observed critically by her stepchildren as well as the old servants of her husband's former wives.

There is no surviving image of the first manor house at Northaw. Thirty years later it was demolished and completely rebuilt.[42] Some local historians believe that the original house was built as a hunting lodge and refurbished for use by the abbots or senior officials of the abbey.[43] The estate, with its small lake, was set among great woodlands, which made the surrounding area a popular hunting ground for courtiers. But its obvious chief asset was its close proximity to London, which lay within a ride of a few hours. It was in a prime location much sought after by those wanting a country retreat convenient to the Court. Edward VI spent most of his childhood at nearby Hunsdon, and both Wolsey and Lord Burghley built palaces in the area.

Bess would be chatelaine at Northaw for the next five years.

CHAPTER 4

FAMILY MATTERS

1547–51

THE MARRIAGE OF BESS TO SIR WILLIAM IN THAT FIRST YEAR of the reign of the boy king was well omened. The entire country was experiencing a new sense of hope.

Bess learned fast. We can see this in her household accounts, produced partially at Northaw and partially at the London house. Within a year she was entering significant sums of money in rents received from her husband's tenants, making the daily disbursements necessary for the efficient administration of her homes, paying bills from suppliers, recording rents on leases held by Sir William and the wages of their servants. Apart from the fact that the financially prudent Sir William would never have allowed his young wife such freedom had she not proved herself capable, it is easy to chart Bess's growing confidence in her position as her account book progresses. At first Sir William makes many of the entries and checks and signs the totals at the end of each month but gradually the accounts become Bess's domain.

For the bride there was the novelty of running a new home – Bess's first household as far as we know; she was probably too young during her short marriage to Robert Barlow to have headed her own establishment. Now she could be proud of her rank in life, and for the first time she had money to spend, with the added pleasure of being able to help members of her family who were not so fortunately placed. But it is important to remember that although Sir William was a successful man, and well off, he was not 'rich', in that he did not have old family money behind him. As a self-made high-flyer, he earned his money in the manner of a modern-day executive and spent what he earned either on his lifestyle or by adding to his lands. There was no 'comfort cushion' of savings. One of their first acquisitions was a great marriage bed, called 'the Pearl Bed'. In a household inventory some years later it was described as:

> Five pieces of hangings . . . eleven foot deep, a bedstead carved and gilded, a tester bed head and double valance of black velvet embroidered with silver, gold, and pearl, with sivines [raspberries] and woodbines [honeysuckle] fringed with gold, silver and black silk, with my Lady's and Sir William Cavendishes arms in the bed head. Five curtains of black and white damask, laid about with gold lace and gold fringe, and gold lace down the middle. A mattress, a featherbed, a wool quilt, a bolster and two pillows, a pair of fustians, two Spanish blankets, a Counterpane of black velvet striped with silver, embroidered with pearls and purles [raised circular decoration of silver or gold wire], and another cover for the bed of black sarcenet quilted . . .[1]

Bess's first child, a daughter, was born ten months after their wedding day. Sir William, ever the accountant, recorded the event punctiliously: 'Frances, my 9th child and the first by the said woman [Elizabeth Hardwick], was born on Monday between the hours of 3 and 4 at afternoon, viz the 18th of June. Anno 2 RE 6.* The dominical letter then G.'[2]

---

*Anno 2 RE 6: year 2 in the reign of Edward VI [i.e. 1548].

The Greys and the Brandons turned out in force for the christening and bishoping.* Whether this was out of allegiance and
affection to Bess or because of Sir William's position at Court is
impossible to determine. It is certainly difficult to reconcile the
attention and kindness unfailingly shown to Bess by Lady Frances
Grey with the proud, haughty and even cruel mother depicted by
her daughter's tutor, Roger Ascham, in his biographical recollection
of Lady Jane Grey. And although Sir William might have been
useful to them, the Greys and the Brandons did not actually need
the Cavendishes. So, given the relationship that continued for many
years between them, it seems a genuinely close friendship existed.
Lady Frances agreed to be the senior godmother, and the child was
named after her.

Katherine Brandon, the widowed Duchess of Suffolk, was the
second godmother. She was the surprisingly youthful stepmother of
Lady Frances to whom, some years earlier, she was to have been
sister-in-law, for as Katherine Willoughby she was betrothed in
early childhood to Lady Frances's brother. Soon after the death of
his wife, the Princess Mary Tudor, Charles Brandon had married
his son's fiancée 'out of hand', causing a minor Court scandal and
much heartache in his family. The bride's former fiancé thus
became her stepson until he died a year later, at about the time
Katherine bore twin sons to her elderly husband. Charles Brandon
had died since then, and it was the elder of these twin boys,
Katherine's thirteen-year-old son Henry Brandon, who was now
Duke of Suffolk, and godfather to baby Frances Cavendish. In the
sixteenth century the role of godparent was not undertaken lightly;
anyone taking it on accepted that it involved an ongoing obligation
to the child.

---

*Bishoping: Confirmation. It was customary for baptism and confirmation to
be performed at the same time if a bishop was present at the baptism. Queen
Elizabeth I, for example, was confirmed at her baptism when she was three
days old.

So Bess, the country girl who only a few years earlier had been forced to turn to her financially straitened mother for help, was now welcomed as an equal in the highest stratum of society. A very lavish sort of hospitality would have been required to entertain guests such as these who were accustomed to and expected the best of everything. But Bess had been fortunate in her childhood placings; her experience in the houses of the Zouche and Grey families stood her in good stead for her role as Lady Cavendish.

We know that it was a lively household, for when her children were grown up they recalled the old 'holidays': feast days, birthdays, Christmas and New Year, which their mother had apparently kept with traditional revelry. 'All the old holidays,' Bess's second son would write, 'with their mirth and rites . . . May games, morris dances, the Lord of the May, the Lady of the May, the fool and the Hobby Horse, also the Whitsun Lord and Lady, carols and wassails at Christmas with good plum porridge and pies . . .'[3] Sir William's half-sister must have been living at Northaw Manor with them for on July 31st Bess hosted a summer wedding when Mary Cavendish 'of Northaw . . . was given 200 marks for her portion' and married Richard Snow.[4] Since the bride's father had left her only £40, the difference was almost certainly made up by Sir William Cavendish. Their brother George Cavendish was present at the wedding, but he was not well placed financially.

While Bess was homemaking, Sir William's choice of godparents for his children over the next years is a strong indicator that he was busy making friends in many different political camps, though with a heavy emphasis on followers of the reformed Church that was so dear to Edward VI. Working constantly around the King, Sir William could see for himself that the boy did not possess a strong constitution. In June 1547, among the wages paid to teachers, jesters and minstrels, Sir William also recorded payments to eight doctors and physicians who were part of the King's entourage.[5] An astute man, Sir William knew that in the event of the death of

Edward VI, there would be political instability. According to Henry VIII's Act of Succession, the heirs to the throne after Edward were his half-sisters, Mary and Elizabeth, followed by his cousin Jane Grey, eldest daughter of the Lady Frances. But a man with his ear to the ground, such as Sir William, would have known that such a transition would not be straightforward. Not only were all the heirs female, but the legitimacy of both Mary and Elizabeth had been legally obscured by their father*, which left opportunities for less closely connected claimants to contest their rights to inherit. There were, too, many well-placed Protestants who were unhappy about the possibility of a counter-reformation if the die-hard Roman Catholic Mary came to the throne; it was suspected that she would attempt to seize and restore all former Church lands. All these possibilities would have been well chewed over in a Court that thrived on gossip and rumour.

As soon as Bess recovered from giving birth she joined her husband in London ('Given to my nurse at my coming from Northaw, two shillings'), where the couple celebrated by entertaining and going about in society.[6] They were entertained by the Greys and also by Thomas, Lord Seymour, brother of the late Queen Jane, and thus uncle to the boy king. His title was Baron Seymour of Sudeley but he was more commonly known by his title, Lord Admiral. His elder brother, Edward Seymour, who was proclaimed the Lord Protector after the death of Henry VIII, had recently become Duke of Somerset and was, in effect, Governor of England until Edward VI came of age.[†]

From the sums paid to messengers and porters for carrying messages and gifts, we know that the Cavendishes were in regular contact with a small, exclusive set. This included the Greys ('Paid

---

*Mary was declared illegitimate when Henry married Anne Boleyn. Elizabeth was similarly treated when her mother was beheaded, and she was always regarded as illegitimate by English Catholics.
†To help identification, these Seymour brothers will in future be referred to as the Lord Admiral and the Lord Protector.

to the horse-keeper who went to Bradgate; twenty six shillings and fourpence' . . . 'given to Patrick when he went to Bradgate; fourpence' . . . 'to a poor man that wrought in the garden at Bradgate; twopence' etc.), as well as the Lord Admiral and his wife (who was the Dowager Queen, Catherine Parr). Other people named in the earliest accounts are Lord and Lady Warwick, who stayed with them on several occasions, the Princess Mary ('Given to Bestenay at my husband's riding to my Lady Mary's grace on the 24th October; one hundred shillings' . . . 'Given to Crompe for riding to my Lady Mary's grace; two shillings and three pence'), Lady Challoner and William Parr (recently created Marquess of Northampton), who was the brother of Catherine Parr and thus also the brother-in-law of the Lord Admiral.

The Cavendishes entertained generously, rewarding their cook with a five-shilling tip for producing an especially fine meal on one occasion when 'my Lord Marquess came to supper'. All their friends were closely connected by marriage, kinship, or political affiliation, and the same names crop up time after time, wherever one researches. By present-day standards, Tudor upper-class society was very limited in numbers.

When they were in London, Sir William and Bess gambled regularly; it was a favourite occupation at Court, and Bess's household accounts reveal that the Cavendishes regularly lost money at the tables of friends: 'lost at play to my lady and my Lord Admiral; 3s/4d'. In order to move in Henry Grey's circles it was necessary for Sir William to play with high stakes. He seemed prepared to drop as much as £2 in an evening, which was a great deal of money in terms of what £2 would then purchase. For example, it was more than the half-year's rent on their London house in Newgate Street, which was leased from the Marquess of Northampton for £3. 16s. 8d. a year. One could buy a half-decent workhorse for £1. As might be expected, Bess was more circumspect than her husband; the amounts recorded by her as 'lost at play' and 'lost at the tables' tended to be of the order of pence, but perhaps she remembered that she could buy a dozen chickens for one shilling and sixpence. No winnings are recorded in the accounts. But even with these losses at gaming the expenditure of the Cavendishes did not exceed their income.

From these household account books left by Bess,[7] one forms the impression of a sensible and confident young wife, comfortable in her marriage, secure in a good income which exceeded their household expenditure, learning from her highly successful husband. They were a vital and busy team of two, probably very good company and actively ambitious.

Bess's first diffident entries in her household accounts expand as she departs from the strict household items to other areas of their lives such as 'paid for information of the Court'.* This is the first instance of Bess paying for intelligence gathering, obviously instigated by Sir William, but it was a practice that she would continue for the remainder of her life. In old age she rarely visited London, but she always made sure she was kept informed of the latest events and Court gossip.

Surviving documents in the Public Record Office also detail occasional instances in the lives of the Cavendishes when things did not go to plan, such as when Sir William attempted to enclose a piece of common land at Northaw to increase his own landholdings. This was a despicable practice followed by many large landowners, which caused untold hardship to the rural poor. In this case the villagers at Northaw fought back; several of them attacked Sir William's surveyor and Sir William took the ringleaders to court. It is heartening to note that although the accused men – William Curle and John Burley – were fined for affray while attempting to protect what they considered to be ancient common grazing lands, on this occasion, at least, the proposed enclosure did

---

*It was not unusual for a sixteenth-century chatelaine to keep household accounts, but few of those which survive are as detailed as Bess's. Doubtless this was due to Sir William's early influence.

not go ahead.[8] But there was still a bill to be paid: 'To my husband's attorney of the starred chamber,* 23 shillings and four pence.' Bess was essentially a pragmatist; whatever happened to her throughout her life, she learned from and built on the experience, never making the same mistake twice. Later she would enclose lands, and even move an entire village for architectural reasons, but she apparently managed it in a manner that did not cause local riots.

The accounts also reveal a more generous side of Sir William. He frequently ordered his wife to give small sums to the children of their servants, or tells her to buy things for members of her family or household: 'Given to my sister Winfield by my husband to buy her a carpet, twenty six shillings and eightpence† . . . Given to Cecily[9] at my husband's command to buy her a petticoat . . . Given to my aunt by my husband'. Sometimes she recorded amounts Sir William had given to beggars, 'given to a poor man' or 'Given at my husband's hand . . . to a man that had his house burned'.

Bess's household accounts show a good income from rents, but a fairly lavish housekeeping bill, too, with dozens of servants who were clearly necessary with two busy households to run. Bess's half-sister Jane Leche, who could have been no older than fifteen in 1548, came as a well-paid lady-in-waiting to Bess at a wage of fifteen shillings each quarter-day. As well as Sir William's secretaries and a major-domo in each establishment (James Crompe and Francis Whitfield), there were references such as 'my butler, Tamis', 'my footman' and 'my porter', a children's nurse, numerous indoor maidservants such as Nan Todd, Cecily, Nell, Johanna, Barbara, 'great Meg [Margaret

---

*The Star Chamber: named for the decoration on its ceiling, this was a court consisting of the King's Privy Counsellors and senior judges. It tried cases of perversions of justice and public order offences, as well as private suits.

†This could be either her eldest sister, Mary, or her half-sister Elizabeth, both of whom married into the Wingfield family.

Crane] and Little Meg', a cook and kitchen staff. There were outside
staff: '. . . the horse keeper . . . the stable boy' and people 'who
wrought in the garden' at Northaw, or 'heaved coal'.

There were several general menservants who carried out regular
commissions, and the names of two of them, Greves and Shawe, are
familiar. Either they or their fathers were among the yeomen who testified on behalf of Mistress Hardwyck at the Inquisition Post Mortem
of Bess's father. This suggests that when Bess married Sir William she
took with her a number of servants who were well known to her
from Derbyshire, probably from her mother's household. In addition
to full-time employees, Bess engaged people from outside, such as a
male embroiderer whose name was 'Angell' (possibly a European
weaver), who often came in to help Bess with large household
embroidery projects or delicate sewing tasks. There were regular,
almost annual, payments to a midwife, and also frequent references
to 'my nurse', who was more than likely a wet-nurse since Bess also
made regular payments to 'the woman who hath my nurse's boy'.

Bess was an indulgent and even affectionate stepmother, and
referred to William's daughters as 'my daughter Cateryn' and 'my
daughter Anne'.* There is no mention of their sister, ten-year-old
Mary, ever being at Northaw, although her name appears regularly in
the accounts each month: 'Given to the woman that hath Mary, ten
shillings' and 'paid for Mary's board, eleven shillings and threepence,'
and occasionally, 'laid out for Mary – twenty five shillings.'[10] These
sums are significant amounts of money for the time and there must
have been some good reason why Mary did not reside with her siblings among her father's new family. Children who were physically or
mentally abnormal were customarily given into outside care and it
seems very likely that this is why Mary is boarded out. The child is
not out of Bess's thoughts, however, for there are other entries: 'Given
to Halle for Mary, the rest of the money that was promised him for

---

*The names Cateryn and Anne as written by Bess are actually Katheryne and Ann
according to their father's journals, so I have used the latter throughout, except
when quoted.

her; fifty three shillings and four pence.' And the following entry: 'For a pretty coat for her; two shillings and sixpence.' Mary missed out on the more lavish wardrobe of the children at Northaw, however:

Item: For my daughter Anne:

A nightingale	4/4d
An ell of cloth to make her sleeves	3/4d
Girdles; red, white and yellow	1/6d
An ounce of satin silk to work it all	2/–
Half an ell of cambric	2/6d
An ounce of lace for her kirtles and her laces	1/4d*

'My daughter Cateryn' and 'my daughter Francys' are similarly treated with purchases of silks and satins for their clothes, and there are other entries which hint at how the girls were dressed: 'a neat waistcoat . . . a red mantle . . . two neat caps . . .' and in the case of the baby Frances, 'a coral for her teeth'.[11] The children were the obvious recipients of the frequent purchases of 'sugar candy' and they were often given pocket money: five shillings at Christmas.

Sir William was a pampered husband by these accounts (although Tudor husbands had a high expectation of wifely duty). Bess purchased his shoes and hose, made his shirts ('for 20 ells of cloth at two shillings the yard, to make shirts for my husband'), made, trimmed and embroidered his doublets, arranged for the skinner to line his jerkins with fur and make his 'buskins'. These buskins were soft leather knee-high boots, necessary on long rides between assignments since everyday woollen hose provided little protection to the legs from the chafe of stirrup leathers. The contents of a drink she prepared for him on a number of occasions – 'for ginger, sugar candy, aniseed and liquorice to make a [posset]

---

*The amounts shown refer to shillings and pence, i.e. 1/6d is one shilling and six pence.

for my husband' – suggest that he suffered from stomach problems, perhaps a gastric ulcer diagnosed by 'my Lord Chancellor's physician' to whom a fee of five shillings was paid for a consultation.

Almost dominating the first account book are the number of entries for materials to make and decorate clothes. Clothes for her stepdaughters – 'given for six yards and a half of satin, for a gown for "Cate"' (Katheryne), who was fourteen and almost a woman (a further five yards of cotton was bought to line the satin gown) – clothes for her husband, but also for herself.

The lifestyle led by the Cavendishes required a rich wardrobe, and it is hardly surprising that Bess's household books are full of the purchase of materials for gowns, ruffs and sleeves, and fashionable trimmings and accoutrements. She obviously delighted in the purchases of jewellery and fine things: 'given to the woman who makes silk hosen . . . paid to Master Dupont for a pearl . . . for four ounces of silver [thread] to edge my sleeves and make my purse . . . Paid to Reynes the goldsmith for my buttons; seven pounds, seven shillings and six pence.' She purchased the best linens, velvets, satins, silks and lace and to decorate her clothes she frequently spent money on 'bone work', bands of material encrusted with embroidery of black silk, or silver and gold wire or thread. In all the portraits we have of her she dresses with elegance and restraint but always luxuriously. One of her favourite gowns was 'mole coloured satin'; it was important both to Bess and her husband that she looked and dressed as befitted her station.

In the earliest surviving image of Bess, painted in about 1560, she wears a fashionable loose-bodied black velvet gown with a high neck. It is a sumptuous garment indicating her rank and importance, and is clearly designed for winter wear. Trimmed with self-coloured bands of bone work, it has a collar of creamy mink. The short puffed sleeves are slashed to reveal that the gown is also lined with this costly fur, and the entire garment is decorated on the front, sleeves and sides with numerous pairs of intricately engraved gold aiglets,* which also act as decorative fastenings. In two portraits of Lady Jane Grey, the sitter wears an almost identical gown to the one worn by Bess in this portrait, except that the fur in the Jane Grey portrait is ermine, which only members of the Royal family and senior aristocracy ('dukes, earls . . . and persons of distinction'), were permitted to wear.†

On her hands and arms Bess wears two gold and enamel bracelets of a popular contemporary design, and four gold dress rings. She wore pearls in all her portraits, and as they are mentioned on a number of occasions in her accounts, and in various inventories, it appears she was especially fond of them. In this portrait she wears them over the standing collar of her bodice as a choker, and two rows of black pearls decorate her small, elaborately wrought, wired 'French hood' headdress of dark red and gold. The fine red embroidery on the sleeves and small ruffed collar of the light-coloured bodice or kirtle is almost certainly her own work. Those long, slim, beringed fingers with their well-shaped and manicured nails were constantly employed at the fine needlework at which she excelled. In common with most chatelaines of her day this would have included helping to make her own household linen: 'paid for cloth that I bought to make a pair of sheets at three shillings an ell, and in the whole 18 ells'.

In the late spring of 1549, twenty-one-year-old Bess was at Northaw awaiting the birth of her second child. Her half-sister Jane was with her, and the two sisters were subsequently joined by their aunt, Marcella Linnacre, who brought with her some luxuries purchased in London. Later, Bess's elder sister Mary also came to stay, and Bess's mother sent gifts of capons and brawn from Derbyshire by the hand of her manservant, Harry, to

---

*Aiglets, sometimes 'aglets', were decorative metal tags at the ends of laces, often engraved gold or silver, and used in place of buttons.
†This style seems to have been worn by several members of the Grey family. There are also portraits of Queen Mary and the Princess Elizabeth wearing similar dresses.

encourage Bess to build up her strength. In the days immediately before and after the birth, a midwife and a nurse were in attendance and the ladies passed their time embroidering new bedlinen for the use of Jane Dudley, 'my Lady Warwick',[12] who had agreed to be a godmother and would stay at Northaw for the christening.[13]

On 10 June a second daughter was born to Bess at 2 in the morning.[14] She was named Temperance, in honour of the Lady Elizabeth (Temperance being the nickname wryly bestowed upon his youngest half-sister by the young King). As well as the Countess of Warwick, Lady Jane Grey stood as a godmother, while the Earl of Shrewsbury[15] was godfather. One can almost plot the fortunes of contemporary Tudor aristocracy by Sir William's choice of godparents for his children. The godfather, Francis, Earl of Shrewsbury, a Privy Counsellor and Earl Marshal of England, continues an unexplained link between the powerful Shrewsbury family and Bess's late father, for John Hardwick named the Earl in his will as one of two 'supervisors' of his estate.

Nor was the choice of godmothers accidental. Since the previous year, the Seymours had fallen from power. In January 1549 the recently widowed Lord Admiral had been arrested on the orders of his brother the Protector and imprisoned in the Tower. The charges were various but one of them was the Lord Admiral's unseemly behaviour towards his quasi-stepdaughter,* the Lady Elizabeth. And following Queen Catherine's death in childbirth, he had tried to persuade the Privy Council to agree to his marriage with the princess.

At the same time he had sent word to Henry Grey (through his gentleman usher, John Harington), that he could arrange a marriage between the Lady Jane Grey and the boy king. Upon this

---

*There was no blood tie. Elizabeth lived for a while with her stepmother Queen Catherine Parr, who married the Lord Admiral soon after Henry VIII's death.

vague assurance, and in return for a deposit of cash against the eventual sum of £2000, Jane Grey became the Admiral's ward and was sent to live at Sudeley, where the Admiral had retained his late wife's attendants to wait upon Jane.[16] These obvious machinations did not go unnoticed by his brother the Protector, or the Privy Council, and the Lord Admiral was arrested for 'disloyal practices' after he made a bungled attempt to kidnap the King which resulted in the death of the boy's pet dog.

The Lord Admiral was a popular man, but the gossip surging around the city after his arrest (possibly 'spin', spread deliberately) was so widespread and damaging that Princess Elizabeth herself was in danger of arrest. She wrote to the Protector, demanding that the Privy Council repudiate the rumour that she was in the Tower and pregnant by the Lord Admiral. Had she been entirely innocent, as she claimed, it was a natural thing for her to have done. 'This City of London,' wrote a contemporary, 'is a whirlpool and a sink of evil rumours where they be bred and from thence spread out into all parts of this realm.'[17] However, Elizabeth's servants Kat Ashley and Thomas Parry were arrested and confirmed, under intense questioning and threats of torture,* that there had been a few unladylike romps. Fortunately the inquisitors were unable to prove that matters had gone any further than some kisses, and slap and tickle, between the infatuated Princess and her so-called stepfather, and Mistress Ashley revealed that such incidents had been initially condoned by Queen Catherine, who regarded them as innocent fun until she discovered her husband and stepdaughter locked in a passionate embrace, when the Queen 'fell out' with them both and Elizabeth was asked to leave.[18]

Elizabeth only just managed to survive this scandal; the Lord Admiral, friend to the Cavendishes, did not. Found guilty of high

---

*Thumbscrews were placed on the table at which Thomas Parry was questioned. The implied threat was sufficient to make him talk.

treason he was beheaded on 20 March 1549. Elizabeth's reaction was cool and does not reflect either the infatuation she appears to have felt for the man or the danger she knew herself to have been in. When news of Seymour's execution was brought to her, Elizabeth told a friend, 'this day died a man of much wit, and very little judgement.'[19]

The Lord Admiral's death provoked a period of unrest and general dissatisfaction with the Protector, who grew more unpopular by the day, and a man in Sir William's position needed to be in London keeping watch on current events. So it is not surprising that immediately after Bess had been churched, the couple removed to Newgate Street, leaving Marcella Linnacre and Jane Leche in charge of the babies at Northaw: 'Delivered to my Aunt Linnacre,' Sir William noted, 'when my wife and I went to London after the christening; ten shillings.'

The execution of his brother would ultimately lead to the downfall of the Lord Protector. In October that year, after mishandling rebellions in Norfolk and the West Country, he was ousted from power and the Protectorate was abolished. After a spell in the Tower, Seymour (who now went by the title Duke of Somerset),* was released, and he again took his place as a Privy Counsellor. Immediately he attempted to regain his previous power, and this led to his rearrest. The man who would eventually replace Seymour as Lord Protector of the boy king was John Dudley, the Earl of Warwick. Initially, though, Dudley was content with the presidency of the Council. Henry Grey, who correctly read the signs, had already taken the precaution of attaching himself to Dudley a year earlier, and the two had been fast friends for some time before Dudley became the most powerful man in England. Moving in Henry Grey's circle, Sir William Cavendish's choice of 'my lady

---

*Edward Seymour built the breathtaking Somerset House as his London home with stones from the charnel house of St Paul's, which he destroyed for this purpose.

Warwick' as first godmother to Temperance, indicates that he, too, was reading the signs and thinking ahead.

That winter the Cavendishes bought a house and some land in Derbyshire. Although they could not have known it at the time, the purchase was to be a life-changing event, and the property concerned would be inextricably linked with the Cavendish name down through the centuries to the present day. The property was at Chatsworth and Bess would have been familiar with it: after all she had grown up within a few hours' ride of it, and the family of her stepfather, Ralph Leche, lived there. It would be remarkable if she had not visited the nearby home of such close relatives. Bess's younger sister Alice Hardwick had also married into the same family, Francis Leche, a nephew of Ralph, and here it is necessary to backtrack somewhat.

Two years earlier, in 1547, Francis Leche had discovered that his wife Alice had been unfaithful to him. It caused a local scandal and he was not a man to wear lightly the horns of a cuckold. In the heat of the discovery he offered the old family property to Thomas Agarde, a friend of the Lord Admiral's, for £700, 'rather than let bastards be his heirs'.[20] The Leche family, including Ralph Leche, who owned some property at Beeley which marched with the Chatsworth land, were aghast when they discovered what Francis had done and clamoured for the bargain to be rescinded. With his temper cooling, Francis realised that he had acted rashly and told Agarde that he had changed his mind, but Agarde refused to back down: a bargain was a bargain, and the law was on his side. Knowing that Agarde had the protection of the Lord Admiral, Francis Leche presented his case to a higher force, the Lord Protector, begging him to intervene so that the property might not be removed from his family.

Having expressed polite distaste at the 'lewd' behaviour of Mistress Alice Leche, and 'without searching the private life of those before us', the Lord Protector ruled in favour of the Leche family. 'Agarde,' he wrote to his brother who had pleaded Agarde's

case, 'has abused you by not declaring his case truly, and if he does
not immediately accomplish our order he shall know the price. We
find that the bargain made by Leche should not disinherit the succession to that land, so as all parties should attain their own.'[21] This
statement, 'he shall know the price', was not a threat to be ignored
coming from such a source, and the unfortunate Agarde now had
on his hands a 'damaged' freehold. Having paid for the property, he
undoubtedly owned it, but this apparently would not protect him
from future claims by members of the Leche family. In the middle
of this matter he died, and it is small wonder that his son and heir,
Francis Agarde, decided to sell Chatsworth back to a member of
the Leche family for whatever he could get.

There are a number of demonstrable occasions in Bess's life
when her mother wrote to tell her of a property for sale at a bargain price,[22] and perhaps this is how Bess got to hear about
Chatsworth. Or perhaps their good friend the late Lord Admiral
had mentioned it to them when he realised that some of the protagonists in the squabble were relatives of Lady Cavendish. In
whatever way they heard of it, on 31 December 1550, 'Sir William
and Dame Elizabeth* Cavendish' purchased the property from
Francis Agarde at the knockdown price of £600.[23] The estate
included 'the manors of Chatsworth and Cromford, and houses
and land there, and in Calton, Edensor, Pilsley, Birchills, Bakewell,
Baslow, Totley, Tideswell, Litton, Dore, Wheston, Abney,
Chesterfield, Beeley, Matlock, Bonsall and Repton'.[24]

The purchase may have been simply a chance one: Sir William
taking advantage of an obvious bargain. But it would have been
absolutely characteristic of Sir William Cavendish to move his assets
and his family further away from London during what promised to be
troubled times should anything happen to the delicate young king.
First in line to the throne was Princess Mary, Roman Catholic and in

---

*Bess is referred to in the deed as Dame Elizabeth, a courtesy title used for all upper-
class women.

close touch with the Pope, who – if she succeeded to the throne – was expected to attempt to return ownership of former Church properties. This was always going to be difficult to achieve, since the buyers of the great tranches of Church lands, comprising almost 30 per cent of all the land in England, had included most of the great families. But it appears Sir William was unwilling to take this chance: almost immediately he began to dispose of the former Church properties he had acquired during the Dissolution, and to buy others. That some of the new acquisitions were also former Church properties did not seem to matter. Probably he wanted to establish a chain of secular buying and selling, in which there could be no doubt of his legal ownership.

There was another consideration: Mary's succession might not go unchallenged. A fervent Protestant faction, headed by John Dudley and Henry Grey, planned to install a Protestant monarch. Given his close connections with Grey, these ambitions may have been known to Sir William, or at the very least he probably suspected what might happen. In the event of the death of Edward VI there was a possibility of civil war with its epicentre in London, only a few hours' ride from Northaw.

It was at just about this time that Bess's baby daughter, Temperance, died. There are few precise dates in the earliest account book, except the quarter-days when rents were received and wages were due, but the child probably died in January or February of 1550 when she would have been six or seven months old. There is no mention of Temperance between December 1549 and the following Lady Day (25 March). She had evidently been ill for some weeks, for there are several payments given to a nurse who was caring for the child after Michaelmas (10 October) in 1549,* and some time later, in about December, there are two successive undated entries which read: 'Given to Bestenay's nurse [Bestenay was Sir William's clerk/secretary]; twelve pence', and 'given when Temperance was sick, five shillings'. Five shillings indicates some serious nursing, or a fee to a senior consultant.

*After the calendar change in 1752, Michaelmas is always celebrated on 29 September.

Because of the high mortality rates, Tudor mothers may have been prepared, to a certain degree, for the possible deaths of their children. Nevertheless, the loss of her second baby would have been a cause of great sorrow to the young mother. We know from letters at a later date, which will be detailed in following chapters, that Bess was an emotional woman. She cried easily when upset, for instance on hearing of the deaths of distant relatives and friends, and even when she heard that a friend was in trouble. And it is noticeable that for several months that summer, many of the household accounts are written in Sir William's hand instead of that of Bess.

She became pregnant again almost immediately, and there was some consolation before the year was out when she gave birth to a healthy son. Sir William wrote: 'Henry, my 11th child, and the third by the same woman, was borne of Tuesday at 12 of the clock at night . . . the 17th day of December [1550] . . .'. The entry is followed by the familiar roll call of famous godparents. Henry Grey (Lord Dorset) and John Dudley (Lord Warwick), arguably now the two most powerful men in the land, stood as godfathers to the child. Equally noticeable is the godmother: the seventeen-year-old Princess Elizabeth, a figurehead for supporters of the Reformed Church. At that time no one could have foreseen the great role that history intended for the daughter of Anne Boleyn, but the lateral working of Sir William's mind is clear to see.

Bess's entries in her household accounts book reveal none of the political turmoil of the time, and are of a strictly practical nature. The costs of her previous lyings-in had amounted to no more than thirteen shillings and fourpence. For Henry's birth she records, in addition to the above, the huge fee of twenty shillings to a Master Mayle, who was probably a surgeon, for he was present when Bess gave birth to 'my boye'. There had been no such entries when Frances and Temperance were born; it is possible that the birth of Temperance had been difficult, and that the Cavendishes were taking no chances this time. Bess also rewarded the nurse with ten shillings and the midwife with three shillings and fourpence. Soon afterwards the Cavendishes put their servants into what came to be known as 'Cavendish blue' livery, to demonstrate the high status of their household.

Bess's mother was widowed again in the autumn of 1550, and in the summer of 1551 she found it necessary to take her son-in-law, Sir William Cavendish, to court on the grounds that some lands 'in Beeley, held of the manor of Chatsworth' which he had acquired, had belonged to her late husband, and were now hers.[25] This, of course, is precisely why Francis Agarde had disposed of the property so precipitately. Still, it seems strange, given the good relationship that existed between Bess and her mother (Elizabeth Leche was a regular visitor to the Cavendish house in London), that legal action was required. Probably it was necessary in order to establish a formal claim, because the boundaries were not precisely drawn up in the deeds.[26]

That summer there were several important changes within their social circle. The sixteen-year-old Duke of Suffolk, Henry Brandon, who had been godfather to little Frances Cavendish, was studying at St John's College in Cambridge with his younger brother Charles when sweating sickness (a virulent form of influenza) broke out. Both boys were hastily removed to the Bishop of Lincoln's palace in Huntingdonshire, but they contracted the infection anyway. Both died on the same day in July, and Charles, who survived his elder brother for only an hour, died the holder of the title.[27] With their deaths the male line of the Brandons died out.[28] The King gave his permission for the title to pass through the female line and on 11 October at Hampton Court Lord and Lady Grey became the Duke and Duchess of Suffolk. At the same time the new Lord Protector, John Dudley, Earl of Warwick, was created Duke of Northumberland.

Although expecting the birth of her fourth child imminently, Bess celebrated Christmas as usual, and among her other household purchases she bought presents, for example a needlecase and a silver thimble at 'twenty pence the piece' and a pair of gloves 'at seven shillings the pair' for her stepdaughter Katheryne.[29] At between two and three o'clock in the morning on 27 December, almost a year to the week of Henry's birth, Bess gave birth to another son, William. Her mother had come to stay with her in the previous month so there were clearly no hard feelings between them over the court case. The baby appears to have had some problem taking his feed, so a Doctor Bartlett was called in on the following day. He diagnosed that the baby had 'a fallen palate' and was paid a fee of three shillings 'for his counsel'. A similar sum was paid to a surgeon named Gorter for advice about the same problem. This time the godparents were Elizabeth, 'my lady Marquess of Northampton',* William Paulett, Earl of Winchester, who was the Lord Treasurer, and William Herbert, Earl of Pembroke.[30]

Bess was still lying-in when the former Protector, Edward Seymour, was executed on 22 January 1552. Henry Grey was one of the judges at the prisoner's trial, and was the supervisor at the execution. We have no way of knowing how Bess reacted to the violent deaths of these people whom she knew so well. It must have made life feel very uncertain, but perhaps, too, it was exciting, then as now, to be young and rich, and involved at the very heart of things.

According to her account books, Bess was again unwell on 2 February when an entry in another hand recorded that a pint of Malmsey (a sweet wine from the Mediterranean) was purchased 'when my lady was sick', but it could not have been very serious, for her friend Lady Port came to dinner the same day.† By mid-

---

*Elizabeth Brook, daughter of Lord Cobham. She married William Parr, Marquess of Northampton, who was brother to Queen Catherine Parr. The Northamptons owned the house in Newgate Street which the Cavendishes rented.
†Lady Port was a member of the Fitzherbert family of Tissington in Derbyshire, and was already a considerable heiress when she married John Port (later Sir John, mayor of Derby) who was brother-in-law to the Earl of Huntington, and also a friend of the Cavendishes.

April Bess was well enough to visit the Court at Whitehall, travelling there by boat, which seems to have been her preferred method of travel in and around London. The Cavendishes' social circle now included other big names: the Pembrokes, the Cobhams and Sir Andrew and Lady Baynton, all of whom would eventually become related through marriages to the Cavendish children.

Throughout his wife's pregnancies during 1550 and 1551, Sir William continued making ambitious plans for the future. In May 1550 he began selling off a few small pieces of land in the south, and he bought the Manor of Ashford in Derbyshire together with 8000 acres of land (borrowing money to do so). On 6 December 1551 he paid Roger Worde, a master mason,* twenty shillings to design him a fine new house at Chatsworth.[31] There was already a 'respectable mansion'[32] there, the former home of the Leche family, and indeed for some years the Cavendishes would live in this original building while their palatial new home was being built nearby.

All that year Sir William steadily shipped furniture and household items from London to Chatsworth: 'all manner of ironwork that pertayneth to two portals sent to Chattsworth by old Alsop [a carrier from Derby]'. Alsop was also paid for conveying a barrel of Rhenish wine, and thirty dozen candles in four baskets, from London to Chatsworth. And on 3 January 1552 an entry in the accounts shows that 'John the waggoner' (Sir William's own servant, not a carrier) was given three shillings and threepence after he took a full cartload from London to Chatsworth. It was not only household items that Sir William shipped to Derbyshire; he and Bess were as keen on the pastimes of hunting and hawking as were their friends: 'paid to Mr Richard Starkey of little St Bartholemew's by Smithfield, for a Gosse Hawk, by my master's commandment,'

---

*There were no 'architects' per se at this time. Owners chose piecemeal from books of plans called 'pattern books', mostly produced in France and Holland, and these basic designs were altered by the owner, and the masons, as required.

wrote Sir William's clerk, 'three pounds, seven shillings and eightpence.'

The existence of two healthy sons undoubtedly helped to spur Sir William's aspirations. Now he turned his attention to other lands that marched with his Derbyshire property, and he was ideally placed to research properties owned by the Crown that were suitable for his scheme. We know that Sir William was liked and trusted by the King, and perhaps he also used his friendship with Henry Grey, who had now become a very important man indeed, to further his ambitious plan to create a vast family estate in Derbyshire.

In every biography of Bess or the Cavendish family Bess is credited with being the instigator of the purchase of Chatsworth, though in fact no documentary evidence exists to support this supposition. It is a reasonable conjecture; Derbyshire was not, after all, a county with which Sir William could have been overly familiar, despite several visits to the county to close down a monastery or two. It was a four- or five-day trip, in good weather, from London, but a longer journey on muddy highways and packhorse trails in the winter months. The land was good for sheep grazing (the woollen industry was of great importance in England), and there were some mines, but not a lot besides.

If there is one characteristic that becomes blindingly obvious when researching Sir William Cavendish, it is that this man did little by accident. He was careful, hardworking and extremely perspicacious. In this instance, however, he must surely have taken some advice from his young wife (Bess was still only twenty-two to his forty-four years) who had local knowledge. Sir William was too smart to have overlooked such an obvious and trusted source of information. But it would have been out of character for Sir William to be badgered into a decision, even by the formidably strong woman that Bess was to become in later life.

Sir William visited Chatsworth several times in 1552 and, indeed, the only surviving letter between him and Bess was written

from there. It is a businesslike postscript to other letters he had
written, which have not survived.

Good Bess,

Having forgotten to write in my letters that you should pay
Otewell Alayne eight pounds for certain oats that we have
bought of him, over and above 40 shillings that I have paid to
him in hand, I heartily pray you, for that he is desirous to receive
the rest at London, to pay him on sight hereof. You know my
store and therefore I have appointed him to have it at your hand,
And thus fare you well. From Chatsworth the XIIIth of April.

All yours, as most worthy, W. C.

The tone of this letter should not be taken as entirely descriptive
of their relationship, however, for earlier that year we know that
Sir William had commissioned a beautiful and costly gift for Bess.
It is mentioned as an expense in his accounts, but in an inventory
of Bess's jewels it is described in detail as 'one book of gold with
ten rubies, 3 [other gemstones] and one diamond, with two pictures in the same.'[33] The portraits inside were of Sir William and
Bess.

The fact that he had sent previous letters from Derbyshire suggests his visit there lasted some weeks. Earlier that month the King
had become ill with measles and smallpox, and the Parliament
which had sat from the start of Edward's reign was dissolved.
Although the King made a recovery by mid-May, the smallpox
remained active in London throughout the summer. Probably it
was this cessation of Court duties that allowed Sir William the
time to pay an extended visit to his new property.

Letters to London would have taken about a week by carrier, for
although the highway from London to Nottingham and Derby was
reasonably well travelled, Chatsworth lay in the heart of the peakland, beyond a vast moor traversed only by packhorse trails. The
writer Daniel Defoe would complain while crossing this moor

nearly two hundred years later, that its 'fifteen or sixteen miles together . . . presents you with neither hedge, house or tree, but a waste and howling wilderness, over which, when strangers travel, they are obliged to take guides, or it would be next to impossible not to lose their way.'[34] Not only strangers lost their way. The local parish registers record the deaths of many local men who went missing on the moor and perished from starvation or hypothermia, or both. John Taylor, the water poet, recorded that even with a guide, 'the ways were so rocky, stony, boggy and mountainous, that it was a day's journey to ride so short a way.' Even 250 years later, in 1809, William Hutchinson warned travellers that, 'the road is extremely dangerous . . . One false step would bring destruction to horse and rider. After a tedious passage . . . we attained the summit of the moor . . . the descent was down a dreadful steep pass, nearly two hundred feet perpendicular. The traveller should be extremely careful, and if his horse gets forward at one mile an hour this is good work'.[35]

Chatsworth in Derbyshire was indeed a long way from Northaw in the gentle woodlands of south Hertfordshire, and not only in distance.

CHAPTER 5

DANGEROUS TIMES

1552–6

WHEN THEY EMBARKED UPON THE AMBITIOUS PROGRAMME of building a great house at Chatsworth, Sir William and Bess probably did not envisage that it would take thirty years to complete. Fortunately, although it no longer exists, there are a number of surviving records which enable us to visualise their new house, including a contemporary oil painting,[1] and a small tapestry picture of it, which is likely to have been worked by Bess.[2]

Set above and parallel to the flood plain of the River Derwent, the new house occupied exactly the same site as that of the main block of the present building. It was already a dated design when it was built, its turrets and battlements giving it the distinct air of a medieval fortress. In counties nearer London new manor houses were beginning to move away from designs that made them look like strongholds in favour of more elegant European renaissance designs.[3] Nevertheless, Bess's Chatsworth had reasonable claims to being the first real 'country house' built in the north of England. Originally two storeys high (Bess would later add another floor consisting of State rooms and a long gallery), and one room thick, it was built of stone from local quarries around a central courtyard.

It had diamond-paned leaded windows and decorative round 'span-dells' over the main entrance depicting the arms of the Hardwick and Cavendish families, as well as carved lion masks. The newness of the building was softened by its perfect setting in a hunting park in a sheltered valley through which the fast-flowing river Derwent rushed, to which Bess gradually added pleasure gardens, orchards and terraces, fish pools and fountains, gazebos and an entrance lodge. The steep hillside behind the house, today clothed in wood-lands, was then bare.

At Greenwich, on 20 June 1552, Sir William Cavendish achieved what he had evidently been planning for a year or more, and prob-ably working out in greater detail during his trips to Chatsworth. He gave all his properties and lands, except those in Derbyshire, to the King. In exchange he received a massive tranche of lands, houses and cottages (including 'villains and natives'), mines and quarries, the bulk of which were situated in Derbyshire. But also included in what was effectively a 'swap' were properties and lands in other counties: Surrey, Nottinghamshire, Leicestershire, Staffordshire, Lincolnshire, Kent, Essex, Dorset, Cornwall, Herefordshire and Northumberland.

The document covering this transfer details the lands he owned before the exchange:

> ... the capital mansion of the Lordship, manor and rectory of Northawe ... and lands in Northawe and Cuffley Herts, the manor of Birhehold, Herts and lands in Chesthunt, Herts. The site of the late priory, cell or rectory of Cardigan, and lands in Tallyngton, Fulbecke, Beckington, Northeraunceby and Calthorpe Lincs, and in Barnaby next Newarke Notts, the manor of Fernefeldes and Harringay and the rectory of Sowermyms, Middlesex, and other lands.[4]

To facilitate a favourable outcome, Sir William sent the Crown surveyors a handsome food hamper while they were at Northaw making their valuation. And those acting on behalf of the King in this transaction must have regarded Sir William's properties highly, for a close-typeset transcript of the list of lands which he received in exchange runs to five A4 pages, and seems today to be an unequal bargain very much in Sir William's favour. Noting that all the properties mentioned were given to 'the said William Cavendish, his heirs and assigns', the document ends that the exchange is 'without fine or fee'.[5] It was a phenomenal bargain and surely a tribute to Sir William's acumen and negotiating skills.

The Cavendishes wasted no time in moving their family and chattels north. Bess spent a good deal of the year 1552 in London, but by that autumn her entire household had been transferred from Northaw to Chatsworth. Aunt Marcella Linnacre and Bess's half-sister Jane (formerly Jane Leche and now Mrs Thomas Kniveton) were living there with the Cavendish children in November, when, following a visit to London by Aunt Linnacre, Bess had cause to reprimand her steward, Francis Whitfield. Having first warned him not to hinder or inconvenience the newly appointed carpenter, Master Neusante, while he was working, she goes on to say:

I pray you, look well to all things at Chatsworth till my Aunt's coming home, which I hope will be shortly. And in the meantime . . . let the brewer make beer forthwith, for my own drinking and your master.* And see that I have a good store of it, for if I lack either good beer or charcoal or wood, I will blame nobody so much as I will do you.

---

*This order by Bess to ensure a good supply of beer sounds decadent by today's standards. But a home brew of light beer, called 'small beer', was the standard drink for light refreshment in all homes. In making this demand Bess was foreshadowing Queen Elizabeth, who on one of her progresses flew into a tremendous rage because there was no 'light' beer available for her to drink, only a more full-bodied type – equivalent to today's real ale. Any Tudor traveller, without knowing the source of local water, was very wise to stick to beer.

That her household was installed in the old manor of the Leche family, rather than the new building, is obvious from the instructions she gives Francis for reparations: 'Cause the floor in my bedchamber to be made even, either with plaster, clay or lime, and all the windows where the glass is broken to be mended. And all the chambers to be made as close and warm as you can.' It sounds as though Aunt Linnacre may have unburdened herself of a few complaints during her visit to London:

> . . . I hear that my sister Jane[6] cannot have things that are needful for her to have amongst you. If it be true, you lack a great deal of honesty, as well as discretion, to deny her anything she hath a mind to, being in case as she has been. I would be loathe to have a stranger so used in my house. And then assure yourself that I cannot like it, to have my sister so used. Like as I would not have an superfluity or waste of anything, so likewise would I have her to have that which is needful and necessary. At my coming home I shall know more, and then I will think as I shall have cause.

She goes on to authorise him to make payments to her nurse and her midwife, as gifts from herself and her boy 'Willie' (now aged eleven months).

> . . . In total you give them twenty-three shillings and four pence. Make my sister Jane privy of it, and then pay it to them forthwith . . . tell my sister Jane that I will give my daughter something on coming home. And praying you not to fail to see all things done accordingly, I bid you farewell from London on the 14th November. Your mistress, Elizabeth Cavendish.

The payments to the midwife, the same reward given at the births of Bess's children, suggest that perhaps Jane had given birth during this period, probably to her daughter Mary. Why else would a midwife be on hand when baby William was eleven months old, for Bess herself had no child in 1552? This would explain Bess's annoyance that her sister had been denied something she needed, 'being in the case as she has been'.

Despite her threat, Bess did not return to Chatsworth for some months, and their housekeeping bill in London that winter and spring was especially high, for they entertained a good deal. Bess's mother came to stay with them, as did her brother James, together with a Derbyshire friend and neighbour, Sir James Folijambe. Her elder sister Jane, and Jane's husband Godfrey Bosville (who had benignly held the wardship of Robert Barlow) came from Yorkshire to stay on a number of occasions. Meanwhile there was constant intercourse between the Cavendishes and the Grey family who now lived at their London mansion in Suffolk Place, and the Parrs – Lord and Lady Northampton – the latter being baby William's godmother.

In February 1553 the King became unwell, and as the weeks went on it must have been acutely obvious to Sir William as he went about his daily tasks at Whitehall that the boy had not long to live. He was in fact suffering from acute pulmonary tuberculosis, for which there was no cure in the sixteenth century. Firmly in the camp of Henry Grey (Duke of Suffolk) and John Dudley (Duke of Northumberland), it is more than possible that Sir William knew of, and was even part of, in some way, the plans of these two powerful men to avert the course of Henry VIII's Act of Succession, under which the throne would pass to Princess Mary. Capitalising on the boy king's obsession that the Reformation must progress, Dudley used his position as Protector, and the affection that the King had for the whole Dudley family, to encourage Edward to draw up a new 'Device' for the succession to the throne. This document overturned his father's instructions and bypassed both Mary and Elizabeth in favour of his cousin, Jane Grey, 'and her heirs male'. It was unconstitutional, but Dudley believed that with sufficient force he could make it work.

With this plan already under way, on Whit Sunday, 21 May 1553, Guildford Dudley, the fourth son of John, Duke of Northumberland, became the reluctant husband of the equally reluctant fifteen-year-old Lady Jane Grey who had been bullied by her parents into the marriage.[7]

It was a triple wedding, a major social event, celebrated at the Dudleys' riverside mansion in London, which was ringed by a large crowd of townsfolk anxious to watch the comings and goings of the great and the good. As well as the marriage of their son Guildford, the Dudleys' youngest daughter Catherine was betrothed to Lord Hastings (heir of the Duke of Huntingdon), and Katherine Grey was betrothed to Lord Herbert, son of the Earl of Pembroke. Almost all the parents of the bridal couples were godparents to one or other of the Cavendish children, and Sir William and Bess would unquestionably have been guests at this great dynastic ceremony.

In June, the dying King's Device for the Succession was presented to Privy Counsellors and leading judges, and was reluctantly passed, although not by unanimous decision. There was covert sympathy for Mary and her superior claim to the throne, even though she was a Catholic. But there was no overwhelming support for any of the women concerned, either in the Act of Succession or in the King's Device, for it was considered impossible for a woman to reign successfully. Unfortunately, apart from Edward VI, not only were all Henry VIII's surviving legitimate offspring female, but so were the surviving children of his two sisters.[8]

On 9 July, three days after the death of the King, Dudley (Duke of Northumberland) boldly proclaimed his daughter-in-law as queen, citing Edward VI's last wishes. Jane Grey no more wanted to take the throne than she had wanted to marry Guildford Dudley, but she had been conditioned throughout her life to submit to her bullying parents' wishes. In one thing only did she stand up to them and her father-in-law. Having been declared Queen, she steadfastly refused to proclaim her husband King.

While the Privy Council were dismayed about Dudley's rough-shod methods and his overturning of the Act of Succession, they found him a difficult man to oppose since he had control of the Tower and its guard. He also had control of the Navy, and in the countryside he appeared to have the support of many landowners who were responsible in times of crisis for mustering small armies, and who, it was assumed, preferred a Protestant heir. Had Dudley captured Princess Mary at the outset, and imprisoned her so that she was not a rallying point, his plan might well have succeeded. He was almost there, but he made that one mistake. Warned by friends, the Princess slipped away to the comparative safety of Norfolk, despite a frantic attempt by Dudley's twenty-year-old son, Robert,* to intercept her, in order to convey her 'to a place of safety'.

As soon as her half-brother's death was declared, Mary pro-claimed herself Queen, and the honest men of East Anglia, a stronghold of the old religion, rallied to her banner; not because she was especially popular but because she was seen as the rightful heir, as Sir Nicholas Throckmorton later wrote:

> And though I liked not the religion
> Which all her life Queen Mary had professed
> Yet in my mind that wicked notion,
> Right heirs for to displace, I did detest.[9]

For nine days England had two Queens: a Protestant one and a Catholic one. Although Sir William Cavendish had carefully main-tained a foot in each camp, there can be no question about which of these two queens he and Bess supported. Like the others in their circle, they stood to gain far more under Queen Jane, but it comes as no great surprise to find that they were not in London when Jane Grey was proclaimed Queen. On 24 June, twelve days after

---

*Later to become Earl of Leicester and the love of Queen Elizabeth's life.

the dying King presented his will to the Privy Counsellors, and fifteen days before the boy's death, Bess's household account book
came to an abrupt end although sufficient pages remained for further entries. The Cavendishes packed up and left London, removing
their entire household to Chatsworth. Bess was five months pregnant. This and the hot summer month ahead gave them sufficient
excuse for their departure. But no one knew better than Sir William
Cavendish that the next weeks were likely to prove difficult and
dangerous.

They watched from afar as the tragic events unfolded. Although
he failed in his attempt to persuade Queen Jane (for such she was
called for those few days) to declare her husband King, John
Dudley nevertheless forced the girl to write letters demanding support from the gentry and known dissenters, reminding them that
under 'ordinances as the late King did establish in his life time, for
the security and wealth of this realm, we are entered into our rightful possession of this Kingdom, as by the last Will of our said
dearest cousin . . .'.[10] He then led an army against Mary, who was
already marching south from Norfolk with her growing band of
supporters, to take possession of her throne.

A few days after he left London with his army, the Privy Council
– emboldened by his absence – declared against Jane Grey and for
Mary, and on 21 July Dudley was defeated and arrested near
Cambridge. Jane Grey and Guildford Dudley were also arrested
and imprisoned in the Tower. On 3 August Mary, by now accompanied by the Princess Elizabeth, was welcomed into London amid
huge celebrations and proclaimed Queen, and on 22 August, a
month after his arrest, John Dudley, the great Duke of
Northumberland, was executed for high treason. Henry Grey was
also arrested at his house at East Sheen and taken to the Tower.

Did Sir William Cavendish fear for his future as members of
the Grey and Dudley factions were rounded up? We do not
know. What we do know from the household accounts is that
while he was very much a member of the Protestant faction prior

to June 1553, he had also made regular visits to, and sent small gifts to Princess Mary over a period of some years. And he would later claim that he had mustered a fighting force of his own at Chatsworth to go to Mary's aid against John Dudley's army, at a personal cost of a thousand marks (£660).[11] This is highly improbable given that Dudley and Grey were among Sir William's closest friends. But he was a wily man, Sir William Cavendish; uncertain that the plan to crown Jane Grey would succeed, he ensured that he and his family were well out of harm's way when the worst happened.

Bess's fifth child was born in November. It was another boy, Charles. And it is surely a measure of the man that within a month of her coronation, Sir William had persuaded the new queen to be godmother to his latest child. All those visits and little gifts made while Mary was living in seclusion now paid off. The two godfathers were a curious mixture. Sir William had almost certainly known Bishop Stephen Gardiner from his days as a young usher in the service of Cardinal Wolsey. Gardiner had always been a great supporter of Mary (and her mother Catherine of Aragon), and he had spent years in prison during Edward's reign because he would not accept all the tenets of the reformed religion. As a result Mary trusted and respected Gardiner utterly, and one can see how Sir William's mind was working here. But the other godfather was none other than Henry Grey, so recently engaged in trying to supplant the Queen with his own daughter, and only just released from the Tower.

This christening raises several points. Since the Queen acted as godmother and Bishop Gardiner as godfather, the service was certain to have been a Catholic one. Sir William pragmatically adopted the attitude of the Vicar of Bray. Neither Sir William nor Bess were intellectuals; there was no agonising for them over the principles of their religious beliefs. The safety of their family and the position Sir William had made for himself were far more important to them than the shade of the Church in which they worshipped. After all, it was only twenty years earlier that they had all worshipped together under the old religion in the very same churches. Given a free choice they would prefer to be Protestants, but Sir William Cavendish and Bess were not made of the stuff of martyrs. The choice of Henry Grey as the second godfather, at that time, is less characteristic.

The christening occurred only two weeks after Lady Jane Grey and her husband Guildford Dudley had been tried and found guilty of high treason. After their trial these two hapless young people were returned to the Tower to await the Queen's pleasure, but, for the sake of her cousin Lady Frances, whom she had always liked, the Queen forgave Henry Grey his traitorous behaviour after Lady Frances pleaded on her knees for her husband's life. Lord Grey was released on payment of a huge fine and allowed to live quietly at one of his houses, at East Sheen near Richmond. Lady Frances, however, continued to live at Mary's Court where she was treated 'with much distinction', to the detriment, and immense irritation of Princess Elizabeth. The two younger Grey daughters, Katherine (her betrothal to the Earl of Pembroke's son was quickly annulled by Pembroke to distance himself from any connection with Henry Grey) and Mary, were maids of honour to the Queen. Curiously, there is no record of Lady Frances ever attempting to plead for clemency for her daughter Jane.[12]

Sir William Cavendish made a clear statement in choosing the out-of-favour Henry Grey as a godparent. It told the Greys that he had not gone over to 'the other side' or deserted them in a time of trouble. It was either the act of a loyal friend, or else Sir William was covering himself in case Henry Grey should ever recover his lost power-base. It gave Grey an opportunity to make a statement, too, by participating in a Catholic service.

This christening ceremony, with its distinguished guests (Sir William does not mention any proxies in his account), implies that Bess was confined in London. There are no surviving household books for this period to prove Bess's whereabouts, and no mention of Sir William in the Calendar of State Papers for that month either. We know from history that there was something akin to panic among parts of the populace when, at roughly the same time as the christening of baby Charles Cavendish took place, it became known that Mary was planning to marry Philip of Spain. Mary's honeymoon period with the people of London had been a brief one. There was great resentment at her immediate attempts to overturn the structure of the Reformed Church (even though this had been predicted), and in August, only weeks after being welcomed to London by jubilant throngs, Mary was surrounded by an extremely hostile mob after her chaplain preached a Catholic service at St Paul's Cross. When news spread of the proposed Spanish marriage, people went in real fear that a Spanish King would also mean the Spanish Inquisition, and there was an exodus of committed Protestants to Germany and the Low Countries.

During that winter of 1553–4 a senior courtier, Sir Thomas Wyatt, son of the famous poet who had been implicated in the trial of Anne Boleyn, hatched a plot to place Elizabeth on the throne and marry her to Edward Courtenay, a descendant of King Edward IV. Contemporary writers confirm the reaction to the threat of a Spaniard on the throne of England: 'At this time many bare such hatred against the Pope's power and the thought of a foreign yoke that Sir Thomas Wyatt and some Kentish men, within ten days of the marriage contracted betwixt Queen Mary and Philip of Spain brake forward into open rebellion.'[13]

Thomas Wyatt and his Kentish army were by no means the full extent of the scheme. In the West Country powerful Protestant landowners such as Sir Peter Carew in Devon and Cornwall, and Sir John St Loe in Somerset and Gloucestershire were secretly mustering private armies with the same intention. And Henry Grey returned to the Midlands to raise an army there.

The plot was betrayed by Edward Courtenay himself. He was a young man who had already spent fifteen years of his life in prison, most of it in solitary confinement, simply because his father had displeased Henry VIII, and he buckled as soon as he was put under pressure. Among the first to suffer the consequences was Henry Grey. Despite his recent appearance as godfather at the Catholic christening service of Charles Cavendish, Grey was as committed to the Protestant cause as it was possible to be, and he wanted no Spaniard on the throne of England. He was preparing to leave Bradgate with his men to ride to Wyatt's support, when a message arrived from Queen Mary offering him command of her forces marching against the rebels. He told the messenger that he would hasten to the Queen's side. 'Ye may see that I am booted and spurred ready to ride, and I will but break my fast and go,' he said. But he intended to throw in his lot with the rebels, banking on the men of Leicestershire rising to the anti-Spanish cause. As he marched south through the Midlands, however, he found no proof of the sympathy which had made itself so evident in the West Country and in Kent, and which he had assumed existed throughout the country. And when they saw how little the cause was supported, even Grey's existing followers began to desert him.

Grey arrived at Coventry on 30 January 1554 and found the gates of the fortified town closed against him. He knew then that the game was up. He paid off his men and sent them home before going into hiding 'in secret places' at Astley Park, one of his manors about five miles from Coventry. By now he was ill with a fever, and he could do little to help himself when he was betrayed by his own gamekeeper, who reported him to Lord Huntingdon. He was arrested, taken to London on 10 February, and a week later was arraigned on a charge of high treason. This time even his wife's eloquence and royal favour could not save him. It was said by some that his judge, the Earl of Arundel (who was brother to Grey's repudiated first wife), was unnecessarily savage, driven by a desire to avenge his sister. But this was the second major mistake made by Grey, and he could not have expected another reprieve.

Lady Jane Grey and her husband Guildford Dudley had played no part in this plan of her father's, but they were regarded by

Mary's advisers as rallying points for further uprisings. A scaffold was hastily erected on Tower Hill and they were summarily executed on 12 February 1554. Eleven days later Henry Grey suffered the same fate.

How can Bess have felt on hearing how this manipulated girl – whom Bess had first known as a bullied nine-year-old child – had groped blindfolded for the block, anxiously crying out to her executioner, 'What must I do? Where is it?' It is not difficult to imagine the frisson of horror she would have experienced, and perhaps her emotions went much deeper since for the remainder of her life Bess kept a portrait of Jane Grey on a table beside her bed. The death of Henry Grey, the bluff, larger-than-life, hunting-mad, gambling friend of Sir William Cavendish would also have affected her and Sir William, as it would affect anyone to lose a close friend in such a horrific manner. And what of the danger to her husband? Sir William had long been known as a member of the Dudley–Grey faction, and he might have been swept up under the Misprision of Treason law, which made it a crime to know that treason is being plotted and not report it, or to have an indirect hand in a treasonable crime. All the couple could hope for was that their long, quiet sojourn in the countryside would count in their favour.

There was still a real chance of civil war as the Wyatt army advanced on London, but with the plot blown and gallows already dangling with the corpses of those convicted of complicity, support from other parts of the country failed to materialise. Wyatt's force was encamped on the south bank of the Thames, but when they attacked, they found London Bridge so well defended that they were forced to travel miles upriver to the next bridge, at Kingston, and approach London from the west. By this time the Queen's men, under the command of the Earl of Pembroke, were ready for them, and Wyatt was defeated. Life in London slowly returned to normal for those not implicated in the rebellion.

For some ten months or so following these dramatic events, it seems that Bess lived quietly at Chatsworth, overseeing the ongoing building work, with Sir William joining her whenever his work at Court allowed. When one examines the fates of some of their closest friends, this was a sensible plan. Their eldest child, Frances, was hardly six years old, yet three of their friends who had acted as godparents since Frances's birth had already been beheaded: Henry Grey, Jane Grey and John Dudley. Prior to that their friend the Lord Admiral and his brother the Protector had been executed. By any standards this is a high percentage of one's acquaintances.

Although it was far from completed, it appears that the Cavendishes were now living in part of the new building, which Sir William modestly described in letters to friends as 'my poor house'.[14] It was far from poor. Chatsworth was already furnished with little expense spared, in what one writer has described as 'splendid magnificence, which must have been unequalled in Derbyshire and neighbouring counties':[15] from the thirteen bedchambers filled with great carved beds and rich hangings embroidered with gold, silver and pearls, to items of household furniture, objects of gold and silver plate, and the tapestries that Bess loved to make and collect (there were fifty-eight tapestries in an inventory taken in 1553). Her own bed was described as 'a bedstead, a tester valance and posts, covered all of black wrought velvet with gold lace and gold fringe [with] curtains of black damask all trimmed with gold lace.'[16] There was also a well-stocked cellar. The fields were filled with sheep and Sir William had forty oxen for drawing his wagons, which had no doubt been employed full time transporting everything to deepest Derbyshire from his other properties.

From contemporary deeds and correspondence we know that between 1553 and 1556 Sir William continued to improve and increase his Derbyshire estate, buying up pieces of land and fighting disputes with neighbours such as Thomas Babington:

... on the 28th of this present month ... [some of your men] came into my ground and ... going to the mountain house found my shepherd's wife with her children in the said house, which

hereto they violently and forcibly entered into . . . and cast out
my said shepherd's wife and her children contrary to the . . .
Queen's statute whereof you are not ignorant . . . Wherefore if it
shall please you to see me tomorrow . . . I shall think myself
more bounden unto you . . .'[17]

Nor did he neglect the decoration of his new house, writing to ask
his friend Sir John Thynne of Longleat about a plasterer, 'which
hath in your hall and in other places of your house made diverse
pendants and other pretty things. If your business be at an end, or
will be by next summer . . . I would pray you that I might have him
into Derbyshire for my hall is yet unmade. And therefore, now
might he devise with my carpenter how he should frame the
same . . .'[18]

Sir William had not renewed the lease on the house at Newgate
Street, which they left at the time of the Jane Grey affair.[19]
Although there are letters from him at Chatsworth, we know
he also spent periods working at the Court because he is often
mentioned in the Acts of the Privy Council, and because some of
his surviving correspondence to friends was written from London.
But Bess disliked being parted from her husband for long periods,
and staying in lodgings was inconvenient. In March 1555,* Bess
was more than eight months pregnant when Sir William wrote to
Sir John Thynne with an urgent request that he might lease his
house at Brentford for a year, or at least 'until my wife shall be
delivered . . . and to confide that if you was not my friend, I would
not so boldly have asked you.' He continued:

Of late I was of a mind to take a house near London . . . [for the]
repose of myself, my wife and my children, but after a long
search by myself and my friends could find none. This put me in

---

*Old calendar. The date on the letter is actually given as 'March 1554' because for
Elizabethans the year ended on March 25th (Lady Day) not Dec 31st.

remembrance of your house at Brentford . . . I make so bold as to
ask you . . . as I do [account you] a very dear friend of mine . . .[20]

Sir John readily agreed to the request and it was at Brentford,
three weeks later, on 31 March 1555, that Bess gave birth to her
daughter Elizabeth. The Marchioness of Northampton and Lady
Katherine Grey were the godmothers, revealing that, despite everything, the Cavendishes remained closely connected with the same
friends, including the Parrs, and what remained of the Grey family.

Sir William and Bess were to use the Brentford house on and off
for some years, whenever they were not at Chatsworth. It was near
enough to London to be convenient for Sir William's work, and far
enough out of town to be away from any immediate dangers,
including infections. Sir William was there in November that year
when he wrote thanking Sir John Thynne 'for the friendship I have
found in you . . . I am now in your house at Brentford where I find
ease and quietness . . . [but with] a month's warning or less I will be
ready to depart . . .'

To everyone's amazement (though Bess was probably close
enough to have known about it), less than a month after the execution of Henry Grey, at the age of thirty-seven, Lady Frances
hurriedly married her twenty-one-year-old former equerry, Adrian
Stokes, recently promoted to the post of 'Master of Horse'. So
proud was she of her young bridegroom that she commissioned
several portraits of them painted side by side. There was a good
reason for the hasty wedding: barely eight months later Lady
Frances gave birth to a daughter, but the child died, as did two further children, both sons. What Queen Mary thought of the liaison
is not known, but the Princess Elizabeth was aghast, referring to
Stokes as her cousin's 'horse-keeper', and she never forgave Lady
Frances this act of *lèse-majesté*.

Bess became pregnant again almost immediately after baby
Elizabeth's birth, and only ten months later her seventh child,
Mary, was born in January 1556 at Chatsworth. There was no

grand christening celebration for Mary; her godparents were local friends and neighbours, Bess's mother, Miss Elizabeth Frecheville (daughter of Bess's old opponent), and Sir George Vernon of nearby Haddon Hall. It was probably a very similar event to Bess's own christening, yet Mary would become – as would Bess herself – one of England's leading peeresses.

CHAPTER 6

'YOUR POOR FRIEND'

1556–8

THE LAST TWO YEARS OF MARY'S SHORT REIGN WERE A
good time to be living away from London and the ghastly parody of
the Inquisition that would earn the Queen the unenviable sobriquet
'Bloody Mary', by which she is still known to every schoolchild.
Hundreds of men and women were burned alive, guilty of the charge
of 'heresy', for which read Protestantism. By 1556 the horrific
burnings had become commonplace and the number sentenced to
die in this manner was only a small proportion of those arrested
for questioning. Under Mary, England became a police state where
anyone with a grudge might inform to the authorities against a
neighbour.

Knowing Bess's preferred lifestyle in later years, one suspects
that she was content to be away from the Court with its deceptions
and dangers, near to her mother and Hardwick, surrounded by her
children and other family members, and able to work about her
lovely new house and its gardens, which had already become an
obsession. Here she was kept busy with all aspects of housewifery
and husbandry, overseeing household matters from cleaning and
cooking to the brewing of beer and the making of cheese. In the

gardens there was fruit to be picked and preserved, herbs to be gathered and dried for cooking and for sweetening rooms and storage chests, vegetables for cooking (although Elizabethans were not keen on green vegetables except in stews – they were thought to encourage 'humours'). From the beehives there was honey, and candles to be made from the wax. From the henhouses there were eggs to gather and fowls for the kitchen. From the fields, cattle and sheep were used as meat in her own kitchens and surplus sold at market; wool clippings were also sold, but some would have been spun in the cottages on the estate. From the woods, venison, game birds, and rabbits and hares were culled and used in the pantry. Bess could have gone on in this manner for many years, contentedly having babies, overseeing the completion of Chatsworth, and dealing with the administration of the Cavendish estates, collection of rents, tending the sick and dutifully writing up her household accounts.

But she was not entirely carefree: Sir William's health had deteriorated drastically just prior to baby Mary's birth. In fact he would never be entirely well again, but by June 1556 he had evidently recovered sufficiently to return to work in London. The couple had accepted an invitation to stay with the Thynnes at Longleat, but soon after his arrival in London Sir William wrote to Sir John and his wife (he referred to the latter, quaintly, as 'and my lady, your bedfellow'), to explain that the visit would have to be postponed until after St Bartholomew's Day, 25 August, due to pressure on his time from the Queen and Council. On 9 July he wrote again, sending a gift of larks for the kitchen, this time writing that he would have to cancel their visit until the following year: 'I am fallen into my old disease and sickness, and am so ill that I shall not be able to ride'.[1] It sounds as though he was a man under considerable stress.

In the spring of 1557, Bess gave birth to her eighth child. 'Lucres, my 16th child, and the 8th by the same woman was born on Shrove Tuesday,' Sir William wrote, 'in the morning between 2 & 3, the second day of March . . .' Again the confinement was at Chatsworth, and again there were no great names as godparents; just family and friends, two godmothers and a godfather (so we know that Lucres was a girl), and one has the impression that this christening was a hurried event. Sir William's health might have been the reason for the lack of ostentatious celebration, or perhaps the baby was sickly, but more likely was a development that was to change the lives and fortunes of himself and Bess. Sir William must have known it was bound to occur sooner or later. There was an audit of his Chamber accounts.

The audit was undoubtedly one of many measures that came about from the Queen's determination to collect money for her adored husband. To all intents, Philip of Spain had deserted Mary several years earlier, when her much-heralded pregnancy proved to be a phantom one, but now he needed money to fund the war the Spanish were waging against the French, and he appealed to Mary for help. Mary had inherited a near-bankrupt country, but she was desperate to win Philip back, even though it meant fighting her Privy Council. She forced through a minting of new coins for general supply, and she despatched Privy Seals across the country asking the great men in each county to loan her £100. In Derbyshire Sir William Cavendish was listed as having refused to comply.[2] These measures enabled Mary to raise 150,000 ducats,* which she sent to Philip. She also promised him the support of the English Navy. The newly minted coins flooded the capital and could not be supported by the Treasury, causing near panic among London merchants who found that the groat in their pockets had been considerably devalued.

Worse was to follow; by the early months of 1557 England found itself being reluctantly drawn into Spain's war with France. After procrastinating as long as they could, the Council finally

---

*A sort of early euro, ducats were valid currency across Europe and worth about one-third of a pound sterling.

agreed to Mary's demands to send Philip six thousand foot and six hundred horse soldiers to stave off a French attack on the Spanish-occupied Netherlands. The Queen's actions brought her the reward for which she hoped. In March that year, just as Bess was giving birth to Lucres, Philip returned to England, obviously deciding that England's support was worth a brief reconciliation with his wife.

As part of the Queen's purge on every department of her administration, Sir William's Privy Chamber accounts were audited. Although he kept account books, he had not rendered a formal statement of these 'for his entire period of office from February 1546 until . . . 1557'.[3] The audit revealed significant errors in each year, dating back to the last year of the reign of Henry VIII, and the total claimed as expenditure by Sir William during that period exceeded the amount that could be accounted for by about six thousand pounds. There was no sinister knock on the door in the middle of the night; instead, the Lord Treasurer, Sir William Paulett,* a friend of many years, and godfather to five-year-old William Cavendish, called on Sir William to tell him frankly that the deficiencies would have to be explained and made good.

Was Sir William Cavendish an embezzler? This topic would be a good one for academic study, for it would take extensive full-time and dedicated research to get to the bottom of it. From the household accounts so dutifully kept by Bess, it can be demonstrated that the annual expenditure on food, clothing, staff wages and entertainments such as gambling was well within their income from rents. No money was taken from the Treasury to fund their lifestyle, then. There was even enough left over, arguably, to pay the wages of the builders employed at Chatsworth.

---

*Paulett, who was Treasurer under four monarchs (Henry VIII, and all three of his children), was a clever, kindly man who owed his unmatched term in office to pragmatism. Asked how he had survived for so long under such diverse ideologies, he said that he was made of willow rather than oak, and bent with the wind. His advice to his friend Cavendish was therefore likely to have been practical.

But in the household accounts there is no mention of how or when the Cavendishes acquired all those lavish assets listed in the 1553 inventory.[4] Where did the contents of those thirteen crowded bedchambers come from? Those costly carved beds with pearl inlay and rich hangings, those tapestries, gold and silver plate whose acquisition is not reflected anywhere in the accounts? Could they have been 'gifts' resulting from favours bestowed by Sir William? Perhaps they were the spoils of his work during the Dissolution, when an unusually lenient approach invited inevitable rewards. Or were they a combination of both? And what about all those pieces of additional land that Sir William kept acquiring, to extend the original Chatsworth estate? How were these funded?

Sir William appears to have built up his estates in a series of swaps, and deals at bargain prices, sometimes in return for favours. But it is clear that there must have been a certain amount of short-term borrowing over the years, from somewhere, in order to purchase bargain properties when they appeared, for though Sir William was now asset-rich, there was no cash available because the Cavendishes had always lived up to their income. Having purchased his post as Treasurer for £1000 (£400 more than he had paid for Chatsworth) it was clearly accepted by both the King and Sir William, according to the custom of the times, that he would earn this sum back through the perquisites of the office. Nor would it have been too difficult for Sir William to justify the fact that his own affairs were sometimes necessarily run in tandem with those of his royal employers.

So the situation is not clear-cut. An examination of the Privy Chamber accounts reveals that the differences in some of the years were surpluses, rather than deficits. This might indicate that care-less bookkeeping was at least partly to blame, rather than deliberate embezzlement (although a cynic might say that it paid a dishonest man to keep a poor set of books). We know that Sir William was a careful man and a very clever man; he must have known these differences existed, whether or not he had benefited by them. But taking into account the manner in which his estates had grown, his ambitious building programme at Chatsworth, all that extravagant gilded and bejewelled furnishing and his well-stocked pastures, even a sympathetic investigator is forced to conclude that there is room for doubt.

In Sir William's defence, the Chamber expenditure had almost always exceeded the annual receipts from the Treasury. Indeed, when he first became Treasurer in 1546, he inherited a deficit of £1848, and within two years he was complaining to the Cofferer Treasurer and Receiver that his department was owed the huge sum of '£14,000 or thereabouts'.[5] Sir William had used his own money, or credit, on occasions to satisfy royal creditors, in effect robbing Peter to pay Paul, doubtless taking it back when the account was in funds.

As a result it may well have become difficult to keep a precise track of how things stood, especially if, as he was to claim, he had a dishonest clerk.[6] But the deficit was a huge sum; more than one-fifth of the annual expenditure of the Privy Chamber.

Sir William claimed that there were some major items of allowable expenditure which he had neglected to enter in the accounts, but he blamed most of the discrepancies on his assistant, Thomas Knot. This clerk had served under Sir William's predecessor, Sir Bryan Tuke, and Sir William had inherited him along with the job. Significantly, as soon as the audit was begun Knot vanished and could not be traced. 'Thomas Knot was . . . in the office wherein I now am, for the space of twenty years,' Sir William stated, '. . . trained and brought up by the said Sir Bryan Tuke, and also hath served under me in the same place and served the full term of XI years. In his doings for that time, looking unto him as thorough . . . I found no cause to question his honesty or truth . . . so in the same his dealings in any renderings for me . . .'[7]

Some of these accounts under investigation survive today in the Public Record Office at Kew, and they were not written in Sir

William's handwriting. Perhaps Sir William made drafts and passed them to Knot who formalised them in a fair hand. Or perhaps Sir William merely glanced at them once a month and authorised them. Sir William further claimed that, following his recent illness, his personal accounts, also prepared by the errant Thomas Knot, were found to be short by an amount in excess of £123. He ended his statement with a personal plea to the Queen, a woman he had personally befriended when she was out of favour: 'I, the said Sir William Cavendish, most humbly beseech Her Majesty, pitying my condition . . . to pardon and allow all things whereof I am most untruly deceived to my great grief. And unto Her Majesty's merciful consideration . . . I most humbly submit myself.' Without her royal intercession, he wrote, he and his wife 'and our innocent children [are] utterly undone and like to end our days in no small penurie.'[8]

Unfortunately for Sir William, the Queen was otherwise engaged. While he was attempting to martial a defence against the inquiries into his stewardship of the royal accounts, the Queen was enjoying a brief second honeymoon, which would lead to a second phantom pregnancy. This, and concern for her husband, who left England in June for Calais (still an English possession at that point), was enough to put the Cavendish affair out of the Queen's mind. Sir William's plea went unanswered.

In mid-summer 1557 Sir William was staying in London when he was summoned to appear before the Star Chamber to answer the charges against him. He immediately sent word to Chatsworth asking Bess to come to him. Leaving baby Lucres to a wet nurse, she set off from Chatsworth on Friday morning, 20 August, with a small party, among whom were two footmen, a guide, six-year-old Henry, now known as 'Master Harry', and Henry's nurse.[9] She took only three days and nights to make the journey, which indicates she travelled with all possible speed, since four nights at least were taken over the distance on most other occasions.

Bess's handwritten expenses for the trip illustrate the vagaries of Tudor travel.[10] Her party had to stop twice while the horses were reshod. On one of these occasions they were at Northampton, then as now famous for its shoemakers. Rather than sit around waiting while the blacksmith did his work, Bess used the time to go shopping. She bought a pair of shoes for two-year-old Elizabeth.* There was a further halt for the repair of broken tack, and at Newport Pagnell one of the horses developed a sore back, which necessitated the purchase of a canvas pad to put under its saddle. There were several ferries to cross on the route, and although it was August, it was evidently cold or damp enough for Bess to require fires in her inn chambers. On the third night the party reached St Albans; the last stage on the journey before London.

Bess was in such a hurry to reach Sir William that she was unwilling to waste an entire night when she was so close to her destination. She took a chamber but used it only for a few hours. After she had rested, she hired some local men to escort her and probably one of her own servants through the night for the remaining miles to London. The rest of her retinue was left to sleep on, to follow her next morning with Master Harry and the luggage. Bess and her escort made one further stop at Barnet – roughly halfway between St Albans and the City. There she spent sixteen pence on ale and wine for the party while the horses were watered and given a breather.[11] Her steward made the final entry for the trip in the new account book which Bess began on the morning of her arrival in London: 'Given to four men which came with my lady from St Albans in the night; ten shillings.'[12]

Elizabethan women habitually travelled in a leisurely fashion. The glimpse we have of Bess's behaviour during this trip – her hasty departure from Chatsworth with just a few servants, her

---

*It is not clear whether or not Elizabeth accompanied her mother on this journey. She is not mentioned anywhere else, nor does she appear in the account book of expenses incurred in London in the following weeks.

shopping trip in Northampton rather than spending time resting at an inn, her ride through the night in order to reach her husband at the earliest possible moment – provides us with the first real hint of the drive that would later manifest itself so forcefully.

The Cavendishes had left Brentford by this time and were renting another house in the city. It was evidently larger than the Newgate Street property since more servants were employed, and it was probably near the Thames, for the cellars sometimes flooded at high tide. There are also more fares paid to boatmen than previously as Sir William and Bess went about their daily occupations. We do not know why Sir William sent for Bess, or why she sped to him in such haste. He was obviously unwell again, for in a letter written to the Privy Council shortly afterwards, he referred to 'my recent illness'. But the housekeeping and entertaining detailed in the accounts during the following weeks do not reflect the household of an invalid. The most likely explanation is that he had just found and moved into this new house and needed Bess to set it up and act as hostess while he won important supporters to his side for his court case. Also he needed his wife at his side at such a difficult time; he could trust no one as he could trust his 'good Bess'.

There was a nurse in the house, Nurse Brown, but she was there to look after Master Harry whose role was to cheer up his father. Harry is first mentioned on the day after Bess arrived in London: 'paid for one pie for Master Harry's breakfast; four pence'.[13] Bess evidently found a bachelor establishment, and one receives the distinct impression from her purchases that as soon as she arrived she rolled up her sleeves and set to work. It was her job to look after her husband, to see that the larder was stocked, that good wholesome food was prepared, that the house was properly cleaned and strewed with fresh rushes. On her first day there she sent out for beef, veal, chickens, rabbits and mutton. There were also purchases of oatmeal, butter, salt, herbs, pepper and mace, damsons, pears and raisins, fresh rushes for the floors, candles, soap and quantities of ale and wine.

On the following day there was a similar shopping list: 6 chickens ('at four pence the piece'), rabbits, half a pound of sugar, a
quarter of pepper ('eightpence' – the price of two chickens), more
spices – mace and nutmeg – herbs, pears and damsons, two pounds
of candles, a basket, two quires of paper (for preparing Sir
William's defence perhaps?), wine for dinner and supper, a bottle of
malmsey and a bottle of sack* as well as ale and beer. Food shopping was done every day; there was no way of keeping food fresh
in the hot summer months, and street markets were open every day
of the week. It seems that Bess may have done some of this shopping herself (a maid would have carried the baskets), for on this
second day while she was out shopping, probably on London
Bridge, she gave twopence to a prisoner at Southwark.

Sir William's appearance before the Star Chamber was set for
10 October but he was not present in person. A few weeks earlier
he had submitted to the court nine books of updated accounts,
together with a letter explaining that he was too ill to attend. On
the day before the hearing the Privy Council returned his books
with a letter. There was no hint that peculation was suspected, but
Sir William was advised that having taken into account all the extra
allowances he had claimed, the deficit over the previous eleven
years, up to October 1556, still amounted to £5237. 5s. 0¾d. He
was politely requested to acknowledge this sum by writing it in the
back of the last account book, and to authorise it with his signature. 'By reason of your sickness for that you cannot attend in
person to answer the further particularities of the said account and
to receive such orders as shall be taken therein,' the letter
instructed, Sir William should send in his place, 'one or two of
your clerks, or such other as you think good, by your letter of
Attorney, to do all such things for you as the case shall require.'[14]

---

*Malmsey was a strong sweet wine from Greece, Spain or Madeira, often prescribed
in convalescence, and sack was a dry white wine imported from Spain and the
Canaries.

He sent Bestenay, his trusted secretary, and two clerks, William Cade and Robert Jeffrey, to present his statement (see Appendix 3), which set out a list of further expenses that he had incurred and believed should be offset against the shortfall. These amounted to over £4500 and, curiously, included the £1000 he had paid King Henry VIII for his appointment as Treasurer of the Chamber. Sir William seemed to be indicating that he had not earned back the cost of his post through perquisites, as was intended. Other items were £200 for outfitting himself appropriately to accompany the King to Boulogne, and the loss of this equipment when he was ordered, at the last minute, to remain in London. A further £200 in monies due to him was 'contrary to the words of my patent, without any offence or suspicion of offence any way committed, taken and kept from me by authority of the Lord Protector and the Earl of Warwick . . .' Another loss of £55 dated from the Lord Protector's committal to the Tower, when Sir William was unable to get repayment for monies advanced to Seymour.

He claimed to have personally paid amounts totalling £1500 to various servants of King Henry VIII, King Edward and Queen Mary. These servants had come to him, he stated, 'complaining with great necessity unto me. And being moved with their often pitiful lamentations and extreme misery I did see them in, daily, I did in consideration thereof . . . lend them part of their wages amounting to the sum before remembered.' He had forfeited this money on the deaths of the two former monarchs. The Royal Family were notorious for seldom remembering to pay their servants, so this statement, at least, was probably accepted at face value. Then there was Sir William's period in Ireland, for which he claimed the agreed daily wage and expenses, totalling £1090, 'whereof hitherto I have no allowance'. And finally there was that dubious one thousand marks which he claimed to have laid out for the men mustered and armed to march against his friend John Dudley, Earl of Northumberland, in defence of Queen Mary, when Jane Grey was crowned Queen. 'Protesting by the truth and duty I

bear her Majesty,' he wrote, staunchly defending this item, 'if I
had been able to bestir a whole world in her defence and for her
good service, it had not been at that time undone.'[15]

In a separate document he made a personal plea to 'your
Lordships, most properly appointed as it were Judges over me'.
Describing himself as 'your humble poor man', he admitted there
was a deficit, but explained that he had been 'most truly deceived,
to my great grief' by Thomas Knot. He promised to satisfy the
amount agreed at the hearing, from the sale of properties and
goods. He further stated that his annual income from his lands
was £500: £300 from lands and properties he owned, and £200
from those leased ('reversions'), stressing that he had little cash. He
reminded them of his long and loyal service, and ended:

> ... now therefore, falling on the knees of a right obedient and
> lamentable servant, ready every hour to take my leave of this
> world, do in the name of my poor wife, my miserable and inno-
> cent children and family, now kneeling and standing before me
> not [including] the number of sorrowful friends present over me,
> appeal by your honourable mouths unto Her Majesty ... heart
> in mouth, [for her] most gracious protection and deference ... if
> my whole house and family and [the] purse ... of me and mine
> are to be saved from submersion ... Your right humble, meek
> and poor sick man. William Cavendish.[16]

That he was truly a sick man can be deduced from his feeble-
looking signature, witnessed by Bestenay, who also wrote out the
long statement and accompanying letter. But for anyone harbouring
suspicions that Sir William's illness might have been a convenient
ploy to avoid having to appear at the trial, proof to the contrary
was not long in presenting itself.

Three days after the hearing, on 13 October, the household
accounts, which previously Bess had kept so assiduously, came to
an abrupt end. She was too fully occupied with other matters to

bother with them. Twelve days later, on 25 October, Sir William
Cavendish died. And late that night, Bess made the final entry in
the pocketbook in which her husband had recorded the births and
christenings of all his children:

> Sir William Cavendish, Knight, my most dear and well beloved
> husband, departed this present life of Monday being the 25th day
> of October, betwixt the hours of 8 and 9 of the same day, at
> night, in the year of Our Lord God, 1557. The Dominical letter
> then C. On whose soul I most humbly beseech the Lord to have
> mercy, and to rid me and his poor children of our great misery.[17]

There are no further household accounts until the following
year, but we know that Bess remained in London after her husband's death, because all her surviving correspondence for that
period is addressed from there. The children, however, were sent
home to Chatsworth.

Sir William was interred in the family tomb at the church of Saint
Botulph-without-Aldersgate in London,* which also contained the
mortal remains of his mother, his first wife, and several of his children from former marriages. The funeral was grand enough to
catch the attention of a contemporary chronicler. Henry Machyn
noted that it was conducted 'with 2 white branches, 12 staff
torches, 3 great tapers, and escutcheons.'[18]

There is every reason to accept that Sir William had been a 'most
dear and well beloved husband'. Bess appears to have looked up to
him, learned from and relied upon him, and she suffered the desolation and misery of any widow. As well she learned, almost before his
tomb was sealed, that his debt did not die with him, and that despite
her husband's statement of appeal, it remained at over £5000.

---

*The church of St Botulph, the patron saint of travellers, was in regular use by 1115.
Daniel Defoe, who was married there in 1683, recorded that at the time of the Great
Plague 5136 people were buried in the churchyard in sixteen weeks.

Bess was now thirty. In the space of ten years she had moved from being an unmarried waiting-gentlewoman to chatelaine of her own great house, with its staff of dependent servants. Thanks to Sir William she had a circle of friends who were the movers and shakers of Tudor England. She had given birth to eight children, the youngest of whom, Lucres, was only six months old when Sir William died.[19] There is no further mention of baby Lucres; she must have died at about the same time as Sir William, which can only have added to Bess's anguish.

With six surviving children under eight years old, three sons and three daughters, not to mention two stepdaughters for whom she obviously cared a good deal, Bess appears to have faced a situation not dissimilar to that faced by her mother when John Hardwick died. But if Sir William, holder of an office where he could readily sell favours to raise money, was floored by the debt, how could Bess possibly meet the obligation without bankrupting herself?

During the next twelve months Bess would prove her resilience and determination, and she would build on what she had learned from her husband. Hardly had she emerged from her 'month's mind' – a period of intensive mourning and lamentation practised in the sixteenth century – when, understanding that her lifestyle and her children's future were under threat and that she stood to lose her beloved Chatsworth, Bess began to fight.

The position in which she had been left, with massive debts owed to the State, was not unique, but it was certainly unusual for a woman to challenge the law of the land. In February 1558 the matter was the subject of legislation by Parliament, who proposed to confiscate lands to recover debts such as that left by her husband. It is referred to in the Calendar of Patent Rolls in connection with Sir William Cavendish's case: 'a search of the Exchequer records having revealed many cases of processes being made against holders of lands of deceased officials, to render accounts'.[20]

The one problem Bess did not have to contend with was the

Office of Wards. Sir William knew a thing or two about tax miti-
gation. He left everything to Bess for her lifetime, only entailing the
house and land at Chatsworth to his eldest son after her death.
There was, consequently, nothing upon which to base a wardship.
Was this entirely Sir William's own idea? Or did Bess's memory of
her mother's terrible experience lead her to persuade him to ensure
history did not repeat itself? We do not know, but it is a likely
explanation.

The income from the Cavendish estates both owned and leased,
as we know from Sir William's statement to the Star Chamber, was
£500 a year. Of this, £300 came from lands that he owned outright
(which now belonged to Bess). Of the remainder, some was income
from properties leased for a specific period, and Bess continued to
hold these leases, but some properties and bonds had been granted
for his lifetime only and reverted on his death.[21] At a reasonable
estimate, her income was probably about £350–£400 a year, a substantial enough sum in those days if she had not the debt to the
Exchequer to consider. There were other debts too, not detailed by
Bess, concerned with borrowings for the purchase of some lands
two years earlier to consolidate the estate. These loans needed to be
serviced.[22]

What were her options? If Bess were to pay half of her entire
income each year against the main debt, it would still take her a
minimum of twenty-six years to repay the capital sum alone. But
that would leave her without adequate funds to maintain her
estates. Then, as now, an enforced sale to repay the Exchequer was
likely to recover only part of the real land and property values.
Another option, which would have to wait until after the obligatory year of mourning was over, was to find a husband who could
afford to pay off the debt. Bess was past her first youth and had a
brood of children. Could such a man be found under the circumstances?

Had she been of lesser mettle, and had she not spent ten years
living with Sir William Cavendish, and learning from him, Bess might

well have been defeated from the start and allowed the properties to be sold. That was the easy way. But the steel in this redoubtable woman now began to make an appearance. If ever Bess sat down and worked things out, decided that no one was going to rob her children of their birthright and that she would instead carry on with her late husband's plans for the advancement of his family, it was surely at this point in her life, for never again would she face such a seemingly impossible challenge. Yet how was she to fight the processes of the State, a lone woman with no official position, few legal rights, and no strong male relative to take up her case?

Bess had several paths open before her. First, she knew from Sir William how the system worked. Second, she had a network of powerful friends and was not shy of asking favours of anyone in a position to offer assistance. The following letter was one of several written by Bess at the time. It was written to Sir John Thynne of Longleat, a leading Protestant and very much part of the Dudley–Grey faction* who formed the closest friends of Sir William and Bess Cavendish.[23] It is not the letter of the shrewd businesswoman Bess was to become, so much as that of a woman who is fighting her corner, but it marked the beginning of Bess's apprenticeship in managing her own affairs.

> Sir, I am now driven to crave your help. I have deferred the time of my sending to you for that I well hoped till now . . . that I should have had no occasion . . . to have troubled you. But now . . . there is a bill in the Parliament House against me. It is a general bill and doth touch many and [if] it pass it will not only undo me and my poor children, but a great number of others. It has been twice read in the Lords' House but it shall be brought up again of Monday or Tuesday, so that it is thought it will be Wednesday or Thursday ere it is brought into the Lords' House.

*He was noted as one of the leading conspirators with Dudley and Grey in 1551.

If it would please you to be here at that time I should think
myself most bounden to you, and though I be in no ways able to
recompense you during my life, I will never be forgetful.

The time is so short that I would not thus boldly have sent for
you unless you might have had more time to have prepared yourself in, but that Master March willed me in any ways to entreat
you to come, which is more than becometh me, all things
considered.

I trust I shall have a great [many] friends, [and] . . . if you will
take the pains to come I shall have many more by your means . . .
And so I take my leave praying you to bear with my rude letter,
in considering what a trouble is able to do.

Your poor friend for ever, E. Cavendish.[24]

Her comment that her behaviour is unbecoming is of special
note. Few non-royal women of her era – if any – are known to have
fought Parliament. And for a recent widow to be in contact with
men outside her family for any reason, let alone on business matters, would have been considered unfeminine and immodest. Bess
was aware of it, but did not allow it to hinder her decision to keep
her husband's estates intact. She was also aware of what she had
taken on, for in another letter she admits she feels 'great fear . . .
and I shall do, until such time as the Parliament ends, which I pray
daily for . . . The bill is so evil liked of the house, and I trust
through the help of you and others, true made my friends, it shall
take small effect and not do me any hurt.' The bill's architect, she
thought, had unwittingly done her a favour; she had more supporters than she might have expected to have, 'for there be few in
the house that they, or their friends, should [not] smart if the Act
should pass'.[25]

Why should men of substance and character like John Thynne
go out of their way to help Bess? She was a widow with a large
family of small children, who stood to lose everything and – now
that Sir William was dead – who could be of little future assistance

whether she won her case or not. There is something missing here that history has not revealed. Bess must surely have possessed some great charm, some essential charisma, or a special ability, to persuade such men to come to her aid when it meant going against the Queen? But they did help her; the bill was duly opposed and lay in abeyance for some years. Bess was still indebted to the State, but at least her properties were not to be seized to pay the debt.

It had been vital for Bess to remain in London, at the centre of things, while this important potential legislation was contested, but by the middle of March 1558 she no longer felt so threatened and wanted nothing so much as to return to her family at Chatsworth. Ill and depressed she made the journey to Derbyshire, and described her time on the road as 'long and foul'. Frequently her horse found it difficult to make its way along highways that were knee-deep in sticky mire. Several times she despaired and considered stopping to rest for a few days, but she pressed on, and was glad she had done so, for, as she wrote to Sir John Thynne a few days after arriving, 'I found my house in all things disordered . . . but for the kindliness of it, I dare compare it to any within this reign . . . I doubt not in a short time to recover my health . . .'[26]

Bess spent the spring of 1558 at Chatsworth, surrounded by her family, recovering from the deaths of Sir William and her baby, and attempting to resolve her financial problems with the aid of a Master Hyde, who had been recommended to her by Sir John. 'I thank him,' she wrote to Sir John. 'He hath taken such pains to bring my disordered affairs to some good order and I shall by his means be able to use my tenants as I trust they will not be able to deceive me. I would I could persuade you that your nearest way to London were to come by Chatsworth . . . wishing you all things as to myself I will cease scribbling. From my poor house at Chatsworth the 31st March [1558].'[27]

On 18 June Bess was back in London, having rented the Thynnes' Brentford house for a year.[28] A few days later she had the children brought down to join her. Parliament was recessed

and though the legislation she so feared was no longer an immediate threat, the huge debt still loomed over her. Her tangled
financial affairs made it necessary to meet Master Hyde on a
regular basis, while she learned how to run her late husband's
estate.

That summer Bess would have heard the widespread rumour
that instead of being pregnant, as formally announced, Queen
Mary was in fact suffering from a fatal dropsy. Her second pregnancy proved no more real than her first, and by August the Queen
lay at Hampton Court, a desperately sick woman, inconsolable
over the loss of Calais, her inability to have effected a counter-
reformation, her husband's absence, and, most of all, her failure to
provide a male heir to the throne. The stomach cancer from which
she was suffering progressed throughout September, by which time
the Queen was so ill that she could no longer even write to her
beloved Philip.[29] By October she had only brief respites from pain
when she was able to make decisions. Officials who had formerly
been so eager to do Mary's bidding, in matters of both business
and conscience, realised that the Protestant heir had not been
well used, and tackled their work with less diligence.

Bess might have glimpsed an opportunity in the Queen's fatal illness. Forgiveness of Sir William's debt was, she knew, within the
gift of the sovereign. There was no point in appealing to Queen
Mary, who had shown no pity for Sir William when he appealed to
her; indeed Bess probably considered that her husband had been
driven to an early death by the actions of the Queen. But the
Queen-in-waiting, the Princess Elizabeth, lived at Hatfield, a mere
couple of hours' ride away from Brentford, just a few miles north-
east of St Albans, on the road that Bess used when travelling to and
from Chatsworth. There was little doubt now that Elizabeth would
inherit the throne when Mary died, for she was the only surviving
child of Henry VIII and was named in the Act of Succession. And
Bess was already acquainted with her. The Princess was, after all,
godmother to Bess's eldest son Henry, and she had been in regular

contact with Sir William Cavendish for some years with regard to her household accounts.

When, on 25 September, Bess closed the London house and returned to Chatsworth, it is likely that she called at Hatfield to pay her respects, just like 'the old acquaintance' to whom Sir Nicholas Throckmorton* refers in his poem describing the events leading up to Elizabeth's accession:

> ... And as we rode there, met us by the way,
> An old acquaintance hoping for advancement,
> A sugared bait, that brought us to our bane
> But chiefly me, who there withall was ta'en.[30]

Bess would have known from Sir William's experiences at Court that this was an appropriate time to make contact, to confirm her support before the Princess was swamped by courtiers defecting from Mary's Court. And Bess had another contact at Hatfield too. Sir William St Loe, a member of Elizabeth's household, was the son of Sir John St Loe, friend and neighbour of Sir John Thynne, and very much a member of the same Protestant set under Dudley and Grey to which William Cavendish had belonged.[31]

During October, while Queen Mary lay dying, Bess was at Chatsworth with her children. The first anniversary of Sir William's death, with its inevitable painful emotional intensity, came and went. But Bess obviously kept abreast with what was happening in London, and on 13 November she was back in the city, just four days before the news broke on 17 November that Queen Mary was dead. Her timing may have been mere coincidence, of course, but the events of the next few months suggest that Bess was in touch with someone at Hatfield House, and her return was well judged. On the morning of Mary's death, a contemporary recorded that, 'between the hours of 11 and 12 aforenoon, the Lady Elizabeth was

---

*Bess's friendship with Throckmorton will be discussed later.

proclaimed Queen Elizabeth, Queen of England, France and Ireland, and defender of the faith . . .' and from mid-afternoon 'all the churches in London did ring, and at night [people] did make bonfires and set tables in the streets, and did eat and drink and make merry.'[32] Rich families placed tables in the streets, laden with ale and wine and food to aid the rejoicing. Clearly this was not a nation in mourning.

Bess had already been in the London area for almost two weeks by then, and was probably lodging at or near Hatfield. It was not until 26 November that she opened up the house at Brentford again and began a new household account book with the words: 'The charges for my house'.[33] The shopping was considerably simpler than in Sir William's day; there was far less red meat consumed. Now, the regular purchases were capons, haddock and mutton, oranges and lemons, salt and walnuts, along with commodities such as white soap, candles, and spices. Prudently Bess reduced her household expenses by almost a third, spending no more than £200 in the year.[34] She sent for the children to join her and received a reply from James Crompe that Master Harry could not leave immediately because 'he hath no boots that will keep out water, so that a pair must be made . . . About Tuesday, God willing, he will be with you.' Crompe also told her about the various schoolmasters who had been engaged for the younger children, including one 'Master Jackson', who would later cause Bess some anguish. For the present, however, Jackson was reported to have done a good job. 'Master William,' Crompe advised, 'will be learned, for he does study and apply his books day and night. There is no need to call him for going to his books.'[35] A week later Bess recorded the cost involved of having her children and some of the servants brought down to Brentford, and the amount she spent on Christmas presents for her half-sister Elizabeth and her Aunt Linnacre, who also came to live with her.

It was an exciting time, with the proclamation of the new Queen and her jubilant arrival in London, followed by the impressive

State funeral of Mary and the new Queen's move from the Tower to Somerset House, and then to the Palace of Westminster. Though few regretted Mary's passing, crowds gathered to watch the pageantry. With her death, the 'Spanish yoke' was removed from the shoulders of Englishmen, and they had a young and beautiful queen, a queen with two English parents.

Christmas at the Court was an especially lively one that year, and was much deprecated by the Spanish Ambassador in his sour reports of the dancing, which went on until long after midnight. It was a youthful court; Elizabeth was twenty-six years old and tasting real freedom for the first time in her life. The people she surrounded herself with were, in the main, also young and heady with success. Many of them were her supporters from Hatfield House.

One of the first appointments Elizabeth made was to confirm Sir William St Loe as Captain of her personal Yeoman Guard, but this exciting news for him was tempered by the death of his father, Sir John St Loe, who died in the same week. If Bess needed a reason to visit, it would have been a natural thing for her to call on Sir William to offer the sympathy of a friend.

We do not know how or when the acquaintanceship of Sir William and Bess Cavendish changed to something more. We do know, however, that over the next few weeks and months, Bess's relationship with Sir William St Loe was to grow ever closer.

CHAPTER 7

SIR WILLIAM ST LOE

1518–58

SIR WILLIAM ST LOE HAS BEEN LARGELY OVERLOOKED AND misrepresented by previous biographers of Bess. 'A fretful delicate man, who had been married twice before and was much older than his bride . . . nobody could call Sir William St Loe a romantic figure', one biographer stated, 'but he had certain sterling qualities.'[1] In an academic examination of Bess, Sir William St Loe is referred to as 'a semi-invalid',[2] and in the first full-length biography of Bess, he was 'a dashing swashbuckler'.[3] At least some of this confusion is due to the fact that Sir William St Loe (1518–65) is often confused with his swashbuckling, not to say downright thuggish uncle, another William St Loe (1504–46), who will – so that the same confusion does not reoccur – henceforward be known as 'Uncle' William.

The William St Loe in whom Bess was interested was only nine years older than she was. Born in 1518, he was the eldest son of Sir John St Loe and his wife Dame Margaret of Sutton Court, Chew Magna, in Somerset.* And because so little has been written about

---

*Sutton Court is one of the oldest manor houses still in occupation. It passed from the St Loe family to the Baber family, and from them to the Stracheys, who still own

him, it is necessary to spend some time investigating the background of this man who would play such a pivotal and exciting role in Bess's story, and to view from a different perspective some national events already covered in Bess's life with Sir William Cavendish.

An old Norman family, the St Loes were first mentioned in England at the Court of Henry I in the year 1100.[4] After this, St Loe men were noted on the periphery of royal service for successive generations and on a number of occasions the head of the family was honoured by being selected as one of the four 'Attendant Knights' to keep watch over the body of a dead king.[5] They were ancient landowners in Somerset, Gloucestershire, and the West Country, and owned numerous town properties in Bristol and Bath.[6] Sir John, whose mother was an Arundell of Wardour Castle,* was appointed the King's Steward and Constable of Thornbury Castle,† in Gloucestershire, before his son William's birth, and later was made Constable of Portbury in Somerset.[7]

The St Loes were traditionally a warrior family, and, like his father, grandfather and great-grandfather, Sir John was empowered to maintain one hundred mounted soldiers, to be ready if and when required by the monarch. He was almost a leftover from a feudal baronage, and his home, Sutton Court, with its thirteenth-century round tower, huge stable yards, outbuildings and surrounding battlemented wall, was a small fortress.

During his lifetime Sir John would hold important local appointments such as Commissioner for the Peace in Somerset and Sheriff of the County. He was made a special commissioner on several occasions when inquiries were being held, and he seemed to have

---

the freehold, though it is now converted into luxury apartments. The village of Chew Magna is situated between Bristol and Wells.
*A different family from the Arundels of Arundel Castle, the Arundells were a West-country family, highly placed in Henry VIII's Court.
†Henry VIII never lived in Thornbury Castle, though he used it occasionally as a progress house, and he spent ten days there in 1535 with Anne Boleyn. Today it is a five-star hotel.

King Henry VIII's trust. Sir John was Member of Parliament for Somerset from 1545 to 1555, and he was the sitting member for Gloucestershire when he died. He was present by the King's invitation at the christening of Prince Edward,[8] was one of the knights appointed by the King to receive Anne of Cleves, and was also an official mourner at the funeral of Edward VI.[9] All these appointments were signal honours bestowed upon a man of contemporary importance.

In 1534 Sir John was sent to Ireland by the specific order of the King, in command of 2000 men.[10] He took with him his ruffian brother, 'Uncle' William, who liked nothing more than a good scrap. The St Loe family were probably glad to see Uncle William go, having supported him with gritted teeth, in recent years, through a murder charge[11] and a brush with the Bishop of Wells over a night-time poaching raid he led in the Palace park,[12] as well as various other lawless escapades. For the next decade, Sir John's name is hardly ever out of despatches to the King from Dublin: 'Sir John Seyntloo took Knockgraffon Castle[13] . . . Sir John Seyntloo prevented the rebels from being succoured during the siege off Maynooth'[14] '. . . the Council determined . . . that Ossary and Seyntloo should go to Munster to win Dungarvon Castle and prevent the Irish on this side of the Shannon from joining O'brene . . . Sir John Seyntloo . . . requested permission to lead an assault on the castle of Dungarvan . . . which the Deputy granted. By four o'clock the same day the Captain yielded the castle and himself as prisoner. On the morrow the whole of his retinue came to the Deputy and Council, and in the church of Our Lady there, were sworn the King's subjects, and to the noble succession of his Majesty and his most dearest wife Queen Anne [Boleyn]'.[15]

Within a few months of landing in Ireland, Sir John was made a Marshal,[16] and in October of the same year he was appointed Commissioner and Chief of the Quorum, based in Kildare. The Earl of Desmond was the enemy, and St Loe seems to have ranged freely from Dublin all over the entire south-east of Ireland, with specific bases in Kilkenny and Waterford, as well as making forays to Limerick, the western capital of Desmond's territory. In November he was ordered to return to London; little fighting went on during the winter months anyway, and both sides tended to snug down as best they could and wait for fighting weather.

Uncle William stayed behind. He found his metier in Ireland, where his natural pugnacity was valued rather than criticised. His name was also frequently mentioned in reports to the King, and his daring assaults on seemingly impregnable fortresses were noted. These exploits have frequently been attributed to his nephew in earlier biographies of Bess (though the boy William was still in the schoolroom at the time). Throughout the fighting in Ireland the one constant factor was the lack of adequate supplies of food, ammunition and wages for the men. Uncle William was a good forager and his men did not go hungry, but in the spring of 1536, having received no pay for over six months his men 'mutinied . . . and refused to tarry in Munster unless they had payment of their wages . . .'[17] He was too good a fighter to lose; the government subsequently found the money for a year's wages for both himself and Sir John, as well as funding three grand captains, three petty captains, 100 mounted men (and their horses), and 300 foot soldiers for each of the brothers. At the same time Uncle William also received 'at the hands of the King' (after a little prompting by Cromwell), the grant of the Castle of Roscarlon in Ireland, some lifetime grants of lands in England[18] and he was appointed 'chief officer of the said Shire [Kilkenny] . . . whereby he is both Captain and Judge'.[19]

One of Uncle William's major successes was to lead the force which, after two days of fierce fighting, took Carrickogynnell, 'a strong castle of hewn marble and another . . . the thickest and best guarded I ever saw in Ireland . . . William Seintloo's retinue, men of high courage and activity adventured the assault and without losing a man took it.' For this and other doughty deeds he was made the 'Seneschal of the liberty of Wexford and all his lands [there] . . . the place being most mete for the defence of Wexford county and the destruction of the Kavanaghes.'[20] But despite the King's approval, Uncle William was regarded by his immediate superiors with caution. He was certainly a courageous fighter, but he was unruly, a disorganised administrator, and a law unto himself; a man to be treated with great circumspection.

Sir John St Loe remained in England for six months. In May he was present at a special meeting of the Privy Council, called by the King, 'to treat of matters relating to the surety of his person, his honour, and the tranquillity of the realm . . .'[21] and within hours of this meeting the Queen, Anne Boleyn, was arrested. Sir John returned to Ireland immediately afterwards but during the next two years he made a number of journeys to England, and there are several recorded meetings between him and the King, as well as his invitation to the christening of Prince Edward. At one point he appeared on a short list of gentlemen with the Marquess of Exeter 'and other knights', selected to lead the King's 'intended army against the rebels in the North'.[22] In November 1536 he was appointed Sheriff of Somerset; an annotation on the document states briefly that he was 'chosen by the King'.[23]

Sir John's closest friends were all powerful men, and included Henry Courtenay (Marquess of Exeter), Lord Mountjoy, Sir Edward Baynton, Lord Henry Grey, William Herbert (Earl of Pembroke), Sir John Thynne and, not least, the great Duke of Somerset (later the Lord Protector), who owned the neighbouring estate of Chew Court.* Like many men in his social stratum St Loe had benefited from the Dissolution, and his portfolio of lands more than doubled during the 1530s. He had four sons, William, Edward, John and Clement, and one daughter, Elizabeth, but all his ambitions were centred on his beloved eldest son William.

---

*Chew Court, formerly owned by the Bishop of Bath and Wells, was sold by Bishop William Barlow to Somerset in 1548. On Somerset's attainder it became Crown property.

William first comes to attention in October 1532, at the age of fourteen, when his tutor, the distinguished scholar and grammarian John Palsgrave,[24] wrote to Sir John:

This Monday ... your servant Thomas Fowlkes informed me you had commissioned him to bring home your son, Master Will Sayntlowe, as the mortality in London was so great, and you supposed I had gone overseas with the King. But as I was not gone, and there is no danger of sickness he [Fowlkes] left it to me to write ...

At Candlemass I mean to go to the University of Cambridge, and keep house at the Blackfriars. There I could have with me your son, Mr Russell's son,* a younger brother of Andrew Baynton,† and Mr Noryce's‡ son, of the King's Privy Chamber ... I go to Cambridge rather than Oxford, because I have a benefice 16 miles off.

Your son, Will Sayntlowe, is the best sped child of his age and time with me. If you withdraw him, either for any tenderness that my lady, his mother, may have towards him, or for any doubts about my honest dealing with such an inheritor as he is, on my faith I promise you, you [will] have killed a schoolmaster, for I will never more teach after Candlemass Day.[25]

Palsgrave's remarks about William's intelligence can be taken at face value, for in surviving letters to the parents of his other pupils the schoolmaster could be frank to the point of offensiveness about the lack of ability in a boy, even when that boy was the illegitimate and esteemed son of the King. Young William was highly intelligent, then, but not an academic, for he is not listed as

---

*Later Sir John Russell, ancestor of the Dukes of Bedford and one of Henry VIII's intimate circle.
†That is, son of Sir Edward Baynton, who was chamberlain to four of Henry's queens, and brother-in-law of Queen Catherine Howard (Lady Baynton was one of Catherine Howard's two sisters).
‡Sir Henry Norrice, who was implicated in the Anne Boleyn trial.

attending either Oxford or Cambridge. In the year after writing the above letter, Master Palsgrave was working in London having been appointed by Cranmer to the comfortable living of St Dunstan-in-the-East.[26] So it appears that Dame Margaret's tender feelings got the better of her, and that William was taken home to the safety of Somerset. The choice of William's tutor, a man closely connected with the royal family, who would ensure classmates whose families were all highly placed in royal service, suggests that Sir John St Loe's forward planning was as careful as that of Sir William Cavendish when the latter chose godparents for his children.

In January 1535 seventeen-year-old William was in Ireland with his father and is mentioned in a letter from Sir John: 'I will be obliged to send strangers with my son, and they will want to know what wages they will receive.'[27] Young William spent a year in Ireland on this occasion, returning to England with his father in November that year; he would later make his own mark serving in Ireland, but he had yet to complete his education. In the previous year William had been betrothed to Jane, the twelve-year-old daughter of his father's closest friend,[28] Sir Edward Baynton of Bromham in Wiltshire, who was a confidant of Henry VIII and Chamberlain to the Queen.[29] However William and Jane had not consummated the marriage by the spring of 1536, when William was sent as a gentleman usher to Henry Courtenay, Marquess of Exeter and 'cousin germaine unto the King'.

For two years William learned how to be a courtier, both at the London house of the Courtenay family, and at their country seat in Devon.[*] It was a princely and gentle household with a dozen gentlemen and half a dozen gentlewomen providing a mini-court, a music teacher, singers, minstrels and falconers; there were twenty-six men simply to look after the gardens. William's time with the Courtenays was a happy one, but he had not long celebrated his twentieth birthday when, in November 1538, the Marquess, 'next

---

[*]Probably Powderham Castle.

unto the crown of any man in England', was arraigned for plotting against the King, sent to the Tower, convicted of treason and summarily executed.[30]

The commissioners sent by the King to take an inventory of the Courtenay estates noted that there were two St Loe men in the household at the time: William's cousin Thomas was also in service, and was described as 'a tall personage; shoots well'. In fact all the St Loe men were exceptionally tall; William's great-grandfather was almost a giant, at over seven foot.* William was described as 'the son and heir of Sir John St Loe, aged 20, married to one of Sir Edward Baynton's daughters, has of his father £10 [allowance].'[31] William was evidently not living with his betrothed wife at this time, for she is not mentioned among the gentlewomen at the castle, although she would have just been reaching her sixteenth birthday. However, the couple's first daughter, Mary, was born a year later in 1539, so their marriage was probably consummated soon after William left the Courtenay household.

In November 1540 Sir John St Loe, newly returned from Ireland, 'and William Seintclo his son and heir', were summoned to Windsor 'to appear before his Majesty',[32] in connection with a complaint by a neighbouring landowner. They were ordered to keep the peace. Sir John's men were known to be unscrupulous in defence of their master and his land, and a certain amount of vandalism had been occurring in Gloucestershire. One St Loe servant was arrested for killing the servant of another landowner in a violent affray arising from a dispute about hunting rights over St Loe lands.[33] The significant outcome of this rap over the knuckles seems to have been that William joined the small permanent army kept by the Crown, and was quickly promoted to the office of captain. In August 1543 he was mentioned in despatches while serving in Boulogne:

*His effigy on the tomb at Chew Magna measures seven foot four inches, while that of his diminutive wife beside him measures only five foot three.

Yesterday . . . was an alarm between the Allemen and the
Englishmen, and the latter were almost into the Allemen's camp
bestowing arrows upon them (and they bestowing shot amongst
us) when by the help of Mr Cromwell, Mr Carew and other
gentlemen we caused them to retire . . . The Alleman colonel who
after the skirmish . . . entered our camp with a dozen 'harcbuzyers'
and seeing my sword drawn offered to shoot me . . . and young
Seintlow, perceiving him to level at me, did the same towards him,
and, as God would, his gun failed to take fire or else he had surely
slain him, and whereat I do not a little rejoice, for if this thing had
taken effect we should not have this year been able to invade
France, so many would have suffered on both sides.[34]

In 1545 young William was serving in Ireland with his father
and his uncle. Uncle William died in 1546,[35] and when Sir John
was permanently recalled to England, young William, now aged
twenty-eight, took over from the previous generation of St Loe men.
   Over the next five years William's name appears regularly in
despatches recording battles between the King's Army and
Desmond's men, and 'Cahir O'Connor and the rebels'. It was
tough, for while the English had better resources and superior
weapons, the Irish fought a guerrilla war, leading the heavily
armoured English into bogs.* William St Loe's good-humoured
fairness made him popular with his brother officers and his men,
and his leadership while in command of the King's forts in Leinster
earned him a knighthood 'for the good service that he hath done in
Ireland . . . and that he shall have in his household 40 able horsemen and 12 pence per diem'. The knighthood was formally
bestowed ('dubbed') in a ceremony held in Dublin in January
1549.[36] Shortly afterwards he wrote a letter to the Lord Justice of
Ireland complaining bitterly that since no corn or other provisions

---

*Some of the English officers who fought in Ireland were subsequently painted with
bare legs to indicate their wading through Irish bogs.

had been received by his men, they would shortly be dead of starvation.[37] His letters to friends in England at this time lack his usual humour, and he appears low-spirited. His father may have worked on his behalf for, at the end of February, Sir William was ordered back to England by the boy king, Edward VI, and instructed to leave his men under the command of Sir Anthony St Leger.[38]

By this time Sir William and his wife, Jane, had two daughters, Mary (born in 1539), and Margaret (born c.1541), evidently conceived during one of his periods of leave. In the autumn of 1549 Jane died, possibly in childbirth, for she is described in a contemporary document as having had '3 fils' although Mary and Margaret are the only two children known to have survived childhood.[39] Sir William returned to Ireland in 1551, where he was appointed Marshal serving under Lord Cobham, with Sir James Croft (who was subsequently made Lord Deputy of Ireland).[40] At the same time Sir William was granted a twenty-one-year lease on a large swathe of lands and properties in West Meath, including the manor and priory of Fowre.[41]

He was ordered home in the spring of 1553 and never again served in Ireland. He was thirty-five, a polished courtier reputed for humour and good manners, hardened by his military experiences. Edward VI saw him as the ideal man to head the personal security of the nineteen-year-old Princess Elizabeth.[42] At the time of this appointment Sir William was granted a twenty-one-year lease 'on the Bishop's Palace of Banwell in Somerset, all the houses and gardens within its site, and numerous lands and two mills at Westgarston, producing forty-four rents worth £53. 7s. 5d.* . . . the keepership of Banwell Park and of the wild beasts there, and allowing for sufficient pasture for these animals, he was to have rights of pasture, and grazing for swine.'[43] In addition, Sir William's elder daughter, fourteen-year-old Mary St Loe, was appointed one

---

*Actual conversion to today's rate £2,700 but in purchasing power £17,325.

of the six maids of honour attending the Princess Elizabeth.[44]
Sir John Harington, who fell in love with Isabella Markham, one of
the six maidens, wrote a poem 'In Praise of Six Gentlewomen
attending the Lady Elizabeth'[45] in which there is a verse about
Mary St Loe, praising her staunch and loyal character.[46]

The death of King Edward VI in the summer of 1553 affected
the entire St Loe family, for they were very much part of the movement to place Jane Grey on the throne. Within days of the King's
death Queen Jane wrote to Sir William's father, 'our trustie and
well-beloved Sir John Saintlowe', commanding him to raise a force
to put down the 'seditious' movement against her, and instructing
him to proceed immediately to Buckinghamshire for this purpose.[47]
Sir John, an ardent Protestant who abhorred the spectre of a
Catholic queen, mustered some two hundred men in the West
Country, including his two younger sons Edward and Clement.[48]
Fortunately he had a somewhat lower profile than others who were
involved, and when Queen Mary's army carried the day, Sir John's
men were rapidly turned round for home and safety. Who could
later say whether they had set out to support Queen Jane or Queen
Mary? Within a matter of months, however, the men were needed
again, as Sir John threw in his lot with Sir Peter Carew and the
West Country supporters of what has become known as the Wyatt
Rebellion.

But Sir William St Loe was far more personally involved in the
Wyatt Rebellion than his father. On 16 November 1553, a
Parliamentary deputation waited on Queen Mary and formally
requested her to choose an English husband, all parties being well
aware that the only suitable Englishman was her kinsman Edward
Courtenay, Earl of Devon. Mary replied that she had already
decided to marry Philip of Spain. Ten days later, a group of
Protestant aristocrats met to discuss this turn of events, and agreed
that the Spanish marriage must be prevented at all costs. The mili-
tias set in place at the time of the aborted Jane Grey uprising could
be quickly re-formed, and would provide sufficient force, if force

was necessary, to stop the marriage. From here it was but a short hop to plotting sedition. The marriage was now promoted between Edward Courtenay and Princess Elizabeth, and having received Courtenay's outline agreement, a plan evolved to march on London, take the capital, depose Mary, and place Elizabeth and Courtenay on the throne. Courtenay had agreed to this, but how much did the Princess Elizabeth know of it? Was she involved with the plotters? It is one of history's great unanswered questions.

The leaders of the plot, apart from Sir Thomas Wyatt of Kent,* were Sir James Croft of Herefordshire (a personal friend of Sir William St Loe from their days serving together in Ireland), Sir Peter Carew and Edward Courtenay in the West Country (both had been friends of Sir William St Loe since his period in service with Edward Courtenay's father in 1538), and Henry Grey, Duke of Suffolk, in Leicestershire (to whom Sir John St Loe had given his allegiance). There were others involved, including Antoine de Noailles, the wily French Ambassador, who knew that a Spanish king on the English throne was not in the best interests of France. A four-pronged attack was agreed upon, with armies from Kent, the West Country, the Midlands and the borders of Wales, due to converge on London on 18 March 1554.

The nineteen-year-old Princess Elizabeth was in an invidious position when all this began, living at Court under Mary's less than welcoming protection, and forced to walk a difficult path by pretending to follow the Catholic religion without sacrificing her Protestant ethics. Despite concern that in her absence her enemies would attempt to further poison Mary's mind against her, Elizabeth requested permission to retire to the country. The Queen gave reluctant assent and Elizabeth removed to Ashridge House, near Great Berkhamsted, Hertfordshire. Before she left Court the French

---

*Son of the poet Sir Thomas Wyatt, who was charged with being one of Anne Boleyn's lovers.

Ambassador noted in his despatches that the Princess spent a considerable amount of time in the company of Sir James Croft. Furthermore, she had caused a great deal of comment at the end of October by having a two-hour meeting with Sir William Pickering (another man who would be implicated as a Wyatt conspirator) in her private rooms.[49] All this occurred before Mary had announced her formal decision to Parliament regarding Philip, but agitation in various parts of the country had begun before that time, and the likelihood is that, as always, Elizabeth was well aware of what was in the wind.

In January 1554 word reached the Queen and her Council that Sir Peter Carew was spreading fear and dissension in Exeter by telling the townspeople that a Spanish king meant a Spanish Inquisition, with burnings, torture, rapine and slaughter. Mary ordered Carew's immediate arrest, but he was forewarned and fled to France. This was a blow to Wyatt, but there were still men in the West Country, such as Sir John St Loe and Sir Edward Rogers, who could lead and secure the West Country in the planned uprising, and Carew continued to work for the cause in France. The French, who had been involved in the plot from the start, had agreed to send reinforcements through Scotland to secure the north. Things began to go wrong when, on 21 January, the unfortunate Edward Courtenay was arrested and interviewed by Bishop Gardiner.

Suspecting that Courtenay would probably not stand up to aggressive questioning, the conspirators met and agreed to bring their plans forward. Their worst fears were justified; according to Ambassador Noailles, the terrified Courtenay immediately confessed everything he knew about the plot. On the following day, 22 January, Sir James Croft galloped up the driveway of Ashridge House. He was on his way from Kent to Herefordshire, where he had agreed to raise his forces a full six weeks earlier than scheduled. His mission at Ashridge was to deliver a message from Wyatt, and to persuade Princess Elizabeth to move away immediately to

Castle Donnington, where she would be safer from any attempt by Mary's men to take her into custody.

Elizabeth was ill with nephritis, a painful kidney infection from which she had suffered intermittently for some years, and was unable to rise from her bed, even supposing she thought it expedient to move from Ashridge. Having sent word of this development to Wyatt, Sir James Croft went on his way. Wyatt evidently did not realise from the message how ill the Princess was, for he subsequently wrote her a letter which was delivered by Lord Russell (as other, previous letters apparently had been)[50] advising her 'that she should get as far from the city as she could, the rather for her safety from strangers'.[51]

Five days later, on 27 January, Sir William St Loe's unmistakable tall figure was observed in Tonbridge, Kent, in the company of three of Wyatt's chief conspirators, Sir Henry Isley and Anthony and William Knevett. St Loe had brought them the Princess's verbal reply to Wyatt. Isley and the Knevett brothers had raised a force of five hundred men, and it was their intention to march towards Rochester on the following day to join Wyatt's army. St Loe's arrival coincided with Isley's noisy proclamation that the sheriff and a local gentleman (who would not come over to their side) were 'traitors to God, the Crown and the commonwealth', as the church bells of Tonbridge pealed the traditional invasion alarm.[52]

Had other parts of the country come to Wyatt's aid, the rebellion might well have succeeded. He raised more than six thousand foot soldiers and five hundred mounted soldiers, and assumed that his fellow conspirators would secure their areas in a similar fashion. At the same time the Privy Council was advised that 'all England was up, between London and Tonbridge every town [was ready] to drive away the Spaniards'.[53] But only Wyatt was ready to move so quickly, and the uprising ultimately failed for several reasons. The authorities had prior knowledge of the plan through Courtenay's confession, which forced the conspirators to move their plan forward so that the operation went off at half-cock, and also the ringleaders had overestimated the amount of support they would receive. Though deeply unhappy about the Spanish marriage, it seems that the general public were not prepared to die en masse to prevent it.

The promised support of armies from the west, the Midlands and the Welsh borders failed to materialise, and on 7 February Wyatt's brave but foolhardy attack on London was put down. He was arrested, along with his men and scores of fellow conspirators. Gallows sprouted up all over London and Kent. The three men Sir William St Loe had met in Tonbridge were among the first of over three hundred to be executed, their bodies left swinging in the winter winds.

Mary had already ordered Elizabeth to return to Court, and explanations that the Princess was too ill to be moved were, not surprisingly, treated with utmost suspicion. On 11 February, doctors sent by the Queen to Ashridge confirmed that Elizabeth was certainly ill, but that it would not be fatal to move her to London.[54] Elizabeth was therefore preparing to leave Ashridge on the following day when news was received that Jane Grey and Guildford Dudley had been executed, and that Edward Courtenay had been committed to the Tower (where he had already spent most of his life). He had been overheard by an eavesdropper to reply to questioning about his involvement in the plot: 'Truly I cannot tell, except I should accuse myself. Let the world judge.'[55]

To hear that Mary had already executed Jane Grey, the person next to her in the Act of Succession, must have been terrifying to Elizabeth. Dressed in stark white, which emphasised the sick yellow pallor of her skin, she was carried in a horse-drawn litter along frozen winter highways, with villagers turning out along every mile of the way to call out their support for her, and bring her nosegays and home-baked pies and cakes. The pace was slow, for every movement caused Elizabeth discomfort, and they were only able to average six miles a day. When she arrived in London on 18 February she was taken to Whitehall, where she was placed in total isolation for two weeks, unable to speak even to Mary, and with only a few members of her retinue allowed for her care.

During this time, ill as she was, Elizabeth must have been aware that many of the Wyatt conspirators were confined in the Tower, and were being hard questioned, probably under torture, for information. One by one they had been found and brought in, among them Henry Grey and his brother Thomas,[56] Lord Cobham and his three sons; Lord John Grey (of Wilton), William Thomas (Clerk of the Privy Council), Sir Nicholas Throckmorton, John Harington, Sir James Croft, Sir Robert Dudley, and dozens more betrayed by Courtenay, until the Tower was crammed full of high-profile State prisoners.

Sir William St Loe, with the rest of Elizabeth's retinue, had found lodgings close to Whitehall while his mistress was held incommunicado. On Saturday 24 February, having been implicated by both Thomas Wyatt and James Croft during their questioning, Sir William was arrested. Taken before the Privy Council, he was duly charged with his involvement, 'which he stoutly denied protesting that he was a true man, both to God and his Prince, defying all traitors and rebels'.[57] Following his examination, St Loe was given into the keeping of the Master of the Horse for the night.

On the following day Sir John Bourne, who was Thomas Wyatt's inquisitor in the Tower, reported to Secretary Petre of the Privy Council:

> We have this morning travailed with Sir Thomas Wyatt touching the Lady Elizabeth and her servant Sir William Saintloo . . . Wyatt affirmeth his former sayings, and says further that Sir James Crofts knoweth more . . . Crofts has been examined [and] confesses with Wyatt, charging Saintloo with the semblable matter . . . Send for Mr Saintloo and examine him, or cause him to be sent here, by us to be examined. Crofts is plain and will tell all. [58]

Sir William was then marched to the Tower. Most men admitted to the Tower as prisoners were defeated by fear from the moment they entered the gate, but St Loe's entrance was noted for its insouciance. 'This morning Sunday 25th of February, was brought into the Tower,' a contemporary wrote admiringly, 'prisoner, Sir William Seintlowe, a man that came in with a wonderful stout courage, nothing at all abashed.'

There is no record of St Loe's 'examination' at the Tower. Although reports to the Privy Council state that he was questioned 'hard' and 'marvellously tossed and examined', we do not know whether this meant that he was tortured or merely questioned aggressively. In order to torture a prisoner, in other words to use the rack, instruments such as thumb screws, or the gruesome 'maiden's kiss', a warrant was required from the Privy Council. Sir William's name does not appear in the warrants listed for the period in the printed Acts of the Privy Council, but this does not mean that he was not tortured, since the lists are incomplete, and also there are some surviving warrants for torture which were never recorded by central government.* Furthermore, the names of Wyatt and Croft do not appear on the lists, yet both later withdrew statements they claimed had been made under duress – in other words under torture or the threat of it. And of course there are methods of inquisition such as sleep deprivation, vicious and threatening behaviour, or the threat of torture – instruments placed in sight of the prisoner, for example, with verbal warnings that torture was about to begin – which were not regarded as torture per se and thus did not require a formal warrant.

What we can be certain of is that Sir William St Loe's chief contribution to history is not his gallantry in Ireland, which earned him a knighthood, nor that he was the third husband of Bess of Hardwick, as so many previous writers have assumed, nor that he subsequently served with some distinction as the Commander of

---

*Jeremy Ashbee, Curator at the Tower of London, advised the author in a letter dated 19 May 2003 that he has seen, in a private collection, writs authorising torture of individuals which do not appear in the published Acts of Privy Council.

Queen Elizabeth's personal guard. It is that, unlike Wyatt and Croft, he said nothing, either willingly or under duress, which could give his questioners anything that could be used against Princess Elizabeth. And it is more than possible that because of this, Elizabeth owed him her life, for had Elizabeth's enemies been able to prove a positive chain of communication between the princess and Wyatt prior to the rebellion, this would have been enough to prove treason.

Wyatt's confession implicated the French Ambassador and Sir James Croft as well as Sir William St Loe. He admitted to being present when the Ambassador spoke to Croft 'to persuade him to hinder the marriage of His Highness [Philip] and the Queen, to raise Elizabeth to the crown, to marry her to Courtenay, and put the Queen to death'.[59] He also claimed that the whole idea had originated with Courtenay, and to have been in communication with Princess Elizabeth on several occasions, naming Sir William St Loe as the go-between. Croft confessed that he had delivered letters to her from Wyatt, and that he had tried to persuade the Princess to 'retire to Donnington'.[60]

Wyatt's statement was put to Elizabeth, together with the information that she was to be taken to the Tower. This resulted in the famous Tide Letter, in which she replied carefully, 'Wyatt might peradventure write me a letter but on my faith I never received the same.'[61] Later, she admitted that she had received an unsolicited message from him, through Croft, advising her to move to a place of greater safety, and also that she sent him word, but, 'not in writing, [but] by Sir William Seyntlowe, that she did thank him [Wyatt] much for his good will, and she would do as she should see cause etc.'[62] This was as much as the inquisitors ever got from Elizabeth. Sir William St Loe told them nothing.

Elizabeth was taken into the Tower on Palm Sunday, 18 March, protesting: 'I come here as no traitor, but as true a woman to the Queen's Majesty as any is now living. And thereon will I take my death.'[63] Wyatt was executed on 6 April. At this point Elizabeth was in genuine fear of her life. Eighteen years earlier her mother

had been executed in the same place, and later she would recall
how 'having no hope of escaping she desired to make her sister only
one request, which was that she might have her head cut off with a
sword, as in France, and not an axe'.[64]

Although it did not form part of his admission, there was a significant body of evidence that Edward Courtenay was 'privy to the
intrigues of the French and Venetian Ambassadors',[65] and a search
of his effects revealed that a cipher had been cut into his guitar 'by
means of which he had corresponded with Carew'.[66] But there
were only suspicions that Elizabeth knew of the plan; nothing could
be proved against her,[67] and lacking demonstrable evidence that
Elizabeth had actually conspired with Courtenay, Wyatt or the
French king, Queen Mary and her Council had no option but reluctantly to order her release. Mary had a soft spot for young
Courtenay, and ignoring the advice of Ambassador Renard and
Bishop Gardiner, she ordered him removed to a castle in the north,
where he lived under minimal supervision.

On 19 May, after being held in the Tower for eight weeks,
Elizabeth was discharged and sent to Woodstock in Oxfordshire,
with an armed guard, under the puritanical supervision of Sir
Henry Bedingfeld.[68] Again there was a massive show of public support during her journey from London to Oxfordshire. People were
genuinely relieved that the Princess had not been executed, which at
one point looked almost certain. And there is no doubt, reading
through the State papers of the time, that, given a shred of real evidence against her, this would have been the outcome. At one point
while Mary was ill, Gardiner, acting on his own initiative, sent a
warrant with instructions for Elizabeth's immediate execution to
the Lieutenant of the Tower. Fortunately Lieutenant Bridges was a
stickler and refused to obey without the Queen's own signature on
the document.[69] Indeed, when Elizabeth saw Bedingfeld and his
hundred men-at-arms escort arriving at the Tower on 19 May she
thought it was the prelude to her own execution and anxiously
asked her ladies 'if the Lady Jane's [Grey] scaffold were removed'.[70]

Evidently, her mind was not put at rest by Bedingfeld. The first stage of her journey was by State barge to Richmond. Her ladies and gentlemen followed and asked permission 'to wait on her' but this was not allowed. All were convinced that Elizabeth was to die and when she was permitted to say goodbye she asked for their prayers, 'for,' she told them, 'this night, I think I must die'.[71] It was several days before she realised she was not under a death sentence.

Bishop Gardiner and Simon Renard, Ambassador to Emperor Charles V, despised and mistrusted Elizabeth. They insisted on numerous occasions that Elizabeth and Courtenay were guilty and must be executed for the Queen's future safety. Renard's letters to the Emperor make clear his frustration at Mary's reluctance to execute Elizabeth, when, as he said, 'it is certain that the enterprise was undertaken in her favour'.[72] In another letter he advised, 'they have removed Courtenay from the Tower and taken him to a castle in the north.* Your Majesty may well believe in what danger the Queen is, as long as both shall live.'[73] The Queen greatly respected the opinions of Gardiner and Renard, but she hesitated to act on their advice because she believed that the people of England would not stand for Elizabeth's execution without positive evidence that the Princess had been involved in the plot. She admitted to them that she, too, was convinced that her half-sister was guilty, and all three of them would have had Elizabeth's head if they could. And Elizabeth knew it. She is said to have scratched on a window pane at Woodstock the following verse:

> *Much suspected, by me,*
> *Nothing proved can be,*
> *Quoth Elizabeth, prisoner.*[74]

---

*On 29 April 1555 Courtenay left England, having been given permission to live in Hungary where he died some years later.

In fact, the only evidence that Elizabeth knew more than she admitted of the plot came from her own mouth a dozen years later, in 1566, when she was being pressed by Parliament to name a successor. The reason she gave for refusing to do so was that her experiences at the time of Wyatt's rebellion had taught her that 'the second person in the realm' was ever at the mercy of any person or group who chose to plot against the sovereign. On that occasion she stated that there were persons present before her in the chamber who had 'tried to make her a party' to their plotting at the time of the rebellion, and 'I had great occasion to hearken to their motions'. Were it not for her honour, she said, she would name them, but, she continued, 'there were occasions in that time I stood in danger of my life . . . so never shall my successor be'.[75] She made a similar statement to the French Ambassador of the day, confirming how close it had all been: 'I learned how to keep silence during the time of Queen Mary, when, had anything been proven against me, I should have lost my life.'[76]

But Elizabeth never forgot those who had helped her during this traumatic period, and even the children of those men and women were on the receiving end of her gratitude: 'Boy Jack,' she wrote many years later when granting a favour to the son of John Harington (who, with his wife Isabella, formerly a maid of honour, had been imprisoned in the Tower with the others), 'I do this because thy father was ready to serve and love us in trouble and thrall.'[77]

Following Elizabeth's release, Sir William St Loe remained in the Tower until 25 June when he was transferred to the Fleet Prison. He and Croft were lucky to escape execution for men with less involvement lost their lives. Seven months later, at a hearing on 28 January 1555, St Loe was ordered to be released, bound to a promise on oath of 'good bearing and order', and payment of a fine of £202. John Harington and Nicholas Throckmorton were treated likewise and fined £100 each, and James Croft £600.[78] When these men and several dozen others left the prison, they were greeted with open celebration in the streets of London, and outside the prison gate there were whoops of acclaim 'and a great shooting off of guns'.[79] Summoned before Queen Mary three weeks later, Sir William was given a military command on the south coast, but the lands in Somerset granted to him by Edward VI were confiscated and returned to the former owner, the Bishop of Bath and Wells.

Sir William was not implicated in a subsequent plot to depose Mary and put Elizabeth on the throne in March 1556, although both his father and his brother Edward were. In the State papers Sir John and Edward St Loe were prominent, listed along with Henry Dudley, Sir Nicholas Throckmorton, Sir James Croft, Sir William Courtenay – all the usual suspects, in fact; some 'thirty knights and many noblemen'.[80] Sir John was confined to his house in the city of London, and along with Sir Anthony Champernowne was bound over, in his own recognizance of the crippling sum of £1000, to attend the Privy Council when called.[81] Edward St Loe was imprisoned in the Fleet. During this time Sir William was in command of a unit in the south of England, and was still there in July 1557 when, because of Mary's support for Philip, there was a possibility of war with France.[82] By summer 1558, however, he was back at Hatfield, serving in the retinue of Princess Elizabeth. And he was still there in November when the news was brought to Elizabeth that Queen Mary had died.

Elizabeth immediately acknowledged her obligation to Sir William St Loe. One of the first appointments she made was to name him as captain of her personal guard. To this honour, a few weeks later, she added a life annuity of 100 marks* each year (backdated to 'Lady Day last'), and granted him several lucrative sinecure posts: 'To Sir William Seyntlow, for life, Chief Butler of England, and Chief Butler of Wales . . . with all profits from the office, and for the better maintenance of his deputies in divers

*£66. 12s. 0d.

ports, an annuity of 50 marks payable out of the customs and price of wines and other issues of that office.'[83]

Both offices carried significant perquisites in return for extremely light duties. The main obligation of the Chief Butler seems to have been that he must attend the coronation banquet and present the new sovereign with 'the first cup of wine', be responsible for supplying the Queen's pantry with fine wines and organise 'deputies' – the equivalent of today's Customs and Excise officers, who imposed duty on imported wines – to send the revenues and accounts to him. It was hardly an arduous post, and the profits of the office, a sort of 'corkage', were substantial. What is more, this post had traditionally been awarded to the most senior members of the old aristocracy. In conferring it upon Sir William, the Queen was actually bestowing on him more honour than is at first obvious. Later, Sir William was given valuable wardships and further grants of land.

As Captain of the Queen's Yeoman Guard, Sir William's duties were no sinecure, of course. He was accountable for the Queen's personal safety at all times, which involved an almost constant attendance at Court, and also for some £10,000, advanced annually by the Treasury to pay for all officials and guards – 'every one of them 40 shillings the month'[84] – who were housed at the Tower of London. He also paid the Lieutenant of the Tower, the gentleman porter and the yeoman warders, and recorded punctiliously that holders of honorary appointments such as Master of the Jewels, the Under-Treasurer of the Mint and the Clerk of the Hanaper had received no salaries, and enclosed signed certificates from them to this effect.

Those other hot-blooded young gentlemen who had actively supported Elizabeth and gone to prison for their pains were rewarded, too, though notably none were appointed to important government positions; Elizabeth sought cooler and wiser heads as her advisers. But Sir Nicholas Throckmorton was made Ambassador to France. John Harington became one of her favourite courtiers and she stood as godmother to his son 'Jack'. Sir

James Croft, who had implicated Elizabeth and St Loe but after-wards withdrew the confession, was made Captain of Berwick Castle in the northern border town of Berwick-upon-Tweed, which was England's first defence against any potential incursions by the Scots. In later life Croft had a distinguished career in Elizabeth's service.

Sir John St Loe died in December 1558, within days of his son's new appointment being conferred. There had been love, pride in each other's achievements, and a great, shared friendship between father and son, so this loss was a significant one to Sir William. But his father's death left him a rich man, and his inheritance added to the lands, properties and positions that he had earned in his own right.[85] Sir William was now forty years old, literally fighting fit and with the world at his feet. He was 'a made man', with a Court position and the clear favour and trust of the Queen. And it was at just about this time that Bess, the thirty-one-year-old widow of Sir William Cavendish, came into his life. However this union was to be marred by the behaviour of his younger brother Edward.

Sir John St Loe's will left two of his younger sons adequately provided for with a reasonable annuity and lifetime tenancies: Clement had £70 a year and a property in Somerset; John had been left £70 a year and a property in Gloucestershire.* Edward, the second eldest son, was left nothing. Since childhood Edward St Loe had caused his parents endless grief by a series of lawless scrapes and efforts to set them against each other. He had also attempted to turn his mother against Sir William by telling lies about him.[86] In 1553 Sir John had given Edward the lease of the manor of Whitchurch and Felton in Somerset at the request of Dame Margaret, but Edward had sold it three years later and quickly run through the proceeds.

*There is no mention of John after his father's death: it is likely he predeceased him.

In the spring of 1558 Edward had been involved in what was locally a major scandal concerning one of Sir John's tenants. John Scutt, gentleman, former tailor to Henry VIII, had lived in the manor of Stanton Drew for some years with his young second wife Bridget, their twelve-year-old son Anthony, and Margaret, the eighteen-year-old daughter of Scutt's first marriage.[87] Scutt was an unpleasant man in his fifties and Sir William St Loe would later state under oath, 'It is well known to the world how wary Scutt's wife was of Scutt, her husband, and what [a] life she led, and how she used him, as Edward Seyntlowe, seeing it daily, could witness.' When John Scutt died very suddenly, Sir William said, '. . . the world both spake and suspected his poisoning'.

Two weeks after Scutt's death, Edward bought from the widow Scutt her lifetime lease in the manors of Stanton Drew, East Cranmer and various other local properties. A fortnight later – barely a month after her husband's death – Edward St Loe and Bridget Scutt were married. The entire district was aghast, but the couple could not afford to wait on proprieties, for Bridget was already nearly three months pregnant with Edward's child. As if this were not enough, the couple had been married only a few months when 'this very lusty young woman' also died suddenly and mysteriously; or 'before her time' as Sir William put it.

Shortly after Scutt's death and before his marriage to Bridget, Edward had visited Sir William at Hatfield and persuaded his brother to purchase the wardship of Bridget's son, Anthony Scutt. He also asked his brother not to accede to their father's wish that William should marry eighteen-year-old Margaret Scutt. This was not difficult for Sir William to agree to, since he had no desire to marry Margaret, despite his father's high opinion of the young woman. However, six months after Bridget's death, Edward married Margaret. Presumably, since there was no blood tie, Margaret's marriage to Edward (her former stepfather by virtue of his marriage to Bridget) did not infringe the prescribed terms of consanguinity, but his family and the neighbourhood were horrified and scandalised by the series of events.

Sir John's long-term opinion of his son Edward is made plain enough by the fact that even eight years before his death, when he drew up his first will, Edward was left only £10 a year, with no property provision whatsoever, considerably less than his two younger brothers.[88] After that date Sir John added no codicils to leave Edward in a better position, or indicate that there had been any revision of his opinion. With all his other relatives Sir John dealt generously. His only daughter, Elizabeth, was left a dowry of 500 marks to marry young Lord Mountjoy as arranged by the two fathers. In addition, he left a sum of £200 that he had agreed to pay Lord Mountjoy if the marriage went ahead. If the Mountjoy marriage did not go ahead, he willed that Elizabeth was to have the dowry and the £200 forfeiture to help her to marry another suitable person. Dame Margaret, Sir John's wife, was left with gold, jewels and plate, and the lifetime tenancy of Tormarton in Gloucestershire, provided she signed a guarantee that when she died she would leave the estate stocked as it was on Sir John's death, with '300 ewes and 500 wethers', for Sir William.[89] In the event, Dame Margaret chose to live in a small dower house in the Chew Valley, so Tormarton became Sir William's principal country seat, and in many contemporary documents he is referred to as 'Sir William Seyntlo of Tormarton', although he never lived there.

Edward was left nothing; not even the £10 a year bequeathed in the first will. Sir John stated that in the event of Sir William's death before his own, then all his property would pass to Edward – but this was merely complying with the law of primogeniture. In Sir John's will there was not a kind word for his second son.

It is perhaps not surprising, given his nature, that Edward St Loe would react violently. And the people who suffered the consequences were his elder brother, Sir William, and Bess, Lady Cavendish.

CHAPTER 8

'MY OWN SWEET BESS'

1559–61

AT SOME POINT DURING THE WINTER OF 1558–9, BESS AND William St Loe fell in love. We know this from Sir William's subsequent letters to her, and although none of Bess's letters to him (to which he refers) have survived, it appears that his affection was fully reciprocated. Also, in his will, written just a few years later, Sir William refers to Bess's 'natural affection' and their 'mutual love'. The likelihood is that this relationship was the passionate love of Bess's life.

His personal wealth and influence aside, what did Sir William St Loe have to offer Bess? From his correspondence with Bess and his friends, it is clear that he had a well-developed, kindly sense of humour, and we have his tutor's opinion that he was above average in intelligence. The late Sir William Cavendish had been more than twenty years Bess's senior, had grown corpulent, and suffered from ill health for the last three or four years of his life, but Sir William St Loe was a physically active man, in the prime of his life, and only nine years older than Bess.

Bess had clearly felt great affection for her late husband, and her marriage had been happy, but dutiful. Certainly she had enjoyed a superior lifestyle, but she had never been free of worries of one sort or another, ever since the death of Robert Barlow. She bore a child almost annually during her second marriage, and from her household account books it is evident that her time was fully occupied with child-rearing, caring for family members, displaying constant prudence in matters of housewifery and the running of her husband's households and servants. She had lost two babies and had nursed Sir William Cavendish during his deteriorating health. As well as the trauma resulting from her husband's death, she had then taken on the management of the Cavendish estates, a role for which she had not been formally prepared or educated, and although she had weathered the immediate problems of the debt to the Exchequer, this matter continued to cause her grave concern. Until Sir William St Loe came into her life there had been few periods in which Bess had been able to simply enjoy herself.

Sir William St Loe teased her and made no secret of his love for her. And while her late husband addressed her as 'Good Bess' in his correspondence, Sir William St Loe addressed her as his 'Sweet love'. She was now a fully mature woman, had tasted independence and probably had come to know herself and what she wanted. St Loe does not affect the role of a supplicant in his affectionate letters to Bess: they are written with all the confidence of a man who knows his love is returned. It would be surprising had Bess not been physically attracted to a man of presence who was so unaffectedly in love with her. From the portrait we have of her at the time,[1] Bess radiates a bloom which is far from matronly. It was characteristic of her, however, that when she fell in love, she showed a degree of acumen and chose a man of means.

Elizabeth's coronation took place in mid-winter. On Thursday 13 January, 1559, following an old tradition, the uncrowned monarch travelled by royal barge from Whitehall to 'take possession of the Tower', the symbolic heart of London. After spending two nights there she set out, on the eve of her coronation day, in a triumphal procession to Westminster. There are two good artistic representations of this historical event,* and Sir William St Loe appears in both, riding ahead of the Yeoman Guard who bring up the rear of the procession in their showy scarlet and black uniforms ('all in red coats . . . with a broad guard [band] of black velvet and cuts [slashes]').[2] In one, they have just issued from the gate of the Tower; Sir William wears a hip-length cloak over his doublet, breeches and hose. There is a jaunty feather in his hat, and his horse – probably one or other of his two favourite horses 'Galantyne' and 'Courtauld'[3] – carries its head high, and is shown with its foreleg lifted, ready to prance, unsettled perhaps by the cheers of the crowds and the chill of the mid-winter day. The air, as we know from contemporary records, was clear, but there were flurries of light snowflakes and the ground was muddy. Behind this tableau there is a huddle of houses, smoke rising from a chimney, and an inn with its signboard swinging.[4] What the illustration cannot show, but we know from written accounts, is that all the bells of London were pealing joyously, and the water conduits ran with wine for several hours.

The Queen, followed by her ladies, travelled a little way ahead of the guard, and was seated in a horse-drawn chariot topped with a canopy. Her gown and mantle were of gold and silver tissue (there were twenty-three yards of material in the mantle alone) and, to ward off the chill, ermine. Far from acting as a distant icon on this long-awaited day, she interacted with her subjects, answering their loyal shouts 'with exceeding liveliness' both in her voice and in her appearance as she returned their good wishes, answering that she wished herself neither prosperity nor safety unless it was for the common good of her people. As the procession reached Cheapside, one of her ladies asked her why she suddenly smiled broadly. She replied, 'Because I have just heard one say in the crowd: "Remember old Harry the Eighth".'[5]

*See picture section.

On Sunday 16 January there was a solemn procession, on foot, from Westminster Palace to the Abbey over newly laid paths that were 'railed-in' and bedecked with blue banners. The Queen's train was borne by her first cousin, Margaret, Countess of Lennox, a woman who would play a major role in Bess's future life. George Talbot, 6th Earl of Shrewsbury, a man who would play an even larger part in Bess's future life, carried the Queen's gloves. And inside the Abbey, behind the dais on which the throne was placed, Sir William St Loe stood guard, confident in the knowledge that in a small room directly beneath the dais, reached by a trapdoor under the throne, he had placed a small reinforcement of yeoman guards.[6]

After the ceremony a State banquet was held at Westminster Hall. Here the Champion of England, Sir Edward Dymock, rode into the hall dressed in full armour, upon a beautiful charger caparisoned in cloth of gold: he flung down his gauntlet and offered to fight anyone who did not recognise the Queen's right to the crown. Next, Sir William St Loe, as Chief Butler of England, ceremoniously offered the first cup of wine to the new sovereign.

In her household book, Bess recorded a payment for her children to watch the procession from a prime vantage point: in the procession stands, which were a feature of the Chepe. There is no charge recorded for her own viewing arrangements, and this is undoubtedly because she was given privileged seating, probably in the Abbey, as an invited guest, and her sponsor was likely to have been Sir William St Loe.

It is not difficult to see what Bess might have found attractive in Sir William, but how was Bess an attractive proposition to him? Well, there was Chatsworth and the estates left by Bess's late husband, which were producing between £350 and £400 a year. But these lands were encumbered by a crippling debt for which any man marrying Bess would become responsible. And then there was the matter of her six children, all under twelve years of age, as well as her two, older stepdaughters, for whom a dowry must be produced. St Loe had two grown daughters of his own to provide for, and the additional responsibility of so many small stepchildren might well have put off a would-be suitor.

The attraction must come back again to Bess herself, and again it is difficult not to conclude that she possessed some charisma or great charm in her demeanour which engaged people like Lady Frances, Sir William Cavendish and now Sir William St Loe, despite her circumstances. Sir William St Loe was not only fascinating and wealthy, but he had the Queen's ear and her favour. In time he could confidently expect to become her Vice-Chamberlain and even a Privy Counsellor (as did Christopher Hatton and others who later captained Elizabeth's personal guard). To put it succinctly, Sir William could have looked far higher for a wife, but he chose Bess Cavendish, and he remained in love with her until the day he died.

In July 1559, soon after the famous *fête-champêtre* and tilt tournament at Greenwich, Sir William announced his betrothal to Lady Cavendish, and immediately her name began to appear on St Loe estate documents. For example, a lease granted to a tenant on some Somerset properties owned by Sir William was to cease 'on the death of Elizabeth, widow of Sir William Cavendish'.[7] The Queen approved the marriage and appointed 27 August for the ceremony. At the time the Queen was also in love, and her passion for her handsome Master of Horse, Robert Dudley (recently created Knight of the Garter), had provoked a good deal of excited gossip, not to say alarm, at Court. 'He does what he likes . . .' the scandalised Spanish Ambassador reported, 'and it is even said that Her Majesty visits him in his chamber, day and night . . . they go so far to say that his wife has a malady in one of her breasts, and the Queen is only waiting for her to die to marry Lord Robert.'[8] Warned by William Cecil, Chief Secretary of State, of the damage she was doing to her reputation, Elizabeth embarked upon a brief public flirtation with forty-three-year-old bachelor Sir William Pickering, who had been a leading player in the Wyatt plot, but no one at Court was really fooled by this obvious feint.

The fact that the Queen 'named the day' suggests that she might have been present at the St Loe wedding ceremony, or it may simply have been that as Captain of the Guard, Sir William required her permission to be absent on a certain date. We do not know the answer, for there is no surviving record of the marriage and we do not know where it took place. But we know when it took place because of a wedding invitation that Sir William sent on 15 August 1559 to Bess's old friend Sir John Thynne at Longleat:

> Saving my promise . . . and not forgetting your friendship, these [lines] are to satisfy you that the day of my marriage is by my Mistress appointed upon Sunday this sevennight [27 August]. At which time both her Ladyship and myself [hope] to see you there. She hath with terrible threatenings commanded me not to forget making of her hearty commendations unto you and to my lady your wife, unto whom I pray you let me be also commended . . . from Somerset this Tuesday 15th August. William Seyntlo.[9]

The newly-weds were certainly in Somerset soon after the wedding. Possibly they were married there, or perhaps Sir William wished to show his bride round his estates. During this visit Bess found that at Sutton Court, where the couple expected to spend time between periods at London and Chatsworth, there was no adequate parlour for her to retire to. With Sir William's permission she ordered one to be built, and the work was set in progress immediately as part of an extension to the existing manor house. Among the decorations which survived for at least three centuries in the panelled and plastered parlour was an arras containing the arms of Hardwick and Cavendish, quartered with those of Sir William's own heritage, St Loe, Poynz, Fitznichols, Rivers, Fitzpayne and Arundell.[10] These heraldic devices can also be seen in a stained-glass window in the north aisle of the local church, St Andrew's at Chew Magna.

In late September the couple were back in London. From there Bess sent her husband's sister Elizabeth 'two chains of gold' costing £21, and a gift of '5 marks' (£4) to his youngest brother, Clement St Loe, who had accompanied them on their bridal visits.[11] The couple had been called back to Court because Sir William was required for an official duty. The French King, Henri II, had been killed in a jousting accident, and as France's ally (at that time), Elizabeth had ordered splendid and solemn obsequies at St Paul's. Sir William was one of the four Attendant Knights appointed along with four peers to be official mourners at the ceremony. He carried the banner, and two of the other three attendants were among his closest friends: Sir Richard Sackville and Sir Edward Warner.[12] Sir William's forebears, as we know, had performed similar duties,[13] and his father had been an Attendant Knight* at the funeral of Edward VI.[14]

Francis, Henri's fifteen-year-old son, now became King of France. And Francis's sixteen-year-old wife, Mary Stuart, Queen of Scotland since she was six days old, was now proclaimed by the French, Queen of France, Scotland and England,† creating a small burr under the skin of every loyal Englishman, not least that of their Queen.

Soon after their return to London in time for Christmas, Bess (now Lady St Loe) was made a Lady of the Privy Chamber.‡ This appointment, undoubtedly a wedding gift from the Queen, was yet a further sign of favour to Sir William St Loe.[15]

Queen Elizabeth had spent a great deal of her troubled young life

---

*Sir William's great-great-grandfather had been one of the three 'Squires to the King's Body' of Henry VI. His grandfather had performed similar duties at the funeral of Henry VII.

†Mary's grandmother, Margaret Tudor, was Henry VIII's elder sister (see Tree: 'Heirs of Henry VII').

‡Maids of honour, unmarried women, were the lowest-ranking women waiting on the Queen. Next in precedence came Ladies-in-Waiting, then Ladies of the Privy Chamber, and finally, the most senior women, the Ladies of the Bedchamber.

in seclusion, deliberately wearing plain and sombre clothes in the hope of convincing Queen Mary of her modest disposition. Now she appeared in colourful splendour, and she encouraged a lively and joyous atmosphere at her Court, welcoming extravagant fashions and the latest dances from the continent. Although she valued the wisdom of older men in her team of advisers and those she placed in top positions, it was understandably mostly young people that Elizabeth gathered round her for her leisure hours.

At thirty-one, Bess was one of the older women waiting on the Queen. Only the most senior-ranking ladies were chosen, for it was a distinctly personal service, attending on a person who was stripping off the emblems of rank and preparing for bed, or washing and dressing each morning. These attendants were with the Queen when she was at her most relaxed and approachable, and though Elizabeth discouraged the talking of 'business' in her privy-chamber, bribes were freely offered for the chance of obtaining one of these sought-after positions. When any of the Queen's attendants retired from service, the Chamberlain was besieged with offers and promises from families who wanted the place for their daughters or wives.

The service was not arduous, and the duties involved caring for the jewellery, folding gowns, laying out a nightgown, tying on sleeves and so forth. More menial tasks than these were performed by servants of the household. The Ladies waited on a rota organised by the Chamberlain, and could technically leave the Court at any time without the Queen's permission. However, if the Queen wished them to remain it was a brave woman who would refuse such a request.

For Bess, the main benefit of the post was obvious. Although the Queen discouraged her ladies from asking favours when she was relaxing, she was well disposed towards them. For the moment Bess's legal advisers had staved off the Exchequer claim, but Bess was always conscious of that large outstanding debt to the State. Her careful deportment was noticed by Robert Dudley, the Queen's life-long love, and he congratulated Sir William on his wife's 'noble and wise government of herself at court'.[16] There was a noticeable *esprit de corps* among the men who had shared imprisonment in the Tower because of their support for the Princess Elizabeth. Bess had known Robert Dudley when he was a youth, and her friendship with the Queen's favourite would continue into their old age.

One person who should have been an obvious choice for the position of Lady of the Bedchamber was a noticeable absentee. Lady Frances (formerly Grey née Brandon) had more right to the position than any other woman in the land for, strictly speaking, she was Elizabeth's heir. But she was never received at Court; Elizabeth never forgave her cousin the sin of marrying her groom for love. However, when, in October 1559, Lady Frances died of an illness from which she had suffered for some months, she was given a State funeral in Westminster Abbey. Her widower, Adrian Stokes, provided an extravagant alabaster tomb for his Lady, and promptly disappeared from history. The two remaining Grey sisters, Katherine and Mary, who had been Ladies of the Bedchamber in Queen Mary's time, were made Ladies of the Privy Chamber – a demotion which infuriated Katherine. Bess, who valued her relationship with the Grey family, remained close to the sisters; she still treasured the piece of jewellery 'set with an agate' that had been given to her by the Lady Frances when she was in her service.[17]

Sir William St Loe was an easy-going man, and he was clearly smitten with Bess. Not only did he encourage his new wife to begin alterations to his ancestral home, but he also underwrote the resumption of building work on Chatsworth, which had come to an abrupt halt for financial reasons after the death of Sir William Cavendish. Aware of, and amused by, her growing obsession with building, he teased her affectionately, calling her 'the chief overseer of my works'.[18]

Bess spent the entire winter of 1559–60 in London with Sir William, while the industrious major-domo, James Crompe, looked after Chatsworth, running the estates, ensuring that the crops were planted and gathered in on time, that the cattle and sheep were tended properly and accounted for, and overseeing the building works. Bess's mother was living at Chatsworth with her sister 'Aunt Linnacre', in charge of the children's welfare and their education by a tutor appropriately called Master Ledger.[19] From there in February 1560 Crompe wrote to tell Bess of estate business and the progress on the ceilings and cornices of the long gallery: '. . . you must have a portal coming into the gallery as Nicholas tells me. Let me know whether he shall do the ceiling first or the portal . . .' He also warned her about a merchant from whom she proposed to order some materials for the house, '. . . take heed how you deal with him for he is a crafty yeoman as I am told'.[20] Meanwhile, he wrote, the books sent for Master William had arrived. Sir William St Loe regarded Bess's children as his own and in his own accounts he recorded the purchase of 'books for the children – 3 Grammars in French,* A *Cosmography of the Levant*; *Psalms* – in French, with notes'. And for himself, a fluent French speaker, he purchased '*Justic Militayrs*'.[21] On another occasion he bought the children an almanac and a book called *Pronunciation*.[22]

In April Bess was back in Chatsworth, straight into her building works. She wrote from there to Sir John Thynne, asking him if he would loan her his plasterer for she was ready to begin 'flowering' her hall. She must have had a momentary mental slip when writing, for she signed herself Elizabeth Cavendish, and then, noticing what she had done, she crossed out Cavendish and wrote above it 'Seyntlo'.[23] A small human experience, shared by countless newly married women.

Little did Bess know it but her pleasant, untroubled lifestyle was already under threat. Without realising it, her bridal visit to Sutton Court and the alterations she had ordered there had created a dangerous enemy. Edward St Loe had had his eye on Sutton Court and

---

*These can only have been the French grammar book written by Sir William's old tutor Palsgrave, since no other French grammar existed at the time.

now made the extraordinary claim that his father had promised the house to his wife Margaret (the former Miss Scutt) as her marital home. Sir William had a larger manor house at Tormarton in Gloucestershire,[24] as well as a house in the city of London, and Bess also had Chatsworth. Edward seems to have assumed that his brother would not be requiring Sutton Court as well, and he was fuming and resentful at what he saw as Bess's intrusion into the home he considered his own.

Sir William had been widowed for over eight years when he met Bess. He had no sons from his first marriage and his service in Ireland had not been without some danger. Edward had probably fallen into the habit of assuming that he was his brother's heir, and this partially explains why he attempted to dissuade Sir William from marrying Margaret Scutt in 1558, only to marry the young woman himself a few months later. Edward was not only attracted to Margaret[25] but probably hoped to prevent his brother from siring a male child. But now Sir William had married a widow with a large family (of whom Sir William appeared inordinately fond), who, furthermore, had a history of fecundity and was still young enough to have more children. Edward could see his chances of inheriting the St Loe lands fading rapidly.

He called on his brother at the London house in February 1560, ostensibly to pay his respects to his new sister-in-law, but there was some bad blood between the two brothers over the alterations at Sutton Court, especially when Edward claimed that his father had promised the property to his wife Margaret 'for her lifetime'. This bequest was not contained in Sir John's last will or mentioned in a previous one.[26] Nor did that careful man make any memorandum or codicil concerning the matter prior to his death. Indeed, upon investigation by Sir William, none of Sir John's closest friends or his executors knew anything of such a promise. More importantly, nor did his widow, the dowager Lady St Loe, who had been left a lifetime tenancy of Tormarton Manor, Gloucestershire. It is just possible that Sir John had promised the lifetime tenancy of

Sutton Court to Margaret Scutt in the event that she were to marry Sir William St Loe, a match which at one time Sir John had tried to promote.

Without question, the property legally belonged to Sir William, but he was not an argumentative man and perhaps he felt his brother had been badly treated. Rather than fight over the matter, he offered Edward the post of steward of Sutton Court, enabling Edward and Margaret to reside there, while being answerable to him.[27] This crumb thrown from the table of the feast was not enough for Edward. He accepted the post but he believed that the rents and the lordship of the manor should be his. He was one of the few people who did not fall under the spell of Bess's charm.

Soon after Edward's visit to the St Loes' London house, Bess was poisoned.

Sir William's mother was staying with Sir William and Bess in London when Bess was taken ill. In a subsequent letter,* Dame Margaret wrote that she was convinced Bess would have died had a remedy not been to hand.[28] Probably this remedy was an emetic; the Elizabethans constantly worried about poison, and kept antidotes available. The Queen's household was not free of this paranoia. A few weeks after this incident – or perhaps it was related, since Bess was a Lady of the Privy Chamber, and her poisoning would have been much gossiped about at Court – Master Secretary Cecil wrote a memorandum about the necessity for caution against any possible attempt to poison the Queen.

> We think it very convenient that your Majesty's apparel and especially all manner of things that touch any part of your Majesty's body be circumspectly looked at. And no person be permitted to come near but those who have the trust and charge thereof . . . No manner of perfume either in apparel or sleeves, gloves or suchlike . . . be presented by a stranger or other

*See p. 155.

person . . . that no foreign meat or dishes being dressed out of Court be brought to your food without knowledge of from whom it cometh . . . May it please your Majesty to take advise of your Physician for receiving twice weekly some preservative . . .[29]

The poison was believed to have been aimed at both Sir William and Bess, but for some unknown reason Sir William seems to have avoided it. Perhaps he was not at home, perhaps the poison was concealed in a garment he did not touch, perhaps he did not eat of a dish that contained the poison.

Once assured of Bess's recovery, Sir William sprang into action. He immediately suspected his brother and began making enquiries among Edward's known associates. With the help of a Mr Mann, who owned a house where Sir William sometimes stayed when he was alone in London, he tracked down a suspect. Hugh Draper, the owner of an inn at Bristol, about twelve miles from Sutton Court, and a man of 'some wealth', was arrested and charged with 'necromancy against my Lady Sentlo'. He was committed to the Tower on 21 March and his entry in the prisoners' list reads:

This man was brought in by the accusation of one John Mann. [He is] an astronomer, . . . suspected of [being] a conjuror or sorcerer, and thereby to practise matter against Sir William Sentlo and my Lady. And in his profession it [appears] that before this time he has been busy and doing with such matters, but he denies any matter . . . touching Sir William Sentlo or my lady. He also [states that it is] long since he so misliked his science, that he burned all his books.[30]

The Lieutenant of the Tower, Edward Warner, was one of Sir William's closest friends. Sir William was a popular man, and his yeoman guards were stationed at the Tower, responsible at times for guarding prisoners. It could not have been a very pleasant incarceration for Master Draper. It was some time before any further evidence came to light and Draper passed his time, as so many other prisoners did, carving graffiti on the walls of his cell; Draper carved an astrological calendar as a device for casting horoscopes. Over it he carved the words, 'Hugh Draper of Bristowe made thys sphere the 30 daye of May . . .'[31] In the light of his statement that he had given up practising magic, it could not have done his defence much good, but the device survives, and is still pointed out to visitors as one of the more interesting graffiti in the Tower.[32]

A few weeks later Bess received an extraordinary letter from Sir William's mother who, after asking how Bess was, went on to write:

> I have been asked what the matter is between my son Seyntlo and his brother Edward. I have made answer I was sure my son Sayntlo would not mislike [Edward] without a great cause. And many hath said to me they hear say Edward should go about to poison his brother and you . . . Here [there] is a great talk of it.
>
> . . . About a month or more [ago] there came a lady hither to me, and was very earnest with me to know whether I heard any such thing: and said she [heard] it at Long's mouth, who brought her letter or token from Bess Sayntlo . . . But I told her I was sure you were poisoned when I was at London . . . which she made it strange she never heard of it before, which I am sure she did. She . . . is [now] at Edward Sayntlo's. Cosdon shall tell you more of her talk to me.
>
> Now I know [for] sure she came hither to hear what I would say, and what she could understand by me. She told me how her cousin Edward had sent to her often to join him, but she would not. I told her what I thought of him, which I am sure she misliked me for . . . she said she was sorry there should be any variance between us, for she did know I have used him very well. But I think she says the contrary to him. I perceive their heads be full of this matter . . .
>
> God send them little power to do my son Sayntlo or you any

hurt. This was the goodwill he [Edward] bore you when he came
up to London to see you, as he said was non other caused his
coming, which I know the contrary, for he liked nothing your
marriage. His good friendship to you, as to me, is all one. The
living God defend us all from such friends.

I pray you, Madam, send me word how this devil's devices
began, and how it came to light. Thanks be to God you know
[about] it. I will trouble you no longer but I pray God send you
both long life, and good health . . . Written the xiii day of June,
by yours most assuredly as long as I shall live,
    Margaret Sayntloe[33]

Dame Margaret was a doting mother to her other children and
it must have cost her an effort to write of her son Edward as a
'devil'. It would be many months before Sir William tracked down
Draper's accomplices, probably through the woman Dame
Margaret wrote of, a cousin of the St Loe brothers, confusingly also
named Elizabeth St Loe (as was Sir William's sister). Eventually,
Francis Cox, who was accused of conspiring with Hugh Draper
and practising 'sorcery', was committed to the Tower and a week
afterwards 'a Mr Ralph Davie and his daughter were committed to
the tower', accused by Sir William, 'that he . . . practised, with the
said daughter, for the poisoning of my lady Sentlo'.[34]

The cousin, Elizabeth St Loe, was likewise committed, and spent
thirty-one weeks in prison and was charged twenty-six shillings
and eight pence a week for her food, five shillings for her servant's
food, and a further five shillings for candles. The quality of her
care, far more lavish than that accorded to other prisoners, leads
one to suspect that Sir William, whose position at the Tower
enabled him to make such arrangements, was too soft-hearted to
allow his cousin to be kept too severely, although she was listed
among the prisoners who 'have neither paid or have been able to
pay their own charges'. The four prisoners each served periods of
between thirty-one and forty-six weeks in the Tower.

The presence in the Tower of Sir William's cousin Elizabeth, with the same name as his wife, has caused a similar confusion in previous biographies of Bess to that caused between Uncle William and Sir William St Loe. All claim that it was Bess who was imprisoned in the Tower. This is incorrect. A year hence, Bess would be in serious trouble, and she was taken to the Tower for questioning, but according to the Tower records she was never kept there as a prisoner. Furthermore, during the period that Mistress Elizabeth St Loe was serving out her sentence, Bess, Lady St Loe, was in attendance at Court, and wrote several letters from Chatsworth and elsewhere.

Curiously, Edward St Loe seems to have escaped any punishment over this affair, despite the fact that the three men in prison were his known associates and that his own mother believed he had been the instigator of the crime. Ralph Davie, in particular, had been a cohort with Edward in other nefarious acts over a number of years.[35] Sir William did not give up, however. He began collecting evidence to sue his brother privately.

Meanwhile, his duty to the Queen took precedence over everything else. Bess understood this, of course, and while Sir William was engaged in escorting the Queen on the first of her many Progresses around the country, Bess went to Derbyshire for the summer. In 1560 the Court travelled to Winchester, Basing and back to Windsor.[36] Sir William and Bess had to be content with communicating by letter and snatching a few days together every now and then. If more than a week went by without hearing from Bess, Sir William became desperate. One such letter was written from Windsor Castle in September 1560, on the day before the Court left for London:

My own, more dearer to me than I am to myself;
    Understand it is no small fear or grief unto me . . . my continual nightly dreams, besides my absence, hath troubled me, but also chiefly that Hugh Alsop cannot satisfy me in what estate

thou or thine is. Therefore, I pray thee, as thou dost love me, let
me shortly hear from thee, for the quieting of my unquiet mind,
how thy own sweet self, with all thine, doeth . . .[37]

There was little Bess liked better than matchmaking. And clearly
before she left London she had done some matchmaking for a
friend of her husband's called Harry Skipwith,[38] with a young lady
called Mistress Neil. All was now all right, Sir William wrote, for
Mistress Neil had opened up her heart to Skipwith who was with
her 'by this time'. And the grateful Skipwith sent Bess 'ten thousand
thanks' for her help. Sir William told his wife how, on the previous
day, the Queen had greatly admired his horse so he had given it to
her. 'Thus wishing myself with thyself', he ended, 'thine who is
wholly and only thine, yea and all thine while life lasteth.'[39]

In a postscript he added that he had visited Eton College, where
Harry and William Cavendish had been entered for the forthcoming winter term. To set her mind at rest he advised that the Almoner
had sent Bess his compliments, and assured Sir William 'no gentleman's children in England shall be better welcome, nor better
looked unto, than our boys. Once again, farewell, my good honest
sweet'.[40]

Sir William's account book gives a vivid picture of his bachelor
life in London. It was a busy and pleasant one. When he and Bess
were both in London they lived in his house in Tuthill Street, but in
Bess's absences he preferred to board at Master Mann's house in
Red Cross Street,* where he lived well and kept a good table without the need to keep a household of servants.[41] He often dined out
with friends such as Lord Cobham, Henry Carey (Lord Hunsdon –
the Queen's maternal cousin and a favourite at Court), Lady
Throckmorton (whose husband Sir Nicholas, the English
Ambassador in Paris, was in regular correspondence with Sir
William, sometimes sending him gifts of gold buttons and aiglets

*Neither Tuthill Street nor Red Cross Street survived the Great Fire of London.

for Bess, and gifts for her children)[42], and a Master Babington (a Derbyshire neighbour, whom Bess referred to as 'cousin').

There are charges for link boys – sixpence, to carry torches to light Sir William's way when he went out to late suppers. He also entertained at Mr Mann's house. When Sir James Croft, for example, came to 'sup' with him on 26 August, a servant was sent out for pears and nuts for dessert, and minstrels were hired to entertain them at a cost of sixpence. On another day when Sir James Croft came to breakfast, the lavish fare cost twelve shillings and ten-pence.[43] Sir William's brother Clement, who had business interests in London, was another frequent guest. Eight serving men took care of Sir William's clothes, his horses, his shopping and his accounts, along with other duties such as carrying messages. With the exception of his valet, the servants did not stay at Mr Mann's house but boarded somewhere nearby, for which he paid them a nightly 'bed and board' allowance.

Being a military man, Sir William was unlikely to be a fop, but his wardrobe was far from austere. For one outfit he paid fourteen shillings and ninepence for two yards of white velvet to make a pair of trunk hose, and a further twenty-seven shillings and sixpence for white satin to line them at eleven shillings the yard. More white satin was bought at equally high cost for the 'panes'* of the trunks, and three yards of a beige colour satin was chosen to make a doublet, which he had lined with sarcenet. The cost of this gorgeous outfit, including the tailor's fee, came to more than £5. Over it he wore a 'white Spanish jerkin' decorated with gold buttons, and he also bespoke some white Spanish buskins. Another similar outfit was made in black velvet and satin, and later he paid a tailor to add some black lace to the velvet coat. With his tall slim figure he must have looked very dashing in his all white and all black ensembles. His washing was done by washerwomen: 'for washing of 2 shirts, 4 handkerchiefs, 1 head kerchief, and 2 pairs of socks on the 16th

---

*Panes: wide bands of ribbon, or material, sewn in parallel onto the garment.

August: 6 pence'.[44] There are frequent payments to seamstresses to repair the lace trimmings on his shirts.

He often travelled between royal palaces by boat, hiring two boats at a time so that his servants and horses could follow him. The river was a busy thoroughfare, the motorway of the day. It was obviously a faster way of travelling from Greenwich to Whitehall, for example, than the long ride south of the river, crossing at London Bridge with its milling hordes.

Sir William was an open-handed man: there are numerous instances of his giving alms to the poor, tips to porters and maids, gratuities to old soldiers that he passed on the road, to a boy that opened a gate for him, to the small son of an innkeeper, or to a man that he asked to watch his luggage 'until the tide came with the barge', and, his secretary recorded, 'a reward to a kitchen boy that tumbled before you, the 4th of September . . . one shilling'.[45]

Once the Court had settled again at Windsor Sir William intended to get away to see Bess, but soon after he wrote the letter telling her he had given his horse to the Queen, the Court was rocked by scandal. On 9 September 1560 Amy Robsart, wife of the Queen's favourite, Sir Robert Dudley, was found by her servants lying at the bottom of a staircase, her neck broken. In view of the gossip that had surged about their relationship since the coronation, it is not difficult to imagine with what horror the Queen received this news. Deeply distressed, she immediately banished Dudley to his house at Kew, which she had given him only months earlier. Meanwhile she ordered an inquiry.

After a few days, a verdict of accidental death was brought in and Dudley was allowed to return to Court. But he would never be free of the stigma concerning the death of his wife, and the suspicion that he was in some way involved followed him throughout his life. It is now believed, given her symptoms, that Amy was suffering from breast cancer. Had she died in her bed of natural causes there is a possibility that after a decent interval Elizabeth might have married Dudley, but the circumstances of Amy's death made that impossible. If she had married Dudley after Amy's death Elizabeth knew that she would be implicated in what many openly described as a murder. Indeed she was already suspected of collusion in some quarters, especially in Paris, from where Sir Nicholas Throckmorton wrote that the rumours concerning the death and Queen Elizabeth's part in it were so malicious, '. . . as I am ashamed to write of them'.[46] There was not a lot the Queen could do but order the Court into deep mourning for a month.[47]

While the crisis ran Sir William could not leave the Court, and when he was finally given leave to go to his wife he was detained in the city by some movement in Bess's case versus the Exchequer. Sir William was determined to remove this problem from his wife: 'I should have been with you this day but for our [Ex]chequer business,' he wrote. He felt it best to stay and deal with the matter, but, he continued,

. . . my hap is evil, my time worse spent, for that my reward is as yet nothing more than fair words, with the like promises. Take it all in good part, and if I should understand the contrary it would trouble me more than my pen can express. I will forbear answering your last letter written to me, for that God willing I will this next week be the messenger myself . . . Farewell my own sweet Bess, from Master Mann's house in Red Cross Street, 12th October, from him who dares not so near his coming home, to term thee as thou art. Yet, thine, William Seyntlo[48]

When he rode north the following week his eight-strong party included his brother Clement and their servants. An additional five horses carried the baggage. He arrived at Chatsworth, after a fast ride, on 21 October. There was no doubting their warm welcome, and they did not arrive empty-handed. The horses had carried baskets of items that were not easy to purchase in Derbyshire: oranges and lemons, plums (out of season), frankincense (for perfuming the air; especially valued during outbreaks of smallpox), a firkin of olives, sturgeon ('the royal fish'), 'certain pothecary wares', and pepper and spices. On a more personal note there were gifts for Bess, wires for her virginals, two dozen black lace points, and 'a Bongrace* of the latest fashion' which cost twenty shillings (the price of a good workhorse). He also carried sixty-three ells† of canvas to Chatsworth, probably by commission of Bess. These items were in addition to other gifts he purchased for her from time to time, such as 'a pair of quartered velvet shoes for my lady and eight dozen ribbon points . . . two ounces of Spanish silk and a dozen coney skins . . . four pairs of Spanish gloves', and 'a knocker for the great gate at Chatsworth'. He frequently despatched gifts to Chatsworth in baskets by carriers.

He had much to tell Bess: the court gossip about the Amy Robsart affair, of course, would have been pounced upon by the ladies of the household, especially Bess, who knew all the protagonists well. But also she would have eagerly listened to the latest developments in their own affair against the Treasury. Sir William had received word that Edward St Loe was causing problems at Sutton Court, collecting and keeping rents due to Sir William, and holding local courts leet and courts baron‡ and sentencing wrongdoers as though he was the landowner. Inevitably it would be necessary for Sir William to go to Somerset and deal with this matter in person.

His other news would have included the fact that the Queen had granted him some new lands at Acton Turville in Gloucestershire,[49] and that in his capacity as Captain of the Guard, he had been granted

---

*Bongrace: a shaped head-dress, covered in velvet and stiffened with a buckram lining.
†An ell was forty-five inches in length: therefore it was one yard and nine inches.
‡Court leet: generally held in the presence of the steward of the manor, in the presence of all male inhabitants of the manor, to elect constables, regulate the quality of bread and beer, and try minor offences such as drunkenness and complaints by neighbours etc. Court baron: held in the presence of the Lord of the Manor, and with local freeholders as jurors, to try cases of debt, trespass, and serious local crimes.

permission to commission a suit of armour from the royal armourer at Greenwich. Intended 'for field and tilt', this armour was built by the celebrated master armourer Erasmus Kirckenar.[50] Sir William's servants collected it by boat. An image survives of this armour, beautifully etched and decorated and, in fact, it provides the only proven facial image of Sir William, apart from the coronation drawings. There was a contemporary conventional portrait painted of Sir William: it was noted twice, once on a table in Bess's bedchamber in an inventory of Chatsworth in 1562, and again in the 1601 Hardwick Hall inventory, when it hung in the chamber which linked the Long Gallery and the Great High Chamber at Hardwick where Bess was then living. But this portrait has long since been lost or mislaid, and we are now left with only this armourer's caricature, a vague image of Sir William with his fashionable moustache and short pointed beard.[*]

Perhaps Sir William was able to give Bess news of her two elder sons, Harry and William – they had almost certainly passed on the road for the boys had left two days earlier in the company of a servant, on their way south to begin their education at Eton.[51] At first they were boarded out with a Master Hills, while black coats, doublets and warmly lined hose were tailored for them locally and appropriate footwear was made. Their minutely detailed accounts show that they had the same preparations to make as any modern-day child going to boarding school: gathering together their trunks of books (a *King's Grammar*, *Marcus Tullius Offices* and *Fabulae Aesopi*), paper, pens and ink, and clothes.

They had already been attending the college for a month before they became boarders on 25 November. 'Paid to the Bursar . . . for the board of Master Henry and Master William and their man for one month . . . 24 shillings.' This did not include 'extras' such as

---

[*]There is a portrait at Hardwick Hall labelled 'Sir William St Loe', but the labelling was done two centuries after Sir William's death. Experts now believe the description to be incorrect and that the subject was probably Matthew Stuart, Earl of Lennox (see Tree: 'Heirs of Henry VIII').

candles for lighting, wood for fires, laundry and mending, the supply of tenterhooks for bed hangings, and the cleaning of their chamber. Eton, it seems, was always an expensive luxury. Sir William was a fond stepfather. When the court was at Windsor it was an easy thing for him to see them, and his account books reveal that on occasion he slipped away from Court in London to visit them as well.

Following his time with Bess, Sir William returned briefly to London, put some affairs in order and then with a goodly escort rode to Somerset. This time he took gifts for his mother, who had removed from Tormarton and was now living in a dower house in the Chew Valley: a yard of crimson lace, some red and white stool-work to make a pair of sleeves, gold and silver thread and some knots of ribbons. Sir William remained in Somerset for just over a week, and what he learned was not pleasant. Then, when he returned to Court, he was received with coolness: '. . . the Queen has found great fault with my long absence,' he wrote to Bess, 'saying she would talk with me further and that she would well chide me . . . I answered that when Her Highness understood the cause she would not be offended. Whereupon she said; "very well, very well."' However, he added, the Queen had not offered him her hand to kiss – as was her usual custom; it was her way of demonstrating her displeasure. Bess arrived in London a month later to join her husband for the twelve nights of festivities marking Christmas 1560.

As a result of his visit to Somerset Sir William ordered his brother to leave Sutton Court, but Edward ignored the command. In January 1561 Sir William and Bess jointly issued a writ against Edward St Loe, alleging that he had acted 'contrary to the trust and confidence' implicit in his position as Steward of Sutton Court, and 'contrary to the natural duty that one brother owes another'. This included his initially entering Sutton Court illegally, taking the profits of the estate as his own, and using the tenants as his own tenants. 'All which the complainants are ready to aver and prove . . .'[52]

Sir William further charged that Edward St Loe:

- had attempted to alienate Sir William and his mother by telling her lies about him; for example Edward had told her that Sir William had discovered the existence of a 'jointure' made by their father, giving Sutton Court to Edward and Margaret for their lives, and that to circumvent this Sir William had entered into a bond with Bess before their marriage, giving her the property and its rents 'without encumbrances'. But there was no such jointure, and no such bond;

- had forged their mother's signature on a letter to Sir William asking him to allow Edward to remain at Sutton Court as Steward;

- had stolen documents and land titles belonging to his late father, and forged others, and with these had laid claim to the manor;

- had 'menaced and threatened the tenants of the said manor' to pay their rents to him 'by such means utterly to defraud your orators';

- had held local 'courts baron' in his own name instead of that of Sir William who was Lord of the Manor;

- had produced Steward's accounts which, when checked by Sir William's agent, Master Lacey of Bristol, were found to be £97. 16s. 3d short.

Edward did not reply to the charges that he had lied and embezzled, but he defended the £97 deficit by counterclaiming he had spent £100 entertaining his brother and his retinue when Sir William visited Sutton Court. Sir William answered dismissively that he stayed at Sutton only one week, where he 'had such presents brought in by friends and tenants, that the said Edward would not spend in half a year'. His brother had 'gained' by his being there rather than being put to any expense, he said. Furthermore, Sir William stated, except for 'those few' servants that waited on him in his chamber, he had 'been at charge for all his horses and men' and they had cost his brother nothing.

Edward swore on oath that he was the possessor of documents proving that Sutton Court was left to his wife, Margaret, for her life, and only after her death to Sir William St Loe and his heirs. Sir William countered that as yet he had not been able to see these documents, but that he believed them to be forgeries.

As the case developed, further skeletons tumbled out of the family cupboard. It was presumably to show the poor calibre of the defendant that Sir William's counsel referred to Edward's past record: his involvement in the mysterious death of John Scutt, and Edward's hasty marriage to the widow who was then three months pregnant with Edward's child, and her sudden and inexplicable death within two months after the marriage, despite her being 'a very lusty young woman'. He also said that Edward had attempted 'by unseemly terms of untruth, to discredit and slander [Bess}, as to make his own unnatural dealings and . . . offences grown out of his own wicked deeds, to be thought by your honour to be her practices'.

On and on went the accusations and counter-accusations in this humdinger of a family soap opera. Edward had charged that in order to persuade Sir William to give her his estates before their marriage, Bess had used 'unnatural' means, such as those she used to recover from poison. This was a clear hint at sorcery or witchcraft – a very dangerous allegation if taken seriously, and Sir William did take it seriously, replying through his counsel that on the contrary his wife:

bore his brother every good will. And so far that, both before and after the marriage, she persuaded Sir William to entail the remainder of all his lands, [in default] of issue of their bodies, to the said Edward. And she ever refused the [rents] thereof, until Sir William . . . perceiving his brother to much unnaturalness and unseemly speeches of him and his wife, did, of very good will towards her, convey the same unto her.

Albeit there is no such likelihood [at present], Sir William may well continue the house by the issue of their bodies, so there need be no such unseemly terms of [his] wife, whom, he must confess, more inwardly has always borne his brother's unkindness towards her, than [told] it to him. And she has been very desirous to do his kin what good she might . . .

As for the matter of the poisoning, she trusts it appears before you to be none of her devices and practises, but that Sir William St Loe, after his wife's poisoning, seeking her safety [which] fell out not by his wife's means but by God's good hap and providence . . . and [she] will be glad to justify before you to her said brother's face, that she never used any such devices or practices, as it pleases him to surmise of her. [53]

Another accusation made against Bess by Edward was that she had caused Sutton Court to fall into 'a state of disorder'. Probably this was the result of the alterations that she had set in motion a year earlier, which remained unfinished because of Edward and Margaret's occupation of the manor. Sir William counterclaimed that it was his brother's poor stewardship that had damaged the house. In addition he was able to produce witnesses to swear that Edward had told friends he intended to destroy the hunting on the estate by killing all the game in several successive days of wanton slaughter.

At the end of it all, the judge was apparently perplexed as to how to rule in this unnatural matter between two brothers. There was no formal police organisation in those days, no detectives to investigate the claims of either party, so that it came down to one man's word against another in court. In the end an unsatisfactory compromise was reached. Edward and Margaret continued to live at Sutton Court, for which they were to pay rent to Sir William and Bess. But a portion of the income from the total rents of the estate was to be returned by Sir William to his brother. The ruling was backdated to their father's death.

Sir William now became concerned about how Bess would be treated in the event of his sudden death without male issue. As things stood Edward would inherit all the St Loe estates and income, and it was obvious that he would not deal kindly with his brother's widow. Sir William therefore made a will which cut out his brother entirely; the property was not entailed and was his to leave where he wished. In the normal course of events a man left everything to the eldest male relative, but Sir William left everything he owned to Bess, and, furthermore, following her death, 'to her heirs forever'.[54] And to ratify this, in case it was challenged, he put in her name everything he owned through a deed of gift.[55]

It was extraordinary in those days for such a large estate to be transferred unconditionally out of a family to a wife. Probably no one except Sir William and Bess knew of this will. Had he made the matter public it is possible that Sir William might have lived longer than he did.

CHAPTER 9

LADY ST LOE IN TROUBLE

1561–5

BESS SPENT THE WINTER OF 1560–61 AT THE COURT, WHERE the main topic of conversation was the death of the frail young French king[1] and the future role of his widow. Mary Stuart was not only Dowager Queen of France and Queen of Scotland, but also styled herself 'Queen of England'.* She was said to be one of the most beautiful women in Europe.

Sir William's close friendship with Sir Nicholas Throckmorton provided him with first-hand information about what was happening at the French court in Orleans where Mary was staying. And from his reports to Cecil of his meetings with her, it is evident that Throckmorton was charmed by the young widowed queen. In one letter he explained that he had advised her, gently, that she had no right to quarter her arms with those of the throne of England, yet even this ardent supporter of Elizabeth felt sympathy for the girl: 'for my part, I see her behaviour to be such, and her wisdom and kingly modesty so great, in that she thinketh herself

---

*See Appendix: 'Selective Tree, Showing the Heirs of Henry VII' for Mary's relationship to Queen Elizabeth.

not too wise', he wrote, 'but is content to be ruled by good counsel and wise men (which is a great virtue in a Prince or Princess, and
which argueth a great judgement and wisdom in her)'.[2] She even
joked with Throckmorton that if only Queen Elizabeth had been a
man, they might have married and resolved all their difficulties.

Mary claimed she had been persuaded by the French to add the
words 'Queen of England' to her title* but Elizabeth would never
forgive Mary for doing so. Indeed, this single error of Mary's may
have changed the entire course of her life and, obliquely, Bess's life
too.

But this was all in the future, and at present Bess was more concerned with the building work going on at Chatsworth, controlled
by her from afar by letters to Crompe and another steward,
William Marchington. These two men ran the estates and reported
to Bess about such things as the feeding of the herds of stock
throughout the winter, hedging and ditching, and tenants' problems. Bess's mother and her aunt were caring for the younger
children and would have written to her separately, but these 'estate
business' letters always contained news of the children's health and
education and it is obvious that Bess had left instructions that she
was to be kept informed at every opportunity: 'at this present [time]
Miss Frances, Miss Elizabeth, Miss Mary and Mrs Knyghton's
children are all well . . . God be praised . . . and all my little
mistresses increase of learning.'

However, running through every piece of correspondence is the
progress – or lack of it – by the builders. Bess replied robustly to
one missive: '. . . If he do tell you he is any penny behind for work
done . . . he doth lie like a false knave . . . and as for the other
mason, that Sir Thomas Folijambe told you of, if he will not apply
his work, you know he is no mete† man for me.' With the coming

---

*It should be remembered that Elizabeth had been crowned 'Queen of England,
France and Ireland' alluding to Calais, formerly held by the English.
†'Mete' = meet, i.e. fit, suitable.

of spring her thoughts had turned to the gardens: '. . . I would have you tell my Aunt Linnacre that I would have the new garden which is by the new house, made a garden this year. I care not whether she bestow any great cost thereof, but to sow it with all kinds of herbs and flowers, and some piece with mallows. I have sent you by this carrier three bundles of garden seeds . . . From the Court this 8th March.'[3]

Just when all seemed to be going smoothly, Bess suddenly found herself in serious trouble from an unexpected quarter, arising from her continued close contact with Lady Katherine and Lady Mary Grey, the two surviving daughters of her friend the Lady Frances. Katherine Grey was now, arguably, heir presumptive to Elizabeth under Henry VIII's Act of Succession. Although she was the most beautiful of the Grey sisters, she was a rackety sort of girl, possessing none of the quiet intelligence or dignity of her late sister Jane. Probably this was why, despite their blood ties, the Queen had little time for Katherine, whom she kept at arm's length, though the girl was tied to the Court by her position as maid of honour and Lady of the Privy Chamber.

Soon after Elizabeth's accession, Katherine's bloodlines had attracted the attention of the Spanish Ambassador, and, believing his approach was made out of genuine friendship, Katherine was either foolish enough, or perhaps ambitious enough, to confide in him of her unhappiness at Court and what she considered ill usage by her cousin the Queen. The Spanish saw Katherine as a possible conduit for returning England to the Catholic faith, for, under Queen Mary, Katherine had obediently embraced the Catholic faith, only to become a Protestant again under Elizabeth. During the winter of 1559, Cecil heard from the British Ambassador to Belgium that the Spanish were hatching a plot to kidnap Lady Katherine and marry her to Philip's halfwitted son Don Carlos. Elizabeth was alarmed enough to take notice. The matter was discussed in Council, where it was reported that Katherine was said to be so unhappy at Court that she would probably leave willingly.[4]

As a consequence, Elizabeth promoted Katherine to the post of Lady of the Bedchamber, where she could keep a closer eye on her.

In fact, Katherine would not have gone willingly to Spain for she was in love. While visiting Hanworth, the home of the formidable Dowager Duchess of Somerset, in the previous year, she had formed an attachment to the Duchess's son, Edward Seymour, Earl of Hertford. Edward Seymour, son of the late Lord Protector, had once been suggested as a husband for Lady Jane Grey. Now, in a changed world, he and Lady Katherine asked permission to marry. The respective mothers were agreeable to the proposed match but as Edward had a remote claim to the throne they both required royal assent. Lady Frances agreed to write and petition the Queen for her permission, but soon afterwards she went into premature labour and died giving birth to a stillborn son before she could complete the letter. Given the Queen's bad feeling towards the Grey family, it is highly doubtful that permission would have been forthcoming anyway. But there was no one else able to speak on the lovers' behalf, except Katherine's uncle, John Grey (whom she did not like to ask), so they were thwarted; a situation that almost always increases passion.

Since her mother's death Katherine had been stuck at court, pining for her lover. Luckily for her she had an ally as feather-brained as herself: Lord Hertford's sister Lady Jane Seymour, who was also a maid of honour. In October 1560 Jane Seymour, impressed by the romance of her brother's situation, and probably not unaware of the potential brilliance of the match, arranged for the two lovers to meet in her tiny private room at Whitehall. There, in Lady Jane's presence, Hertford and Katherine were secretly betrothed, and he promised to marry her, also secretly, at his London home – Hertford House – on the very next occasion that the Queen left London.

The couple did not have to wait long. In late November 1560 the Queen and her Court left the Palace of Westminster for a hunting trip at Eltham, which was to last some days.[5] Katherine claimed she

The earliest known portrait of Bess *c.*1560, still at Hardwick Hall

Hardwick Hall. Bess was born in the original house in 1527, but it is shown here after Bess had remodelled it half a century later

Edward VI's coronation procession in 1547, in which Sir William Cavendish took part. It shows the procession leaving the Tower, proceeding along East Cheap, passing Bow Church into Cheapside. Note the decorated spectator stands en route. It then passed St Paul's (still with its original steeple), along the Strand past Charing Cross to Westminster. Sir William's house in Newgate Street would be in the left foreground of this picture

Sir William Cavendish, Bess's second husband, *c.*1550

The London Bess would have known well: Cheapside, with St Paul's in the background (the original steeple collapsed in 1561). On the left, next to the bell tower of Bow Church, is a permanent gallery for watching processions. In the centre is the Standard water conduit, and in the distance Edward I's cross

King Edward VI. His patronage gave
impetus to Sir William Cavendish's
ambitious plans

Portrait believed to be of Jane Grey.
Her jacket is almost identical to that worn
by Bess (see earliest portrait of Bess),
except that it is ermine, a 'royal' fur

A portrait thought to be of Lady Frances
Brandon, Duchess of Suffolk, mother of
Jane and Katherine Grey

London Bridge in Bess's time – the only bridge across the Thames. The severed heads of wrongdoers were exhibited on poles (drawn out of scale here, for emphasis)

Well-dressed passengers being ferried across the Thames, with London Bridge in the background

Chatsworth House built by Bess and Sir William Cavendish in 1552.
This painting by Richard Wilson is after a contemporary original by Siberechts

A needlework cushion depicting Chatsworth House. It is mentioned in
Bess's inventory of 1601 and is almost certainly her own work

Queen Mary I. She had little patience with errors in Sir William Cavendish's accounts

Elizabeth I: The coronation portrait, 1559. Bess first met the Queen when Elizabeth was twenty years old and she stood as godmother to Bess's eldest son Henry. Their friendship was lifelong

The 10th Lord Cobham and his wife Frances (standing), with their children. Frances and Bess were best friends for many years

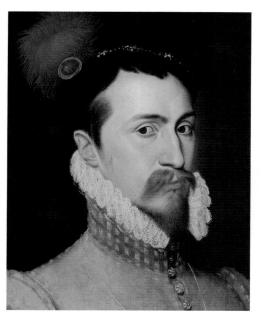

Robert Dudley, Earl of Leicester, c.1564. The love of Queen Elizabeth's life, and a great supporter of Bess

Sir Thomas Wyatt: leader of a rebellion to oust Queen Mary and place the Protestant Princess Elizabeth on the throne

Sir Francis Walsingham. Initially he was Elizabeth's ambassador to France, but from 1573 he was Principal Secretary and ran England's first secret service

William Cecil, later Lord Burghley, Elizabeth's devoted chief minister. He was swept up in the perennial quarrels of the Shrewsburys had a toothache, and Jane, who was consumptive and often ill, said she felt too unwell that day to travel. No sooner had the Court departed than the two young women hurriedly left the Palace by the back entrance, the orchard stairs which led to the river. They then walked 'along by the sands to the Earl's house in Cannon Row'[6] and arrived there before noon. Jane had organised everything, but the clergyman did not appear, so she went out and found another priest on the street.[7] After performing the short marriage service the priest left, and the newly-weds immediately retired to bed for a few hours while Lady Jane occupied herself elsewhere in the house. After this, the two women returned quickly to the Palace because the maids of honour had to account for any absences to the Chamberlain.

For a while it was all very romantic with secret trysts between the newly-weds whenever these could be arranged, but three months after the clandestine wedding Lady Jane Seymour died and thereafter it became far more difficult for the couple to meet. In April the Queen ordered Lord Hertford to accompany William Cecil's son, who was going to France to finish his education. Before his departure, the couple snatched a stolen hour together during which Katherine told her husband she thought she might be pregnant. He promised that if she found this to be so, she was to write to him, and he would try to return at once.

When she was sure of her condition, Katherine wrote asking Hertford to fulfil his promise and come to her aid, but he was unable to do so. By late July, Katherine was well into the seventh month of her pregnancy as she set off with the Court on the Queen's summer Progress to East Anglia. On Saturday 9 August she came to a realisation that she could not keep her secret for much longer. Desperate to confide in someone, she chose her mother's old friend, Bess, Lady St Loe, whom she had known since she was seven years old, and who had always been a part of Katherine's life, even through the worst times of the execution of her father and sister.[8] Indeed one historian suggests that Lady Jane and Lady Katherine Grey were bridesmaids at Bess's wedding to Sir William Cavendish,[9] and though this is a possibility, it can only be regarded as conjecture since there are no records of that marriage ceremony except Sir William's journalised memorandum of the occasion. Now here was Katherine Grey in trouble, and here also was Lady St Loe, an old family friend, attending the Queen that summer as a Lady of the Privy Chamber, and noted by the Queen to be 'most privy' with Lady Katherine.

Katherine cornered Bess as the two women were retiring late that night and duly confessed her circumstances. To the girl's alarm, instead of offering sympathy and wise counsel, the older woman burst into floods of anxious tears. Bess, who had seen Katherine's father and sister go to the block, understood instantly what Katherine apparently did not. Under the Royal Marriage Act of 1536, it was treason for anyone of royal blood to marry without the consent of the sovereign.

Bess knew the Queen well enough by now to realise that the affair would not go unpunished. The fact that Katherine had chosen a Seymour as a husband could not have helped: that tiresome, troublesome and ambitious family with its uncomfortably close connections to the House of Tudor. And not only had Katherine behaved extremely foolishly on her own account, but now she had involved Bess. In a highly agitated state, Bess told Katherine 'she was very sorry that she had done so [married] without the consent of the Queen's Majesty, or any of her other friends'.[10] Then, advising the girl to go to bed while she thought about the matter, she hurried away to her own chamber, no doubt to unburden herself to her husband.

Next morning, Lady Katherine thought she noticed little groups of people looking at her and talking about her. It did not occur to her that by now, at almost eight months pregnant, her shape alone might have been sufficient to cause gossip, and she surmised that Lady St Loe had betrayed her. She panicked and decided to approach Sir Robert Dudley who had the Queen's ear and total confidence. He was the son of her father's old ally and not only a family friend but, through Jane Grey's marriage to Guildford Dudley, he was a kinsman, a sort of brother-in-law once removed. If she could win his support, she reasoned, she might be sure of the Queen's sympathy.

Waiting until the Court had retired for the night, Katherine stole into Sir Robert's bedchamber. Kneeling at the side of his bed she woke him up to tell him of her plight and beg him to intercede for her with the Queen. Dudley was as dismayed as Bess St Loe had been. He had no wish to be dragged into this sordid predicament, and he certainly wanted no misunderstandings about the presence of a pregnant young woman in his bedchamber in the middle of the night, kinswoman or not. He sent Katherine away, and next morning he told the Queen what he knew. Predictably, Elizabeth erupted in spectacular fashion. When William Cecil was told, he was convinced that it was part of a plot to replace Elizabeth with another of the Grey sisters.

Lady Katherine was arrested and sent back to London where she was committed to the Tower. The day after her arrival there, on 17 August, Sir Edward Warner received orders to question Lady Katherine 'straightly' concerning:

... how many knew of the love between her and Edward Seymour ... from the beginning. And let her know she shall have no manner of favour lest she shall show the truth, not only what Ladies and gentlemen were privy, but also what Lords and gentlemen. For it doth now appear that sundry persons have dealt therein ...

You shall also send to Alderman Lodge, secretly, for [Lady] Sentlow, and shall put her in awe of divers matters confessed by the Lady Katherine, and also deal with her that she may confess to you all her knowledge in the same matters.

It is certain that there hath been great practises and purposes, and since the death of the Lady Jane [Seymour] she [Lady St

Loe] hath been most privy [with Lady Katherine] . . . And as you
shall see occasion so you may keep [Lady] Sentlow 2 or 3 nights
more or less, and let her be restored to Lodges or kept still with
you as you shall think mete . . .'[11]

Bess was ordered to return to London where she was questioned.
Sir William St Loe, who was a close friend of Bess's inquisitor,
Sir Edward Warner, would have undoubtedly advised his wife to
tell Warner everything she knew. By remaining silent she could
not help Lady Katherine, and she would draw down the Queen's
displeasure upon herself. There is no record of where this inquisition took place – probably it was at the Tower, but Bess is not
listed as a prisoner there – nor is there any record of the interview.
It is certain that the experience would have been a traumatic one;
Bess had seen too many of her friends sent to prison for years,
and worse, for falling foul of the monarch, to take it lightly. But
since her involvement is not referred to again in State papers,
it may be assumed that Bess was acquitted of any suspicion of
collusion.

Lord Hertford was brought home from France and committed to
the Tower. There is a full report of his questioning: Hertford
described the priest who had married them, 'a man of mean stature
and fair complexion with an auburn beard and middle age', wearing a falling collar such as German preachers wore. He described
the day of the marriage, recalling that after the ceremony, which
was conducted by the Book of Common Prayer, his sister Jane had
paid off the priest because he (Hertford) had insufficient money
on him. His sister had remained in the chamber with them for a
quarter of an hour, 'but then, perceiving them ready to go to bed
withdrew herself, leaving them alone . . . and they went naked into
bed, in the same chamber where they were married, for about 2
hours. Afterwards, he lay with the Lady Katherine in the Queen's
houses, both at Westminster and Greenwich, in her chamber,
nobody being privy . . .'[12]

The Queen's inquisitors found not a scrap of evidence of any plot against Elizabeth. But equally, the couple could produce no evidence that the marriage had actually taken place before they hopped into bed. There was no certificate of marriage. The document of jointure which they claimed Hertford had given Lady Katherine together with a hundred crowns, before his departure for France, had been 'put away in a safe place', but she had mislaid it while moving about during the Progress. The priest could not be traced, and their sole witness, Lady Jane Seymour, was dead. The Queen told the Privy Council it was her belief that Lady Katherine's claims to the throne had been invalidated by her father's treason.

Katherine gave birth to a son, Edward, Lord Beauchamp, on 24 September 1561, and in May of the following year the Archbishop of Canterbury, who had carefully examined all the evidence, pronounced that there was 'no marriage' between Lady Katherine and Edward Seymour. This was an important verdict, for had the marriage been proven, a legitimate son would have had a strong claim to the throne. Instead the couple were found guilty of 'fornication', fined heavily and sentenced to imprisonment during Her Majesty's pleasure. Sir Edward Warner was not strict with them, and the couple were allowed to visit each other in the Tower. Lady Katherine lived in comfortable circumstances in a suite of rooms with eight or nine servants and a child's nurse. A year later, to the Queen's impotent rage, another son, Thomas, was born to the couple.

Sir Edward Warner, Sir William St Loe's friend, received a short prison sentence and lost his prestigious post. Hertford was ordered to pay the staggering sum of £15,000, and, together with his elder son Edward, was packed off, in social disgrace, to live with his mother, who must have been reeling from the ruinous penalties imposed on their estates.* Lady Katherine remained in the Tower

---

*In fact the sum of £15,000 was later reduced to £10,000 of which Lord Hertford had paid only £4000 when he died many years later.

with baby Thomas, pining and refusing to eat, and sending out piteous letters begging for clemency. Eventually, after plague broke out in London, she was transferred to the custody of her uncle John Grey in the country, and after his death to another relative. After several years had passed, and as the drama of the affair receded, her friends began to hope that the Queen might be ready to forgive. At this precise moment, Lady Mary, Katherine's younger sister, who had a deformed spine and was very undersized ('almost a dwarf'), chose also to marry in secret. Her husband, Thomas Keyes, a giant of a man, was the gatekeeper at Whitehall. 'Here is an unhappy chance, and monstrous,' William Cecil wrote anxiously to Sir Thomas Smith on 21 August 1565. 'The Sergeant Porter being the biggest gentleman at Court, hath married secretly the Lady Mary Grey, least [i.e. shortest] of all the Court.'

As in her sister's case, when the matter was discovered the officiating priest could not be traced, but Lady Mary at least had some witnesses to her marriage. She could not therefore be charged with fornication, but she had failed to get royal permission for the marriage. Her husband was imprisoned, and Mary spent years in miserable detention of one form or another. The Queen had no intention of allowing another potential claimant to the throne to spring from the Grey family. Lady Katherine died at the age of twenty-seven, probably from anorexia. She had refused to eat properly for over a year, perhaps hoping that her frailty and illness would draw the Queen's sympathy. It did not. Both her children were raised by their father and will turn up again, later in the story.

Lady Mary remained in custody until the death of her husband four years after Lady Katherine's death. She was then released, but within eighteen months she too died, in some poverty, in 1578. It is probable that Bess had some hand in the burial of this curiously impecunious and forgotten heir presumptive to the throne of England (for, amazingly, such Mary Grey was, under Henry VIII's Act of Succession). Bess was in London at the time of Lady Mary's death, when the last surviving daughter of Bess's friend the Lady Frances and Henry Grey was inexplicably buried at St Botulph's without Aldersgate alongside the tomb of Sir William Cavendish.

Following her questioning in August 1561 about the Hertford–Grey marriage, Bess remained in London for some months. It was unusual for Bess to spend so long away from Chatsworth, but possibly it was considered unwise for her to return home because smallpox had broken out in parts of Derbyshire, although Chatsworth remained mercifully free of it and her mother wrote that the children were all well and safe.[13] Whatever the reason, Bess was still in London in October, writing to Francis Whitfield to instruct him to have the porch completed before the battlements, and adding a maternal note: 'tell Bess Knowles and Frank [Frances] I say that if they play their virginals that they are good girls.'[14]

Though she often spent long periods away from her children they were never far from Bess's thoughts. That November, still in London, she was negotiating with Sir George Pierrepoint, who was a neighbour with an estate near Nottingham (within a day's ride of Hardwick), to marry thirteen-year-old Frances to his son, Henry. Sir George wrote to her, thanking her for the 'great pains' she had taken with him, 'accepting everything (though it were never so rewardingly handled) in so gentle sort as you did, which doth, and will, cause me to love you the better while I live, if I were able to do you . . . some service.'[15] He and his wife had met Frances, he said, and they liked her.[16] The marriage was to be formalised in the following year, but it was arranged meanwhile that Frances should serve as a gentlewoman in Lady Pierrepoint's household, at Holme Pierrepoint, just as Bess had done with Lady Zouche at the same age. This would give all parties an opportunity to see if they got on. The young couple were subsequently married in 1562, and it proved a successful and fruitful union.[17]

That same autumn Bess had also arranged the future of her stepdaughter twenty-one-year-old Ann Cavendish. In September 1561 an indenture was drawn up to confirm that in the event of

Bess's death, Ann's guardians would become Sir Edward Rogers (comptroller of the Queen's Household), Sir Edward Warner, Sir William St Loe and other prominent men. Sir William agreed to 'sustain' Ann 'in meat, drink and apparel suitable to her estate and degree, till she marry'. He further agreed that within a year of the date of the indenture, he would offer a 'convenient husband and marriage'. If Ann chose to marry the person proposed, who must first be approved 'by her mother' Bess, then Sir William would provide Ann with a dowry of 1000 marks.* Should Ann choose to remain unmarried, she was to have the money as a preferment, unless she remained single only because she refused to marry a man deemed suitable by Bess, in which case Ann's preferment would be reduced to 600 marks.[18] It appears the girl was worried about being forced into a marriage against her will, and that this document was Bess's way of proving to Ann that she had only her best interests at heart. In the event, in 1562 Ann Cavendish married the man suggested by Sir William and Bess. He was Sir Henry Baynton, the younger brother of Sir William St Loe's first wife, and this marriage would also prove to be a long and happy one.[19]

In July 1563, soldiers returning from a skirmish with the French brought the plague to London. It was a bad outbreak, with people dying at the rate of four hundred a week in the capital,[20] and an estimated twenty-one thousand people died of the disease that year. Sir William and Bess were at Oatlands, where Elizabeth and the Court retreated as the infection raged: both escaped infection. The Queen, however, developed a fever and collapsed in a coma which lasted four hours. When she was revived she was still very ill and was thought to have smallpox; she asked her Council to make Lord Robert Dudley Protector of the Realm, if she died. She said she 'loved him dearly, and had long done so; but called God to witness that nothing unseemly had ever passed between them'.[21] In the event it was not smallpox and she made a recovery after several weeks' convalescence.

*£666 sterling.

But there was a good reason for the St Loes to remain in London that year, because their suit with the Exchequer, concerning the £5000-odd deficit in Sir William Cavendish's accounts, was finally brought to court. Sir William had petitioned the Queen, prior to the hearing, to look upon the matter with lenience.

As a result, Elizabeth pardoned and released the couple from the debt, on payment of a fine of £1000, to be paid to the Exchequer by Sir William on behalf of his wife and her son Henry.[22] Sir William had probably used up any favours the Queen may have considered she still owed him, for she was never overgenerous where money was involved. Having been left with a bankrupt kingdom and a debased currency, she could not afford to be. But for Bess the burden of worry had been removed, and her beloved Chatsworth was at last out of danger.

From just these few incidents, it is clear that Sir William was not reticent about spending his money on Bess's behalf – a thousand pounds paid to the Exchequer, nearly seven hundred pounds provided as a dowry for Ann Cavendish, and these sums were in addition to the cost of building works at Chatsworth that he had paid for. Following the court case, Bess returned to Chatsworth, but this separation of the St Loes did not harm their marriage. Whenever he wrote to Bess, Sir William reiterated his feeling for her: 'your loving husband with aching heart until we meet . . .'[23] His letters also contain details of small domestic trivia which add to our understanding of their lives. On one occasion, when he had returned to London after a leave, he wrote to urge her to send by carrier a piece of luggage that his manservant had forgotten to load. It contained his linen: '. . . there be hand towels and other things therein that I [need] when I shall lie at Whitehall. My men have neither shirt nor any other thing to shift, until that come.'

As a military man reliant on his horses, Sir William was an expert horse manager. When he was away from Chatsworth he did not fail to send instructions to his wife on how to look after her stables:

Trust none of your men to ride any of your [stabled] horses, but only James Crompe or William Marchington. And neither of them without good cause serve speedily to be done. For nags there be plenty enough about the house to serve other purposes. One handful of oats to every gelding at a watering will be sufficient to see that they are not laboured. You must cause someone to oversee the horsekeeper... he is very well learned in loitering...

A short postscript shows that Sir William was as careful a landowner as was his wife. It seems Mr Agarde, from whom the Cavendishes had originally purchased the property, had been fishing in one of their rivers. 'If you think good, lease your fishing in [the river] Dove unto Agard. We are the losers by suffering it as we have done.'24

In the autumn of 1563 Sir William was returned as Member of Parliament for Derbyshire, though there is no record that he was ever active in the House, and his correspondence shows that he was always preoccupied with his duties as Captain of the Guard. In all likelihood it was a protective move against a possibility of Cavendish or St Loe lands ever again being threatened by unsympathetic legislation. In the following year Sir William was also made Commissioner for the Peace in Derbyshire and Gloucestershire. One advantage of these added responsibilities may have been that he could demonstrate a need to leave the Court on a more frequent basis. It also indicates the amount of respect that Bess had earned in the county; Sir William was an outsider, totally unknown in Derbyshire, and his election was undoubtedly due to her influence rather than his own.

It is surprising that Bess, who conceived so easily during her marriage to Sir William Cavendish, had no child by St Loe, since they were obviously close and happy together. St Loe had children by his first wife, so fertility was not in question for either of them. Furthermore, from Sir William's statements to the court in

1561, when he was fighting his brother, it is clear that he still hoped for a son. Possibly, one or other of the couple had become infertile because of infection, or perhaps Bess had been damaged in delivering her last child, Lucres, who had died as an infant. A woman who had already undergone as many childbirths as Bess might well have taken some precautions to prevent pregnancy, but there was no foolproof system for birth control in the sixteenth century. Whatever the reason, there is no suggestion that Bess was ever pregnant during her marriage to Sir William St Loe.

In 1564 Bess's third son, Charles, joined his two older brothers at Eton while his sisters continued their education at home. The lives of Sir William and Bess moved into a tranquil phase, and Bess spent the summer and autumn months at Chatsworth where the building and furbishing programme upon which she had embarked four years earlier seems finally to have come to an end.

Sir William was able to join her that autumn for an extended stay. 'I am glad you are in good health and I trust the sight of your new finished building will continue it,' wrote Sir William's cousin, who had visited them from Corfe in Dorset. He agreed it was no bad thing for Sir William to spend some time at Chatsworth in order to convey an impression of 'negligent waiting', implying that Sir William was hoping for some preferment and did not wish to appear too anxious. Even when she was at Court with her busy and active husband Bess was not always able to spend as much time with him as she wished, and she jealously guarded the times he was able to spend with her away from the pressures at Court. Her correspondent goes on to suggest politely that she might allow Sir William to spend a little more time with his friends: 'it would stand you in hand to forbear him more than you have.'[25]

It seems that Bess simply enjoyed spending time with her husband. In her fourth and last marriage there is similar evidence that initially Bess was jealous when she and her husband had to be apart for any length of time. This was not due to loneliness; Bess had a large household and like Sir William she made friends easily. Her closest woman friend was Frances, Lady Cobham who, like Bess, was an avid needlewoman. Lady Cobham was nearly eight months pregnant in October 1564 when she wrote hinting that Bess had spent far too long at Chatsworth. Addressing Bess as 'her I love dearly and most desire to see', Lady Cobham wrote: 'I wish you had good cause to come and lay in these parts, as I could wish, then you would be as great a stranger in Derbyshire as you now are in London.' Writing of her forthcoming confinement, Lady Cobham requested anxiously, 'I pray you pray for me. I know I shall speed the better for a good woman's prayers,' and then went on to discuss the needlework that they were both working on. It was to be a New Year gift for the Queen. Lady Cobham was making the sleeves 'of a wideness that will best suit the Queen . . . they are fine and strange. I have sent you inclosed the braid, and lengths of a caulle for the Queen of the same work, for you to suit with the sleeves . . . The fashion is much altered since you were here. Ten yards is enough for the ruffs of the neck and hands.'[26]

Lady Cobham was safely delivered of a second son a few weeks later but it was December before Bess returned to the Court, where Robert Dudley had recently been created Earl of Leicester. The Court was always at its most enjoyable during the twelve nights of celebrations over Christmas and New Year, and Bess was still in London about 6 February when she received a letter from her brother James Hardwick, accompanied by one from their mother, asking if Bess could advance James a loan, in return for the security of his coalmine at Hethe, or the purchase of some lands he owned in Auldwerk. James was in debt and seriously ill with bronchitis, 'but as soon as the weather is fair I must see you, if I be anything well,' he wrote. The letter from her mother recommended the lands James mentioned as 'very good land . . . I think is very good for you, daughter . . . [and] it is worth much to my comfort that you should have it before any other.'[27]

At this point Bess decided to brave the winter roads and return to Chatsworth. Maybe she wanted to discuss the matter of a loan with her brother, or to view the properties he proposed giving her as security, or even selling to her, or perhaps she simply wished to see her children.

She could not have been many days at Chatsworth when some totally unexpected news was brought to her by a messenger. Sir William St Loe had been taken suddenly and seriously ill in London.[28] What must have made Bess's blood run cold was the astonishing intelligence that Edward St Loe was staying with him at the time. It is safe to assume that Bess would never have left her husband alone in London had he been unwell when she decided to travel to Derbyshire and she immediately set out on a frantic return dash back to London.

But she was too late. Sir William St Loe had been ill for only three days and was very likely dead even before Bess received the message. She may have met one of his servants on the London road, as she hurried south and he galloped through the mire towards Derbyshire with the tragic news.

When she arrived in London she found that for several days prior to, and on the very day of Sir William's death, Edward St Loe had been at his brother's bedside. And soon afterwards, Edward claimed that he was in possession of an indenture, signed by Sir William before his death, agreeing that Edward and Margaret St Loe had a legal right to Sutton Court. 'Shortly after the sealing and delivery of this indenture,' Edward St Loe's lawyer stated in court, 'the said Sir William Seyntlowe deceased in the City of London, his said [wife] then being in the county of Derby, above one hundred and twenty miles from the city . . . Edward Seyntlowe being with the said Sir William at the day of his death.'[29]

There was something very suspicious about Sir William's sudden death in the presence of his brother with whom he had been at loggerheads for several years, especially in view of Edward's history – the sudden and inexplicable deaths of John and Brigid Scutt, not to mention the subsequent attempt to poison Bess, for which even his own mother blamed Edward. Equally doubtful was the mysterious indenture, supposedly giving Edward and his wife Margaret the lifetime 'right and interest' in Sutton Court. Sir William had fought a similar assertion for five years. Edward claimed that Sir William had kept an identical copy of this deed, but the grieving Bess found no trace of such a document among her husband's belongings.

Just as in the cases of John and Bridget Scutt, there was nothing about Sir William's death to prove that Edward had had a hand in it, although few would blame Bess for suspecting that water given to her husband had been poisoned. It would have been uncharacteristic of Bess not to have this matter investigated to the best of her ability, but she must have found no evidence of poisoning for she did not even mention the matter in a subsequent court appearance. Again, the lack of an organised police force helped the wicked (if wickedness there had been). The law was imposed by members of the judiciary, with the physical assistance, where necessary, of county sheriffs. Wrongdoers were brought to the attention of quarter sessions by those who felt they had been wronged and the matter was then judged solely upon the evidence brought by the complainant and the defence of the accused.

Lacking any evidence, there was nothing Bess could do, other than arrange her husband's funeral, and in February 1565 Sir William was buried at the church of Great St Helen's at Bishopsgate, alongside his father.[30]

Bess spent some weeks in London, but visits to the Court were necessarily painful. A replacement Captain of the Guard was appointed immediately, of course, and a month later, on 25 March, Sir Nicholas Throckmorton was granted the lifetime post of Chief Butler previously held by his great friend the late Sir William St Loe.[31] On the same day Bess wrote to her 'cousin' Henry Babington asking for more time to consider the settlement of her lands. She was unable to make any new arrangements, she wrote, for she had just learned that her late husband's will, in which he had left everything he owned to her and her heirs 'for ever', to the exclusion of his own family, was being contested. The complainant was Margaret, the younger daughter of Sir William's first marriage, now married to Thomas Norton, son of a rich merchant family in Bristol.

With her natural grief, and this latest problem, Bess would have taken only a passing interest in the current Court gossip that the Scottish Queen had fallen in love with Henry, Lord Darnley. Darnley was the elder son of Margaret, Countess of Lennox, a friend whom Bess had met while serving in the Queen's Privy Chamber. Margaret Lennox was daughter of Princess Margaret Tudor (elder of the two sisters of Henry VIII).* As a granddaughter of Henry VII, the Lady Margaret had a claim to the English throne to the same degree as that of the Lady Frances Grey, albeit a claim that had been legally invalidated by Henry VIII's Act of Succession, which bypassed Scottish claimants. Margaret's late husband, Matthew Stuart, 4th Earl of Lennox, was descended from King James II of Scotland. Lord Darnley was therefore also a cousin to the Scottish Queen.

But of more pressing concern to Bess was the fact that after less than seven years of happy marriage she was alone, yet again. And what is more, she was being forced, as she had been on the two previous occasions, to fight for her rights.

---

*By her first marriage, the Princess Margaret Tudor was wife to the King of Scotland, James IV, and mother of James V. By her second marriage, to Archibald Douglas, 6th Earl of Angus, she gave birth to Margaret Douglas, who married the 4th Earl of Lennox.

CHAPTER 10

A VERY ELIGIBLE WIDOW

1565–9

UNLIKE MANY SIXTEENTH-CENTURY WILLS WHICH ARE complicated and rambling, Sir William St Loe's was laudably brief. Taking two paragraphs to commend his soul to his maker, confirm his belief in the resurrection of the body, and add the usual clause that he was 'in perfect health and memory, thanks be to God', he willed his estate as follows:

> In consideration of the natural affection, mutual love, and assured good will, which I have ever perceived and found in my most entirely beloved wife, Dame Elizabeth St Lowe, I do give and bequeath unto her, the said Elizabeth, all and all manner [of] my leases, farms, plate jewels, hangings, implements of household, debts, goods and chattels, whatsoever, to have, hold, use and enjoy to her own proper use, and behalf. Which said Elizabeth my wife I do ordain and make my sole and whole Executrix of this my last Will and Testament.[1]

Sir William's younger daughter Margaret immediately contested the will, clearly urged on by Edward, since she used the precise phrase used by Edward in a later court case: that it was unnatural for her father to leave his own children 'not one groat . . . Margaret Norton, alias St Lowe* is seeking and demanding that justice be done on her behalf instantly'.

In the event, the Court of Probate upheld the will, but one does have some sympathy for Sir William's two daughters. Why had Sir William not left them anything? He was a rich and unusually generous man. The probable answer is that he had already endowed his daughters with suitable dowries and believed that they were adequately provided for within their marriages. Also, this will was never intended to be his final one; he had made it hurriedly some years earlier in order to protect Bess at a time when he thought it possible that Edward might attempt to kill him or have him killed. In the end his death came so unexpectedly and so swiftly that he had no time to make any adjustments concerning his daughters, even supposing he had wanted to. But in leaving everything to Bess he did not help her reputation. Her legacy was the talk of the Court that summer; Sir William's elder daughter Mary St Loe was well known and liked, and received much sympathy. It was said that she had been 'cruelly robbed' by Bess of her inheritance.[2]

Edward levelled similar accusations against Bess to anyone who would listen. It began a legend about Bess which would follow her all her life and beyond (in much the same way that the supposed 'murder' of his wife Amy haunted Robert Dudley), that she had deliberately set out to get the 'ancient inheritance' of the St Loes to the detriment of Sir William's blood family.[3] It is therefore important to remember Sir William's written and sworn statement to the court when he sued his brother over Sutton Court, that Bess had wanted Edward to have the St Loe lands.[†]

---

*Margaret Norton, née Margaret St Loe, should not be confused with Edward's wife Margaret St Loe, née Scutt. In the event it was Margaret Scutt St Loe who benefited by the court's decision.
†Extract from Sir William's statement (see Chapter 8): '. . . his wife bore his brother every good will. And so far that, both before and after the marriage, she persuaded

Edward decided to make a fight of it. Refusing to stand by the agreement reached with his brother after the previous judgement, he stopped paying rent to Bess. Bess then declined to make payments against the backdated sums that Sir William had agreed to pay to Edward, and the whole matter went back to the courts. As her evidence, Bess offered the probated wills made by her husband, and his father, as well as the deed of gift made by Sir William four years before his death. Edward presented the indenture apparently signed on Sir William's deathbed, which Bess never accepted as genuine, although the signature was apparently convincing enough to the judiciary.

The case was brought to court in Somerset within two months of Sir William's death. Bess insisted on having the same judge who had tried the previous hearings to avoid the need for covering old ground. Edward cleverly attempted to turn this to his own advantage. He stated to the court that he had made various offers to Lady St Loe for a compromise through her friends, one of whom was Sir John Thynne. '. . . the Complainant utterly declined,' he said, 'saying she would have the matter heard by your Lordship; as though she had special confidence of your Lordship's favour and friendship to her, above that of her friends.'[4]

Insisting that he had only agreed to the former compromise, which had been greatly to his detriment, 'hoping to procure the goodwill of his brother', Edward maintained he had lost the previous case 'by the slanderous and wicked tales and devices of the Complainant [Bess], which were void of all truth and thereby the more easily to procure the overthrow and utter spoil of her husband, and his house, to her gain, and to the utter undoing of this defendant (Edward).'

Sir William to entail the remainder of all his lands, [in default] of issue of their bodies, to the said Edward. And she ever refused the [rents] thereof, until Sir William . . . perceiving his brother to much unnaturalness and unseemly speeches of him and his wife, did, of very good will towards her, convey the same unto her . . .'

... the said Sir William died, not leaving to this defendant, nor yet to any of his own children or friends, the value of one groat, either in goods or lands, but all unnaturally given and bestowed upon this Complainant, clearly forgetting the satisfaction of legacies due to his brother and sister* by the last Will and Testament of Sir John St Loe, his father lately deceased.

... Sir William had the trust, and only charge thereof, to him committed, being his father's only executor, who left to him the chief and only possessions and inheritance, which had long continued in his family. All which is now spoiled and utterly wasted by the only procurement of the Complainant, to the clear disinheritance of the Defendant, of a great part thereof being entailed to the heirs male, of great antiquity.

The Complainant continues her malice towards him . . . [so] he refused to pay the order legally passed of the pension of £35, because the money had to be sent to London from his house in Somerset 4 times a year, which cost him a good portion of the yearly rent . . .[5]

Bess's plaint was that the manor had been legally conveyed to her by her husband, and that no entailed properties 'of great antiquity' were involved in his gift to her, because such entailed properties had not belonged to Sir William to give. But in the long and tedious arguments one senses the fight going out of her as the case dragged on. The matter was not completely cleared until two years later, when the judge ruled that the deed signed by Sir William St Loe on the day of his death gave Edward's wife, Margaret St Loe, a lifetime interest in the Manor of Sutton Court, with the property reverting to Bess, or Bess's heirs, after Margaret's death, not to the St Loe family as Edward St Loe wanted. During the course of the hearings

---

*The word 'sister' in this context clearly refers to Edward's wife, Sir William St Loe's sister-in-law. Sir William's only sister, Elizabeth St Loe, did not contest the will.

Edward St Loe was sent to serve the Queen's Majesty in 'the remote
north places of Ireland' and there he would remain for two years.[6]
Whether or not Bess had any involvement in his posting is
unknown.

Meanwhile, Bess was free at last to consider her future. She was
now thirty-eight years old. Of her six children, the three boys were
away at school, her eldest daughter, seventeen-year-old Frances,
was married, and only the two youngest girls, Elizabeth aged ten,
and Mary, aged nine, were still at home. Bess now had under her
own control the combined Cavendish and St Loe fortunes, as well
as her widow's dower from the Barlow family. By any standards she
was a rich woman, and she had a consuming passion: the advancement of her children. She decided to spend some of her money on
Chatsworth, adding a third floor, to consist entirely of magnificent
State rooms suitable to entertain a monarch.

She spent the remaining months of 1565 at Chatsworth, where,
in the New Year, an inventory was taken. Only a fragment remains
of this inventory, which is clearly incomplete because no clothes or
jewels are mentioned, and only one book (*Psalms*), though we know
from Sir William's accounts that there were other books in the
house. In fact, with the exception of one poignant entry among the
items in her bedchamber, no articles of a personal nature are
recorded. But set against the panelled and beautifully plastered
room, the rich colours of the soft furnishings must have glowed as
Bess sat and gazed at the portraits of family and friends she had lost.

In My Lady's Chamber:

1 bed of red cloth trimmed with silver lace; 5 curtains of Mocado
Red
1 'cwylk' of Red Sennet on red flage and white flage
2 quilts on a down bed & 3 bolsters
1 great chair, green checked silk & 1 little chair, black velvet
2 leather chairs

1 pr [fire] Andirons; 1 pr tongs; 1 fire shovel

3 tables, on which [pictures] of; Sir William Cavendish, my master [Sir William St Loe], another of my lady [Bess], and another of my Lady Jane [Grey].

3 curtains of silk hanging over the tables

1 long cushion of black velvet; 1 long cushion of blue taffeta

6 pieces of hanging of blue cloth & 6 great coffers

1 square board [table]

1 cupboard; 1 long cloth for the cupboard

2 curtains green satin for the windows.[7]

We know from another inventory, taken a year later, that Bess still owned 'one book of gold with 10 rubies, 3 sasers & one diamond with two pictures in the same' that had been bought for her by Sir William Cavendish (the 'two pictures' were of Sir William Cavendish and Bess). And from this same 1567 inventory we know that among her pieces of jewellery, Bess still treasured the jewel of gold and agate given her by the Lady Frances Grey, and another ring containing a seal.

In August 1566 Bess was back at Court, attending in the Queen's Bedchamber with her friends Frances Cobham, Blanche Parry and another woman who was to become a lifelong friend, Lady Dorothy Stafford.[8] Sir William's friends had all rallied round her and one, Sir Richard Sackville, had even instructed his steward that he had given his hunting quota of venison at Clympton Park to Lady St Loe.[9]

It is not possible to know whether Bess actively looked for another husband; she hardly needed to. But that winter it was widely rumoured that she was to marry Henry Cobham, brother-in-law of her best friend. By January 1567, while reporting the Twelfth Night festivities to his master, a servant of Lord Lennox wrote: '. . . Either Lord Darcy, or Sir John Thynne shall marry my Lady St Loe, and not Lord Cobham.'[10]

In fact Bess attached herself to no one in particular. When she was at Court she carried out her duties with dignity and circum-spection, and at other times she stayed quietly at Chatsworth overseeing her latest building work. World affairs seem to trouble her little but she could not have remained unaware that the Queen of Scotland, having fallen in love with Lord Darnley had married him and lived to regret it.

Henry Darnley was handsome and aristocratic; he was also debauched, cruel and arrogant. Although granted the title King of Scotland by Mary, Darnley wanted this title to be his 'for life', so that in the event of Mary's death he and his heirs would rule Scotland. By the spring of 1566 he had convinced himself that David Rizzio, Mary's Italian secretary and confidant, was advising her against his, Darnley's, ambitions. With a group of thugs he broke into an after-supper card game and butchered Rizzio in front of Mary and the other players; she was almost six months pregnant at the time. Despite this, her child, James, was born safely in June of that year, and a few months later Mary began seeking a divorce.

In February 1567 Darnley was murdered by the Earl of Bothwell, although Bothwell's guilt could not be established at the mock trial held soon afterwards. Bothwell then abducted the Queen and held her in captivity – it was said she did not object overmuch, having fallen in love with him despite the fact that he had raped and impregnated her. The pair were subsequently mar-ried, and Mary is on record as saying that she would follow Bothwell to the end of the world in her petticoat.[11] There was enough material here to keep even Elizabeth's gossip-ridden Court open-mouthed. As she listened, Bess could not possibly have fore-seen that these events would affect her life.

That same winter, in January 1567, Gertrude, the wife of George Talbot, 6th Earl of Shrewsbury, died.[12] Again, the episode seemed to have no connection with Bess, but nine months later the wid-ower began paying court to Lady St Loe. No detail survives of their courtship, but the two had probably known each other, or about each other, for most of their lives. Chatsworth and Hardwick were not much more than twenty miles from the Earl's home, Sheffield Castle. The Earl's father, Francis, was mentioned in Bess's father's will, and the names of George Talbot and the Earls of Shrewsbury crop up over the intervening years in several title deeds which also bear Bess's name. He was also godfather to Temperance.

A portrait of George Talbot in his prime shows him as a commanding figure: a serious-looking man, lantern-jawed, with a stern, slightly frowning expression. He has short dark hair and wears a long silky beard and moustache; his side-whiskers are just beginning to turn grey. The best-known surviving portrait of him was painted in 1582, almost fifteen years after his marriage to Bess. By that time he was fifty-four and looked ten years older than that. He had become a thin, long-faced man, with a gloomy expression, thin compressed lips and deep lines of care etched into his forehead and round the mouth and eyes. Gone was the lavishly embroidered white satin peascod waistcoat of his youth, and in its place a simple black coat, worn with an exquisite lace-edged ruff. The years between had been traumatic for him, and Bess has been blamed for this decline. However, today's reader might like to consider that any man caught up in the lives of the three most fascinating women of the Elizabethan age – the Queen herself, Mary, Queen of Scots and Bess of Hardwick – ran the risk of being slightly scorched.

Born in 1528, George Talbot had succeeded to the title Earl of Shrewsbury in the second year of Elizabeth's reign when he was thirty-two. His first marriage was a dynastic arrangement* (he was eleven at the time of his betrothal), but it was apparently a contented enough partnership. He spent long periods away from his wife Gertrude, daughter of the Earl of Rutland, in command of 'the armies in the north', though he evidently returned home often enough to sire four healthy sons and three daughters during the twenty-one-year marriage. He was a Knight of the Garter,

---

*The marriage of George, Lord Talbot and 'Gartrid' (Gertrude), daughter of Lord Rutland, took place on 28 April 1539.

the Lord Lieutenant of the counties of Yorkshire, Derbyshire and Nottinghamshire, Chief Justice in Eyre, and Chamberlain of the Receipt of the Exchequer, in addition to other less important offices.

The Talbots were immensely rich, old nobility, and owned vast expanses of land in Derbyshire, Nottinghamshire, Shropshire, Staffordshire and Yorkshire as well as a number of large properties such as the castle and manor house at his principal residence in Sheffield, Wingfield Manor, Worksop Manor, Buxton Hall, Welbeck Abbey and Rufford Abbey (the latter two had been acquired by the 5th Earl, at the time of the Dissolution). The family also held some valuable leases from the Crown, among which were Tutbury Castle and Abbey in Staffordshire – built in the reign of William the Conqueror and once owned by John of Gaunt. And there were a number of houses in the city of London, the main one being Cold Harbour House in Thames Street near London Bridge; another, 'the lyttel house', was near Charing Cross. And there was a house in Broad Street which was mostly let.* Later, the Earl would acquire a house outside the city, in the village of Chelsea, at what is now Cheyne Walk. In terms of landholding, Shrewsbury was arguably the richest man in the country, leading one biographer to describe him as 'a prince, whose princedom was north of the Trent.'[13] In a surviving set of accounts made seventeen years after the Earl's death, the Steward reported receipts in one year of £45,446.

Shrewsbury did not need Bess's lands, but the Talbots were acquisitive by nature and even if the main attraction was Bess herself, the Earl would not have overlooked her significant land holdings in Derbyshire and the West Country. In particular, the Barlow lands in Bess's portfolio had coal and lead mines, which would be welcome additions to the core business of the Earl's coal

---

*This street in the old city cannot now be identified; it was probably destroyed in the Great Fire.

and smelting interests. For Bess's part, few women would have rejected a proposal by the Earl of Shrewsbury. Not only was he a personable man, but his power, position and title made him irresistible. For Bess, the title 'Countess of Shrewsbury' would have dangled invitingly; and not least was the knowledge of what such a marriage could mean to her children's prospects, a subject dear to her heart.

The Earl had probably not yet declared himself in the autumn of 1567 when Bess encountered a domestic problem which offended her a great deal. Perhaps some of her distress was due to the fact that the potential scandal might affect her budding relationship with the Earl, but so concerned was she that she turned to the Queen for help. As a result William Cecil wrote on behalf of the Privy Council to the Archbishop of Canterbury, explaining that 'Lady St Loo, widow, having retained as schoolmaster, Henry Jackson, late a scholar of Merton College, Oxford, is disturbed by scandalous reports raised against her family by him. You are to examine the matter thoroughly and speedily, with the assistance of the Solicitor-General, Mr Oseley, and Mr Peter Osborn, or any other Ecclesiastical Commissioners, that the lady's good name may be preserved. If he has unjustly defamed her, he is to be severely punished.'[14]

On the following day the Queen intervened personally:

September 29th 1567

The Queen to the Archbishop of Canterbury.

We understand you have examined the pretended contract devised by Henry Jackson against Lady St Loo, who has long served with credit in our Court.

As such a slanderous device should be severely punished, we require you, with the aid of some of the Commissioners for ecclesiastical causes, to proceed to extreme punishment, by corporal or otherwise, openly or privately, and that speedily, that our servant may be restored to her good name . . .[15]

What was this slander which so upset Bess and threatened her reputation so badly that it was worth involving the Queen? The surviving correspondence does not provide details. Henry Jackson taught Bess's children for several years while she was married to William St Loe.[16] As a gentleman tutor, Jackson would have been considered a member of the household at Chatsworth, dining with the family and privy to a good deal of family business. There has never been even a hint that Bess was ever sexually indiscreet. The strongest probability is that Jackson fell out with Bess over what he regarded as the contractual terms of his employment, and, while unemployed and disillusioned, began to repeat what Edward St Loe had said about her 'appropriation' of the St Loe estates to the detriment of the St Loe family.

After leaving Chatsworth, Jackson tutored at Merton College, and by the autumn of 1567, when this affair blew up, he was a minor canon of St Paul's Cathedral, hence the Archbishop's involvement. Many years later, when Bess and her fourth husband had irrevocably fallen out, the Earl would write that when he first took up with Bess, her name was a 'byword' at Court, and that he should have been warned by this. The gossip did not prevent him from taking Bess's side at the time, however, and like Sir William St Loe, George Talbot, Earl of Shrewsbury, appears to have fallen headlong in love with her.

Another imputation, repeated by successive biographers, concerns the marriage of two of Bess's children to two of Shrewsbury's children. An eighteenth-century hagiographer of the Shrewsbury family, who appears to have believed wholeheartedly in Edward St Loe's evidence, stated: 'In an evil hour the Earl of Shrewsbury made a proposal of marriage. Before she [Bess] would consent to be raised to the bed of the first Peer of the Realm, she stipulated that he should give his daughter to her eldest son, and that Gilbert Talbot, his second son should espouse her youngest daughter [Mary, then aged eleven].'[17]

In fact there is no way of knowing whether or not Bess made the marriage of their children a condition for her own hand, and this statement is pure hypothesis. But we do know that this type of intermarriage was not a new idea to the Earl. Five years earlier, he had chosen to ally himself with the Earl of Pembroke by marrying his eldest son, Francis, Lord Talbot, to Pembroke's eldest daughter, Anne Herbert. At the same time the Earl of Pembroke's son and heir, Henry, married Catherine, eldest daughter of George Talbot.[18] The properties of the Shrewsburys and Pembrokes were thus all nicely tied up. Furthermore, the Earl of Shrewsbury's daughter Grace (now proposed as wife to Bess's heir, Henry Cavendish), although only eight years old, had already endured one matrimonial disappointment. Two years earlier her father had arranged for her to marry Lord Dacre's heir, but the proposed bridegroom on that occasion disobliged by dying at the age of seven. The tender age of his daughter did not weigh with the Earl, who treated his children as marriage pawns, just as he himself had been.

The family which would appear to have had most to gain by the proposed marriage of Bess's heir to the Earl's daughter is the Earl's rather than Bess's, for it would put Cavendish lands into Shrewsbury hands. And in marrying Bess, Shrewsbury stood to gain control of the combined Cavendish and St Loe lands, which although entailed to Bess's heirs on her death became legally his lands during her lifetime. Bess made some stipulations about keeping Chatsworth House and a few other properties over which she wished to exercise a measure of personal control during her lifetime, but her requests did not appear unreasonable to the Earl and he readily agreed to them. Moreover, in the marriage jointure, which she was experienced enough to require, several Shrewsbury properties – the rents of the manors of Handsworth, Bolsterstone and Over Ewedon – were made over to her for her lifetime.

The marriages of the four children duly went ahead at the Church of St Peter and St Paul, Sheffield (now Sheffield Cathedral) on 9 February 1568.[19] Henry Cavendish (seventeen years old) married

Grace Talbot (eight), and Gilbert Talbot (fifteen) married Mary Cavendish (twelve).

Soon afterwards – the precise date or place is unknown, but it was between 9 February and 25 March 1568 – George Talbot, the 6th Earl of Shrewsbury, married Bess, the widowed Lady St Loe. We know this, for one of the first things the Earl and his Countess did after their marriage was to purchase Margaret St Loe's life interest in the manor of Sutton Court at Chew in Somerset at a cost of £500.[20] The sale was recorded without a date, but it occurred prior to Lady Day in 1568.[21] It was a sweet revenge for Bess, who promptly rented the property out to good tenants. Soon after the sale was completed Edward St Loe returned from Ireland: he and Margaret moved from Somerset to Wiltshire where they purchased a small manor house.

At this date there was only one Duke in the land, the great Duke of Norfolk, so that by her marriage to the premier-ranking Earl, Bess became one of the most prominent women at Court. It was a dizzying rise from her expectations at birth.

From the first, the Shrewsbury marriage promised to be a successful one. The Earl was apparently delighted with his wife, who was the same age as himself.* In letters to her when he left her to visit his other estates, he addressed her as 'My none' (probably a corruption of 'mine own', as in 'mine own Bess'), and this gradually became 'my sweet None,' or sometimes 'my own sweetheart' or 'my own dear heart'.

> My dear None,
>   Being here arrived at Wingfield late yesternight from Rofford, though very weary in toiling about, yet thinking you would be desirous to hear from me, scribbled these few lines to let you understand that I was in health, and wished you anights with me.

*Bess was about six months older than the Earl.

... I mind tomorrow, God willing, to be with you at Chatsworth; and in the meantime, as occurrences befall to me you shall be the partaker of them. I thank you sweet None for your baked capon, and chiefest of all for remembering of me. It will be late tomorrow before my coming to Chatsworth, seven or eight of the clock at the soonest. And so farewell my true one, this 28th June.

Your faithful husband,

G. Shrewsbury[22]

The couple did not attend the Court in that first summer of their marriage, but in the autumn they sent the Queen a gift of some venison with Bess's nephew, Anthony Wingfield.* In a letter from Elizabeth Wingfield, her younger half-sister, Bess learned that the Queen had spoken to Anthony for an hour, 'of my lord and you, so carefully that I think your honours have no friend living that could have more consideration, nor show more love and affection'. At the end of the conversation the Queen had asked Anthony when Lady Shrewsbury intended to come to Court. When he said he did not know, the Queen said: 'I am assured that if she have her own will she would not be long before she would see me. I have been glad to see my Lady St Loe, but am now more desirous to see my Lady Shrewsbury. I hope my Lady hath known my good opinion of her . . . I assure you, there is no Lady in this land that I better love and like.'[23]

Between the death of Sir William St Loe and Bess's marriage to Shrewsbury, great matters of State had been occurring. The marriage of Mary, Queen of Scots to the Earl of Bothwell (the suspected, though unproven, assassin of Lord Darnley) had evoked the wrath of Scottish nobles. Mary and Bothwell had been married only five weeks when her kingdom was threatened by revolt. After Bothwell left her to muster an army, Mary was taken into custody.

*Son of Bess's half-sister Elizabeth, née Leche.

He made several half-hearted attempts to rescue her, but the couple never saw each other again and later she miscarried twins. She was eventually required to abdicate in favour of her year-old son James, on the evidence of the so-called 'Casket Letters', which, if genuine* linked her to the murder of her former husband.[24] On 28 May 1568 the deposed Queen escaped from her island prison at the Castle of Lochleven and fled to Carlisle in England, where she begged asylum and placed herself under Elizabeth's protection.

The Queen immediately despatched Sir Francis Knollys† to Carlisle to act as Mary's vice-chamberlain. In due course he reported back, obviously captivated by Mary. Elizabeth was not, at that point, especially averse to Mary but the effect of Mary's charm on most of the men who met her was not lost on Elizabeth, and it made her wary. A few months earlier, Sir Nicholas Throckmorton, who had known Mary in France, had been sent to Scotland during the time of the Scottish Queen's troubles and was one of several such men who were totally captivated by her. It was at least partially due to Throckmorton's influence and diplomacy that Mary managed to survive that period of captivity.

In a gesture of queenly solidarity, Elizabeth advised the Scottish government that she would refuse to acknowledge the infant James as King of Scotland while his mother lived. However, when the Privy Council met to discuss the matter of the refugee, Elizabeth was strongly counselled not to allow Mary to leave for France or Spain, nor, at present, to meet with her. Cecil was particularly concerned that Mary might become a rallying point for English Catholics. Since Mary could not be sent back to Scotland, and they

---

*Sixteen letters, claimed to have been written in Mary's own hand, to Bothwell, and taken from a silver casket in her rooms after her arrest. Extracts from these letters were used in contemporary reports, and contemporary copies of some of the letters survive, but the originals were said to have been destroyed in 1585.
†Knollys was husband to Elizabeth's first cousin (a Boleyn relation), Lady Catherine née Carey. Catherine's brother Henry, Lord Hunsdon, had been a great friend of Sir William St Loe.

could not let her travel to the mainland of Europe, it was decided for the time being to hold her in confinement, giving as a reason the fact that she was still under suspicion of being involved in the murder of Lord Darnley.

Protesting strongly, Mary was escorted to the Castle of Bolton in the care of Lord Scrope, Warden of the West Marshes, and Sir Francis Knollys (both men were related to the Queen by marriage), while a court met at York to consider all the evidence at considerable length. Mary soon realised that she had exchanged one form of captivity for another; yet she was confident that all would come right, and that Elizabeth would free her and help her to claim back her throne in Scotland.

Meanwhile, the Earl of Shrewsbury and his new countess were undoubtedly thrilled at the Queen's comments about them to Anthony Wingfield. When Shrewsbury was summoned to Court he travelled to London with alacrity. Bess did not accompany him; she remained with her beloved eldest daughter, Frances, now nineteen years old and awaiting the birth of her first child.

It seems that the Queen had already worked out a new role for the Earl of Shrewsbury. If she had drawn up a specification for Custodian of Mary, Queen of Scots, the Earl would have met every criterion for the position. Although a prisoner, Mary was a still an anointed queen and needed to be treated as such – suitable accommodation was therefore required for her and for the members of her household, and Shrewsbury had a number of large properties, any one of which could house Mary and her retinue; he was a rich man and could afford to pay for the necessary additional servants and security required; he was happily married and therefore less likely to fall in love with Mary, as did many men who came into contact with her; his loyalty and sense of duty was unquestioned; and he and his wife were staunch Protestants.

By early December 1568 the Earl was stuck at Court, unable to leave without the Queen's permission. In a letter he tells Bess that he had just been on the point of sending one of his servants to Chatsworth because he had not heard from her, 'which drove me in the dumps . . .' when her messenger arrived with her hamper of home-made pies and venison. He was careful to tell her he had given some of her puddings to her friends 'Lady Cobham and . . . my Lord of Leicester, and the rest I have reserved unto myself to eat in my chamber.' Her letter had advised him that his son Ned (Edward) had been sick, but that she had nursed him and he was now out of danger. 'I thank God I have such an one that is so careful over me and mine,' Shrewsbury wrote tenderly;

> . . . God send me soon home to possess my greatest joy. If you think it is you, you are not deceived . . . I live in hope to be with you before you can answer . . . This present Monday in the morning, I [found] the Queen in the garden, at good leisure . . . With as good words as I could wish [she declared] that ere long I should well perceive that she did trust me as she did few. She would not tell me wherein, but I doubt [not] it was about the custody of the Scot's Queen . . . I think before Sunday these matters will come to some pass, that we shall know how long our abode [here] shall be. But howsoever it falls out, I will not fail to be with you before Christmas, or else you shall come to me.
>
> The plague is dispersed far abroad in London, so that the Queen keeps her Christmas here, and goes not to Greenwich as was meant. My Lady Cobham, your dear friend, wishes your presence here. She loves you well, I tell her I have cause to love you best . . . And as the pen writes so the heart thinks, that of all earthly joys that have happened to me, I thank God chiefest for you. For with you I have all the joy and content of mind, and without you death is more pleasant to me than life, if I thought I should be long from you.
>
> And therefore, good wife, do as I will do; hope shortly for our meeting. Fare well my dear sweet None, from Hampton Court, this Monday at midnight, for it is every night so late before I go

to my bed, being at play in the Privy Chamber . . . where I lost almost a hundred pounds . . . your faithful husband till death. G. Shrewsbury.

The Queen was as good as her word. Ten days later the Earl was created a Privy Counsellor and made the custodian of the Scottish Queen. The Earl wrote to Bess the same day, 13 December, to advise her that it was 'now certain the Scots Queen comes to Tutbury, to my charge'. Elsewhere in the letter he bemoans his inability to get away from Court, even now, and in answer to her request that he return home soon, he replies that he does not think he can get there until Christmas Eve. 'What my desire is thereunto, I refer to your construction. If I so judge of time, methinks time is longer since my coming here without you, my only joy, than I did since I married you, and such faithful affection, which I never tasted so deeply of before . . . Your black man is in health; your faithful husband until my end. G. Shrewsbury.'[25]

The Earl returned to Chatsworth on Christmas Eve as he promised, but he was back at Hampton Court on 26 January 1569 where the Queen's written instructions were handed to him. He had been chosen, the document read, 'in consequence of his approved loyalty and faithfulness, and the ancient state of blood from which he is descended, to have custody of the Queen of Scots'. He was to treat his prisoner, 'being a Queen, of our blood, with the reverence and honour mete for a person of his state and calling, and for her degree'. She was to be accorded all the ceremony due to her position, 'nor by this removing [to Tutbury] have her state amended'. But while assuring all this, he must have a care that his charge did not escape, nor meet with anyone likely to help her to escape.

He was to vet her household and 'reduce the number, omitting those who are superfluous . . . Her diet must be kept at the former rate, and payments made by the clerk who was sent for that purpose from [London]. Should she be sick or wish to speak with his wife the Countess, he shall permit the latter to come to her but very rarely and no other gentlewoman shall be permitted to visit except his own, ordinary servants.' He was also warned that he must not allow Mary to practise her charm on him, in order to win his support, and to assist him in this he was to be made privy to the 'apparent presumptions against her for murdering her husband, and unlawful marriage with the principal murderer, Bothwell. He shall be informed of other particulars too long to be written here . . .'[26] One can only assume this means the Casket Letters. On the back of this document, the Earl has scribbled some queries about how long Mary's imprisonment was likely to be, his concern about some people in the neighbourhood of Tutbury who were 'corrupted with Popery', and for further details concerning the precise conditions of access for his beloved wife to the prisoner.

The Queen had settled on Tutbury Castle as a suitable place to hold Mary, but when Bess and the Earl had visited the Castle together on 7 January during his Christmas visit to Chatsworth, Bess had been appalled. Used for years only as a hunting lodge it was virtually unfurnished, cold, dank, and totally unfit to house a royal prisoner with any degree of comfort. Bess suggested to the Earl that Sheffield Castle would be a far better place to hold Mary, while Tutbury was made ready. The Earl hastened to London and the Queen agreed to his suggestion, but before he could return home again a letter written weeks earlier arrived at Chatsworth from Robert Dudley. It contained the Privy Council's instructions that Tutbury *was* to be used to confine Mary.

Bess replied to Leicester immediately pointing out that the instructions had been despatched on 14 January and not received until 6 p.m. on the twentieth.

My Lord, I was much grieved because there was no more haste with delivery of the said letters, considering the weighty and great causes depending thereon. . . . My humble duty and service to be showed in the despatch of such things as the Queen's Majesty requires to have in readiness within Tutbury Castle, the house being unready in many respects for the receiving of the Scottish Queen coming suddenly.

I have caused workmen to make forthwith in readiness all such things . . . most needful to be done before her coming. And, God willing, I shall cause three or four lodgings to be furnished with hangings and other necessities. And rather than I should not with true and faithful heart answer the trust reposed by the Queen's Majesty, I will lack furniture of lodging for myself . . .

Tutbury this 21st January [1569],
Elizabeth Shrewsbury[27]

Bess stripped Sheffield Castle of its best tapestries and furniture and shipped them to Tutbury. Sheffield was thus rendered uninhabitable and Tutbury was once again settled upon. Meanwhile Bess also provided many items from Chatsworth, while the Earl's next letter advised that the Queen had agreed to send some suitable furnishings and plate from the Tower of London.[28] These included nineteen large tapestries; four great and twelve small 'Turkey Carpets' and four beds with feather mattresses and bolsters, with hangings and cushions in crimson and gold.

There was then the question of Mary's removal from Bolton Castle to Tutbury to be considered. The Queen's insistence that Mary must not be subjected to any discomfort caused disquiet to those in charge; how could a four-day journey in the middle of winter be otherwise?[29] The heavily escorted party left Bolton on 25 January and took longer than estimated, because one of Mary's ladies was taken ill at Rotherham, and Mary refused to go on without her. Knollys, whose wife Catherine had just died, was desperate to complete the journey so that he might return home to his children, but Mary would not be hurried. The party finally arrived at Tutbury on 4 February where Bess was waiting with the Earl to greet the royal 'guest'.

One wonders what Bess made of the twenty-six-year-old Queen, still widely regarded as one of the most beautiful women in Europe, despite her damaged reputation. Sadly, Bess left no record of her opinions, but in the early days the relationship between Bess and Mary was a courteous and friendly one. On her arrival the Earl gave Mary a message from Queen Elizabeth, which she received 'with temperate words' and 'in a modest manner'. After she had rested, the Earl spoke to her about reducing her household, and 'she was content that her attendants (presently 60) should be reduced to 30, besides her women and grooms of the chamber'.[30] In return, Mary required that a 'cloth of state' be erected over her chair to signify her royal estate, and asked that she be provided with horses and grooms 'at her Majesty's charge'.[31] She had only ten horses on her arrival at Tutbury and considered that more would be required.

Three weeks later, a servant of Queen Elizabeth on his way to Ireland detoured to visit the Earl. Hearing of his arrival, Mary asked that he be brought before her. He duly reported that she first apologised for her English (Mary having left Scotland at the age of six, her first language was French), and told him that Harry Knollys had been teaching her.

> I asked, since the weather did cut off all exercises abroad, how she passed the time within. She said that all the day she wrought with her needle, and that the diversity of colours made the work seem less tedious, and [she] continued so long at it till very pain did make her give over. And with that laid her hand upon her left side and complained of an old grief, newly increased there . . .[32]

Later, Harry Knollys (brother of the recently widowed Sir Francis) and the visitor were able to talk. Knollys told him that Mary had been afraid to leave Bolton Castle, believing that Cecil was her enemy, and had suspected an attempt would be made to kill her on the road. The messenger ended his report with a warning: 'If I . . . might give advice, there should be very few subjects in this land have access to, or conference with this lady . . . She has an alluring grace, a pretty Scottish accent, and a searching wit, clouded with mildness . . . joy is a lively infective sense, and carries many persuasions to the heart, which rules all the rest.'[33]

Although initially Shrewsbury was pleased at having been given the honour of guarding the Scottish Queen, he would soon realise that it involved far more than he had envisaged. It was, in fact, a poisoned chalice. He could not manage to reduce the number of her servants, and within weeks was already starting to complain to Cecil that 'the Queen of Scots coming to my charge will soon make me grey-headed'.[34]

In those early days, however, neither he nor Bess could have realised that he would have the care of Mary for over fifteen years, and that their guardianship of the Scottish queen would lead to the breakdown of their marriage.

A DIFFICULT GUEST

1569–73

WHEN THEY BECAME CUSTODIANS OF THE SCOTTISH QUEEN, life for the Shrewsburys changed irrevocably. Previously they had divided their time between Chatsworth and Sheffield Castle, with the Earl occasionally making visits to his other estates as necessary. Now he was stuck at the austere Tutbury, and in order to be with him and assist in looking after Mary, Bess had to desert her precious Chatsworth. Neither the Earl nor Bess enjoyed this arrangement, but initially they assumed it would be of a limited duration, and consoled themselves that when it was all over they would be suitably rewarded by the Queen's favour.

Tutbury was a dismal place. Its value to the Shrewsburys was in its land and the hunting it afforded, but it was seldom used, and its neglect was self-evident. It had been chosen as Mary's prison with security rather than comfort in mind, for the old fortified building had only one, easily guarded entrance. This is how Mary described it in a letter to Bertrand de la Mothe Fénèlon, the French Ambassador:

I am in a walled enclosure, on the top of a hill, exposed to all the winds and inclemencies of heaven. Within the said enclosure, resembling that of a wood of Vincennes, there is a very old hunting lodge, built of timber and plaster. Cracked in all parts, the plaster – adhering nowhere to the woodwork – [is] broken in numerous places.

The said lodge is . . . situated so low that the rampart of earth, which is behind the wall, is on a level with the highest point of the building, so that the sun can never shine upon it on that side, nor any fresh air come into it. For which reason it is so damp that you cannot put any piece of furniture in that part, without its being, in three or four days, covered with mould . . . in short the greater part of it is rather like a dungeon for base and abject criminals, than the habitation fit for a person of my quality . . . and out of those who have sat up with me at night during my illnesses, scarcely one has escaped without fluxation, cold or some disorder . . .[1]

She went on to complain that the 'garden' allocated for her exercise was no more than a 'potato patch . . . fitter to keep pigs in. The house, having no drains to the privies, is subject to a continual stench. Every Saturday they are obliged to empty them and [from] the one beneath my window . . . I receive a disagreeable perfume.'

It was hardly surprising that Bess panicked when she heard they were to live at Tutbury while they guarded Mary. Apart from her natural instincts as a hostess and homemaker, Bess loved warmth and personal comfort, and throughout her adult life surrounded herself with every luxury she could afford. Furthermore, it is evident from the Earl's weekly reports that, unable to leave their charge for even half a day, the Shrewsburys were almost as much prisoners as was Mary. News of the Court and the outside world came in letters from friends and family. Bess's eldest son, Henry (eighteen), now living at Court, had been taken under the paternal wing of Lord Leicester, for whom he acted as a page. 'The more I am acquainted with him, the more I like him,' Robert Leicester reported, to Bess's great satisfaction.[2]

Bess was now forty-one; her family was already dispersed. Henry was at Court, William (seventeen) had just entered Clare Hall College, Cambridge,[3] and Charles (fifteen) was at Eton. Frances, her eldest daughter, was happily married with a daughter of her own ('Bessie', who was adored by her grandmother), and Bess's two unmarried daughters, Elizabeth (fourteen) and Mary (thirteen) were almost certainly away from home, serving in a noble household as Bess had done. Notably, when the Cavendish children wrote home for help or supplies, to submit their accounts, or tell their news, it was not their mother to whom they appealed but 'Aunt Linnacre', who could always be relied upon to be at Chatsworth, whereas their mother could not.[4]

The Earl quickly found himself beleaguered with petty requests from Mary's household, and while he left matters concerning the Queen's diet and personal needs to Bess, upon whom he relied heavily, he fretted continually about the expense involved. The forty-five shillings a week provided for the Queen's food would not buy everything Mary expected and demanded. Nor did the amount allowed for her stables cover the costs of horses for her and her ladies and gentlemen. The Earl, a compulsive worrier, wrote to Cecil for assistance in this respect. 'I have for some time, to avoid troubling Her Majesty, allowed this Queen's stable at my own cost,' he explained, '. . . to keep her better occupied abroad while the weather serves.'[5]

Mary was a good horsewoman and riding was her main exercise. But even these brief periods of relative freedom for her caused the Earl concern, for unless the rides took on the appearance of a royal progress with an armed force, he was constantly on the alert, fearing an attempt by Catholic supporters to snatch her away. Yet another anxiety was the fact that the massive household had already used up all the local supplies of wood and coal, corn, hay and fresh food, so that carts had to be sent further and further afield for stores. He therefore asked permission to move Mary to his manor at Wingfield.

Bess was practical, and worried less than her husband. Also she was more intimately involved with Mary, who took to spending a good deal of her day in Bess's comfortable chamber. There, the two women, together with the most senior ladies of Mary's court, Mary Seton and Agnes, Lady Livingstone, sat and chatted over their sewing. Bess was a good needlewoman and Mary was an outstanding one. They took pleasure designing new work from pattern books, which Mary had brought with her; some were motifs charged with meaning and symbolism to those who knew what to look for. They also designed and made new gowns and discussed the latest hairstyles. Mary's lady-in-waiting, Mary Seton, was very skilled at dressing hair, and Mary's hair – black in colour and cut short during her escape from Scotland, needed false pieces to look its best. Sometimes, however, Mary wore wigs of different colours. Their feminine chatter, the Earl comfortably reported to Cecil, was of 'indifferent, trifling matters'.

According to Mary, the Countess of Shrewsbury was so affectionate towards her 'that had I been her own Queen she could not have done more for me'. Bess apparently promised Mary that if at any time her life was in danger, or if she was ordered to be removed from Shrewsbury's care, Bess would help to give her some means of escape.[6] She also claimed that Bess repeated pejorative gossip about Queen Elizabeth and her relationships with men (especially Robert Dudley) and her servants, and that at one point she ordered her son Charles Cavendish to swear in Mary's presence that he would reside at Court specifically to gather information for Mary. She said, furthermore, that Bess smuggled out letters for her, in cipher.

If Mary's version of the extent of their early relationship is to be believed, Bess was playing a dangerous game. While swearing loyalty to Queen Elizabeth (and meaning it), she was pretending to Mary that she supported her. Like Shrewsbury, Cecil, Leicester and Mary herself, Bess knew that in the event of the death of Elizabeth, Mary was the most likely contender for the throne. Indeed, Mary took care to remind Shrewsbury of this fact from time to time. On several occasions when Elizabeth was seriously ill, rumours of her imminent death were in circulation. Had Shrewsbury and Bess been overly severe, Elizabeth's death would make their situation an unenviable one. So it appears that Bess's friendship, and the 'kind' treatment meted out to Mary, may have been the pragmatic equivalent of an insurance policy.

Mary confided her health problems to Bess. 'She has complained almost this fortnight of her grief of the spleen,' the Earl reported to William Cecil, 'which my physician here informs me (being here to minister to me) he understands from hers is *obstructo splenis cum flatu hypondriaco*. Whereof . . . by reason of great pains through windy matter ascending to the head and other parts, she is ready to swoon.'[7] The doctor was at Tutbury because the Earl had suffered a painful attack of gout*, but in spite of this, he reported, 'I have not been absent from her [Mary] half a day since she came.'[8] As soon as both he and the Scottish Queen were fit to travel, he wrote, he hoped to transfer her to Wingfield, a move already approved by the Queen. But 'meantime,' the Earl wrote, 'I must humbly desire by you a convenient sum of money that things may be bought aforehand for ready payment.' He had not yet realised that it was intended that he foot the bill for many of the week-to-week costs of keeping Mary in captivity. In addition to an allowance for Mary's 'diet', the Earl was given '6d a day for 40 persons' to be used at his own discretion, to cover all aspects of keeping Mary's household. It had seemed sufficient when explained to him, but in practice Shrewsbury found it quite inadequate, and month after month he had to dig deeper into his own coffers.

Queen Elizabeth obviously read the Earl's reports, but she consistently ignored his repeated requests for an increase in the monthly allowance, merely querying the fact that Mary was free to wander

---

*The Earl and so many other men of his acquaintance (the Cecils, the Earl of Leicester, Gilbert Talbot, to name but a few) suffered from what the Elizabethans called 'gout' that I doubt the ailment was the one we describe by that name. It seems to have been a catch-all name for sundry conditions including arthritis, cardiac conditions and rheumatism as well as kidney complaints.

about the castle. How was it, she wondered, that the Scottish Queen was free to wander in and out of the Countess's chamber each day; was this not a security risk? The Earl bristled at the implication. It could hardly be avoided unless he locked all the doors, he responded, in which case Mary would realise she was being kept 'a straight prisoner'. He was ready to obey any command Her Majesty made, he argued, but surely no one of any understanding 'can think that I or my wife would be glad of such tedious hourly attendance, to the want of our own liberties, as we fain would have?'[9]

On 10 April 1569 – a little over two months after Mary's arrival at Tutbury, Bess set off for Wingfield Manor to prepare it for occupation. Ten days later the Earl joined her with Mary and her household. The journey had been quiet, to his immense relief, with no demonstrations of any sort en route. Wingfield was a considerable improvement on Tutbury. It was built in 1440 and added to during the reign of Henry VIII when large properties began to resemble domestic dwellings rather than castles, so that some allowances had been made for the physical comfort of the inhabitants. Situated on a hill, with a steep approach on two sides and a four-storey tower at its south-west corner, the manor was built round two square courtyards. Its best feature was a huge Great Hall lit with a magnificent oriel window at one end and Gothic windows along two sides, making it unusually light. Even Mary described it appreciatively as 'a palace'. She was given a suite of rooms on the west side of the north court. The chambers were small by her standards, but they were considered the most beautiful rooms in the house because of the glorious views over the orchards, which would have been a froth of springtime blossom when Mary was taken there. The Earl and Countess had a suite of rooms over the entrance porch so that they could see anyone arriving or departing.

During the previous months it had been suggested to Mary by various supporters that if she obtained a divorce or annulment of her marriage to Bothwell, a marriage to the Duke of Norfolk would be regarded as more suitable, and would have many advantages.

Indeed, somewhat surprisingly, since she had once sworn to follow him anywhere in her underclothes, Mary had already agreed to dump Bothwell, who was a prisoner in Denmark.* Or rather, she had indicated that she was content for the marriage to be annulled, on the grounds that Bothwell had not had his first marriage properly dissolved before marrying her. Although the thrice married Norfolk was a physically puny man, he was immensely rich and powerful, and commanded the loyalty of the major Catholic families in the north. This was what made him attractive to Mary. For his part, Norfolk saw that as King of Scotland he could dominate the Privy Council and trounce both Leicester and Cecil, both of whom he disliked. Mary began addressing her letters to him, and speaking of him, as 'My Norfolk'.

Several members of the Privy Council, including Cecil and Lord Leicester, were aware of these daydreams of Mary's concerning Norfolk, and if they did not encourage them, at least they appear to have accepted them. Better for Mary to marry an Englishman, the thinking went, than a French or Spanish prince who might raise an army on their borders. Despite being asked to reduce her household, Mary had increased it, which made it more difficult for Shrewsbury to police comings and goings. Mary used this to advantage, corresponding secretly about the Norfolk proposal with a number of contacts, among them the Duke of Alva† (who was plotting an invasion of England).

---

*Pursued by the Scottish authorities to answer charges concerning Darnley's murder, Bothwell escaped to Norway. There he fell into the custody of some relatives of a former mistress whom he had mistreated, and some creditors, and was handed over to the military. He was then taken to Denmark and kept in solitary confinement for ten years in appalling conditions which drove him to insanity and an early death.
†A Spanish general and statesman of great repute, Alva was given a dukedom for his military successes as a young man. He was feared throughout Europe for his ruthless savagery, and in 1567 he was sent to the Netherlands by Philip with 'unlimited powers' to subdue the people and convert the country to Catholicism. Immediately, he set up the 'Bloody Council' and when he left there five years later he boasted he had executed 18,000 men.

A few days after her arrival at Wingfield Mary was allowed to see a visitor from Scotland. She received him in one of the tower rooms, but the news he carried – how she was regarded in Scotland (as a murderous adulteress), the poor treatment of her supporters, and the fact that there were no plans in hand for her to return – upset her. 'She wept and lamented exceedingly till she went to bed,' Shrewsbury reported. 'She marvelled her good sister would see her so used, and like words. Her lips and whole face was greatly swollen – she would eat nothing at supper, but sat weeping, notwithstanding all the persuasion that my wife and I used that she should trust Her Majesty's goodness . . . She heard all we said very quietly but we could not appease her weeping.'[10]

The fits of weeping were to become commonplace. Mary often burst into hysterical tears when things did not go her way, to Shrewsbury's great discomfiture. In May the Earl wrote to Cecil in great indignation that on the previous night his captive had actually come to his bedchamber, after the household had retired, 'weeping and complaining that one of her servants is stopped from visiting her; she spoke with much grief and passion . . .'[11] She blamed Cecil for this withdrawal of privilege and regarded him as her chief enemy. She was correct, of course: he was. Cecil's entire loyalty was to Elizabeth and he saw Mary as a considerable danger to the peace of the realm: 'The greatest offence,' he stated, 'is the Queen of Scots' challenge to the Queen of England's title, [and her] delay in making any reparation as she was bound to do.'[12]

On the occasion when the visitor from Scotland was given permission to see Mary, she sent thanks to Cecil through the Earl who further reported that 'she is in great hope of some notable goodness at Her Majesty's hand.' But he had also noted a worrying trend: 'The daily repair of Scots to her so increases that, though lodged in the town, the company going and coming being 80 persons . . . my expenses greatly exceed [the allowance].' Because of these visitors he had had to employ more guards out of his own pocket. His

letters asking for reimbursement were to become as frequent as
Mary's fits of weeping.

At the end of May 1569, Mary became seriously ill. Bess suggested they should move her, by horse litter, eight miles away, to the
far greater comforts that Chatsworth could afford 'for 5 or 6 days,
till her lodging here be made sweet . . . returning again next
week'.[13] This problem of keeping the house 'sweet' was a major one
with such a large number of people making use of the elementary
sanitary arrangements that had been designed for a family and a
few servants. Now there was Mary's own huge household, as well
as the Shrewsbury servants, and a large corps of guards. Although
the majority of Mary's servants were boarded out, they provided
her 'court'* during the day, with inevitable consequences.

As Mary recovered she asked if she could visit the nearby spa at
Buxton, where Shrewsbury had a house and owned the mineral
springs. Bess had probably mentioned this spa to Mary; it was
renowned for its healing properties for painful joint conditions.
Shrewsbury thought he, too, would benefit from a visit to Buxton.
He advised his wife that he doubted it would be allowed, but nev-
ertheless he wrote to ask permission, also using the opportunity to
request an additional £500 to pay for fresh provisions 'for this
Queen'. When the allotted date came for Mary's return to
Wingfield, there had as yet been no reply from London about
Buxton, so Shrewsbury decided to return her to Wingfield as
planned rather than risk the Queen's displeasure.

On the day set for the removal, he woke with 'a great pain
between his shoulders and in his back, likewise in his legs'.[14] After
a hot bath he felt slightly better, though unable to ride and he

---

*Mary's 'court' now included a Master of Household, an Usher of the Chamber, a
Master of Horse, two pages, four maids, a dozen 'ladies and gentlemen' and their
personal servants, a secretary, two doctors, a priest, an embroiderer and seamstress,
a tailor, two wardrobe keepers and six varlets, fourteen sundry servitors, three cooks,
a baker and a pastry cook, two pantry men, a farrier and grooms, three lackeys and
four stableboys.

therefore travelled in a horse-drawn litter. Mary also travelled in a litter and Bess rode between them. By the time the party arrived at Wingfield, the Earl had contracted a severe chill. Hot and feverish, he drank almost a quart of small beer, which, said his doctor, inflamed his body 'full of vapours' which passed from his stomach to his head. For a few hours he was so ill it was thought he could not survive the attack. 'Both myself and those about me doubted my life that night,' he wrote, and such was the pain that 'I wished rather to die than live'.[15]

While doing everything she could to comfort her husband, Bess was also mindful of his obligations concerning the prisoner. She immediately sent a fast messenger to Cecil: 'most sorrowfully, yet of duty, I must advise you that my Lord is fallen into an extreme sickness'. It was, she reported, 'a dangerous palsy', however, she had given orders, until she received further instructions from Cecil, 'that the former order of watch and ward shall be more diligently kept'.[16]

This note caused consternation in London; the Queen immediately sent a message to Sir John Zouche, who lived near Wingfield, ordering him to go to Shrewsbury's assistance. 'Do your best to recover him to health and meantime assist him with your counsel and presence, [and] due attendance on the Queen of Scots ... behaving yourself to her with such reverence as she may know you are a gentleman of good blood and consideration, as we know you are. And when Lord Talbot comes [there], advise him in directing his father's officers and servants.'[17] A similar instruction went to Sir Ralph Sadler, with the additional note that 'if you see him [Shrewsbury] in peril, you shall take order in our name for the custody of the Queen of Scots, requiring the Countess and all her family to take your direction ...'[18] She also wrote to Henry Hastings, the Earl of Huntingdon, suggesting that he might take over as long-term custodian should Shrewsbury not be able to continue in that position, and stressing that Mary must have no unauthorised visitors and send no messages, and that Huntingdon was to do his best to cut down the number of her servants to thirty.[19]

The Earl was incapacitated for some days, but within a week the crisis was over. Bess wrote to Cecil telling him of her husband's recovery and then rode the short distance to Chatsworth, to supervise the lying-in of a young relative. The Earl wrote to her ('My own sweetheart') saying that he was already well enough to attend to business. He sent her £50 of the £53 she had requested, saying he would let her have the rest when he could. The Scottish Queen was such a drain on his purse, he grumbled, that he was never in pocket and he had been let down by people who owed him money. Meanwhile he was arranging to have two barrels of 'the first' wine sent to Chatsworth and did not forget to mention that he was 'longing' for his 'sweetheart'.[20]

The Earl's sudden and severe illness, only eighteen months after their marriage, must have come as a shock to Bess, who had already lost three husbands. She had not forgotten those former partners in her marriage to the Earl, and though she left nothing in writing, her emotions can be seen in her embroidery. In one panel she used symbols to represent the names of Barlow, Cavendish and St Loe, with a pattern of tears falling on to quicklime, surmounted by a Latin quotation which translates as, 'Tears witness that the quenched flames live'. This motto had been used by the widowed Catherine de Medici, and may have been suggested to Bess by Mary.[21]

It is not known precisely how much of the work on the surviving tapestries at Hardwick* was done by Bess. We know from her account books that she sometimes employed professional embroiderers to assist her, but 'never more than one at a time', as she would later insist to her husband during a discussion about expen-

---

*There is a further collection at Oxburgh Hall, Norfolk, including one large piece of embroidery worked and signed by both Queen Mary and Bess ('Elizabeth Talbot').

diture. There are also pieces containing her cipher 'ES' which were evidently her own work. There is too much emphasis on the purchase of needlework supplies in her account books for Bess not to have been an avid needlewoman. For Mary, however, with time aplenty, embroidery was a compulsion, and she contributed a great deal of exquisite work to the Hardwick collection during her long years of imprisonment at the various homes of the Shrewsburys. Biblical and classical themes were favourites, and in one famous set of tapestries representing goddesses and their virtues there is a distinct resemblance in the faces of Zenobia and Penelope to a portrait of Bess made soon after she became Countess of Shrewsbury. All these complicated works were encrusted with mythical beasts and flowers, and crowned with mottoes, coats of arms and heraldic devices such as the Cavendish stags, and the twined serpent design adopted by Bess at about this time and used throughout her life thereafter.

Mary's hopes for a marriage with Norfolk were destined to fail when the Scots voted overwhelmingly that her marriage to Bothwell was legal and binding. And when Norfolk went to Court he walked into the blinding fury of an outraged Elizabeth who, it seems, was among the last to learn of the proposed marriage. Nor was Norfolk the only one to suffer from the Queen's tempestuous outburst. She castigated Shrewsbury as well. 'I have found no reliance on my Lord of Shrewsbury in my hour of need, for all the fine speeches he made me formerly,' she announced angrily, ordering that Mary be returned to Tutbury. And she sent the Earl of Huntingdon, as a pointed insult, to 'assist' Shrewsbury in his task.

Shrewsbury was shocked and hurt that his trust, responsibility and loyalty had been called into question. He reacted with bitterness, but he had no alternative but to tag along behind the strutting Huntingdon as Mary's rooms were searched by men brandishing pistols. Mary's household was reduced to thirty persons, without her approval, and a number of the Shrewsbury servants who were suspected of being sympathetic to her were summarily dismissed on Huntingdon's command. The guard was doubled (at Shrewsbury's expense), and Huntingdon was openly patronising about Mary's previous treatment under the Shrewsburys, and was particularly suspicious of Bess's relationship with her. He did not trouble to withhold his opinion that the Earl and Countess had treated the Scots Queen with 'too much affection'.

Mary, who saw that her new keeper was a different man from Shrewsbury, hated and feared him, and was astonished when he dared suggest Lord Leicester (his own brother-in-law) as a husband for her. She is said to have told her ladies that she had no intention of marrying Elizabeth's cast-off lover (though of course Leicester was not cast off, and Elizabeth would never have allowed such a match). With the help of one of Bess's servants Mary smuggled out a letter to the French ambassador Bertrand de la Mothe Fénèlon, begging him to speak on her behalf to the Queen, of her fear of Huntingdon:

> I entreat that you will make the Spanish Ambassador accompany you . . . for my life is in danger while in their hands [Lord Huntingdon and his men] . . . Keep secret this letter, so that no one knows of it, or I shall be guarded more strictly than ever; and give your letters to this bearer secretly, for my Lord Shrewsbury's ships* . . . will serve me greatly, but if it is known you [will] ruin me!

In a frantic postscript she added:

> Since writing this letter, Huntingdon has returned, having from the Queen the absolute charge of me. The Earl of Shrewsbury, at my request, has prevented him from taking me away, until a

---

*A number of aristocrats owned ships and used them as privateers and for overseas trading ventures. The Earl had three ships: two of them – the largest was named *The Talbot* – were used to ferry slate, and coal and iron from his mines, and glass, around the northern ports. The third ship was named *The Bark Talbot* (or perhaps *The Barque Talbot*), and was employed in trading ventures and privateering expeditions.

second order arrives [from the Queen]. I entreat you to represent the violation of the law of nations, by placing me in the hands of one who is a competitor to the crown as well as I am. I beg also that you will write . . . by the ship of the Earl of Shrewsbury, by this bearer, and let it be secret.[22]

While Shrewsbury wallowed in aggrieved misery, Bess fumed that the effort and expense they had so far incurred was so little appreciated. And although the Earl could not leave his captive without permission, there was nothing stopping her from going to London. She persuaded Shrewsbury that she should go to the Court and explain their position to Cecil to whom she was 'my singular good friend and so I trust you will continue'.[23] Bess had already begun to realise the fruitless nature of Shrewsbury's role as Mary's jailer. She no longer regarded the position as desirable; but she did not want Shrewsbury relieved of his important position while under a cloud.

When Mary learned that Bess had gone to London she remembered confidences shared over their needlework which might easily rebound on her. She was also aware of her hostess's redoubtable nature and the fact that Bess would put her husband's interests before Mary's. She hastily wrote to Cecil asking him not to listen to 'the schemes and accusations of the Countess who is now with you'. She asked the Earl to forward this as a sealed note to Cecil, and the Earl enclosed it with a letter of his own, in which he wrote:

I hear to my grief that suspicion is had of overmuch goodwill, borne by my wife to this Queen, and of untrue dealings by my men. For my wife this must I say [that] she has not otherwise dealt with this Queen than I have been privy unto, and that I have had liking of. And hath so dealt that I have been the more able to discharge the trust committed unto me. And if she, for her dutiful service to Her Majesty, and true meaning unto me, shall be suspected . . . she and I may think ourselves unfortunate.

And when I perceive her Majesty is led to understand that by my wife's persuasion I am the more desirous to continue this charge, I speak before God that so far from her persuading me to continue, she has been in hand with me as far as she dares, and more than I thought well of, since my sickness, to procure my discharge.

I am not to be led by her, otherwise than I think well of, [but] if I had not found myself well recovered, I would have been a humble suitor for my despatch.[24]

Bess had private interviews with Cecil, Walsingham and the Queen, and she remained in London for some weeks, where a contemporary noted that the Countess of Shrewsbury's 'carriage was so graceful, discreet, wise and obliging, that the whole Court was much taken with her'.[25] During her time there she and Shrewsbury corresponded; he addressed her as 'My own sweetheart'[26] and Bess called him, 'My jewel'.[27] Her business in London is not mentioned in either letter; however, when Huntingdon made his next move, saying that his continued residence at the house of Lord Shrewsbury was untenable, and confidently requesting that either he be removed from his present post, or that Mary be transferred to his own house at Asheby, neither of his options were accepted. Instead, another 'assistant keeper' was sent to Tutbury, Walter Devereux, Viscount Hereford, to ease the tension between Shrewsbury and Huntingdon. Hereford did what he was sent to do, but after a short time he requested a release from his tedious duties. As one historian put it, 'it was no employment for a Devereaux'.[28]

The year 1569 – the first year of Mary's imprisonment under Shrewsbury – ended with the first serious attempt to liberate her. The leaders of this 'northern uprising', Thomas Percy, Earl of Northumberland and Charles Neville, Earl of Westmorland, were supporters of the Duke of Norfolk. With their small but determined army they marched towards York and Tutbury. Shrewsbury and Huntingdon received orders to remove their charge to the walled town of Coventry, where it was thought that a long siege could be resisted, if necessary. Mary was at Coventry for only a few weeks before the northern army was suppressed without a battle being fought, and in January Mary and her keepers returned to a bitterly cold and damp Tutbury, the most hated of all her places of imprisonment.

A lengthy official inquiry followed, held in tandem with the trials of the principals. One witness, Thomas Bishop, reported that several months earlier he had met the Earl and Countess of Shrewsbury, near Wingfield. They were riding out together 'for their past time abroad', in the company of the Earls of Northumberland and Westmorland. Bishop testified that he had fallen in with the party, and that, significantly, all their talk was of the Duke of Norfolk, who had been committed to the Tower on 11 October 1569. Although there was never any suggestion that the Shrewsburys had conspired with Northumberland and Westmorland, it was thought that they might have been 'used' by their honoured guests to obtain information about Mary's captivity.

Each small criticism of Shrewsbury and his care of the Scottish Queen injured his sense of loyalty, his dutiful nature and his self-esteem. Already nervous and stressed, this latest development made him testy and short-tempered, which rebounded on Bess and inevitably upon his captive, whose limited outdoor privileges were gradually withdrawn.

As the winter gave way to spring, matters improved. Huntingdon was removed, and in mid-May 1570 permission was granted for Mary to be transferred to Chatsworth, while Tutbury was 'cleansed and sweetened'. A more relaxed regimen came into force. Cecil wrote that the Queen might 'take the ayre about your howss on horseback [in] your Lordship's company . . . and not to pass from your howss above one or twoo myles, except it be on ye moors'.[29] At Chatsworth, for the first time in many months, Mary was again allowed a few visitors. Having learned the hard way, Shrewsbury had become a far more careful jailer by this time, and as a result he was able to frustrate a plot to rescue Mary.

Prior to the northern rising there had been another plan to release Mary, concocted by a cousin of the Earl of Northumberland, Leonard Dacre (whose dead brother had once been the proposed bridegroom of Shrewsbury's small daughter Grace). This plan had been squashed by Norfolk who, still hoping to marry Mary, thought that an escape would ruin all hope of ever gaining Elizabeth's approval to the match.

Now this old scheme was resurrected by a number of young men of the county under the leadership of Sir Thomas Gerard, a Catholic squire. Those involved were few: the brothers Francis and George Rolleston, John Hall (a former servant of the Earl of Shrewsbury) and two men from Lancashire, Sir Thomas and Sir Edward Stanley. The idea was that while riding out over the high moor, as she often did, Mary would be snatched. She would then be taken to the coast, and from there by boat to the Isle of Man, where she would be able to negotiate with Elizabeth from a position of strength. One morning at 5 a.m. the two Rolleston brothers met Mary's Master of Household, John Beaton, on the bleak and chilly 'high moor' above Chatsworth to coordinate the escape. Beaton was not convinced that the kidnap idea would work; the guards were too many and the plotters too few. He favoured Mary escaping at night by being let down on a rope from a window. Mary was still only in her twenties, and, despite her reported illnesses, she was strong. She had certainly endured worse, in her recent colourful career, than being lowered from a window on a rope.

Eventually, Bess got to hear of the plan and told Shrewsbury. The Rolleston brothers were arrested and sent to prison. Beaton died suddenly and was buried in the churchyard in the nearby village of Edensor before Cecil's men could question him. But it appears that the plan did not have Mary's approval anyway. When Beaton approached her about it, she turned it down, saying that she still had confidence that Elizabeth would restore her 'to her former dignity', following requests from the Kings of France and Spain.[30] Not that Mary had given up hope of marrying Norfolk; she still managed to maintain a secret correspondence with him: 'I pray you, think and hold me in your good grace . . . daily,' she wrote. '[And I] shall pray God to send you happy and hasty deliverance of all troubles. I shall not have any advancement or rest without you.'[31]

To the chagrin of the Shrewsburys, two members of their household were found to have been involved in the escape plan. John Hall, gentleman, told the Privy Council that he had been in the Earl's service for four years but he had left 'because he misliked the Earl's marriage, as divers of his other friends did'.[32] The other man, Hersey Lassells, said that both Mary and her major-domo Beaton had offered him bribes to perform commissions for the Queen, but he had refused because he had a patent of twenty marks a year from Lord Shrewsbury. He said that he had 'made Lady Shrewsbury privy' of the approach by Beaton, and the Countess had instructed him to promise to do what he was asked, but to come to her at once and tell her. But he admitted he had not told Lady Shrewsbury when Mary gave him a gold ring set with an agate as a token to show to the Duke of Norfolk.[33]

Once again Bess found herself suspected of conspiring with the Scottish Queen. She wrote in her defence that she had been suspicious of Lassells, and had questioned him over a period of some weeks in an attempt to extract information on the Scottish Queen's 'doings and devices'. Lassells was young and conceited, she wrote, and believed that Queen Mary liked him. Bess said that Mary had merely 'pretended a good will unto him', but the real incentive she offered to Lassells was her promise that if he helped her to escape 'she would make him a lord'. Having found out all that she could, but believing it to be of little substance, Bess dismissed the man from her service lest he should corrupt other servants. 'I assure your Lordship, on my faith,' she wrote to Cecil, 'that I was never

made privy nor knew of any dealings between her and the Duke of
Norfolk, done by either the said Lassells or by any other living
creature.'[34] It was certainly not the last occasion on which Mary's
charm would 'turn' Shrewsbury servants.

Despite all these events, Queen Elizabeth's attitude appears to
have softened towards Mary. By midsummer 1570 she was as close
as she would ever come to releasing her. She wrote to Shrewsbury
that Mary's supporters had complained to her that Mary was not
permitted 'to take the air abroad. Although we can find no fault
with you, for a due regard to her being in your charge, yet we are
content, that in your company she may ride and take the air for
health . . . We would be ready to satisfy all requests made for more
licence for her liberty there, but that we have frequent advertise-
ments . . . to convey her away [while she is] riding abroad . . . As
such peril be prevented by your circumspection, we are pleased
that she be permitted to have any liberty to take the air, being convenient for her health.'[35]

Mary was now allowed to ride, hawk and hunt, and send and
receive some letters. One, for example, was written by Mary to
Margaret, Countess of Lennox, her former mother-in-law, asking
her not to believe false reports made against her by her enemies.
Mary claimed to be utterly innocent of the death of Darnley, and
asked for advice about having her son, the Countess's grandson,
brought into England. And she promised always 'to love you as my
aunt, and respect you as my mother-in-law'.[36]

Mary's chambers at Chatsworth were directly above what is
now the Painted Hall in the present-day building, overlooking the
river and the glorious peakland. It was a brief period of relative
pleasure in her long imprisonment, and almost the only time that
she was housed in real comfort. A local legend, and one that has
been passed down through generations of the Cavendish family, is
that Mary's favourite place to take the air during the period of this
newly relaxed regime was what is still known as 'Queen Mary's
Bower'. The square stone building, with a garden on its roof and

the arms of Shrewsbury on a lintel, stands in a dry hollow now, but in Bess's day it was surrounded by a small moat fed by the River Derwent. It was part of the complex of fishponds whose edges were lined with walks and trees, and its purpose was that of 'a prospect tower in the pools and . . . a fishing station'. These ponds or water gardens, one of which was a long canal, were decorative but practical; stocked with carp they ensured constant supplies of fresh fish for the table.

No evidence has been found to support the old belief that Mary Queen of Scots and her ladies used this building to take the air. Indeed, in one history of Chatsworth's gardens a historian points out that the building was never even referred to as 'Queen Mary's Bower' in any published work until the eighteenth century.[37] However, while it might be true to say that no evidence exists to prove that Queen Mary used the structure, it is equally true to say that there is no evidence to prove that she did not use it. It would certainly have been a practical and pleasant place for her to spend a few hours in the open air. And since there was only one entrance to the building, across water, it would have enabled her to be securely guarded from a discreet distance while affording her an unusual degree of privacy.

In September Queen Elizabeth wrote to Shrewsbury that she was pleased with the manner in which he had conducted his trust, but warning that she heard constant rumours of plans for 'the escape and conveyance away of the said Queen'.[38] There was no hint of censure, but she reminded him yet again of the importance of his task. This was not surprising since the Pope had recently described Elizabeth as a heretic and invited Catholics to depose her, almost the equivalent of an Islamic *fatwa*. This ensured that the regime of religious tolerance that Elizabeth wanted was essentially doomed. Catholics were again regarded as enemies of the State, and Mary was their figurehead.

That winter Mary was moved to Sheffield Castle, then spent the following spring and summer at Tutbury before being returned to

Sheffield in August 1571. It was during this year that Bess began to spend periods of time at Chatsworth, away from her husband and away from Mary. Letters to Bess from the Earl speak of 'longing to hear from you' and hoping she felt the same as he did. He commiserated when Bess fell ill, and at the same time reported his own episodes of 'great pain' from attacks of gout.[39] He wrote to the Queen requesting permission to come to Court, but this was not allowed.

Gradually a pattern of living apart was established, and Bess settled into the more pleasurable life of running her great house and managing her household for longer and longer periods. As well as her mother*, her aunt Linnacre, and several sisters or stepsisters, there were a number of young gentlewomen serving in her household. One of these was a young kinswoman introduced by her late husband's nephew, Richard Cavendish, who had married into the Baynton family (as had Sir William St Loe and Ann Cavendish).† Cavendish had written that his brother, 'having a daughter of 18 years is very desirous to place her in service with your Ladyship, by reason of such honourable reports as he has received of you'.[40] Another, Elizabeth Smyth, wrote after she left Bess's service to marry, to confide that Bess had 'always been like a mother' to her.[41]

Bess's summer at Chatsworth that year enabled her to live as the great lady she had become, with her aunt and various other ladies of her family and some well-bred maidens providing the same sort of light services for her that she had once given to Lady Zouche and Lady Frances. And there are some surviving letters from the period revealing Bess as an inveterate matchmaker on behalf of her young protégés, promoting unions within the families of Barlow, Chaworth, Baynton, Pierrepoint – all names familiar from her past.

---

*The last mention I can find of Bess's mother, Elizabeth Leche, is in 1570.
†Bess's stepdaughter, Ann was the daughter of Sir William Cavendish by his first wife. Sir William St Loe arranged Ann's marriage into the Baynton family. St Loe's first wife was Jane Baynton and his two daughters, Mary and Margaret, were brought up in the Baynton household after their mother's death.

Her two pages at this time were Anthony Barlow (the grandson of her first husband's brother), and ten-year-old Anthony Babington (the son and heir of Catholic friends), who would come to a ghastly end on account of the Scottish Queen.

Not unnaturally, Bess 'doted' on her first grandchild 'Bessie' (Elizabeth) Pierrepoint, the daughter of her own firstborn, Frances, but there is evidence that throughout her life Bess was always drawn to babies and small children. At the age of four, little Bessie would become a handmaiden, and a great favourite, in the retinue of Mary Queen of Scots, who called the child 'Mignonne' and made pretty clothes for her.

Another matter of importance to Bess at this time concerned her ancestral home, Hardwick Hall. Her brother James was married but had no legitimate children to pass the estate on to. He suffered from an acute bronchial problem and, perhaps as a consequence of his poor health, was an incompetent manager. It is doubtful, in fact, that the estate had ever recovered from the long wardship during his childhood, and James was once again in financial difficulties. Not for the first time he turned to his rich and powerful sister for help. If Bess could not lend him some money, at any rate of interest, James wrote, Hardwick Hall would have to be sold. Bess loaned him money, characteristically secured by a mortgage on the house, and leased his coal and ore mines. Although she was happily settled in her beloved Chatsworth, which was entailed to Henry after her death, she had two younger sons to provide with homes, and perhaps she had some faint idea of using Hardwick as a dower property for her old age. But she intended to work the mines, having learned how her husband profited from his. Only the tie of Shrewsbury's guardianship of Mary, Queen of Scots spoiled what was otherwise a golden period of contentment for Bess.

In September 1571 the Duke of Norfolk, who had been freed in the previous year, was rearrested and placed in the Tower upon evidence that he had sent letters and gold to Scottish nobles who 'sided with the Scottish Queen'. When his house was searched a letter was found from Mary, Queen of Scots to him; it provided proof that the pair had been in correspondence for some time, and were involved in a plan to secure Mary's release. 'His servants,' a correspondent wrote to Bess from the Court, 'were racked for the denying of the most manifest truths.'[42]

The Earl's life still centred round his captive, to the neglect of his own estates, and some of the problems of guardianship affected Bess. Norfolk's rearrest coincided with a discovery by the Earl of one of Mary's message channels, and he had copies made of her secret coded letters before allowing them to be delivered. He sent the copies to Cecil, who had now been ennobled as Lord Burghley.[*] Burghley replied that although the letters had not yet all been deciphered, the Queen was pleased with the new development. With knowledge gained through the letters the Earl formally interviewed Mary, who categorically denied having communicated with Norfolk. But the Earl had seen the evidence for himself, and knew that she was lying to him; and he knew, furthermore, that she was also corresponding with the Pope and with the King of France.[43] His knowledge hardened his heart towards Mary and he savagely cut her personal household 'to ten persons I thought good to stay till Her Majesty's pleasure be known . . . partly for that they dare [not], for danger of their lives pass into Scotland'.[44]

During this crisis Bess had returned from Chatsworth to Sheffield to help her husband, because following Norfolk's arrest Mary was again in close confinement, allowed to take exercise only 'on the leads' of the roof, and in the totally enclosed court-yard. 'Myself or my wife be always in her company,' Shrewsbury reported, 'for avoiding all other's talk either to herself or any of hers.'[45] Even when Mary claimed she was becoming seriously ill for lack of adequate fresh air and subsided into tears and melancholy, the Earl – recalling her lies to him – would not yield. 'I perceive her principal drift was, and is, to have some liberty out of these gates,

[*]Cecil will be referred to henceforward as Lord Burghley.

which in no wise will I consent to, because I see no small peril therein.'[46] He was duly rewarded when Lord Leicester (referring to himself as 'your poor kinsman') wrote to tell Shrewsbury how grateful the Queen was for all his care of the prisoner.[47]

A few weeks later, in January 1572, Shrewsbury was given a brief respite from his arduous work as Mary's jailer, but it was not a break he enjoyed. He was summoned to London to preside as Lord High Steward at Norfolk's trial for treason. Sir Ralph Sadler was appointed Mary's temporary guardian, and Bess remained at Sheffield with Mary during her husband's absence. Mary wanted nothing to do with Sadler, but Bess was seldom away from the Queen's side, anyway.[48] The Earl wept as he pronounced the death sentence on Norfolk, a man whom he had respected and admired, but his tears were nothing compared with Mary's when she heard. Fearing Mary's reaction, Sadler asked Bess to break the news, but when Bess went to her she found the Queen had already learned of the verdict from a servant and was in floods of distraught tears.

Bess tried to rally the Queen by being unemotional. To Mary's tearful confidence that she feared her letters to Norfolk had caused his downfall, Bess replied practically that nothing Queen Mary had written would have done the Duke either good or harm, pointing out that 'if his offences had not been plainly proved against him, those noblemen who passed sentence on his trial would not for all the good on earth have condemned him'. In other words he had been tried by his peers upon his own behaviour, not Mary's. But Bess's unsympathetic attitude annoyed Mary, and a new coolness entered the relationship of the two women.

No date had been set for Norfolk's execution, and Queen Elizabeth prevaricated on a number of occasions when the death warrant was sent for her signature. In an attempt to prolong the Duke's life Mary embarked on a series of fasting days every Monday, Wednesday and Friday, when she spent the entire day on her knees praying for the Duke's deliverance. Sadler was thoroughly unnerved by all this and wrote to Burghley saying that he knew Lady Shrewsbury was longing for her husband's return, but that her longing was no greater than his own. 'I was never so weary of any service as I am of this, saving I know it is my duty,' he wrote. When Shrewsbury returned to Sheffield he found Mary very depressed, and she told him that she would give her body, her son and her country for her liberty. Though neither of them was aware of it, she had as yet served less than a fifth of the time she would spend as his prisoner. A few days later three letters, written by Mary in code, were found under a stone outside the castle, awaiting collection by her supporters.

After some weeks Bess went back to Chatsworth, and shortly afterwards there was another bungling attempt to rescue Mary from Sheffield. She dropped from a window but was quickly apprehended, and her conspirator, Sir Harry Percy, was arrested. Gilbert Talbot, the Earl's second son, reported from the Court that as a result he had been asked questions about the security at Sheffield by a member of the Council. He had replied that 'there good numbers of men, continually armed, watched her night and day, both under her windows and over her chamber, and on every side. So that unless she could transform herself into a flea or a mouse it was impossible for her to escape.'[49]

The Earl sent Gilbert's letter to Bess at Chatsworth, asking for her comments before he replied to Burghley, saying that he would use one of her 'favourites', Anthony Barlow, to carry the message to London. He still missed her company: 'Farewell my only joy,' he wrote. 'This Saturday I pray you keep your promise. You said you would be with me in a fortnight at the furthest. Therefore, let me hear from you when I shall send your horse my sweet heart.'[50]

This was how relations stood between Shrewsbury and Bess when on 22 April the Earl signed an important deed of gift. By this gift, although Bess would retain her life interest, lands that she had brought to her marriage with Shrewsbury were now settled upon her sons William and Charles (Chatsworth was already entailed to Henry). This was not done out of pure altruism. Apparently the

Earl owed Bess 'a great sum of money', made up of debts which Bess had incurred on his behalf, money which the Earl was bound to pay the two younger Cavendish sons when they came of age* under the marriage settlement, and 'other diverse weighty considerations'.[51] Bess would benefit from this arrangement by about £1000 a year in rents, and not only did Shrewsbury not have to find the cash to pay off his stepsons on their majority, but they paid him a cash sum in settlement, thus easing his cash flow problems.

In June 1572 the Shrewsburys were together on a rare visit to London where Shrewsbury was summoned to witness Norfolk's execution. It was not a duty he relished, even though he stood to gain from the Duke's death, for he succeeded to the prestigious title which Norfolk forfeited, that of Earl Marshal of England. A letter from Sheffield brought the Shrewsburys up to date with the news. Queen Mary had sunk into a decline after hearing of Norfolk's execution: 'Her majesty [Mary] gets worse every hour. Nothing remains in her stomach; she has vomited 10 or 12 times last night, noting but phlegm . . .' If they did not get help speedily, her doctors feared it would arrive too late.[52]

Bess remained at Court while the Earl returned hastily to Sheffield; he could not afford for Mary to die while in his care for fear that he might be suspected of having had her poisoned. From Sheffield he wrote to Burghley that Mary's heart was filled 'with a deadly hate against the Queen's Majesty' and that she was very stormy and 'hostile' towards him. On a more personal matter, almost certainly at Bess's instigation, he wrote: 'I have just heard of Lord Wharton's death and that the Earl of Sussex has the wardship of his son. His house and lands are near mine and my wife has a daughter of his age whom I mind to prefer in marriage. If his Lordship will part with this young gentleman I will give as much as another for this marriage. Pray be a means betwixt us to obtain this request which my wife and I earnestly desire.'[53]

---

*William Cavendish was twenty-one in 1572.

When the Queen left for her Progress in July, Bess travelled with the royal train as far as St Albans and then proceeded north. Gilbert Talbot wrote to tell his father that his stepmother had made a very favourable impression upon the entire Court and that he had discussed her with Lord Leicester. 'I never knew a man more joyful for his friends than he, at my Lady's noble and wise government of herself . . . saying he heartily thanked God for so good a friend and kinsman as your Lordship, and that you are matched with so noble and good a wife.'54

The Earl, clearly delighted, reported to Bess, who was once again ensconced at Chatsworth:

My dear None, of all joys I have under God the greatest is your self. To think that I possess so faithful a one that I know loves me so dearly, is all, and the greatest comfort that this earth can give . . . And where you advise in your letter you willed me to beware which I did, that I should not [reveal] to this lady anything of the matter . . . I asked her in quick manner, 'whether she writ any letters to her friends . . .' She affirms of her honour that she has not. But howsoever it is that she has written, therein, I may safely answer I make small account thereof.

I thank you my sweet heart you are so willing to come when I [wish]. Therefore dear heart, send me word how I might send for you. And till I have your company I shall think long of my only joy & therefore appoint a day. And in the meantime I shall content me with your will, and long daily for your coming. I read your letters closely, and I like them so well they could not be amended. I have sent them up to Gilbert & have written to him how happy he is to have such a mother as you are.

Farewell my only joy, this Tuesday evening, Your faithful one, G. Shrewsbury55

In October 1572 the Earl received news that Queen Elizabeth was ill with smallpox, and he wrote to Burghley in a state of agitation. The Queen had already suffered an attack of this dreaded virus in 1563, and since one infection normally provided lifelong immunity, her illness came as a shock. Mary had pointedly reminded Shrewsbury on several occasions that should Elizabeth die, she was heir to the throne and that when that day came she would remember his care of her. It was not Lord Burghley who replied, however, but the Queen herself. 'My faithful Shrewsbury,' Elizabeth wrote, calmly dismissing his anxiety, 'let no grief touch your heart for fear of my disease . . .' It was true that about fourteen days earlier she had been struck with a 'distemper' and a fever. Some red spots had appeared on her face, which her doctors had feared were smallpox, but after four or five days all trace of them had vanished and she was already recovered. 'At this day, we thank God, we are so free from any token or mark of any such disease, that none can conjecture any such thing.'[56]

That winter there was a further attempt to discredit the Shrewsburys with the Queen. Rumours spread that security at Sheffield was lax and that Bess was far too intimate with the Scottish Queen. The reverse was true; so good was their security that Mary's supporters realised the only way they could effect a rescue was to have her removed from the Earl's diligent charge. Hence the whispering campaign.

Bess heard of these rumours through her numerous correspondents at Court,[57] and Shrewsbury was bitterly hurt, once again, to learn in a letter from his son Gilbert that many people – including the Queen herself – believed he was 'a secret favourer of the Queen of Scots'.[58] By this time he had begun to think as his wife did. The job of guarding Mary had turned into a thankless full-time burden, leaving him no free time to look after his own affairs. His efforts were not appreciated and, even worse, the money infrequently doled out to him proved insufficient to provide adequate care for Mary and her court, which had become a permanent drain on his own exchequer. The constant anxiety about a possible escape, the fact that Elizabeth might be told something about him to his disadvantage and the lack of his own freedom was taking a toll on his health. The stress was causing him to become fractious and peevish, not helped by the fact that Bess spent more and more time away from him at Chatsworth. Despite everything, however, he could not find it in himself to resign his post. He still hoped instead for an honourable discharge, with some mark of appreciation of his sacrifices.

He wrote to Burghley, suggesting that another custodian might be sought for Mary, and to stress his own poor health he outlined a plan he had drawn up for the care of his prisoner in the event of his death. As for the rumours about his care of Mary, he said, 'my services and fidelity are such as I am persuaded Her Majesty condemns those who so untruly surmise against my wife first, and now myself, either of us undutifully dealing with this Queen, or myself of any carelessness in regard of my charge . . . As for my riding abroad sometimes (not far from my charge) in respect of my health only; it has been well known to your Lordship from the first. Nevertheless, henceforward, Her Majesty's command for my continual attendance upon this lady shall be obeyed.'[59] His suggestion that Mary be removed from his care was not accepted, and eventually the rumours that had caused his letter were traced to two chaplains who had livings on Shrewsbury's estates. They were suitably punished.

During the summer of 1573 Mary was again ill, and when she recovered she requested that she be allowed to visit Buxton spa to aid her convalescence. The Earl, who had also been ill, reinforced the request, saying that he too would benefit from the expedition. The Queen wrote that she was reluctant, but felt that she could not 'in honour' deny the request. Bess had obviously been making further changes at Chatsworth because Burghley, who was also deeply involved in a building programme of his own, sent his regards to her, and added that he wished he was at Chatsworth where he expected to see 'a great alteration to my good liking'.[60]

The Buxton trip went off as planned. Bess joined the party and after a few days Burghley joined them to try to obtain some relief from the pain of arthritis in his hands. It was a pleasant interlude while it lasted. Queen Elizabeth was on her summer Progress when she learned that her chief minister was consorting at a spa with the Scottish Queen, and she threw one of her spectacular jealous tempers, unfairly storming that Burghley had gone to her rival to ingratiate himself. As soon as he heard about this Burghley hurriedly returned to Court.

Although they were now spending a fair amount of time apart from each other, and despite the tribulations surrounding the guardianship of Mary, there is plenty of evidence that four years into their marriage, the relationship between the Shrewsburys was as comfortable and successful as the unusual circumstances allowed.

CHAPTER 12

A DANGEROUS MATCH

1574–5

AT THE START OF 1574 BESS'S DAUGHTER ELIZABETH WAS eighteen years old and still unmarried. This was certainly not her mother's fault. Bess had made numerous attempts to find Elizabeth, her last unmarried child, a suitable husband, the most recent having been a proposed match with the son of Katherine, the youthful Dowager Duchess of Suffolk, by Katherine's second marriage to Mr Richard Bertie. The Duchess had been a friend since the early days of Bess's marriage to Sir William Cavendish, and was godmother to Frances Cavendish. But Bess's suggestion to join their children was not taken up because the young man had already formed an attachment.

Shrewsbury confided in a letter to Burghley that Bess had caused him to approach other parents on his stepdaughter's behalf: 'Lord Rutland, Lord Sussex, Lord Wharton, and sundry others.'[1] There was no fault with Elizabeth; she was a mild-mannered, obedient girl, reasonably attractive, with an impeccable background and first-class connections. Her family could never have predicted the troubles that her marriage would ultimately cause.

That spring of 1574 was relatively uneventful for the Shrewsburys. The Scottish Queen gave no trouble except for asking for some pigeons to keep as pets (though Shrewsbury suspected that they were more likely to be employed as messengers). There being no obvious problems at home Bess went south to visit Katherine Bertie. There was another visitor staying at Huntingdon at the same time: Bess's friend Margaret, Countess of Lennox, niece of King Henry VIII, and mother of the murdered Lord Darnley.[2] One topic that was certainly discussed by the three women was a possible marriage partner for Bess's daughter, and young Mr Bertie being unavailable, Margaret Lennox's younger son made an even more attractive alternative.

The Earl wrote to Bess while she was away, saying that he had high hopes of a rumour 'of this Queen's going from me'. As usual he addressed her affectionately and it is a reply to her letter enquiring about his comfort. The letter, which even includes a small tease, proves that the relationship between the couple was as close and loving as ever, and this is important because of later assertions that their marriage was already in trouble:

> My sweetheart,
> . . . the true and faithful love you bear me is more comfortable to me than anything I can think of. I give God thanks daily for the benefice He has bestowed upon me. The greatest cause I have to give Him thanks is that he has sent me you in my old years, to comfort me with all your comforts . . . I thank you for the fat capon. It shall be baked and kept cold and untouched until my sweetheart comes. Guess who it is? . . . Farewell my sweet true None and faithful wife, all yours, G. Shrewsbury.[3]

As time went on Shrewsbury would discover that there was no truth in the rumour that the Scots Queen was to be returned to Scotland, but it cheered the Earl for a while to think he might soon be free of his troublesome charge.

Later that summer the Countess of Lennox applied for leave from the Queen to travel to her estate at Settrington in Yorkshire, and thereafter perhaps to visit her royal grandson, James, in Scotland. Rumours flew about the Court that she proposed to bring the child back to England, but she denied this and was granted a reluctant permission for the trip, provided that she went nowhere near Chatsworth or Sheffield. Queen Elizabeth had never really liked Margaret Lennox, and she wanted no opportunity for a rapprochement between her and her former daughter-in-law, the Scottish Queen.

Bess knew of her friend's plans: most likely the matter had been discussed when they had met at Huntingdon in the spring. In September Katherine Bertie advised Bess that the Countess was about to set out from Huntingdon, where she had rested on her way north. Bess immediately repeated an earlier invitation to the Countess to spend a few nights at Chatsworth. Lady Lennox was already en route when she received this message, and she replied giving the reasons why it was not possible for her to come to Chatsworth as she had intended. Bess discussed the problem with Shrewsbury and they decided to ask the Countess to stay instead at their house at Rufford Abbey in Nottinghamshire, on the outskirts of Sherwood Forest. Here the Earl's father had built a small mansion in the grounds of a twelfth-century Cistercian abbey that he had acquired during the Dissolution.* Lady Lennox later wrote to Lord Leicester that Rufford being 'not one mile out of my way, and a much fairer way, as is well to be proved', she could hardly refuse the invitation.

Travelling with the Countess was her sole surviving son, the slender, fair and delicate nineteen-year-old Charles Stuart, younger brother of the late Henry Darnley erstwhile husband of Mary, Queen of Scots. Darnley had predeceased his father, so when the 4th Earl of Lennox died his title and estates were granted to his second son, Charles, by the Earl of Mar (then Regent of Scotland).

---

*Three centuries later, D. H. Lawrence would use Rufford as the setting for his sensational book *Lady Chatterley's Lover*.

However, when Regent Morton succeeded Mar, he repealed this grant on the grounds of primogeniture, ruling that the lands legally belonged to Lord Darnley's heir, the boy king, James VI of Scotland. From that point Margaret Lennox and her son received not one penny from the estates, though her son Charles was still known as the 5th Earl of Lennox.

Despite his lack of money and estates, Bess appears to have made no secret of the fact that she was interested in Charles Stuart as a husband for Elizabeth. Shrewsbury knew this, for he told Burghley that the two mothers had discussed the possibility 'for the best part of a year';[4] but her real interest probably dated from that visit at Huntingdon. Nor was the invitation to the Countess and her son to stay at Rufford concealed in any way, for soon after the invitation was accepted Shrewsbury mentioned the fact quite casually in his weekly report to Burghley.

As soon as all was arranged, Bess gathered up Elizabeth and set off for Rufford to greet her guests. Shortly after her arrival there in mid-October, Margaret Lennox became ill and took to her bed for five days. Bess, apparently, was kept busy nursing her guest, and during this time the young couple were left very much to their own devices. Unused to such freedom they wandered about the great estate until they fell deeply in love. As one writer put it, 'it would have been easy for them to lose themselves in Rufford – especially as no-one was trying to find them'.[5] By the end of five days Charles Stuart and Elizabeth Cavendish had pledged themselves to each other, and the two mothers had no objections to make. Indeed they were delighted that their offspring had fallen in so well with what was clearly their original design.

Successive historians have assumed the illness of Lady Lennox was feigned, but why should this have been necessary? Aristocratic Tudor parents routinely arranged their children's marriages. The reason could only be that the mothers knew full well that they would very likely need an excuse to show how the marriage had come about when the matter became public knowledge. And young love was a better reason to offer than dynastic ambition. The wedding went ahead within days, in the chapel of Rufford Abbey.

It has been said that the Earl knew nothing of this matter and was angry when he learned of it. The reverse is true; he was pleased. 'I wished the match,' he wrote to Burghley, 'and put my helping hand to further it, and was contented . . . this taking effect I shall be well at quiet for there are few noblemen's sons in England that she [Bess] has not prayed me to deal for, at one time or another . . . and now this comes, unlooked for, without thanks to me.'[6] It is true that he was not party to the actual ceremony, which occurred so fast he only learned about it after it was accomplished.

But the matter was not as simple as Shrewsbury hoped it would be. When the Queen heard of the marriage she flew into another of her famous tempers, for Charles Stuart was a direct descendant of Henry VII. And even though his lineage was through the female line, this still gave him an indisputable claim to the throne of England after that of Mary, Queen of Scots and her son James. In addition, he was Mary's brother-in-law, and his children would be her nieces and nephews. He should not have married without Elizabeth's consent, and it is inconceivable that Margaret Lennox, the young man himself and Bess were not aware of this important fact, especially when one considers that the Countess was not even allowed to undertake a journey to Yorkshire without royal permission.

There is no other explanation for the Countess of Lennox and Bess having flagrantly disregarded the Royal Marriage Act, and taken this perilous course of action, but the fact that they thought the long-term advantages worth the risk. For Bess, the marriage was everything she wanted for one of her daughters: a senior title, elevation to semi-royal circles and the tempting possibility that from the union might come a potential male heir to the throne. Undoubtedly it was financial expediency that had persuaded Margaret Lennox to take such a dangerous step. In marrying her son to Bess's daughter, Lady Lennox had allied herself with a family beneath her own royal status, but with real wealth and power. Bess evidently loaned Lady Lennox a significant sum of money, for scattered among the latter's records of repayments of debts to the Crown, there are four annual repayments of £500 to Bess Shrewsbury.[7] And as well as the money loaned by her mother, Elizabeth Cavendish brought to her marriage a dowry of £3000.

Burghley wrote immediately warning Shrewsbury that the incident was likely to cause major trouble and Shrewsbury replied by return in a long letter dated 4 November 1574, explaining how it had all come about: how they had felt obliged to offer their friend lodging on her journey, how the Countess had fallen ill, how the young couple, having met, had fallen in love to the extent that Charles Stuart was 'sick with love', and 'swore he would have no other wife but Elizabeth Cavendish'. He finished his letter: 'I have written for your Lordship's full knowledge, so that you may deal with what shall be more or less imagined, or preferred to Her Majesty against me and my wife.' He stressed that the idea of the marriage was 'not secret nor hid from the world . . . it has been talk between them more than a year past, and not thought worthy of Her Majesty's hearing'.[8]

Shrewsbury clearly hoped his explanation (perhaps dictated by Bess) would end the matter, but to suggest that the Queen would have no interest in the marriage of a young man with a claim to the throne of England was arrant nonsense. Others of lesser importance had been incarcerated in the Tower for years for similar conduct. Bess had a son and stepson at Court, Charles and Gilbert, and their letters home in late November, detailing Court gossip and the Queen's attitude to the marriage, did not make cheerful reading for the Shrewsburys.

On 2 December Shrewsbury wrote two further letters from Sheffield, and there was a distinct note of alarm in both. In the first, addressed to Lord Burghley, he wrote, 'I am advised that the late marriage of my wife's daughter is not well taken in the Court, and there are some conjectures, more than well brought to her

Majesty's ears, in ill part against my wife.' He begs Burghley, from friendship and knowledge of his and his wife's duty and service over the years, to speak well in their favour whenever he heard such talk. To the Queen the Earl wrote:

> May it please your Majesty, I understand of late your Majesty's displeasure is sought against my wife for the marriage of her daughter to my Lady Lennox's son. I must confess to your Majesty, the truth is it was dealt with suddenly and without my knowledge. But as I dare undertake and assure your Majesty for my wife, she finding her daughter disappointed of young Bertie . . . and [seeing] that the other young gentleman was inclined to love with a few days acquaintance, did her best to further her daughter to this match, without having any other intent or respect relevant to your Majesty.
>
> I wrote of this matter to my Lord of Leicester a good while ago at great length. I heard nothing from him that I knew was done about the same, and thought not to trouble your Majesty therewith, because I take it to be of no such importance . . .
>
> I have always found your Majesty to be a good and gracious Sovereign, so do I comfort myself that wisdom can find out right well what causes move thereunto, and therefore I am not afraid that any doubtful opinion or displeasure will remain with your Majesty of me or my wife, whom your Majesty and your Council have many times tried in times of utmost danger. We never had any other thought, but as your Majesty's most true and faithful servants.'[9]

It was an unhappy time for the Shrewsburys. Margaret Lennox was ordered to return to London in mid-November, and she set off at once with her son and new daughter-in-law, Elizabeth, the new Lady Lennox (who travelled in her mother's comfortable horse-drawn litter). But the journey was strung out for weeks with one excuse after another: the roads were bad; the mules were lame because of the poor travelling conditions; the river fords were swollen with winter rains and dangerous to cross. By delaying her arrival the Countess hoped to give the Queen time to come to terms with the marriage, but by 12 December she could find no further excuses and made an appearance at Court. The French Ambassador who saw her that day wrote that the Countess was very afraid that she and her son would be sent to the Tower. The Queen treated her kinswoman with cold anger and made it clear the matter was far from closed. In desperation the Countess appealed to the one person to whom the Queen might listen: the Earl of Leicester. She had not realised, she wrote to him, that the Queen would be offended by her staying at Rufford Abbey with the Countess of Shrewsbury: 'I neither went to Chatsworth (which was the place her Majesty did mislike of) nor yet near Sheffield, by thirty miles at the least. And surely, my Lord, touching the marriage, of other dealings or longer practices was there none, but the sudden affection of my son.'[10]

Unfortunately, the Earl of Shrewsbury's and Margaret Lennox's accounts did not quite tally. Shrewsbury had already told Burghley that the Countess and his wife had been discussing the idea of a marriage for many months, while Margaret Lennox was claiming there had been 'no other dealings or longer practices' and that it had all happened because of 'a sudden affection'. There were other minor anomalies in the stories of the protagonists, and Queen Elizabeth concluded that there had been a conspiracy. On 27 December 1574 the Countess was arrested, and the young couple were confined to their house in Hackney. Lady Shrewsbury was ordered to London for questioning.

As she entered the Tower, Margaret Lennox wailed to her jailer that she had now been cast into prison three times, 'not for matters of treason, but for love matters. First when Thomas Howard, son to the Duke of Norfolk, was in love with me; then for the love of Henry Darnley, my son, to Queen Mary of Scotland, and lastly for the love of Charles, my younger son, to Elizabeth Cavendish.'

On the first occasion, as a young woman, she had been secretly betrothed to Lord Thomas Howard, son of the Duke of Norfolk and a relative of Anne Boleyn. Queen Anne had favoured the match, but when she fell from favour in 1536 so did members of her family. The betrothal was 'discovered', and Lord Thomas was suspected of aspiring 'to the dignity of the Imperial Crown of this realm' by having traitorously contracted himself 'by crafty, fair and flattering words to and with the Lady Margaret Douglas', daughter of the Queen of Scotland and sister of Henry VIII.[11] Indeed, this matter caused the drawing up of the earliest known Royal Marriage Act, by which any member of the royal family marrying 'without the King's consent . . . shall be held guilty of high treason'. After composing some love-sick poetry, Lord Thomas died in the Tower of 'prison fever', and Margaret was released from custody soon after the birth of Edward VI when the succession was considered secure.

The second time Margaret Lennox found herself in the Tower had been at the time of the marriage of her son Henry, Lord Darnley, to Mary, Queen of Scots in 1565. Although history tells us that this marriage had come about more by the joint conniving of Lord Leicester and Sir William Cecil than by the devices of the Countess, her property was still confiscated as a punishment.

Bess could not have received the summons until the New Year, by which time Shrewsbury had already corresponded several times with Burghley. On 27 December the Earl wrote insisting that the Lady Margaret Lennox was 'a subject in all respects worthy of Her Majesty's favour, and for the duty I bear to Her Majesty I am bound methinks, to commend her as I find her. Yea, and to entreat you, and all my Lords of the Council, for her, to save her from blemish'.[12] He argued that the real problem was not the actual marriage of his stepdaughter, which could in no way be construed as 'contemptuous to the Queen', for he pointed out, warming to his subject, marriage was a basic right which 'any subject may by law claim . . . It is not the marriage matter, nor the hatred some bear to my Lady Lennox, my wife, or to me that makes this great ado, and occupies heads with so many devices. It is a greater matter, which I leave to conjecture, not doubting your Lordship's wisdom has foreseen it.'[13]

Indeed the Queen and her advisers could see what Bess herself undoubtedly realised – that a child of this union could conceivably sit on the throne of England. After all, Elizabeth herself had once stood third in the line of succession behind her two siblings before a chain of unlikely circumstances had made her Queen. Jane Grey's claim to the throne through the female line was not dissimilar to that of Charles Stuart. The Lennox–Cavendish marriage was not only regarded as imprudent, but because Queen Elizabeth was childless it was seen as a potential danger to the future peace of the realm.

Bess's informal role as joint custodian of Mary, Queen of Scots was a further complication in the matter, for now Bess's daughter became sister-in-law to the Scottish Queen, and aunt to James VI of Scotland. Bess and Queen Mary had so far enjoyed a reasonable relationship, indeed, as we have already seen, Bess's enemies at Court had frequently accused her of being far too close to her captive, and far too lenient. Lady Lennox, on the other hand, had openly expressed her hatred of her former daughter-in-law. When Queen Elizabeth asked her what her feelings were towards Mary who was, after all, the mother of her grandson and her niece, the Countess replied, 'I was but made of flesh and blood and could never forget the murder of my child ... by my faith I could not think I could ever forget it ...' Yet Queen Elizabeth had never trusted Margaret Lennox, whose late husband, the Earl, had ruled Scotland for a brief period, acting as Regent for his grandson. Lady Lennox was now poor, but she was of royal blood and she was ambitious, as she had twice proved.

Despite being ordered to London, there is no surviving record that Bess spent any time in the Tower in January 1575, as is claimed by some biographers, if, indeed, she went to London at all that winter. More likely she pleaded to be allowed to remain at Sheffield to be present at her youngest daughter's lying-in at Sheffield Castle. In early February 1575, Mary (Cavendish) Talbot, the nineteen-year-old wife of Shrewsbury's second son, Gilbert, gave birth to a son at Sheffield Castle and Bess was present. Gilbert and Mary had been married in 1568 when they were barely teenagers, but they had probably only lived together as man and wife for a year or so at this point. The child was named George after his grandfather, and his birth was cause for celebration. He was the first male child born to one of Shrewsbury's sons, and a possible heir to the Shrewsbury title since the marriage of the Earl's first son, Francis Talbot, was so far barren. For Bess it was another beloved grandchild, and she had always loved babies. But the happy occasion served to annoy the Queen.

Walsingham and Burghley were still involved in the questioning of a number of servants from the Shrewsbury household who confessed under torture, and in some cases under the threat of torture, that they had helped or supported the Scottish Queen by carrying her messages.[14] One of them implicated Lady Cobham – Bess's best friend – as being a 'favourer' of the Scottish Queen at the Court[15] causing Frances Cobham to hastily and tactfully remove herself to Kent. On receiving news of the birth of little George Talbot, the Queen reacted angrily, railing that the number of unauthorised people who had undoubtedly entered Sheffield Castle to attend at the birth of the child created a security risk. Reading into this a condemnation of his guardianship of Mary, the Earl coldly denied any laxity:

> The dislike Her Majesty [has] of my son Gilbert's wife brought to bed in my house, because women and strangers [might] repair hither, makes me heartily sorry. Nevertheless, the midwife excepted, none such have, or do at any time, come within her [Queen Mary's] sight. And at the first, to avoid such resort, I myself, with two of my children, christened the child.[16]

The Queen would have been even more angry had she learned that Mary, Queen of Scots had stood as a godparent to the child. But her vexation did not extend to all members of the Shrewsbury family, it seems. That spring the Earl's eldest daughter, Catherine, wife of the Earl of Pembroke, became seriously ill at Baynards Castle near the Shrewsburys' house at Thames Street in the city. The Queen went twice to sit with the invalid and remained for several hours, staying 'very late both times'. Catherine's sister-in-law, Anne Talbot, was staying there and wrote to tell Bess about it: 'the last time it was 10 of the clock at night, and when her Majesty went from hence, being so great a mist as the divers barges and boats that waited for her lost their way and landed in wrong places. But thanks be to God, Her Majesty came home without cold or fear.'[17]

Margaret Lennox was released from the Tower in March, but both she and the newly-weds were still confined to the Lennox house in Hackney throughout that summer while the official inquiry dragged on.[18] Bess knew that she was not yet clear from the Queen's anger, but she had several friends at Court who were constantly working on her behalf, especially Lady Sussex, who suggested Bess might bring the Queen round by sending her an expensive gift; not gold or plate, she cautioned, but a cloak of watchet (blue) or peach satin, 'embroidered with some pretty flowers and lined with sundry colours made with gold spangles; such fantastical things will be more expected than cups or jewels'.[19] With time, the matter faded into the background. Queen Elizabeth knew Bess pretty well by now; she knew that Bess was ambitious for herself and her family, but equally that her loyalty was unquestioned. Had there been any real doubt about this, the Queen of Scots would have been removed from Shrewsbury's care.

Meanwhile, at Chatsworth Bess busied herself with family and estate matters. The affectionate letters between herself and Shrewsbury show that Bess visited him at Sheffield on a regular basis. In one letter she teases Shrewsbury that he has forgotten his None since she has not heard from him for some time.[20] He hastens to reassure her: 'My dear heart, as you wish to be with me, so assuredly I am desirous to have you.'[21] The main contents of their letters to each other are, however, about domestic matters. Bess has 'great need of a plumber'; she has plenty of malt for brewing ale but needs some hops. She also wants some oats, and her horses sent over to Chatsworth so that she can come to Sheffield. On other occasions they write to each other about a quantity of iron that she had asked for, and the offal from slaughtered beasts which she feared was being wasted, or oats from the store at Sheffield that were needed at Chatsworth. In one letter, written before he moved Mary to enable the castle to be cleaned, the Earl chides Bess gently about the ever-ongoing work at Chatsworth:

> . . . as for yourself I cannot like to have you undo yourself, and hindrance of my works, to bestow my men in work there, and you to keep so many men as you do, considering my building I begin to have. I shall not be able to furnish you with corn and beef as I have done till that be finished . . . I am glad your [fore-man] will be advised by you to send for his wife, for their being here for the 12 days therein. Do as you like best & it shall please me.
>
> I pray you take orders for the plate and damask and diaper napkins and sheets that there may be brought, for there is neither damask nor diaper napkins in the house. I am much in doubt it will be Thursday next before we can remove . . . Farewell my only love, from Sheffield this Friday at 10 of the clock.
>
> Your faithful husband, G Shrewsbury
>
> Wishing myself with you. You are not forgotten here by your friends, they well [mislike] for you to be so long away.[22]

They were both busy people, wholly taken up with the running of their estates in a profitable manner. And in addition they had individual commitments – Shrewsbury's custody of the captive

Queen, and Bess's building works at Chatsworth. Bess's determination to run her estates profitably is highlighted by a supplication to the Queen in August 1575 from tenants of the Peak villages. Some enclosed pastures 'and the common way through the forest', which by tradition had been open to them for free grazing 'from the feast of St Ellen to the feast of St Michael,' were now withdrawn.[23] They claimed that there was no way they could complain about this other than by direct appeal to the Queen. Bess's relationship with the Queen being what it was, it is probable that she backed down on this occasion.

Bess routinely stayed at Sheffield to oversee the 'cleansing' of the castle while her husband took Mary to another house. A number of letters written by Bess from Sheffield indicate that she was at Sheffield for a period of some days or weeks in almost every month throughout the summer and autumn of 1575. In one letter to Shrewsbury in November 1575, for example, Bess forwards a request from her son William Cavendish. Lady Mary Sidney had asked William if she could borrow the Shrewsburys' house 'at Cold Harbour'.* Lady Mary never appeared in public because she had been grossly disfigured by an attack of smallpox contracted while she was nursing the Queen through the disease. As a result the Queen was inordinately fond of her, and the two women often met privately. Bess saw the loan of the house as a way of earning back the Queen's favour. 'My None,' she wrote,

> I see my Lady Sydney is desirous to have your house this winter.
> If it please you that she have it, upon condition that if you come
> to London yourself then you may have it upon 2 days warning,
> to be made ready for you, it were not amiss. I am of the opinion

---

*According to John Stow's *Survey of London* published in 1603, Cold Harbour was once the property of Edward the Black Prince, and was later given by King Henry VII to his mother Margaret Beaufort. When she died, Henry VIII gave it to Francis, Earl of Shrewsbury.

that you shall not come there before Easter. God grant you may
be there then in good sort. I will set my works in as good order
as I can, and come to you of Saturday come sennight, and sooner
if you see cause . . . Farewell, my dear None.[24]

As the year 1575 drew to a close there was friction between
twenty-three-year-old Gilbert Talbot and his father. He and his
wife and ten-month-old George, 'your lyttel fellow . . . who is very,
very well, thanks be to God', had been given Goodrich Castle in
Hereford by Shrewsbury, but it was badly and sparsely furnished.
The Earl had provided some poor items of furniture and hangings
from Sheffield Castle, but Gilbert thought these 'mean and inadequate' and his father had refused to let them have items of good
furniture which Bess had earmarked for them. Gilbert told Bess
that the few items she had sent them from Chatsworth – a bed,
some hangings and tapestries – were worth more than everything
else in the house. He complained that his father had provided the
cheapest cotton for Mary to make sheets. But worse than all this
was a marked change in his father that worried him.

My Lord is continually pestered with his unwonted business;
and is very often in exceeding choler of sleight occasion; a great
grief to them who love him to see him hurt himself so much . . .
I have great hope in your Ladyship's at your coming, and in all
my life I never longed for anything so much as to be from hence.
Truly Madam, I rather wish myself a ploughman, than here to
continue.[25]

The Earl increasingly came to blame Gilbert's close relationship
with Charles Cavendish for the disagreements between himself and
his son. Gilbert and Charles had been educated together as boys
and they would remain closer than many real brothers all their
lives. Mary, too, was seen by Shrewsbury as a pernicious influence, encouraging Gilbert to defy his father. On one occasion

Shrewsbury wrote complaining about Charles who had been caught poaching. 'I would have you provide for Charles, your son,' Shrewsbury wrote to Bess. 'He is easily led to folly for within two nights after you went from me, his man Morton enticed his master, Blythe and my armourer to go a-stealing in Stavely Park in the night . . . I would wish you to advise him from these doings, lest some mishap might [lead] thereby to his harm and to your grief.'[26]

But Shrewsbury's main worry was cash. Though he was one of the richest men in the land, his wealth was in land and fixed assets, and the continual cash outlay for the upkeep of the Scottish Queen was beginning to bite. He had to pay for the massive guard around any of his properties inhabited by Queen Mary, and Mary's personal demands were also exacting. 'Two tons of wine, in a month, were not enough for her and her suite,' he complained to Burghley, 'besides that is occupied for her bathing and such like purposes.' In one month alone, in his 1575 accounts, he spent £300 on behalf of Mary, for purchases including hogsheads of French wine, damask, fine linen for sheeting, live quails in cages, writing paper, sweets and comfitures. Elizabeth's response to the complaint was the instruction that Mary's household must be reduced from thirty to half that number, and that, accordingly, she intended to reduce the budget 'for the Scottish Queen's diet' from £52 to £30 a week. She totally ignored the Earl's appeals for the back payments still owed to him.

Only a fragment survives of a letter written by Shrewsbury at the time, in which he expresses himself forcefully to his sovereign about his unhappy situation as guardian of the Scottish Queen:

When I received her into my charge at your Majesty's hands I understood very well it was a most dangerous service, and thought hard for any man to perform without some great mischief to himself at least. And as it seemed most hard and fearful to others, and every man shrank from it, so much the gladder was I to take it upon me, thereby to make appear to your

Majesty my zealous mind to serve you in a place of greatest peril.
And I thought it was the best use your Majesty could make of
me. I demanded not great allowance, nor did stick for anything,
as all men use to do.

My Lords of your Council, upon good deliberation, assigned,
by your Majesty's commandment a portion of fifty and two
pounds every week (less by the half than your Majesty paid,
before she [Mary] came to me), which I took and would not in
that doubtful time have refused your Majesty, since service of
trust so committed to me . . .[27]

He had never expected great recompense, he wrote, 'nor did
stick for anything, as all men use to do'. Had his lands and his life
had been demanded, he would gladly have offered them to serve
her Majesty. But the sum allocated was totally inadequate, he
argued, and even this amount had often gone unpaid, to his great
financial detriment.

Part of the problem seemed to be that he was only allowed to
claim his 'expenses' every six months. Subsequently, he asked
Walsingham if he could make monthly claims but Walsingham
replied that the Queen would dislike this. 'Her Majesty's disposition is such that willingly she would not be often troubled with the
signature of bills,' he wrote, advising that it was best to continue
with the half-yearly accounts, 'whereof, from time to time, and
also for the half-year past, I will do my best endeavour'.[28] No one
knew better than Walsingham how financially damaging it could
be to spend one's own money on State business. He would beggar
himself and his family in the formation and running of England's
first secret intelligence agency.

The suggestion of a reduction in the allowance may have been
one pressure too many for Shrewsbury. He was not a man of robust
health: he was progressively racked with gout and arthritis, and he
often suffered from other illnesses described as fevers and 'distempers'. His continual worry about money was added to by the

attitude of the Queen and Council whereby any unproven stray rumour at Court concerning his guardianship of the Scottish Queen could bring disapproval and suspicion upon him and his family. And finally there was the lack of his personal freedom, and the fact that he and Bess were so often apart. Small wonder he became increasingly sour and snappy.

But sometimes his behaviour, and even his correspondence during this period border on the irrational. Despite the fact that he was not in great favour with the Queen or the Council, for example, in mid-December 1575 he wrote baldly proposing his third son Edward as a husband for Burghley's daughter Elizabeth. Burghley diplomatically refused 'for the present'. He wrote, gently, that his daughter was still 'young in years . . . I have determined not to treat of marriage for her until she shall be above 15 or 16, and if I live longer than I expect to, [not] before she was near 18 or 20.' But apart from this, he explained, the Queen was suspicious that he favoured Queen Mary, and had still not forgiven him for his visit to Buxton. In the current circumstances it would be foolhardy to link his name with one so closely connected with the captive queen.[29]

There was, in fact, a noticeable change in the Earl's personality during the second half of 1575. From that date onwards he became not just careful with money, but obsessed with penny-pinching, and there was a new fretful irascibility about him, coupled with mild paranoia towards his wife, and a certainty that he was always right. Today, such a sudden and dramatic personality change would lead to questions about his health, even suspicions that he might have suffered a small stroke. Shrewsbury complained to Bess that he felt unwell at this time which he blamed on having eaten too many herrings.[30] But he was still addressing Bess as 'Dear Heart', 'My None' and 'my only love' and ending his letters with his usual 'your loving', or 'your faithful husband.' Clearly, then, the fault did not lie within his marriage; but whatever the cause, his increasingly mulish behaviour, which began at this point, would escalate and eventually alienate him from every member of his family, including Bess.

Meanwhile, however, there had been yet another important family event at Chatsworth,[31] when Bess's daughter Elizabeth, Lady Lennox, gave birth to a daughter, whom she named Arbella. Gilbert and Mary Talbot were godparents. All members of the Cavendish, Shrewsbury and Lennox families would have preferred the child to have been a boy, but the baby's sex would have been a relief to Queen Elizabeth and Lord Burghley. Nevertheless, here was a child with royal Stuart blood, who could be groomed for a great marriage – a possible bride for the boy king James of Scotland, for example. And that would make Bess grandmother to a Queen.

CHAPTER 13

RAISING ARBELLA

1576–8

NOTWITHSTANDING MARY, QUEEN OF SCOTS' SUSPECTED complaisance over the death of her husband Lord Darnley, baby Arbella's mother and grandmother Lennox were gratified, shortly after the child's birth on or about 10 November 1575, to receive a message of congratulations and good wishes to her new niece from Queen Mary. Two letters of reply were sent, one from Margaret Lennox and one from Elizabeth Lennox, and each thanked the Queen for her kind message regarding 'our little daughter here, who some day may serve your highness'.[1] The Dowager Countess had once sworn that she could never forget Queen's Mary's part in the murder of her elder son, but now, for Arbella's sake, she began sending her small gifts and signing herself, 'your Majesty's most humble and loving mother, and Aunt. M.L.'

The first tragedy in Arbella's star-crossed life occurred when she was barely six months old: her father died of consumption in April 1576. Charles Stuart had never been physically robust, and perhaps this was part of the reason why his mother was so desperate to see him married that she was prepared to risk imprisonment to accomplish it. Now (basing her argument on the fact that Henry, Lord

Darnley predeceased his father, and that after the death of the Earl
of Lennox his title descended to their surviving son), the
redoubtable Countess insisted that her granddaughter Arbella was
the true heir to the Lennox title and Scottish estates. The Scottish
Regent disagreed, responding that the Lennox estates had
descended directly to Lord Darnley's son James, and as a consequence were now the property of the Crown of Scotland.

The two grandmothers were not able to obtain Queen
Elizabeth's support for the claim, but they somehow persuaded
Mary, Queen of Scots to draw up a will in which she granted 'to my
niece Arbella, the Earldom of Lennox held by her late father; and
enjoin my son, as my heir and successor to obey my will in this particular'. Although this will was never signed, Mary's wish was
evident from it. But as a recent biographer of Arbella commented,
'in this, as in so many other things, James would disappoint his
mother'.[2]

Perhaps the death of Charles Stuart softened Queen Elizabeth's
attitude to the Lennox marriage. Certainly she appears to have
relented towards Bess by the following month, when Lord Leicester
wrote to Shrewsbury about Bess spending time with the Scottish
Queen: 'I find the Queen's Majesty well pleased that she [Lady
Shrewsbury] may repair at all times, and not forbear the company
of that Queen, having not only good opinion of my Lady's wisdom
and discretion, but thinks how convenient it is for that Queen to be
accompanied, and pass the time with your lady, than [with] meaner
persons.'[3]

Any comfort Shrewsbury may have felt at this news was dis-
pelled within weeks when his eldest daughter, Catherine Herbert,
Countess of Pembroke, died, aged twenty-two, after an illness of
nearly two years. Catherine had been a special favourite at
Court, and the Queen had even loaned the Pembrokes one of
her own ships to travel to the continent in search of a cure.
Shrewsbury's heir, Francis, was married to Anne, daughter of the
1st Earl of Pembroke, but Catherine's death meant the end to

Shrewsbury's hopes of a grandson heading the senior branch of that family.

In the early months of 1577, Bess went to Court for the first time in several years. Two of Shrewsbury's sons informed their father that her visit had been a great success. The Queen herself spoke of Lord and Lady Shrewsbury to Francis Talbot, assuring him that 'neither of their loves was lost unto her' and that she returned their love 'with the like again, and other good words to that effect'.[4] Leicester then wrote to Shrewsbury: 'without flattery, I do assure your Lordship that I have not seen Her Majesty make more of anybody, than she has done of my Lady'.[5] Shrewsbury was at Buxton at the time, having received permission to take Queen Mary there for three weeks. He was now instructed to remove her to Tutbury, but, taking advantage of his wife's restored favour, he wrote advising that Tutbury's situation would be unhealthy for the captive Queen, and requested permission to take her back to Sheffield instead.[6] This was granted.

Bess had two aims in visiting the Court. First, she petitioned the Queen to write to the Scottish government in support of Arbella's claim to the Lennox title and lands. Second, she hoped to persuade the Queen to stay at Chatsworth at the end of her summer Progress. The Queen's tour was scheduled to end with visits to Grafton, Northampton, Leicester, Asheby (Lord Huntingdon's home) and Buxton. A royal visit to Chatsworth would have justified all Bess's building works, even though such marks of esteem had been known to be the financial undoing of many aristocratic hosts. The Queen and Council considered the matter, but eventually the entire plan was changed and it was decided to end the Progress at Grafton.[7] While this was disappointing there was also some good news. Time and good living had taken a toll on the Earl of Leicester. Now approaching middle age, he was overweight and suffering from a variety of minor afflictions. His physicians 'fully resolved . . . he must drink and use the Buxton waters 20 days together', even if the Queen could not go there. And Leicester, whose support in any matter was almost as good as a royal command, accepted Bess's invitation to spend a few nights at Chatsworth following his visit to Buxton.

On 5 May 1577 Shrewsbury wrote to the Council asking for permission to move Mary to Chatsworth for three weeks while Sheffield was spring-cleaned. When he advised Bess of this plan she replied in a long letter, which pointed out that there were no suitable provisions at Chatsworth for the prisoner, and Shrewsbury had not sent any by cart, 'which makes me think you mind [intend] not to come'. She wrote mainly of estate business and family news: 'my son Gilbert has been very ill in his head ever since he came from Sheffield, I think his old disease.* But he is now, I thank God, somewhat better.' There was even a rare touch of humour: 'you promised to send me money before this time . . . but I see [it is] "out of sight, out of mind" with you'. She was sure that the Queen would grant permission for the move to Chatsworth, cautioned Shrewsbury to have everything in readiness, and ended her letter with the words, 'God send my jewel [Shrewsbury] health.' What makes this letter memorable is Bess's postscript, which has caused considerable debate among historians:

> I have sent you some lettuce for that you love them. And every second day some is sent to your charge [Queen Mary] and you; I have nothing else to send. Let me hear how you, your charge and love, do, and commend me I pray. It were well you sent four or five pieces of the great hangings, that they might be put up, and some carpets. I wish you would have everything in readiness that you might come within three or four days . . . Write to Baldwin [major-domo of the Earl's house in London] to call on my Lord Treasurer [Burghley] for answer of your letters.[8]

---

*Gilbert often suffered from 'distempers' as did his father.

Was Bess echoing an old tease when she referred to Mary as her husband's 'charge and love', or was there more to it? Did she really suspect the Earl had deeper feelings for his captive? Mary's fabled charm failed with only a very few men, and there are numerous letters among Shrewsbury's reports to Burghley and Walsingham in which he denies falling victim to the wiles of the Scottish Queen, such as one that year where he begs to be allowed to come to Court to clear his name of 'reports that there is a want of respect due to my charge here, and that I am too much at the devotion of this lady, and so the less to be trusted'.

It sounds as though it may have been a subject that was as much discussed in the Shrewsbury bedchamber as at Court. In view of remarks Bess would make to Gilbert later that year, and her reported remark to the Queen in her visit to Court in 1577, there is good reason to think that Bess was jealous of the relationship between Shrewsbury and Queen Mary. If so, it was almost certainly unjustified, but human relationships are rarely straightforward. When Bess was asked by the Queen to say how Queen Mary was faring, she replied: 'Madam, she cannot do ill while she is with my husband, and I begin to grow jealous, they are so great together.'[9]

In June 1577 Lord Leicester began his long-awaited visit to Buxton spa. He arrived with his brother and a few gentlemen ('the house was too small to accommodate more', he wrote to Burghley), to take the waters, and planned to spend two or three nights at Chatsworth before returning to London. On 13 June Leicester wrote to Shrewsbury from Buxton, playfully suggesting that Shrewsbury would benefit from spending some time at his own spa, 'but not if you do as we hear you did last time.' He had heard that the Earl had travelled daily from Sheffield Castle 'taking great journeys abroad of 10 or 12 miles a day', eating liberally with a great company of friends. Leicester boasted that he and his brother dined sparingly, with one or two dishes at most, and that they took only moderate exercise on horseback. But he ended with his sincere thanks, saying that Lord and Lady Shrewsbury had dealt nobly with him in every way.[10]

The lists of 'food sent unto Buxton' for the Earl's visit survives, and it certainly does not seem to bear out Leicester's claim that he was dining moderately. The day before his arrival the drayman took over a hogshead of clear wine, two hogsheads of beer and two hogsheads of ale. After that, on each day of his stay, Bess sent fresh foods over by wagon. Among the supplies sent on the first day of the visit were '1 buck, 24 rabbits, 4 fat capons, 12 quails'. This basic fare was accompanied by venison pasties, bread, lard, butter, salad herbs and oil. On the following day she sent turkeys, capons, partridges and peascods, together with a flagon of best wine, quince apples and clotted cream, and marchpanes. Friday was a fast day, when no red meat was eaten, so she sent baskets of trout and grayling with four fat capons and six partridges. By the end of the first week the wine, beer and ale needed to be replenished. This was the pattern for the entire period of the Earl's visit.

This was not simply the largesse of a generous hostess to an old friend, for, as usual, Bess had an agenda. Leicester was one of the most powerful men in the realm, and he understood that such liberal entertainment placed him under an obligation. And he knew what Bess wanted – to gain the Queen's support for the claims of her daughter Elizabeth and granddaughter Arbella. This is made clear by a letter dated 30 June 1577 written to Bess by Gilbert Talbot, who had been sent to Buxton to represent the Shrewsburys during Leicester's visit:

I showed the letter of my Lady Lennox your daughter, to my Lord of Leicester, who said that he thought it were far better for him to defer her suit unto to Her Majesty till his own coming to the court, than . . . to write to her before. For he thinks Her Majesty will suppose his letter, if he should write, were but at your Ladyship's request . . . and so it do no great good. But at his meeting your Ladyship [at Chatsworth] he will, he says, advise in what sort [manner] your Ladyship should write to the Queen's Majesty, which he will carry unto her. And that he will be as earnest a solicitor therein, as ever he was for any thing in his life. And so he doubts not to prevail to your Ladyship's contention.[11]

Leicester had, though, written to inform the Queen of his more than generous reception at Buxton, and this provoked the Queen into writing to Shrewsbury in a positive orgy of gratitude on Leicester's behalf.

Being given to understand from our cousin of Leicester how honourably he was not only received by you and the Countess at Chatsworth, and his diet by you both discharged at Buxton, but also presented him with a very rare present, we should do him great wrong (holding him in that place of favour we do) in case we should not let you understand in how thankful sort we accept the same at both your hands. Not as done unto him, but to our own self, reputing him as another our self.

And therefore you may assure yourselves that we, taking upon us the debt not as his but our own, will take care accordingly to discharge the same, in such honourable sort, as so well-deserving creditors as you are, shall never have cause to think you have met with an ungrateful debtor.

In this acknowledgment of new debts we may not forget our old debt. The same being as great as a sovereign can owe to a subject. When through your loyal, and most careful looking to the charge committed to you, both we and our realm enjoy a peaceable government; the best good happe that to any prince on earth can befall. This good happe then growing from you, you might think yourselves most unhappy if you served under such a prince as should not be ready graciously to consider of it as thankfully to acknowledge the same. Whereof you may make full account to your comfort, when time shall serve. Given under our signet at our manor of Greenwich the 25th day of June 1577. Elizabeth[12]

Shrewsbury's reply reveals his simple pride that the sacrifices made by him and his wife had been acknowledged as helping to secure the peace of the realm. And his handwritten endorsement on the Queen's letter, 'to be kept as the most precious jewel', hints that perhaps he also saw it as an insurance policy against a future fall from grace.

But housed in the State papers is another letter. It was also written to the Shrewsburys by Queen Elizabeth, at the same time as the above letter, on the same subject. But it is less formal, and delightfully conveys her humour as well as her playful affection for Leicester. She begins much as in the earlier letter, thanking the couple profusely for the care they have given Leicester, acknowledging that she is greatly in their debt. 'Wherein lies the danger,' she continues mischievously. For unless they reduce Lord Leicester's large allowance of food, she fears the debt may grow to be so great that she will not be able to discharge the same 'and so become bankrupt'. She then proceeds to suggest a more appropriate diet, which she hopes they will not exceed under any circumstances:

... allow him by the day two ounces of flesh (I refer the quality to yourselves) and for his dinner the twentieth part of a pint of wine to comfort his stomach, and as much ... water as he likes.

On festival days, as is fit for a man of his quality, you may enlarge his diet by allowing him for his dinner the shoulder of a wren, and for his supper a leg of the same, besides his ordinary ounces of flesh. The like proportion you should allow to [his] brother, Warwick ... whose body is already so replete, that the wren's leg be abated, for that light suppers agree best ... You shall inviolably observe this order, and so may you right well assure yourselves of a most thankful debtor to so well-deserving creditors.[13]

Both letters are curiously possessive. Even the first, rather formal one gives the impression of having been written by a wife thanking a hostess for entertaining her husband, or a mother on behalf of her son. No wonder Leicester was courted; he was as near to being a royal consort as it was possible to get.

Leicester arrived at Chatsworth in a horse-drawn litter because a boil on the calf of his leg made riding uncomfortable. Bess teased him that Buxton was not known for sending 'sound men halting home'. He stayed three days, and in a letter from Richard Topcliffe, at whose home Leicester halted on his way to London, Bess learned that her late guest was praising her hospitality and wishing he might have prolonged his visit 'by another three weeks'.[14] For Bess it was all she could have hoped for; it was how she and Sir William Cavendish had intended Chatsworth to be used: for the entertainment of influential persons with a view to furthering their family aspirations. During his visit, Leicester was able to visit Mary, Queen of Scots for a short time.[15] We do not know where this meeting took place; it was probably at Sheffield, but it might be that Mary was transported to Chatsworth so that the Earl could be present, with his wife, during Lord Leicester's visit.

After Leicester's departure Bess went to stay at Sheffield and within days the Shrewsburys had a violent disagreement. It blew up over a minor incident, and, as in most domestic arguments, the opponents, hurt and angry, each stood on their dignity. This was not the start of the Shrewsburys' great estrangement; but the interesting thing about this quarrel is that we know exactly what each of the protagonists said, thought and felt. Although Shrewsbury was a good, loyal, dutiful and upright man, he was a severe parent who found it difficult to demonstrate the paternal affection he undoubtedly felt. Bess listened sympathetically to the complaints made about their father by her stepchildren, and tried to help them, sometimes by lending them money. As a result she enjoyed a warm and affectionate relationship with them, especially Gilbert, who was also her son-in-law. On this occasion he acted as a go-between and faithfully recorded every word his father said about the dis-agreement with Bess.

The quarrel began in late July after Bess had arranged for a group of workers to carry out a task at Sheffield Manor Lodge. In Gilbert's letter the workers are described as 'embroiderers' but this title would have included upholsterers, tapestry repairers and hang-ers. John Dickenson, Keeper of the Earl's Wardrobe, refused them overnight lodging there, probably because he thought they were a security risk. The Lodge was only a short distance from the Turret House, a three-storey stone building erected in 1574 by the Earl to accommodate Mary and her court, and at the top of the Turret House was a large, flat, leaden roof where Mary took her daily exercise when she was being kept in close confinement. The embroiderers complained to Bess's groom, Owen, who argued with Dickenson. The Earl, when advised of the matter, naturally sided with his own man, and when Bess became involved sparks flew.

Shrewsbury apparently left Sheffield Castle immediately after the heated exchange between himself and Bess. A day later Gilbert rode over to Bolsover to meet his father, who had taken a rare over-night leave from Sheffield in order to attend to some estate busi-ness. As the two men rested their horses on the return journey, Shrewsbury asked Gilbert if he had spoken with his stepmother since the previous day. Gilbert answered that he had, and at his father's request told him what they spoken of. The following repre-sents extracts (with minor alterations to grammar and punctuation), beginning with Shrewsbury's query as to how Gilbert found his stepmother. Gilbert wrote that he had replied:

> Truly Sir, with as grieved a mind as ever I saw woman in my life, she told me your Lordship was vehemently offended with her . . . with many words and shows of your anger of evil will towards her. Whereby her Ladyship said she could not doubt that all your Lordship's [former] love and affection is clean turned to the con-trary. And her Ladyship further said she had given you no cause

to be offended. Her Ladyship, hearing that the embroiderers were kept out of the Lodge by John Dickenson's command, said to your Lordship, in the morning: 'Did you give commandment that the embroiderers should be kept out of the lodge?' And you answered her: 'No'. Then her Ladyship said, 'They were kept from their beds yesternight. And he that did so says John Dickenson had given express commandment.' Which you told her was a lie.

Shrewsbury reacted 'sharply' according to Gilbert. 'He . . . uttered cruel words against them [the embroiderers], over-long to trouble your ladyship with, and being alighted from his horse said, "Let us be going; I shall have enough to do when I come home."' Gilbert said: 'I think my Lady be at Chatsworth by this time.' To which Shrewsbury asked, 'What, is she gone from Sheffield?' and Gilbert answered affirmatively, 'By eleven of the clock.' His father was astonished: 'Is her malice such she would not tarry for my coming?' he asked.

Gilbert explained, 'Her ladyship told me you were quite contented at your first coming that she should go yesterday' but his father denied any knowledge of this arrangement, and Gilbert continued, 'My Lady further told me that when your Lordship was contented for her departure that day, that your Lordship had business in the Peak and would shortly come there and lie at Chatsworth.' Shrewsbury was now greatly offended and said, 'Her going away, thus, gives me small cause to go to Chatsworth . . . All the house can discern her Ladyship's stomach against me by her leaving before my coming.' Seeing that his father was now very angry, Gilbert told him,

Her Ladyship had very great and earnest business at Chatsworth . . . with certain freeholders for Sir Thomas Stanhope . . . I pray your Lordship give me leave to tell plainly what I gathered by my Lady. I see she is so grieved and vexed in mind, as I protest to God I never saw any woman more in my life.

And after she had told me how, without any cause at all, your Lordship uttered most cruel and bitter speeches against her, when she all the time never uttered any undutiful words . . . she plainly declared unto me that she thought your Lordship's heart was withdrawn from her, and all your affection and love turned to hate and evil will. Her Ladyship believes this is contrary to what she deserves. In manifold ways she has . . . so infinitely made proof of her . . . dear affection and love for you, both in health and sickness . . . and she has wished your griefs upon herself, to unburden and quiet you of them. When she told me of this, her dear love towards you, and nowhere had your Lordship requited her, she was in such perplexity as I never saw a woman. She now believes your Lordship thinks himself most happy when she is absent from you, and most unhappy when she is with you.

'At this', Gilbert wrote, 'I assure your Ladyship he melted . . .' Shrewsbury replied, 'I know. Her love hath been great to me. And my love hath been, and is, as great to her. But what can a man do more for his wife than I have done, and daily do for her?' Gilbert told his father:

My Lord, she were to blame if she considered not these things; but I gather plainly by her speech to me that she thinks your heart is hardened against her, as I have once or twice already told your Lordship. And that you love them who love her not, and believe those about you, which hate her. At her departure, her Ladyship told me that she truly thought your Lordship gladder of her absence than presence.

Shrewsbury replied, 'Gilbert, you know the contrary. And how often have I cursed the building at Chatsworth for want of her company by her going away? I would not have done so to her.'[16] 'After this,' Gilbert continued in his epic letter, 'he talked not much, but I know it pinched him . . . Yesternight, not having talked with any but myself, I know that his heart desires reconciliation if he knew which way to bring it to pass. The living God grant it and make his heart turn to your comfort in all things.'[17]

Most historians have dated the eventual sensational break-up of the Shrewsburys' marriage from the Lennox marriage, but this letter is actually the first account of any disagreement between the couple and it is a detailed account. Although this is a condensed version of Gilbert's full report, the Lennox marriage is never mentioned, and the matter seems to be one of simple domestic disharmony. There is, in fact, no discernible evidence that Bess's involvement in the Lennox marriage contributed to the permanent estrangement of the Shrewsburys that was to come.

Although as a dutiful wife Bess deferred to the Earl when she was at Sheffield, she was used to being in sole control at Chatsworth. In overriding her orders to the embroiderers at Sheffield, she felt that Dickenson diminished her status in the eyes of her husband's employees. Just as Shrewsbury was embarrassed to learn that his household would have noted Bess's sudden departure before his own return. Bess's remarks to Gilbert about her husband smack rather of a petulant 'you-don't-love-me-any-more' retort, than anything more serious, although perhaps there is a hint, yet again, of sexual jealousy. But if Bess seriously thought that her husband was giving too much time and attention to Mary, Queen of Scots, surely the solution lay in her own hands? She had only to spend more time with him at Sheffield, and less at Chatsworth. Yet at Sheffield the atmosphere was unpleasant and life restricted; at Chatsworth she found peace and independence to live as she wanted to live.

The Earl was not well and was fractious because of the constant pain he was suffering. The gout in his hands had even affected his handwriting, appallingly bad at best, but virtually unreadable at this point ('for reason of a great ache, which has vexed me in the wrist of my right hand a long time, I am able to write no better,' he wrote to the Queen). Allied to the normal problems of administering his vast estates, he had also become enmeshed in a serious quarrel between two neighbouring landowners (Sir Thomas Stanhope and Sir John Zouche) at the request of the Privy Council. There was the on-going financial worry and stress concerned with the imprisonment of the Scottish Queen, as well as the constant attempts by Mary to plan an escape, and correspond with supporters.

Mary had various ways of communicating with her supporters: writing in alum (a form of so called 'invisible writing') was easily discovered, so she advised her correspondents not to use this method. She preferred instead that they should write 'between the lines of a new book' sent to her 'between the fourth, eighth, twelfth and sixteenth leaf'. Green ribbons were to be attached to any books used in this manner so they could be identified among the others. Another form of communication was writing on the bolts of fine cloth such as white taffeta, lawn and other delicate materials. She advised that a half-yard should be added to the bolt so that she knew any bolts arriving with an odd half a yard were communications. Another hiding place was in the cork heels of her ladies' slippers.[18] Some of her methods of smuggling notes were known about, and when Mary complained that she had been robbed of her jewels in a burglary in May 1576, Burghley and Walsingham were of the opinion that it was more likely Mary had smuggled them out to her supporters to fund an escape plan. Naturally the blame for this fell on Shrewsbury, who felt he could do nothing right. It is perhaps not surprising that he was short-tempered and difficult to deal with.

When Gilbert wrote to Bess a week later, on 1 August,[19] the quarrel was still unresolved. He had told his father that as a gesture of conciliation, because the Earl so disapproved of him, Bess had offered to dismiss her groom, Owen. However she was perplexed as to what reason she could give the man for letting him go since he was an excellent employee. The Earl merely growled that he doubted she would accept a new man of his choosing. The couple were to be brought together again by a family tragedy which would put all their differences into perspective.

Gilbert's son George was two and a half years old and apparently in excellent health. He is mentioned in letters as greeting his grandfather warmly when the Earl returned to Sheffield from Bolsover, and continually asking after Bess whom he called 'Lady Danmode[r]' [Lady Grandmother]. Bess was held up to the little boy if he was naughty. 'If I have any spice,' Gilbert wrote affectionately, 'I tell him Lady Grandmother is come and will see him, which he will then either quickly hide, or quickly eat . . .' In his letter of 1 August Gilbert advised Bess in a postscript that 'George is very well, I thank God.'

Bess was then kept busy for some days entertaining another eminent visitor. When Lord Burghley informed Shrewsbury that he intended to pay a further visit to Buxton, Shrewsbury immediately invited him to stay at Wingfield and Chatsworth during his trip. Shrewsbury visited Buxton while Burghley was there in the first week of August to treat the pain in his hands from gout. But any hopes the Earl entertained of long, cosy discussions with the Lord Treasurer were dashed when news was received of an escape attempt by Queen Mary from Sheffield, and Shrewsbury had to rush back to his castle to deal with the matter. The small emergency also prevented Lord Burghley from meeting the Scottish Queen. Having heard that Leicester had met her, he requested the same privilege, but was refused. He spent two days at Chatsworth and left on 7 August 1577.[20] Three days later, little George Talbot suffered a sudden convulsion and died the same night.

Both grandparents were shattered by this loss. For Shrewsbury little George was his only grandson and represented the continuation of his line. But clearly he loved the child, describing him in a letter to Walsingham as 'my dearest jewel under God next to my sovereign'. For Bess also there were dynastic implications but she too had adored the child. After his funeral she returned to Chatsworth and was inconsolable. Shrewsbury reluctantly accepted that George's death was the will of God, 'who only lent him', he wrote to Burghley. '[But] my wife (although she acknowledges no less) is not well able to rule her passions, and has driven herself into such a case by her continual weeping.' Fearing she would make herself seriously ill by her bouts of crying he requested permission to move Queen Mary to Chatsworth, in order that he might be with his wife and provide what consolation he could.[21] This was granted.

But it is small wonder that two months later Bess cancelled a much looked forward to visit by her daughters Elizabeth and Mary and baby Arbella, because there was illness at Chatsworth. She was not prepared to take any chances with little Arbella. In the autumn Shrewsbury and his captive returned to Sheffield, and Bess remained at Chatsworth. And just as Shrewsbury's children applied to Bess for help in resolving quarrels with their father, so did her own children seek help from Shrewsbury in disagreements with their mother. Bess was furious with her third son Charles when he injured the eye of the gentleman servant of a friend in a mock sword fight. Charles wrote to Shrewsbury:

> I beseech you to appease my Lady's mislike to me through this crooked misfortune, which was but ill luck . . . He fell, which amazed me greatly, for if ever in my life I played more cooler or with better discretion, both the man's master and myself be greatly deceived. But God be thanked he is well amended and in no danger . . . I humbly beseech your earnest means to my mother, for I protest I desire not to live to have the least frown from her, much less to be in her disgrace, and except it be done by your Lordship, whose wisdom I know can temper this [mis-conception] of hers, I shall rest in doubt not to be restored to her favour, which I hold dear above all things.[22]

In January of the following year, 1578, Shrewsbury was still involved in trying to resolve the Stanhope–Zouche affair, a matter in which Stanhope had accused Zouche of embezzling funds made available for the local musters. It may seem surprising that despite her early association with the Zouche family, Bess sided with

Stanhope, as did Shrewsbury. Bess had discovered that Zouche had been one of the chief rumour-mongers at the time of the Lennox marriage, and this had done Bess a good deal of harm at Court. In one series of letters Stanhope begs the Earl to go to London and speak on his behalf to the Privy Council and the Queen. Shrewsbury would have liked nothing better but he could not get permission to leave his charge for a visit to the Court, so on 12 January Stanhope asked that Lady Shrewsbury should go instead:

> Your Lordship knows that women with women can work best, especially one such as my Lady [Shrewsbury] whose wisdom and discreet course can sufficiently deal with the best of them, be this with her Majesty or the Council or the other ladies about her Highness. And so may she prepare the way for all things, and return so instructed, and leave such a plot for you behind her, and work your friends for you, in such good order, as at your coming there shall be no difficulty at all, but that everything must go as you desire. This was my Lord of Leicester's advice and speech to me in the summer.[23]

In the event it was March before Bess went to London, and by then there was another reason for her visit. Following an affable supper entertaining the Earl of Leicester, Margaret, the dowager Countess of Lennox suddenly dropped dead. The news came as a shock to Bess; the two women were of an age, and had been friends and confidantes for years. Lady Lennox had worked tirelessly on Arbella's behalf, and as she lived mainly in and about the Court it had been convenient for Bess to leave these matters to her, unless applied to for assistance. Her demise left only Bess to fight on Arbella's behalf.

With her grandmother's death Arbella moved one step nearer the throne; the Scottish Regent refused to acknowledge the child's mother as her guardian and Queen Elizabeth quickly stepped in and made Arbella her ward. This caused Elizabeth Lennox great distress, thinking that her child might be taken from her, but she was granted custody of Arbella. In a letter dated 17 March 1578, written from Sheffield, Bess thanked the Queen for her 'especial and gracious goodness to grant unto my poor daughter Lennox, the custody of her child, notwithstanding that there were divers means used to influence your Highness to the contrary'.[24]

Though Queen Elizabeth had never liked Margaret Lennox, she could not allow a kinswoman with a claim to the throne to die as a pauper without damaging her own stature. Since the Lennox marriage, Bess had been regarded as a kinswoman to the Dowager Countess, and accordingly she hurried down from Derbyshire to appear as one of the principal mourners at the royal funeral. The Queen organised the glorious tomb in Westminster Abbey, decorated with the figures of the Countess's dead children – six who died in infancy, Henry, Lord Darnley (depicted with the crown of Scotland floating over his head), and Charles, the father of Arbella.

Bess comfortably assumed that Arbella would at least inherit her Lennox grandmother's English estates, but she was in for a shock. Elizabeth confiscated the greater part of these, ostensibly to pay for the State funeral expenses and to pay off Margaret Lennox's debts, leaving only a small property for Arbella, which produced less than £300 a year.[25] The Queen also awarded a 'pension' for Elizabeth Lennox of £400 a year and £200 for Arbella. These sums would have been considered very reasonable had the child been the daughter of a courtier, but they were inadequate to enable a girl who was a princess in all but title to fulfil her destiny. Worse news was to come from Scotland concerning the Lennox Earldom and Scottish estates. In May 1578, a few weeks after the funeral of the Dowager Countess, the Lennox title was formally conferred on a brother of the 4th Earl of Lennox, the ageing and childless Bishop of Caithness – an uncle to the late Henry Darnley and Charles Lennox.

In her will, the Dowager Countess specifically left her Court jewels to Arbella, naming and describing over twenty items and referring to other items which she could not recall to memory at the time; the pieces included set-piece jewels such as large identifiable diamonds, rubies and emeralds, as well as gold and crystal bijouterie. They were to be kept by the executor of Margaret Lennox's will for Arbella, and given to her when she reached the age of fourteen. In September of the following year, Queen Mary – clearly prompted by Bess – wrote to the executor ordering him as 'sole executor to our dearest mother-in-law and aunt . . . to deliver in to the hands and custody of our right well beloved cousin Elizabeth, Countess of Shrewsbury, all and every such jewel as the said Lady Margaret delivered and committed . . . for the use of her grandchild if God send her life until fourteen years of age . . . if not, then for the use of our dear and only son, the Prince of Scotland.'[26] Bess had obviously become suspicious, and rightly so, for soon afterwards the executor was robbed – or claimed he was robbed – of the jewels, while on a journey in Scotland. Most of them surfaced some time later among the possessions of King James of Scotland.

These missing jewels were yet another problem for Bess to resolve on her granddaughter's behalf, and she became engaged in what was to be a prolonged struggle to obtain Arbella's rightful estate. She persuaded Shrewsbury to write to the Earl of Leicester, begging him to persuade the Queen to write to King James on Arbella's behalf, and countersigned the letter, adding that:

Unless her Highness would vouchsafe her gracious letters in most earnest sort to that King on her little ward's behalf . . . we cannot but be in some despair of prevailing . . . The Bishop of Caithness, to whom it seems that the King has granted the Earldom is a very old man, sickly and without child. I cannot but think [it] is encompassed for him to that end that D'Aubigny* in France,

---

*A cousin of Arbella's, Esme Stuart, Lord d'Aubigny, who lived at the French court.

being the next heir male, should succeed him, for I well remember that the Duke of Guise and d'Aumale have written to the Scottish Queen on D'Aubigny's behalf.

Besides I have heard my wife say that old Lady Lennox told her long ago of this D'Aubigny's seeking to prevent the infant [succeeding]. Which I leave to your Lordship's consideration upon your Lordship's informing her thereof. We have no other hope but her Majesty.[27]

Meanwhile, just to make the point, a portrait was commissioned of two-year-old Arbella. Dressed in full miniature Court dress, stiff with pearls, and wearing a gold chain and shield containing the motto of the old Countess of Lennox – 'I endure in order to succeed'[28] – the tiny sitter is defiantly described as 'Arbella, Countess of Lennox'.

CHAPTER 14

ENOUGH TO ALIENATE THE HEART

1578–81

IN THE AUTUMN OF 1578 BESS WAS FIFTY-ONE YEARS OLD
and there was plague in the city of London. Nevertheless, Shrewsbury
wrote to Burghley that he had sent his wife to Court to see the
Queen and do her duty for both of them. He hoped she might persuade the Queen to increase the allowance provided for Mary's
keep and pay him the backlog of expenses he had claimed, which
remained unpaid. But when she set out on 7 October 1578 for
London, Bess's priority was Arbella.[1]

At the first reports of infection, Elizabeth Lennox had taken her
child out of the city to stay with friends in a house near Dunstable.
Bess joined them there for four or five days and sent ahead to
bespeak suitable accommodation in Richmond where the Court
had fled to escape the infection. She arranged to take her daughter
and granddaughter back to Chatsworth with her on her return
journey, for she was taking no chances where this especially precious child was concerned.

There was no suitable accommodation to be had in Richmond,
but on hearing of Bess's difficulty Lord Leicester offered her a small
suite, 'one very good chamber, with some other little room,' in his

own rooms, which were the best at Court. 'Here,' Bess wrote to Burghley on 24 October 1578, 'I rest very glad, for that I would rather have, albeit never so little, a corner within the Court, than greater easement further off.'[2]

Bess's personal mission was to persuade the Queen to increase the allowance of £200 per annum for Arbella, to pay for the sort of superior education that a girl of her rank merited, and perhaps to agree to return the Lennox Yorkshire property from the Crown. The Queen had no intention of doing either, since there were already far too many calls on the treasury, and because she never entirely trusted Bess's motives concerning Arbella. But, as always, Elizabeth was unfailingly kind to Bess; she treated her petition with gentleness and diplomacy – possibly for Leicester's sake, since he was evidently supporting the application.

The Queen's leniency even spilled on to Bess's children and stepchildren. On May Day that year (1578), the Queen had risen earlier than usual and, still dressed in her nightgown, went to look out of her window at Greenwich, which overlooked the tilt-yard. Walking underneath her window was Gilbert Talbot, who, sensing a movement instinctively looked up. To his horror he found himself looking straight at the Queen in a state of undress. She started back, 'very disconcerted', and Gilbert – knowing Elizabeth's insistence on her regal state – was worried that he would be banished from Court. Later that morning, in the presence chamber, the Queen saw Gilbert again, and as she passed him she smilingly gave him a sharp rap on the head with her fan, telling the Lord Chamberlain how she had been embarrassed earlier that day.[3]

Apart from Leicester's support, there was perhaps another reason for the Queen's approachability. Bess arguably knew the adult Mary better than any other woman. She was the only woman – members of the Scottish Queen's retinue apart – who spent any time with Mary during her fifteen years of captivity, and for several years the time the two women spent together on a daily basis appears to have been considerable. There have been books written about the relationship between the two queens and the effect each had on the other even though they never met, but in a personal sense Bess's life was far more affected by Mary's confinement. It is a safe guess that when Bess visited the Court, the Queen would have questioned Bess closely about the Scottish Queen: what she said, thought, looked like, dressed like, and her general demeanour. Away from the Queen, Bess must have been lionised in London society for, her social rank notwithstanding, what a dinner guest to have – someone who could talk knowledgeably at first hand about the enigmatic Queen Mary who was the source of so much gossip, rumour and innuendo.

Once again Bess made her mark on that glittering Court, and again Leicester wrote to Shrewsbury remarking that everyone had been impressed by his wife's remarkable wisdom and her noble bearing. She was unable to stay for the twelve nights of rejoicing at Christmas that she always enjoyed, because she had promised Shrewsbury she would join him for the holidays at Sheffield and help to entertain the Scottish Queen. She was therefore reluctantly forced to return home on 20 December, her mission unaccomplished.

'I came hither on Christmas Eve,' she wrote to Sir Francis Walsingham on 29 December 1578 from Sheffield Castle, 'and left my little Arbell at Chatsworth. She endured very well with travel, [though] I was forced to take long journeys to be here with my Lord afore the day.' Since her arrival, Bess reported, the Scottish Queen had kept to her bed, except for Christmas Day. 'She is grown lean and sickly and says want of exercise brings her into that weak state . . . I hope there will be advised consideration in believing her.'[4]

There is no mention of Arbella's mother but the child remained in Derbyshire from this date, and it is probable that Elizabeth Lennox decided to make her home at Chatsworth for economic reasons. As a young widow with an income of £400 a year, Elizabeth would have been expected to remarry, but there is no evidence that she made any attempt to do so. Throughout 1579

Bess presented one petition after another in an attempt to obtain 'justice' for Arbella. At one point she arranged for her second son, William, to present a request to the Queen that the two annual pensions of £400 and £200, paid to her daughter Elizabeth and Arbella respectively, should 'continue as long as the crown held the Lennox lands'. There was no positive response to this petition and the year ended badly for Arbella's supporters when the old Bishop of Caithness died. As Bess feared and had predicted, the Lennox title was conferred on the young, brilliant and personable Esme Stuart, Lord d'Aubigny, who was now living in Scotland. The boy king James was so besotted with him – his first real friend – that it was not unusual for him to kiss him in public. There was consolation for Bess when she received news that her son William had been knighted. Nothing pleased Bess more than to hear of the advancement of one of her children.

But her relationship with Shrewsbury was still deteriorating. He was becoming obsessed with the conviction that he was facing financial ruin because of his expenditure as custodian of Mary, and there is no doubt that he was treated badly by Elizabeth in this regard. He wrote to Burghley: 'I am left by birth and my ancestors a true loyal subject, and in it will I ever live and die, and live I may (if it so please the Lord God) to do Her Majesty some service. Therefore I hope she will not leave me to ruin myself . . . so that very shortly I may become in case therewith never after able to do either prince or country [a] service . . .'[5] But in his anguish the Earl rounded on those nearest to him in an orgy of economies, and never missed an opportunity to complain that Bess and his children were needlessly extravagant.

One thing he never mentioned as a prime possible cause of his financial difficulties was the new 'great house' he was having built at Worksop. Work upon this prodigy house had begun in 1577,[6] and Bess *was* probably involved to some degree, since the building was designed by Robert Smythson, a master mason who had worked for many years for the Thynnes at Longleat, and more recently for Bess.

The main building at Worksop had been an uncompleted shell of a manor house, begun by Shrewsbury's father and left abandoned at his death. Chatsworth was now all but finished, and Bess had plenty of spare energy for a new project. But it is doubtful that she was responsible for Worksop since, in all his complaints about her extravagances, Shrewsbury never once mentioned this house, which was built on the scale of a palace.[7] With all the financial problems Shrewsbury complains of – and in consideration of the number of houses he already owned and could never use – this additional huge outlay seems a somewhat superfluous, even frivolous, project to have undertaken at the time. He did not need another house; he already owned castles at Pontefract, Tutbury and Sheffield, manor houses at Handsworth, Wingfield and the converted Rufford Abbey (scene of the betrothal of Charles and Elizabeth Lennox), hunting lodges at Tutbury, Sheffield and Worksop, and a commodious house at Buxton, besides other properties.

Perhaps Shrewsbury wanted something of his own that would outshine Chatsworth. If so, he chose the right man to build it. Smythson's innovative designs at Longleat and Wollaton, and eventually at Hardwick, were influenced by the grace of the European Renaissance. With emphasis on symmetrical balance, and light – through an extravagant use of glass – Smythson created an ethereal look, which, by comparison, outdated Chatsworth.

Undoubtedly the building of Worksop exacerbated Shrewsbury's financial difficulties. Now his letters to Burghley and the Council became even more frequent and full of complaints and pitiful pleas about the costs of maintaining his prisoner. They were plainly justified, even prompting Walsingham to take the Earl's side against the Queen. From Richmond, Walsingham wrote:

I am sorry I cannot procure from the Queen such resolution touching the allowance for the Scottish Queen's diet, as I think her Majesty ought to yield [but] Her Majesty acknowledges herself as much bound unto you as a Prince may be to a subject. I find her rather disposed to gratify you with some suit. Two causes presently cause her to deal more straightly, the one – her great charge about Ireland amounting to £10,000 a month, the other, a request made a good while since from Scotland to borrow money for discharging the King's debts.[8]

While the sympathy, explanations and offers of compensation in terms of favours were no doubt gratifying, it did not help Shrewsbury's cash flow. He estimated he was spending £1000 a year on extras such as spices, wine and fuel that were not covered by the allowance provided for Mary and her retainers. There was another £1000 a year spent in 'the loss of plate, the buying of pewter and all manner of household stuff, which by them is exceedingly spoiled and wilfully wasted'.[9] He was allowed sixpence a day each for twenty-four guards at Sheffield, but he employed double that number. And in addition to the ordinary wages of his own household servants, he was paying them an extra £400 a year 'to secure their loyalty', so that they would not be lured into helping the captive.[10] And then, in the spring of 1580, he received a reprimand from the Queen after he took a few days off to attend to some estate business away from Sheffield.

Shrewsbury, by nature a pessimist and a worrier, was now a bitter, disillusioned and angry man, sliding gradually into paranoia. To these destructive emotions were added the constant pain he suffered from gout and arthritis.[11] Bess took the brunt, and he blamed her for many of his ills, the more so because she was not constantly at his side as a dutiful wife. By the standards and mores of the times Shrewsbury was possibly justified, although many aristocratic couples lived apart for long periods while a husband was at Court. But whether he had right on his side or not, the gentle consideration Shrewsbury had shown Bess in the first years of their marriage was completely gone from their relationship by the spring of 1580. She could do nothing to please him and the marriage began to fall apart.

Shrewsbury's first wife had been dutiful and obedient, a colour-less woman who left no mark on history other than a pretty poem on her tomb, but she provided a benchmark for her husband, defin-ing for him the measure of wifely duty. His assumption that all women were like his dead Gertrude was where Shrewsbury went wrong with Bess. Bess could be both dutiful and obedient, but not if it affected her position and financial stability, or, more impor-tantly, the wealth she had carefully accumulated for her children, and their future.

This strong and intelligent woman had no difficulty in compart-mentalising her life, and now she separated her duty and love as mother to her children by Sir William Cavendish from that of her role as wife to Shrewsbury. It was plain to her that Shrewsbury was being used by Queen Elizabeth in the matter of the Scottish pris-oner. Probably she told him so, sharply. But Shrewsbury's sense of duty to his monarch was so ingrained that all he would do was to make feeble complaints and hope to be rescued. Bess seems to have decided to let him get on with it, while ensuring that her own affairs were run competently. She was quite capable of running two lives. The problem was that Shrewsbury did not want half a wife.

In May that year the disagreements left the confines of the Shrewsburys' homes when the Earl began openly grumbling to his friends and correspondents about Bess. He claimed that she was extravagant, always building and making additions to Chatsworth, or buying land to enrich her Cavendish children (these accusations were certainly true), yet, he complained, she constantly came to him asking for money. To be fair to Bess, this was her right under their marriage agreement: the Earl had the rights, rents and income from most of her Barlow, Cavendish and St Loe properties in return for providing for her livelihood and giving her an allowance. Shrewsbury also charged that Bess was no comfort to him, she was always away at Chatsworth, and that she alienated his children from him and encouraged them in extravagance. Their friends and family were drawn into the squabble, causing one friend to write despairingly to another: 'I cannot perceive that his Lordship will be by any persuasion reconciled with her Ladyship.'[12]

In one fit of bad temper, Shrewsbury insisted on little Arbella being returned to Chatsworth from Sheffield Lodge, where the child had been living for a while with Gilbert and Mary Talbot. Mary was pregnant, and the violence of the incident upset her so much that she fled to her mother at Chatsworth. Shrewsbury immediately banned Gilbert from visiting his wife there, on pain of his stopping Gilbert's £200 annual allowance.

Bess evidently gave as good as she got, since Shrewsbury charges her several times with having a 'wicked tongue'. It was hardly possible for any woman of her day to argue a point heatedly without being branded 'a shrew', and when Shrewsbury compared Bess with his saintly and obedient first wife he regarded Bess's behaviour as that of a fishwife. Their domestic disagreements were noisy and bitter, neither prepared to give way, each believing they were right and attempting to justify themselves.

It is hard to explain what happened between this couple who, such a short time earlier, had been so happy and so affectionate for over a decade. Shrewsbury, remember, had often thanked God for sending Bess to comfort him in his old age (though in fact he was only fifty-two, the same age as Bess). He had also admitted to his son Gilbert, in their conversation at Bolsover that 'her love hath been great to me, and my love hath been, and is, as great to her'. In fact, there seems to have been no great single dispute of any significance, just a gradual withering away of tolerance and affection, mainly on Shrewsbury's part, for Bess seemed genuinely bewildered by the change in her husband, insisting to Gilbert that the Earl used 'cruel and bitter speeches, against her, when she all the time never uttered any undutiful words'.[13]

One of Bess's gentlewomen, Frances Battell, who had served Bess for several years, wrote about the matter to a friend and claimed that the Shrewsburys' differences had first begun when

Bess spoke her mind to the servants of the Queen of Scots. By this time Mary no longer trusted Bess, and had come to dislike her. The feeling was mutual, although Bess recognised that Mary could still be important to Arbella and so she was circumspect. The servants of each woman, not unnaturally, took up partisan stances, and since members of both households regularly took meals together in the great hall, together with Shrewsbury and Bess, this may have been an uncomfortable arrangement at times.

Frances Battell recalled an occasion when they were all discussing Queen Mary's situation, and one of Mary's gentlemen voiced the opinion that Queen Mary ought to be Queen of England. No one replied to this daring statement at first, but then Bess spoke up. 'It would be better,' she said hotly, 'that the Scottish Queen were hanged before this should come to pass.' Later Bess told her ladies that she regretted speaking so hastily but that the comment had made her angry and she had felt duty bound to answer it.

Battell wrote that Shrewsbury took great offence at his wife's behaviour, and 'since that time her Lord deals hardly with her. My Lord wrote only one letter to my Lady this half year, and that was all about me and that it was a shame for him to keep me, and with many words that are too much to write of.' If her Lord continued his 'hard speech of me', Battell continued, she would not be able to stay in Bess's service because it was now so unpleasant, even though she would be sorry to part from her 'kind Mistress'. What Lord Shrewsbury chiefly held against her, Battell stated, was that she had told him openly that she pitied her mistress for her situation – 'which is to be pitied, and lamentable it is'.[14]

If the evidence of this eyewitness is taken at face value, it is scarcely surprising that Bess was jealous of Mary. Shrewsbury was clearly prepared to side openly with his royal prisoner against his wife in public. All the same, this seems more like a symptom than a cause. We know from the letters of both Robert Leicester and Gilbert Talbot that Shrewsbury was rude to Bess in front of their

servants and household on a number of occasions, which humiliated her. Bess also complained that Shrewsbury now reserved the
gentler side of his nature for dealing with his captive. This is a situation that few wives would tolerate, yet Shrewsbury insisted that
he had no love for the Scottish Queen. 'Amongst other false accusations,' he wrote to Queen Elizabeth, 'your Honour knows that I
have been [accused] of some undutiful [behaviour with] the Queen
of Scots. But I am very well able to prove that she has shown herself an enemy to me, and to my fortune. And that, I trust, will
sufficiently clear me.'[15]

It is difficult to know whom to believe in this tangle of accusation, counter-accusation, bitterness and aggression. But one thing
is certain: at the heart of it all was the Queen of Scots, who seems
to have worked at alienating Shrewsbury and his wife – and she
had succeeded. It was in Mary's interests to divide and rule; Bess
was a far stronger person than Shrewsbury and in her absence
Shrewsbury was easier to manage. He could be charmed, cajoled
and beguiled, and at times he was charmed, cajoled and beguiled.
But Bess could not be charmed once she and Mary had fallen out,
and when she left Sheffield for good, not only were the terms of
Mary's imprisonment less restrictive, but it was also easier for her
people to smuggle letters in and out. It is impossible to read the
hundreds of letters emanating from this trio of personalities without concluding that Mary was the wedge which insinuated itself
between husband and wife.

The Earl now began to lard even his letters to the Queen with
criticisms of his wife. In June 1580, he recruited the help of the Earl
of Leicester, who was spending a few days at the spa at Buxton,
asking Leicester to go to Chatsworth and speak to his wife, and
attempt to make her conform to Shrewsbury's idea of wifely duty.
Leicester bravely complied with the request, but only after the
Queen had agreed that he should try to reconcile the couple.
Afterwards, Leicester wrote to Shrewsbury about his interview with
Bess, explaining that he had found her in great distress, claiming

tearfully that she was not to blame for the troubles between them, but that 'others' had worked to turn Shrewsbury against her. Leicester told her that the Queen was sorry that the couple were estranged, but Bess insisted that the fault did not lie with her.

When Bess asked Leicester for a specific account of how she was supposed to have offended, he repeated Shrewsbury's claim that she had threatened her husband that she 'knew things about him' that would harm him if she were to make them public. The implication was that these were connected with the royal prisoner.

Leicester told her he was astonished that 'so wise a woman' as Bess would treat her husband this way. Bess does not seem to have disputed the fact that she had made the threat, only the idea that she would have broadcast it: 'I think there is no creature able to say it of me, neither have I ever had the thought to deal that way with him . . . God forbid that I should use any such speeches against him,' she replied. Leicester was convinced that Bess had no intention of publicly speaking out against her husband, but she was, he wrote to Shrewsbury, aggrieved that the Earl was traducing her and her children to his friends, and felt she was badly used in a number of other ways:

One was that she had been, as it were, slighted before your servants, and that you openly made an exclamation of her to her own face, coming from chapel, which she grieved at, and [still] does.

Then I told her further that I had heard she had sent your Lordship a message, upon a very small cause, by which she showed herself not to owe you any further obedience or duty, that her love was gone etc. To this she seemed much troubled, and told me it was not so. But this much was true, [she said]; 'that your Lordship, sending the little Arbella to me, being a thing I desired much to the contrary, and that she might stay still with my daughter Talbot. And did use his commandment for her abode with me. I answered him [that he] dealt hardly with

me, and did use me strangely in many things, not as though I
were his wife, but in such sort as were enough to alienate the
heart and duty of any wife.

And, said she, I think I willed my son Talbot [Gilbert] to write
such words of grief, finding his so extreme, and unnatural [in]
dealing with me. And my son is here, though a prisoner only,
coming to take his leave of me, and his wife . . . [before] taking
his journey to London.[16]

At this point Bess led Leicester to her daughter's chamber, where
he found Gilbert and Mary Talbot. Gilbert told him that he was
forced to come to Chatsworth secretly, late at night, to see his pregnant wife, so that his father did not know of the visits. On this
occasion he had called to say goodbye to her before departing for
the Court. He was so clearly anxious about Leicester's seeing him
there, that Leicester tactfully left after only a few minutes.

I have reported . . . as near as I can, what was the chief matter
that passed between my Lady and me. So must I say in truth I
found her most desirous and most willing to have your good
favour, above any worldly thing . . .

Touching the mislike you have of my Lord Talbot for his going
to Chatsworth, truly my Lord, all things duly considered, your
Lordship doth hardly need to be offended for that matter, his
wife being there, and with child . . . truly my Lord he is bent in all
obedience and duty to serve you and obey you . . . and your
Lordship I know, will not refuse willingly the fount of the blessing of God, which is the comfort of your own flesh and blood,
your child, and him that must succeed you . . . Her Majesty has
also conceived a very good opinion of him [Gilbert]; he is only
now shadowed and darkened by the want of your Lordship's
father-like countenance and favour . . .

Good my Lord, think it sometimes what I was bold enough to
say at Buxton touching this matter. I am sure there never was any

who spoke with a more sincere mind towards you and your house . . . neither shall you ever find any kinsman or friend that has been more careful for both of you . . . than I have been. From Richmond, 26 June [1580].[17]

In his reply, Shrewsbury completely ignored what Leicester had to say regarding Bess's explanations, and wrote that he rejoiced that Leicester had now heard his wife's 'lies' from her own lips. He went on to explain why he had forbidden Gilbert to visit Chatsworth:

I have forbade him for coming to my wicked and malicious wife, who has set me at nought in his own hearing, that – contrary to my commandment – hath both gone and sent unto her daily by his wife's persuasion. Yea, and hath both written and carried letters to no mean personages on my wife's behalf . . . He hath been a costly child to me . . . [and now] he takes the way to spoil himself in London . . .'[18]

Shrewsbury then applied to move his prisoner to Chatsworth but this was refused. Queen Elizabeth was unwell with a strange pain in the head and a stitch over the stomach, he was told, and she 'was resolutely bent against the going to Chatsworth'.[19] Burghley wrote separately to explain that he had received intelligence 'that it is earnestly intended within the realm and without, that very shortly the Queen there should either by slight or force, escape from you.'[20] So, despite Leicester's valiant attempt at mediation, the immediate dispute was never resolved, and it lay between the couple, festering, although they appear to have maintained a semblance of being together for another year or so.

Gilbert and Mary's baby was born, a daughter whom they called Mary after her mother, and the Scottish Queen stood as godmother. Bess continued to make occasional dutiful visits to Sheffield, usually when Mary was moved, so that it could be cleaned and sweetened, repairs made to broken windows, and the rat catchers brought in.[21]

The threat of escape, about which Burghley warned, seems to have dispersed quickly, for at the end of July permission was given for a visit by Queen Mary to Buxton spa. Although Buxton would appear to be a less secure venue than Chatsworth, the Earl assured the Privy Council that surveillance at his Buxton house was strict, and that the only correspondence Mary would receive was from the French Ambassador. But she had a bad start to her journey to Buxton; almost as soon as she was seated on her horse it shied, and 'she fell and hurt her back, which she still complains of', the Earl reported, 'notwithstanding she applies the baths once or twice a day.'[22]

Despite his seemingly endless streams of letters to the Queen, Burghley, Walsingham and anyone on the Privy Council he thought might help, the allowance for the Scottish Queen's 'diet' was not increased. In fact, to Shrewsbury's utter bewilderment, on 29 January 1581 the Queen reduced it, from over £50 a week to £32, and ordered him to cut Mary's retinue by half.

It is impossible to explain why the Queen should have treated Shrewsbury in such a cavalier manner. The only explanation is that she genuinely thought that Shrewsbury had plenty of money, that despite his appeals these amounts were really not terribly important to him. In the event she continued to exploit his loyalty. Walsingham was startled enough to write to the Queen: 'Pray God the abatement of the charges [allowed] that noble man that hath custody of the bosom serpent, have not lessened his care in keeping her.'[23] If Shrewsbury could not afford to guard his prisoner adequately, he pointed out, she would escape. 'How can my Lord maintain his people about him, and if she not be seen unto, she will escape. I beseech your Majesty, let not the pinching and sparing of a thousand pounds ∴. work such extremities. And [even] if no such thing were to happen, I would not keep so dangerous a guest to gain as much money as my Lord . . .'[24] But when Walsingham subsequently attempted to see the Queen to plead Shrewsbury's case, he was refused an audience. And after being kept waiting for over two weeks, he realised that he was wasting his time.

Sending for Gilbert, who was in 'lodgings in Westminster at the sign of the half moon, in a grocer's house', Walsingham told him it was obvious that the Queen would not be moved in the matter. He advised him to tell his father it was useless to keep badgering her about the allowances still outstanding. She had not the resources to pay him, chiefly because of a £20,000 sum she had to pay to Scotland and other 'infinite daily sums' to which she was committed.

He suggested that instead Shrewsbury should write to the Queen, Lord Leicester, Lord Burghley and several other members of the Privy Council, telling them that he requested that the Scottish Queen be removed from his keeping forthwith, and that in respect of the sums outstanding he would take instead some grants in lands and farms. He should remind the Queen of his utmost loyalty for over eleven years, Walsingham counselled, and point out that his service had gone completely without reward, where many who had provided lesser services had been handsomely recompensed.[25]

Shrewsbury could not believe that it was the Queen's real intention to treat him so poorly, and so did not accept this sensible advice from Walsingham. Instead, he wrote again, begging to be allowed to come to Court to explain matters. Meanwhile he made an attempt to remove some of Mary's servants, and cut down on costs by drastically reducing the number of dishes served. Mary smuggled out messages to her supporters, and soon Elizabeth had an uncomfortable interview with the French Ambassador in which she was virtually accused of trying to starve Mary to death. Hitherto, Mary was used to choosing from umpteen dishes – up to sixteen – at mealtimes. Now Lord Leicester wrote hastily to the Shrewsburys to warn them of Mary's claim that on Easter Day 'she had but two dishes, and in both the meat was bad'. He urged Shrewsbury to respond immediately; 'your Lordship should answer that you were cut off your allowance and therefore could yield no better'.[26]

In despair, the Earl wrote asking Walsingham for the going price of silver in London because he feared he must sell some of his plate to meet the demands of his creditors.[27] Now instead of constantly bombarding the Queen for the monies owed him, his requests are piteous pleas to be allowed to come to Court and see her. Privately, though, he instructed his London agent to continue to press Burghley regarding the outstanding amounts still owing to him. With all these financial pressures, the monthly allowance that he made to Bess under their marriage agreement, in respect of lands of hers that came under his control, was one of the first things to suffer. As far as he was concerned she always appeared to have enough money to spend on buying land for her sons, and was unlikely to starve.

Inevitably this became yet a further cause for rancour between husband and wife, and Bess now began writing to the same set of people complaining of the Earl's treatment. There is a rebuttal dated 12 October 1581, written in the Earl's illegible hand, declaring that all the accusations made by his wife against him concerning money are untrue. He claims grandly that he had paid off her debts, and lists them, but they total only £24.[28] He also lists lands and tenements, which he had allowed the Countess 'to own and enjoy'. These were Chatsworth and 'all the lands which she had from her husband Sir William Cavendish. All the lands which she had by conveyance of Sir William Seyntloe. All her stocks of sheep and cattle and many other things . . . all of which she doth enjoy by the Earl's permission.'[29]

One can imagine Bess's reaction to this. Her husband had reneged on contracted promises regarding her annual allowance. He was keeping for himself the rents of many of the properties she had brought into their marriage, while pointing out how generous he was in allowing her to occupy her own property. Meanwhile, he was maligning her to their influential friends. It comes as no surprise to learn, a month later, in a letter from Shrewsbury to his London agent, that Bess is pressing him hard for money: 'the old song,' he comments sourly.[30] Bess's periodic visits to her husband had become very joyless affairs by this time. And she was grieving, too, because her only brother James Hardwick* had recently died aged fifty-five, a bankrupt in the Fleet prison. Hardwick was duly seized by the Lord Chancellor's department, although thanks to her foresight in securing loans with mortgages Bess was a major creditor.[31] Indeed, at this point, the main reason she was pressing the Earl for the money he owed her was to buy Hardwick back from the Crown, and she complained to Burghley that the Earl would not repay her.[32]

As the winter set in, the Scottish Queen's health worsened, and she became ill enough to cause concern to her own and Shrewsbury's doctors. As a result, the clerk of the Privy Council, Robert Beale (Walsingham's brother-in-law), was sent in late November to judge for himself how serious matters were. Bess had been summoned to Sheffield and was waiting with Shrewsbury to meet Beale; together they warned him against Mary's 'deviousness'. There was a delay of some days before Mary finally summoned Beale to her chamber in the early evening. As he crossed the threshold, all the candles were mysteriously doused, leaving the room in total darkness apart from the glow from a fire. In a feeble, wispy voice, Mary listed her complaints, whispering that she was so ill she could hardly eat and drink, and she expected not to live much longer. And all the while Beale could hear her ladies, sobbing softly somewhere in the gloom.

Unable to see how ill the prisoner really was, unnerved by the entire episode, and recalling the warnings of her deviousness, he did not know whether to be concerned because Mary *was* dying, or worried that he had been tricked. He returned and told the Shrewsburys what had happened and asked Bess if she would go

---

*James Hardwick had been married twice; his second wife Elizabeth Araker survived him but he had no legitimate issue, only one bastard son, to whom he gave his name (William Hardwick of Williamsthorpe).

and check on the Queen. She did so, returning shortly afterwards to say that she had found Mary fast asleep. Later, at Beale's request, Bess went to see her again. 'She found her complaining as before,' Beale reported. 'Howbeit, seeing her face, she says is not much altered . . . in her opinion she has known the Scottish Queen far worse than she presently was.'[33] Eventually Beale did get to see Queen Mary in daylight; he recorded that he found her pale and wan, crippled with rheumatism and overweight from lack of exercise.

At least Beale's visit had the effect of relaxing the close confinement, which was a relief to everyone including Shrewsbury. Not wanting to be accused of killing Mary by neglect, Elizabeth agreed to several of Mary's demands:[34] that she might be allowed to go two or three miles outside of the park; that she might be allowed a coach and six horses in which to take exercise; that the household regimen might be more relaxed so that entertainments, such as a play or a masque, could be held occasionally, to break the tedium for all concerned; and that she might change a few of her older servants who had become tired in her service. Elizabeth agreed to all these, but she did not accede to Mary's final request, that Shrewsbury's long overdue expenses in connection with her captivity be repaid.

Mary's health improved.

CHAPTER 15

DISCORD

1582–4

THE FOLLOWING YEAR SAW SOME MAJOR REVERSES IN THE houses of both Cavendish and Shrewsbury. Hardly had 1582 begun before the Earl of Shrewsbury was writing to Lords Burghley and Leicester to advise that, 'It has pleased God to call to his mercy out of this transitory world my daughter [Elizabeth] Lennox, this present Sunday being 21 January . . . about 3 o'clock in the morning.' She was twenty-six years of age and had been taken ill during a Twelfth Night party at Sheffield. Shrewsbury explained that her dying wish was that the Queen would take pity on her little daughter, Arbella, and in her will* she specifically asked Lords Burghley and Leicester to present this last wish as a petition to the Queen. He added, 'my wife taketh my daughter Lennox's death so grievously that she neither doth, nor can think of, anything but lamenting and weeping'.[1]

Later, when Bess wrote to Burghley, she was still very distressed

---

*In her will Elizabeth Lennox left 'my best jewel set with great diamonds' to the Queen, her 'white sables' to Bess, and a gold salt cellar to Shrewsbury for being such a good father to her.

'by the death of my daughter . . . whom it pleased God . . . to take out of this world in her best time . . . I doubt not in mercy, for her good, but to my no small grief . . . whom I cannot yet remember but with a sorrowful, troubled mind'.[2] Her purpose in writing, however, was to plead on her orphan granddaughter's behalf who, formerly, 'had been where her mother was during her life,' but now Bess could not bear to be parted from the child 'nor in any place where I may not see her and daily hear of her . . . of whom I have special care, not only as a natural mother has of her best beloved child, but much more greater in respect of how she is in blood to her Majesty, albeit one of the poorest . . .' wherefore, it was necessary for her to establish a nursery and staff 'fit for her calling'. She reminded him of the allowance made by the Queen to her late daughter of £400 annually, in lieu of the confiscated Lennox estates, and the £200 the Queen similarly made little Arbella. 'I hope her Majesty, upon my humble suit will let that por- tion which her Majesty bestowed upon my daughter Lennox, and my jewel Arbella, remain wholly to the child, for her better educa- tion. For the servants that are to look after her, and her masters that are to train her up in all good learning and virtue, will require no small charges.'[3]

Shrewsbury had been pressing the Queen to allow him to come to Court, and for a while it seemed that the Queen had agreed and was merely seeking a mutually convenient date. Then, to his dis- appointment he was advised that his visit was postponed until later in the year. He therefore requested permission to take Queen Mary to Chatsworth, 'for that my daughter Talbot will be near her lying- in time' and also to allow the time 'to sweeten my house that my children may come to me'.[4]

This permission was apparently not granted, and Mary Talbot's lying-in duly commenced at Sheffield Lodge, with Bess in attendance. Within a few days of her arrival at Sheffield, there was some sort of domestic crisis, for Shrewsbury ordered his wife back to Chatsworth, and he returned to Sheffield Castle. On the following day Mary

Talbot went into labour and produced a healthy girl, whom she called Elizabeth, a name already over-used in the family. Shrewsbury reported grumpily: 'I am removed to the castle, and am most quiet when I have the fewest women here.' There is a hint of what may have caused this latest quarrel when he adds that his wife had pressed him to hire some of the men who had formerly served Elizabeth Lennox, but he had refused, snapping nastily, 'I have too many spies in my house already.'[5]

Shrewsbury was undoubtedly suffering from a persecution complex but there was some truth in this statement concerning spies; even though the one we know about had nothing to do with Bess. That same month Walsingham's agents in Paris had been watching Shrewsbury's former secretary Thomas Morgan, who resigned his post at Sheffield at his own request. Walsingham ordered his agents to shadow the man suspecting that he had been 'turned' to the cause of the Scottish Queen, and it was no great surprise when he learned that Morgan had sailed for France. Suspicions hardened when Morgan covertly despatched 'a Welsh boy, about the age of 17 years with letters for England via Calais'. Walsingham was warned to look out for the youth at Dover: 'he is full-faced, apparelled in a black cloak, black hose and sky-colour nether hose.'[6] Intercepted messages confirmed Morgan's role as Mary's agent in France, a position he held for the remainder of her life.

A very brief and unexplained softening in Shrewsbury's attitude towards Bess is revealed in a letter written on 15 May 1582 to Thomas Baldwin, his London agent, advising that his wife needed a new horse litter. He instructed Baldwin to tell Gilbert to ensure that this vehicle should be 'a very handsome one', and was to be acquired with all possible speed, '. . . immediately after Whitsun, if not before'.[7] He confirmed that he was going to Buxton on 18 May with the Scottish Queen, and that he had once again requested permission to come to Court. He was so confident of obtaining a favourable reply to this request that he instructed Baldwin to prepare Cold Harbour House for his arrival. But there is no further mention of his anticipated visit a month later, when he told Baldwin he could not buy some suggested land because his children were 'so costly'. Nor could he pay off the debts of his heir, Lord Francis, about which Baldwin had advised him. Work had almost stopped at Worksop, and it was perhaps indiscreet for Bess at this time to embark on a new building at Chatsworth, albeit a small one. She commissioned Robert Smythson to design and build a lookout tower on the hill in the north-eastern corner of her park wall. The Stand Tower (now known as the Hunting Tower) is one of the few features to survive at Chatsworth from Bess's time.[8]

In July 1582 there was another family tragedy when Margaret,* the wife of Bess's third son, Charles Cavendish, died. The young couple had been married little more than a year when Margaret died after giving birth to a son they named William.† Charles, who was knighted that year, lived at Stoke Manor, a few miles from Chatsworth. In her moving letter of condolence to Margaret's parents, Bess begged them to continue to regard Charles as their own son.[9] Shrewsbury mentioned all these family matters in his reports to Burghley, but he was never sympathetic about Bess's family bereavements; his usual reaction was one of irritation because she cried a great deal, which he appears to have considered self-indulgent. He does not comment on Bess's reaction when, at the end of August, his own son and heir, Lord Francis, contracted plague and died shortly after arriving at Belvoir Castle, where he had gone to visit his uncle.

Losing his eldest son – the child who had been trained to inherit the Shrewsbury estates – was a body blow to a man already over-

---

*Margaret was the daughter of Thomas Kitson, a rich London merchant whose country house was Hengrave Hall, Norfolk. Kitson was knighted in 1578 when he entertained the Queen and her train for three days at Hengrave, during her summer Progress. He left no sons so his great fortune was divided between his two daughters. Charles inherited Margaret's share.
†This William died in infancy. Another son, by Charles's second wife, was also called William, and he would become the 1st Duke of Newcastle.

burdened with stress. His second son, Gilbert, now became his heir and succeeded to the courtesy title of Lord Talbot, but Gilbert had proved a great disappointment to his father, mainly because he had always sided with Bess in the Shrewsburys' marital disputes. Indeed father and son were estranged at this time, and what especially irked Shrewsbury was the fact that, barring accidents, Gilbert's wife (Bess's youngest daughter Mary, whom the Earl had come to dislike because she always took her mother's side and encouraged her husband to do so) now seemed likely to become the next Countess of Shrewsbury.

After ten years of making requests, and just prior to the news of his son's death, Shrewsbury was finally granted permission to travel to Court and a temporary custodian was appointed for the duration of his absence. At last, the Earl believed, he could put his case about the cost of his custody of the Scottish Queen, and he was confident that his problems would all be resolved. His departure was delayed by the death of Lord Francis, and by the funeral. But then, just before he was due to leave Sheffield, the Queen withdrew her permission when she discovered that Shrewsbury had allowed a French diplomat to visit his prisoner.

Walsingham's spy network had learned that Mary had sent messages out with this visitor: letters in cipher to the King of Spain, to the Duc de Guise, and to her network of Catholic supporters who were busily organising yet another escape plan. Rumours flared that this could only have happened with Shrewsbury's connivance; only he had the power to admit visitors, after all. It was then discovered that Shrewsbury had made two visits with Mary to Buxton that year, when he had received royal assent for only one visit.

Disloyalty was out of character for Shrewsbury; no one seriously believed he would knowingly have allowed Mary to correspond with enemies of England, or risk her escaping. So these aberrations, which so worried the Privy Council, were likely to have been acts of kindness, allowed because he was naive about human nature; and the terms of her imprisonment had, after all, been relaxed. But it also shows that Shrewsbury *was* vulnerable to Mary's charm and wiles; and that Bess's hints of his 'closeness' to his royal prisoner were justified.

Shrewsbury was almost as much a prisoner as Queen Mary. Both suffered regular periods of ill health, and because of Bess's frequent absences (her own decision) Shrewsbury saw far more of his beautiful prisoner than he did of his wife. Since Mary was reliant on the Earl's goodwill for everything that made her life tolerable, it is reasonable to assume that she would have exerted herself to win his co-operation. So it would be surprising if Shrewsbury and Mary had not become reasonably close during the fifteen and a half years they were thrown together.

A few weeks later, another blow descended on Shrewsbury. Among the letters of condolence for the death of Lord Francis was one from the Earl of Pembroke, brother of Francis's widow, Lady Anne, requesting that his sister's 'widow's jointure' be paid directly to him. Indeed, he asked if – according to the terms of the original agreement between the two fathers – the one-third could be increased 'if that were possible'.[10] Had everything gone according to Shrewsbury's original plans his eldest daughter Catherine would have become Countess of Pembroke, but both she and her husband had been dead for seven years. And now, instead of the Shrewsbury family having the use of the generous dowry Anne Herbert had brought to her marriage with Francis, he would have to pay her jointure, which he could ill afford.

Once again Shrewsbury's misery rebounded on Bess, and when she went to London that December she told her friends of his bad treatment of her, of his withholding of her allowance, and openly blamed her husband's sympathetic relationship with his prisoner as a major cause of the breakdown of the marriage.[11] When Shrewsbury heard about this (probably through Leicester who vainly attempted to help both parties), he immediately suspected Bess of telling the Queen the same things. So he ordered his son Henry to call on the Vice-Chamberlain, Sir Christopher Hatton, with the draft of a letter he had written to the Queen. It was another rant about his wife's behaviour, and Henry reported back that Hatton's reaction was unfavourable, judging the letter 'too sharp' to present to the Queen.

'Where your Lordship writes that your wife's speeches are both infamous and wicked, but are better heard than yours,' Hatton had advised, '[this] will drive Her Majesty into choler, for she has always said . . . she would take it in very bad part that you should flatly condemn her of partiality towards your wife.' Furthermore, Hatton had told Henry that, since Lord Shrewsbury was dealing with a matter of such importance 'and with so perilous an adversary as your wife, he would wish you not to write anything that may move her [the Queen] to anger'. He thought it was quite possible that the Queen might show Shrewsbury's letter to Bess and ask her to answer the charges; 'she that has so perilous a head . . . as your wife has, who would no doubt reply: "Now your Majesty may plainly see that my Lord doth seek nothing else but the destruction of me and mine, for he says only the disgrace of his enemies will satisfy him."'[12]

The main cause of this latest crisis was that rumours about a relationship between the Earl and his prisoner, including one that she had conceived Shrewsbury's child, were being widely circulated in London and it was not long before the story reached the ears of Queen Mary herself. She sent for Shrewsbury and between them they concluded that Bess and her two sons were responsible. Mary wrote to the French Ambassador begging him to see Queen Elizabeth to demand 'that she see justice done to me against the Countess of Shrewsbury and her children, touching the scandalous reports which they have circulated about me . . . I shall never have any pleasure until their wickedness is known.'[13] But this charge of spreading rumours was only one of the sources of dispute between Bess and her husband.

The Shrewsburys came together again in the early summer of 1583, when Bess visited Sheffield soon after the birth of a son,

John, to Gilbert and Mary. It was a joyful occasion, and according to Bess's later testimony they parted amicably, the Earl showing 'not the least mislike, but with many fair words and promises assured her that he would in a few days send for her again'. The baby died and the Earl never did send for Bess; in fact, within a month he actually prohibited her from visiting Sheffield or any of his houses.

In the meantime, the couple quarrelled again because Shrewsbury continued to withhold Bess's allowance while still collecting rents from her properties, and he advised Thomas Baldwin that his latest dispute with his wife was 'to be settled by arbitration.'[14] Since the death in prison of James Hardwick two years earlier, Hardwick Hall had been in chancery*, with the Lord Chancellor acting as auditor for the estate. In 1583 Bess managed to purchase the house, lands and properties outright, for £9,500.[15] Probably the fact that Bess could raise so much money, while he was financially straitened, renewed the Earl's grievance and he refused even to see Bess to discuss her complaints. She travelled to London and, from lodgings in Chancery Lane, on 26 August she wrote to him:

My Lord,

The innocency of my own heart is such, and my desire so infinite to procure your good [opinion], that I will leave no ways unsought to attain your favour, which long you have restrained from me. And in all duties of a wife I beseech you not to run with a settled condemnation of me, for my heart cannot accuse itself against you. Neither is there anything alleged against me that deserves separation.

My Lord, how I have tended your happiness [in] every way, were superfluous to write, for I take God to witness, my life [has] ever been adventured for you. And my heart, notwith-

*Coming under the jurisdiction of the High Court of Justice.

standing what I have suffered, thirsts after your prosperity, and desires nothing so much as to have your love.

Alas! My Lord, what benefits it you to seek my trouble and desolation, or wherein does it serve you to let me live thus, absent from you? If you will say because I now love you not, I know, my Lord that hatred must grow from something and how I have deserved your indignation is invisible to me. If you will say that I, or mine, have touched you in duty of allegiance, first I protest there is no such thing. And what can you have more than that Her Majesty justified you, and us? The Lords at the Council, I and my sons clear you; or how can it be thought that I should forget myself so greatly, being your wife, and my daughter wife to your eldest son?

My Lord I beseech you to give me liberty to come unto you. I doubt not but in every particular to satisfy you, as my innocence will manifestly appear. And then I trust you will quiet my heart, receiving me into your favour, for you only may do it.[16]

The address in Chancery Lane might offer a clue to this extremely conciliatory letter. It could, of course, be a perfectly genuine plea from a wife who feels herself wronged, who retains an affection for her estranged husband, and wishes to be restored to hearth and home. On the other hand, it might have been written at the suggestion of a smart lawyer as demonstrable evidence that the couple's separation was none of her doing. Bess had long ago recognised the value of top legal assistance, and such devices – pleas for 'conjugal restitution' – have survived into the present day.

Shrewsbury vigorously denied any blame for the breakdown of the marriage. He wrote to his contacts at Court, Burghley, Leicester and Walsingham, putting his case and attempting to obtain their support. Just as anyone might today, caught up in the domestic squabbles of friends, they shied off uneasily, replying carefully. Walsingham had a good excuse: he was genuinely ill and could not deal with lengthy correspondence. Burghley was overbusy. Leicester replied diplomatically but firmly:

> . . . concerning the unkindness of my Lady, your wife's, dealing,
> truly my Lord I am sorry with all my heart for it. I know it must
> be a great grief to you that any cause of division or mislike
> should grow that way. And the more where so great a love and
> good will was, and heretofore has been between you. I may
> [only] lament it, for it is not for me, or any other, to enter into
> those causes [disputes] between you . . .[17]

He pointedly reminded the Earl in another letter that Bess was 'a
very wise woman'.[18] Lord Leicester's letters are addressed from the
palace of Nonsuch where he was staying with the Court. He must
have known that it was only a matter of time before Shrewsbury
discovered that Leicester had loaned Bess his grand London house
for the duration of her stay at Court, inviting her 'with many compliments' to 'use it as though it were her own'.[19] Why should
Leicester make such a generous gesture that risked making an
enemy of Shrewsbury? The answer is that Leicester and Bess were
planning a family alliance.

As a result of their discussions, in March 1584, eight-year-old
Arbella became the betrothed 'wife' of Leicester's two-year-old son,
Lord Denbigh. Bess and Leicester obviously had their eye to the
future here. Bess may have reasoned that with Leicester's support
Elizabeth might be persuaded to declare Arbella as her heir. From
Leicester's viewpoint his son's marriage to Arbella could place the
child on the throne of England (something he had almost certainly
once hoped for himself). Neither party thought to advise the Queen
of this match until after the ceremony, though they must have been
only too well aware of the fury that would rain down upon their
heads when it became known. Both having weathered royal storms
in the past, they evidently decided it was worth the risk.

On this occasion Elizabeth and Mary, Queen of Scots were in
total agreement. Mary wrote to the French Ambassador that 'noth-

ing has ever alienated the Countess of Shrewsbury from me more than this imaginary hope, which she has conceived, of setting this crown on the head of Arbella her granddaughter, by means of marrying her to the son of the Earl of Leicester'.[20] Queen Elizabeth's wrath fell mostly on Leicester, but it was to be of a short duration. The betrothal plans came to nothing, for less than four months later, in July 1584, little Lord Denbigh, the prospective bridegroom, died of a convulsion.

Leicester was on a Progress with the Queen when he received the news of his son's death, and he left abruptly, not even stopping to ask permission, to go to his wife who was permanently *persona non grata* at Elizabeth's Court.* When he rejoined the Court Leicester was a broken man; he had genuinely loved his son, who was described on his tomb as 'the noble imp', and with the child went all Leicester's hopes and plans for the future and his dreams of dynasty. The Queen could not remain angry with him in these circumstances.

In reply to Shrewsbury's letter of condolence Leicester wrote that his son's death was a great loss to him, especially as he had no other sons,† and, now that he was growing old, he was unlikely to have any more. Perhaps this loss was the reason why he was tempted to advise Shrewsbury not to come between his son and daughter-in-law, Gilbert and Mary Talbot. In response to a plea from his son backed up by Burghley, Shrewsbury had allowed Gilbert to sell some St Loe lands in Somerset and Gloucestershire to pay off his debts.[21] In a subsequent interview he told Gilbert that he loved him better than all other children, but that it would please him if Gilbert would separate from his wife. But Gilbert

---

*Queen Elizabeth forgave Leicester for secretly marrying Lettice Knollys, but Lettice was banned from Court.
†This was not strictly true. Leicester had a son by Lady Douglas Sheffield after a secret marriage in 1573, which Leicester repudiated for fear of Elizabeth's wrath. This boy – Sir Robert Dudley, later Duke of Northumberland and Earl of Warwick – became a man Leicester would have been proud to call his son.

had no wish to separate from Mary and he took the problem to Leicester, who warned Shrewsbury that he was likely to lose his son's allegiance if he persisted in the matter. 'God forbid,' Leicester wrote, 'for it is heavy in the sight of God for any man to seek separation between man and wife.'[22]

Shrewsbury felt himself justified, however, especially in the light of the most recent family squabble. The problems between himself and his son, he replied, had not been Gilbert's fault; 'it is his wife's wicked persuasion and her mother's together, for I think neither barrel better herring of them both . . . but,' he conceded grudgingly, 'I would [not] have him hate his wife, though I do detest her mother.'[23] In the following month, August 1584, he wrote again to Leicester, indignantly claiming that he had been 'denied a night's lodging in his own house' by his wife's son, Sir William Cavendish. Sir William had forbidden him entry to Chatsworth and had used lewd language to him, in front of his servants, 'greatly to my dishonour', and as a result he had decided to take the matter to common law.

At the time of their marriage, Shrewsbury wrote, his wife had cajoled him into settling many of her lands upon herself and her children, and in doing so 'I lost . . . the advantage from those lands which by her I do possess, the lands of Barlow, Cavendish and St Loe'. These lands, he wrote, he had bestowed upon Bess 'in trust . . . for her benefit', but by their recent differences, 'she has forfeited that trust'.[24] It is clear that what Shrewsbury actually wanted, and believed himself entitled to, was to be rid of Bess, whom he had come to hate, but to keep all the lands and possessions she had brought into the marriage. No wonder Bess fought back.

Shrewsbury fought, too. Savagely. Even before he wrote the above letter to Leicester he had directed his agents and bailiffs to instruct the tenants of the St Loe properties in Somerset and Gloucestershire to pay their rents to him, and not to Bess, 'at their utmost peril'.[25] He then wrote to Burghley complaining that Bess had left *his* house at Chatsworth, taking many precious household items with her, to Hardwick Hall, which was now the home of her son Sir William Cavendish.[26]

What really happened was that, having been warned in advance by a member of staff at Sheffield, that Shrewsbury was preparing to ride to Chatsworth for a showdown, Bess had fled to Hardwick taking with her the most valuable pieces of plate and tapestry and leaving her son to protect her other property as best he could. She had good reason to fear her husband by this time. In the previous few weeks the Earl's men, led by one Nicholas Booth, one of Shrewsbury's bailiffs, had conducted a campaign of terror upon Bess's sons, her servants and their tenants. First Charles was attacked and forced to lock himself in a church where he had to climb into the steeple to avoid being beaten up. Later, some of the walls around his manor at Stoke were broken down and his servants were set upon and thrashed. Law-abiding tenants who had paid their rents to Bess's agent on time were punished for 'non-payment' by having their animals and property confiscated by the Earl's men, and in some cases their property was relet over their heads.[27] Bess could do little but write to Burghley, begging him to write to her husband who, she thought, would take more notice of a letter from Burghley than from 'any other living person'.

Before Burghley could write, Shrewsbury arrived at the main door of Chatsworth at the head of a force of forty men armed with guns and knives, and it was clear that he was after far more than 'a night's lodging'. His intention, as Sir William well understood, was forcibly to occupy the house. When Shrewsbury beat on the locked door and demanded entry on behalf of himself and his stepson Henry Cavendish, Sir William, armed with a pistol and a halberd, refused. Shrewsbury's men then attacked, breaking windows and forcing the barred doors, before carrying away whatever items of plate they could lay hands on.[28] William waited a few nights; then he went to Sheffield with his own force of armed men and took back some of the things that had been removed from Chatsworth.[29] And when the Earl made no attempt to retaliate, he went back on another night and removed most of the remaining items.[30] As soon as Leicester heard of the incident he wrote reminding Shrewsbury of the good relationship he and Bess had once shared: 'Who bare more affection in this world to his wife than you did [for] a long while?' he asked, while admonishing him gently for his behaviour in storming Chatsworth; 'in my opinion it was . . . very foolish.'[31]

This matter inevitably became the talk of the Court that year of 1584, as had most of the events in the ongoing saga between the Shrewsburys. The Earl immediately blamed his stepsons William and Charles for spreading 'vile rumours' about him. But we know that at least some of the stories to which the Earl objected were released into the public domain by his own son. For example, in the late spring of 1584 Gilbert had visited his father at the still uncompleted great house at Worksop, where Shrewsbury had quietly taken Queen Mary for a visit. When he arrived there Gilbert found to his surprise that his father had another guest – Gilbert's uncle, the Earl of Rutland. Rutland was brother to Shrewsbury's first wife, so at first sight there should have been nothing unusual about his entertaining his brother-in-law. But Rutland was also a well-known Catholic zealot, who made no secret of the fact that he supported a Catholic restoration.

It was curious for Shrewsbury to have entertained such a person, especially in view of the fact that he was fully aware of the constant threat by Catholic sympathisers to rescue Mary. Indeed, following the discovery of the Throckmorton plot* in November of the previous year, many of Shrewsbury's letters dwelt in an obsessive manner on his suspicion of local Jesuits. Yet because Rutland was 'kin', Shrewsbury did not consider him a danger; again it highlights a curious naivety in Shrewsbury. Anyway, it was the last straw as

---

*This plot, named after Francis Throckmorton (a Catholic cousin to Sir Nicholas) involved an invasion by Spain to rescue Mary, which was discovered in November 1583. Letters from Mary to the French Ambassador and others prove not only that she was aware of the details of the plan but also that, following Bess's physical split with Shrewsbury, Mary had many lines of clandestine contact open.

far as the Queen and the Privy Council were concerned. Although Shrewsbury had been a loyal and trustworthy servant, and was never regarded in any other light, it was concluded that he was no longer to be relied upon to guard the Scottish Queen.

He was allowed to take Mary to Buxton in June and July 1584, as already planned. This was something she had looked forward to for months; the spa treatment eased her pains, and she always welcomed any diversion in her imprisonment. When he returned to Sheffield from Buxton, Shrewsbury found to his satisfaction that permission had been granted, at long last, for him to visit the Court. Sir Ralph Sadler was appointed temporary custodian and it was arranged that Mary would stay at Wingfield during Shrewsbury's absence. Never suspecting that the arrangement was to be permanent, Shrewsbury pointed out that Sadler would find it far easier to police Mary at Sheffield than Wingfield, and, knowing both properties, Sadler agreed: 'I would rather choose to keep this Queen here with sixty men, than at Wingfield with three hundred.'[32] Nevertheless, the two men obeyed their orders, and on 4 August 1584 they escorted Mary and her suite to Wingfield. Two days later Shrewsbury bade her farewell. The following week Elizabeth signed the instrument which removed Mary, Queen of Scots from Shrewsbury's keeping after fifteen and a half years. They would not meet again until Mary was on trial for her life.

As soon as he arrived in London, Shrewsbury attended a Privy Council meeting at Oatlands, but before he would agree to take his seat on the Council, he demanded abrasively whether any of those present knew 'of any manner of disloyalty or undutifulness in his discharge of his custody of the Scottish Queen'. Having been assured that his loyalty was never in question, he was persuaded to participate in the day's business, but it was noted that his effort was mostly directed at trying to prevent his stepson Sir Charles Cavendish from being elected a Knight of the Shire of Derby, while ensuring that his own sons were chosen.

He also swore a formal complaint against Sir William Cavendish over the incident at Chatsworth. Without being given an opportunity to defend himself, Sir William was immediately arrested and sent to the Fleet Prison for 'insolent behaviour'.[33] Bess had arrived in London by this time and had engaged legal counsel before the matter was brought before a judge. When both sides of the story were heard, William was released. By this time Shrewsbury had returned to Sheffield.

There is abundant evidence that the Queen and Lords Leicester and Burghley had seen for themselves during his visit to Court that Shrewsbury was a man of deteriorating mental health. While consistently taking Bess's side, the Queen was demonstrably gentle with Shrewsbury, calling him 'her good old man', and even providing a footstool beside the throne so that he could sit while she spent long sessions chatting with him.[34] According to the Spanish Ambassador, Shrewsbury thanked the Queen for delivering him from 'two devils, the Scottish Queen and his wife,' but as Elizabeth had not delivered Shrewsbury from his wife, this story may be apocryphal.

At Michaelmas 1584, the Earl's London agent, Thomas Baldwin, brought a legal action on his master's behalf, against an Islington innkeeper who was telling his guests 'openly, that the Earl of Shrewsbury had gotten the Queen of Scots with child, and that he knew where the child was buried'.[35] Perhaps this is at the root of Shrewsbury's letter to his sons Edward and Henry, who were at Court, having recently returned from a long tour of France. In his letter, Shrewsbury requested his sons to enquire what people in London thought and said of him, accusing Bess of setting her sons 'to give evil speeches' against him. He instructed Edward and Henry to 'be stout' in dealing with their stepbrothers.[36]

There is no evidence that either Bess or her sons were guilty of spreading the 'illegitimate child' stories, although given Shrewsbury's treatment of them, it would be surprising if they retained any respect or affection for him. A man called Babsthorpe had published a book which contained the accusation,* so perhaps Bess, Sir William and

Sir Charles Cavendish heard the story and simply did not bother to deny it. But there were other rumours about Shrewsbury circulating at the time which may well have been true, such as one that claimed that while staying at Worksop Manor the Scottish Queen had been allowed to walk freely, and unguarded, in Sherwood Forest. Again, this story was most likely originated by Gilbert; apart from Lord Rutland, he was the only person known to have stayed at Worksop Manor during Mary's two short visits there.

In fact, the rumours that Mary had carried Shrewsbury's child were not new. Four years earlier, in 1580, in a document annotated in his own hand, Lord Burghley listed a number of such stories which had been released 'by authority'. These included, among other things, the claims that Mary's supporter, the Duc de Guise, was planning to invade England, that Lord Burghley and Lord Leicester were to be assassinated, and that 'the Queen of Scots was with child by the Earl of Shrewsbury'.[37] Indeed the 'illegitimate child' story had first been spread as far back as 1572, as official spin to discredit Mary.

We also know from Mary's own pen, that she had quite deliberately placed the blame for spreading this last rumour upon Bess, to discredit her. 'You will have been able to understand from my said letters,' she wrote to the French Ambassador, Castelnau de Mauvisière, 'my intention to implicate indirectly the Countess of Shrewsbury, against whom if I am once without fear of opening my mouth, I feel sure that she and all her courtiers would have reason to repent having so cruelly and traitorously attacked me.'[38] This woman who spent her life plotting and machinating (not entirely without justification, it must be said) was patently capable of poisoning Shrewsbury against Bess. She even wrote to Bess about the matter and, as she advised one correspondent, Bess

---

*Shrewsbury received permission to sue Babsthorpe, although Elizabeth tried to prevent it, using a *scandalum magnatum* statute.

had replied, 'with very many words and much anger . . . [and] declared that she had never heard anything of the same, either by me, or any other. Whereupon she was ready to give her oath to the Queen her sovereign . . .'[39]

There was one further attempt by Queen Mary to damage Bess, and this was contained in an extraordinary letter Mary addressed to Queen Elizabeth, which begins: 'I call God to witness that what the Countess of Shrewsbury has said of you to me is as nearly as possible what follows.' What follows is a catalogue of scandalous stories about Elizabeth and her supposed lovers, such as the Earl of Oxford (Edward de Vere) and Sir Christopher Hatton. About the latter, Mary claimed, Bess had told her 'that you literally pursued him, displaying your love for him so publicly that he was obliged to withdraw, and that you gave young Killigrew a box on the ear because he did not bring Hatton back when sent in pursuit'. She claimed that Bess had tried to engineer a marriage between Hatton and her daughter Elizabeth, but Hatton was too afraid of the Queen to negotiate.

Another man accused of being the Queen's lover, Mary wrote, was Jean de Simier, who had been the Duc d'Alençon's envoy in the French marriage negotiations. And Mary's pen seems to have been dipped in venom as she relates that Bess had told her that Elizabeth was, 'so vain and had such a good opinion of your beauty, as if you were some goddess' that Elizabeth encouraged and believed in the most flagrant flattery, such as that she was 'as glorious as the sun', and that while Elizabeth basked in such words her courtiers sniggered at her behind their hands. Mary says Bess also told her that Elizabeth was a cruel mistress, and had broken the finger of an attendant while in a rage, and pretended a chandelier had fallen on him. But perhaps the worst accusation, and the one which seems to bear some truth, is that Bess had tried unsuccessfully to obtain Mary's agreement for the marriage of Arbella to King James of Scotland.[40]

Had Elizabeth ever received this letter, and had she believed it, it would certainly have meant the end of any ambitions Bess had for her children. Not only was Elizabeth's iconic virginal status questioned, but there is the inference that she was a ridiculous figure in the eyes of her courtiers (which is arrant nonsense). In the event, though, it appears that the letter was merely drafted and never sent. It was probably collected up with Mary's papers before she was executed, or perhaps it *was* despatched, only to be intercepted by Walsingham's intelligence network. It ended up among Burghley's papers.

It is easy to believe that Bess may have allowed herself to be carried away in a catty feminine gossiping session over her needle-work during the early days of her relationship with Mary. And it is also possible to believe that Bess connived at the proposal of a marriage between Arbella and King James, although it is just as likely that Margaret Lennox conceived this idea. However, some of the incidents of which Bess stands accused in this letter, if they ever occurred, could have taken place only long after the two women ceased to be friends, when it is doubtful that Bess would have been so indiscreet with Mary. It is more likely that Mary heard some of the stories from her other informants. Such rumours about people in high places were not exactly uncommon; among Bess's papers is a letter from one of her correspondents reporting that a man called Marsham had spread gossip that Queen Elizabeth had two children by the Earl of Leicester, 'and for that is likely to lose both his ears or pay £100 fine'.[41]

In November 1584 the Queen of Scots rejoiced when news was received that the Privy Council had agreed to her demands that Bess and her sons should be 'examined . . . to confirm or refute the rumours and language they have previously maintained, that in the cause of reason and justice they may be punished as an example'. Shrewsbury was also pleased, believing that his complaints were to be fully vindicated and his reputation restored.

Bess and her sons duly appeared before the Council. Under oath they denied being the source of rumours that the Queen of Scots was pregnant by Lord Shrewsbury, indeed they held them 'as very false, scandalous lies, maliciously invented and set on foot . . . in this kingdom and others, that the said Queen of Scotland had one or several children by the Earl of Shrewsbury . . . protesting that they were not the authors, inventors or reporters of it'.[42] They also offered to face anyone who accused them of being involved, and to prove the charges were a lie. Then they swore, still under oath, and on their knees, that while in the custody of Lord Shrewsbury, Mary, Queen of Scots 'had never deported herself otherwise in honour and chastity than became a Queen and a princess of her quality'.[43] Perhaps knowing that the pregnancy story had been spread as government propaganda for nearly a decade, certain members of the Council felt that this was sufficient exploration of the matter.

The statement by Bess was enough for one of Queen Mary's secretaries, Claude Nau, to write, inexplicably, 'I have obtained right from the Countess of Shrewsbury, in the presence of the said Queen [Elizabeth] for the false rumours that she caused to be sown against the honour of Her Majesty, which she has publicly retracted.'[44] Perhaps this was intended as a placebo to comfort Mary for it was not as it happened; in fact, Bess and her sons were totally exonerated of all blame.

CHAPTER 16

NO WINNERS

1585–6

FIFTY-SEVEN WAS CONSIDERED ALMOST OLD AGE IN
Elizabethan times but Bess was more fortunate than most; apart
from some stiffness in her joints in damp and cold weather she
remained fit and active. She was regarded at Court as a formidable
personality, not only for her wisdom and dignity of bearing but
because she was articulate and stood up for her rights, and not least
because she was able to marshal powerful support. She had
achieved much for a woman of her time, and would go on to
achieve more, but this was not a happy period in her life.

Her eldest son, Henry, married to Shrewsbury's daughter, Grace
Talbot, was a great disappointment to her. Although Bess was friendly
with Grace[1] and, judging from their letters, they held each other in
mutual affection, she regarded Henry as a wastrel, and a poor heir to
everything for which she had worked. 'My bad son Henry' she once
called him, and he reminded her of her dead brother James,* having

---

*Although James Hardwick had no legitimate children he named an illegitimate son,
John Hardwick, as his heir. Bess maintained some contact with this nephew and his
name appears in her accounts in the 1590s.

nothing of the dynast about him, and no thoughts for furthering the future of his family: the goal to which she and his father had aspired. Instead of taking an interest in his heritage, Henry preferred to travel and to gamble,[2] spending as little time with his wife as he could. He had sired bastard children all over the county of Derbyshire, but not one child was born in wedlock to carry on his line. Henry knew of his mother's opinion of him, and this was probably why he lent support to his stepfather amidst the couple's perennial bickering. But there was nothing Bess could do about Henry; it was he to whom Chatsworth – Bess's beloved Chatsworth – was entailed.

In fact, Henry was probably a better man than he sounds. He was a music lover and kept his own group of musicians, and, having a good eye for a horse, he was a successful owner and trainer.[3] He was MP for Derbyshire in 1572, and though he had not stuck to this, his stepfather and father-in-law, the Earl of Shrewsbury, thought he was twice the man of either of his brothers and had told the Queen so while Henry was serving in the army in the Low Countries in 1578. The Earl gave Tutbury Abbey, a cheerless place by all accounts, to Henry and Grace as their marital home. It was not far from the castle where Mary, Queen of Scots was now imprisoned under the guardianship of Sir Amias Paulet. Paulet was always suspicious of Henry and Grace. They had grown up regarding his prisoner almost as a member of the family, and Paulet frankly told Burghley that he would prefer them moved from such close proximity.

Bess's two younger sons fitted her ideal more closely. Her second and favourite son, Sir William Cavendish, was married to Anne Keighley, and they now lived in Hardwick Hall. For years William, of whom Bess's steward once said there was never any need to drive him to his books, had become the equivalent of Bess's personal assistant, and she probably could not have achieved what she went on to achieve without his able support.

Sir Charles, who lived a few miles from Chatsworth at Stoke

Manor, had been widowed after a year, and left with a motherless baby who died in infancy. Of Bess's three sons, Charles seems to have had the pleasantest personality. Educated to believe he would inherit little, he was lucky to have married well and had no financial problems, though the loss of his wife hit him hard. He was brave, well mannered, insouciant and affectionate. His best friend was Gilbert Talbot, to whom he was steadfastly loyal, and upon whom he was a good influence, despite Shrewsbury's dislike of the close relationship.[4]

Of Bess's two surviving daughters, Frances, married to Sir Henry Pierrepoint, had five children. The eldest of these, Bess's namesake Elizabeth 'Bessie' Pierrepoint, had been in the Scottish Queen's service since the age of four. According to Mary, the child – whom she called '*Mignonne*' – had been her 'bedfellow' (children routinely shared the beds of adults in the family), and had been as carefully and virtuously brought up as if she was her own daughter. When Mary's guardianship passed from Shrewsbury, Bessie accompanied her royal mistress to Wingfield and Tutbury Castle, but now she was seventeen, and a marriage was being promoted between her and a son of Lord Percy, the Earl of Northumberland. Bessie had always been a great favourite of the captive Queen, who stated that 'she would be no impediment to the marriage' and would release the girl who, she said, looked younger than her age and 'was inclined to fatness, yet her marriage might increase her stature and take away the inclination . . .'[5] Furthermore, Mary privately told her jailer Amias Paulet, she did not wish to give the Countess of Shrewsbury any cause to tell people that the Scottish Queen had ruined her granddaughter's life by depriving her of the chance of a brilliant marriage.[6]

Mary, Lady Talbot, married to Gilbert, her husband's estranged heir, had provided Bess with three granddaughters but no surviving grandson so far, to replace poor little George.

Bess was an involved grandmother, holding her grandchildren in deep affection, taking an interest in their academic achievements and often sending them small gifts when she could not see them in person. But it was the orphan Arbella who embodied all Bess's remaining ambitions. She had lived with Bess since her mother's death, and in 1585 she was nine years old. According to Mary, Queen of Scots, Bess had consulted an astrologer who had foretold that Arbella would marry King James of Scotland and ultimately become Queen of England.[7] Whether this is true, and if so whether Bess believed this or not, she certainly ensured that Arbella was educated as a princess by the best tutors available. From family letters, we know that Arbella was a good and virtuous child, intelligent, articulate, musically gifted and a linguist: by the time she was thirteen Arbella could 'read French out of Italian, and English out of both'. As well as precocity in the schoolroom, she enjoyed the outdoor pursuits of riding, hunting and archery; her childhood and education were similar, in fact, to that of the young Princess Elizabeth.

But of all the problems in Bess's life as she neared her sixtieth birthday, the main one – and the one that try as she might she could not resolve – was her disastrous marriage to George, Earl of Shrewsbury.

From the symptoms – a very gradual mental deterioration and personality change – the Earl seems to have been suffering the early stages of an age-related dementia, perhaps caused by what we now recognise as small ischaemic strokes. Although he was the same age as Bess he had been in almost constant ill health for about six or seven years, and his letters are full of his ills. These ailments are always blamed on 'the gout', and the extreme pain and swellings on his body that he complained of are typical of that illness and of arthritis. But there were other symptoms which cannot be ascribed to gout: his sudden outbursts of intimidating bad temper and emotional instability, his memory losses, the invention or exaggeration of events to fill the loss (such as his armed attack on Chatsworth which he appeared to regard as a mild-mannered request for a night's lodging), and what can only be described as a paranoid obsession centred on his wife, her two younger sons, her daughter Mary and his own son Gilbert.

He believed that these members of his family were conspiring to rob him of his money, that they were spreading scandalous lies about him to ruin his reputation, and – now that he could no longer blame the cost of keeping Mary, Queen of Scots – that their wilful extravagance was driving him into bankruptcy. As well as prohibiting Bess from setting foot in any of his houses, he had driven her out of Chatsworth and withheld her allowance – money that was legally hers under their marriage contract, and a good proportion of which derived from properties that she had brought into their union. Other 'enemies' also presented themselves: in one curious incident a rumour spread in Scotland that the Earl of Shrewsbury had a fleet of a dozen ships at sea, 'which rob practically every man they meet'. He was furious when he heard about it and branded all Scotsmen 'lying villains'.[8]

Anyone with a husband, parent or beloved relative with similar symptoms will sympathise with Bess's predicament. Even today, with a battery of helpful medications and greater understanding, it is a distressing condition, and it is difficult to accept major personality changes when the person looks and appears outwardly normal for some considerable time – even years. The behaviour of the Queen and her courtiers and government towards Shrewsbury when he was at Court, and in the letters written to him afterwards, indicate that they were well aware that Shrewsbury had a problem. They were gentle with him, fending off his constant complaints and petitions with kindness rather than irritation, but, noticeably, they consistently came down on the side of Bess in her defence against him.

This support might have been of some comfort to Bess, but it did not help her in any practical sense. The Earl's servants took him at his word when he spoke of wanting to take revenge on her and her sons, with the result that her tenants were now terrorised in their homes. Bess said she was now literally too afraid to return to

Chatsworth, and therefore remained at Hardwick Hall with her son William and his wife. Although at this time Hardwick was more substantial than the half-timbered house in which Bess had grown up, it was not what she had become used to. James Hardwick had begun to extend the house but, typically, had left the work half finished.

Bess had seen Chatsworth raised from the first footings upwards, had overseen every step of the building and décor – had spent thirty years – more than half her life, on its aggrandisement. There was not a stone of it she did not know about and she missed it. Hardwick was inconvenient for the sort of living and entertainment Bess was used to, with its central hall stretching from the front to the back, rather than from end to end which would have given it length and grandeur. It had not been designed so much as 'grown' – a chamber fitted in here, a wing added there, as occasion demanded. And having stood empty following her brother's death, it was dank and unwelcoming. Bess was depressed enough to write uncharacteristically to Walsingham that all she hoped for now was 'to find some friends for meat and drink, and so to end my life'. However, she was an optimist by nature and, true to form, it was not long before she embarked upon a project to extend and beautify the former manor into something that would reflect her usual lifestyle and serve as a fitting setting for her little 'jewel', Arbella. This began as a modest programme – the building of a new great hall – but later she would embark upon a complete remodelling and extensive additions.

Shrewsbury had not recovered from the fact that the Council had exonerated Bess and her sons of spreading rumours about him and the Scottish Queen. Refusing to accept the decision, he brought a private suit against Bess, among other things charging that she had 'animated her sons, not only with force to keep me from a night's lodging in one of my houses [Chatsworth], but also with slanderous speeches and sinister practices to dishonour me'. But the gist of his suit concerned property matters. He hoped to discredit the deed of gift made in 1572 under which he had transferred to the younger Cavendish sons ownership of certain lands brought into the marriage by Bess. When he made the gift, Shrewsbury had owed Bess money, so the land was transferred partly in lieu of this debt, and the balance was paid to Shrewsbury in cash in her sons' names. As was her lifelong practice, however, Bess had retained a life interest in the lands, which provided her with an annual income in rents.

Initially, Shewsbury claimed the document was a forgery. It is entirely possible that he genuinely did not recall signing it, but it patently contained the Earl's signature, although notably there were no witnesses, which was unusual. When it was judged to be a genuine document, Shrewsbury claimed he had been ill when he had signed it, and had not known what he was signing. But he had sent a letter to Lord Burghley dated the same day as the deed, in which he wrote of various matters concerning the Scottish Queen, in a perfectly normal hand and not mentioning any ill health.

Bess was also able to show that her sons had borrowed the money paid to Shrewsbury in respect of the settlement of this deed, and indeed that they were still paying off the debt. Other sums Shrewsbury claimed that Bess had had from him over the years – often, he claimed, extracted over his sick bed without his knowledge – were hugely exaggerated, and Bess was able to show that not only were the amounts he listed excessive, but they were perfectly legitimate drawings, mostly part of the monies due to her under their marriage settlement.

In fact the Earl's 'suit', backed up by sworn documents presented by his counsel, offered not a scintilla of detail to support his wild accusations about his wife. They merely echoed, yet again, his general dissatisfaction about Bess's 'misbehaviour' of which he had complained since the onset of his illness at the beginning of the decade (and possibly for eighteen months prior to that when he had first begun displaying uncharacteristic emotional outbursts).

The matter was heard by three of the Earl's peers. In what was a man's world, surely these men, Lord Chancellor Bromley, and two Chief Justices – given even a vestige of doubt – would have come down on the side of one of the most powerful Peers of the Realm, who, having been guardian of the Scottish Queen for sixteen years, was now plagued by a wife he accused of being a 'shrew'? They did not. In fact they vindicated Bess on every count. Furthermore, they recommended that the Earl should take his wife back into his home, should pay her £2000 in rents he had collected that year on properties that were hers, and that in return she should pay him, in future, £500 per annum for lands she occupied that were the Earl's.

Bewildered, hurt and angry, Shrewsbury wrote to the Queen from Chelsea, protesting that the only defence presented by the Countess had been 'that of my wife's servants and a secret instrument written in her own hand without witness, [whereas] I had many warrants duly registered and copied'. He had no option but to accept the verdict, but he refused to accede to the suggestion that he should take his wife back into his home, and advised that he was not able to wait upon Her Majesty, 'being now so grieved with the colic and the stone' that he wished only to return home. He then begged her (a hint that he had so far received no reward for his guardianship of the Scottish Queen), 'to give me some remembrance of your good liking for my long service'.[9]

A few weeks later Lord Leicester replied to him at the Queen's request, pleading with Shrewsbury to accept the Council's decision. In the letter, Leicester wrote that the Queen had pointed out that as Sovereign Head of State she sought to give justice to all persons, especially 'in this cause of my Lady your wife, whom you have long and for many years very lovingly and honourably entertained till within these few years that the breach between her and the Queen of Scots fell out'. The Queen was convinced that it was through Mary's machinations 'though not directly with yourself', that the Shrewsburys had been driven apart.

. . . and yet your Lordship not meaning to do it for that Queen's sake, but other matters laid before you, to withdraw your love from my lady.

Her Majesty . . . never yet heard or could find sufficient matter laid against her [Bess], to cause so hard and extreme a breach to be made between a man and his wife.

. . . My Lord, you must not think that Her Majesty doth this for special favour more to my Lady than to you, but . . . she doth think my Lady hath received some hard dealing, and doth not find sufficient material to charge her touching yourself, that she should be so turned away.[10]

The second matter [concerns] such deeds and grants as your Lordship has conveyed to my Lady, . . . which her Highness did commit to the grave consideration of the Lord Chancellor and other learned judges . . . They all think the meaning [intention] of your Lordship was that my lady should enjoy all these gifts.[11]

Shrewsbury took this hard, and replied bitterly: 'Her Majesty has set down this hard sentence against me, to my perpetual infamy and dishonour, to be ruled and overrun by my wife, so bad and wicked a woman. Yet her Majesty will see that I will obey her commandment, though no curse or plague on earth could be more grievous to me . . . It is too much to make me my wife's pensioner.'[12]

Bess spent the summer and autumn of 1585 at Court, which made Shrewsbury suspicious. He wrote to the Queen that the aim of his Countess was to bring him into disrepute with her, when all he was guilty of was having disloyal servants who gossiped about him. The Queen should punish Bess for her slanders, he wrote, and banish her from Court. Meanwhile, he positively encouraged his own servants to be impertinent to Bess, to such an extent that she eventually complained to Walsingham about the 'ill-conduct of Copley', Shrewsbury's London steward, a man with whom she had had a long and satisfactory working relationship and whom she had always formerly addressed as 'Good Copley'.

In September Gilbert Talbot applied to his father for financial assistance, on Bess's advice. Gilbert was now in debt to the tune of over £5000, could no longer hold off his creditors and wrote in desperation: 'most humbly beseeching your Lordship, on my knees, to

pardon my fault of spending hitherto . . . but rather than remain
still so far behind hand as I am . . . I would wish to end my life'.[13]
Shrewsbury retorted unsympathetically that it was a good comeup-
pance for a son who had sided with his stepmother against his own
father. However, he suggested that if Bess would sell him a property
called Sutton for £2300 he would give this to Gilbert to pay off his
debts. Bess was doubtful about this offer, shrewdly surmising that it
was a ruse of Shrewsbury's to make her part with a prime property
at a knock-down price. She offered instead to sell Shrewsbury some
other lands in Derbyshire which she had previously earmarked for
her son Charles. These lands, she said, might be sold off to pay
Gilbert's debts, but in any case she would match pound for pound
any sum Shrewsbury would donate for this purpose.

When Gilbert relayed this offer to his father, he found that Bess
had correctly summed up his father's real intentions. Shrewsbury
wrote admitting he had no intention of helping Gilbert financially,
and that he had simply been testing to see what his wife would do
about Sutton. As for Gilbert's debts, he wrote: 'in the last year you
have had in money and lead, and by my toleration, nearly £2000,
besides your maintenance and allowance £800 money. These are no
small matters and how you should so spend all this money and
bring yourself so far into debt I cannot but marvel.'[14]

On and on it went, this interminable dispute between husband
and wife, fuelled by Shrewsbury's obsession with letter-writing.
Almost weekly the Queen, Lords Burghley and Leicester, Walsingham,
and indeed anyone connected with Bess,* were on the receiving

*I located thirty-four surviving letters written in the twenty-two weeks from April to
August 1586, concerning the Shrewsburys' marital problems. Of these fifteen are
from Shrewsbury to the Queen, Burghley, Walsingham, Leicester and Bess. Four
were written by the Queen, three by Bess, and the rest are from other correspondents
to Shrewsbury. Further letters concerning this matter, which either have not survived or I have not traced, are referred to within these letters. Shrewsbury's behaviour
during this period was not unusual: any twenty-two weeks between 1584 and 1586
would probably reflect a similar pattern.

end of a long screed from Shrewsbury in his barely decipherable hand. He ordered Leicester to cease trying to effect a rapprochement between them; he stated to Walsingham that the grief caused by his wife was of 'the like whereof hath [never] been offered to a man of my cut by a woman of so base a parentage and her children . . . ';[15] and he told Burghley how sorry he was to learn that his wife was still at Court, pestering the Queen with complaints about him. As before, his allegations were all of a general nature, rather than specific, such as in the following – typical – letter written to Bess:

Wife. The offences and faults you have committed against me . . . no good wife would do. Though you desire to be charged particularly, that you may know your faults, I need not to express them, they be so manifest to the world. And if I would hide them, your behaviour and conditions have laid them open.

There cannot be any wife more forgetful of her duty, and less careful to please her husband than you have been, nor any more bounden, nor have received greater benefits by her husband than you . . . In that I loved you and did many good things for you and was loath that the world should see your behaviour, it may be judged that I would still so have continued, if you had not sought all means both at home and abroad to offend me . . . [but] your insatiable greedy appetite did betray you.

Your own living at my hands would not content you, nor yet a greater part of mine, which for my quietness I could have been contented to give you, but this was short of the mark you shot at, and [still] do . . . As for our cohabitation, you went away volun-tarily, not turned away by me as you say . . .[16]

In another letter he accused Bess of telling the Queen that he had been 'ruled' by Mary, Queen of Scots, which he angrily denied, and he also denied that Bess was more respected locally than he was himself. Bess sent a polite and patient reply to this letter, which brought the response, 'your fair words are nought but form . . . they appear beautiful but they are mixed with poison'.[17]

With all the problems of State (this domestic squabble took place against the background of the problems in the Low Countries and Drake's magnificent adventures against the Spaniards), it is amazing that Queen Elizabeth, Lords Burghley and Leicester, and Francis Walsingham found time to read, let alone reply to Shrewsbury's storm of letters. And yet the Queen wrote to him frequently, calling him her 'good old man', and repeatedly asking him to allow his wife to have access to him 'which she has now wanted for a long time'. Why did Bess lobby so hard to be reunited with a husband who had become so unpleasant to her? Obviously she wanted to be allowed to return to Chatsworth and live in peace there. And it is just possible that, despite everything (Shrewsbury had refused to comply with any of the recommendations of the court hearing: he had not paid Bess the £2000; would not allow her in his presence or in any of his houses; and continued to persecute Bess, her sons and their servants and tenants), Bess still retained the affection for Shrewsbury that she professed she did.

In November 1585, acting on Burghley's advice, the Queen commissioned Sir Francis Willoughby* of Wollaton Manor, and Sir John Manners† of Haddon Hall, to preside over a full investigation of the Shrewsbury matrimonial problems, with instructions to examine 'the allegations on both sides'.[18] This commission would spend six months deliberating on the matter.

In April 1586 Shrewsbury joined the Court at Oatlands to take part in the annual St George's Day service. He then returned to Sheffield and had not long arrived there when he received the results of the commission's findings. He had been totally confident

---

*Willoughby had been a connection of the Dudleys and was an old friend of Bess and Sir William Cavendish.
†Shrewsbury's brother-in-law by his first marriage, and one of Bess's closest friends in old age. Haddon Hall had passed to the Manners family as a result of Dorothy Vernon's marriage to Sir John.

that an in-depth inquiry would uphold his complaints about his wife and her children, would convict her of malicious slander, and return to him all the lands and titles that he had conveyed to his wife on their marriage, as well as the items of plate he claimed she had 'stolen' from Chatsworth. Once again he was disappointed.

This time, to ensure that the Earl accepted the report and recommendations of the commission, the documents were counter-signed by Lord Burghley and Walsingham, and they ratified the decisions reached a year earlier, as follows:

1. That the Earl content himself with £500 of land assigned to him by the Queen's former order.
2. That the Earl pay the Cavendishes the £2000 claimed by them in respect of profits of the lands at variance.
3. All suits against the said Countess and her sons should cease . . . nor is he to enter into any action against the Countess etc for matters past.
4. The Earl is not to displace any of the Countesses tenants.[19]

This schedule was conveyed to Shrewsbury accompanied by a personally written letter from the Queen, who wrote kindly, but firmly, of

... an earnest desire since the first dislike fallen out between you and the Countess your wife, to set all matters as well of unkindness between you yourselves, and her younger sons, by our mediation brought to some good end and accord . . .

The place we hold requires . . . that we do not suffer in our realm two persons of your degree and quality to live in such a kind of discord. As also for the special care we have of yourself, knowing that these variances have greatly disquieted you, whose years require repose, especially of the mind. We have of late thought . . . that no such effects have followed our mediation in that behalf, as we looked for (although we hope for better here-after), especially touching that unkindness.

Calling unto us the Lord Chancellor . . . together with our
cousin of Leicester to deal between you . . . and our Lord
Treasurer, and our Secretary whom we appointed this last winter
[we ordered them] to proceed in the same cause, with your son
Henry Talbot and your servant Copley, for that [the] former
order by us intended was not brought to a quiet end . . . Which
our pleasure is to be observed, as is specified and contained in a
schedule hereinclosed, subscribed by the said Lord Chancellor,
Lord Treasurer and our Secretary.

Elizabeth R. Greenwich, 12th May 1586.[20]

The Queen's reference here to Shrewsbury being 'disquieted' –
'you, whose years require repose, especially in the mind', seem to
confirm her opinion of the cause of the problems. Bess was the
same age but there was no question of her needing repose; in fact,
she was still actively serving in the royal bedchamber on occasion.
Walsingham wrote as well, advising the Earl to comply with the
'findings'. Burghley also wrote that week, but on a different subject.
He begged Shrewsbury to help Gilbert, who would have to go
abroad if his debts were not soon discharged. Gilbert had told him
he could not face his father because he feared the latter's violent
temper, and at Bess's suggestion had asked Burghley to intercede for
him, because of his father's admiration and respect for him.
Although Gilbert thought that the Earl might suspect Bess's hand in
this, which would put him 'in greater peril' of his father's anger, he
had no other options.[21]

As soon as he received the results of the commission Shrewsbury
hurried back to London. There he continued barracking Burghley,
Walsingham and Sir Thomas Bromley, this time charging that his
wife, 'now she has so apparently manifest her devilish disposition
to the utter ruin and destruction of my house and name' had bribed
them to gain their favour.[22] Had they not considered Shrewsbury's
illness a mental one, these men would surely have taken great
offence at such a charge. But the only response was one from

Walsingham, firmly denying that the Countess had used her money to buy favours at Court. In fact Bess constantly sent gifts to influential people, as indeed did Shrewsbury, but this was no more than working the system. Despite all their efforts Shrewsbury made it abundantly clear that he did not accept the commission's decision.

Bess was still living at Court in July 1586 when the Queen issued a formal decree that the Earl of Shrewsbury must allow his wife to occupy and enjoy all her properties, paying her husband the amount of £500 a year for this privilege. The Earl was now hoist by his own petard, for he had formerly insisted that the lands he had taken over from his wife were worth only £500 a year. Now he grumbled that he would lose £2000 a year by the Queen's ruling.

But the Council soon had other things to think about, for later that month plague struck the city.[23] Elizabeth and a few attendants were at Oatlands and remained there, and the Court decamped to Richmond. In periods such as this, it was hopeless to try to get any response to letters, and Shrewsbury's letters went unanswered. Bess remained with the Court on this occasion for at least six months, serving in the Privy Chamber and the Bedchamber, and, to Shrewsbury's annoyance, this gave her an intimate access to the Queen completely denied to him.

He continued to write bitter and vindictive letters to Bess. She always replied politely and patiently:

> My Lord, I hold myself most unfortunate that upon so light occasion it pleases you to write in that form to me, for what new offence is committed since her Majesty reconciled us? ... My Lord, I know not how justly you can term me insatiable in my desire of gaining, for my losses hath been so great with my charges, that makes me desire honestly to discharge my debt with my children's lands, which you have no need of.
>
> ... I am greedy of nobody's lands, else neither look for the seven hundred pounds you have of those lands, but would keep the rest, which by all law, order and conscience they ought to

possess . . . To speak truly I assure you, my Lord, my meaning is
not to molest or grieve you . . . Can it be thought greediness to
demand nothing? For I desire no more than Her Majesty's order
gives, and wish your happy days to be many and good – whereas
it pleased you to [countermand] her Majesty's written order . . .

So beseeching the Almighty to make you better conceive of me
without offence . . . Richmond this Thursday, Yr obedient and
faithful wife, E. Shrewsbury.[24]

To this letter the Earl had responded: 'You ask what new offence
is committed since her Majesty reconciled us? . . . I answer that
there is no creature more happy or fortunate than you have been,
for, where you were defamed, and to the world a byword, when you
were St Loe's widow, I covered those imperfections by my marriage
with you, and brought you to all the honour you have, and to the
most part of that wealth you now enjoy.'[25] He then presented as
his next salvo a list of pieces of plate and 'valuable' household items
which he insisted were his property, and demanded their return.

Of the thirty-four items listed, Bess noted that more than 75 per
cent had been her own property at Chatsworth, and she was able to
demonstrate their appearance on inventories dated prior to her
marriage to the Earl. Others, such as a gold cup that was given to
her at the time of 'the Scottish Queen's lying at Coventry', cost £70,
which she claimed she had accepted in part payment of a debt of
£200 owed her by the Earl, and a writing desk, 'not worth 30
shillings and stolen by a footboy', had been a gift to her from Lady
Pembroke. There was also a 'great basin and ewer fashioned like a
ship valued at £100', which Bess stated was: 'bought by the Earl for
the Countess to give away [as a gift] which she did. As his Lordship
well knows.' Further sundry items, she claimed, had been bought
for her by the Earl in lieu of money he owed her for sheep and
cattle.

In returning the annotated schedule, she commented in an
accompanying letter that the items demanded by her husband were

'of small value, and mere trifles for so great and rich a nobleman to bestow on his wife in 19 years.' And during that same time, she counterclaimed, the Earl had received many items from her, such as 'better than £1000 worth of linen consumed by him, being carried to sundry of his Lordship's houses to serve his Lordship's turn'.[26]

The Queen now decided that it was time to bang heads together over this wearisome business. On 7 August the Earl and Countess of Shrewsbury were called before Burghley, Bromley and Walsingham to go through the findings of the former commission, and ordered to come to some form of mutual agreement. After much debate a schedule was drawn up and signed by each of them. The Queen was advised of this satisfactory conclusion and, relieved, 'she called the Earl and his wife before her and in many good words thanked the Earl for she knew he had conformed to this for her sake and at her request . . . and they showed themselves very well content . . . and in good sort departed together, very comfortable to the sight of all their friends, both lords and ladies and many others'.[27] The Earl was bound over to keep to his agreement under the penalty of otherwise paying a massive fine of £40,000.

Under the agreement, Bess was to go with Shrewsbury from the Court, that very day, to the Chelsea house. And on the following day she was to go to Wingfield Manor for a month, taking with her some servants of the Earl (though none of her own) for her comfort. The Earl was to join her at Wingfield for six days, and after that she might return to Chatsworth. The Earl agreed to meet all the expenses of the household at Wingfield. The Earl agreed that 'if the Countess shall behave herself well towards him, as she promises to do, the Earl will send for her to his house . . . to remain with him a week or more at a time'. He agreed to forgive William and Charles Cavendish, but only after they had been sent for and humbled before him, on their knees promising never again to give the Earl 'any cause for offence' and agreeing to return certain items of plate and hangings which he claimed belonged to him.[28]

This is what happened, initially, but within days of Bess leaving
for the country Shrewsbury was busy again, writing to Burghley
that though he had agreed to allow his wife access to his houses
at Chelsea and Wingfield, yet he had never agreed to 'bed and
board' with her, nor should he be burdened with the costs of her
living at Wingfield. In a letter written to Bess soon after this, he
reminded her that: 'You pressed Her Majesty . . . that you might
come to my house at Chelsea, which I granted, and at your coming
I told you [that] you were welcome upon the Queen's commandment. But, though you were cleared in Her Majesty's sight for all
offences, yet I had not cleared you, nor could trust you till you did
confess that you had offended me . . . my goods you shall restore to
me before we come together. And if you cannot be content to do
this I protest before God, I will never have you come upon me,
whatever shall.'[29]

One of the causes he gives in this long and rambling letter is that
when he had been seriously ill, years earlier, he had made her his
sole executrix. He claimed that while he was ill she had sold or
transferred the deeds of some of the St Loe lands to friends of hers
'so that if I had then died, the same might have been embezzled . . .
as the case of St Loo. But when I perceived how things stood I put
you out of my will.'[30]

A few weeks later the Earl presented a schedule purporting to
show what his wife and her sons owed him, including back wages
to her servants at Chatsworth, and his legal costs which had
amounted to over £1000 a year. The demand totalled £22,700. He
also wrote to Gilbert saying that he would allow Bess to come to
him, but Gilbert's wife would never be admitted. Weeks later,
when he demanded to know why his wife had not called on him as
she had said she wished to do, Bess had already made clear her only
reason for not coming to him was her fear of his 'extreme
temper . . . I will in all duty and humbleness subject myself to any
other means of correction,' she wrote. She was willing to be dis-
possessed of any 'earthly benefits in present or future', or accept

any other method of chastisement which her husband pleased, so long as he did not subject her to 'the extreme anguish of words, which would deprive me of all joy or comfort of life or worldly things'.[31]

By September the Earl's letters were becoming less frequent and as a result the constant squabbling came to a merciful though unsatisfactory cessation. The reason soon became obvious. By October the Queen, her advisers, and the Earl of Shrewsbury in his position as Earl Marshal of England were all caught up in preparations for the trial of Mary, Queen of Scots, on a charge of high treason.

CHAPTER 17

DEATH OF A QUEEN

1586–90

AFTER WILLIAM OF ORANGE WAS ASSASSINATED IN 1584 AT the instigation of King Philip II of Spain, the town of Ghent fell to the Spaniards. Following urgent representations by the Dutch, and the subsequent surrender of Antwerp, Queen Elizabeth took the Netherlands under her protection to ensure the stability of Europe and the future security of her own realm. The French refused to become involved in a war with Spain, so Elizabeth had little alternative but to make a stand, for if Spain were allowed to completely overrun the Low Countries, as they evidently planned, Spain's armies and her Navy would be ideally placed to invade England.

Elizabeth ordered Drake to attack the Spanish in the Americas and on the high seas, and in December 1585 she sent Leicester as her Lieutenant General at the head of a great army to take the Netherlands back from the Spanish army of occupation. It was not a success. Leicester was unwell, unfit and ageing; he was not a good choice for this important role. The cost of maintaining the Army drained money from the exchequer at a rate that caused Elizabeth to refer to it despairingly as 'a sieve that spends as it receives, to little purpose', and in one of the battles, at Zutphen, Sir

Philip Sidney, Walsingham's son-in-law and icon of chivalry at Elizabeth's Court, was mortally wounded.

There was a very real danger at this point that Spain would invade England. In addition, there were the machinations of Mary, Queen of Scots, who, during the spring of 1586, had become involved in a plot to assassinate Elizabeth. These serious, ongoing affairs of State make the intervention by Elizabeth and her senior ministers in the domestic affairs of the Shrewsburys during the period from 1584 to 1586 all the more surprising. Elizabeth would have been justified in saying 'a plague on both your houses' and leaving them to it, but it seems that all those involved felt genuine affection and concern for both parties. Even during the worst times, the letters to Shrewsbury from the Queen, Burghley, Leicester and Walsingham were unfailingly kind though, noticeably, they had continued to support Bess.

There was nothing new in plots against Elizabeth, of course, or in Queen Mary's part in them; sooner or later Walsingham's fine-tuned intelligence network got to hear of them. For example, prior to his death in 1583 the Duke of Lennox – the same Esme Stuart who had been given the Lennox title which Bess tried to claim for Arbella – had been writing secretly to Queen Mary for several years. He was the kingpin of a complicated plan in the early 1580s which involved financial and military support by the Pope and the King of Spain to invade England, rescue Mary, topple Elizabeth and restore the Catholic religion. 'Courage!' he wrote to Mary. 'I ask nothing of you, only that if this enterprise be successful your son should still be acknowledged as King.'[1]

Such schemes were never regarded lightly by Walsingham or his fellow Counsellors, but other than ensure Mary's closer confinement and apprehend the conspirators, as in the case of Throckmorton, or deflect the plots, as in the case of Lennox, there was little they could do to stop Mary or diminish her role as a rallying point. She could, and did, claim that it was not her fault that her supporters wished to rescue her, and that she played no active part. What was different about this latest plot was that during its course, Walsingham was able to obtain Mary's admission in writing that she agreed to the assassination of Elizabeth and the invasion of England by Spanish troops.

After being removed from the care of Shrewsbury in September 1584, Mary lived for three months at Wingfield Manor in the care of Sir Ralph Sadler. In January 1585 she was moved back to dank old Tutbury, under the guardianship of Sir Amias Paulet, a severe puritanical man who regarded Mary as a deceitful woman, saw her much-vaunted charm as 'wiles', and passionately loathed her religion. Under Paulet, Mary's sixteen years in Shrewsbury's care must have been recalled almost with affection, for Paulet carried out to the letter his instructions that the prisoner was to be kept in the strictest possible confinement.

By the end of 1585 Tutbury's middens had become so offensive and dangerous that their cleansing became imperative, and on Christmas Eve, Mary and her court were moved to Chartley Castle, a property situated seven miles north-east of Stafford which belonged to Robert Devereux, the young Earl of Essex. Mary's health had suffered in the damp and unsanitary conditions at Tutbury, and the long cold winter journey made her ill. She was bedridden at Chartley for almost two months.

At the time of the move, due to Paulet's effective policing, Mary had not been able to communicate with her supporters in France and Scotland for a year. But on her arrival at Chartley her attendants discovered an ingenious system by which a limited amount of secret correspondence could be sent and received. Mary was thrilled but what she did not know was that Walsingham had set up the system, and, in what must rank as one of the earliest known acts of entrapment, Mary became embroiled in a plot to assassinate Elizabeth. This plot has become known in history as the Babington Plot.

Anthony Babington was the son of an ancient and wealthy Derbyshire family whose name often appears in Cavendish and

Shrewsbury deeds, letters and general documentation. The families were friends and at the age of ten, young Anthony was serving Bess as a page at Chatsworth, and later he spent two or three years at Sheffield as page to Shrewsbury. During the four or five years in which Anthony Babington served the Shrewsburys, he came into contact with Queen Mary, particularly at Chatsworth where security was less strict. Mary habitually encouraged children to visit her, and no harm was seen in allowing her this small privilege. No doubt the romantic youth dreamed of being her knight errant. Another Shrewsbury employee serving at Sheffield at the same time as Babington was Thomas Morgan, then secretary to the Earl. But by 1585 Morgan was in Paris acting as Mary's agent, and constantly shadowed by Walsingham's agents.

While touring France after his marriage at the age of eighteen, Anthony Babington was contacted by Thomas Morgan, and subsequently introduced by him to other Marian supporters. This was noted by Walsingham's agents. Babington then returned to England, where his likeable personality, intelligence and wealth made him popular at Court. He was soon involved with a clique of young Catholic noblemen who assisted Jesuit priests in moving secretly about the country. Later he became part of the chain which passed a series of letters to Mary.[2] Babington's initial idea had been to free Mary from her long imprisonment, but his romantic and naive intention somehow became merged into a more sinister agenda.

Since January 1586 letters between Mary and her supporters had been 'smuggled' in and out of Chartley in a watertight container in beer barrels, with the assistance of the local brewer – referred to sarcastically as 'the honest fellow' by Paulet, who was aware that the honest fellow was in the pay of Walsingham as well as Queen Mary. As a consequence, after being decoded by cipher expert Thomas Phelippes, all Mary's communications were read by Paulet, Walsingham and Burghley before being copied and sent on to their intended recipients.

Walsingham, always jealous of Elizabeth's safety, had orches-
trated this scheme in December of the previous year when a priest
named Robert Gifford had been apprehended carrying an introduction to Mary, and confessed that he knew of a plot to rescue
Mary and assassinate Elizabeth. He was not punished because he
was 'turned' and became a highly successful double agent. Once
Walsingham had Gifford in place, he allowed Mary the secret
method of communication in the hope that she would betray her
real feelings about Elizabeth in writing, and, since Mary had no
idea that her letters were being read, he succeeded in a spectacular
fashion.

On a lighter note, Mary's secretary Nau used the same 'barrel
method' on a few occasions to correspond with Mary's lady-in-
waiting Bessie Pierrepoint, with whom he had fallen desperately in
love and wished to marry. Bessie had now left Mary's service and
was serving at Elizabeth's Court. Having once been proposed as
wife to the son of an Earl, she had no wish to lower her sights and
become the wife of a secretary, so, even though he was a royal secretary and was approved by her father, Bessie refused him.* Queen
Mary was offended, and wrote that there was too much of her
grandmother about Bessie's behaviour, despite her own pains in
bringing her up so carefully. She would therefore 'be sorry to have
her bestowed on any man that I would wish good to'.[3]

Mary was delighted that she was once again in contact with her
supporters, and also with the sheer intrigue of the system, which
brightened her long days, and her health improved dramatically.
That spring, in exchange for assistance from Spain to effect her
release, she had offered that if her son had not become a Catholic
before her death, 'I will cede . . . to the King [Philip] your Master,
my right to the succession of this [English] throne'. She begged

---

*It would be seventeen years before Bessie married. She was by then thirty-five, and
James I had just come to the throne of England. Her husband was a member of the
Erskine family, and was created Viscount Fenton, and later Earl of Kellie.

that her offer be kept secret for, if it became known, her dowry from the French would be stopped, it would cause a breach in her relationship with her son, and it would bring about her 'ruin and destruction in England'.[4]

On 3 June she was able to be carried in a chair to the ponds to watch some duck hunting. By July she was allowed to ride in the park at Chartley, and she even wrote to one of the conspirators: 'God . . . has not yet set [me] so low but that [I am] able to handle a crossbow for killing a doe, and to gallop after hounds on horse-back'.[5] Galloping a horse requires reasonable physical fitness – with or without the archery – and her ability to do this is at odds with the frail and crippled figure often depicted at this period by Mary's supporters and some biographers.

It was in June that Anthony Babington began using the 'barrel' system to communicate with Mary. On 14 July Mary received a letter from him which detailed the four strands of the plot. First, Spanish and Papal troops would invade England in sufficient strength to overcome all opposition; second, English Catholics would rally to help the invaders; third, Mary would be released; and fourth, Elizabeth (referred to as 'usurping Competitor') would be assassinated by six noblemen, Babington and five others, 'who will undertake the tragical execution.'[6]

Against Claude Nau's advice Mary replied to this letter on 17 July with equal care:

> . . . the affairs being thus prepared, and forces in readiness both within and without the realm, then it shall be time to set the six gentlemen to work, taking orders that upon the accomplishing of their design I may be transported out of this place.[7]

Her letter was so detailed that she even asked that fresh horses should be kept standing by after Elizabeth's assassination to gallop to Mary with all speed to let her know the murder had been carried out successfully.

There is nothing equivocal here. The communication system set in place by Walsingham may seem morally questionable (though it can be argued that the end justified the means), but the plan was written out by Babington and the reply was written by Mary; there was no trickery involved in the contents of the letters. Mary accepted that England would have to be invaded by Spain, and that Elizabeth would have to be assassinated, in order that she, Mary, could be freed. In doing so she placed her own head on the block, no matter what methods Walsingham used. Thomas Phelippes recognised this and on the back of the copy he made of the deciphered letter for Walsingham, he drew a tiny set of gallows.

As soon as the 'gallows letter' was intercepted, Babington and his co-conspirators were arrested. Mary was kept in ignorance of these events and was delighted in early August to be allowed to join the buck hunt at Tixall, some five miles away from Chartley. Mary was fit enough to have to stop her horse several times on this five-mile ride, in order to allow Sir Amias Paulet (who had been unwell) to catch her up, and she was clearly enjoying the outing. In fact, it was merely a ruse to allow her rooms to be searched, and her papers confiscated, in her absence.

At the gates of Tixall Park a group of men headed by the Queen's emissary, Sir Thomas Gorges, waited for her. Sir Thomas was gaily dressed in a richly embroidered green doublet, which Mary at first thought was worn in her honour. But instead of greeting her as she expected, he told Mary that her part in the conspiracy had been discovered, and that her servants were to be removed from her. Her two secretaries, Nau and Curle, were arrested, and Mary never saw them again. Both men later broke down under questioning and verified that the copy letters (made by Phelippes the code-breaker) were true copies of letters written by their mistress. Mary was kept in isolation at Tixall Castle for a fortnight before being returned to Chartley, where she found her rooms in the sort of disarray that follows a particularly aggressive burglary. A month later, on 21 September, she was sent with a small nucleus of her former court to Fotheringhay Castle, about twenty miles south-west of Peterborough in Northamptonshire.

Babington and three of his fellow conspirators died a horrible death.* What is more Babington was forced to watch one of his co-conspirators die first, knowing that he was about to meet the same fate himself. Such ferocious cruelty was inflicted on him that even hard-bitten Londoners, baying for the blood of the plotters, were sickened by the butchery. Elizabeth was, as always, tuned to public reaction and recognised that people were averse to such 'diabolical torture'. So on her orders, the following day when they went to the scaffold, the remaining plotters received the normal treatment reserved for traitors, and were hanged until they were dead before being drawn and quartered.

Yet even with incontrovertible evidence of Mary's collusion in the proposed assassination plot, such was the Queen's belief in the sanctity of monarchy, coupled perhaps with a natural reluctance to emulate what had been done to her own mother, that Burghley and Walsingham had to work hard to persuade Elizabeth to consent to send Mary to a trial. Eventually she capitulated, and the hearing was set for the second week in October. The most senior ministers, commissioners and Peers of the Realm were summoned to the hearing at Fotheringhay. Among these, in his capacity as Earl Marshal of England, was Shrewsbury.

During the trial, Shrewsbury lodged at the home of his son Henry Talbot, an estate called Orton Longeville situated within a few miles of Fotheringhay.[8] The trial was scheduled to begin on Saturday 11 October but it took some days for Burghley and Walsingham to persuade Mary that she should appear. This she steadfastly refused to do, until her resolution was undermined by a letter from Elizabeth which stated: 'You have planned in divers

---

*According to the writer, Camden (*History of the Annals of England*, 1615), they were hanged, but cut down before they were dead so they could watch while 'their privies were cut off' and they were disembowelled before being 'quartered'.

ways . . . to take my life and to ruin my kingdom by the shedding of blood . . . I never proceeded so harshly against you, on the contrary I have maintained you, and preserved your life with the same care as I use for myself.' It was in Mary's best interests, Elizabeth continued, that she appear before the court and respond to the charges. 'But answer fully and you may receive greater favour from it.'[9]

On 15 October Queen Mary appeared before the court in a room above the Great Hall at Fotheringhay Castle. Here, for the first time, she came face to face with the most ardent anti-Marians: Walsingham, Burghley, Sir James Croft and Sir Christopher Hatton.* There was a solid battery of Council members and twenty-six earls, barons and senior justices. 'Many counsellors', Mary commented, 'but not one for me.'

She was, indeed, expected to defend herself, though she had no defence to make, for she had undoubtedly written the letter in which were the incriminating words. However, she had not been given details of the prosecution's case, so initially she answered with a lie, testifying that she had never corresponded with Babington. This was quickly and easily disposed of. After this she cleverly and bravely stood up to her interlocutors for two days, stating that when, as a young woman, she had styled herself 'Queen of England', she had merely been following the instructions of the French government, and arguing the legal technicalities of her position as 'an absolute Queen' who could not be made subject to the laws of a country which held her an unwilling prisoner. But her written words had already condemned her, and these were compounded by the confessions of Babington and his co-conspirators, as well as those of Nau and Curle.[10]

Had the Princess Elizabeth written down her reply to Thomas Wyatt all those years ago instead of entrusting a verbal message to

---

*Throughout the two days of the trial, Mary asked Paulet to identify various men whose names she knew well from her correspondence.

Sir William St Loe, she would have then been in exactly the position in which Mary now stood. And had Mary followed Claude Nau's advice not to reply to Babington in writing, Walsingham would have had no evidence upon which to convict her. History turns upon such small decisions.

After a two-day hearing, Mary's judges returned to London to consider the verdict in the Star Chamber on 25 October. Shrewsbury wrote to Burghley from Orton Longville advising that he was too ill to travel to London: 'I am weak and must make much of myself, for I must look for when the bell will knell for me.' Burghley wrote that as the Queen had especially requested his presence, 'I would advise you not to be absent'.[11]

On the following day Burghley wrote more sympathetically, saying he was grieved to hear of the seriousness of Shrewsbury's condition and that he had spoken again to the Queen, who was 'very sorry that your Lordship should be absent at that day, lest there might be some malicious sinister interpretation [of it].' In consideration of the widespread rumours of Shrewsbury's relationship with Mary, malicious interpretations of his absence were surely inevitable? However, Burghley continued, if it proved impossible to attend, Shrewsbury must send him a letter confirming the opinion he had stated to Burghley at Fotheringhay, that the Scottish Queen was guilty and had not proved her innocence. After the hearing, Burghley wrote again to tell Shrewsbury that he was the only important person not present, but, 'by reading your Lordship's letter, your sentence did conform to the general sentence of all the rest of the commissioners,* and then it was ordered that ... this sentence should be put in ... a record to the which we should all put our names and seals.'[12]

There was only ever going to be one outcome, of course, though it was not a unanimous verdict. One man, Lord Zouche – of the

*Several days later Shrewsbury was asked to resubmit this letter, using words sent by Burghley, but containing the same date as Shrewsbury's original letter.

same family in which Bess had served as a girl – was courageous
enough to state that he was not satisfied with the verdict. Even so,
declaring a verdict of guilty was one thing; persuading Elizabeth to
agree to the execution of her 'sister Queen' was another. On the one
hand she was pressured to execute Mary by her Council, by the
commissioners, and by her subjects, while on the other hand she
was begged by envoys from Scotland and France to be merciful.
Eventually, however, after several months of deliberation Elizabeth
was persuaded to sign the death warrant in early February 1587.

Bughley knew that even though she had signed the warrant the
Queen would be reluctant to act on it, and he feared she might
withdraw her permission. He therefore produced a letter which he
had had signed by members of the Privy Council, and this authorised Shrewsbury and the Clerk of the Council, Robert Beale, to
carry the death warrant to Fotheringhay and to ensure that the execution took place without further delay. The two men arrived
during the late evening of 7 February to find that Mary had already
retired to bed. However, on being told the matter was urgent she
dressed, and received them in her room. Mary was now a plump
middle-aged woman, lame in one leg from rheumatism. Only ves-
tiges remained of her legendary beauty; yet she retained an air of
calm majesty.

Shrewsbury, who knew her so well, reportedly had some difficulty in finding his voice as he gave her the news that the death
sentence was to be carried out. He probably read from a script
written out for him by Burghley, which stated that Mary had
brought this situation upon herself by 'her many attempts both for
the destruction of the Queen's person and the invasion of this
realm; the hope and comforts she hath given to the Prince Palatine,
traitors of this realm both abroad and here at home . . . she is justly
condemned to die. The whole realm hath often times vehemently
required that justice might be done, which Her Majesty cannot
longer delay.'[13] Beale then read out the death warrant stamped
with the great seal and signed by Elizabeth. Mary had been told in

November that she had been found guilty, and had expected no less a sentence, so now she had only one question: when was the execution to take place? Shrewsbury answered that it was to be 'tomorrow morning at eight o'clock'.

It was obviously a shock, but Mary remained outwardly calm. It was left to her doctor to plead with Shrewsbury to give his mistress more time to prepare herself. He reminded the Earl of all the kindnesses he had shown Mary in past years, but Shrewsbury dared not change the instructions he had been given, and said there could be no delay.

On the following morning, an hour later than Shrewsbury had decreed, Mary, Queen of Scots came to the block. She had persuaded herself that she was dying as a martyr for her religion, rather than for a treasonable act, and she was possibly the most tranquil person in that great crowded chamber as she entered it, quite alone. The Earl of Kent had arrived along with a few other gentlemen, and he and Shrewsbury, as the official witnesses, were seated prominently on stools at one end of a square platform, which also contained the block. Mary smiled a little as she approached them, and asked that her ladies might be allowed to enter the room to assist her as she disrobed. Kent refused brusquely, but Shrewsbury explained they had been disallowed for two reasons – one was that they might scream and cry out and disrupt the proceedings as well as making things worse for the Queen herself; and secondly it was feared that they might try to dip their handkerchiefs in her blood as mementoes. Mary gave him her solemn word that they would do neither, and Shrewsbury agreed that two of her ladies and five of her gentlemen might be admitted.[14]

Poor Shrewsbury. It was he who had the responsibility of signalling to the executioner when to strike the blow against this woman who had shared his home for sixteen years, and whom he had seen in weakness and strength, gaiety and despair. And he had to watch as the first blow merely sliced into the back of Mary's head, causing her to moan. A second blow was needed to sever the head from the body. When all was over and the executioner held up Mary's head, Kent called out loudly, 'Such be the end of all the Queen's enemies, and all the Gospel's enemies.' Shrewsbury could not speak, even to utter the obligatory 'Amen', and it was noted that tears were coursing down his face. His son Henry, with whom he had stayed the previous night, set off for London immediately to carry the news to Burghley. By the next day the execution was known about at Court, and when the Queen heard she became hysterical, alternately weeping torrents of noisy tears and throwing furious rages.

Walsingham absented himself from Court and was said to be 'ill' at home. Burghley and Leicester were banished. Letters from Burghley begging the Queen to allow him to come and sit at her feet were returned unopened, marked 'not received'. It was four months before he was forgiven, and for weeks Elizabeth would not speak to any of the members of the Privy Council who had put their signatures to the document ordering the execution to take place. Eventually she came to accept that they had only acted out of loyalty and, albeit mistakenly, in her interests. Most of the men concerned were aged, and there was no question of anyone seeking self-advancement; they were already at the pinnacle of their chosen careers, and Shrewsbury was entirely loyal and harmless. But she remained deeply angry that they had acted without her express sanction, and although the deed could not be recalled, she saw no harm in making them suffer.

At the end of March, Walsingham was back at Court, reporting to his correspondents that 'behind my back Her Majesty gives out very hard speeches of myself'.[15] Shrewsbury was ordered to Court where Bess was in attendance in the Privy Chamber and the Bedchamber. Shrewsbury kicked his heels for some days before being called into the presence. By this time he would have been fully aware of the Queen's fury towards all those concerned in the summary execution of Queen Mary, and anxious to give his side of the story.

But this was not why he had been summoned; the Queen wanted to discuss his marriage. Bess had complained that Shrewsbury was still collecting her rents and not paying her any allowance. After exchanging the barest civilities with Shrewsbury, the Queen sent for Walsingham and Shrewsbury's hated daughter-in-law Mary Talbot, wife of Gilbert, who were waiting together in an ante-room. Mary was commanded 'to say what her mother desired of my Lord'.[16] Mary complied willingly, stating that all her 'old, distressed mother' wished for was to resume married life with the Earl and that she 'longed to see him'. Shrewsbury became agitated and said he was unwilling to live with his wife, who had wickedly maligned him. But the Queen had the last word; couching her wishes as a request, she obtained a grudging agreement from the Earl that he would convey his wife to Wingfield in an honourable manner. It was also agreed that he and his wife would 'keep house together and my Lord shall allow her £300 yearly and certain other provisions* for housekeeping. His Lordship shall resort thither as often as his health and leisure permit, and he is sometimes to send her to any other of his houses where he may be.'[17] Of course there was nothing new here, and one is forced to wonder why anyone thought the Earl would keep his word, since he had reneged on similar agreements made on previous occasions.

Chastened by the Queen's cool demeanour towards him over the execution of the Scottish Queen, Shrewsbury initially acquiesced. On 22 April Bess went to live at Wingfield, and the Earl made arrangements to visit her in mid-May. He spent about ten days there, and to ensure this great sacrifice was not wasted, he wrote to Walsingham advising him that he was staying with the Countess 'according to Her Majesty's request'.[18] Walsingham replied that the Queen had already heard from another source that the Shrewsburys were together at Wingfield, 'whereof she showed a

---

*Shrewsbury agreed to provide 'towards her household charges . . . twenty quarters of wheat, twenty quarters of malt, twenty beeves and forty muttons'.

very good liking for your Lordship's carefulness to satisfy her request'.[19] Unfortunately we have no record of what passed between husband and wife during that period, but if Bess hoped to win Shrewsbury back, she failed. It was probably a difficult and uncomfortable time for both parties.

The Earl was back in Sheffield in June when Burghley wrote with yet another request that Shrewsbury help to relieve Gilbert's debts. Burghley reminded the Earl of a private conversation they had had in his coach two years earlier, when Shrewsbury had promised to help his son. 'Think it is your honour, that your son live in honour and reputation. I myself have a son or two. I assure your Lordship that which they expend in honest sort to be my comfort, as it was my own expense. We fathers must take comfort of our children, to see and provide for them, to live agreeable to our comfort. But my good Lord, accept that my writing is meant as well for the honour of an Earl of Shrewsbury as for a Lord Talbot.'[20] Gilbert was not the only one of Shrewsbury's sons in severe financial difficulties. Henry Talbot, too, found he could not live on the allowance made by his father, and that summer he was another supplicant, asking for permission to be allowed to lease some of his properties to raise money to pay his debts.

The Earl's response was predictable: he did nothing to help either son, or to pay Bess's living expenses at Wingfield and, despite his apparent compliance with the Queen's orders, he continued to malign his wife and her daughter. He wrote to Gilbert telling him not to expect 'any more at my hands than I have already allowed you whereof I know you might live well, and clear from any danger as I did, if you had that government over your wife and her pomp and courtlike manner of life was somewhat assuaged . . . I wish you had but half so much [money] as she and her mother have spent in seeking through malice, my overthrow and dishonour, and I in defending my just cause.'[21]

From a study of her letters and suits over a period of four years, it appears that Bess genuinely wished to be reconciled with her husband, despite his illness. But, equally, it must have been evident to this intelligent woman that she was not going to win Shrewsbury round, even without Mary, Queen of Scots to complicate matters between them. She now began to devote her energies to building projects at Hardwick and another family matter of some significance.

With the death of the Queen of Scots, only one person, King James of Scotland, stood nearer to the English throne than did the Lady Arbella Stuart. In the summer of 1587 the Queen invited eleven-year-old Arbella to Court, and the girl went with Gilbert and Mary Talbot. Sir Charles Cavendish was staying with them and soon after her arrival, Sir Charles wrote to his mother that Arbella had made her curtsey at Court and that Her Majesty had twice spoken to her but had not questioned her about her books as expected. She had also had dined several times in the Queen's presence at Theobalds, Burghley's country estate.[22]

Sir Walter Ralegh was present at one of these dinners to which Arbella was invited, escorted by Charles. Burghley 'highly commended' Arbella to Sir Walter, saying that she spoke French and Italian, played several instruments, danced well, sewed and wrote 'very fair'. He said he wished she were fifteen years old (of marriageable age) and cuffed Sir Walter playfully. Ralegh entered into the spirit of the evening, and agreed, whispering, 'it would be a happy thing'.[23] Indeed, Burghley paid Arbella a marked attention throughout that supper, and he did so again on the following afternoon 'in his Great Chamber, publicly . . . And,' Sir Charles wrote confidently to Bess, 'since he has asked . . . she shall come again.'

The Queen had not formally recognised Arbella's claim, but it seems that Burghley was hedging his bets. Although not yet in her teens, Arbella had already been suggested in marriage to a number of notables – Leicester's son, and Esme Stuart, for example. And if we are to believe Mary, Queen of Scots, Bess had even suggested King James of Scotland as well. In his despatch to Paris during Arbella's visit to Court, the French Ambassador wrote that if King James were to be excluded from the succession because of his foreign birth (Scotland), then Arbella was the natural inheritor of the throne of England.[24]

(Indeed, in 1588, just prior to the launch of the Spanish Armada, there was a serious proposition by King Philip, through his envoy Mendoza, that Arbella should marry the Duke of Palma's son.* This so alarmed King James that he wrote to Elizabeth insisting that Arbella should not be allowed to marry anyone without his express consent. The girl was certainly a personage to be watched, especially after the Queen told the French Ambassador's wife during a dinner at which Arbella was present, 'look to her well. She will one day be even as I am and a lady mistress. But I will have gone before.')

Arbella was special to Bess but she loved all her grandchildren, her 'jewels', as she always referred to them, so Charles also wrote of four-year-old Alathea, Gilbert and Mary's youngest daughter, who had charmed the Court: 'she is so merry and talkative, and as pretty a child as any is'. It was a long chatty letter, full of details of the décor at Theobalds, and Court and family news: Sir William, he reported, was ill with a crick in the neck, and Mary was now recovered from her indisposition and had also been to Theobalds where the Queen had been 'exceedingly gracious' to her. The Queen 'talked much about your Ladyship', and said she 'would speak to the Lords [Burghley and Leicester] herself' about Bess's problems with Shrewsbury 'and promised these things should be finished'.[25]

Despite this promise, little further was done at any official level and six months later Bess was still writing to tell Burghley that her husband was not providing the money for her living expenses, as ordered, and had visited her only three times during that year. Nor had he provided the basic necessities of living at Wingfield, such as firewood for the great fireplaces, as he had promised the Queen he would.

In fact, the Earl was bedridden, suffering from gout in his feet,

---

*Palma was Commander in Chief of Spain's armies, and was regarded as the greatest general of the age.

which made it impossible to walk, and arthritis in his hands which he told Burghley was now 'almost comfortless'. Nevertheless, in November the Queen wrote asking Shrewsbury to muster soldiers from among his tenants to aid the Earl of Huntingdon, her lieutenant in the north, who was raising an army in the event of a possible attack by the Scots in revenge for the execution of Queen Mary. Shrewsbury replied that he had feared no recovery from his illness until the warmer weather in the spring, but that the Queen's request had 'quickened his vital spirits' and given him new strength. Burghley tried again to obtain some financial help for Gilbert's debt, which was, 'as a cancer growing. You charge him [Gilbert] with being in league with his "fast friend" your wife, but I know that he has always laboured for her reconciliation with you.'[26] But it was as useless as ever to attempt to bring Shrewsbury round; he was completely obsessed with the belief that the extravagance of his children was bringing him to bankruptcy, and that they were constantly encouraged in this extravagance by his wicked wife. This did not prevent the Earl from enjoying a noble lifestyle at Sheffield. That Christmas, in one week, his reduced household consumed '3 quarters of wheat, 441 gallons of beer, 12 sheep, 10 capons, 26 hens, 7 pigs, 6 geese, 7 cygnets, 1 turkey and 118 rabbits'.[27]

The death of Mary, Queen of Scots had not improved relations with Spain and during the winter Elizabeth and her ministers received incontrovertible intelligence that Spain was preparing to attack England with a great fleet of ships. In February 1588 Walsingham wrote to Shrewsbury that the latest reports suggested the Armada would 'be ready to set forth by the end of March'.[28] By April there was a general awareness that England was going to have to fight Spain for survival, and Shrewsbury received precise instructions, as Earl Marshal of England, about mustering of men and their deployment, pointing out some 'defaults' in his arrangements to date. The letter was signed by Lord Chancellor Hatton, Lords Burghley, Leicester and Howard, and Sir Francis Walsingham and Sir Thomas Heneage, all members of the Privy Council who were undoubtedly aware that Shrewsbury was in no fit state, either physically or mentally, to be of real assistance. Yet the office of Earl Marshal was a lifetime appointment. Leicester was Shrewsbury's deputy, and it is evident from surviving documents that in the spring of 1588 it was Leicester who was acting as Earl Marshal and not Shrewsbury.[29]

By June a state of national emergency existed, and Shrewsbury was ordered, as Lord Lieutenant of Derbyshire and Staffordshire, to assemble the gentlemen of the counties and get them to furnish as many men as they could for the imminent defence of 'country, liberty, wife, children, lands . . . and for the profession of the true and sincere religion of Christ'.[30] In July, Gilbert advised his father not to come to London unless specifically sent for. Gilbert had hoped that his father's offices might revert to him for the period of the emergency, but his great champion Lord Burghley was ill, and so could not help to propel this scheme. Shrewsbury found some occupation, during this tense time, seeking out and apprehending Jesuits in Derbyshire.

This pursuit became another obsession, but he could also still act with great courtesy and presence. He wrote to the Queen offering his services to resist the invasion, saying that though he realised he was old, the Queen's quarrel with Spain would make him young again, and though he was lame in body he was 'lusty in heart to lend her greatest enemy one blow, and to live and die in her service'.[31]

Queen Elizabeth received this letter on the eve of the most critical hour of her reign. After a heavy engagement in the Solent on 4 August, the damaged but undefeated Armada moved up the English Channel to anchor on 6 August in the treacherous currents of the roads off Calais while they waited for promised reinforcements. On 15 August the Queen inspected the English Army at Tilbury and made her stirring rallying call. She had originally intended to go to Dover, but Leicester would not allow her to put herself in such danger.

That night, Leicester reported to Shrewsbury that the Queen's speech had 'so inflamed the hearts' of everyone present that 'I think the weakest person among them is able to match the proudest Spaniard'.[32] Elizabeth was obviously moved by Shrewsbury's eve-of-battle letter, and when all danger was passed, she replied affectionately, addressing the Earl as 'My very good old man' and thanking him.

Only a few days later, at the moment of her greatest triumph, the Queen lost the man whom she trusted above all others, and on whom she had come totally to depend. Robert Leicester, who had been in poor health for some time* died on 4 September 1588, aged fifty-five, while on his way to take the waters at Buxton. He had always been a friend to the Shrewsburys, helping both of them and never taking sides throughout the years of strife. The loss of a direct intimate channel to Queen Elizabeth, as well as a friend, was a double blow to both Bess and the Earl.

Shrewsbury's letter of congratulation to the Queen on the victory over the Spanish fleet, sent before he heard of Leicester's death, was answered sombrely:

> although we do accept and acknowledge your careful mind and good will, yet we desire rather to forbear the remembrance thereof, of a thing whereof we can admit no comfort, otherwise by submitting our will to God's inevitable appointment. Who, notwithstanding His goodness by the former prosperous news, hath nevertheless been pleased to keep us in exercise by the loss of a personage so dear unto us.[33]

Despite the alarms that summer, Arbella had been summoned to Court again in June 1588. Now in her thirteenth year, she was courted and petted, but she also made some enemies if an account written fifteen years afterwards is to be believed. On her way to chapel one day, Arbella apparently took a position at the head of the

*Probably a heart condition.

procession, in the place of a princess, ahead of ladies of rank. When asked to step back by the Master of Ceremonies, she is said to have insisted that this place was 'the very lowest position that could be given her'.[34] The Earl of Essex (nineteen-year-old stepbrother to that 'noble imp' to whom as a baby Arbella had been betrothed), the Queen's latest favourite, came to Arbella's aid by 'saluting' her publicly when people stood aghast at such arrogance. Later, the Queen described Arbella as 'an eaglet of her own kind'[35], implying that she was prepared to overlook the regrettable lapse, but nevertheless ordered the girl back home to her grandmother's care. It would be three years before Arbella was summoned to Court again.

Given the state of the country at the time (it was in the weeks leading up to the Armada invasion), and bearing in mind her value as a potential hostage to an invading force, it is likely that the Queen considered Arbella would be safer in Derbyshire with her grandmother. Elizabeth might also have been irritated, for the chapel incident coincided with the withdrawal of the proposal of the possible marriage with Palma's son. Furthermore, she is known to have been suspicious at the amount of attention shown to Arbella by the young Earl of Essex. So it was probably a combination of all these things which persuaded Elizabeth that young Arbella was simply too troublesome to have around her Court.

Bess remained at Wingfield throughout that summer of the Armada as she had promised the Queen she would, but in the autumn she took Arbella and moved to Hardwick, where she could see how her building works were progressing.

During the previous year the three-storeyed east wing had been built to include a gallery on the top floor and a suite of rooms for Bess, and eventually a second great chamber called 'The Forest Great Chamber'* was added on the top floor, with access, via a

---

*The name derives from the frieze of 'forest folk' (deer and other animals prancing amidst trees). The lifelike trees were real tree-trunks, covered in plaster and painted.

stairwell in a tower, to the leaded roof, which provided a walking area. It was an ideal place to stand and watch any hunting that was taking place at Hardwick. When Bess visited in 1588, the west wing was being rebuilt. The four storeys of this wing included a room known as 'my lady's old bedchamber', so it is obvious that existing parts of the old house were incorporated into the new design.

The Hill Great Chamber on the top floor of the west wing was the grandest room in the house. Designed for the formal entertaining of guests of the highest rank, it had spectacular views over the surrounding countryside from three sides of the room. Its bright and modern decoration, with an impressive painted overmantel of the giants Gog and Magog, led to the room often being called 'The Giants' Chamber'. Between the giants is the winged figure Desire. Those who were *au fait* with allegory knew that this was based on a Dutch engraving depicting Desire and Hope leading Patience on a triumphal chariot, with Fortune dragging behind, shackled. Modern-day scholars believe that 'this can be read as a comment on Bess's situation. She is Patience, who desires to triumph over the iniquities of her husband, and defeat cruel Fortune, who had put so many obstacles in her way'.[36] But this message was only clear to those who were familiar with the original work. Perhaps the light she was able to achieve in this room, arguably one of the most impressive rooms Bess ever built in her life, formed her ideas for a new project; one which would be associated with her name through four centuries, but one which lay in the future for her at that point.

Bess did not visit Hardwick often that year. Although it was only an hour's ride from Wingfield,* under her agreement with the

---

*Hardwick is approximately seven miles from Wingfield. This has led researchers to wonder whether the old Hall at Hardwick was ever visited by Mary, Queen of Scots while taking exercise during the time she was imprisoned at Wingfield.

Queen she was supposed to remain at Wingfield waiting for her husband. Meanwhile, though Shrewsbury visited rarely, every move Bess made was reported to the Earl by his bailiff, William Dickenson, or William's sons Gilbert and John. Perhaps knowing when his wife had ridden over to Hardwick helped Shrewsbury in some way to feel he had a measure of control over her.[37]

Bess was well aware she was being watched, for she too had her agents among the servants. She knew, from her steward Nicholas Kinnersley, that during one such absence Gilbert Dickenson had turned up and questioned her servants about her movements. When had the Countess left Wingfield, he asked, and when she was due back? 'What is the meaning of the questions ... I know not,' Kinnersley wrote to Bess, 'except it be to bring my Lord words of your absence here so that he might come upon you sudden and find you away'.[38] Bess already knew that a boy dressed in a green coat had come from Sheffield Manor late one night and asked similar questions of the stable hands.

She also knew, that autumn, that the relationship between her husband and his housekeeper, Eleanor Britton, was far more than that of master and servant. Probably the information that the Earl 'doated' upon Mistress Britton came via Gilbert and Mary, who kept in constant touch with Bess, writing her long letters containing the latest news from Court and elsewhere, and always signing themselves, 'Your Ladyship's most humble and obedient loving children'.

Eleanor Britton was not new to the Earl's employment. Gilbert would later testify that she had worked for the Earl for eleven years prior to his death (since just about the time that the Shrewsbury marriage began to fall apart, in fact), but her name first crops up in a letter from Bailiff Dickenson in 1586. On that occasion Dickenson complained that she had baked some venison pasties with so much wine that they had broken up on his way to Sheffield. It sounds as though Shrewsbury may have found a jolly lass with whom to console himself in his last years. Eleanor Britton had probably been the Earl's mistress for a number of years, hence Shrewsbury's continued resistance to returning to his wife. And perhaps it is no coincidence that the Queen wrote to Shrewsbury again that December, urging him to allow Bess to see him sometimes which, she wrote, was his wife's dearest wish.

Surviving papers reveal the mountain of work involved in the administration of the Earl's estates, with leases, tenancies, disputes over grazing and other commoners' rights, the mining and sale of lead and coal, as well as his persistent persecution of local Catholics. In his last years, Shrewsbury's management was inconsistent. Often in great pain, he apparently spent much of his time working on the design for his own tomb.* The effigy lying on the marble sarcophagus depicts the Earl as the warrior he had perhaps been in his youth, wearing plate armour. It is bareheaded, with the helmet placed alongside, and at its feet is the inevitable Talbot.† Four years earlier he had commissioned John Foxe the martyrologist[39] to draft a long memorial inscription in Latin, omitting any reference to the Earl's second wife – the Earl undoubtedly supplied the content for the text.[40] This was carved on to a massive stone with a blank space left for the date of death to be added. Shrewsbury observed mournfully that he would not be surprised if his children forgot to complete the inscription. In this he guessed correctly.

In May 1589, following the death of Peter Barlow of Barlow, the late owner of the Barlow estates, Shrewsbury held a meeting at Worksop with Barlow's son and heir Anthony Barlow and the executors and, as a result, purchased the Barlow estates.[41] It was from this estate that Bess had been receiving the 'widow's third' dower ever since the death of her first husband forty-five years earlier. But the effects of the dower obligations, several wardships, and perhaps periods of bad management, too, had brought the

*In what is now Sheffield Cathedral.
†A Norman breed of hunting dog.

once healthy Barlow lands into a parlous position. The Barlow estate abutted some of Shrewsbury's land and included some profitable lead mines, the products from which could be exploited by Shrewsbury's ships and sales network. The price he paid was high, £8000, and he also took over debts totalling £7000, as well as responsibility for meeting Bess's dower payments until her death.[42] 'Queer what a dear purchase Barley is', Gilbert would write wonderingly, when he came to check the details after his father's death.

Bess's various sources of income from previous husbands had given her financial independence, which can only have been an irritant to Shrewsbury during their marital disputes. There seems little doubt that Shrewsbury purchased the Barlow estates, despite the disadvantageous price, in order to get back at his wife in some way, and perhaps to secure a measure of control over her revenues.

In July, Gilbert and Mary Talbot wrote a long, dutiful letter to Bess containing Court news, and ending with the welcome information that the Queen had particularly asked after Lady Arbella.[43] But still Arbella was not invited to Court.

That winter Shrewsbury and Bess were now sixty-two years old, but whereas Bess was as vigorous as ever, the Earl regarded himself as, and was perceived as, an old man. It was a bitterly cold winter, and Shrewsbury suffered torments of pain. In February, a 'humble and faithful poor friend', who did not sign his name, wrote to tell Shrewsbury of a rumour that the Countess and Arbella were intending to spend the summer in London. 'My Lord, if you could find the means she might bring all her train with her, young and old . . .' and this, the writer pointed out, would mean Shrewsbury would not have to see her, or be troubled with her in Derbyshire for many months, which 'I would think it the better for your Lordship'.[44]

Bess did not go to Court that year, 1590; as for Shrewsbury, most things were already beyond him. Living in a small house at Hanworth with his housekeeper and mistress, his children banned from calling on him by his own decree, and separated from all who might have otherwise cared for his welfare, he was gradually fading from life. Somewhat surprisingly, after refusing to speak to Gilbert's wife Mary for years, in the spring of 1590 he suddenly wrote her a friendly letter when he heard she was ill. Gilbert endorsed it wonderingly – 'My father's kind letter to my wife.'[45] Shrewsbury reported that he was ill, and still so weakened by gout that he was unable to stand without support.[46] The death, a month later, of Sir Francis Walsingham, worn out in his devoted service to Elizabeth, and in debt having spent his entire fortune running his intelligence network,[*] robbed Shrewsbury of one of his most devoted correspondents. Such letters as he and Burghley wrote to each other that summer were those of old men swapping tales of symptoms, ill health and medications.

By August Shrewsbury was totally bedridden, and on 24 September he seemed to be rambling when he told an old and loyal servant 'with almost tears in his eyes that he feared the Lady Arbella would bring much trouble in his house by his wife's and her daughter's devices . . . my wife and her daughter are dealing with the heralds about matters which must be kept from me, for at this time I am a great block in their way. I know Gilbert Talbot will be too much ruled by them – for they do with him what they [wish] and so I have told his friends, but they will not help . . . I will go to the Queen this next spring if I go but two miles a day.'

The Queen was against Gilbert, he said, because of those matters in which his son had taken Bess's side against the Earl in respect of Lady Arbella, who was treated by his wife and her daughter as a superior being, 'but now it is otherwise . . . for they have been advised by their friends that it was misliked'.[47]

Even during this last stage of Shrewsbury's life Bess was still agitating with the great and the good to effect a reconciliation. On

---

[*]Walsingham had to be buried at night to save the expense of a costly funeral, and against the possibility of a creditor kidnapping the body and holding it to ransom.

12 October that year the Earl received a letter from the Bishop of
Coventry and Lichfield, following a visit made by the prelate to
Sheffield. The Bishop reminded the Earl that during their discussions he had already advised him to return to his wife. Now he
urged Shrewsbury again, for his own sake, to return to Bess. He
cited the teachings of St Paul:

> . . . and this doctrine Christ himself confirmed, when he forbade
> all men to put away their wives unless for adultery, a thing never
> suspected in my Lady your wife . . . It must . . . remain a great
> clog and burden to your conscience to live asunder from the
> Countess without her own good liking and consent thereto . . .
>
> Some will say in your Lordship's behalf that the Countess is a
> sharp and bitter shrew . . . indeed, My Lord, I have heard some
> say so, but if shrewdness or sharpness may be a just cause for
> separation between a man and wife, I think very few men in
> England would keep their wives long . . . it is a common jest that
> there is but one shrew in all the world and every man hath
> her . . .
>
> Peradventure, some of your friends will object greater matter
> against her; as that she has sought to overthrow your whole
> house. But those that say so I think are not your Lordship's
> friends, but rather Her Ladyship's enemies, and their speech car-
> ries no resemblance of the truth.[48]

But by then it was already too late to make representations to
Shrewsbury. There are a number of surviving letters that were written to him in October and early November 1590, but none written
by him, for during this period he was seriously ill at Sheffield. He
died at seven o'clock on the morning of 18 November 1590, and
Eleanor Britton and her nephew immediately began gathering up as
many portable items of value as they could lay hands on.

News of Shrewsbury's death would not have reached the Queen
and her Court for several days. In the meantime, on 19 November, a

courtier wrote to Gilbert to tell him what had happened that very day. Mary Talbot had been at Court with their favourite daughter, six-year-old Alathea, a highly intelligent and 'forward' child, and 'If I should write how much her Majesty did this day make of the little lady your daughter . . . often kissing [her], which her Majesty seldom useth to any, and then amending her dressing with pins, and . . . carrying her to her own barge, and so into the Privy lodgings, and so homeward . . . you would scarcely believe me. Her Majesty said, as true it is, that she is very like my lady her grandmother [Bess]. She behaved herself with such modesty as I pray God she may possess at twenty years old'.[49]

This sign of almost excessive favour shown to Bess's granddaughter is further evidence that Bess still enjoyed the Queen's confidence, and her friendship. Some previous biographers have written of clashes of temperament between these two strong women, and of the Queen losing patience with Bess, but though I searched diligently for evidence of this, I could find none whatsoever. Nor are any sources cited for this conjecture by previous biographers. It seems fair to conclude that the earliest suggestions of this were ventured by her first biographer some 200 years after her death, and must have been copied from one book to another until it became received wisdom. It would certainly have been out of character for Bess, who was a clever woman and sure-footed in her personal relationships, and if she had disagreed with Elizabeth she was far too sensible to have done so openly. Her demeanour, in her own letters to the Queen and in her behaviour at Court, according to reports by others, was always modest, loyal and exemplary. Undoubtedly she flattered the Queen, and we know she gave costly and sumptuous gifts. It is more likely that Bess attempted to exploit the Queen's almost maternal feeling towards her subjects in pleading for her help with Shrewsbury and his all too obvious mood swings.

Whatever the truth of Bess's feelings towards Shrewsbury, his death freed her in many ways. She was free of the obsessive and wearisome delusions of a mentally ill husband that had dogged her life for seven or eight years, and this can only have come as a relief. She was again mistress of her own lands and incomes from the Barlow, Cavendish and St Loe estates. And as the widow of the late Earl, she was further entitled to one-third of the income from the Shrewsbury estates (said to be £3000 per annum in the mid-1590s),[50] as well as her entitlement under her pre-nuptial agreement – the marriage jointure – which gave her a life interest in a number of properties belonging to the Shrewsbury estate.

No copy of the marriage jointure has survived; however, we know from the properties which Bess used during the remainder of her life that she was clearly entitled to live in, and exploit, Bolsover Castle and its coal mines, and Wingfield Manor (where she had spent the last few years – ostensibly, at least – in the hope that she would be reconciled with her husband), together with its lead mines, glass works and forge.[51] There were several other smaller Shrewsbury properties in Derbyshire and Yorkshire. And in addition she had Shrewsbury House at Chelsea.

Next to Queen Elizabeth herself, Bess was now the richest – and therefore the second most powerful – woman in England.

Sir William St Loe in his tilt armour, 1560

Sir William St Loe. A detail from a drawing of the coronation process by an unknown herald

Sir William St Loe, Captain of the Queen's personal Yeoman Guard, leads his men from the Tower at the coronation procession in 1559

Lady Katherine, Jane Grey's sister, with her son Edward, Lord Beauchamp.
Bess's friendship with the Grey sisters would get her into trouble

A needlework cushion of the sacrifice of Isaac, with the figures wearing Elizabethan court dress.
The women (*right*) were thought to be Bess and her ladies

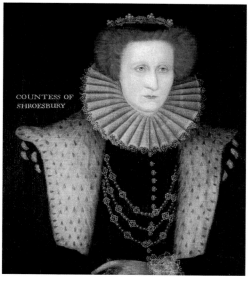

A portrait of Bess, aged forty, painted shortly after her marriage to the Earl of Shrewsbury

Detail of tapestry at Hardwick with the head of Zenobia, the warrior queen of ancient Syria, looking remarkably like Bess

George, 6th Earl of Shrewsbury, Earl Marshal of England and Bess's fourth husband, c.1567

Margaret Douglas, Countess of Lennox. Granddaughter of King Henry VII, and mother of Henry, Lord Darnley, the murdered husband of Mary, Queen of Scots

Margaret Douglas, Countess of Lennox, with her family. The effigy on the bier is that of Lord Darnley; the small boy in the foreground is King James VI of Scotland, son of Mary, Queen of Scots and Lord Darnley. Behind the Countess is Charles Stuart, Bess's son-in-law and the father of Arbella

Mary, Queen of Scots, when she was Queen of France, the most beautiful princess in Christendom

A page of ciphers used by Mary, Queen of Scots for secret correspondence, while she was imprisoned by the Shrewsburys. Both the Shrewsburys appear on the list

Contemporary drawing of the execution of Mary, Queen of Scots. Bess's husband (shown seated in right-hand chair at top of page) wept openly at the death of his former prisoner

Tutbury Castle, one of the Shrewsburys' massive homes, where Mary, Queen of Scots was imprisoned for various periods from 1569

Elizabeth, Countess of Hardwick, *c.*1585. [inset] George, 6th Earl of Shrewsbury, 1582.
A martyr to 'gout', he became a pernickety and bitter old man.
Compare his appearance here with his earlier portrait

The 7th Earl and Countess of Shrewsbury: Gilbert Talbot and his wife Mary Cavendish, Bess's youngest daughter

The Lady Arbella Stuart. Bess called her 'my jewell', but the rebellious orphan became the bane of Bess's old age

Sir William Cavendish, Bess's second (and favourite) son who inherited her estates and became the 1st Earl of Devonshire

Robert Cecil, later Lord Salisbury. He took over from his father, Lord Burghley, and was a staunch friend and supporter of Bess and her family

The only known image of Bess in old age, c.1601

The Long Gallery at Hardwick

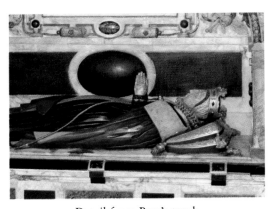

Detail from Bess's tomb

Bess of Hardwick's
magnificent tomb
in Derby Cathedral

CHAPTER 18

THE DOWAGER COUNTESS

1590–2

WITHIN TWO DAYS OF HIS FATHER'S DEATH, GILBERT
Shrewsbury was astonished to find that he had inherited an estate
that was starved of cash.[1] The huge sums the 6th Earl had expended
in sixteen years of guarding Mary, Queen of Scots, had undoubtedly begun a downward slide of his former wealth. The annual
allowances to his wife and children, although not excessive given
the station of the recipients (and the payments were not always
made), drained over £4000 each year from cash reserves. Added to
this, the crippling building costs of Worksop Manor, his new house
in London with its own tennis court, some loss-making purchases
(such as the Barlow estate), and the poor management of his estates
generally for the last half decade had brought the 6th Earl to the
poor financial state which he had so often bewailed, but no one had
believed.

Five years earlier, in desperation, Gilbert had tried unsuccessfully
to persuade his father to make a settlement upon himself and his
brothers. At that time he had assessed his father's income at
£10,000 a year,[2] and since the old Earl had not been known for

spending, except for the building of Worksop, it followed that he must have hoarded his money.

Gilbert knew what to look for. One huge deep chest, which stood at the side of the late Earl's bed, and was moved about with him when he travelled, should have contained up to £8000 in silver. Gilbert found it empty. There were also two black coffers in which the Earl always kept his gold: 'one,' Gilbert stated, 'would contain about £10,000 in gold'. It was found to contain only £200 and some empty moneybags; the other coffer was completely empty.[3]

Even if there was no saved cash there should have been, at the very least, money from rents received during the past quarter. Gilbert called in auditors after concluding that 'a great store of money was in great quantities stolen'.[4]

Nor was money the only missing asset. Sheffield had been stripped of virtually every portable item of value. All the family jewellery – rings, bracelets, gold chains, a watch, brooches of diamonds and rubies, and crystal had gone, as had gold coins, gold and silver objects such as basins and models in gold, a valuable striking clock, rooms-full of furniture and bedding, cattle and even the leases of land and properties, the whole worth many thousands of pounds.

Gilbert did not have to look far for the culprit. Eleanor Britton had left Sheffield immediately the old Earl breathed his last. She was found living with her nephew, Thomas, in her own richly appointed house which was stuffed with 'gifts' from the old Earl.

Gilbert made a brief raid on Mrs Britton's house and confiscated what he could lay hands on, but it was a token incident, and he was forced to resort to the law and issue a suit against 'these impudent clamorous persons' for the return of a long list of items which had, he claimed, been 'unscrupulously appropriated . . . My Lord my father was generally esteemed to be mean with his money, plate and jewels, whereof [Eleanor Britton] by opportunity of her attendance, and his indisposition and weakness, for a year before his death, embezzled so great a quantity of it, it was found that what remained was not much more than sufficient to defray the trappings for his funeral.'[5] Eleanor Britton was 'a stranger' who had come from Norfolk eleven years earlier, he continued, and even though everyone knew she had been the Earl's mistress for some years, 'she had no reason to expect so great a recompense as she pretends to be given to her'.[6]

He claimed that Britton had sent a huge quantity of valuable plate to London to be repaired or exchanged, but that it had never come back to his father. Mistress Britton boldly countersued for the return of the confiscated goods, insisting that the late Earl had given her everything she had removed from Sheffield. And indeed, he may well have done so, such was his mental state and his absolute dependence on Britton at the end. He had refused to admit any of his children or other relatives in his final months. And though he was known never to part with lands or other capital assets, his will made in May 1590, six months before his death, left lands and farms to loyal members of staff such as Dickenson, and he left money to various charities. The will was properly signed and witnessed.[7]

Having tried threats, which had no effect, Gilbert tried cajolery. If Mistress Britton would return everything, he offered, he would give her a new russet gown, £1000 in gold, and find good horses for her and her men.[8] Needless to say, since Eleanor Britton now had the money to fight Gilbert in the courts, his offer was rejected. The matter was still being contested five years later, but he never managed to recover all the items he believed had been stolen.

Worse was to come for Gilbert. The will named his two younger brothers, Edward and Henry, as executors, with Lord Burghley, Lord Derby and a few other trusted contemporaries as supervisors. Gilbert, so long estranged, was mentioned only in passing, although of course he was the sole heir to all the entailed properties and could not be disinherited, and the late Earl had specifically bequeathed a thousand pounds each to Gilbert's three daughters. When the extent of the financial problem was realised, both

Edward and Henry declined to accept the role of executor. Bess was asked to be sole executrix at the suggestion of the supervisors, though this would have appalled her dead husband. Had she been allowed to carry out this task, Bess's aptitude for financial order and administration would probably have helped Gilbert; but now that he had the title Earl of Shrewsbury, he had no intention of being reliant on his stepmother. He contested the matter and Bess could not be bothered to fight it. Gilbert therefore took on the duties of sole executor.

The Earl's body had been embalmed and his funeral did not take place until 10 January 1591. It was on the scale of a State funeral, as befitted a man regarded by many as a prince of the Peakland. Despite the lack of money in the estate, and the animosity his father had shown to him in life, Gilbert seems to have been determined that this funeral would be remembered in the area for centuries to come. With the assistance of the Heralds he drew on the records of funerals such as those of Mary, Queen of Scots and the Earls of Derby and Rutland when making the arrangements.[9] Bess played little part in the organisation of this event, but, accompanied by Arbella, she attended the service, the two women waiting inside the church of St Peter and St Paul until the great procession arrived there. Nothing like it had ever been seen before, according to a contemporary writer, 'and the assembly to see the same was marvellous, both of nobility, gentry and country folks, and poor people without number'.[10] It is reckoned that 20,000 people watched or attended, and that of these some 8000 poor onlookers received the funeral dole of bread and one penny, although as many again wished for the dole and could not be served. Three men were killed when a tree they had climbed fell and crushed them.

By the date of his father's funeral Gilbert had fallen out with almost every member of his family and many of his former friends. He had quarrelled with his two younger brothers almost immediately – as families often will when an estate is involved. Later he would claim that his brothers had cheated him out of £10,000 when he 'compounded' with them over his father's estate.[11] After one violent argument he formally accused his brother Edward of attempting to murder him with poisoned gloves.[12] Gilbert had undoubtedly suffered a grievous blow. He had been in debt for years, and probably these debts had been allowed to run on by his creditors because of Gilbert's great expectations. Now it appeared that he had inherited no money and further debts, and Gilbert had lost his sense of humour.

There are quarrels recorded with his mother's family, the Manners of Rutland and Haddon Hall in Derbyshire, over lands that had come to the Shrewsburys on her marriage; with his neighbours, such as Mr Wortley of Wortley, over land boundaries; with his own tenants, when he pursued an aggressive policy of increasing rents across the board; with Lady Talbot (the former Anne Herbert, widow of the late Francis, Lord Talbot, Gilbert's elder brother), over the nonpayment of her widow's dower; and with Bess, when he withheld not only the monies due to her as widow of the Earl of Shrewsbury but the dower monies from the Barlow estates. There was also disagreement between Gilbert and John Stanhope, a friend at Court. Initially Stanhope had written of his sadness on hearing of the old Earl's death, but offering his hearty congratulations to Gilbert on succeeding to the title. And at Gilbert's request, Stanhope watched out for Gilbert's interests in the matter of his succeeding to the honorary titles, especially that of Earl Marshal of England, held by Gilbert's father and grandfather.[13] But Stanhope was to become Gilbert's bitterest enemy. Charles Cavendish was almost the only person with whom Gilbert did not fall out.

Bess had befriended Gilbert for years, and had supported him and her daughter when the old Earl had refused to do so. This had taken the form of small cash gifts; she had never paid Gilbert's debts nor encouraged him in his excessive expenditure. Now, despite all the letters professing love, friendship and loyalty that Gilbert and Mary had written to Bess for the past decade, Gilbert

began to regard Bess in much the same light as he had formerly
regarded his father – as a hindrance to his aims in life: her rights as
a widow entitled her to one-third of his income.

When she learned of Gilbert's situation, Bess seems to have made
an honest attempt to come to some sort of 'good agreement' with
him. She had two meetings with Gilbert's agents, but the agreements they reached were not upheld by Gilbert. At the request of
Gilbert and Mary, a third meeting was arranged, in which they
were represented by Jarvis* Markham, a kinsman whom Bess
respected. Bess began by telling Markham that there seemed to be
little point in her agreeing to anything, since Gilbert had twice
reneged on the articles they had formerly agreed. Markham assured
her that he would be bound in the sum of £6000 to ensure the Earl
accepted any agreement made at this third meeting, and that she
would be paid before the end of March.

So Bess signed an agreement on 12 March 1591 detailing what
she was owed in respect of monies, lead and cattle, compromising
for the sake of a settlement. She expected to be recompensed on the
last day of March. But the date went by and she heard nothing, and
when on 12 April an old servant of Burghley's called on her on his
way to Court, she wrote a letter for him to deliver to Burghley,
explaining the situation. It was not a complaint, nor was she asking
Burghley to do anything, she was simply acquainting him with
facts. Some days earlier, she wrote, she had received a report that
Gilbert intended to pick a quarrel with her, so that he could 'break
off the agreement, though he neither misliked the sum, nor [the]
days of payment; the sum being so small in respect of my dues
that in reason he had to conclude . . . but by pretending some other
matter, he will seek to bring me in the end to nothing'. And she
concluded, 'I will be loath to speak to him [a] fourth time.'[14]

Her only redress was through the courts, and, having fought
her husband over her allowances for a decade, she was obliged

---

*Probably Gervais, a name frequently used by the Markham family.

once more to embark on a similar persistent battle with her stepson over her dower payments. Her position was now stronger, the death of the old Earl having returned to her all the Cavendish and St Loe lands that she either owned outright, or in which she had a life interest, as well as some Shrewsbury properties which had come to her as part of her marriage jointure.

But even during her husband's life she had never been poor. Bess was always adept at managing her money, no matter how little or how much she had at any one time and, just as the old Earl had claimed, she could always find enough to buy lands and properties for her children, or to commission new building projects. Her disputes with him were really about the fact that, being a hard-headed businesswoman, she wanted what was due to her under contract, even if she did not need it. It seems that she used a form of cost-centre accounting, ensuring that the revenues from an estate met the expenses of that estate, so that she could quickly spot any loss-making ventures. When she complained that the Earl had not provided firewood for Wingfield, for example, it was not that she could not afford firewood, but that the Earl was legally committed to provide it (as well as the £300 per annum expenses he had agreed to), and he did not do so. And, being Bess, she was not prepared to let him off the debt.

During the latter half of 1590, even while the old Earl was dying, Bess had not only been involved in extensive rebuilding at the Old Hall at Hardwick but was even then planning to embark upon an extravagant new building. She was also using excess revenues to offer short-term loans at good rates of interest to neighbouring landowners and her tenants in Somerset, who were hard-pressed due to poor harvests caused by an excessively cold winter followed by a wet summer.[15] She was a fair but firm landlord, and a determined adversary when crossed. To one West Country tenant she wrote, after examining his claim about the terms of his tenancy during the time of her husband's management: 'there is nothing awful done unto you; neither during my time has there ever been . . . nor before it . . . If you call the matter in question by law I shall be ready to answer it.' Advising her tenant to get his lawyer to talk to one of her sons, or her legal representatives, she ended: 'I doubt not but to satisfy you thoroughly. I have written to one Mr Baber* of Bristol, one of my learned counsels, to be ready to meet you . . .'[16]

That same year Bess acquired lands at Edensor, adjoining Chatsworth, from the Duke of Cumberland, who had defaulted on a loan she had made him to finance a merchant venture. Another property she acquired in the same way was Thomas Shakerley's lands at Little Longstone, 'and all his lands in the Peak', for the sum of £3000.

The Old Hall at Hardwick had by now taken on a completely new appearance, for during the past two years Bess had built a new wing and raised the entire building to four storeys, more than doubling its size. The front entrance led into a two-storey hall, with light from 'screens' at both ends, but despite all her work she was not content with it; she could not make it into the sort of house she really wanted. She had a life interest in two major properties: Chatsworth House, which was entailed to Henry, her disappointing eldest son, now aged forty (he had no legal heir and was presently touring in the Orient); and Wingfield Manor, where she had lived on and off for the past few years. But neither of these properties belonged to her outright, and it would have been surprising if the pragmatic and businesslike Bess had been prepared to go on investing money into houses that she could not pass on to her chosen heirs. The money she had invested in the Old Hall, on the other hand, she was not worried about, for it would eventually go to her favourite son, William, along with all those properties and chattels that were Bess's to give. He was a good, dutiful son who had never put a foot wrong and, what is more, he had a healthy son William.

---

*Attorney-at-law, Francis Baber (1565–1643) leased Sutton Court at Chew from the Shrewsburys.

Whatever hopes Bess had for founding a Cavendish dynasty were now firmly rooted in William and his family.

Bess had vision, energy and money. Now, it seems, she wanted a home of her own that was designed all of a piece, and in which she could spend a comfortable old age, yet which would offer a fit setting for the granddaughter who might yet become a Queen, and where the great and the good – not excluding Queen Elizabeth – could be entertained. She may have recalled the captivating, ethereal appearance of Longleat, with its well-illuminated rooms, for it was Smythson whom she consulted to design her a new house adjacent to the Old Hall.

Smythson's plans for the new house at Hardwick predate the old Earl's death. It is difficult to explain how Bess could have justified such an extravagant new project while complaining about the non-payment of her allowances, but she ordered the foundations dug in November 1590. She obviously knew that her husband was nearing the end of his life by then, and indeed the Earl died while the foundations were still being excavated. For years the Earl had considered himself an old man, but Bess had not finished with life and she looked forward to an exciting future. She had the new house to build, and Arbella's potential prospects were unlimited.

Today we would say that Arbella had grown up in a dysfunctional household. She had been orphaned at an early age, and throughout her childhood her grandparents had been constantly at war. Technically, Arbella lived with her loving but strict grandmother, even sleeping in her grandmother's bedchamber. Her contact with her grumpy grandfather Shrewsbury was limited, but there was that occasion when, as a three-year-old, Arbella was staying with Gilbert and Mary's family at Sheffield and the old Earl had thrown the child out and returned her to Chatsworth in a fit of rage, which must have been a frightening experience.

It is also likely that Arbella was at Chatsworth at the time when, for fear of the Earl's threats, her grandmother had to flee to Hardwick with the Cavendish family silver (a prudent move as it turns out, since it was thereby saved from Eleanor Britton). Arbella had spent a fair amount of time with Gilbert and Mary Talbot and their daughters Alathea, Mary and Elizabeth, and at other times she had spent periods with her uncles William and Charles Cavendish and their families. And sometimes, when her grandmother had been away on business matters, she had been left alone in the care of the servants and waiting gentlewomen. It could not be considered a very happy childhood – passed around as she had been – and her two visits to Court, when Arbella was petted and made much of, were probably regarded by her as high points in her life. In November 1591, however, all the unhappiness of Arbella's childhood seemed behind her when her grandmother told her they were going to London for a long visit.

The purpose of Bess's trip to London that winter was not simply to allow sixteen-year-old Arbella to experience the Christmas festivities at Court. The idea of a match between Arbella and Rainutio Farnese, son of the Duke of Palma, had been first floated several years earlier, but had been dropped when the Armada was launched. In the late summer of 1591, while Spain and England were attempting to repair diplomatic relations, the Farnese marriage proposal was revived. Burghley knew of it as early as August, when the Palma family asked for a miniature of Arbella. But by October it was being discussed more openly.[17]

Bess must have known, too. It would be a remarkable coincidence if, knowing nothing of the negotiations, Bess had suddenly begun planning a lengthy and costly stay in London. Such a marriage, though a good one, would put an end to any hopes she harboured of the English throne for Arbella, but if the Queen really favoured the match and the bride was sent to Spain as an English 'princess', then it would be to Arbella's benefit. Bess had long endeavoured to get an increase in Arbella's small State pension of £200, and she never gave up hoping that Elizabeth might declare Arbella her heir.

So the visit was conducted in considerable style, with no expense spared. Indeed, in its size and grandeur, the retinue almost resembled a royal Progress. Sir William and Sir Charles Cavendish and their respective families joined them, and Bess's account book provides details of the expenses of the entire party, including forty retainers who served the three families.

They travelled in leisurely stages. Bess and Arbella were in a great lumbering coach, pulled by teams of heavy horses. Her sons and their families travelled in their own coaches – Sir Charles had a light London coach, which probably provided a more comfortable ride, but needed constant repairs. The most senior of Bess's ladies, Mrs Digby, Mrs Abrahall and Jane Kniveton – the half-sister who had been in Bess's service for decades – travelled in horse-drawn litters. Others, such as needlewomen and Bess's stewards and secretary, rode hackney horses (forty-three horses were stabled at one overnight stop, at a cost of sixpence per horse).[18] This is a significant number of people and horses, and undoubtedly caused heads to turn and no little commotion as they passed through villages and hamlets on the high road.

Their route south lay through Nottingham, Leicester, Market Harborough, Northampton, Stony Stratford, Dunstable, St Albans and Barnet, and they took a week over it, in contrast to the times when Bess had dashed to London on horseback in three days to join Sir William Cavendish or Sir William St Loe in times of crisis. But this journey was intended to be one of pleasure and enjoyment, despite the temperatures – for sixteenth-century winters were far colder than those of the twentieth century. Horse-riders had the benefit of heat generated by their own exertions and the body heat of their horse, but unheated coaches and horse litters afforded minimal protection against icy temperatures, which is why they travelled in short stages.

Bess was in her element on this journey, surrounded by family and servitors; en route she dispensed charity with a liberal hand. To the poor in each town she invariably gave forty shillings. In the evenings waits and musicians were well paid to entertain the party while they ate. Church bells pealed in every large town through which they passed, to welcome her arrival and signal her departure. Indeed, to ensure the bells rang out a servant clad in the distinctive blue Cavendish livery rode ahead to arrange it and reward the bell-ringers appropriately.

The size of her luggage train – twelve wagons – indicates that Bess always intended to make her London visit a long one, and weeks beforehand her steward had already despatched ahead other wagonloads of furnishings, bed hangings, linen and plate. A flock of forty sheep and two fat oxen were sent south, to graze in nearby fields until required for the kitchen. Household supplies such as firewood were laid down. And travelling with Bess was a full complement of household staff: the butler, cooks and kitchen staff, who would ensure the excellence of Bess's entertaining. All this was necessary because Bess's visit was to last for nearly nine months, until the end of July 1592.

She did not intend to live at Court, or even in the city, but in the clean and healthy fresh air of rural Chelsea, at Shrewsbury House,* next to the old Palace of Chelsea which had once formed part of Queen Catherine Parr's dower. Bess opened up Shrewsbury House properly for the first time in years, and had even extended it to provide accommodation for her large party. The village of Chelsea lay some distance from London by horse, but by boat it was an easy and fast journey to any of the Thames-side palaces: Westminster, Whitehall and Greenwich downstream, and Richmond and Hampton Court upstream. The city had grown since the time when Bess had been a young housewife living there with Sir William Cavendish. Then it was still hardly larger than Roman London, and stretched from the Tower to St Paul's. Now, buildings crowded along the river bank beyond Westminster towards Chelsea, and downstream of the Tower for a mile or so in the opposite direction. Shrewsbury House

---

*Identified as standing upon the site of the present numbers 43–45 Cheyne Walk, Chelsea.

was a brick house, built around a quadrangle, and is thought to have had only three wings during Bess's time, though originally it had a fourth side, fronting the river. It was said to have had a long gallery 120 feet long, wainscoted in dark oak.[19]

Almost the first thing Bess did on arrival was to summon tailors and haberdashers to make suitable Court wardrobes. Her accounts reveal that bolts of sumptuous velvets, satins, silks and taffeta were purchased in fifty-yard lengths. This material was not only for gowns for Bess and Arbella, but also to make a New Year gift for the Queen. Customarily all courtiers presented the Queen with a New Year gift, and they vied with each other to find one that the Queen would especially notice. Bess seldom presented gold or silver items or a purse of gold coins as many did; instead she gave an item of clothing, a beautifully worked cloak, or a pair of sleeves stiff with pearls. In that December of 1591 she paid the Queen's tailor, Johns, £59. 14s. to make a gown, which was then embroidered by Parr, an embroiderer, at a cost of another £50.

There is a formal portrait of sixteen-year old Arbella made at this time. She is dressed in a white satin gown with black trimming, wearing magnificent ropes of pearls – probably her grandmother's, although Bess did give Arbella some jewels of her own as well.[*] The Lennox jewels, which, according to the will of her paternal grandmother, Margaret Lennox, should have gone to Arbella, were now known to be in Scotland, but King James showed no intention of repatriating them. In 1590 Bess had made a determined effort through Walsingham and Burghley to get these jewels for Arbella, but these representations, as in previous similar attempts, had failed. The English Ambassador reported to Burghley that he had several times approached the King and requested 'that the jewels appertaining to the Lady Arbella might be restored to her . . . nevertheless I am still

---

[*]In an inventory of her jewel coffer in 1593, Bess included several items which she superscribed 'given to my girl Arbella'. Also recorded in her account book is the purchase of '5 little jewels at 14s a piece' and 'another little one of a bee' which would be more suitable for a young girl than for Bess herself.

deferred'. By now Bess had given up the reds, blues and greens of her earlier gowns, and seems to have decided that black was the most suitable colour for the clothes of a sixty-year-old widow. There are vast quantities of black taffeta, black damask, black lace and black velvet to make gowns and headdresses, which were set off with snowy white lace and gauzy ruffs, cuffs and trimmings.

When all was ready, they took a boat to Whitehall, an ambitious conception of Cardinal Wolsey's which had been subsequently extended in a jumble of buildings from Westminster almost to what is now Trafalgar Square. It covered twenty-three acres, and boasted two thousand rooms. The huge gardens contained a tilt-yard, a tennis court built for Henry VIII, a cockpit, and Elizabeth's privy gardens beneath the windows of her suite. Close to these private apartments Elizabeth had constructed a massive banqueting hall, painted white (hence the name), which had become the centre of Court life.

The location was the same, but for Bess the Court was much changed since her previous visit. Many familiar old faces were missing: Leicester of course had been dead these three years, Walsingham had died during the previous summer and Sir Christopher Hatton[*] had died of diabetes and kidney failure (said to be in debt to the Queen to the tune of £56,000)[20] while Bess was on her journey to London. Lord Burghley, weakened by gout and other illnesses, had retired from active duty with the Queen's regretful blessing,[†] though he never retired from serving Elizabeth in reality.

There were new favourites at Court now: Leicester's stepson, Robert Devereux,[‡] the handsome young Earl of Essex (though the

---

[*]Sir Christopher Hatton had been a favourite of the Queen since she saw him performing as a young man in a Court masque. Rumour said he was the Queen's lover, and reading his passionate letters to her one can see why. He was a long-term favourite, showered by the Queen with gifts of money, properties and senior State appointments. Elizabeth referred to him as her 'bellwether'.

[†]In a letter dated 10 May 1591, Elizabeth amusingly, yet movingly, discharged her 'disconsolate, and retired sprite the hermit of Theobalds', from further attendance.

[‡]In 1590 Essex had secretly married Frances, daughter of Walsingham and the widow of Sir Philip Sidney. He was banished for a few months but was soon basking in Elizabeth's favour.

Queen was cross with him that winter over his behaviour in France, and he was made to kick his heels); and Sir Walter Ralegh, the great rival to Essex. Both of these young men were known to Bess, and she was in correspondence with each of them over inconsequential matters, such as their recommendations for people applying to join her service. Burghley's able son, Robert Cecil, had taken over as the *éminence grise* of Elizabeth's administration, and Bess made a point of making friends with him, too. These men formed the new power base around Elizabeth, but unlike Elizabeth's near contemporaries, Burghley, Walsingham, Leicester, Bromley, Hatton et al., the new men did not work together in harmony, and were constantly jealous of their own positions and advancement. For Bess, the change meant not just the loss of old friends, but the absence of powerful representatives watching out for her interests at Court, so it would have been out of character had she not found time to make new contacts during her time there.

Perhaps the Christmas gaieties were slightly less vivacious than those she recalled, for the wars in the Low Countries and the cost of defeating the Armada had greatly depleted the Exchequer. But there was dancing, at which the Queen still excelled, and there were music and masques and gambling and games. During the twelve days of feasting and religious observance the Lord of Misrule took the ambience of the Court back to the Queen's childhood in the days of Henry VIII, with gales of hilarity. In Bess's accounts there is a payment of twenty shillings to the Queen's jester, Ramsey, as a New Year tip, and a similar amount to Shenton, the fool. Plays were performed, and it is believed possible that one of Shakespeare's early plays* was put on for the Queen that Christmas; Shakespeare himself may even have performed in it. He was first mentioned as an actor in 1592,[21] and when his *Henry VI* played to packed houses at the Rose at Bankside some 16,344

---

*Plays known to have been written by Shakespeare prior to 1592 are: *Henry VI*, *Richard III*, *Two Gentlemen of Verona* and *Titus Andronicus*.

people paid to see it from the galleries alone, a figure which may be doubled to account for those who watched from the pit. Bess may not have been a regular theatregoer (as her son William was), but the fact that a former Earl of Shrewsbury was a leading character in this play might have intrigued her sufficiently to attend a performance.

In response to requests from the Palma family in Spain, there were several miniatures painted of Arbella during this London visit, one by the greatest miniaturist of all, Nicholas Hilliard, and another by Hilliard's able assistant, Rowland Lockey.[22] These exquisite works of art were the forerunners of photography, a portable way of circulating an image, and particularly useful when State marriages were being negotiated. Throughout that winter of 1591–2 the Farnese marriage was being promoted hard by the Spanish Ambassador. The Queen enjoyed manipulating foreign ambassadors, and this may have been simply a tease, for in view of recent events it seems unlikely that she would have allowed the Spanish to gain control of a potential claimant to the English throne. And it was surely no coincidence, that Christmas, that King James of Scotland should write a personal letter to Arbella from Holyrood, acknowledging for the first time their close kinship, or as he put it, 'the strict band of nature and blood, whereby we are linked to [one] another'.[23] This was an encouraging development for Bess and Arbella.

When she was not staying at Court, Bess entertained lavishly at Chelsea, and it is from the gratuities paid to the servants of her important visitors that we know who came to dine and gossip: Lady Warwick; Lady Walsingham; 'the Lady Marquess' of Northampton; Lady Sheffield;* Lady Southampton (whose husband

---

*Lady Douglas Sheffield and Robert Leicester went through a secret form of marriage which, to avoid the Queen's anger, Leicester never acknowledged. Years later he married Lettice Knollys, so he could never confess either the earlier marriage or the 'base-born' son without bastardising his son by Knollys – 'the noble imp' who was once betrothed to Arbella.

was Shakespeare's patron); Sir Fulke Greville; the Lord Chancellor; Charles Howard, the Lord Admiral; Sir William Cordell, the Master of the Rolls; Thomas Sackville (Lord Buckhurst), the Lord Treasurer; and Sir John Harington, the Queen's favourite godson.* Harington later wrote about Arbella during this period, recalling her 'good judgement . . . free from pride, vanity or affectation and the greatest sobriety in her fashion of apparel and behaviour that may be. All of which I have been myself an eye witness . . . at Chelsea, where she made me read the tale of Drusilla in *Orlando* unto her, and censured it with a gravity beyond her years'.[24]

Many of these important people were friends, but there were plenty of beloved old acquaintances of lesser importance who came to see Bess: Anthony Wingfield, for example, husband to Bess's half-sister Elizabeth Leche and a Gentleman Usher to the Queen. Wingfield carried out countless commissions at Court for Bess for decades and was one of her most frequent correspondents. Roger Manners of Haddon Hall near Chatsworth, a kinsman of the Earl of Shrewsbury and a neighbour, was a visitor; and Bess's oldest and dearest friend, the ailing Lady Cobham, called. It was probably the last time the two women ever saw each other. Bess also entertained friends who were not necessarily part of the Court scene: the first to call was a cousin Mary Scudamore, swiftly followed by old Lady Bacon and old Lady Cheek (both came to borrow money, and got it).

When the Court left Whitehall for Greenwich at Easter, Bess had further to travel but it did not stop her regular attendance. Although it is known that they met on a number of occasions during that winter of 1591–2, there is no surviving account of

---

*The son of the Sir John Harington, who went to the Tower with Elizabeth at the time of the Wyatt rebellion, and his wife Isabella (Markham). He spent years translating *Orlando Furioso* into English, and was banished from Court when some lurid early sections were passed round among the Queen's maids of honour. He completed the work in 1592 and, after presenting a magnificently bound copy of the work to the Queen, he was forgiven.

Bess's discussions with the Queen. Elizabeth had nearly always been kind to Bess, and knew her extremely well; after all, Bess had served in the Privy Chamber and the Bedchamber, on and off, for thirty years. As a young princess, Elizabeth had stood as godmother to Bess's son Henry, an obligation she never treated lightly, although Bess would surely have noted that her Henry was not regarded in the same affectionate manner as was John 'Boy Jack' Harington.

There had been a few disagreements between Bess and the Queen over the years: the Katherine Grey fiasco, hardly Bess's fault; and the marriage of Elizabeth Cavendish to the Earl of Lennox, and the secret betrothal of Arbella to Leicester's son – which were very much Bess's business. And perhaps there had been a coolness over some of the contents of the Scottish Queen's letters to Elizabeth, but the Queen trusted Bess's loyalty, and Bess was never long out of favour. Throughout the long years of wrangling with the old Earl of Shrewsbury, Elizabeth had unfailingly supported her, always referred to her kindly in letters, and spoken of her with affection and respect to Gilbert and Mary Talbot, Sir Charles Cavendish and the Wingfields. She had also regularly sent Bess a New Year gift – not by any means an axiomatic response to a gift given to her – and on occasion these gifts were more than mere tokens. One year she sent Bess a 'standing cup of 40 ounces [of silver]', an item of higher value than the Queen ordinarily gave to her courtiers.[*]

In fact, in the complete absence of any evidence to the contrary, there is no reason to suppose that these two mature women, who had many shared experiences, and were among very few survivors of their generation, were not pleased to see each other, and were not as good friends as their relative positions in life allowed them to be. Certainly they had many old friends in common, a few still living though many dead. Only one thing might have stood in the way of complete trust and friendship: Bess's aspirations for Arbella.

---

[*]Bess was given this cup in 1599, and she bequeathed it to Sir John Manners.

In this, it is likely that Elizabeth, wisely, always suspected Bess's motives.

The affairs of the Dowager Countess were, in any case, not centre stage in the spring of 1592, when all the Court could think about was an unfolding scandal. Bess Throckmorton, one of Elizabeth's ladies-in-waiting, requested leave to visit her brother in February. When she returned to her duties in April, her drastically altered appearance seemed to confirm widespread gossip that she had given birth to a child by Sir Walter Ralegh. The rumours were true; her son had been born in March. Sir Walter was away at sea that spring, but by the time he returned in June the story had come out that when her pregnancy was discovered, he and Bess Throckmorton had secretly married before he sailed. Elizabeth was incensed that one of her ladies had so disgraced herself, and was deeply wounded by Ralegh's betrayal, after he had been a chief favourite for a decade. She sent the couple to the Tower, and although they were subsequently forgiven, it was effectively the end of Ralegh's career, leaving the way clear for Robert Devereux, Earl of Essex.

It is possible that even after nine months in London Bess did not intend to return to Derbyshire; after all nothing had been decided about Arbella. But in July, London experienced the worst outbreak of plague for many years, and this forced a virtual exodus from the city. Elizabeth went on a Progress to the West Country, staying at Sudeley Castle near Cheltenham, then on to Bath and Oxford. Sudeley must have disturbed a flock of memories, for it had once been the home of her stepmother, Queen Catherine Parr, and her last husband, the Lord Admiral, who was long suspected of having been the teenage Elizabeth's lover.

By the time Bess quit Chelsea for Hardwick on the last day of July 1592, twelve days after she had paid her last visit to the Court, her accounts[25] show that she had spent a whopping £6360 during her London sojourn. It was a huge sum, larger, even, than the great debt to the State which had so weighed Bess down after the death of Sir William Cavendish. Every penny is meticulously accounted for, from lampreys at sixpence and oysters at fivepence, to the amounts paid to boatmen to convey Bess and her party to Court, or to visit one or other of the great houses in the city. Seldom did she travel alone, so that two or three vessels were hired when she visited, and when she left the Court at Greenwich for the final time, she travelled back to Chelsea in the luxurious barge owned by the Bishop of Bristol ('given to 2 of my Lord Bishop of Bristol's barge men; five shillings'), accompanied by her ladies and gentlemen who were in a flotilla of six boats. That same day she hired ten 'hackneys' to transport her servants and various goods back to Chelsea, 'at two shillings and fourpence a piece; 23s 4pence'. Her litter horses were twice ferried across the water at a cost of twenty pence, presumably to carry her to and from the Thames.[26] There were generous tips to palace servants during the five weeks she lived at Court in June and July 1592, and there were large sums paid to her lawyers 'about my Lady's law matters'. There were gratuities paid to a midwife and nurse, ten shillings each, when Bess's lady-in-waiting and long-time confidante, Mistress Elizabeth Digby,[*] gave birth. And when the child was christened Bess gave £4 and Arbella gave £2 to the baby's mother. A magnificent wedding gift of £50 was given when one of her ladies-in-waiting, Anne Cooper, married Bess's Clerk Comptroller in April that year. There were countless small gifts to her servants, and tips to tradesmen who gave good service. Bess was an appreciative and generous employer but she expected give and take and carried no passengers. And the poor were not forgotten: several times she gave 'twenty shillings to the poor of Chelsea'.[27]

Bess was born to shop, it seems, although she spent wisely and insisted on good value. As well as the bolts of materials to make clothes, there were the accessories: perfumed gloves and shoes made of costly Spanish leather, furs and fur trimmings (powdered ermine,

---

[*]Elizabeth Digby was married to John Digby, a gentleman in Bess's service. After Bess's death he became Sheriff of Nottinghamshire, and was knighted.

undoubtedly for Arbella, who with her royal connection was entitled to wear the royal fur), lace and gauzy lawn to make elaborate ruffs, jewellery and embroidered panels, pearls and crystals, hair decorations and headdresses. In the best-known portrait of Bess she wears no jewellery except five hefty ropes of pearls in graduated colours, but her jewel casket contained such items as 'a cross of diamonds; a girdle of goldsmith's work of gold, pearls and emeralds; a ring with a great ruby; a chain of gold, pearls and a pomander; a great diamond . . .'[28]

Nor was her new house forgotten; Bess shopped for the New Hall at Hardwick as enthusiastically as any woman today would shop in London when decorating a new home. Among her purchases was a set of tapestries, seventeen of them, sixteen of which were known as the Gideon Tapestries. They had formerly belonged to Sir Christopher Hatton, but his heir[*] was forced to sell them, along with other valuable items, to make ends meet. These tapestries were destined for the long gallery at Hardwick and because the Hatton coat of arms was woven into the corners, and would have to be removed and replaced with her own arms, Bess paid only £321. 6s. 1d. for them, having knocked £5 off the asking price.[†] There were other tapestry purchases such as the Tobias tapestries, and some featuring forest scenes. And she bought large quantities of gold and silver plate, as well as bolts of cloth-of-silver and cloth-of-gold, together with needles and gold and silver needle-cases and thimbles. It was as if the Earl's death had removed all restraint in

---

[*]Hatton died unmarried and his estates (and debts) were inherited by his sister's son, Sir William Newport. Sir William subsequently changed his name to Hatton by deed poll.

[†]The purchases of the tapestries are recorded in Bess's account books: 'July 9th in the 34th year of E.R. [1592]; Bought of Sir William Hatton . . . for one piece of Arras of the story of Abraham containing forty Flemish ells at fourteen shillings the ell – twenty eight pounds. For 16 pieces of Arras containing one thousand ells and a half of Arras, of the story of Gideon, at six shillings sixpence the Flemish ell, cometh to three hundred twenty six pounds fifteen shillings and nine pence, whereof the making of new arms was abated five pounds, likewise one stick and a half in [unreadable word] – coming to nine shillings and so the residue paid is £321. 6s. 1d'.

Bess's spending habits. Now she had no one to answer to in anything she chose to do. The number of tips and gratuities she dispensed reveal that despite her business acumen, Bess was a kind woman. Perhaps she recalled her own periods of financial difficulties.

The main reason for Bess's trip to London, Arbella's future, remained unresolved, although the Farnese marriage proposal was still on the table. The youthful Arbella was probably more interested in the dashing Earl of Essex, who, had he not married a year earlier, might well have had Arbella in his sights. Even so there was a considerable amount of gossip about Arbella and Robert Devereux during her visit to Court in 1592, which years later Arbella would refute as 'slanderous'. In a recent biography of Arbella the point is made that Arbella and Essex had much in common, 'both setting great store by their noble birth, both erudite, both with a streak of hysteria never far below the surface, both potentially self-destructive, both all too apt, when things went wrong, to hurl wild accusations at a third party'.[29] Whatever the truth about their relationship, Essex would remain a friend of Arbella until his untimely death.

On the return journey, Bess travelled most of the way comfortably ensconced in her new horse litter, a copy of one made for the Queen. It was covered in Bess's favourite colour, a 'tawny coloured' velvet and tuft taffeta, with gold silk fringes and with parchment panels. She had commissioned it while she was at Chelsea, and was so pleased with it that she gave the builder a 'special reward'.

While the main part of her train travelled on to Derbyshire, including the guarded wagon which contained all the gold and silver plate purchases, Bess diverted to visit family or friends. When she reached Northamptonshire she visited Holmby, formerly the home of Sir Christopher Hatton and now owned by his hard-pushed heir, Sir William, who had sold Bess the Gideon Tapestries and a large quantity of gold and silver plate from his uncle's debt-ridden estate. By the following day she was already at Leicester.

At Nottingham she stayed two nights – Thursday and Friday – at Holme Pierrepoint with her beloved 'Frank' (her eldest daughter Frances) and Sir Henry Pierrepoint. This couple had been happily married for thirty years, and here the talk was of a family wedding which had been promoted by Bess and the best friend of her old age, Sir John Manners. Bess's granddaughter Grace* was duly betrothed to the son of John Manners, and Bess provided a dowry of £700. The wedding was to be held in the following week at Chatsworth, when Bess gave the couple £100 to buy plate for their new home. Later in the year, when the newly-weds visited her at Hardwick Old Hall, Bess gave them another £20.

From Holme Pierrepoint Bess travelled to Wollaton, near Nottingham, the new home of another old acquaintance, Sir Francis Willoughby,† who had once sat on the tribunal to determine the truth of the affairs between her and George Shrewsbury. Willoughby's house had been designed by Smythson and finished four years earlier, but the designer had been hindered by the flamboyant additions demanded by his client. Nevertheless, Bess was undoubtedly curious to see this latest of the great prodigy houses designed by Smythson, especially since she had 'loaned' her Master Mason, Thomas Acres, to Willoughby during its construction.[30]

The building had placed the wealthy Sir Francis in financial embarrassment, and during Bess's visit to Wollaton he asked her for a loan of £3050. Bess knew how debts between friends went unpaid and ruined relationships, and wisely insisted on security in the form of deeds to various properties, to be held in Arbella's name during the period the loan remained unpaid. Meanwhile Bess earned interest of £300 a year.

---

*Second daughter of Sir Henry and Frances Pierrepoint. Her elder sister was 'Bessie', who had been companion to Mary, Queen of Scots, and had never lived at home since the age of four.
†Sir Francis Willoughby had been the ward of the Duke of Suffolk, first cousin to the Grey sisters, and was related to both the Seymours and Dudleys. Bess had probably known him for almost fifty years at the time of this visit.

Willoughby died in 1596 and the payments fell into arrears. A year later one of his heirs attempted to redeem the mortgaged assets by offering Bess £3050, with a year's interest. Bess was able to prove that a clause concerning the period of redemption had been contravened, and Arbella had therefore become the owner by default. The claimant declared in a petition to Secretary Robert Cecil that the property was now valued at £15,000, and that other heirs beside himself had been disadvantaged by the Countess of Shrewsbury's dealings.[31] But Bess had the law on her side, and it was a typically shrewd investment by her, if not strictly ethical. Arbella thus became a woman of property, which would undoubtedly help in any marriage negotiations.

Willoughby was only one in a long line of courtiers, including Hatton and Shrewsbury, to name only two, who were beggared by their ambition and loyalty to Queen Elizabeth, and in most cases there was a palatial new house involved. Bess now found herself in the position of financing some of the great men at Court, where she was generally credited as having a masculine understanding of business and finance, which was a great compliment.

Somehow, this elderly woman managed to have her great houses, and the respect of the Queen and members of the Court, without ever getting into debt. For her time she was a phenomenon.

CHAPTER 19

MORE WINDOW THAN WALL

1592–9

ON 5 AUGUST 1592, WHEN BESS ARRIVED BACK AT HARDWICK,[1] she moved into the Old Hall, where the extensive additions were nearing completion. In her long absence the new rooms had been glazed, fireplaces had been installed, the new kitchens, two Great Chambers and a suite of State rooms were completed and ready for use. Even so, the house may have felt somewhat crowded at times, for William's growing family* and household also lived there, and it can only have been difficult for William's wife, Anne – who had grown used to being chatelaine – to give way to Bess's dominating presence and another woman's preferences.

But Bess never intended the arrangement to be a permanent one. From her windows at the Old Hall she could see across to her new house, where the walls had already reached the level of the top floor. No doubt the speed with which the building had gone up was helped by the fact that the materials were all available from local sources. Timber from the woods at Heath, Pentridge, Teversall and

---

*They were to have six children – three boys and three girls – between 1583 and 1598.

Crich Chase, for Bess did not wish to denude the new deerpark at Hardwick; sandstone and limestone from nearby quarries, and mortar made from limestone quarried at Crich (near Wingfield). Lead for the roof, water tanks, conduits and other drainage came from mines at Barlow, which Bess had given to William Cavendish. The iron came from Wingfield, where there was a large forge; alabaster came from Tutbury, presently occupied by Henry Cavendish and his long-suffering wife Grace Talbot, and black marble was quarried at Ashford in the Water.[2] Glass supplies proved a problem at one point as Gilbert Talbot was the main local supplier, so Bess set up a 'glasshouse' and found glaziers to make her own glass. She employed two competent overseers, but for at least some of the time Bess herself seems to have been the driving force of the small army of 'stone-getters' and stone-breakers, masons and sculptors, builders and craftsmen, carpenters and artists, painters and artisans, 'sayers' and glaziers. After many years of building projects, but more particularly after her experiences at Chatsworth, she knew exactly what she wanted. Her slight, upright figure, dressed in black with white ruffs and trimming must have been a familiar sight to the builders as she picked her way round the site, observing progress, making comments and giving instructions. There were always problems to be resolved, such as the cutting of large quantities of 'blackstone'; and when Thomas Acres devised a mechanised method for doing this Bess rewarded him: 'Paid unto Acres upon a bill for the making of an engine for the sawing of blackstone: 10 shillings.' He was later able to improve the design of the waterwheel which drove this machine, and Bess was so delighted that she gave his wife a present of twenty shillings, 'to buy a gown . . . in respect of her husband's device of sawing blackstone . . .'[3]

The names of 375 workmen appear in the building account books; many had worked at Chatsworth, and probably spent their entire working lives in Bess's employment. Robert Smythson's name is missing; he was not involved in the contruction.* But Bess's lively interest in the building process is illustrated by her close examination of these accounts. This is someone who knew about everything that occurred on the site, and she checked the accounts weekly, signing her name in her large, characteristically firm signature: 'E. Shrouesbury'. If she did not approve, she made appropriate comments, such as one in May 1595: 'Because the walls rise and be not well, nor all of one colour, they must be whited at the plasterer's charge'.

She often altered her household accounts in the same way. For example, one entry appears in a clerk's hand, in respect of a nephew who had been working in Bess's service: 'Given to George Kniveton,† not in respect of his services but for his mother's sake,‡ over and above his wages at his go . . .' Bess has scored through the incomplete phrase of what was clearly intended to be 'at his going'. One can imagine her grabbing the pen from the clerk, and scribbling fiercely in her own hand: 'at *my putting him away* . . . £11.'⁴ On another occasion she wrote: 'Given to Gurney [a tirewoman]** at her going away, not for good service but for charity: 40 shillings.'⁵ And when David 'Davey' Flud, the clerk of works who had worked for Bess at Chatsworth, made errors in his arithmetic, Bess crossed them out and corrected them before signing. One week he made three attempts to reach a total, and each was incorrect. Bess's pen scores through the page as she makes the corrections, and the following week one finds the following in her own hand: 'Memorandum: Sir Harry Jenkinson†† enters to take

---

*Smythson's plans include a central staircase that was altered during construction, so we know the drawing is a design and not a subsequent survey.
†Bess also employed a painter called John Kniveton, who painted medallions of emperors on the wainscoting, but whether he is related to George is not known. All we know about George Kniveton is that he died near Jerusalem.
‡Jane Kniveton, Bess's favourite half-sister, who was a lady-in-waiting to Bess for many years.
**A dresser who looked after a lady's wardrobe.
††The Reverend Sir Henry Jenkinson was also Bess's chaplain.

charge of the workmen and keeping of the books...
E. Shrouesbury.'[6]

The style of interior decoration can only have been Bess's own.
She had evolved it over many years of building experience, learning
by mistakes, and observing what had been done at other great
houses and palaces. In the plasterwork, woodcarving and in stone,
convoluted allegories and the constant repetition of the Cavendish
and Hardwick arms proclaim the great estate to which Bess had
risen. There were other heraldic devices, even those of the Queen
herself (into which Bess incorporated her own initials), over the
fireplace in the breathtaking Great High Chamber, said to be a
compliment in case the Queen should ever visit Hardwick. There
was grace in the proportions, but Bess gave full rein to her ideal of
interior decoration with the confidence of someone whose taste
would never be queried.

Bess had been home only a matter of weeks when she received
worrying news from Burghley. A Jesuit had revealed, under torture,
a plan to kidnap Arbella. The principals apparently believed that
Arbella was 'certain' to be proclaimed Queen should Elizabeth die
and schemed 'to convey her with stealth into Flanders; which, if it
be done, she shall shortly visit Spain.'[7] Burghley, who always
realised Arbella's potential in connection with the throne (even
though the Queen chose to ignore it), warned Bess to check the
neighbourhood for Jesuits and Catholics.

Bess replied, 'My good Lord, . . . I was at the first much troubled
to think that so wicked and mischievous practises should be devised
to entrap my poor Arbella and me . . . but will use such diligent
care . . . to prevent whatsoever shall be attempted by any wicked
persons against the child'.[8] Having had the district searched for
'traitorous and naughty persons', Bess advised that there was a
seminary about a mile from Hardwick, but that there was only one
man of whom she was really suspicious. He had been Arbella's
tutor for the past three and half years.

Bess related to Burghley how, when they visited Chatsworth, this man, Morley-the-tutor, had told Arbella he wished to leave her employment. At first he attempted to get Arbella to give him an annuity, or a lease of land 'worth £40 a year', alleging he was much penalised, financially and otherwise, by having left the university (Cambridge) to turn private tutor. Arbella said she could not oblige, so he went to Bess who listened stony-faced before she sent him away empty-handed. On the following day Morley returned, telling Arbella he would work for no recompense if only he could remain in her employment. Ever practical, Bess was immediately suspicious of any man who offered to work for no money,* especially following his remarks of the previous day. She was fair-minded, though, and admitted that she 'could not accuse him of papistry'.

Meanwhile, she advised Burghley, she was maintaining tight security around her grandchild, whom she always called Arbell: 'I will not have any unknown or suspected person come to my house ... my house is furnished with sufficient company. Arbell walks not late; at such time as she shall take the air it shall be near the house, and well attended on. She goeth not to anybody's house at all. I see her almost every hour in the day; [and] she lieth in my bedchamber . . .'[9] But, she adds, 'I will be more precise than I have been.' The letter is written in the hand of William Cavendish, signed by Bess, who explains that she cannot write herself because she is suffering from a great pain in the head, which might have been neuralgia or migraine. This letter suggests that seventeen-year-old Arbella was almost as much Bess's prisoner as her aunt the Queen of Scots had once been, and within days Bess and Arbella left Hardwick for another visit to Chatsworth.

With the plot discovered, its machinery became useless, and the

---

*Bess's suspicions may have been more justified than she ever knew. In a recent biography of Arbella, the author Sarah Gristwood explores the theory that Morley-the-tutor may have been Christopher Marlowe, the playwright and well-known government spy. Marlowe/Morley; Barlow/ Barley – names were often spelled phonetically in the sixteenth century.

sense of alarm faded. In early December news was received from London that the great Spanish general, the Duke of Palma, had died. His son was no longer considered of any particular diplomatic value, so the Farnese marriage negotiations were terminated. There is no evidence that this was either welcome or unwelcome news to either Bess or Arbella, and soon afterwards they returned to the Old Hall at Hardwick for the remainder of the winter. No doubt Bess wanted to enjoy the celebrations in the light and beautiful Hill Great Chamber; there was nothing like it at Chatsworth. And perhaps she wanted to keep Christmas and New Year in her usual style, with her favourite son and his family around her. We know from a letter written years later by Sir William that in his mother's home, 'holidays' – feast days, birthdays, Christmas and New Year – were always kept with traditional revelry. 'All the old holidays,' he wrote, 'with their mirth and rites . . . May games, Morris dances, the Lord of the May, the Lady of the May, the fool and the Hobby Horse, also the Whitsun Lord and Lady, carols and wassails at Christmas with good plum porridge and pies . . .'[10]

Bess's ability to enjoy herself and provide enjoyment and entertainment for her children, retainers and tenants has been previously overlooked, as has her obvious warm affection for her husbands, children and grandchildren, and her passionate grieving at the loss of loved ones when, according to Shrewsbury, she was 'not well able to rule her passions, and has driven herself into such a case by her continual weeping'. There are few records which mention these characteristics, in contrast to the many proofs of her businesslike attitude that have been preserved. But the evidence is there, in St Loe's letters and in the letters and even the reported speech of the Earl of Shrewsbury, and they depict a far more rounded, warm and passionate personality than previously suggested.

Her generosity to her family has also been missed, yet her household account books are awash with examples of gifts of money bestowed upon her children and grandchildren. Even in 1593, when she and Gilbert were estranged, she loaned him £1000 to help him during a difficult period, and when Gilbert and Mary called at Hardwick, she gave him and Mary an 'outright gift' of £100, together with £5 to each of their three daughters. Both William and Charles had an annual allowance of £400, besides the properties she had bought in their names, and there were frequent gifts of £100 here and £50 there. The black sheep Henry had no annual allowance; but every time he called on his mother she gave 'poor Harry' £20 or £10. She also bailed him out on a number of occasions: 'to Henry; for a lease sold to Charles £200' and '. . . to purchase two obligations of Harry's £310'. Frances and Henry Pierrepoint were also given the odd gift of £500 or £300, and the grandchildren were always treated when they were brought over to Hardwick to visit their grandmother: 'to little Will and Charles Cavendish 4 angels each . . . To their nurse 10 shillings.' Cash gifts were constantly handed out by Bess, and it seems that no family member ever called at Hardwick without being given a gift of £5 or £10. Often she dipped into her money coffers simply because she enjoyed sharing with her family.

Soon after the seasonal celebrations came to an end Bess made another important acquisition when she purchased the manors of Owlcotes, Heath, Rowthorn, and Stainsby for the sum of £3,350,[11] about a third of her annual income.* Both her father and grandfather had farmed these manors, leasing them in fealty from the Savage family, who had owned them for over two centuries. Now this substantial parcel of lands became Bess's outright, and it is obvious that this remarkable woman, blessed with good health and energy, now sixty-five, was still wheeler-dealing, making acquisitions, lending money, running her considerable estates with a sure-footed flair beyond that of most of her male

---

*There are various theories about Bess's annual income. Pamela Kettle in *Oldcotes* (p.12), suggests it was £60,000 and this theory appears in early biographies. But I lean towards David Durant's statement that it was about £10,000 (discounting income from the lands and properties she had already settled on her children). It was still a massive sum.

contemporaries, and building for the future. She also controlled her large family and households so that even when they were at odds with her (generally because she would not give them what they wanted), they always respected her.

In business matters she seems to have made few mistakes, and if, on occasion, she found that a mine or some lands could not easily be run at a profit, she leased them out, took the rents and let someone else worry about making the investment pay. She hardly ever sold land, and it almost goes without saying that she would have realised the value of the building materials available on her estates – iron and lead, brick, stone and slate, and glass, at a time when the very rich were just about to embark on a building boom of the great country houses which characterise the early English renaissance. All these assets were duly exploited and eventually Gilbert Talbot found he had no market for his glass: Bess's glazier, Sylvester Smith, had not only flooded the local area, but had set up better sales outlets and transport systems to London.

Bess was not brought up to expect this kind of life, nor had she been educated to it, as a male heir would have been. She had absorbed her knowledge autodidactically from Cavendish, St Loe and Shrewsbury, but she applied her knowledge to far greater practical use than any of these men ever did. She surrounded herself with good and intelligent servants, and she seems, from her correspondence, to have had the measure of them all. She was, in fact, a Tudor entrepreneur, aided considerably by her second and favourite son, William Cavendish. She could trust him absolutely and he worked extremely hard under his mother's direction. As well as William, Bess relied on Timothy Pusey, who was to Bess what William Cecil was to Queen Elizabeth.

Had Bess's estates been formalised into a modern-day company this triumvirate would have been respectively, Bess – Chairman and Managing Director, William – Assistant Managing Director, and Timothy Pusey – Company Secretary, and they made a formidable and successful team. Beneath this top management structure was a layer of middle management: the day-to-day administration of Bess's estates was handled by seventeen on-site bailiffs. The business had a number of divisions: sheep and cattle-farming, mining and foundries, quarries and glass-making, property rentals and leaseholds, and money-lending. Her 'head office' staff, as well as William Cavendish and Pusey, consisted of a battery of trusted lawyers and several good accountants. But Bess always checked every detail personally: her bold signature appears at the foot of most pages in the account books.

Pusey – who was only ever known in Bess's accounts, and in her letters to him, as 'Tymothy' – had worked for Bess for some years prior to taking over officially as steward. Not only was he a brilliant accountant and bookkeeper, but he had a legal background, which was an invaluable asset to Bess who was always requiring deeds, transfers and settlements to be drawn up. She knew the power of the law, and increasingly used it to her advantage. Why did Bess go on with her acquisitions and deals and money-making schemes? She did not need more money, and her own future and that of her offspring was secure now. The simple explanation is that she enjoyed it. She was a woman ahead of her time, and she revelled in the challenges and rewards of dealing with, and perhaps besting, men.

Bess achieved most of her greatest successes at a time when the country was in recession. Years of financing armies in Ireland, helping the Protestants in the Netherlands to gain independence from the Spanish, and England's own war with the Spanish, albeit victorious, had emptied the nation's coffers. Rumours abounded that Philip was building a new Armada, while at home crippled and maimed war veterans begged in their thousands on the streets. At the same time four cold winters and wet summers caused farming and agricultural incomes to slump, all of which added, at the end of the 1590s, to a widespread sense of public disillusionment. It was during these years that Bess most thrived.

The new Hardwick Hall was still far from completion, but Bess liked what she saw of it so much that she hardly changed the original design. It is plainer than other Smythson houses, but that was un-doubtedly Bess's preference, and it has even more window area. Work to enhance the old Hall was still continuing, and the ink was scarcely dry on the deed of sale of the lands bought from Edward Savage, when Bess contacted Smythson again, this time with the intention of building a house at Owlcotes (now called Oldcotes) for William Cavendish and his family. Work began on this house in March 1593.[12]

Although no trace of Oldcotes survives, Smythson's drawings and plans are extant, and from these we know that the house he designed for Bess at Oldcotes was smaller than Hardwick, two-storeyed, with two three-storeyed towers and a three-storeyed central block. Nor did it have the ethereal expanse of glass, but it was a house of great character in the Smythson tradition. Bess left the management of building Oldcotes to William, for whom it was intended, and in the seven years or so that building work was going on at Oldcotes she mentions it in her accounts on only four occasions when she either gave William money to pay bills for it, or visited the site herself.

Gilbert and Mary Shrewsbury were living at Cold Harbour House, in London, that winter of 1593 and Charles Cavendish was staying with them. It was at this time that a regrettable and damag-ing quarrel began between Gilbert and John Stanhope. The two men had been friends at Court for years, and like many feuds it seemed to begin from almost nothing. Twenty years earlier, John Stanhope's brother Thomas, who owned the Stanhope family home at Shelford in Nottinghamshire, had thrown a weir across the River Trent to improve his fishing. This had led to a feud between the Stanhopes and the Zouche family, in which Bess and the old Earl had – to their irritation – unwittingly become embroiled. It had died down years ago, but Gilbert now raised the matter of the weir again, objecting to it ostensibly on behalf of local people. The matter was nothing to do with him for although he owned lands in Nottinghamshire, the weir did not affect these, nor did he have any jurisdiction in the county. However, his father and grandfather had been Lord Lieutenants of Nottinghamshire and therein, it appears, was the rub.

Gilbert had expected to step into all the honours and titles of his late father, but many of these had been granted to the Earl when, as a young man, he had served his country in an active sense. Not all of his titles were automatically conferred on Gilbert, who, it must be said, had done nothing to earn them. Indeed, so far, his entire life seems to have been spent acquiring huge debts and expecting his stepmother to fight his battles with his father and keep his creditors off his back. He was, in modern parlance, a spoiled rich kid who had got himself into debt.

Gilbert *was* made Lord Lieutenant of Derbyshire since his inherited title made that almost a foregone conclusion. He was also made a Knight of the Garter a year or so after his father's death. But his expectations of becoming Earl Marshal of England and Lord Lieutenant of Nottinghamshire as his father had been before him were doomed to be disappointed. John Stanhope had offered to watch out for Gilbert's interests at Court in these matters, but when the election was announced, his brother, Sir Thomas Stanhope, was named as candidate for the Lord Lieutenancy of Nottinghamshire. John Stanhope had already risen far, and enjoyed the Queen's favour and respect. This was rarely given lightly, so it can be assumed that Stanhope was a man of ability. Gilbert, rightly or wrongly, assumed that Stanhope had pressed his brother's ambitions over his, Gilbert's. Bypassing Stanhope, he wrote about it to Lord Burghley in September 1592: '. . . so long as her Majesty for any respect whatsoever, shall not hold me worthy of the place, I will not desire it. Only with all humble earnestness I must crave, that I may not be forced to swallow up such indignities in my country, as never any of my ancestors did, and which would make me contemptible in the world.'[13] When it was made obvious to Gilbert that he would not be considered for the Nottinghamshire Lieutenancy, he fielded two candidates of his own.

It was the start of a long vendetta. That winter, under the guise of coming to the aid of local country people who were affected by the weir, Gilbert's local agent twice attacked and damaged the weir with gangs of men armed with staves and picks. By March 1593 the relationship between the Stanhope family and Gilbert Shrewsbury had deteriorated to open enmity, and in the general unpleasantness Charles Cavendish felt obliged to defend his best friend's good name. He challenged Stanhope to a duel by rapiers 'against injurious expressions used by him' concerning Gilbert.[14] On the afternoon of 16 March, John Stanhope sent his 'second' to Charles Cavendish, accepting the challenge and appointing the meeting at Lambeth Bridge at 7 a.m. on the following day. Charles was an extremely accomplished swordsman, and he stipulated that they should fight in shirtsleeves, and that their supporters (Charles named his 'cousin Jarvis Markham'), should 'hover' in boats on the water so as not to give any unfair advantage to either party. This was duly agreed by the respective seconds.

Charles, who had recently made a second marriage (to Catherine Ogle),* was waiting at the appointed place and time, but when John Stanhope appeared he was wearing a bulky doublet, which he explained by saying he had caught a cold. Upon examination by the seconds, the doublet was found 'to be of great thickness, and so hard quilted' that the point of a knife could not penetrate it. On being asked to remove the garment, Stanhope refused; whereupon Sir Charles mockingly offered his own waistcoat to keep Stanhope warm, saying that he would, however, still engage to fight in his shirtsleeves. Despite the studied insult, Stanhope insisted upon keeping the doublet, and the two seconds agreed that this made it an unequal match. Upon which, honour satisfied, and having watched Stanhope depart in his boat, Sir Charles returned to Cold Harbour and his wife.[15]

The Stanhope family did not leave the matter there; they took the case of the weir to the Star Chamber, and won. This did not settle anything, and the feud deepened. A group of Talbot and

*Catherine was the daughter of Baron Ogle, and sister to Jane, Edward Talbot's wife.

Cavendish retainers ambushed John Stanhope and four of his men outside the Three Tuns Inn in Fleet Street. They tumbled down some stairs with swords drawn, yelling, 'yonder comes Stanhope, to it, to it,' and an old Stanhope servant was badly injured in the fray. Mary wrote that Gilbert would not dine away from home while in London, for fear of being poisoned by one of the three Stanhope brothers. While she could not challenge the Stanhopes to a duel, as her favourite brother Charles had done, she could declare her opinion. She sent a messenger to say to Sir Thomas: 'my Lady commandeth me to say,' he intoned, 'that you be more wretched, vile and miserable than any creature living; and for your wickedness, become more ugly in shape than the vilest creature in the world . . . that she doth in no ways wish your death; but to this end that all the plagues and miseries that befall any man may light upon such a caitiff* as you are . . .'[16] Indeed this was an abridged version of the message, for the messenger could not bring himself to repeat some of the more offensive phrases.

Stanhope sent a draft of the insulting remarks to Lord Burghley, 'with a letter of heinous complaint'.[17] Eventually it came to the Queen's ears, and she was distinctly unamused. She could do without brawling courtiers, and she directed her sympathy to the man she knew best, John Stanhope. This development was quickly transmitted to Bess: 'The Queen here daily bears more and more a bad conceit of the Earl of Shrewsbury, and his countess, for the sake of the Lady Arbella, which has been evinced in a late quarrel between his Lordship and the Stanhopes.'[18] And Gilbert received a note from his servant Alexander Ratcliff, which informed him that the Queen had said: 'It is not my Lord [Gilbert]'s doing but my Lady [Mary]'s; my Lady leads my Lord in all things, as she likes'.[19] How the old Earl would have relished this vindication of his opinion.

Bess would not have been amused either; not only had she admonished Charles previously about brawling with swords, but

*Caitiff: a despicable or cowardly person.

she could see that Gilbert and Charles were damaging their positions by attacking a rising man in Elizabeth's inner circle. Even
worse, they were damaging Arbella's position. She had learned
early, from old Sir William Cavendish, how the Court worked:
gifts, flattery and favours went further than fights and mischief. If
these failed, she always relied on a direct petition to the Queen or
a senior member of the Council, and then, eventually, and as a last
resort, she would take a case to the court of the Star Chamber. But
retaining the Queen's favour was paramount to survival.

In May, Bess left Hardwick Old Hall and went to live at
Chatsworth for a year; perhaps sharing her home with an active
young family and another woman did not appeal. She returned to
Hardwick a number of times during that year, but only for brief
visits when she stayed with William and Anne while she checked on
the progress of the building works.

The relationship between Gilbert and Bess failed to improve,
and finally, failing to get any satisfaction in the matter of her
widow's 'third' payments, and together with Sir Francis Leake,
who led a group of some of the Earl's tenants up in arms because of
precipitate rent rises and other matters, Bess laid a formal complaint against Gilbert which was heard by the Privy Council.[20] It is
therefore not surprising to find Gilbert now castigating Bess in his
correspondence in much the same manner as his late father had
done.

While all this was going on, at a time when one would think
Gilbert might be looking to his own family for friendship and support, he challenged his brother Edward to a duel with rapier and
dagger when they quarrelled over a lease Gilbert claimed Edward
had fraudulently obtained from the old Earl.[21] 'I say that you have
lied in your throat,' he wrote, 'and if you find yourself aggrieved (in
such sort, as in honour of your birth, you ought) I will not fail to be
found, with two gentlemen . . . on such a day and hour, and with
such weapons and garments, as my two servants shall conclude
with you . . .'[22] Edward sensibly refused to meet Gilbert, calmly

stating that he could not bring himself to fight with his own flesh and blood.

Soon afterwards Gilbert charged that Edward had hired an apothecary named Wood to supply him with poison to impregnate Gilbert's gloves.[23] Edward, who was in regular touch with Bess, may have consulted her about the matter. She, after all, had been involved in a similar case with Edward St Loe many years earlier. Subsequently, Edward Talbot took the matter to court, and sued his brother and Wood. Apothecary Wood swore on oath that Edward had promised him an annuity of £100 to poison Gilbert. However, Edward won his case, and Wood was found guilty of slander, sentenced to be pilloried and have one ear cut off and three letters branded on his forehead. He continued to implicate Mary, 'my Lady Shrewsbury', however, and she was called before the Master of the Rolls, but released after questioning.

After that, bad blood lay between Gilbert and both his brothers for half a decade and more. Gilbert's only real friend was Charles Cavendish, with whom he had been in the schoolroom at Sheffield and Chatsworth, but he also made overtures of friendship to Henry Cavendish, whom Bess had more or less banished from her sight as a wastrel. Perhaps it was a case of 'my enemy's enemy must be my friend'.

But Gilbert was an unhappy man. He had waited years to come into his own and found, when he did, that he was not rich, as he had expected. He had made enemies with former influential friends, including Stanhope and Bess. And as his father had been before him, Gilbert was bested in any argument by his more intelligent wife. Mary had been hated by George Shrewsbury, who blamed her for all his son's problems almost from the day of their youthful marriage. Although charming, and an erudite reporter of Elizabeth's Court, Gilbert was a weak man at heart, whereas Mary, like her mother, was a forceful personality. She lacked Bess's diplomacy and political acumen, but then Mary had never lived in fear of her life and had been brought up in a protected environment, so she had never had to learn tact. In fact, by the end of the 1590s Mary had become a disillusioned and nagging wife.

Both Gilbert and Mary were profligate with money, living a glittering and elaborate lifestyle as befitted their rank as Earl and Countess, regardless of the fact that they did not have the money to support it. Bess might have steered them on to the right lines, but they saw little of Bess who, to her dismay, temporarily lost contact with her daughter and three Talbot granddaughters. This she minded more than anything.

On 10 November 1595 there was an unusual excitement at the Old Hall at Hardwick when the Queen's favourite, the Earl of Essex, and his men spent two days there.[24] Arbella and Essex had been friends since her unfortunate contretemps in the Royal Chapel procession years earlier, and this visit coincided with Arbella's twentieth birthday celebrations.* It is not too difficult to believe that Bess offered the invitation with the specific intention of using the Earl's visit to remind the Queen about her granddaughter's situation. Arbella had been away from Court for more than three years at this point, and would soon be regarded as having been left on the shelf. If this was Bess's intention, the stratagem worked: the following spring Arbella was summoned to Court. Bess did not go with her; Arbella was chaperoned by the inseparable trio of Gilbert, Mary and Charles. And, what is more, Gilbert was finally given an official State appointment.

In fact he was Queen Elizabeth's second choice, for Essex had been nominated for the post at first. But in the spring of 1596 Essex sailed for Spain in uneasy joint command, with Sir Walter Ralegh, of the English fleet, on a mission to destroy the new Armada being built at Cadiz. In his absence, Gilbert was commissioned to head a mission to Paris, to confer upon the French King

---

*Although the precise date of Arbella's birth is unknown, the letter written by old Lady Lennox advising Mary, Queen of Scots of the birth was dated 10 November 1575. Given Arbella's perceived importance, it is most likely that this letter was written the same day.

the ancient Order of the Garter, to ratify a new treaty against Spain, and to present the new English Ambassador, Sir Walter Mildmay, at the French Court.[25]

Henri IV of France, though raised as a Huguenot, had become a Catholic in order to make his throne more secure. Elizabeth had been suitably disgusted, but Henri's casual response was the enigmatic one-liner 'Paris is worth a Mass'. When Henri began actively seeking an annulment of his marriage to his barren wife (Marguerite de Valois), he discussed the possibility of a marriage to Arbella with his Minister, Sully. He said he would have no objection to the Infanta of Spain '. . . nor would I refuse Princess Arbella of England, if, since it is said the crown of England really belongs to her, she were only declared presumptive heiress of it'. Rumours continued to circulate in European courts about Henri IV and Arbella; in Vatican correspondence it was written that 'Queen Elizabeth has promised him a near cousin of her own, whom she loves much and intends to make her heir and successor'.[26] But following Henri's conversion to Catholicism there had been no further discussions at the English Court about a match between him and Arbella.

During Gilbert's absence, his enemy John Stanhope was knighted and appointed Treasurer of the Chamber (a position once held by Sir William Cavendish under Henry VIII, Edward VI and Queen Mary). But this did not take the edge off the fact that Gilbert's mission to France was deemed a success, and he returned to London justifiably pleased with himself. Mary Talbot was jubilant and made the mistake of using the occasion to ask the Queen to allow two of her daughters to be appointed maids of honour to their cousin, the Lady Arbella.

It was bad timing, an error the more astute Bess would not have made. Essex and Ralegh had succeeded in destroying the new Armada at Cadiz, a feat of derring-do that thrilled the nation. Essex was hailed as a hero and cheered to the rooftops wherever he appeared, but Elizabeth was disgruntled because they had missed the Spanish treasure fleet. The Spanish had scuttled it in a protected port rather than allow it to fall into the hands of the English. With her exchequer coffers empty, Elizabeth had hoped for spoils as well as glory and she was in no mood for generous gestures. She pointedly informed Mary Talbot that only princesses of the blood were entitled to have maids-of-honour, and for good measure she ordered the entire Talbot party to leave the Court.

While Bess's children and older grandchildren jockeyed for positions at Court, Bess was more than content to remain in Derbyshire, leading the quiet but busy country life that had always suited her, overseeing her building concerns, and sitting at the hub of her small 'court' that was a miniature version of the royal one. Her accounts show that she employed scores of servants – at one time seventy-four are on the payroll – all dressed in Cavendish blue, or 'mallard colour' livery,[27] and ready to fulfil her slightest whim. She also had her ladies-in-waiting and young gentlemen ushers and pages; she had her secretaries, stewards and chaplain. And she had the company of her younger grandchildren, William and Anne's children, whom she adored. Most of them were called 'my juwyl' (jewel) at one time or another in correspondence, and it is probably significant that as soon as Bess moved to the new house, William's children were taught in the nursery on the ground floor there. Why, when they lived so close, was their schoolroom not in the Old Hall? The reason can only be that Bess liked having the children around, even though she was always fully occupied with matters of business, and far from bored. From what we know of the activities that went on at Hardwick, it was a house full of noise and life, and having brought up six children of her own, probably Bess enjoyed the sounds they made, as well as the close bond that grandparents can have with their grandchildren. William's eldest son, also William, but called Wylkyn in the family in order to distinguish between father and son, was a splendid heir. He was intelligent and active, and excelled at riding and fencing, though he was not as keen on the schoolroom as his father had been. When he was eleven years old, he and his father made a signed agreement that in exchange for 'a rapier, a dagger, an embroidered girdle, and a pair of spurs' Wylkyn would undertake to speak in Latin to his cousin Arbella from November until Shrove Tuesday.[28]

The Hardwick account books show that there was a good deal of entertaining, and although Bess did not employ her own musicians, there are frequent payments to visiting groups and musicians in the employ of friends such as the Earl of Essex and the Earl of Rutland. There were concerts given by local waits (street singers) and plays were performed, too: in 1596 the Queen's Players visited and gave a performance at Hardwick, and the companies of actors employed by friends or kinsmen – Lord Thomas Howard, Baron Ogle,* and the Earls of Huntingdon and Pembroke – also came at various times to put on performances and masques there.

At last, after long years of waiting and planning, Bess moved into the new Hardwick Hall on Monday 4 October 1597, a full two years before it was completed. It was at just about the time of her seventieth birthday; indeed, it is more than likely that it *was* her seventieth birthday,[†] for there were certainly celebrations that day, with musicians playing. Much work remained to be done and she would have had to put up, for a long time yet, with the noise of workmen and artisans. Why, when the Old Hall was now a comfortable home? No better explanation offers itself for this particular choice of day, in what otherwise seems a precipitous move, and what a previous biographer has described as 'a rush job on a sudden decision of Bess's'.[29] Finally she was able to hang all those tapestries, place all that furniture and plate that she had been buying for years. Cartloads of Bess's favourite pieces were trundled over from Chatsworth. Chatsworth was still far from emptied, as the inventory taken in 1601 reveals, but the depletions caused

*Charles's wife was Baron Ogle's daughter. Edward Talbot's wife was her sister.
†See Appendix 1 for discussion.

Henry some concern, for later there are letters from him to his mother about it.

Arbella, back after her season at Court, moved in with her grandmother and together they occupied a suite of rooms which consisted of 'my Ladies withdrawing chamber; my Ladies chamber and pallet, the little room within the dressing room, the maid's chamber and closet within; Lady Arbella's chamber and a little closet'. Arbella now had her own chamber, which she called her study, but in the 1601 inventory all it contained was a bed. Another bed, described as 'my Lady Arbella's bed', with its blue and white canopy, was still located in her grandmother's bedchamber. Although Elizabethan beds were large, and being thickly curtained against draughts, allowed a good deal of privacy, it is hardly surprising that at twenty-two years old, Arbella had begun to fret about what life held for her. At the same age Bess had been married twice and had several children. Arbella was alternately flattered and fêted at Court, and then treated as a child or quasi-prisoner at home, which must have been extremely frustrating. But there was no gainsaying her grandmother's wishes. Years later, Arbella would refer to this time as 'that unpleasant life she had led in the house of her grandmother, with whose severity and age she, being a young lady, could hardly agree'.[30] For the moment Arbella was marooned, again, in her grandmother's new house.

How did this intelligent and well-educated young woman pass her time? We know she continued her studies, and set aside a time each day for her books. She still had a tutor who had replaced Morley-the-tutor; James Starkey was a chaplain who also taught William's children. Arbella continued to study Spanish (in case marriage should take her to Spain), and Hebrew (perhaps in order to read ancient manuscripts from the original); she also read Virgil, Plutarch and other classics. We know that games were often played at Hardwick; in the Great High Chamber, there are game boards inlaid into the top of the massive table. Arbella was a musician, and played the lute, viol and the virginals, an early form of spinet, which Bess had made her own daughters learn, and probably also played herself. As well, Arbella enjoyed dancing and was a keen needlewoman.

There were acres of beautiful gardens with pavilions for quiet relaxation and freedom from company, as well as woodland walks, but even here Arbella would have been aware of her grandmother's presence. There are few places from where she would not have seen the final touch to the structure of Hardwick Hall, which even today is a breathtaking architectural feature – the giant stone initials ES (for Elizabeth Shrewsbury, or 'Shrouesbury' as she always signed herself), surmounted by the coronet of a countess and garlanded with a delicate stone scroll were, and remain, a constant reminder of whose house it was. These features were mounted on three sides of each of the six great corner towers,* creating effective balustrades on the roof and, silhouetted against the sky, could be seen for miles.

Bess, who had spent years building Chatsworth only to effectively lose it to Shrewsbury during his lifetime, and knowing that it would go eventually to her undeserving and estranged son Henry, was taking no chances with this house. It was smaller than her other two houses, having only forty-six rooms (excluding service rooms) compared to the ninety-seven rooms at Chatsworth, and fifty-five in the Old Hall.[31] Of these forty-six rooms, fourteen were bedchambers, but the Old Hall was used for additional guests of lesser importance. Nor was the new Hardwick Hall finished internally to such a high standard as Chatsworth, where the fine plaster decorations had taken decades to complete and many of the rooms were beautifully panelled. But it was state-of-the-art design, with acres of glass giving it an ethereal appearance, and the rooms were large, grand and flooded with light. Symmetry was paramount here, quite unlike the part-timbered Old Hall across the way, which

---

*The towers, similar to those at Wollaton, proved something of a nuisance, the upper rooms of these being accessible only from the roof leads.

had been built piecemeal, a wing here, a wing there. The new
Hardwick Hall was delicate and unfussy. Where necessary, regardless of cost, Bess used expensive glass over the brickwork of
chimneys to make false windows, simply to ensure overall symmetry. When Robert Cecil was asked about Hardwick, he is said
to have replied: 'Hardwick Hall? More window than wall', a quip
that has rippled down the centuries in its revised form. Apart from
Smythson's original drawing, which Bess altered slightly, Hardwick
Hall owed nothing to anyone but Bess. It was hers, and would
ever after be identified as hers.

The great hero of the Armada, Sir Francis Drake, died in Panama
in January 1596 from dysentery. He was in command of a raiding
fleet bound for the Spanish Main, where he had hoped to divert
King Philip's ships away from England, and also intended to relieve
him of Spanish treasure. In the year following Drake's death, the
Queen gave permission for a fleet of privately owned ships to sail
for Pernambuco, with tacit approval to wage war on the Spanish.

Bess became involved in this venture when in October 1597 she
was visited by Hercules Folijambe, whose brother James Folijambe
had been a close friend of the late James Hardwick. Hercules had
a reputation as an adventurer and seafarer, and had been offered
the command of the galleon *Constance* in the private fleet of
twenty ships. He was so confident that he would make his fortune
that he approached Bess with a proposition to borrow money to
pay for a crew and provision and arm his ship. Bess was interested,
but as usual she wanted security for her money, so he sold her
some of his lands outright, and mortgaged others in Chesterfield,
and she handed over £1000 in cash. Sadly for Folijambe, the mission was a failure, and he lost everything: all his properties were
forfeited to Bess in lieu.[32]

Bess could hardly put a foot wrong in those years; everything she
did increased her estates and her income. She even purchased from
the Queen: 'for divers lands and parsonages . . . £12,855. 15s. 11d.
Remains in the hands of my son William Cavendish £514. 8s.

2¾d.'[33] Her account books are full of the names of neighbours to whom she made loans, and often these were quite significant amounts: Markham, Leake, Saville, Ferrers, Sacheverall, Fitzherbert – all borrowed monies at one time or other, but the loans were always protected by land or property mortgages as security.

The departure of Bess and Arbella and their household left the Old Hall free for William and Anne and their children, and no one must have welcomed this more than Anne Cavendish. She also had Oldcotes to look forward to, when that building was completed. But she was destined never to live in Oldcotes; only four months after Bess moved across to the New Hall, Anne died, in February 1598, after giving birth to a son, James. She was buried in Ault Hucknall churchyard, close to her son Gilbert, who had died in the previous autumn at six years old. Little James was a great favourite of his grandmother, and her affection is illustrated not in diary form, or letters, but in the entries in her household accounts, such as one when he was three years old, which stated: 'paid to the joiner for a little chair for James – 12 pence, and a little stool for him 12 pence'. James is also mentioned in Bess's will, made in 1601, but like his brother Gilbert, little James was destined to die in childhood. Of all Sir William's sons, only William (Wylkyn), born in 1590, who dressed like his father in doublet and hose with a small dagger in his belt, survived to adulthood.

Bess did not forget Charles. He was also given money to build a new house, at Kirkby-in-Ashby in Nottinghamshire. It was not far from Hardwick, but Bess was never involved with it as she was with Oldcotes. She gave Charles £400 towards building costs in 1597, but the house was never completed.[34] Charles already owned Stoke Manor in Derbyshire where he had lived with his first wife. When, to the relief of his mother, he married again, it was a good match. Catherine was the daughter of Lord Ogle, and as part of the marriage settlement the couple had Ogle Castle. Charles also had a legal agreement with Gilbert (dated as early as 1588) that on Bess's death he could have first refusal on Bolsover Castle, and in the same year as work began at Kirkby, he rented Welbeck Abbey, near Worksop, from Gilbert.*

The deaths of six-year-old Gilbert Cavendish and his mother Anne were the first in a series of losses that struck at the heart of everything Bess was working for: the advancement of her family. Within a year of their mother's death, two of the three daughters of William and Anne Cavendish also died, probably in an epidemic, so that of William's six children, only William, Frances and baby James were left.

In August Bess heard that Lord Burghley had died. The Queen had visited her old friend many times at his London house on the Strand where he lay dying. She spoonfed him his meals of porridge and broth and said she had no wish to live on without him; 'you are, in all things, to me Alpha and Omega', she told him, which made him weep. His last message to his son Robert was: 'Serve God by serving the Queen, for all other service is indeed bondage to the devil'.[35] After Burghley's death, the Queen was inconsolable for weeks and would break down at the mere mention of his name. He was the only man for whom she was ever seen to cry in public. A month later, her great enemy, King Philip of Spain, died 'after fifty days of intense pain'. With Philip's death the world seemed a safer place to Elizabeth for his son lacked his father's historical hatred of England.

Bess mourned Burghley, too. He had always been a stalwart sup-porter and friend of hers, and had given her incalculable assistance throughout the forty years they had known each other. And he had done this without ever betraying his friendship with George Shrewsbury, which was a significant achievement given the enmity that Shrewsbury felt towards his wife in his final years. Bess had

---

*So many of Bess's descendants became Dukes and they owned so many great houses near Nottingham (including Welbeck), that the area was dubbed by locals 'the Dukeries', a name by which it is still known.

few really important contacts at Court now, though she was certainly in correspondence with Ralegh and Essex. However, she always ensured that her agents in London kept her abreast of Court and foreign news and gossip, and she maintained contact with various officials. These she looked after by sending gifts with visitors to the Court: a fat stag, venison pasties or small items of plate.

It seems that despite her disagreement with Gilbert, Bess somehow maintained a relationship with her daughter Mary. In a carefully worded letter dated 28 February 1598 she wrote to them both that she was sorry to hear Mary had a bad cold, and that she herself had suffered one. She also asked when they were coming to stay with her, implying that they were still on occasional visiting terms. She wrote, as any mother would, that the air at Hardwick would do them good and sent her blessing; 'the same to our three jewels', she wrote, referring to her granddaughters, Mary (now eighteen), Elizabeth (sixteen) and Alathea (fourteen).

The old vendetta between Gilbert Shrewsbury and the Stanhopes erupted into violence again; perhaps it had never died down. It was not Gilbert who was the victim, however, but his champion and friend, forty-five-year-old Charles Cavendish. John Stanhope had clearly never forgotten, nor forgiven, the taunts by Charles about his padded doublet when they had met to fight six years earlier. On a June morning in 1599 Charles set out to visit the brick kiln near what was still a building site at Kirkby-in-Ashby, less than half a mile from where he was staying with his wife Catherine. With him Charles had his brother-in-law Henry, his page, Lance Ogle, who was obviously a young member of his wife's family, and a groom. When a group of twenty horsemen appeared on a hillside in the distance, he assumed it was his neighbour Sir John Byron out hunting.

Suddenly, however, the horsemen began galloping towards him and he realised that they meant him no good. Having not anticipated any fast work, he was riding a small horse, but he clapped his spurs to its side intending to try to get to the cover of his new building. The horse fell, and Charles could not even draw his sword before he was shot twice at close range by two men wielding pistols. One of the bullets 'hit him in the inside of his thigh, but missed the bone, and yet lyeth in the flesh, near the point of his buttock. He has also divers small Shot in several parts of his thigh and body . . . which are thought to come out of the same pistol . . . Sir Charles is hurt also in the head, and on the hand . . . but those not dangerous hurts'.[36] His companions had now caught up and, between them, the three men and a boy, armed with rapiers and a small dagger only, managed to unhorse six of the attackers, two of whom were killed in the fight; one ran off badly injured 'and is now thought dead'. The sound of the violent struggle finally reached the ears of workmen at the building site, and though unarmed they rushed to investigate. Sir John Stanhope, who had taken no active part, but had obviously led the attack, was seen making a getaway in the vanguard of those 'running away'.

Needless to say, any bullet wound was potentially lethal in the days before antibiotics, and Lady Catherine would have called in a surgeon immediately, but for some reason the bullet could not be removed. When Bess was told, as always concerned when one of her children was ill, she called in a surgeon from Chesterfield, but the bullet remained. Charles recovered slowly, but a year later the injury was evidently still giving trouble, for the Queen heard about it and sent her own surgeon to investigate and try to help by a little probing for the bullet. Curiously, it appears that Stanhope was never penalised for what looks like a cowardly attack, and he remained at his post as Treasurer of the Queen's Chamber. Later he was made vice-chamberlain, and was admitted to the Privy Council on the same day as Gilbert Talbot. Perhaps the extant papers which record this story are only one side of it, otherwise Stanhope's lack of punishment is inexplicable. However, the experience certainly affected Charles: the building at Kirkby was halted and never restarted. Years later, after his mother's death, he removed the building materials and used them to rebuild Bolsover Castle.

The Shrewsburys were at Court that Christmas of 1599, and there was good news awaiting their arrival in November. A letter from a friend advised that the Queen had spoken well of them, and had listened to 'some of the truth of the dispute with Edward Talbot'.

Besides Hardwick and Oldcotes, Bess was building in Derby, where she had commissioned the building of an almshouse for twelve old people. It was completed in 1600 and Bess endowed it in perpetuity, so that the residents would receive an annual stipend of thirty-three shillings and fourpence, as well as a suit of clothes upon which was a badge containing the initials 'E.S.'. Hardwick was nearing completion by this time but there were still some outstanding jobs to finish. To Bess's annoyance, despite her instructions to pour boiling water on the mortar to prevent it freezing, the excessive cold before Christmas eventually halted all work until the coming spring.

CHAPTER 20

'IN PERFECT HEALTH AND GOOD MEMORY'

1600–02

BESS HAD NOT SEEN THE QUEEN FOR EIGHT YEARS BUT SHE had never failed to send a costly New Year gift to London, and she made sure that Arbella continued the custom. In January 1600 Bess received a letter from Lady Dorothy Stafford, who had served Elizabeth for thirty-seven years, even 'lying in the bedchamber'. The two women had known each other since Bess became a Lady of the Privy Chamber after her marriage to Sir William St Loe, and they had remained friends through the years. In this letter Lady Stafford thanked Bess on behalf of the Queen, saying that her mistress had taken a special liking to Arbella's gift. It was 'a scarf or head-veil of lawn cut work, flourished with silver and silks of various colours', and,

> ... it pleased her Majesty to tell me that whereas in certain former letters of your ladyship's, your desire was that her Majesty would have that respect of my Lady Arbella that she might be carefully restored to her Majesty's good liking, that according to the contents of these letters, her Majesty told me,

that she would be careful of her, and withal has returned a token
to my Lady Arbella.[1]

Now that she no longer travelled to London, Bess realised that
the Queen probably gave little thought to Arbella; she was – to
use one of Bess's own expressions – 'out of sight, out of mind'. So
this written promise that the Queen 'would be careful' was what
she had hoped for.

In the spring there was an attempt at a rapprochement between
Bess and the Shrewsburys, when Charles wrote from Leicester that
Mary and Gilbert intended to call at Hardwick on their way home
from London, and stay 'one day at least with your ladyship'.[2] No
reconciliation was effected, and some weeks later Bess complained
to Robert Cecil that under the pretence of a grant of lands, Gilbert
had attempted to incorporate some properties she owned that were,
she wrote, 'dearly obtained by me'.[3] She had already conveyed the
lands to her children, but Gilbert had included them with other
properties that he owned and transferred them in the names of
two of his servants. Perhaps in the muddle left by his father Gilbert
made a genuine error, but Bess did not think so, since a few weeks
earlier he had accused his two brothers of doing exactly the same
thing. By incorporating these properties in a document 'signed with
his great seal', he was attempting to provide written evidence of
new ownership that might, at some future date, obfuscate the real
ownership. Bess was on to it, however; she presented the facts and
begged Robert Cecil 'to the best construction' of them. Not only
would an admonitory letter from Cecil curb Gilbert, but it was
faster – and less costly – than the process of law.

Although she could no longer represent herself in person at
Court, Bess maintained a regular correspondence with Robert
Cecil, who appears to have held her in affection as well as respect,
perhaps because he had grown up knowing her as a friend of his
father. Certainly Cecil was known to favour Arbella as a possible
successor to Elizabeth and now that the Queen, at sixty-seven, was

beginning to fail, the question of the succession was of great importance.

During that winter of 1600–1601 Bess and Arbella waited on every letter from Court for the latest news about their friend the Earl of Essex who was in serious trouble. Essex had begun life at Court with every possible advantage: his close family connection with Robert Leicester, his handsome appearance, personal charm, courtly manner and physical bravery all marked young Robert Devereux out for the Queen's favour. Subsequently she had showered upon him every possible honour, office, title and gift, as well as her own affection. She forgave him when he caused dissension in her Court by setting himself up as the figurehead of a rival faction to Robert Cecil, and when he became the sworn enemy of her other favourite, Walter Ralegh. She was infinitely patient with his youth and passion, and she forgave him on numerous other occasions when he transgressed. In 1597 she had given him the much-coveted post of Earl Marshal of England. It would be true to say that he had the world at his feet.

But the Queen's signal favour was not enough for Essex; at thirty years old, at the height of his powers, he had an eye to his future, and Elizabeth was ageing fast. He made secret overtures to King James of Scotland and increasingly began to act on his own initiative in matters of State. When called to account by the Queen, he publicly insulted her and turned his back on her. Even this she eventually forgave, and in 1599 he was given command of the Irish expedition force, an army of 15,000 men over which Essex had more power than had ever been given to any previous Governor General. Everything went wrong. Essex became ill with dysentery and probably a kidney stone, and, surprisingly, he was a poor commander. His men were killed by the hundreds in battles, died of disease or simply deserted, until he had only 4000 left. The Queen was appalled, but she sent him reinforcements of 2000 men. Eventually, rather than fight a major battle he knew he could not win, Essex met his opponent, the Earl of Tyrone (Hugh O'Neill), and negotiated a peace treaty which was disadvantageous to England. Elizabeth was livid and wrote at once ordering him to wage war against Tyrone.

The Queen had forgiven Essex so many times that he was confident she would do so again, despite the fact that his ignominious failure had cost a staggering £300,000 and the lives of thousands of men. Deserting his army, he hurried back to London where he discovered she was at Nonsuch. After crossing the Thames by ferry, travel-stained, soaked through from heavy rain and with muddy boots, he arrogantly strode past the Queen's guards, through the Privy Chambers and entered her bedchamber (as he had obviously been used to do). The Queen had just risen from her bed and had not yet begun her *toilette*.

Although she was vigorous and wiry, still danced, and dressed magnificently from a wardrobe containing three thousand dresses, Elizabeth was now showing her age. Even riding her horse left her stiff and numb. A contemporary account describes her as 'very majestic, her face oblong, fair but wrinkled, her eyes small, jet black and pleasant, her nose a little hooked, her lips narrow and her teeth black. Her hair was of an auburn colour, but false; her bosom was uncovered as all English ladies do until they marry'.[4] The French Ambassador had also noted the bare royal bosom that season, and in his report distressingly described it as 'somewhat wrinkled'.[5] To maintain her majestic image as Gloriana, Elizabeth necessarily spent long hours being made up and dressed for her public.

When Essex burst in on her she was understandably at first flustered that this young and supremely handsome man should catch her with her unmade face showing every wrinkle, and her thin and wispy white hair without her red hairpiece. She was not alone, of course – there were Ladies of the Bedchamber present, and ladies and gentlemen waiting in the adjacent Privy Chamber to witness that the Queen listened to Essex, gave him her hand to kiss, and sent him away kindly enough. Only subsequently did she allow herself the luxury of anger because she had been caught at such a disadvantage. Essex was ordered confined to his magnificent London house (formerly Leicester House where Bess had once stayed). Eventually, his act of *lèse-majesté* probably cost Essex his life, for the Queen never really forgave him. When they next met, Essex knelt before her, but she took hold of him by his belt and shook him violently and berated him. Those watching reported with awe that 'her choler did outrun all reason . . . [and] there was no doubt whose daughter she was . . .'[6]

Months later, in June 1600, a special commission was convened at York House, chaired by Lord Egerton, Lord Keeper of the Great Seal of England. Here Essex was finally asked to explain why he had treasonably ignored the Queen's order to fight Tyrone. He proclaimed that he would tear his heart from his chest rather than commit an act disloyal to the Queen. The charge of treason was subsequently dropped, but he was found guilty of disobedience and dereliction of duty, stripped of all his titles and kept under house arrest for the remainder of the year.

By January 1601 his plight had provoked massive public sympathy. Essex had been regarded as a national hero since his exploits in Cadiz in 1596 and was acclaimed by cheers and clapping wherever he went. The full facts of his failure in Ireland were not yet known by the masses, so his popularity remained undimmed. During that winter, pamphlets proclaiming his innocence were widely distributed, and graffiti insulting to the Queen appeared on walls all over London. Cecil was said to have 'poisoned the Queen's mind' against Essex. Even the clergy became involved, and congregations in churches throughout the country were urged to pray that the Queen might show clemency to the Earl.

At this point that wily statesman Robert Cecil deliberately circulated a false rumour that Essex was to be moved to the Tower. Alarmed, Essex allowed himself to be convinced by his supporters that he could rally the city to himself. On 8 February, after rumours had eddied for days, he broke out of Essex House and with two hundred men rode through the city attempting to stage a coup. It was an act of utter stupidity, which ended with his surrender to the Earl of Nottingham. He was charged with treason and this time he was indeed imprisoned in the Tower.

Only eleven days later, on 19 February, Essex was brought to trial, convicted, and sentenced to death. Cecil could move with lightning speed when he chose and he was taking no chances with this declared enemy of his. He need not have worried; a year earlier Elizabeth might have forgiven Essex, might have intervened and insisted on some form of clemency such as lifelong banishment. But she could never feel the same about him once he had seen the old woman behind her glorious façade, nor would she ever forgive the fact that he had attempted to take her crown.

In the first days of their affectionate relationship Elizabeth was said to have given Essex a ring from her finger. It was of gold, with a cameo of Elizabeth, possibly the one now in the Chapter House Museum at Westminster Abbey. She told Essex that if he ever returned the ring to her she would grant him any request. A legend persists that a few days before his death, Essex smuggled this 'boon' ring out of the Tower to his friend Lady Scrope, asking her to take the ring to the Queen. By mistake it was taken to Lady Scrope's sister, the Countess of Nottingham, wife of the man who had accepted the surrender of Essex and was his bitter rival. The ring never reached the Queen. There is no existing evidence to support this story, but there is historical evidence that even while Essex was trying to raise London against her, Elizabeth attempted to go out alone into Fleet Street to see if anyone would dare to attack her person. It was an act of typical courage by Elizabeth, and she had to be forcibly restrained by her Councillors, 'with much ado', from carrying out her intention.

Lady Essex, of whom the Queen was fond, begged for her husband's life to no avail. After attending a play by Shakespeare on Shrove Tuesday night, the Queen signed the death warrant. On the following morning, Ash Wednesday, 25 February 1601, Essex went to the block. He was the last of Elizabeth's favourites; she was never seen to grieve for him.

All of these events were relayed to Hardwick by Bess's network of correspondents, which included first-hand accounts from Lord Keeper Egerton, who chaired the commission which first examined Essex. Only a little over two years earlier, Lord Essex had been an honoured guest at Hardwick. His power at Court had made him a target for anyone hoping to curry favour with the Queen, Bess among them. There are several surviving letters between her and Essex during the intervening period, indicating that the relationship was maintained and valued. Later, Arbella would reveal that she was desperately grieved at the death of Essex. Had he not already been already married (to Philip Sidney's widow), Essex might well have married Arbella for her lineage alone, though he was evidently also attracted to her physically and had several times 'stolen' kisses. But that February of 1601, Bess and Arbella could only follow the fortunes of their friend Essex through letters and reports by the occasional visitor en route from Court. Bess had seen it all before, of course – numbers of her friends over the years had raised themselves too high and had suffered the ultimate penalty.

Bess was now seventy-four, still in good health and as busy as she had ever been. But she did not ignore the inevitable, and, against the possibility of a sudden demise, she had an elaborate tomb built from a design by Smythson. In her accounts are the details of the costs, including a payment to the vicar for organising the stone, labourers to prepare the site, the 'chief stone-getter' and his men, and for teams of horses to drag forty loads of stone to Derby from the quarries. On 27 April 1601 it was 'finished and wanting nothing but setting up' in the place she had designated: All Hallows Church in Derby (now Derby Cathedral). She also wrote her will, in which she attested that she was 'in my perfect health and good memory, I thank my most merciful Father', and she made William her heir and sole executor. To William's son Wylkyn she left a 'Cup of Lapis Lazuli with cover, all garnished with gold and enamelled, as an heirloom to go with my house at Hardwick, and to stand entailed at my decease, as the furniture [at Hardwick] stands entailed'.

Henry, who was still living discontentedly at Tutbury, and to whom Chatsworth was entailed by his father's will, was left the contents of Chatsworth House (though she had already removed the most valuable furnishings to Hardwick). She left Henry's wife, 'my daughter Grace, 100 angels to buy a ring to wear for me'.* To Arbella, 'my very loving grandchild', she left a crystal looking-glass framed with silver and gilt and set with lapis lazuli and agate; a sable, the head being of gold set with stone; a white ermine sable with a gold enamelled head; 'all my pearls and jewels' except those individually bequeathed; 'and I give to her a thousand pounds in money'.[7]

Her eldest daughter Frances and 'my beloved son Henry Pierrepoint' (who was asked to be a supervisor of the will) were provided for, but Bess's other two children were specifically disinherited because of 'unkindness offered me by my son-in-law the Earl of Shrewsbury, and my daughter his wife, and likewise my son Charles Cavendish . . .' However, she offered them her forgiveness for the wrongs they had done her, and left them her blessing.

Assuming she might die before the Queen, Bess left her 'a cup of gold' worth £200; but the gift had strings. Bess begged that the Queen would be 'good and gracious' to Arbella, 'a poor orphan', and also to 'all my children', reminding the Queen of 'my former faithful service' and the Queen's 'former gracious usage towards me'.[8]

Eighteen people witnessed Bess's will; most were members of her household. She was taking no chances that it might be contested. One is tempted to wonder whether she was using it as a form of weapon to bring Charles, Mary and Gilbert back into line. Having already given her children lands and houses sufficient to

---

*An angel was worth six shillings and eightpence.

live in luxury, what other method did she have for disciplining them than threatening to cut them out of the eventual sharing out of her great fortune? Bess was no different from a present-day self-made tycoon who cannot see why their children, despite having been given far greater advantages, cannot accomplish as much as they have, or even simply capitalise on their good fortune.

Together with her account books, the great inventory listing Bess's possessions at Chatsworth and the two houses at Hardwick which formed part of her will in 1601 provides a vivid picture of Bess's life and a virtual tour of her houses. Each room is named, and every piece listed. It is an astonishing record of acquired riches, even though it does not include her jewellery and personal objects of significant value which appear in jewellery lists of previous dates, or those mentioned in her will: the looking-glass framed in silver gilt and set with lapis lazuli and agates, for example, the ropes of huge pearls for which she was famous, and her rings of 'great' diamonds, rubies, and emeralds. And that precious lapis cup. These items must surely have been housed within the various small coffers in her bedchamber, 'a little gilt coffer, a little coffer covered with leather, a little coffer covered with black velvet, three flat coffers covered with leather, a box painted and gilded with my Lord and Lady's arms on it, a yellow cotton to cover it, another box covered in green velvet'. These small coffers were not to be confused with the two great iron-bound coffers which held land deeds and her store of gold and silver coins.

Chatsworth was seldom used at this point, but it was still furnished and maintained. By now William had remarried; his second wife was Elizabeth Wortley, the daughter of a family friend who was also one of Gilbert's many legal opponents. William, Elizabeth and the children had moved to Oldcotes, leaving his chamber in the Old Hall at Hardwick almost empty at the time of the inventory. The other rooms in the Old Hall were kept furnished and used to house visitors when the new house was full. The workshops at the Old Hall served both properties, and there was also a bakehouse, brewhouse, dairy, chandlery, smithy and still house. The two Halls at Hardwick were almost a small village.[9]

We know from letters and reports of visitors that Bess increasingly suffered from rheumatism or arthritis, and occasionally used a stick as she walked about her houses and gardens checking everything was in order. She must have had a little dog, too, for there was a tethering ring on one leg of her writing desk, where she habitually hitched the leash.[10] But those large windows, which were so splendid architecturally, made the house particularly cold and draughty in the winter, especially perched as it was on a hilltop, and Bess always had a fire in her bedchamber, which she kept insulated against draughts and winter chills. And, rather than the opulent satins and velvets which featured in the guest rooms, her bed was hung with warm bed-curtains of finely woven scarlet wool. The window curtains were also scarlet. And a second pair of bed-hangings were kept to be used over the scarlet ones in exceptionally cold weather; when these were all fastened round her bed, it must have been cosy to the point of stuffiness.

Bess's ageing bones evidently felt the cold a good deal, for in her chamber were three 'coverlets' to hang across the two windows and the doors in winter months. Eight warm rugs protected her un-shod feet, two great tapestries fifteen foot deep, 'with personages and forest work', hung against the walls. And in addition to the 'featherbed', bolster and pillows, there were twelve warm blankets.

As well as her own great scarlet-caparisoned tester bed, Bess's bedchamber housed Arbella's smaller bed with its gilt knobs and two blue and white curtains suspended from a crown-like canopy – a sort of half-tester. Besides the beds there was Bess's writing desk, a folding table and a chair and some stools, and the great iron-bound money and deed coffers. At the time of the inventory she seems to have been doing most of her work in this room, for she had no study, though other 'desks' were listed, which were probably portable writing slopes that could be carried from room to room and placed on any table.

In the winter months, the ageing Countess probably spent a good deal of time in her bedchamber for it is not a large room compared with the others in the house, which would have made it easier to keep warm. Six books are listed in the inventory: 'Calvin upon Job (covered in russet velvet), the Resolutions, Saloman's Proverbs, a book of meditations, and two other books'.*

The lack of a library at Hardwick in Bess's day has been noted critically by some writers, yet Bess never pretended to be an academic. She received only the usual education given to a girl child, but she was careful to ensure her daughters and granddaughters were educated to a higher standard than was the norm. Nor were books in such ready supply; there was no mass market, and books were costly items. Sir William St Loe, we know, bought books for himself and for Bess's children. We know that her son, Sir William Cavendish, was an avid reader, and his account books reveal that he purchased numbers of books, including Stow's *Chronicles*, Guazzo's *Dialogues*, and Gilbert's classic work on *Magnets and Magnetism*, as well as Italian and Latin works. Arbella, though, was considered a learned woman and a bookworm. Her tutor wrote of conversations between them as she 'worked at her books'. Yet there is no list of books in Arbella's room either. Perhaps, like the jewels and other precious items, books were normally kept in boxes and so were not included in the inventory.

A small room off Bess's bedchamber was used to house the close stool – a rudimentary ensuite toilet – and the main door led to her much larger 'withdrawing chamber', where she received family and friends, or sat with her ladies and gentlemen. Listed in the 1601 inventory, besides her own gilded and black leather chair and wooden footstool, is a little chair of wrought cloth-of-gold with gold and red silk fringe, a chair of 'Turkie work' [presumably

---

*While this book was being researched, another contemporary book was discovered at Hardwick. It had been dropped or hidden behind the panelling in Bess's bedchamber – it was a small catechism of the sort children used.

covered in Turkish silk carpeting or tapestry], 'two chairs for children' and a large number of stools: 'five stools of Turkie work, a little stool of green cloth, two black leather stools, three inlaid stools, two inlaid forms . . .' – enough seating for about twenty people.

Bess's household, like the Court in London, contained many young people, and many of her ladies and gentlemen were far younger than she was. Perhaps, as one biographer claimed, Bess drew energy from this pool of youth; or perhaps she employed young people for Arbella's sake. If so, it does not seem to have worked, since Arbella was morose and depressed following the death of Essex. News of her misery even reached the Court, where she was said to be 'heartbroken'.[11] Arbella may well have been emotionally involved with Essex; it is impossible to say, since no correspondence between the two has survived. But an equally acceptable explanation is that Arbella was depressed at what she regarded as a form of imprisonment, and that she had relied on Essex to help her to get out of Hardwick.

So she moped about, working with her tutor, often quarrelling with her grandmother who, impatient with Arbella's restless moodiness, berated her. When the women of the family met to discuss wedding plans for Arbella's much younger cousin* with all the pleasure that such an occasion brings, it served only to increase Arbella's moodiness. Despite all the prestigious propositions of marriage that had surrounded her name in the past, and the brilliant future for which she had been educated and led to believe was her birthright, here she was in her middle twenties, an 'old maid' in the sight of the world, trapped in her grandmother's house and with nothing to look forward to.

To be fair to Bess, she had done everything possible to find her granddaughter a husband, even at the cost of inviting the Queen's

---

*Nineteen-year-old Lady Elizabeth Talbot, daughter of Gilbert and Mary, was to marry Henry Grey, heir (after his father) to his uncle Henry Grey, 6th Earl of Kent.

disapproval. Bess truly loved Arbella. She was the only person spoken of in affectionate terms in Bess's will (apart from little James Cavendish), and she often gave her granddaughter costly gifts and treats. But what Arbella wanted was a life of her own, and this Bess was unable to give her, since the Queen had made it abundantly clear that Arbella's marriage was State business, not Bess's. Inevitably, the once affectionate relationship between Bess and Arbella began to break down. Bess, fulfilled and always busy, could not understand why her granddaughter was not equally content. Arbella's life was, after all, not an unusual one for an unmarried daughter, and it was more luxurious than most. Perhaps Arbella was chaperoned more closely than some at times, but this had been prescribed by the Queen, and the girl had many friends in the local area.

So Bess sometimes spoke to Arbella sharply, and was not above administering an occasional slap, or even tweaking her nose. Arbella felt humiliated and tearfully told her tutor and chaplain that she spent most of her time now thinking of ways 'to get from home, by reason that she was hardly used in despiteful and disgraceful words'. In writing of this, Starkey said that her distress 'seemed not feigned, for oftentimes, being at her books she would break forth into tears'.[12] Arbella now regarded Bess as her jailer, and blamed her for all her unhappiness.

Eventually, Arbella's desperation drove her to an act of folly. Having concluded that marriage was the only way of escape for her (as it was for the majority of women in the Elizabethan era), and since her grandmother seemed unable to find her a husband, she decided to find her own. Later Arbella would describe herself as being 'neither credulous, nor a fool', yet she apparently gave no thought to the fact that her actions transgressed the Royal Marriage Act. Nor that her choice of husband was an extraordinarily dangerous one, for he was Edward Seymour, seventeen-year-old grandson of that hapless couple, Lord Hertford and his long-dead wife, Lady Katherine Grey.

CHAPTER 21

SHARPER THAN A SERPENT'S TOOTH*

1602–03

THROUGH HIS GREAT-GRANDMOTHER THE LADY FRANCES Brandon, young Edward Seymour was a direct descendant of Henry VII. His father, Edward, Lord Beauchamp, though born in the Tower and declared illegitimate, had a recognised claim to the throne. Allied to Arbella's own claim through her father, a union between the two was potentially explosive. The story of Lord Hertford and Lady Katherine was merely romantic history to Arbella – but to Bess, who knew the protagonists as close personal friends and had experienced the pain and the danger of it all, Arbella's proposition would have been like putting a match to dry kindling.

Later, Arbella would state that it was entirely her own idea to send a messenger to Lord Hertford, proposing the marriage as though it came from her uncles William and Henry Cavendish. From the written instructions she gave to her courier it is evident

---

*'How sharper than a serpent's tooth it is to have a thankless child.' William Shakespeare: *King Lear*, I. iv.

that she knew the history of Jane and Katherine Grey and the Hertford marriage. It seems remarkable that she could not recognise the similarity of her own situation to that of Lady Katherine. She obviously knew that her grandmother would never sanction her scheme, since before embarking upon it she took the precaution of sending her money and jewels away from Hardwick to a friend in Yorkshire, fearing that everything would be confiscated if her plan was discovered.[1] She had many sympathisers among her local friends, and chief among these were her Uncle Henry, who, being something of a black sheep, was not a frequent visitor to Hardwick, and a young 'cousin', Mr George Chaworth,* who was besotted enough to wear a 'gage' – Arbella's glove – in his cap. Arbella used her network to smuggle messages and run secret errands, and in all likelihood now identified herself with her aunt, Mary, Queen of Scots.

By December 1602, Arbella was ready to make her move. Her intended courier, James Starkey – her tutor and chaplain – who had gone to London on an extended visit to his family, decided at the last minute that he could not get involved after all. He sent a message via Arbella's aunt, Frances Pierrepoint (who probably did not realise its significance), that he was 'not available until Easter'.

Arbella then approached John Dodderidge, a trusted servant at Hardwick (he was one of the witnesses of Bess's will), and asked him to deliver a message to Lord Hertford. When he heard the message Dodderidge advised caution, saying that Arbella's grandmother would never approve it without the Queen's knowledge and sanction. Eventually Arbella persuaded him, against his better judgement, to keep the message secret from her grandmother, telling him that he was representing her uncles Henry and William; indeed that he must keep her own involvement secret when he met Lord Hertford.

---

*George Chaworth was a second cousin of Robert Barlow, Bess's first husband. Bess referred to him in letters as 'cousin'.

On Christmas Day, while the Hardwick household was too busy celebrating the winter solstice to miss him, she despatched Dodderidge with her carefully worded instructions. We know Henry Cavendish was involved to some degree, for he waited near the gate at Hardwick with a horse, and saw Dodderidge on his way. Dodderidge had applied for leave to visit his family to cover his absence, and he reached Lord Hertford's house, eight miles north of London, on the evening of 30 December.

The Seymour family were probably feasting, for the Twelve Nights of Christmas were unfailingly 'kept' by Tudor aristocracy. Lord Hertford was so surprised at being asked to speak secretly with a retainer that he would only agree to hear Dodderidge's message in front of witnesses, and what he heard made him increasingly incredulous. Poor Dodderidge – who must have been cold and tired after his long midwinter journey – was made to repeat his message and answer pertinent questions before being taken off and locked up for the night. Lord Hertford had paid a heavy price for daring to marry Katherine Grey. Many years passed before he regained the Queen's approval by the lavish entertainment offered her and her entourage at Elvetham, his property in Hampshire.* But when in 1595 he petitioned that his marriage to Katherine Grey might be legally recognised for the sake of his grandchildren, he and his two sons were arrested and clapped in the Tower. So he was taking no more risks, and at once sent a message to the Court explaining what Dodderidge had said.

Arbella had instructed Dodderidge to say that Henry and Sir William Cavendish wished to propose a marriage between their niece Arbella and Edward Seymour (who was at least a decade younger than Arbella). To this end Lord Hertford himself or Edward's father (Lord Beauchamp) must come to Hardwick with

---

*For this entertainment Lord Hertford had a lake dug in the shape of a crescent, large enough to float a small sailing ship upon it. In the lake were three islands, each containing a pavilion, and from these issued forth musicians, fireworks, actors, masques and 'other sports'.

Edward at once and in disguise, to minimise the danger of a leak. 'If they come as themselves they shall be shut out the gates, I locked up, and my grandmother will . . . advertise and complain to the Queen', Arbella warned.[2] So they must pretend to be total strangers and appear as 'an ancient, grave man' accompanied by his 'son or nephew', preferably from the north of England, calling to offer to sell some land. They were to identify themselves to her by carrying 'all the testimonies they can, [such] as some picture or handwriting of the Lady Jane Grey whose hand I know – she sent her sister a book at her death which [is] the very best they could bring – or of the Lady Katherine, or Queen Jane Seymour, or any of that family, which we know they, and none but they, have.[3]

Who else but Bess could have told Arbella about that note from Jane Grey who had been dead for almost fifty years? Jane wrote it on the Sunday before her execution, on a blank page in her Greek bible, which she had left to her sister Katherine.[4] In this inscription Jane wrote that the bible 'will teach you to live, and learn you to die' and other good advice which, as history proved, was wasted on Katherine.[5] It suggests that Bess often spoke to Arbella of the Grey sisters and their sad history. We know that Bess treasured a picture of Jane Grey, which stood on a table at her bedside for years in the same bedchamber that she still shared with Arbella. And Arbella's statement that she was familiar with Jane Grey's handwriting suggests that she had perhaps seen letters between Bess and Jane Grey, although none are known to have survived. Overall, though, Arbella's ridiculous scheme sounds as though it was concocted by a young woman who viewed life as a romantic story.

The Queen's poor health was causing concern to her courtiers that Christmas, especially since she still steadfastly refused to name her successor. When Cecil heard about Arbella's plan, he sensed a plot to take the throne after Elizabeth's death. Elizabeth, too, was uneasy; she had no love for the Seymours. It was Jane Seymour who had replaced her own mother as Queen, and perhaps Elizabeth recalled those long-ago days when as a young princess,

Thomas Seymour, the Lord Admiral, had almost been her own downfall. When asked if she would consider naming Edward Seymour, Lord Beauchamp (father of Arbella's proposed husband) as a successor, she had famously snapped: 'I will have no rascal's son in my seat.' The Arbella situation was deemed so urgent that a royal commissioner, Sir Henry Brounker, was despatched to Hardwick immediately. He left Court the same morning – New Year's Eve 1602 – with instructions to find out the truth, though he was primed to deal gently with the Dowager Countess, for Dodderidge was adamant that his mistress knew nothing of the matter.

Sir Henry Brounker arrived at Hardwick on 3 January 1603. His report advised that he found the family alone, with no visitors. 'My Lady of Shrewsbury, after she had my name, sent for me into her [long] gallery* where she was walking with the Lady Arbella and her son, William Cavendish. I told her Ladyship in the hearing of her grandchild that your Highness having occasion to send me to see her Ladyship, and to commend your Majesty unto her with all gracious favour . . .'

Royal commissioners were not sent without a good reason, and after Brounker had delivered the Queen's message, Bess was so relieved that Brounker had difficulty in preventing her from falling to her knees in gratitude. Having got the preliminaries over, Brounker suggested that Bess and he should walk to the end of the gallery to talk privately. There he handed her a letter from the Queen, which advised that she wished Arbella to speak in confidence with Sir Henry. 'In the reading thereof, I observed some change of countenance, which gave me occasion again to comfort her with the assurance of your Majesty's good opinion and favour,' Brounker wrote. Arbella then went off with Sir Henry, leaving Bess and Sir William to wonder what could be the true purpose of this visit.

*The Long Gallery is 167 feet long and up to 40 feet wide in places.

Arbella denied everything, but she was a poor liar, and Sir Henry could see by 'the coming and going of her colour that she was somewhat troubled'. After she had changed her story several times, he suggested she should write it down. She wrote a page of nonsense, which irritated Sir Henry, and he produced Dodderidge's confession and waved it at her. 'It is so openly confessed,' he warned, '[that] there is no denial', and he advised her to make another attempt. Arbella hedged because she did not know what Dodderidge had said about her uncles, Henry and William, and was clearly concerned about involving them. In fact, Dodderidge swore he had never spoken to either man, and only had Arbella's word of their involvement, but that he had received a horse from Henry Cavendish.

Arbella's next effort was yet another tissue of obfuscation. This 'made me believe her wits were somewhat distracted,' Sir Henry wrote, 'either with fear of her grandmother, or conceit of her own folly.' When he told her this, Arbella tearfully suggested that Sir Henry should write down what he wished her to say, and that she would sign it.[6] Perplexed, Sir Henry went back to see Bess and told her the entire story. It must have been shocking for her to hear that her favourite son had been implicated, and Sir Henry reported that the old lady was so distressed and angry that it was only with great restraint that she was held back from striking Arbella. And despite Sir Henry's calming assurances that she still had the Queen's favour, Bess remained very upset. Sir Henry departed, carrying, as well as Arbella's 'confession', her letter to the Queen;

May it please your most excellent Majesty,
Sir Henry Brounker has charged me with many things in your Majesty's [name], the most wherof I acknowledge to be true, and am heartily sorry that I have given your Majesty the least cause of offence. The particulars, and the manner of handling, I have, to avoid your Majesty's trouble delivered to Sir Henry Brounker. I humbly prostrate my self at your Majesty's feet, craving pardon for what is passed, and of your princely clemency to signify . . .

your gracious remission to me by your Highnesses letter to my lady my grandmother, whose discomfort I shall be until then . . . Your Majesty's most humble and dutiful handmaid,
   Arbella Stuart.[7]

Bess also wrote to the Queen, confirming that she had been ignorant of Arbella's scheme, and to state that she now felt she had no control over her wayward granddaughter. '. . . I am desirous, and most humbly beseech your Majesty, that she may be placed elsewhere, to learn to be more considerate, and that after it may please your Majesty either to accept of her service about your royal person, or to bestow her in marriage, which in all humility and duty, I do crave your Majesty, for I cannot now assure myself of her, as I have done'.[8]

Brounker was delayed on his return journey to London because his horse slipped and fell on him, but he was back at Court on 13 January and reported that in his opinion the matter was a storm in a teacup; Arbella was not a danger. More than likely, she was held too strictly at Hardwick, and he believed she had been led astray by 'base companions' who encouraged her to think her plan was feasible. He totally vindicated Lord Hertford, who was, he said, 'guiltless'.

Arbella could not know this, of course, and she sent a panicky letter to John Hacker, Mary Talbot's steward. Arbella had spent a lot of her childhood and youth with her aunt Mary, and probably regarded her as a surrogate mother. In this letter she asked Hacker to 'beseech' her aunt to come down to Hardwick, 'with the like speed she would do if my Lady my Grandmother were in extremity . . . the matters I would impart to her, and will neither for love or fear impart to any other, until I have talked with her, import us all – and especially her and me – more than the death of any one of us.'[9] The letter was intercepted by Timothy Pusey, Bess's trusted aide.

The remark that the matter was of import 'especially to her and me' suggests that Mary Talbot was involved in Arbella's plan, although no other evidence to this effect has ever surfaced. A copy was made of the intercepted letter, and this was rushed to Robert Cecil, while a reply was delivered to Arbella purporting to come from Mary Talbot, in which she apologised that she was otherwise occupied: 'I cannot come to you now'. Other notes written by Arbella to her supporters in the neighbourhood of Hardwick were likewise not delivered, and they all bear the unmistakable hand-writing of Timothy Pusey. Bess had closed all avenues for Arbella, who now had even less freedom than before.

Bess's letter of appeal was answered not by the Queen, but by her vice-chamberlain, Sir John Stanhope, who must have relished the fact that the Cavendish family was in trouble. He wrote that the Queen wished Arbella to remain at Hardwick, but that she might be held less strictly. To Arbella it must have seemed a patronising letter, for Stanhope ridiculed the difference in years between Arbella and Edward Seymour, and intimated that the idea had always been foolish, with no hope of success. It cautioned her that she must in future 'live in good sort with so good a parent and so worthy a matron' as her grandmother, because any similar behaviour in the future would not be regarded with such tolerance. It was a letter to make Arbella scream with frustration.

The relationship between Arbella and her grandmother having reached an all-time low, Arbella wrote again to the Queen, saying all she had wanted was some liberty, and begging to be allowed to come to Court to serve. Bess also wrote to the Queen; hers was the letter of a woman at her wit's end about what to do for the best. The 'bad persuasions' of Arbella's friends had 'so estranged her mind and natural affection from me,' she wrote despairingly, 'that she holds me the greatest enemy she has.'

Bess and Arbella were not on speaking terms by this time, and at the end of January Arbella wrote her grandmother a 2500-word letter, taunting her with a secret lover who would help her to escape from her imprisonment. It was a fiction, invented by Arbella to alarm Bess, and it worked. Unsure how it was possible for Arbella to have been in contact with such a person, but not knowing what to believe, Bess wrote a third time to the Queen, advising that Arbella had warned her that 'she could be taken off my hands' if she only gave the word.

Arbella then wrote to Cecil and Stanhope on 6 February 1603, more or less demanding that her grandmother be informed that it was the Queen's pleasure that she might freely choose her own servants and 'that I should . . . have the company of some young lady or gentlewoman for my recreation, and scholars, music, hunting, hawking, [a] variety of any lawful disport I can procure, or my friends will afford me.'[10] It harked back to the days of the Shrewsburys' arguments, where each protagonist used the Queen and the Council as unwilling arbitrators in a private quarrel.

The uncomfortable situation at Hardwick, though noted, seemed of diminishing importance in London that February. The Queen's closest friend, her cousin the Countess of Nottingham, died and Elizabeth became so depressed that her own health was affected. Having caught a chill, she deteriorated rapidly. King James wrote to Cecil in the same month saying he had heard that Arbella had been 'lately moved by the persuasion of Jesuits to change her religion'. Cecil delicately ridiculed this report, replying that he would take a wager that it was untrue, especially as Arbella was surrounded by good Protestants such as her grandmother and her chaplain and tutor, James Starkey. But Starkey, who had heard of Dodderidge's arrest, must have been waiting for the knock at his own door. Believing he could be implicated in a charge of treason he chose to hang himself, leaving a note which confessed to his involvement in Arbella's scheme to marry Edward Seymour, and ending: 'If I had a thousand lives I would willingly spend them all to redeem the least part of her reputation.'[11]

Starkey's suicide coincided with the arrival of Bess's third letter, and was enough to warrant Sir Henry Brounker paying another visit to Hardwick, this time to grill Arbella intensely about her self-confessed secret lover. Arbella teased him, saying coolly that she meant King James of Scotland. Such perverse behaviour was beyond Bess's comprehension. Not knowing how ill the Queen was, Bess wrote to her again, pleading that Arbella be removed, for Arbella's sake as much as her own. Arbella had now threatened a hunger strike unless she was allowed to live as she demanded.

That her granddaughter had been driven beyond the limits of her endurance seemed not to occur to Bess; 'Arbella is so wilfully bent,' she wrote despairingly to Cecil, 'that she has made a vow not to eat or drink in this house at Hardwick, or where I am, until she may hear from her Majesty. So that for preservation of her life, I am enforced to suffer her to go to a house of mine called Oldcotes, two miles from here. I am wearied of my life, and therefore humbly beseech Her Majesty to have compassion on me . . . there is so little reason in most of her doings, that I cannot tell what to make of it. A few more weeks as I have suffered of late will make an end of me . . . I see her mind is the cause of all.'[12]

Arbella's sanity would be brought into question later in her life; indeed, her most recent biographer suggests she may have suffered from porphyria.* It is hardly surprising that the pragmatic Bess had come to the conclusion that her granddaughter was mentally disturbed; she had witnessed Arbella's year-long melancholia following the death of Essex, and her extraordinary scheme concerning Edward Seymour. Even Brounker thought 'her wits were thoroughly disordered', and her behaviour since his visit in January had been part manic and part depressed; one day she was in floods of despairing tears, the next she was smilingly threatening to escape with her secret lover, or to starve herself to death. She studiously ignored attempts by members of the household to bring her into conversation, and spent hours scribbling letters that were sometimes dozens of pages long, and in which she vented her anger, despair and desire to take control of

---

*Some of Arbella's symptoms are those of porphyria: 'transient mental breakdown which may be interpreted by observers as hysteria, which can be mild or severe, but despite the severity of an attack the patient can recover very rapidly.' Mary, Queen of Scots is also thought to have suffered from this disease, but the best-known royal sufferer is George III.

her own life. One letter to Brounker was so rambling and lengthy that he suggested so much writing had caused 'a distemper of her brain'. Some of Arbella's writing is wild and unhinged; but it was clearly cathartic for her, a psychological release for a well-educated woman who felt there was no one in whom she could confide.

Bess could not know it when she wrote her letters, but she would never again hear from the Queen. Elizabeth had not yet taken to her deathbed, but she was already dying. The story was put about that she was broken-hearted at the loss of the Countess of Nottingham, but her chill became an infection, which led to abscesses in her throat, and this deteriorated into what sounds like pneumonia. When Lady Nottingham's brother, Robert Carey, visited the Queen at Richmond in the week after his sister's death, he was shocked at his cousin's appearance. 'I am not well, Robin,' she told him flatly. 'And in her discourse', he said, 'she fetched . . . forty or fifty great sighs. I was grieved . . . to see her in such plight, for in all my lifetime before I never knew her fetch a sigh but when the Queen of Scots was beheaded.'[13] Later her long slim fingers swelled so much that her Coronation Ring, embedded in the flesh, caused her great pain. A decision was taken to cut it off, but this distressed her; 'all the fabric of my reign,' she wrote, 'little by little, is beginning to fail.'[14]

Meanwhile, at Hardwick, there was another crisis brewing. In March Arbella returned from Oldcotes, where she had spent the past weeks concocting another plan to escape from her grandmother. Once again her uncle Henry Cavendish was involved. On Shrove Tuesday she received a letter, which she read and overtly threw into the fire. Bess was suspicious but said nothing.

The following day, Ash Wednesday (9 March in 1603), was a significant date since Essex had been executed on Ash Wednesday two years earlier. Arbella wrote to Sir Henry Brounker reminding him of Essex and:

> . . . this fatal day, Ash Wednesday, and the new dropping of tears of some, might make you remember – if it were possible you could

forget ... And were not I unthankfully forgetful, if I should not
remember my noble friend, who graced me ... [an] unproved prisoner and undeserved exile, in his greatest and happy fortunes ...
eclipsing part of Her Majesty's favours from him; which were so
dear, so welcome to him? ... I am constrained to renew these
melancholy thoughts, by the smarting feeling of my great loss, who
may well say I never had, nor never shall have, the like friend ...[15]

That same day Arbella sent her page, Richard Owen,* and
another servant, Henry Dove, to an inn at Mansfield where Henry
Cavendish was waiting for her instructions regarding the escape
scheduled for the following day, Thursday. He was almost certainly the writer of the letter that Arbella had burned. The plan was
that Henry would wait at Ault Hucknall church where, under the
pretext of taking a walk in the park, Arbella would meet him at
noon; an escort of armed men was to hide in the woods nearby.
Richard Owen returned to Hardwick, and Henry Dove remained
with Henry Cavendish.

By suppertime on Ash Wednesday, Bess had received a report
that her son Henry had been seen acting suspiciously. He was
staying at the Mansfield Inn in the company of John Stapleton, a
well-known Catholic. Stapleton was 'son and heir to Stapleton of
Carleton in Yorkshire', Bess explained later. 'It is 8 years since I saw
him. He hath written to me many times to know if he might come
[to Hardwick] but I disliking him would not suffer him.' These two
gentlemen were accompanied by a party of thirty or forty horsemen, all armed with daggers and pistols, and one of the horses had
a small pillion seat 'to carry a woman behind him', and the rider
had attempted to hide this with his cloak.

On Thursday morning, Henry Cavendish and Stapleton rode
into Ault Hucknall with eight of their men, leaving the remainder

---

*Possibly the son of the groom Owen, whom Shrewsbury had once insisted Bess
should dismiss.

hiding in and around the area, some at Rowthorne, where 'Stapleton hath lurked three days, as I heard even now', Bess wrote. She was alarmed enough at the report to disperse her own men in and around the village to watch and listen, and it is to them that we owe the next part of the story. They heard a villager ask Dove what Henry and his men were doing there, and he answered, 'to take my Lady Arbella away'. Henry and Stapleton called on the parson, Mr Chapman, and told him 'they were desirous to speak with Lady Arbella for her good, and they desired to have the key of the steeple to see if my lady Arbella did come to them'. Reverend Chapman was wary, and pretended to have difficulty finding the key, but Mrs Chapman forthrightly burst out: 'If you had been here on Saturday last you might have seen her for she was at the church.' At this Stapleton took off his hat and threw it on the ground.[16]

The two men were invited into the parsonage for refreshments, and soon afterwards two of Arbella's servants, Richard Owen and her embroiderer Freek, arrived with a message. Arbella had set off for her walk at noon, but had been stopped by a member of the household who had reminded her that it was time to eat. Realising it would be unwise to make an issue of it, Arbella sent word that they would have to try again on another day. There was some discussion among the men, who said it would be two weeks before they could remuster.

Henry and Stapleton then mounted their horses and rode off, appearing at 2 p.m. at the porter's lodge at the main gate of Hardwick. They were alone, but Bess knew that 'well-armed' men were hidden nearby, so her gates remained locked. Henry sent in a message that they wished to visit his niece, but Bess refused to allow Stapleton through the gates, 'for I have disliked him of long, for many respects', she wrote later to Sir Henry Brounker. However, she continued:

. . . for that Arbell was desirous to speak with my bad son Henry I was content to suffer him to come into my house and speak with her, rather than she to go to him, but sent word not to remain here above two hours . . . Arbell and Henry Cavendish had not talked, as I think, a dozen words together, [before] they both came down and offered to go out of my gates. One of my servants entreated them not to . . . go out until they had my consent. Arbell seemed unwilling to stay, yet at length, by persuasion did stay until word was brought to me. When I understood of it, I sent word to her that I did not think it good she should speak with Stapleton, and wished her to forbear it, for I thought Stapleton no fit man for her to converse with.[17]

Demanding of her grandmother whether she was now a true prisoner, Arbella said she would soon see, and walked out of the house towards the porter's lodge. On Bess's orders the porter refused to open the gate, so Arbella exchanged a few words with Stapleton through the gate, telling him to return to Mansfield and stay there until he heard from her. She then asked Henry to return on the following day but Bess forbade it, 'so I think he will not come,' she wrote. The two men then left. There was very little Henry could do, in fact. Had he stormed the house with his band of armed men, his mother, as well as people whom he and Arbella respected, would inevitably have been hurt. Once again the strategy had not been thought through. Henry was 'no sooner gone out of my gates', when Arbella announced that she intended to take a walk, 'which', wrote Bess, 'I thought not convenient'. She had won the day simply because she had been able to impose her will over Henry and Arbella, but knew she could not guarantee Arbella's safekeeping in the future: 'she being here one day, I fear I shall not have her here the morrow if I should suffer her to go out of the gates. In my opinion it were best she were removed . . .'[18]

At the end of what must have been a very trying and emotionally fraught day, Bess sat down and wrote a full report of everything that had happened and despatched it at once by a fast rider to Sir Henry Brounker. On learning of the Stapleton involvement, Robert

Cecil – always paranoid about a Catholic plot – feared that the attempt to 'rescue' Arbella might, after all, be part of an attempt to marry her to a claimant to the throne. Perhaps there *had* been a secret lover. It was particularly sinister at a time when the Queen was probably dying, though few people besides himself and Elizabeth's attendants knew this. Once again Brounker rushed up to Hardwick, but Arbella refused to see him. She locked herself in her room, sending him a note which said that she would not come out 'till I be absolutely cleared and free every way, and have my just desires granted and allowed'.[19] After Brounker left, the Privy Council sent messages to Sir John Manners at Haddon Hall, and Sir Francis Leake at Rufford Abbey, requiring them to lend assistance to the Dowager Countess in looking after Arbella. They were neighbours and old friends of Bess, as well as being connected by marriage.

By this time Bess had taken as much as she was prepared to stand. On 20 March she amended her will, adding a codicil to revoke the bequests she had formerly made to Arbella and Henry, 'and resolved that neither . . . of them shall have any benefit by any such gift or legacy'.

At 2 o'clock on the morning of 24 March 1603, Queen Elizabeth died. On the previous evening, Robert Cecil and Lords Nottingham and Egerton had begged her to name her successor but she was already beyond speech. However she did, so they claimed, make a little sign with her hands and fingers, which they took to indicate a crown. This was interpreted as her wish that King James should be her successor, and it was indeed convenient, for by the greatest good fortune Cecil had already arranged relays of fresh horses posted along the road from London to Scotland, and for Robert Carey* to stand by, ready to ride with the news to the Scottish King.

As soon as Elizabeth had breathed her last, a ring was dropped

---

*Robert Carey was a younger son of Lord Hunsdon (Elizabeth's maternal cousin), and the brother of Lady Nottingham and Lady Scrope. It was Carey who had been the bearer of the letter written by Elizabeth to King James, advising that his mother had been executed contrary to her wishes.

from her bedchamber window as a signal to Carey, who was waiting below, ready for his epic ride. One version of this event says that this ring was a sapphire one, given by Carey to his sister Lady Scrope, who was in the Queen's chamber with instructions to drop it as a secret signal that the Queen had died. However, there was no need for secret signals since Carey was standing by under Cecil's specific orders. Another version is that the mother-of-pearl, gold, ruby and diamond ring that Elizabeth wore every day was taken from her finger. And that it was this ring, bearing the initial E in diamonds, and the initial R for Regina in blue enamel, which was taken to James, so that he could be sure that Elizabeth was truly dead. This remarkable ring survives today and was recently on exhibition at Greenwich for the first time in living memory.[20] It was designed as a locket and opens to reveal miniature enamelled busts of Elizabeth and Anne Boleyn. There is something very touching in the knowledge that, although Elizabeth never mentioned her mother after coming to the throne, she nevertheless carried this secret daily reminder of her.

To avoid possible public disorder, news of the Queen's illness had been suppressed by order of the Privy Council. Rumours had inevitably leaked, but the news of her death was received quietly, and on the following day King James VI of Scotland was proclaimed King James I of England. It was a peaceful transition, smoother than anyone in the Privy Council had dared hope. They had feared a possible uprising featuring rival claimants, especially when Edward Seymour, Lord Beauchamp, left London secretly on the evening before Elizabeth's death. But there were no riots, no dissent at all. Indeed, the only galloping horsemen were those hastening to Scotland to introduce themselves to the new King, just as the roads to Hatfield had once been crowded at the time of Elizabeth's accession.

Edward Seymour, Lord Beauchamp, may well have had something planned, for according to rumours he was in the West Country and – backed by the French – had mustered a force of up to 10,000 men, ready to support his claim to the throne, and that of Arbella, against James of Scotland. However, Frances Pierrepoint wrote to her mother that a visitor from London had just told them 'that all things in the southern parts proceed peaceably; only my Lord Beauchamp is said to make some assemblies which he [the visitor] hopeth will suddenly dissolve into smoke, his [Beauchamp's] forces being feeble to make headway against so great an union'.[21] Nothing further was heard of this matter, but in the State papers is a report that Lord Beauchamp had yielded to pressure from his father Lord Hertford, who threatened to have himself carried to London, crippled as he was, and pledge his son's name to the proclamation of the new King.[22] Reading this, the researcher is tempted to wonder whether Beauchamp was not, after all, somehow involved in the marriage proposals Arbella had made concerning his son.

An uneasy quiet settled at Hardwick, as if Bess and Arbella were each waiting to see how they would be affected. They did not have long to wait. In early April the King wrote to Henry Grey, 6th Earl of Kent, and asked him to take Arbella in. 'We are desirous to free our cousin the Lady Arbella from that unpleasant life which she hath led in the house of her Grandmother, with whose severity and age, she – being a young lady – could hardly agree'.[23]

Henry Grey was a distant kinsman to Arbella. Her cousin Elizabeth (daughter of Mary and Gilbert Talbot) was married to the Earl's nephew and eventual successor, and the popular young couple lived with the Earl on the Earl's estate, Wrest Park near Bedford. It is likely that the King had been prompted to make this request by Robert Cecil, at Gilbert Talbot's urging, since Gilbert was at Whitehall at the time. Whatever prompted it, a request from a new King was unlikely to be refused; an invitation to Arbella to visit her cousin at Wrest Park was duly received, and she packed and departed south, to the great relief of all parties.

Bess had been constrained by orders from the Queen concerning Arbella's movements and marital prospects; Arbella had regarded

Bess's care as smothering and ambitious – and not without some justification. But it was a sad end to Bess's dreams and ambitions for her granddaughter, and she considered the episode a poor and ungrateful reward for the love and care she had lavished on Arbella since her birth.

Arbella was the highest-ranking female relative of Queen Elizabeth, and, as such, she was invited to attend the State funeral on 28 April as the Principal Mourner. She petulantly refused on the grounds that since she had not been allowed into the Queen's presence during the latter's lifetime, she refused to be brought upon the stage now 'as a public spectacle'.[24]

The account books indicate that life at Hardwick quickly resumed normality after Arbella's departure, but Bess was not untouched by recent events. She was six years older than Queen Elizabeth, and had known her ever since the time when, as a vulnerable teenage princess, she had stood as godmother to Henry Cavendish. The death of such a vital personality, who had played a key role in Bess's life for over forty years, and who had wielded an almost omnipotent power, was bound to cause shock and a sense of personal loss, as well as provoking thoughts of Bess's own mortality, since she had outlived almost everyone in her own generation.

Added to this, Bess had been subjected to upsetting tantrums for months, terminating in the emotional trauma of Arbella's departure, which everyone felt was likely to be a permanent separation. There was bound to be an effect. Even today, when life expectancy is more than twice that of an Elizabethan, the elderly are not resilient to profound emotional shock. At the age of seventy-six Bess still possessed an indomitable spirit, but the events of the previous six months caused her at last to start feeling her age.

CHAPTER 22

END OF AN ERA

1603–08

EVEN AFTER THE DEATHS OF QUEEN ELIZABETH AND HER friends, Bess managed to remain in touch with the latest news, gossip and legislation from the Court; it was not unusual for three or four letters to arrive in the same week containing identical information. One of her most useful and informed correspondents was Dr James Montague, Dean of the Chapel Royal, to whom Bess gave gifts of 'above three hundred pounds' in one year.[1] Her letters to Robert Cecil and others on business matters were as cogent and decisive as ever, but from 1603 there is a creeping sense of Bess starting to become an observer of the lives of others rather than an initiator of events. The trauma of the events of the past months – Henry and Arbella's betrayal of her, as she saw it, and the Queen's death – had been a watershed.

Visitors to Hardwick variously reported that Bess was 'well for her age', 'increasingly frail', or suffering from hip pain and 'walking with the aid of a stick'. William Cavendish took over more and more of his mother's work, and obviously had her total confidence, which was not well received by his siblings who saw him, rather, as feathering his own nest. As a Member of Parliament, William was a frequent visitor to London, and in a position to keep his mother well informed. He had a precise mind and, like his father, had a good head for figures. He was clever in business matters, but he lacked his mother's ability as an entrepreneur, and, more than that, her humanity. Bess, though, regarded William and his children as the future of the Cavendish family and everything she had worked for.

From letters and visitors' reports we know that Bess kept abreast of events which affected the lives of Henry, Mary and Charles, though she did not interfere and was not directly involved in them. Thus she knew that Gilbert and Mary did not join the trek to Edinburgh. As soon as the death of Queen Elizabeth was confirmed, and probably acting on Cecil's advice, Gilbert wrote to King James, saying that he would be honoured to serve him, and hoped there would be no lack of trust because of his father's role in the life of the King's mother. And he tentatively suggested the King might like to break his journey south by staying with him and his wife at their house at Worksop.

A week later the King wrote to reassure him: 'Assuring you that as you have uttered your tender affection and most dutiful care to serve us, whereof we never had any distrust . . . We will at all occasions make it known to you how far we respected your friendly courage in all the process of that which is past, since the decease of our late dearest sister the Queen [Elizabeth].' He ended his letter by accepting Gilbert's invitation to stay at Worksop.[2] This was more than Gilbert had hoped for and he was cock-a-hoop at the opportunity to gain the new King's favour so early in the reign. He immediately wrote to the local gentry advising that the King was coming to Worksop, and inviting them to be part of the company, adding that he would 'not refuse any fat capons, and hens, partridges, or the like'.[3] It was to be a sort of up-market 'bring-your-own' party.

On 20 April Gilbert and Mary welcomed the new King and his entourage to the great Smythson-designed house, which Mary,

Queen of Scots had twice visited. Probably more than any other single factor, Worksop had been responsible for the old Earl's financial difficulties at the end of his life. Yet how pleased he would have been that it was to be used to entertain the monarch. Sadly for Bess, who is said to have designed the Great High Chamber at Hardwick specifically with a royal visit in mind, her wish was never gratified.

The King was happy to dawdle at Worksop. He could not, by tradition, take possession of Whitehall until after Elizabeth's funeral had taken place later the same week. Bess would have heard immediately – as would the entire county and beyond – of the lavish entertainment provided by Gilbert and Mary, and aware of the poor state of their finances she must have winced, knowing that they were incurring further debt in the hope of what they might gain in favours in the future. She had seen it all before.

The cost of this royal visit might have been the reason why, a few days after the King left Worksop, Gilbert asked a friend of Bess, Sir John Bentley, to try to effect a reconciliation between himself and his mother-in-law, 'who in the end,' Bentley reported, 'seems to have agreed'.[4] Nothing came of this initiative, for in the following January there is a letter to Gilbert from Sir Francis Leake in which Leake 'hopes that the opportunity for a reconciliation with the Dowager Countess will soon occur'.[5]

The funeral of Queen Elizabeth took place on a spring day. Her body had been embalmed and transported by State barge from Richmond to Whitehall. There, watched over by relays of lords and ladies, it lay in state on a black velvet bed until 28 April. Thousands lined the procession route, just as their parents and grandparents had done at her coronation. The Elizabethan chronicler John Stow reported that Westminster was crammed, 'the streets, houses, windows, leads [roofs] and gutters' all packed with a silent, expectant multitude. There was a long procession of a thousand participants, but it was Elizabeth's coffin the public wanted to see. It was borne on a horse-drawn chariot draped in black velvet. Alongside marched a dozen noblemen – six either side – clad in black mourning robes and carrying long poles from which flew banners depicting the arms of England, the lion of England, the dragon of Wales, the Tudor grey-hound, the fleur-de-lis of France, and other heraldic devices. The banners provided the only spot of colour that day.

What drew everyone's rapt attention, however, was the life-size wax effigy of Elizabeth which lay on top of her coffin. Many appeared to think it was the Queen herself they saw. As the vehicle passed, Stow wrote, 'there was such a general sighing, groaning, and weeping as the like hath not been seen or known of in the memory of man.' He might have been describing the twentieth-century reaction to the funeral of Diana, Princess of Wales. There had been crowded streets for the funerals of Henry VIII, Edward VI, 'Bloody' Mary and other royals, but these had been mere pageants by comparison. Elizabeth had lived in the hearts of her people for forty-five years and her death was felt personally. She symbolised the spirit of the age, and with her death this age had ended. They did not yet know it, but the term Elizabethan would remain synonymous with English pride and renaissance through four centuries.

On the following day King James entered London with what appeared to observers to be a motley court of Scotsmen, which – according to Horace Walpole – initiated a new nursery rhyme:

> Hark, hark, the dogs do bark,
> The beggars are coming to town,
> Some in rags, and some in tags,
> And some in velvet gowns . . .

Like Bess, Gilbert and Mary appreciated Arbella's potential role in history. They were genuinely fond of her, as indeed they would be having often cared for her along with their own children when she was growing up. While the King was at Worksop they spoke to him about Arbella's situation and found he was disposed to be magnanimous to this cousin whom he had formerly considered a rival for the English throne. Her history may also have plucked some string of mutual accord, for James too had lived a sad child-hood – far more traumatic than Arbella's. He had been only a year old when his mother's lover, Bothwell, had murdered his father, Darnley, and he had been removed from his mother soon after-wards, before he could even walk. He had grown up in the chilly care, for want of a better word, of an elderly relative whose only motivation was to rule Scotland through the boy. There had been no love in his young life, except in his intense teenage friendship with Esme Stuart, and any feelings James may have harboured for his mother had been stifled by pejorative propaganda long before he began communicating with her during her imprisonment.

Maybe James welcomed the support of a kinswoman in whom he could trust, for his journey south had been haunted by the mocking buzz phrase 'King Elizabeth; Queen James.' Within a short time of the King's arrival in London, he wrote again to the Earl of Kent to say that Mary, Countess of Shrewsbury had informed him 'of the great desire which our cousin, the Lady Arbella hath, to come to our presence . . . We do well approve these desires of hers and for that purpose are well pleased she do repair to our Court at Greenwich, in the company of her Aunt.'[6]

Arbella stayed at Court with Mary for only a few weeks. By mid-June she was staying at Sheen with the family of Helena, the Marchioness of Northampton,* an old friend of the late Queen, who had taken Arbella's place as Principal Mourner at Elizabeth's funeral.

From Sheen on 14 June Arbella wrote to Robert Cecil, begging him to remind the King 'of my maintenance'. She told him she had many debts and that '£2000 would not exceed my necessity'. The

---

*The Marchioness of Northampton was the third wife of William Parr (brother to Queen Catherine Parr, and good friend of Sir William Cavendish and Bess during the early years of their marriage). Formerly Helena Snakenburg, she came to London in the entourage of Princess Cecilia of Sweden, and she and the widowed Parr fell madly in love. Parr died within twelve months of their marriage.

£200-a-year State pension that had been paid to Arbella since baby-hood came to an end with Elizabeth's death. Bess had always supplemented this £200, so Arbella had never had to economise, but she appears to have frittered away £2000 in a remarkably short time. We know that Arbella had sent 'money and jewels' away from Hardwick before trying to arrange the Hertford marriage in December 1602, so she was obviously not destitute when she left home. But after she left Hardwick Arbella had no income whatso-ever, only the knowledge that after her grandmother's death she would have the rents from the lands Bess had taken in lieu of mort-gage from Sir Francis Willoughby a decade earlier. These properties had been purchased in Arbella's name and the ownership could not be taken away from her, but Bess had retained a life interest in the income.

When Cecil wrote to Bess asking her to help her granddaughter he found her coldly uncooperative. Subsequently he persuaded the King to grant her £660 pounds outright, and later an annual pen-sion of £800.[7] This seemed like riches indeed, but Arbella would quickly find that her £800 did not stretch as far as £200 had done when her grandmother was keeping her.

In July the new Queen, Anne of Denmark, arrived in London. Like her husband she had broken her journey at Worksop,[*] and Arbella had been a prominent member of the welcoming party. Almost immediately she was given the sought-after role of Trainbearer to the Queen, and to her great satisfaction – and prob-ably to Bess's when she heard of it – Arbella was treated with the greatest honour and deference. She related well to the Queen, who was exactly the same age, and at formal functions Arbella was always seated next to the Royal Family, and took precedence over all other women at Court. She played a prominent role in the coronation, though it was an abbreviated affair because a

---

[*]There is a story that Bess invited the new Queen to break her journey south by stay-ing at Hardwick, but that this was gracefully declined because of Bess's relationship with Mary, Queen of Scots.

particularly virulent attack of plague had closed the city to visitors. Arbella's course now seemed set fair. She was in constant correspondence with her uncle and aunt, Gilbert and Mary, and it pleased her to use her influence on their behalf. It was soon rumoured that Mary was to be made a Lady of the Bedchamber.[8]

Arbella was now in her element. True, there were a few grumbles in her letters about 'this everlasting hunting' (the King's favourite occupation), and the lack of time available for her books, but she was enjoying life. Indeed, thanks to her grandmother, she was perfectly suited to just this role.

In November, a plot was discovered to kill both the King and Henry, Prince of Wales, and, with the help of Spain, place Arbella on the throne. Arbella was never personally suspected of involvement, but some famous names were. It was called the Main Plot (to distinguish it from a lesser plot of a few months earlier, called the Bye Plot), and its ringleaders included Sir Walter Ralegh, who defended himself with consummate brilliancy, Lord Grey of Wilton, Lord Cobham,* and Sir Griffin Markham.[9] The forced confessions of lesser conspirators also implicated Bess's son Henry, who was summoned to London for questioning.[10]

Bess would have heard all this news at Hardwick four or five days after it had happened, but she was involved with her own problems of a more domestic variety. William was in London attending Parliament, and in his absence Bess had quarrelled with William's wife, Elizabeth. The latter had taken to her bed at Oldcotes, and was said to be 'very sick'.[11] The two women were only reconciled after Bess apologised. As Christmas 1603 drew near, while London was agog with the trial of Sir Walter Ralegh, Bess was again more concerned with parochial matters when one of her granddaughters, Mary Talbot, was betrothed to William Herbert, the 3rd Earl of Pembroke. It was an excellent match, and

---

*This Lord Cobham was the son of Bess's 'best friend', and was Bess's godson. He was described as 'a most silly Lord, but one degree from a fool'.

soon afterwards, when William Stewart, Privy Counsellor and a friend of Gilbert, called at Hardwick, he found Bess 'in good disposition'. However, she was still feeling hurt and not receptive to the idea of reconciliation with either Gilbert or Mary, or with Arbella,[12] despite the fact that the latter, because of the increasing favour shown to her by the King, had now become an important personage at Court.[13]

Nor was Bess disposed to help her son Henry when, on 3 April 1604, Lord Burghley wrote to Bess to tell her that though Henry had been cleared of any involvement in the Main Plot, he was deeply in debt, physically unwell and depressed. Having been cut out of his mother's will Henry could not afford to furnish Chatsworth, which would be a great empty shell without its most valuable contents, and his only resort would be to sell his life interest in it. He had produced no legitimate offspring despite siring innumerable children in the county, which had earned him a thoroughly bad reputation and brought shame upon the family. But it was Henry's behaviour in the Arbella matter that had finally hardened Bess's heart against him. She replied to Cecil:

> I wish he had lived [differently] so that he were clear of all faults attributed to him . . . Had it been so, I might have taken less grief for his undutiful and unnatural dealings. I could sooner be persuaded of his innocence, had I not been openly informed (as I know you and others of the Council are), of his former acting in the same manner.
>
> No friend should sooner persuade me to do [good] for him than yourself. But I have been so badly dealt with by him, and others who sought my overthrow . . . that I must crave pardon if I refuse to do for those who – not only in this matter but in many others – have sought to hurt me . . .[14]

This was a difficult letter for any mother to have to write about her eldest son, especially for Bess, to whom her family meant everything. It could be construed as mere miserliness, but we know from her household books that Bess was not a mean but a generous person. Every week money was doled out at the gates of Hardwick and Chatsworth to the poor, and the books are scattered with charitable references. The poor people in her Derby almshouse were always well looked after, and so were the administrators. Her servants, too, were treated kindly and given gifts for birthdays, holidays and marriages and on the few occasions when she travelled to her other properties, she freely distributed largesse. But she would not pay Henry's debts, either from hurt at his behaviour over the Arbella affair, or a total disapproval of his lifestyle which had wasted his significant inheritance, or both.

Henry returned to Tutbury in despair, and it was left to his wife, Grace, to care for him and try to get some relief for their massive debts from her brother Gilbert. Grace was a quiet, self-effacing woman, who probably put up with her husband's escapades because of what was clearly her own barren state. Bess liked Grace, who was not only her daughter-in-law but her stepdaughter; she had known Grace since she was an eight-year-old bride at the double marriage of the children of the late Earl and herself. When Edward Talbot wrote to his sister Grace to ask if it was true that Henry had offered his life interest in Chatsworth to Gilbert in exchange for Gilbert settling his debts, Grace passed on a message from her husband: 'Assure my brother that I am, and ever will be, sorry to do anything that may be hurtful either to him or to the house wherof I came . . . except great and extreme necessity doth enforce me to, which now – God knows – is great. And we are hardly dealt with, both by my old Lady [Bess] and my Lord [Gilbert] . . .'

In fact Gilbert was so hard-up that he had told Henry he could not help him in the matter of his creditors, 'without they will take their payment in words'.

Edward Talbot had always been close to Bess, and would remain an affectionate and dutiful stepson until the end of her life, often writing to her, paying her visits, and exchanging small gifts.

Edward was Gilbert's heir,[*] and was understandably concerned at the manner in which Gilbert and Mary had run down the Shrewsbury estates and at reports of their extravagance and their indebtedness. 'The Earls jewels and plate are laid to pawn,' one correspondent wrote, 'and there are as many suitors every day at his chamber, as at the most noble men at court, but they only come to crave their debts. Also that there is nothing the Earl can do in Parliament, nor like to be anything he can learn.'[15] At one point Gilbert was not even able to make the annual payment of his daughter's marriage settlement, and the poor bride was forced to write reminding her father that her husband had need of it.

In the summer of 1604, Sir William Cavendish joined Arbella at Court, where uncle and niece were reconciled. And when their cousin, William Kniveton, subsequently wrote to his mother, Jane Kniveton, at Hardwick, he not only passed on Arbella's regards to her grandmother, but also enclosed a short note from her. It was the first time, since their parting, that there had been any communication between the two women. Gilbert was also in London, Kniveton reported, 'in his old state for all I hear, and no better'.[16] It is not clear whether this referred to the Earl's gout, which he suffered from just as his father had done, or his finances.

There was a happy event in June when Bess's old friend, John Manners of Haddon Hall, wrote to advise her of the birth of a mutual great-grandson. The child, John, was the first son born to George and Grace Manners; Grace (formerly Pierrepoint) was the daughter of Bess's eldest daughter, Frances. Nothing gave Bess greater pleasure than seeing the network of her children and grandchildren spreading into families of influence and respect.

William remained at Court until July because Arbella had agreed to help him gain a peerage. She spoke to the King about this on four separate occasions, and even recruited the support of

---

[*]Some years after the death of little George, Gilbert and Mary had had a second son, John, but he had died as an infant.

twelve-year-old Henry, Prince of Wales. It did not come about during that session, but William reported to Bess that he was hopeful the matter would be dealt with in the next parliament. However, one of Gilbert's correspondents reported waspishly: 'Mr Cavendish . . . waits hard on my Lady Arbella for his barony; but I am confidently assured he will not prevail . . . Although we may be assured that my lady hath a promise of the king for one of her uncles to be [made] a baron . . . it is not likely to be Mr William [*sic.* William was knighted many years earlier], for he is very sparing in his gratuity.'[17] When he returned home, still without his peerage, William told his mother that during his visit to London Arbella had received several proposals, but she 'will not hear of marriage'.[18]

Arbella was no better at managing her money than her uncles Henry and Gilbert. She soon found she could not live on her income and her debts mounted steadily. Perhaps this, and a genuine desire to help Mary and Gilbert, was at the bottom of her agreement to assist in getting a peerage for William. She knew that it would delight her grandmother and perhaps, in turn, bring her back into favour. Also, it seems, Arbella was genuinely homesick; in several letters to Gilbert and Mary she asked for news of events and people at Hardwick. She even offered, after hearing that Bess was inclined to 'a good and reasonable settlement between herself and her divided family',[19] to try to intercede with Bess on Gilbert's behalf. At Christmas she begged the Shrewsburys to invite Henry and Grace Cavendish to Sheffield for Christmas, because they had no money to celebrate the holidays at Tutbury. And when in the early months of 1605 Bess was reported to be very ill, Arbella asked permission to leave the Court to go to her. The King was delighted at the idea of a reconciliation and personally wrote a letter to Bess, asking her – for his sake – to treat Arbella kindly, with her 'former bounty and love'.

Bess may have been physically unwell, but there was nothing wrong with her wits, and in view of what had formerly occurred between herself and Arbella, she narrowed her eyes at this

patronage. She welcomed Arbella, but coolly, and instead of replying directly to the King, she wrote to James Montague, Dean of the
Chapel Royal, asking him to read the letter aloud to the King.

She found it 'very strange', she wrote, that her granddaughter
should come to Hardwick doubting her reception or entertainment, indeed, she was surprised Arbella was so keen to return to
Hardwick at all when she had once so earnestly desired to leave it.
Arbella was doubly welcome because of the King's recommenda-
tion, she wrote, yet in response to the King's request for her to be
bountiful, she believed she had already demonstrated her 'good-
meaning and kindness' to Arbella. The properties she had
purchased for Arbella [from Sir Francis Willoughby] would eventually provide her granddaughter with £700 a year, and she had
also given her 'as much money as would buy a hundred pounds a year
more'. This statement was pointed cynicism, since these amounts
precisely equalled the £800 State pension that the King had
awarded Arbella. However, Bess continued, she had now given
Arbella a gift of a gold cup worth £100, and £300 in cash, which
she considered kind, 'considering my poor ability'.[20] Her granddaughter would always find a welcome at Hardwick, she finished,
but she had other grandchildren who were in greater need of her
bounty than Arbella.

The point Bess made was not lost on the King for he is said to
have smiled wryly when the letter was read to him. The visit had
the effect of reconciling the two women, but they would never
again be close, despite Arbella's best efforts to return to being her
grandmother's darling. Bess had been far too hurt ever to entirely
forgive her granddaughter.

When, later that year, the Gunpowder Plot was discovered, Gilbert
was implicated and taken in for questioning and, just as Henry
Cavendish had been, was completely vindicated after a short stay in
the Tower. But there was also gossip about Mary Talbot's involvement. It was known that she favoured Catholicism and wore a
crucifix, and her close relationship with Sir Walter Ralegh and his

wife Bess Throckmorton was not regarded as a wholesome friendship. Mary defiantly issued a writ against the perpetrators of the
rumours, Lady Anne Markham and Edmund Lascelles, who
retracted their accusations and apologised.[21]

When Arbella returned to London it was to attend the christening of the baby princess, Mary. Arbella was to be the chief
godmother along with the Countess of Northumberland, and the
Queen's brother, Duke Ulick of Holstein, who was in England on a
visit, was godfather.[22] The ceremony was held on 19 April, and to
mark the occasion a number of peerages were bestowed: Robert
Cecil was made a baron, and the King gave Arbella a blank Patent,
advising her to fill in the name of whomever she wished 'to be created . . . at your pleasure.' Sir William Cavendish thus became Lord
Cavendish, and was one of eight barons who carried the canopy
over the child at the baptism. However, Arbella's assistance was evidently not given entirely out of family affection; there was a price
to be paid. In the account books of William Cavendish, his clerk
recorded vaguely that 'after my Lord's creation' his master had
'paid over . . . the sum of £2000' at the house of Sir William
Bowyer.[23] It is not clear to whom this payment was made, but
Arbella seems the most likely recipient.

In June 1605 Bess received a letter from the Lord Chancellor
asking her to answer a bill in Chancery, filed by Gilbert, in which
he claimed that Bess had laid waste to great areas of his lands 'not
meant for her', by cutting down woodlands, mining and digging
coal. Gilbert already owed Bess £4000 in respect of her dower
rights so Bess fought the matter hard. She had become so accustomed to fighting for her rights that she knew the law extremely
well and knew how to defend herself. The lands in contention, she
stated, were hers by right during the term of her life, having been
conveyed to her by her husband, 'by his voluntary act, and not by
the procurement of the defendant . . . for the quiet enjoyment of her
jointure'. And that 'as to the supposed wastes, spoils and damages
in the bill' this was part of her 'quiet enjoyment'.[24] She won her

case, but she was furious with Gilbert. A month later when Sir John Harpur visited Hardwick he reported to Gilbert that he had found Bess 'well for her years', though suffering from pain in her hip and 'both impatient and mindful of your suit against her'.[25] In August, Gilbert's cousin, Roger Manners, found Bess 'still very angry' with Gilbert, and showing no inclination to forgive him.[26]

There was no softening towards her son Henry, either, though he was allowed to visit her once or twice, each time – according to the account books – being given £10 from her iron-bound money coffers. Letters from Grace to Bess to thank her for her kindness to them often contained a gift of a pie or some produce from Tutbury; Grace had little else to give. From a letter Henry wrote at the turn of the year 1605 to 1606, it is safe to assume Bess had sent a New Year gift to Tutbury:

> With our most humble and dutiful thanks for your La[dyship]'s bountiful goodness towards us at all times, my wife and I have made bold to present your honourable good Ladyship with such poor and humble thanks with a simple New Year's gift, as this place can afford. Beseeching that according to your Ladyship's accustomed goodness you were brought safe then in good part, and now we shall pray most [fervently] to God almighty to send your Hon Ladyship many happy and healthful new years. And so humbly craving your Ladyship's daily blessing to us both, now most humbly take our leave. Tutbury the last [day] of December, [1605]. Your Ladyship's humble and obedient son, Henry Cavendish

The renewed contact did not tempt Bess to change her will, for, as with Arbella, Bess had been too hurt to forgive Henry for what she regarded as his betrayal of her. However, Henry was not very perceptive; in a letter to Gilbert, he wrote that he still had hope that his mother would hand over the contents of Chatsworth to him.[27]

During the early months of 1606 Bess became ill again, and was confined to her room for weeks. Her family now began to realise that, indestructible as she had always seemed, Bess could not live for ever. She was now seventy-eight, ancient by sixteenth-century standards, but in fact no one appeared to know exactly how old she was,[*] and in one letter Gilbert referred to her as being eighty-four years old.[28] She may even have exaggerated her age to invite more admiration, as people of a great age are often inclined to do. There is certainly plenty of evidence that Mary, Charles and Henry wished to be reconciled with their mother, but perhaps Charles, who was not in financial difficulties, had the only truly unselfish motive.

In September 1606 an ideal opportunity for reconciliation occurred when Gilbert and Mary's youngest daughter Alathea married Thomas Howard, Earl of Arundel.[29] It was as brilliant a match as that of her sister Mary, and one that Bess welcomed warmly.

With her other children, Frances and William, and also with her stepchildren and all her grandchildren, Bess remained loving and supportive, bestowing gifts of plate and properties from time to time, and welcoming their visits along with those of her many friends. The Earl of Rutland, a family connection[†] always greatly esteemed by the late Earl, wrote to Bess telling her he had heard recently from his cousin, Edward Talbot, who had been to stay at Hardwick and found Bess in good health. Rutland was pleased at this news and thanked Bess heartily for 'your good favours and love towards him'.[30]

In the following spring Bess received welcome news that Alathea had dutifully conceived, and the Earl of Arundel wrote ('to my honourable and most worthy Grandmother') thanking her for her favour and kindness, indicating that she had sent a gift of some sort. Later Bess was asked to be godmother to the child, a son,

---

[*]Not everyone was as punctilious as old Sir William Cavendish. With no formal recording of births, ignorance of precise birth dates was not uncommon.
[†]The old Earl's first wife was daughter of a former Earl of Rutland.

James Howard (Lord Maltravers), to whom the King had agreed to be godfather (the first time he had ever stood as godfather). Bess could not make the journey, so Arbella stood as her proxy at the christening. To mark the event Bess sent to Mary Talbot the 'Ermen sable' with the head 'enamelled in gold', which she had originally bequeathed to Arbella. Mary thanked her mother profusely 'for the Armen . . . which I shall keep as a great jewel, both in respect of your ladyship and of her from whom your Ladyship had it.* There can be nothing wrought in metal with more life'.[31] All Bess's grand-daughters had now married well and were happy. In September the Dowager Countess of Pembroke wrote from the Savoy Palace, praising her daughter-in-law Mary Talbot, and the Pembrokes were noted at Court for their great happiness and sense of fun.

As a result of these family events, Bess and Mary were reconciled by the summer of 1607, and there are a number of letters between them in which Mary solicitously enquires about the severe hip pain, from which Bess now suffered almost constantly. Bess's letters to Mary are also mostly concerned with the health and activities of family members such as Gilbert, who increasingly suffered from gout, and she also enquired after James, baby son of Alathea and the Earl of Arundel, whom Bess called 'little sweet Lord Maltravers'.[32] But despite these friendly intimacies, Bess was suspicious of Mary's leanings further and further towards the Catholic faith, and she was not disposed to leave her any of her hard-earned money to be squandered, as the present Earl and Countess had done with the Shrewsbury inheritance.

In August 1607 Bess added a second codicil to her will, which was witnessed by twelve people. Its sole purpose was to confirm her earlier resolution to disinherit Arbella and Henry. Arbella might

---

*Because ermine had been a 'royal fur' until part way through Elizabeth's reign, this item is likely to have been given by a royal benefactor, possibly the Lady Frances, Jane Grey, the Countess of Lennox, or even Queen Elizabeth. However, Bess's daughter Elizabeth left sables to Bess in her will, and these could be the same items.

flit about at Court believing that she had won her grandmother over, and Henry might live in hope of being left the furniture at Chatsworth, but Bess could not find it in herself to forgive either of them. There may have been, too, a horror of their debts and their casual attitude to money. Both had been given privileges Bess could never have dreamed of, but they had never taken advantage of their education and capitalised on it. Just like her brother James, they spent happily with no thought for the future. Why, she evidently reasoned, throw good money after bad? Even Charles, who could hardly be prised away from his best friend Gilbert, spent lavishly, though he did not run into debt. Only William watched and harvested his money, making it work as she had done.

In September Gilbert wrote Cecil a letter that might easily have come from his father years earlier. It complained of his health and his wife's behaviour:

My last [letter] pitifully complained of the gout's pinching me, and now you write of Tyrone and the rest . . . flying into Spain. But what is it to me who am neither fit for counsel nor execution, but rather to live in a coalpit or a cell? . . . My wife has gone to see her mother. When she returns I will show her what you write of those who are so resolute against crosses,* and wish she could in part follow their rare and excellent example.[33]

In mid-December Gilbert and Mary visited Hardwick together. It was the first time Bess and Gilbert had met in many years and Gilbert reported to Robert Cecil, now Lord Salisbury, that he had found his mother-in-law in good health, and that there had not been a word of 'any former suits or unkindness, but only compliment, courtesy and kindness'. They had found her very aged, he wrote, yet she still retained her 'great wit'.[34] This news was warmly

_____
*Mary blatantly wore a crucifix around her neck.

welcomed by Cecil, and also by the daughters of Gilbert and Mary, who had never been estranged from their grandmother and seem to have loved her a good deal.[35]

It was the coldest winter anyone could remember. By the end of December the entire country was in the grip of an iron-hard freeze that would last for almost two months. The Thames was frozen over to such a thickness that horses could be safely ridden from bank to bank, and there was a Frost Fair on the frozen river 'the like of which has not been seen in living memory'.

On New Year's Eve Mary Talbot sent a gift over to Hardwick; it was a cushion for Bess to lean on when she said her daily prayer.[36] The messenger reported back to Mary that Bess 'looked pretty well, and spoke heartily', but in her letter of thanks Bess told her daughter that she was in worse health than she had been at the time of their visit two weeks earlier. By the following day she had taken to her bed.

On 3 January 1608 Henry Cavendish's wife, Grace, wrote anxiously to Sir John Harpur, a trusted friend of Gilbert's, about negotiations that had taken place between her husband and his brother William during the previous week. William Cavendish had been in London on business since early December, accompanied by his son 'Wylkyn' who was to meet his prospective bride, Christian Bruce, the twelve-year-old daughter of Lord Kinloss. Though he could ill afford the journey, Henry had gone to London at his brother's request, specifically in order to discuss the sale of Henry's life interest in Chatsworth, since he now accepted that Bess was unlikely to change her mind about the contents of the house.

The brothers met for dinner at Sir Henry Maynard's on 27 December,[37] and as a result of their discussions, Grace wrote, 'Lord Cavendish offered £5000 for Chatsworth and £500 a year' during Bess's life. Henry had asked for £6000 and, in view of Bess's age and health, for £500 a year 'for four years certain'. Grace asked John Harpur for his opinion about these negotiations.[38] Harpur, who was said to be 'devoted body and soul' to Gilbert, replied the same day that the Dowager Countess was ill and believed to be in some danger. Therefore he cautioned Grace to tell her husband not to agree to anything until he had checked with Gilbert.[39]

Bess had a sore throat and bronchial complications. Dr Hunton of Sheffield, who had been Bess's physician for over a decade, was called in and he treated her with various types of treacle for her throat and cough, and hot plasters to encourage sweating. The intensely cold weather combined with her age inevitably made it difficult for her to rally, and as she deteriorated her household became very concerned.

On 4 January Gilbert wrote to Henry intimating that the end was not far off for Bess. Even during their visit in mid-December, he reported, he and Mary had found her old and frail. They had noticed that Bess ate little, and was unable to walk from one room to another without becoming noticeably unwell. Since then they had received a thank-you note from her on New Year's Eve, saying she was 'worse'. Within the last day Mrs Digby had sent 'a secret message' saying that Bess was now so ill that Mrs Digby was afraid to leave her, day or night.

'I have heard,' he added ominously:

. . . that direction is given to some at Wortley, to be in readiness to drive away all sheep and cattle at Ewden* instantly upon her Ladyship's death.

These being the reasons that move me thus to advise you. Consider how like it is that when she is thought to be in danger, your good brother [William] will think it time to work with you [concerning Chatsworth] to that effect. And – God forgive me if

---

*The property at Over Ewden was Shrewsbury land that had been part of Bess's marriage settlement. Bess obviously wished to ensure that when the land reverted to Gilbert on her death, no Cavendish stock was inadvertently misappropriated. She had done the same thing a year earlier when a friend (Mr Beresford) died leaving 'a great quantity of lead, wool, sheep and some cattle'. On that occasion she asked Sir John Manners to check that the chattels were not spirited away before the legal heir could take possession of them.

I judge amiss – I verily think that, till of late, he hath been in some hope to have seen your end before hers, by reason of your sickliness and discontentment of mind. To conclude, I wish and advise you to take no hold of any offer that shall be made unto you.

You have not been forgot to my Lady [Mary Talbot], neither for yourself nor for Chatsworth, but we have forborne to write to you thereof, knowing that one of your brother's principal means [is] to keep us all so divided one from another.[40]

Henry, also ill in bed, replied on 8 January saying he had duly turned down William's proposal.

I know my entail as well as any lawyer can beat it into my head. And I know the foundation to be weak and easily over-thrown. My brother's offers would allow my debts to be paid, and given me his friendship and no expectations of suits or law brabbles between us; then an increase of £500 for four years, which would have served me well. But out of affection for you I have set all this aside, and refused the offers. But in conse-quence, my wife and I need your help. We have always been tractable to you and made four journeys to London to our great charge. We heard of your being at Hardwick lately and [that you] mean to return. We hope that you and my mother will bear us in remembrance.[41]

News of Bess's condition had been sent to London. William and Wylkyn were still at Court on 6 January 1608 where the Twelfth Night was always marked by riotous celebration. The King of Denmark was visiting his sister, Queen Anne, and she had ordered a masque to be performed in his honour. This 'golden play' was called *The Masque of Beauty,* and Arbella appeared in it clothed in silks and jewels estimated to be worth over £100,000, eclipsing even the Queen in magnificence. No one was allowed to attend this party who could not throw £300 on the gaming table;* no wonder Arbella was constantly having to borrow money.

But William did not stay for the masque; the messenger from Hardwick must have arrived in London about 7 January, and William rushed northwards, skittering back over icy rutted roads and through snowdrifts to his mother's deathbed. He was home by the middle of January when, as the faithful Timothy Pusey recorded, propped up in her chair before the fire, Bess sent for William early one morning, and told him she thought she was dying. By then she was probably suffering the early stages of pneumonia.

William spent a great deal of time with his mother in those last days, and when he was not with her she constantly and fretfully asked for him. He was the future; she trusted him to continue her life's work as she could not trust Henry, or Charles, or Mary. As the days dragged on and her condition worsened, she occasionally became confused. One day she fancied that the well at Hardwick had been poisoned and yet, she insisted querulously, she knew her broth had been made with that water. Perhaps she was recalling the death of Sir William St Loe and her suspicions that this had been the cause of his sudden death.

One morning she told William that she had been lying awake all night thinking 'of matters that might concern him much, that perhaps he never thought of'. She demanded that he tell the Chancellor of Lichfield that she had made her will, and that it must not be interfered with. As the sole executor, knowing that his mother's will had been well witnessed and registered in London, William must have felt it safe to ignore the request. After a few days Bess asked if he had done as she had asked, and notwithstanding his explanation, she was 'offended' when he said he had not.[42] Her mind was

---

*Inflation was minimal throughout Elizabeth's reign; Bess would have remembered how extravagant it had seemed when Sir William Cavendish lost £2 in a night's play with the Lord Admiral.

obviously ranging over all her affairs, and she began to give him instructions about minor bequests and last wishes, which, for the most part, he dutifully appended as a memorandum to her will:

> That the said Countess, being in perfect mind and remembrance did by Word add to her Will, formerly made in writing, as followeth: First she charges her son William, Lord Cavendish, to bestow one hundred pounds on Something that the profit thereof might be bestowed, as occasion should require, for repairing her Alms Houses at Derby, for ever. Also she told the said Lord Cavendish her son, that she would have him give to her daughter Shrewsbury from her, the Pearl Bed, with all that belonged to it in that chamber, except the hangings [tapestries] . . .

Other bequests were added in the form of a nuncupative codicil when they came into Bess's head, as she tied up the ends of her life. Frances and Charles visited her and 'she wept with joy' to see them, telling Mrs Digby after they had left that 'she had more liking for [them] than for Sir William'.[43] To Robert Cecil, Lord Salisbury, she left a cup of gold valued at £100, and £100 in cash was to be given to her friend and waiting gentlewoman, Elizabeth Digby. There were sundry cash sums left to people like the Dean of His Majesty's chapel, and servants whom she held in particular affection who were not dealt with in her original will. But there were also some verbal bequests to her children, witnessed by Mrs Digby, which William seems, inexplicably, to have neglected to write down: £4000 to Charles, to buy land for his two sons (William and Charles), and 2000 marks to Frances.

On 2 February Dr Hunton moved into Hardwick to care for Bess and make her as comfortable as possible with his herbal remedies and hot 'plaisters'. For eleven days the doctor nursed her, while she fought for her life. Her naturally strong constitution, like that of Queen Elizabeth, would not give in easily. Outside her windows the world was unnaturally hushed by a deep blanket of snow, and although the normal running of the great house went on, it, too, was quiet and expectant, while every soul within its walls waited for news from upstairs.

On 13 February, with the end only hours away, the inseparable trio of Charles, Mary and Gilbert were either sent for or arrived at Hardwick of their own volition. Arbella was not present. All Bess's children were now past what was considered middle age: William was fifty-six, Charles fifty-four, and Mary fifty-two. They gathered uneasily before the fire in a small room between Bess's bedchamber and her withdrawing room, while Mrs Digby moved quietly in and out. There was little she could do for Bess now, except keep the bedchamber warm and comfortable.

When in the late afternoon Mary was summoned to the bedside, William became very agitated. Mrs Digby later described him as 'fearful' and 'unwilling' that Mary should have 'any private conference' with her mother. He asked Mrs Digby to 'use some means' to get Mary away from Bess, and she concluded that he was worried that Bess might change her will, and leave further bequests, or perhaps mention bequests that he had forgotten to note down. Mrs Digby told him that 'supper was coming up and therefore [Mary] would not have time for anything'.[44]

It would have been already dark when, at 5 o'clock on that cold mid-winter evening, Bess of Hardwick breathed her last, hardly the distance of an arrow's flight from the house where she was born.

On the following day, as soon as he and Mary arrived back at Sheffield, Gilbert wrote to Robert Cecil to let him know of Bess's death. Mary had obviously been able to speak with her mother, for Gilbert reported that 'the old lady . . . had that great blessing of sense and memory, even to the end', and he ended his letter by sending 'the remembrance of my wife, who vexes herself with extreme grief and many tears'.[45]

At Hardwick, William began the tedious duties of an executor. His first act was to pay off Dr Hunton, to whom he gave forty marks for his final services to Bess. By a curious coincidence it was the exact sum originally bequeathed to Bess under her father's will: 'I will that each of my five daughters have 40 marks of good and lawful money of England to their marriage when they be of age.'

Bess Hardwick had come a long way, and done great things with that modest stake in life.

CHAPTER 23

A LONG ARM . . .

1608 et seq.

AS SOON AS THE NEWS OF BESS'S DEATH REACHED HER, Arbella set out from London to join the Shrewsburys at Sheffield.[1] From there she visited Hardwick and spent some time alone beside her grandmother's coffin which was shrouded and draped in black velvet. Bess's embalmed body would lie in state for over two months, awaiting two public funeral services (one was possibly a form of memorial service in London) which had yet to be arranged.

Mary Talbot mourned her mother hard, and probably because of the estrangement that had existed between the two women for half a decade until recent months, her grief was unexpected to Gilbert. He wrote to Robert Cecil that he was 'surprised at the distress of his wife at the death of her mother', but that he was 'hoping to set some workmen on soon' to help take her mind off her sadness.[2] The Dowager Countess of Arundel heard the news from Alathea and wrote to Gilbert to say she was sorry to hear of Mary's extreme anguish, regretting that Alathea could not come to her mother as she was ill with a fever.

To the frustration of his siblings William worked slowly and carefully at administering the estate, and kept his own counsel. On 1 March, two weeks after Bess's death, and after a short memorial service (without a committal) had been held in Derby, Gilbert wrote with clear irritation to Cecil, saying that Arbella was still with them at Sheffield 'ill at ease', still waiting for news which never came. 'We are strangers to all my Lord Cavendishes proceedings, and do neither know anything of the old Lady's Will as yet, nor the time when the funerals are intended, but we hear that she was more publicly buried* at Derby than I have heard the like, where a solemn service was intended afterwards'.[3]

Gilbert decided to move more swiftly. Within days he had sent instructions to his bailiffs concerning the Shrewsbury lands held by Bess until her death: 'the tenants are to be instructed to have their rent ready to pay to the Earl at the next rent day'.[4] At Wingfield he instructed Henry Butler that beginning with Bess's steward, he was 'to expel everyone except servants'.[5]

When William finally announced the date of Bess's funeral as 4 May, it was 'so close to St Georges Day',† when Knights of the Garter were obliged to join in ceremonial procession with the sovereign, that Gilbert had to write and beg special leave not to attend the Garter service. 'I can hardly with my infirm body perform so long a journey forward and backward in so short a time without some damage,' he wrote to Cecil. He felt sure he would hardly be missed among so many people, especially since the only duty required of him was 'a short march in a purple robe'.[6] However, it seems that Gilbert did not attend Bess's funeral, so either he did not get the necessary licence to absent himself from the Garter Procession, or perhaps he was ill with gout.

Recalling her late husband's funeral, Bess used her will as a long arm from the grave to direct her own: 'I especially will and require

---

*Bess was not 'buried' until two months later; this is a point of speech to convey the extravagant style of the service.
†23 April.

that my funeral be not over sumptuous, or otherwise performed with too much vain and idle charge.'*

During her lifetime she had commissioned a family vault to be constructed below St Katherine's Quire in the south aisle of the medieval church of All Saints (in the sixteenth century known locally as 'All Hallows'). Bess had seen and approved this vault, as well as her own elaborate tomb which was compatible with her station in life. The tomb was designed by Smythson and included a painted life-size effigy. Bess knew that the funeral ceremonials for a countess were already prescribed by the College of Heralds and choreographed according to the social rank and the lineage of the deceased. So she left the massive sum of £2000 to cover the not over-sumptuous funeral expenses, which was to include the proper housing of her family and household in Derby. A further sum of £1000 was to be shared among her servants, 'to be paid . . . [with]in ten days after the finishing of my said funeral', and the residents of her Alms House in Derby were given 20 shillings each and a mourning gown. In total the expenses of the funeral appear in the Cavendish account books at £3257,[7] a staggering sum that greatly exceeds the costs of the funerals of even the Earl of Leicester and Lord Burghley.

Some delay in the funeral service was inevitable, since notice had to be given to important people who had to come from other parts of the country for such a prestigious event. But there was another matter which required William and other members of the family to be in London in April – the marriage of eighteen-year old 'Wylkyn' (or to be correct, Sir 'Wylkyn', for he had been knighted by this time) could not be put off. Bess had been involved in the negotiations as she had in the marriages of all her children and

---

*I have not found any eyewitness account of Bess's funeral, but Lawrence Stone in *Crisis of the Aristocracy* (Clarendon Press, 1965), p.575, states that on that day, 'some of her servants, a prey to conflicting emotions . . . and anxiety about the future, indulged themselves very freely, and there were orgiastic scenes below stairs at the Old Hall.' No citation is given, and I have not been able to validate this.

grandchildren – and was more than likely pushing the matter hard from her deathbed to ensure that it went ahead as she wished. She knew from first-hand experience the important role of marriage in building and securing a family fortune, and this latest match was a dynastic union advantageous to both parties. One contemporary report suggested that the Cavendish family would benefit by a dowry of £100,000.[8] It may have been Bess's own instruction that her death must not be allowed to interfere with the arrangements.

The child bride, Christian Bruce, was heir to the Scottish Earl of Kinloss (a close friend of King James), and she was a favourite handmaiden of the Queen. The snag in this arrangement was that Wylkyn was an unwilling bridegroom. He was already in love with one of the younger ladies of Bess's household, Margaret Chatterton, and indeed had already seduced, or had been seduced by, her.[9]

Somehow, Wylkyn was cajoled or browbeaten into agreeing to the marriage, and the younger generation of Cavendishes and Talbots gathered in London for their cousin's nuptials. Arbella was prominent among them, and reported to be very friendly with 'my lady Cavendish the Baroness' (Elizabeth, William's second wife, and stepmother to Wylkyn), both of them dancing and rejoicing at a pre-wedding supper party. Alathea and Thomas Howard, the Earl and Countess of Arundel, were there with their baby son, whom even Henry Cavendish described as 'sweet little Lord Maltravers', just as Bess had done a few months earlier. Alathea's sister Mary, and Mary's husband William Herbert, Earl of Pembroke, also attended, as did Henry Cavendish. Not surprisingly, in view of the bad feeling running between them, neither Gilbert, Mary nor Charles were present but Henry wrote to tell them how touched he was that on hearing that he and Grace were staying in Shrewsbury House in Broad Street, 'Lady Pembroke [Gilbert and Mary's daughter, Mary] came to welcome her aunt and me, poor soul, to London'.[10]

Henry wrote a detailed report of the wedding, which took place on 10 April, to Gilbert and Mary:

. . . The bride is metely handsome, as they say, of red hair and about 12 years of age. Helas, poor Wylkyn, he desired and deserved a woman already grown, and may evil stay 12 weeks for a wife, much less 12 months. They were bedded together, to his great punishment, some 2 hours. The next morning I waited on my lady Arbella at White Hall, and . . . I told her I thought it was she made the match, which her ladyship denied, but not very earnestly . . . I told her my betters would think as I did, and ten thousand others besides.[11]

Queen Anne, having not been consulted about the matter, disapproved of the marriage; indeed at first she hardly knew what to make of it, since it had been kept secret until the day before the ceremony. Like Henry Cavendish, she came to believe that Arbella was in some way responsible, and this began a marked coolness between the two former friends.

Immediately after the public 'bedding' – a wholly symbolic affair in view of the age of the bride – Wylkyn was allowed to set up his own establishment in London with a tutor and companion, Thomas Hobbes. Here, William Cavendish showed a spark of understanding and sympathy for his son – or maybe it was a quid pro quo of Wylkyn's – because at the time Hobbes, who eventually became a notable philosopher and author, was simply an Oxford graduate, only two years older than Wylkyn, who had been recommended to Lord Cavendish by the Master of Magdalen.

In the evening, after the wedding celebrations had ended, as Henry Cavendish sat in his bedchamber 'at my book, most earnestly', his brother William's servant called at Shrewsbury House and served him with a subpoena to appear in Chancery Court on 14 April. Having only seen his brother a few hours earlier, Henry was bewildered. 'It seemed very strange to me. At the first, I thought it was something about the Lady our mother's Will. But I am assured . . . by skilful men . . . that it cannot be so, but that it is something touching my entail'.

When he had been able to read the document, Henry found it '. . . as full of lies as lines; pretending that I go about to cut off my entail to disinherit my rightful heirs . . . I am so unfit for these law matters [and] this one matter drives me into such agony, discontentment and perturbation of mind, as will lessen my time . . . I hope my cruel brother will not have his will of me altogether to his liking.'[12] He ended his letter to Gilbert and Mary with a wistful statement that he would greatly miss their presence and support, and that of his brother Charles, in London, for brother William was 'too wily' and skilful an opponent for him to deal with alone.

This was the opening salvo in the inevitable squabbles between Bess's children over her great estate. During the case between Henry and William, Henry (aided by Gilbert) attempted to overturn the codicil which had disinherited him of the contents of Chatsworth, but Bess had made sure that her wishes would be carried out. Timothy Pusey testified that Bess had justifiable cause to disinherit Henry, and that the changes had not been made at William's urging.[13] It was some time before William and Henry settled their differences, but eventually, out of necessity, Henry sold his life-interest in Chatsworth to William for £8000.[14] Henry had no legal heirs, and the property would have reverted to William eventually, provided he outlived Henry, which seemed likely. Meanwhile, William did not want Chatsworth to go to rack and ruin under his feckless brother's control. There was also a danger that Henry might decide to sell his life interest to someone else, though the potential buyer whom William most feared, Gilbert, Earl of Shrewsbury, could not have afforded to buy it.

The bequests made verbally by Bess on her deathbed were fought over and contested bitterly. Everyone, except William, expected more than they got, and William was blamed within the family for having been left so much to everyone else's disadvantage. Mary had hoped that her reconciliation with her mother would have worked in her favour and was upset to learn that she had been left only the great Pearl bed and her husband the sum of £3000. When she wrote to tell her sister-in-law Grace this, Grace was already aware of it, but to Grace £3000 probably sounded like riches. Arbella was left £1000, Wylkyn and Frances, the two survivors of Sir William's six children, were left 2000 marks each. These monetary bequests were, of course, in addition to all those lands and properties that Bess had purchased in her children's and grandchildren's names, which passed to them outright after her death.

In the wrangling, Bess's epitaph seems to have been forgotten, just as George Shrewsbury's children forgot to add the date of his death to his tomb. The Latin text* that eventually complemented Bess's effigy was not carved and fixed to her tomb until 1677†, almost seventy years after her death. It is perhaps not surprising that by then her precise age had been forgotten and she was described as having died at the age of eighty-seven when she was in fact eighty.

Under William's firm control the Cavendish family continued to prosper, and Bess's descendants pursued her policy of advantageous marriages and the consequent absorption of the lands and fortunes of other great families. This made the Cavendishes not only immensely powerful, but able to withstand the upheavals during and after the Civil War‡ and other tides of ill-fortune. There have been many charges levelled against Bess in the succeeding four centuries: chiefly that she was a hard-hearted shrew, out for what she could get. The terms 'termagant' and harridan' have even been applied to her by respected historians, but the surviving documentation does not support these opinions. In fact, there is far more evidence that she was an affectionate and caring woman, rather than the reverse, and that she was shrewd rather than shrewish.

---

*The text provides the names of Bess's father, four husbands, all of her children and some grandchildren. Of Bess herself it states only that 'she built magnificent buildings at Chatsworth, Hardwick and Oldcotes' and the date of her death.
†One of Bess's grandsons is described as 'the Duke of Newcastle', a title not conferred on him until some time after the restoration of Charles II, so the inscription must be after that date.
‡The Civil War lasted from 1642 to 1648, but the Restoration did not occur until 1660.

Although we know nothing about the relationship in her first marriage, it is certain that she inspired her second husband, Sir William Cavendish, with sufficient respect for her ability to leave her a lifetime controlling interest in all his properties. Had Bess been a normal woman of her time he would have made one of his nephews or friends the executors and guardians of his heir. Such a course would have been usual and would have surprised no one.

We know also that Bess could inspire ardent devotion, evidenced by loving letters both from Sir William St Loe and from George, Earl of Shrewsbury. It is true that Shrewsbury changed his opinion a decade after their marriage, but this must be regarded in the light of his failing health, allied to the stress of keeping Mary, Queen of Scots (who was certainly not innocent of coming between man and wife), financial worries, and the fact that in his latter years he came under the thrall of another dominating woman, his rapacious mistress Eleanor Britton.

Thousands of documents, only a few of which have been able to be detailed in this book, reveal Bess as an intelligent, affectionate, diligent and loyal woman, who was also smart enough to look out for herself and her children. In a man's world this was not necessarily viewed sympathetically. In adversity Bess fought back as a male counterpart would – more cleverly than most, in fact – and a man bested by a woman in those days, as Lord Shrewsbury patently was, could only excuse his own weakness by branding a woman as a shrew.

My conclusion, having lived daily with Bess for almost five years, is that she was a woman ahead of her time, just as her contemporary Elizabeth I was also a woman ahead of her time. Bess's tomb, in the staggering beauty of Derby Cathedral, depicts her at the time of her death, just as Queen Elizabeth's funeral effigy presents not Gloriana at the height of her power, but a dignified and tired old woman. But to think of Bess in these terms is to overlook the fact that she made her way because she was once a feisty young woman who fought her corner shrewdly and relentlessly, every step

of the way, and made few mistakes. She did not have the advantage
of great beauty to aid her, as other women in history who succeeded through advantageous marriages did, which can only mean
that Bess had extraordinary charm or charisma.

For several centuries the two great lines of the Cavendish family
flourished on the foundation left by Bess. For at least part of that
time Charles's line was in the ascendancy,[15] and together they were
arguably one of the most powerful families in the country. Today,
Bess's direct family through William's descendants – the senior
line – still control the Cavendish estates from Chatsworth. The
assets have been passed down through the male line, but, aptly for
a family which was moulded by a woman, the Cavendishes are
noted for the strong women they have both produced and married:
Christian Bruce (bride of the unhappy Wylkyn), who proved an
able successor to Bess, and rescued the estate from her husband's
extravagances; Georgiana Spencer, the 6th Duchess of Devonshire
about whom a bestselling biography was recently published; and
the present Dowager Duchess, Deborah ('Debo') Mitford, to name
a few.

Each in her own way helped to keep alive Bess's original vision,
and it has proved a remarkable and enduring heritage.

APPENDIX 1

Discussion of Bess of Hardwick's Date of Birth

The following facts are supported by contemporary documents:

1. Bess married Robert Barlow in the spring of 1543,* and was of 'tender years' – under sixteen – at the date of the marriage, which took place shortly before Robert's father died on 28 May 1543.

2. Robert Barlow, Bess's first husband, died 24 December 1544.

3. According to the Inquisition Post Mortem inquiry on John Hardwick in September 1530, Bess's brother James Hardwick was born in April 1526. Allow for their mother's lying-in of one month, plus nine months for Bess's gestation, and Bess could not have been born prior to March 1527. However it must have been after June that year, or she would not have still been 'of tender years' in May 1543 when she married.

4. Bess's father died 29 January 1528 and was already very ill on 6 January, at which time, according to his will, he thought it was possible that his wife might be pregnant. It is doubtful, then, that that child, Alice, could have been conceived later than late December, since John Hardwick was already ill by then.

5. Alice's birth at full term could not have been any later than mid August 1528, but it might have been earlier than this.†

---

*See document C1/1101 at Public Record Office, Kew. Statement made by Bess ('Mistress Elizabeth Barley') in her court case to obtain her Barlow dower rights.
†It was unusual for a woman to conceive again immediately (i.e. within a month) after a birth, because of the custom of abstaining from sex until she had been churched, and the initial period of breast-feeding.

To summarise: if she had been born before June 1527 Bess could not have been under sixteen in May 1543 when she married. And allowing time for a month's lying-in by Elizabeth Hardwick after Bess, and an appropriate time for Alice's conception, Bess could not reasonably have been born after the end of October.

The conclusion, based on the above facts, is that Bess was born between June and the end of October in 1527. This would mean Bess attained her sixteenth birthday sometime between June and October of 1543, and thus would have been only fifteen years old in May 1543, when she married Robert Barlow.

There are no references to Bess's birthdays in her existing correspondence or her accounts. But the liklihood is that when she moved into her newly built, and still far from complete, Hardwick Hall on 4 October, 1597, she did so to commemorate her seventieth birthday.

APPENDIX 2

The Office of Wards

This Crown Office, as all-powerful as the Inland Revenue and VAT offices are today, had evolved from the medieval practice of Knight Service in the days before the State kept large, trained armed forces in permanent readiness. All land was technically the property of the Crown and was apportioned by the Crown, to be held and enjoyed by favoured property owners in return for the provision of a mounted knight (sometimes with foot supporters) when an army was needed to deal with local or national emergencies. When the thrifty Henry VII came to the throne, he identified wardship as a significant source of revenues, and updated the powers of the old Office of Wards. His son, Henry VIII, constantly seeking money to support his extravagant lifestyle, further strengthened the laws concerning wardships.

The iniquitous effect of these changes was that during Henry VIII's reign (and for some time afterwards), should a landowner die before his heir reached his twenty-first birthday, all lands and properties were taken over by the Office of Wards, to be administered during the ward's minority. During the period of wardship, all the income and profits of the estate went to the Crown, although sometimes the property, or part of it, might be rented back to the heirs. More often – a far worse fate – the wardship was auctioned, or sold, by the Crown to wealthy neighbouring landowners. Sometimes the buyers were friends, who kept the estates in good heart and looked after the education of the young ward. But often the ward and family of the deceased were left at the mercy of rapacious or manipulative speculators, whose sole interest was to make as much as could be leached from a lucrative property while the wardship lasted, and in many cases to arrange the marriage of a defenceless ward to a member of his own family so that property would eventually come into their own ownership.

Generally, significant landowners were men, and holders of wardships were also, usually, men. But there were occasionally women holders of wardships. Bess of Hardwick was one, and another was the pious Elizabethan diarist Lady Margaret Hoby, who actively lobbied to get lucrative wardships. These were much sought-after, being a perfectly legitimate manner of earning extra income.

The law on wardships was greatly improved under Queen Elizabeth when in 1561 the Court of Wards came under the benign and efficient influence of William Cecil, who was to be its Master for thirty-seven years.

APPENDIX 3

Sir William Cavendish's Statement to the Star Chamber, August 1557

ITEM: it may please Her Majesty to consider if the King her father not fully two years before his death received of me One Thousand pounds for the office of the Treasurership of the Chamber, whereunto it pleased her here to call me. By taking of nothing there, being first by his Special Commandment appointed to serve at Boulogne, [France,] I lost £200 at the least in my provision to furnish me any way meet to serve the place and calling, according to my bounden devotion to his Majesty's Honour. And being fully furnished as before, my stuff being gone and I ready to set towards Boulogne, I was stayed by my calling into the said office of the Treasurership of the Chamber. The commodities and ordinary benefits wherof, were immediately after the King's death, by great extremity and contrary to the words of my patent, [without] offence or suspicion of offence any way committed, taken and kept from me by an authority of the Protector and The Earle of Warwick afterwards Duke of Northumberland. Wherein I did also lose to my undoing from those years in [which] my ordinary benefits were against all order and right taken from me [. . . under] accounting my benefits to be one way and other yearly, £100 over and besides £100 in my [system] to pursue my said office, and benefit of the same.

Notwithstanding it, it pleased her Majesty, at the time upon the declaration of my grieved wrong, extreme payment and losses sustained as before, to write the most gracious and favourable letter unto my Lord Treasurer, it [now] is for my belief for which cause among numbers of others I am specially bounden over, and besides my natural devoted duty, [during] my Life to pray for Her Highness.

ITEM: Of my charged remaining here at London by the commandment of the Lord Protector and others of the honourable
Council at the time, to make provision of WyteHall for the
[unreadable phrase] for the Earl and his life provision, sent northwards to the forty third [. . .], and also unto Boulogne for my
payment and travel money. I was promised a [. . .] reward by the
day, accounting for the time I served [£55. 40s. 50d.]. Nothing was
answered or recompensed by reason the protectors at the time were
committed to the Tower, which among other things I most humbly
beseech her Maj to confide towards my relief.

ITEM: I am like and stand in danger without her Maj's great favour
to lose the sum of DDD£ [£1500] at sundry times and beforehand
lent unto diverse the King her fathers poor servants, and since that
time King Edward, and also her graces servant, complaining then
great necessity unto me and being moved with their often pitiful
lamentations and extreme misery did I daily see them, I did in consideration thereof before these days lend and pay them part of their
wage amounting to the sum before remembered which, by their
deaths, without Her gracious mercy, I lost.

ITEM: That it may please your Maj to confere that the King her
father sent me among others such as Baron Welshe and John Myne
with commissions into Ireland. Wherein I remained one whole year
and was promised [. . .] the day in reward, over and beyond
[amounts] allowed and payed to cash . . . amounting for that time
to [£1090]. Whereof hitherto I have no allowance.

ITEM: I remained in London . . . in Commission with Sir Walter
Myldemay the space of 12 weeks to take the account of the
wardrobe of the robes and was promised for my time and trouble
xiijs iijd [13s. 4d.] a day . . . whereof I have had no allowance.

ITEM: Where at the beginning of Her Majesties exertions and happy reign I heard and saw the danger intended towards her by the unnatural enterprise of the late Duke of Northumberland and his inherent infamy about all things under God in Her Grace's person, I did according to my bounden duty advise such a number of men as I could, then or after to come toward her defence. Protesting by the truth and duty I bear toward Her Majesty, if I had been able to bestir a whole world in her defence and for her good service it had not been at that time undone. But being unable to extend my due service according to my heart I moved and hired as many whose regard stood me in one thousand marks, which I never meant to ask one penny allowance, had not this extreme payment loss, and other charge sums remembered, constrained me. Thereto most humbly beseeching Her Maj's courteous and [uniformed] inclination to mercy. Have consideration of me my wife and poor children.

William Cavendish

What Happened to Bess's Children and Grandchildren

Readers might wish to know what became of some of the numerous colourful personalities who peopled Bess's life.

Cavendish, Charles: Bess's third and youngest son who made his home at Welbeck. His second marriage also proved a happy one. He had commanded a regiment in 1578 when Queen Elizabeth sent assistance to the Low Countries, and for this service he was rewarded with a knighthood in 1582. He was also elected to Parliament for two terms in 1597 and 1601. After George Shrewsbury's death, Charles was estranged from his mother because of his friendship and absolute loyalty to Gilbert, the 7th Earl, with whom Charles had been educated and had toured Europe as a youth, and he was hardly reconciled before her death, although she did leave his two sons £4000. Charles died in 1617 aged sixty-three, within a year of the death of his lifelong friend Gilbert, 7th Earl of Shrewsbury. Charles's elder surviving son, yet another William (called 'Will' Cavendish by Bess to distinguish him from her son William, and William's son 'Wylkyn'), became Viscount Mansfield in 1620, Earl of Newcastle in 1628, and Duke of Newcastle in 1665. His descendants eventually became Dukes of Newcastle, Dukes of Portland and the Barons Ogle.

Cavendish, Henry: Bess's eldest son, and heir to the Chatsworth estates of his father Sir William Cavendish after his mother's death. The cross of Henry's life was the marriage to Grace Talbot arranged by their parents while both were still children. Grace was a dumpy little woman, shown in her only portrait wearing black, sitting beside her virginals with an open book of music. Henry was keen on music, but he was also a roving adventurer; a man of his time. He once stormed at his wife before their servants that she was a harlot, which seems extremely unlikely behaviour for this mild-mannered, thoroughly dutiful woman.

Henry had no children by his wife Grace, but he made up for this by siring bastards all over the county, of whom he recognised and gave his name to four. One of these, Henry Cavendish, who some-times visited Bess at Hardwick, was made Henry's heir, though Chatsworth (which was entailed in legitimate tail male) could not be passed on. It may have been this fact, as much as his debts, which decided Henry to sell Chatsworth to his brother William Cavendish for £8000 and buy some lands at Doveridge. Henry (senior) died in 1616, the same year as Gilbert, Earl of Shrewsbury. Henry Cavendish the younger lived at Doveridge, and was a grandson that Bess would have respected – after all he carried her bloodline. He founded the line which would become the Barons Waterpark.

Cavendish, William: Bess's second and favourite son and her heir. Having been made Baron Cavendish in 1605, three years prior to his mother's death, he went on to become the 1st Earl of Devonshire in 1618.

There has not been space in this book to explore William, who was a complex personality. He was a tall, thin, good-looking man, with reddish-fair curly hair and blue eyes. In the best portrait of him, painted at about the time of Bess's death, he wears an elabo-rate red Court costume, trimmed with silver and lace, and a feather-trimmed hat. He comes across in correspondence as a humourless, ambitious man, intent on his duty to the family estates. He was devoted to his children, yet he married his reluctant son Wylkyn to the twelve-year-old Christian without a qualm – his main concern being that the bride's family might back out at the last minute because of royal disapproval. However, he made up for it by appointing as tutor and companion the brilliant young Thomas Hobbes, who accompanied Wylkyn on a tour of Europe.

Although he did not have the entrepreneurial skills of his mother, William was a speculator of sorts, in that he invested £1000 a year in the East India Company for fifteen years, and was also involved in a company which traded with Russia, the Bermuda Company, and in the English pioneer settlement in Virginia. We know from his accounts that he was an avid patron of the theatre in London. Frustratingly, he does not give the names of the plays he went to see, but he sometimes paid for a stool to sit close to the stage. It seems he enjoyed music and singing, for among his other purchases are song books of madrigals, lute strings and a treble viol. There is a corroborative entry in Bess's own accounts: 'given to them that plays of music with Will – 20 shillings'. He was also a smoker, a habit he picked up quickly from Francis Drake.

He was created Earl of Devonshire in 1618, in consideration of which he paid £10,000 to the Crown. In August of the following year, the Prince of Wales, later Charles I, who was staying at Welbeck with William's nephew, the Earl of Newcastle, came over to Hardwick and dined there – while Court musicians played outside the window of 'my Lady's Chamber'. After his mother's death, William wielded an almost semi-feudal power over the great estates she had created in the heart of England. He died in 1625, having outlived both his brothers and Gilbert, his step-brother.

Cavendish, William ('Wylkyn'): Bess's grandson; born in 1590, he grew up mostly at Hardwick and Oldcotes. He was eighteen when his grandmother died and was probably close to her from the number of times his name is mentioned in her account books. Within weeks of her death he was married to Christian Bruce, daughter of Lord Kinloss, and later they had two sons – William, who became the 3rd Earl, and Charles, who was killed fighting on the Royalist side in the Civil War – and a daughter, Ann. Although the image painted by his uncle Henry Cavendish of eighteen-year-old Wylkyn portrays him as embarrassed by his marriage to

twelve-year-old Christian Bruce, it was not an unhappy arrangement in the long run.

Wylkyn became fast friends with his young tutor, Hobbes, and
they had a splendid time together in the period before Wylkyn had
to go home and consummate his marriage. In that time Wylkyn
managed to acquire a reputation as a rake and learned how to
spend money like a prince. Hobbes did his best to curb the worst
excesses and took responsibility for Wylkyn's privy purse. John
Aubrey, biographer of Hobbes, wrote that 'his lord, who was a
waster, sent him up and down to borrow money, and to get gentlemen to be bound for him, being ashamed to speak for himself'.[*] In
1610 the two men left for a year's Grand Tour in Europe, but there
is no evidence that this helped Wylkyn to mature.

Wylkyn survived his father as 2nd Earl for only three years, and
died at the early age of thirty-eight from 'excessive indulgence in
good living', so it was said. Perhaps it was just as well he did not live
longer, for he was as extravagant as his father had been careful. He
had borrowed heavily, at punitive interest rates, against his expectations, and when he succeeded his father even the massive Cavendish
annual income could hardly keep up with his debts and the cost of
his princely lifestyle. Had he survived there might have been nothing
at all to hand on to his son, for just before Wylkyn died, a bill had
already been presented to break the Cavendish entail in order to sell
lands to pay off his creditors. Fortunately, the red-haired Christian
Bruce, who was noted for her wit and wisdom as an adult, was as
careful and ruthless as Bess had been. It was Christian who nursed
the estates back into solvency for her son. Christian's grandson, the
4th Earl, was created Duke of Devonshire in 1694, for helping to
bring William of Orange to the throne. It was this first Duke who
razed Bess's Chatsworth and built the house that exists today on the
original foundations laid by Bess and Sir William Cavendish.

[*]Mark Girouard, *Hardwick Hall* (National Trust Handbook), Revised Edition, 2002,
p.36.

Hobbes lived with the Cavendish family for the remainder of his life, becoming in turn tutor to Wylkyn's son, the 3rd Earl, whose name, somewhat predictably, was also William. Hobbes was buried in Ault Hucknall churchyard.

Stuart, Arbella: After her grandmother's death, Arbella remained at Court until 1610, when she was planning to withdraw and buy a house in the country, possibly for financial reasons. Although she had lost the close friendship of the Queen, the King always treated her with the greatest courtesy and told her that should she wish to marry, she could choose any man within his kingdom. Soon afterwards, William Seymour, the younger brother of Edward (to whom Arbella had herself proposed marriage), approached her with an offer of marriage though he was twelve years her junior.

Arbella dutifully fell in love with her young swain, but when the King was advised he refused permission since the match of two potential claimants to the English throne was far too dangerous to allow. Arbella pretended to give up the idea, but covertly she pressed William to proceed with their plan, and on 22 June 1610 they married secretly at four o'clock in the morning in her chamber at Greenwich Palace. The marriage was soon discovered and the pair were imprisoned, Arbella being placed in the custody of Sir Thomas Parry at Lambeth, and Seymour confined in the Tower.

In March 1611 Arbella was sent north to be confined in the care of the Bishop of Durham. A day after the party left London, Arbella became ill, probably feigned, and she was taken to a house at Barnet. The King agreed that the party could remain there until Arbella recovered. Arbella contacted William Seymour and set up a plan for them to escape to France by ship from Blackwall. In June, a few days before the journey to Durham was to recommence, she slipped out of the house disguised as a man and rode to London, where she was to meet up with her husband. His escape from the Tower did not go as smoothly and he could not meet her at the arranged time. She was obliged to sail with the tide, without him, but ordered the captain to drift about in the English Channel, hoping that William would catch her up. In fact, William got to France without any problems, but Arbella's ship was captured by a naval pinnace sent to recapture her.

This time Arbella was consigned to the Tower (housed in the Bell Tower where her father-in-law, Edward, Lord Beauchamp, had been born). The King, like Bess before him, was hurt and angry at Arbella's betrayal of his former kindness and never forgave her. It did not take long for Robert Cecil's intelligence network to discover that Arbella had been aided and financed by her aunt Mary, Countess of Shrewsbury. Mary's conversion to Catholicism had become well known for she made no secret of it, openly collecting and wearing Catholic symbols and relics. James now began to suspect a plot to convert Arbella and place her on the throne as a Catholic queen. Mary was also sent to the Tower, pending trial, and was released the following year. Arbella – though she was never formally tried – was obviously intended to be a life prisoner. After four years Arbella realised this and lost the will to live. She went on a hunger strike, refusing food and, when she became ill, all care and medication. She died aged thirty-nine in September 1615.

In 1867, when a search was made of royal remains in Westminster Abbey, Arbella's coffin was found lying on top of that of Mary, Queen of Scots, in a vault directly beneath Mary's tomb.

Talbot, Alathea: Outlived her two sisters and thus eventually became the sole heiress of Gilbert, 7th Earl of Shrewsbury and his wife Mary (née Cavendish). She was, unusually for her day, interested in science and was a published author. She was painted by Rubens and lived for a time in Venice, bringing back to London a gondola, which she used on the Thames. During the Civil War, Alathea and her husband were Royalist supporters and lived on the continent, though they were apart for most of the time, without money and separated from their children.

Talbot, Elizabeth: Bess's granddaughter, second daughter of Gilbert and Mary Shrewsbury. Married to the 8th Earl of Kent. Author of a medical treatise, *A Choice Manual of Rare & Select Secrets in Physick and Chirurgery*, which was published two years after her death in 1651. She was said by John Aubrey to have taken the historian John Seldon as a lover.

Talbot, Gilbert: Bess's stepson, and, because he married Bess's daughter Mary, also her son-in-law. He and Mary lost both their sons in infancy and he tended to regard 'Will' Cavendish, son of Charles Cavendish, as the son he never had, making him executor to the Shrewsbury estates though Will was only twenty-three years old at the time. Gilbert died in 1616.

Talbot, Mary (née Cavendish): Bess's youngest surviving daughter, Mary married Gilbert Talbot, who became her stepbrother when their parents married shortly afterwards. On the death of George, the 6th Earl, Mary became the Countess of Shrewsbury, as her mother had been before her. Her marriage was a happy enough partnership for the first twenty years, but, as with her mother, she was the stronger of the couple and the latter years of the marriage were not comfortable for either Mary or Gilbert. Within two years after her mother's death Mary was writing to her steward that she must have £1200 before Michaelmas to pay a debt to a Mr Basset, and that she also owed her daughter and son-in-law, the Earl and Countess of Pembroke, £3000; 'I know not which way to turn'.[*] Mary was as redoubtable as her mother, with a waspish tongue, a better education, and far more arrogance than Bess. I have found a number of occasions where, because she had the same title as her mother, Countess of Shrewsbury, some of the things which Mary said and did – which earned considerable odium – have been mistakenly attributed to Bess by historians.

[*]*Calendar of Shrewsbury and Talbot Papers at Lambeth*, vol. O, p.332, f.97.

Mary's genuine affection for her niece Arbella led to her being imprisoned in the Tower for over a year for assisting Arbella to escape to France to join her husband, William Seymour. Under questioning, she proved 'obstinately Catholic', and contemptuous of her interlocutors, refusing to answer on two grounds: first that she was a peeress and had a right to be tried by her peers, and second that she had made a promise never to talk of the subject. For her obstinacy she was fined £20,000 (a sum so vast that it was never likely to be paid) and returned to the Tower. She was finally released in December 1615 on compassionate grounds when Gilbert, Earl of Shrewsbury fell dangerously ill. She nursed him faithfully, but he died some months later in 1616.

In 1618 Mary was again called before a court to answer rumours that Arbella (though dead for three years) had borne a child to William Seymour, and that the baby had been smuggled out of the Tower. Again, Mary refused to answer the questions, and again she was sent to the Tower, told it was for 'life', though she was in fact released five years later in 1623, at the age of almost seventy. The Crown took Worksop Manor from her in lieu of the £20,000 fine. She died in 1632 at the age of seventy-six.

APPENDIX 5

Extract from Tree Showing the Relationship between the Brandons and the Hardwicks

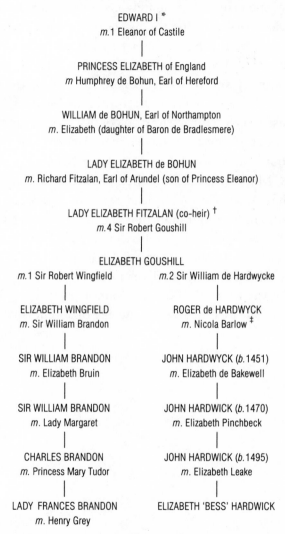

EDWARD I *
*m.*1 Eleanor of Castile

PRINCESS ELIZABETH of England
m Humphrey de Bohun, Earl of Hereford

WILLIAM de BOHUN, Earl of Northampton
m. Elizabeth (daughter of Baron de Bradlesmere)

LADY ELIZABETH de BOHUN
m. Richard Fitzalan, Earl of Arundel (son of Princess Eleanor)

LADY ELIZABETH FITZALAN (co-heir) †
*m.*4 Sir Robert Goushill

ELIZABETH GOUSHILL
*m.*1 Sir Robert Wingfield   *m.*2 Sir William de Hardwycke

ELIZABETH WINGFIELD   ROGER de HARDWYCK
m. Sir William Brandon   *m.* Nicola Barlow ‡

SIR WILLIAM BRANDON   JOHN HARDWYCK (*b.*1451)
m. Elizabeth Bruin   *m.* Elizabeth de Bakewell

SIR WILLIAM BRANDON   JOHN HARDWICK (*b.*1470)
m. Lady Margaret   *m.* Elizabeth Pinchbeck

CHARLES BRANDON   JOHN HARDWICK (*b.*1495)
m. Princess Mary Tudor   *m.* Elizabeth Leake

LADY FRANCES BRANDON   ELIZABETH 'BESS' HARDWICK
m. Henry Grey

*By his second wife, Princess Margaret of France, came the line that produced Henry VII and his heirs, so Bess was also distantly related to Queen Elizabeth. And because of their fascination with genealogy, both would have been aware of this.
†By her first husband, Thomas Mowbray, Duke of Norfolk, through a daughter and son, she produced the Tudor and Grey families, a second strand of kinship between Bess and Queen Elizabeth.
‡Daughter of Robert Barlow, of Barlow in Derbyshire; Bess married into this family.

This tree has been compiled from information in the papers of Rev'd Joseph Hunter, FSA, Manuscripts Department, British Library.

APPENDIX 6

The Stepchildren of Bess of Hardwick*

1. FROM HER MARRIAGE TO SIR WILLIAM CAVENDISH:

The children of his first marriage to Margaret Bostock:

Elizabeth (1534–died young)
Katheryne (1535–) *m.* Thomas Broke, son of Lord Cobham
John (1537–died young)
Mary (1539–still alive in 1557 but died soon after)
Ann (1540–) *m.* Henry, son of Sir Henry Baynton

The children of his second marriage to Elizabeth Parris, widow:

Susan (1544–died young)
John (1545–died young)
Daughter (1546–stillborn)

2. FROM HER MARRIAGE TO SIR WILLIAM ST LOE:

The children of his first marriage to Jane, daughter of Sir Edward Baynton and niece of Queen Katherine Howard:

Mary (1539–) one of Princess Elizabeth's maids of honour
Margaret (*c.*1541–) *m.* Thomas Norton of Bristol

3. FROM HER MARRIAGE TO GEORGE TALBOT, 6TH EARL OF SHREWSBURY:

The children of his first marriage to Gertrude Manners, daughter of 1st Earl of Rutland:

Francis (*c.*1550–82) *m.* Anne Herbert, daughter of 1st Earl of Pembroke
Gilbert (7th Earl) (1552–1616) *m.* Mary Cavendish *(see Bess of Hardwick Tree)*
Catherine (*c.*1553–76) *m.* Henry, 2nd Earl of Pembroke
Mary (*c.*1555–) *m.* Sir George Saville Bt.
Grace (*c.*1560–) *m.* Henry Cavendish *(see Bess of Hardwick Tree)*
Edward (8th Earl) (1561–1617) *m.* Jane Ogle, daughter of 7th Baron Ogle
Henry (1563–96) *m.* Elizabeth Raynor

*Stepchildren's names in bold print feature in the text.

SELECTIVE TREE SHOWING THE HEIRS OF HENRY VII

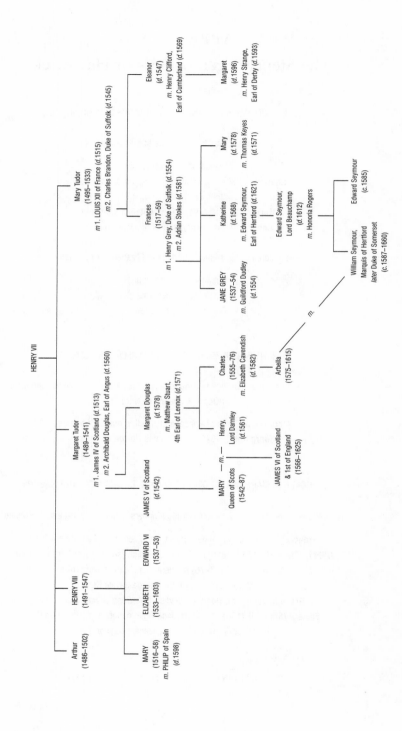

HENRY VII

Arthur
(1486–1502)

HENRY VIII
(1491–1547)

MARY
(1516–58)
m. PHILIP of Spain
(d.1598)

ELIZABETH
(1533–1603)

EDWARD VI
(1537–53)

Margaret Tudor
(1489–1541)
m 1. James IV of Scotland (d.1513)
m 2. Archibald Douglas, Earl of Angus (d.1560)

JAMES V of Scotland
(d.1542)

Margaret Douglas
(d.1578)
m. Matthew Stuart,
4th Earl of Lennox (d.1571)

MARY —— m. —— Henry,
Queen of Scots   Lord Darnley
(1542–87)   (d.1561)

JAMES VI of Scotland
& 1st of England
(1566–1625)

Charles
(1555–76)
m. Elizabeth Cavendish
(d.1582)

Arbella
(1575–1615)

m.

Mary Tudor
(1495–1533)
m 1. LOUIS XII of France (d.1515)
m 2. Charles Brandon, Duke of Suffolk (d.1545)

Frances
(1517–59)
m 1. Henry Grey, Duke of Suffolk (d.1554)
m 2. Adrian Stokes (d.1581)

JANE GREY
(1537–54)
m. Guildford Dudley
(d.1554)

Katherine
(d.1568)
m. Edward Seymour,
Earl of Hertford (d.1621)

Mary
(d.1578)
m. Thomas Keyes
(d.1571)

Edward Seymour,
Lord Beauchamp
(d.1612)
m. Honoria Rogers

William Seymour,
Marquis of Hertford
later Duke of Somerset
(c.1587–1660)

Edward Seymour
(c.1585)

Eleanor
(d.1547)
m. Henry Clifford,
Earl of Cumberland (d.1569)

Margaret
(d.1596)
m. Henry Strange,
Earl of Derby (d.1593)

NOTES

ABBREVIATIONS USED IN THE NOTES AND BIBLIOGRAPHY

APC	Acts of the Privy Council
BL	British Library
CHA	Chatsworth House Archives
CPR	Calendar of Patent Rolls
CSP	Calendar of State Papers
CST	Calendar of Shrewsbury and Talbot Papers at Lambeth Palace and College of Arms
DAJ	*Derbyshire Archaeological Journal*
DNB	Dictionary of National Biography
Folger	Folger Shakespeare Library
HMC	Historical Manuscripts Commission
IPM	Inquisition Post Mortem
L&P	Letters and Papers, Henry VIII
PRO	Public Record Office at Kew, London
SAJ	*Archaeologia, Journal of the Society of Antiquaries*
TCA	Talbot Papers in the College of Arms
TTS	*Transactions of the Thoroton Society*

1: MERRIE ENGLAND

1 John Hardwick was born in 1495. See Hardwick family tree pp. x–xi.
2 Patrick Collinson (ed), *The Sixteenth Century*, see article by J. A. Sharpe, 'Economy and Society', p.32.
3 See Appendix 1 for discussion on Bess's date of birth.
4 SAJ: 12/6/1913. 'Bess of Hardwick's Building and Building Accounts' by Basil Stallybrass, pp.1–2. '. . . at that time there were probably more timbered than stone buildings in Derbyshire'; also BL MSS: Harl.1093, ff.27, 28, 36 and 96. A survey conducted in 1570.
5 DAJ: vol. CVII (1987), pp. 41–54, 'Hardwick before Bess – the origins and Early History of the Hardwick family' by David Crook. Also TTS: vol. XXVI (1922), 'Hardwick Hall' by Harry Gill pp.1–17.
6 John Hardwick's Inquisition Post Mortem and will. PRO: E/150/743/8.

7   Ibid.
8   DAJ: vol. CVII (1987), pp. 41–54, op. cit.
9   David Cressey, *Birth, Marriage and Death*, p.167.
10 See Appendix 1.
11 PRO: E/150/743/8.
12 Cox, 'Notes on Churches of Derbyshire', vol. I, p.246.
13 PRO: E150/743/8.
14 DAJ: vol. XXX (1908), 'Elizabeth Hardwick – Countess of Shrewsbury', p.231; also, Williams, *Bess of Hardwick*, p.1. The Leakes would ultimately become the Barons Deincourt of Sutton, and also Earls of Scarsdale.
15 PRO: C/142/50/102. Deposition re Hardwyck taken 8 September 1530.
16 Average life expectancy was 30–35 years. See Collinson, *The Sixteenth Century*, p.32.
17 PRO: E150/743/8. John Hardwyck's will states that on 6 January 1528 he 'gave the aforesaid [lands and properties] ... to Edward Willoughby kt, John Leeke Esq [his brother in law], Henry Marmyon esq, Thomas Leeke, gent [his father-in-law], Robert Peret, Clerk and Ralph Spalton, yeoman and Edward Bareford Esq.'
18 Ibid.
19 PRO: C142/50/102, 25 November, 1529.
20 The testators were: 'Richard Haselhurst of Spenkenhill, gent, Edmund Wotton, gent, John [unreadable], gent, John Browne, gent, Godfrey Ashe, yeoman, Richard Woodhouse, yeoman, John Shawe, yeoman, Robert More, yeoman, Thomas Greves, yeoman, Thomas Bretysford, yeoman, William Presse, yeoman, Anthony Walton, yeoman and William Downe, yeoman'. Some of these men, and/or their sons, were working in Bess's household 20 years later when she was Lady Cavendish.
21 Durant, *Bess of Hardwick*, p.6.
22 Marriages among the gentry and upper classes tended to be by 'special licence', performed in a private chapel or in the large houses of relatives, so the few marriages recorded in 16th-century church registers tend to be mainly those of working-class couples. We know from extant documentary sources that Elizabeth remarried, but we do not know the exact date or where the marriage took place.
23 For example see Carrington, *Selections from the Stewards' Accounts at Haddon Hall from 1549–1671* (Bembrose, 1890).
24 He is known to have had an annuity of £6. 13s. 4d., and some leases of lands in other counties from which he would have received rents.
25 The earliest surviving portrait of Bess (*c.*1560) shows her with red curly hair, only partially tamed into the straight parted style she had attempted to adopt. Her eyebrows and lashes are fair and her eyes are blue.
26 Elizabeth then had at least five surviving children by John Hardwick –

Mary, Jane, James, Bess and Alice – and three, Elizabeth, Jane and Margaret, by Ralph Leche. As previously explained, we do not know the names or dates of the deaths of the other two daughters who were alive when John Hardwick wrote his will in January 1528. But it is possible that there were at one point ten children growing up at Hardwick.

27 Examples of her work exist at Hardwick and the V&A, London.

28 See William Shakespeare, *The Life of King Henry VIII* (Act III), in which the character Wolsey describes Anne Boleyn as 'a spleeny Lutheran'. Even later in the century the term 'Lutherans' (i.e. followers of Martin Luther) was more widely used to describe followers of the Reformed Church than the word Protestant.

2: CHILD BRIDE, CHILD WIDOW

1 Byrne, *The Lisle Letters*, vol. III, p.19.
2 Ibid. Lady Honor Lisle to her daughter, vol III, p.20.
3 CHA: Nathaniel Johnson, 'Lives of the Earls of Shrewsbury', a bound unpublished manuscript in seven oversized volumes. See vol. V, p.259.
4 PRO: C1/1101 – record of a hearing held in October 1546 re Bess's dower rights.
5 PRO: Ward 9/152.
6 PRO: E150/743/8.
7 Munby, *How Much Is That Worth?*, p.13. A pound consisted of 240 pennies, and a mark of 160 pennies (or 13 shillings and four pence).
8 PRO: STAC 2/19/310.
9 Although unusual, there are cases of this. William St Loe, for example, served in the household of the Courtenay family with his first wife in 1538. See chapter 7.
10 Cressey, *Birth, Marriage and Death*, pp.287–8.
11 BL: Harl. 1093, f.7.
12 PRO: C1/1101.
13 Ibid.
14 Ibid.
15 Those I have been able to identify were heard as follows: (i) 28 March 1545; (ii) Holy Trinity (May or June) 1545; (iii) 3 November 1545; In Octase of St Hilary (Jan–March) 1546; and (iv) in the Easter Term (*c.* April) 1546. And the one whereby she obtained the major part, but not all, of her entitlement in October 1546.
16 PRO: C1/1101.
17 CHA: Rolls 691; drawer 367.
18 Lady Frances also had a sister, Lady Eleanor Brandon (see 'Heirs of Henry VII' family tree, p.498).
19 Through Margaret Tudor, the elder of Henry VIII's two sisters. The English, however, preferred to ignore the Scottish claimants.
20 CSP: L&P 1539 no. 572, pp.200–201
21 The new Queen, Anne Boleyn, had tactfully made her apologies,

knowing that the sympathy of the Grey family had all been reserved for her rival, Queen Catherine.

22 CHA: Inventory August 1567.
23 Bess's height is deduced from the life-size image on her tomb which she approved several years before her death in 1608. The other details are from portraits.
24 Byrne, *The Lisle Letters*. vol. II, p.177 fn.1, and p.209 '. . . my kinsman, Henry Caundishe, this bearer . . . honest and tall . . .'

3: LADY CAVENDISH

1 Weir, *Children of England*, pp. 45–6.
2 Ascham, *The Schoolmaster*, p.33.
3 Collins, *Historical Collections of the Noble Families of Cavendish*, p.11. The entries used here were transcribed in the 18th century from the notebook. A number of writers and historians saw this notebook, and quoted from it (e.g. see article on Sir William Cavendish in the DAJ, vol. XXIX (1927) which differs very slightly from Collins' transcription), but the notebook itself, described by one writer as 'a pocket-book', has disappeared from the library at Welbeck (where it was last seen in 1943), and was still missing in 2004.
4 The family originally came from Cavendish in Suffolk, where one of Sir William's ancestors, John Cavendish, is thought to have slain the rebel Wat Tyler during the reign of Richard II.
5 George married first a Mistress Spring of Lavenham, Suffolk, and secondly, Margery Kemp of Spains Hall, Essex, the niece of Sir Thomas More. They had two sons, William and Henry; William sold the house called Cavendish.
6 Thomas never married. He became a Knight of St John of Jerusalem and died in the Holy Land.
7 Burke's *Peerage*, 106th edn., vol. V, p.837.
8 From the will of Thomas Cavendish, quoted in Collins, *Historical Collections of the Noble Families of Cavendish*, p.7.
9 note to come
10 *DNB*: vol. 9, p.363.
11 Weir, *Henry VIII and his Court*, p.238.
12 Collins, *Historical Collections of the Noble Families of Cavendish*, p.4.
13 CSP: L&P May 1535, p.98. Also extract from handwritten notes by local historian, Gerald Millington: 'William Cavendish was granted a copyhold of "Northawe, alias Northall, alias Nynne" in 1535'.
14 Daughter of Edmund Bostock of Whatcross in Cheshire.
15 Richardson, *History of the Court of Augmentations*, p.55.
16 Ibid. p.40.
17 Ibid. p.8.
18 CSP: L&P January 1536, p.93 ('in Cromwell's own hand').
19 CSP: L&P June 1536, p.495.

20 PRO: E101/424/10. Part of the accounts produced by Sir William Cavendish for the Court of Augmentations. The handwriting is very stylised and is not that of Sir William, but probably that of his clerk, Robert Bestnay.

21 CSP: L&P September 1536, pp.166, 170–1 and 181.

22 Bess's household account books in Folger Xd.428; and at CHA.

23 CSP: L&P 1538, p.514.

24 CSP: L&P 1538, p.281.

25 Quoted in Collins, *Historical Collections of the Noble Families of Cavendish*, p.9. The 'grant in fee' was not ratified until February 1540; see CSP: L&P February 1540; p.115.

26 PRO: E117/14/44.

27 CSP: L&P August 1549, p.494.

28 Sir Anthony St Leger to the King, 6 May 1542, CSP: L&P May 1542, p.182.

29 DAJ: vol. XXIX (1927), p.91. She was born Elizabeth Parker, daughter of Thomas Parker of Postingford in Suffolk.

30 PRO: E101/424/10. Information contained in William Cavendish's statement to the Star Chamber in October 1557.

31 Lacey, *Henry VIII*, p.206.

32 PRO: E101/424/10. William Cavendish's statement to the Star Chamber in 1557.

33 APC: New Series I/356.

34 Payne Collier, *Trevelyan Papers* (Camdem Society, 1857), p.195.

35 According to his accounts, Sir William's important work of recording the minutiae of the expenses of the King's chamber went on without any significant gaps, such as time for a honeymoon that month. It is possible that his deputy Robert Oliver may have carried on the work in Sir William's absence, but Sir William would doubtless have remembered the censure at his earlier lapse.

36 Pritchard, *Shakespeare's England*, p.152.

37 Ibid.

38 Ibid.

39 Fynes Moryson, *An Itinerary* (London, 1617); Pritchard, *Shakespeare's England*, p.154.

40 CHA: Sir William St Loe's account book, 1560.

41 CST: Lambeth, vol. M, p.260 f.75; also Lodge, *Illustrations of British History*, vol. II, p.580.

42 Ambrose Dudley, the Earl of Warwick, 'received the manor of Northaw from Elizabeth 1st in 1576 and built his fine house Nyn Hall on the site of the previous manor house'. Information supplied by Val Higgs, local historian; letter to author 28/11/2002.

43 Brian Warren, local historian, in letter to author 08/09/2004, points out that although Enfield Chase lies only a mile away, there were already three royal hunting lodges nearby. He is not convinced Northaw was built as a hunting lodge.

4: FAMILY MATTERS

1 Levey, *Of Household Stuff: the 1601 Inventories of Bess of Hardwick*, pp.33–4.
2 Collins, *Historical Collections of the Noble Families of Cavendish*, p.11.
3 Gristwood, *Arbella – England's Lost Queen*, p.85.
4 BL: MSS Dept; Private papers of Revd J. Hunter, f.159.
5 'Household Book of Edward VI', in Payne Collier, *The Trevelyan Papers*, pp.195–6.
6 Folger Xd.428. Household Book of Lady Cavendish.
7 Folger Xd.428. The earliest household books, covering Autumn 1548–50, are now in the Folger Shakespeare Library in Washington DC. Those covering 1551–60 are in the archives of Chatsworth House, Derbyshire (CHA). The folios in the Folger book are not separately numbered or dated. All quotes in this chapter which are not separately identified in the notes will be found in the Folger housekeeping book.
8 PRO: STAC 3/1/49.
9 Cecily was obviously a valued member of the household, for Bess often bought her shoes and petticoats. She may have been a companion/maid to Sir William's daughters from his first marriage.
10 Folger Xd.428, Bess's household accounts from 1548.
11 Ibid.
12 Jane Dudley, Countess of Warwick, was the daughter and heir of Sir Edward Guildford who had once held the wardship of John Dudley.
13 Folger Xd.428, Bess's household accounts from 1548.
14 Collins, *Historical Collections of the Noble Families of Cavendish*, p.11.
15 Francis, the 5th Earl of Shrewsbury.
16 Later she was sent to live with Lady Seymour, mother of Edward and Thomas Seymour, at her London house.
17 Holinshed, *The Chronicles of England, Scotland and Ireland*, p.26.
18 Haynes (ed.), *The State Papers of William Cecil, Lord Burghley*, (Bowyer, 1740), MDCCXI. On Bodleian film: ESTC 18th Century; Reel 429 1. p.26. Note: Elizabeth went to stay at the home of Sir Anthony and Lady Denny at Cheshunt.
19 Quoted in Chamberlin, *The Sayings of Queen Elizabeth*, p.3.
20 CSP: Edward VI, August 1548, pp.61–2. Correspondence between the Duke of Somerset and Lord Seymour.
21 Ibid.
22 Folger Xd.428 (48) 'if you could acquire the land . . . it were much to my comfort if you could send as much money as you think it to be worth . . . if you were minded to buy some land in Hallam I assure you it is very good land . . .
23 BL: Additional MS 5861.
24 CHA: document numbered H/240/15. 'Indenture dated 10 May 1547 by which Francis Leyche of Chatsworth sold to Thomas Agarde of Becktie in Ireland his estates in Derbyshire and Staffordshire for £700.

There is a further indenture dated 31 December 1550 by which Francis Agarde (son and heir of Thomas Agarde) sold to Sir William Cavendish and Dame Elizabeth his wife, the manors of Chatsworth and Cromford.' See also PRO: C1/1208/23.

25 PRO: C1/1208/21–22. Also C142/90/31 and E150/758/4. Also CHA: Inquisition Post Mortem of Ralph Leche, dated 24 February 1551.

26 There was another court action at the same time, regarding ownership of border lands of the Chatsworth estate, between the Cavendishes (both named on the suit) and John Wykes and his wife Anne née Leche. See PRO: C1/1208/23.

27 *DNB*: vol. 6, p.222.

28 This left Lady Frances Grey next in line of blood.

29 CHA: account books 1551–1553, p.11, 29 December 1551.

30 Collins, *Historical Collections of the Noble Families of Cavendish*, p.11. William Herbert was married to Lord Northampton's sister.

31 James Lees-Milne, *Tudor Renaissance*, p.101.

32 Hall Ford, *The History of Chesterfield*, p.375.

33 CHA: 2-page inventory of Bess's jewels dated August 1567.

34 Defoe, *A Tour through the Whole Island of Great Britain*, 3 vols (G. Strahan, 1728). Quoted by Hey, *Packmen, Carriers and Packhorse Roads*, p.8.

35 Ibid., pp. 8–10.

5: DANGEROUS TIMES

1 The painting at Chatsworth is thought to be an 18th-century copy by Richard Wilson of a painting by the artist Jan Siberechts c.1692. Or it may be that Wilson simply made some additions to the original painting.

2 Bess's arms appear around the decorative border of this work, and it is so similar to other works known to be by her that it is generally accepted to be her needlework.

3 Cardinal Wolsey had already recognised this and incorporated many new Italian architectural features at Hampton Court.

4 PRO: E/305/20/H4.

5 CPR: 23 June 1552 (the deed was actually signed on 15 June 1552); see also PRO: E/305/20/H4.

6 In Hunter, *A History of Hallamshire*, this Jane is assumed to be Bess's full sister, Mistress Bosville of Gunthwaite in Yorkshire. However I think it is more likely to be her half-sister Jane Kniveton (née Leche), who had been living with Bess for almost four years and was paid fifteen shillings a quarter as wages.

7 Her reluctance was partly due to the fact that Guildford was already betrothed to her cousin, Margaret Clifford (daughter of Jane's aunt Eleanor, née Brandon), and partly that Jane herself was contracted to marry Edward Seymour, son of the executed Lord Protector.

8 Mary Tudor, from her marriage to Charles Brandon, was mother to

the Lady Frances and grandmother to Jane, Katherine and Mary Grey
and Margaret Clifford. Margaret Tudor, through her first marriage to
the King of Scotland, was grandmother of Mary, Queen of Scots.
Margaret married twice, and through her second marriage, to
Archibald Douglas, there were two possible heirs with an indirect
claim: her grandsons Henry Stuart, Lord Darnley and his brother
Charles Stuart, the latter of whom would play a major role later in
Bess's life. See Selective Tree, p.498.

9 Nichols, *Chronicle of Queen Jane and two Years of Queen Mary*, vol.
   II, p.272.
10 Ellis, *Original Letters*, vol. 1, p.183.
11 PRO: E101/424/10.
12 *DNB:* vol. 23, p.185.
13 Camden, *History of the Annals of England*: see 'Introduction' (no
   page numbers).
14 Longleat: Thynne Papers, vol. II, f.227, Sir W. Cavendish to Sir John
   Thynne 3 March 1555, and vol. II, f.250, ditto, 24 June 1556.
15 Durant, *Bess of Hardwick*, p.27.
16 Levey, *Of Household Stuff*, p.10 and p.27.This item is included in the
   1601 Inventory of Hardwick Hall, but is known to date from the time
   of Bess's marriage to Sir William Cavendish.
17 Folger Xd.428 (14) Sir William Cavendish to Sir Humphrey
   Bradburne and Thomas Babington, 25 August 1555.
18 Longleat: Thynne Papers, vol. III.
19 Longleat: Thynne Papers, vol. II, f.227, Sir W. Cavendish to Sir John
   Thynne 3 March 1554/5.
20 Ibid.

6: 'YOUR POOR FRIEND'

1 Longleat: Thynne Papers, vol. II, f.252.
2 BL: MSS Dept, Private papers of Revd J. Hunter.
3 Richardson, *History of the Court of Augmentations,* p.123.
4 See previous chapter.
5 Richardson, *History of the Court of Augmentations,* p.156.
6 Payne Collier, *Trevelyan Papers*, part II, pp.21–138
7 PRO: E101/424/10.
8 Ibid.
9 CHA: Kitchen accounts 20 August 1557–1 March 1559. Since they
   reached Leicester on the first night they must have started out in the
   morning.
10 CHA: Household Accounts 1557–59. Hardwick MS 1, f.1r and f.1v.
11 Ibid.
12 Ibid.
13 Ibid.
14 APC: 9 October 1559.
15 PRO: E101/424/10.

16 Ibid.
17 Collins, *Historical Collections of the Noble Families of Cavendish*, p.12.
18 Nichols (ed.), *Diary of Henry Machyn – Citizen and Merchant Taylor of London 1550–1563*, p.156.
19 Collins, *Historical Collections of the Noble Families of Cavendish*, p.12.
20 CPR: 1563, m25, p.496, refers to the Cavendish case of 1558.
21 PRO: State Papers 46/33/288.
22 Ibid.
23 Tytler, *England under the Reigns of Edward VI and Mary*, p.37.
24 Longleat: Thynne Papers, vol. III, ff.12–14.
25 Longleat: Thynne Papers, vol. III, f.15.
26 Longleat: Thynne Papers, vol. IV, f.243, to Sir John Thynne. 15 March 1558.
27 Longleat: Thynne Papers, vol. IV, f.246, to Sir John Thynne 31 March 1558.
28 CHA: Hardwick MS 3, f.20.
29 CSP: (Spanish), vol. XIII, p.398.
30 Strickland, *Life of Queen Elizabeth*, p.102.
31 Longleat: Thynne Papers, vol. III, f.27.
32 Nichols (ed.), *Diary of Henry Machyn*, p.178.
33 CHA: Hardwick MS 3.
34 Durant: *Bess of Hardwick*, p.33.
35 Folger Xd.428 (18). James Crompe to Lady Cavendish.

7: SIR WILLIAM ST LOE

1 Williams, *Bess of Hardwick*, p.40.
2 Hogrefe, *Women of Action in Tudor England*, p.63.
3 Rawson, *Bess of Hardwick and her Circle*, p.15.
4 Wood, *The Ancient Parish of Chew Magna*, p.111.
5 Henry VI and Henry VII.
6 Calendar of Inquisitions: C Series II, vol. 22 (83).
7 Oldfield, T. H. B., *History of The House of Commons* (Baldwin, Cradock and Joy, 1816), p.330.
8 CSP: L&P 29 Henry VIII (1537), p.137.
9 CSP: L&P 31 Henry VIII (1539), p.201.
10 CSP: L&P 26 Henry VIII (1534), John Hussee to Lord Lisle 20 September, p.455.
11 CSP: L&P 19–20 Henry VIII (1528), p.864.
12 *Star Chamber Cases* 1524, vol. III, no. 219, p.81: The Bishop of Bath and Wells vs Seyntlaw.
13 CSP: L&P June 1535, p.348.
14 Ibid.
15 CSP: L&P 1535, p.79. Skeffington to Henry VIII.
16 CSP: L&P,1535, p.234. Skeffington to Henry VIII.
17 HMC: State Papers of Henry VIII (1536), vol. 1, p.391 et seq.

18 CSP: L&P 29 Henry VIII (1538), pp.199 and 386. Also HMC: Carew MSS 1537, p.116. The lands are fully detailed in HMC: *Appendix to Seventh Report of the Keeper of Public Records in Ireland*, p.39. (In a curious twist, in 1538, 'Uncle' William St Loe offered these lands to one Thomas Agarde – the very same Thomas Agarde who later purchased the Chatsworth Estate from Bess's brother-in-law, and whose son sold it to Sir William Cavendish.)

19 CSP: L&P 29 Henry VIII (1538), p.iii et seq.

20 CSP: L&P 30 Henry VIII (1539), p.35.

21 CSP: L&P 27 Henry VIII (1536), p.348.

22 CSP: L&P 28 Henry VIII (1536), p.249.

23 CSP: L&P 28 Henry VIII (1536), p.491.

24 John Palsgrave is regarded as one of the leading scholars of his day. As a young man he was a close friend of Sir Thomas More, and was fluent in Latin and Greek. He was tutor to Henry VIII's highly intelligent younger sister Princess Mary, and was a member of her retinue when, in 1514, she went to France to marry Louis XII 'amid scenes of medieval splendour'. During this time he wrote two books on French grammar. Later he tutored her son Henry (by Charles Brandon, Duke of Suffolk). On hearing that there was no book introducing a student to the French language, Brandon suggested to Palsgrave that he write one – which he did in 1523 (*The Introductory to Wryte and Pronounce French*). Later still he taught Henry Fitzroy, Earl of Richmond, son of the King and 'Bessie' Blount (daughter of Lord Mountjoy). At the time there was a real possibility that Henry would make Fitzroy his heir. Palsgrave lost this salaried Court position because of a personality conflict with Wolsey after a search of Palsgrave's study while he was out revealed a written indictment of Wolsey. He is chiefly remembered for his translation from Latin of *The Comedy of Acolastus* by Fulonius.

25 CSP: L&P 24 Henry VIII, pp.621–2.

26 Carver (ed.), *The Comedy of Acolastus*, translated from Latin by John Palsgrave, Introduction, pp.l and li.

27 CSP: L&P 26 Henry VIII (17 January 1535).

28 His first marriage took place in or before 1534 (when he was not quite 16), see IPM of Edward and Isabella Wadham in 1534 (PRO C142/64/139), in which the manors of Churchill and Pucklestone were left to Sir John St Loe for his life, 'and in remainder to William St Loe and his wife Jane'.

29 Henry used to stay at the Bayntons' home in Wiltshire (see CSP: L&P 26 August 1535, p.58), and Baynton was one of the King's hunting cronies.

30 CSP: L&P 30 Henry VIII (1538), pp.293–4.

31 Ibid., 'The Marquess of Exeter's servants'.

32 APC: 1540, pp.84–5.

33 The complainant was Thomas Kemys.

34 CSP: L&P 35 Henry VIII (1543), p.44.

35 CSP: L&P 37 Henry VIII (1546), vol. 1, p.20. 'Mr William Seyntlo is dead and the Senechalship of Wexford is therefore void . . . the King favours Brereton [to replace him].' This William St Loe was born at Tormarton in Gloucestershire in 1504, the younger brother of Sir John St Loe, father of Sir William St Loe. He was 44 years old when he died.

36 Ibid.

37 Joseph Hunter, 'Biographical Memoir of Sir William St Loe', in *Retrospective Review* 2nd Series, vol. II, 1828, p.316; letter dated 20 April 1549.

38 APC: Febuary 1549, p.401.

39 Harleian Society, *Wiltshire Visitations 1623*. See under Baynton family of Bromham.

40 CSP: Ireland, February 18, 1551.

41 HMC: *Calendar of the Public Records of Ireland* (8th Report) appendix 9: no.787, July 1551.

42 Strype, *Annals of the Reformation*, vol. III, p.96.

43 Hembrey, *The Bishops of Bath and Wells 1540–1640*, pp.125–6.

44 Markham, *Life of Sir John Harington*, p.11

45 The six maids of honour were: Isabella Markham, who later married John Harington the writer of the poem; Elinor Norwich; Honora Grey, daughter of Lord Grey of Wilton; Mary St Loe; Bridget Skipwith; and Margaret Willoughby, who afterwards married Sir Mathew Arundell of Wardour, was mother of Sir Thomas Arundell and became a cousin to the St Loe family through her marriage. John Harington and Isabella Markham married in 1553 or 1554 for they were incarcerated in the Tower in 1554 as man and wife, at the time of the Princess's imprisonment.

46 Hughey, *The Arundel Harington Manuscript*, p.300.

47 HMC: Index to 2nd Report (1553), p.153.

48 Sir William St Loe was then in the service of Princess Elizabeth. Sir John's youngest son John St Loe had died.

49 Somerset, *Elizabeth I*, p.37.

50 Holinshed, *The Chronicles of England, Scotland and Ireland*, p.320: 'they had already found by the confession of the son of the Lord Privy Seal, who was arrested in his father's house, that this young man had received letters from Wyatt during the time of the Rebellion which were addressed to Elizabeth'.

51 CSP: (Spanish), vol. XII, p.140, 8 March 1554.

52 PRO: SP11/3/f.32, Sir Robert Southwell to the Council, 24 February 1554, also CSP: p.51. All three men were executed after the failure of the Wyatt rebellion.

53 CSP: Febuary 1554, p.51.

54 CSP: vol. III, f.21, report by Lord Howard.

55 Nichols, *Chronicle of Queen Jane and Two Years of Queen Mary*, p.59.

56 Ibid., p.60.

57 Foxe, *Book of Martyrs*, p.119

58 CSP: February 1554, p.51. The inquisitors were Sir John Bourne, Sir Richard Southwell, Sir Thomas Pope and Sir John Bridges. See also Tytler, *England under the reigns of Edward VI and Mary*, vol. II, pp.313–14, and Loades, *Two Tudor Conspiracies*, p.92

59 Tytler, *England under the reigns of Edward VI and Mary*, p.306.

60 Ibid.

61 PRO: SP/11/4/2. This is the famous 'Tide Letter'.

62 Nichols, *Chronicle of Queen Jane and Two Years of Queen Mary*, p.70.

63 Ibid., p.71.

64 Strickland, *Queen Elizabeth*, vol. I, p.32 (she cites *Mémoires de Castelnau*, p.65).

65 Tytler, *England under the reigns of Edward VI and Mary*, pp.328, 330. The French had agreed to make simultaneous attacks from bases in Scotland and Calais, and the Venetian Ambassador later told Simon Renard (Ambassador to Charles V) that he had known all about the plot, and the names of the conspirators, for two months before the rebellion began.

66 Ibid., p.320.

67 Nichols, *Chronicle of Queen Jane*, pp.72–3. See also Tytler, *England under the reigns of Edward VI and Mary*, vol. II, pp.320 et seq.

68 Elizabeth forgave Bedingfeld, telling him shortly after she was made Queen that if she ever needed a prisoner to be looked after carefully and strictly she would send for him.

69 Strickland, *Queen Elizabeth*, p.71.

70 Ibid.

71 Ibid., p.72.

72 Holinshed, *The Chronicles of England, Scotland and Ireland*, p.310.

73 Tytler, *England under the reigns of Edward VI and Mary*, p.400.

74 Holinshed, *The Chronicles of England Scotland and Ireland*, p.133.

75 Somerset, *Elizabeth I*, quoting from CSP: (Spanish), vol. XI, 314. Also PRO: 31/3/21, ff.144–5; Neale, *The Elizabethan House of Commons*, p.148; and BL: Stowe MS.354, f.18.

76 Chamberlin, *Sayings of Queen Elizabeth*, p.160.

77 Ibid., p.38.

78 APC: 28 January 1555, p.90.

79 Bayley, *The Tower of London*, p.208.

80 CSP: 1556, p.154. And PRO: SP11/7/23.

81 Loades, *The Reign of Mary Tudor*, p.224.

82 CSP: July 1557, p.288.

83 CPR: 1 Elizabeth December 1559, pp.258, 323, 352.

84 PRO: AO1/283/1068.

85 His principal seat at Tormarton, Gloucestershire, was leased out; it was a medieval manor, and in the 17th and 18th centuries visitors to

the ruins were shown the dungeons there, with iron rings and chains set into the wall 4 feet from the ground. These were said to have been installed by the de River family (ancestors of Sir William) to 'imprison villains'. See John Aubrey, *Wiltshire Topographical Collections* (London, 1659).

86 CHA: Replication of Sir William Loe, 1561, drawer 143, f.3, and PRO: C/159/9, ff.1–4.

87 Wiltshire Fleet of Fines 1553, no. 463. And *Notes and Queries*, vol. iv, p.118: 'John Scutt, gentleman, and Bridget Scutt, his wife, were tenants of Sir John St Loe . . .' Also, CPR: 1559, p.338; also, Wood, *The Ancient Parish of Chew Magna*, p.138–9: 'Margaret St Loe was the daughter of the Scutts of Stanton Drew'.

88 PRO: E/328/241; and CHA: drawer 144. The sums detailed here were not written into Sir John's final will written in August 1551, but they were detailed in an earlier will, (dated 17 June 1544 and witnessed by Sir Edward Baynton), which probably formed the annex to the final will mentioned by Sir John.

89 Ibid.

8: 'MY OWN SWEET BESS'

1 Portrait now at Hardwick Hall, dated *c.*1560.
2 BL: Cotton MSS, f.5.
3 CHA: Mentioned in Sir William St Loe's book of accounts 1559–60.
4 Rowse, 'The Coronation of Elizabeth I' (1953); a reproduction of this article appeared in *History Today*, May 2003, pp.18 et seq.
5 Chamberlin, *The Sayings of Queen Elizabeth*, p.300.
6 Rowse, 'The Coronation of Elizabeth I' (1953), reproduced in *History Today*, May 2003, pp.18 et seq.
7 Nottingham University Library: Portland papers, Ref: 157/DD/P/ 114/13, 20 July 1559.
8 CSP: (Spanish), 1559, p.27.
9 Longleat: Thynne Papers, vol. III, f.27.
10 BL: MSS Dept, Private papers of Revd J. Hunter, f.159; and, Collinson's *History of Somerset*. Also private papers in the author's library. The work for this parlour was apparently begun in 1559, and the only possible time slot after the marriage was late August/ early September.
11 Folger Xd.428 (133).
12 BL: MSS Dept, Private papers of Revd J. Hunter, f.159.
13 *Archaeologia*: vols. XVI and XXXI–XXXIII, 'Henry VI'.
14 *Archaeologia*: vol. XII, p.389.
15 BL: Lansdowne MS/3, f.191 and f.193.
16 Lodge, *Illustrations of British History*, vol. II, p.149.
17 CHA: Inventory of Bess's jewels, dated August 1567.
18 Folger Xd.428 (75).

19 Folger Xd.428 (19).

20 Ibid.

31 CHA: Sir William St Loe's accounts 1560, f.21.

22 Ibid., f.61.

23 Longleat: Thynne Papers, 25 April 1560.

24 This had been left to him by Sir John's cousins the Wadhams, and is mentioned in chapter 7.

25 After Sir William's death, Edward St Loe became 'respectable'. His marriage was a long and apparently happy one.

26 PRO: E/328/241.

27 PRO: C3/159/9 (4). Replication of Sir William and Lady St Loe to the answer of Edward St Loe, defendant.

28 Folger Xd.428 (74). 'I was sure you were poisoned when I was at London and if you had not had a present remedy you had died'.

29 CSP: 1560, p.368.

30 Bayley, *History and Antiquities of the Tower of London*, Appendix to Part II, p.1.

31 The city of Bristol was usually spelled Bristowe in 16th-century documents.

32 Jeremy Ashbee, Curator, Tower of London, to the author, 19/05/03.

33 Folger Xd.428 (74).

34 Bayley, *History and Antiquities of the Tower of London*, Appendix to Part II, p.1.

35 CHA: drawer 243/3. 'Sir William St Loe's replication.'

36 The Queen stayed at the house of Lord Paulett (the Lord Treasurer) in Basing and was so impressed with the house, that she told the old man that if he were younger, 'I could find it in my heart to have him to my husband before any man in England.' Nichols, *Progresses of Queen Elizabeth*, p.87.

37 Folger Xd.428 (75), September 1560.

38 The fourth son of Sir Henry Skipwith.

39 Folger Xd.428 (75), September 1560.

40 Ibid.

41 CHA: Sir William St Loe's account book, October 1560: 'For charges at Master Mann's house, nine days 9th–17th October; £4.17s.0d. For washing ten shirts at that time: 20d. Given to the servants of the house there at the same time: 2s.'

42 BL: Addl MS.35830, f.77. Sir William sometimes replied in fluent French.

43 This breakfast consisted of 'bread, beer, wine, beef, mutton, chickens, lamb and fruit'. CHA: Sir William St Loe's account book, f.25.

44 CHA: account book of Sir William St Loe 1560–61. All the details of his clothing, purchases and London activities are extracted from this source; ff.25 et seq.

45 Ibid., f.32.

46 Strickland, *Queen Elizabeth I*, p.141.

47 Derek Wilson, *Sweet Robin* – a biography of Robert Dudley. See p.121 et seq. for a detailed account of the death of Amy Robsart.
48 Folger Xd.428 (76).
49 Rudder, *History of Gloucestershire*, p.216 (modern reprint of the 1779 publication).
50 CHA: Sir William St Loe's account book, October 1560. This has been confirmed by material about the Royal Armoury at the V&A Museum.
51 J. Hunter (ed.), *Retrospective Review*, vol. II, second series, 1828: 'Expenses of two brothers at Eton', p.149 et seq.
52 PRO: C3/159/9, f.4, 'Replication of Sir William Sentelowe and his wife Dame Elizabeth', *c.* January 1561.
53 CHA: drawer 143 (3). 'Sir Wm and Dame Elizabeth St Loe vs Edward St Loe.'
54 PRO: C3/159/9/1 and PROB 11/48 (244) Morisson. The will was made and signed on 1 March 1563.
55 PRO: C3/170/13 (2). The Answer of Edward St Loe to the bill of complaint. 'Sir William St Loe . . . had in his life time conveyed all his goods by a deed of gift to the use of the complainant.'

9: LADY ST LOE IN TROUBLE

1 Francis died on 5 December 1560, a month short of his seventeenth birthday. He was succeeded by his brother Charles.
2 CSP: (Foreign) Elizabeth, vol. IV, p.201.
3 Folger Xd.428 (83).
4 CSP: (Foreign) Elizabeth, 1559, p.443.
5 Ellis, *Original Letters*, vol. 1, p.272.
6 Ibid. In some documents this is spelled Chanon Row.
7 BL: Harl. 6286, p.50. A volume consisting of documents concerning the trial of Katherine Grey and her marriage to the Earl of Hertford. This includes the full statements made by Katherine and Edward Seymour to Edward Warner, Lieutenant of the Tower.
8 HMC: Salisbury Papers, vol. 1, p.153.
9 Wilson, *Queen Elizabeth's Maids of Honour*, p.27.
10 BL: Harl. 6286, p.49. Unless otherwise stated, the information provided for this episode is taken from Lady Katherine's statement to Edward Warner, which is now in the British Library manuscripts department.
11 CSP: Elizabeth, 1561, p.369. Also HMC: Salisbury Papers, vol. 1, pp.87–8 and 153.
12 BL: Harl. 6286, p.49.
13 Folger Xd.428 (47), Elizabeth Leche, 29 September 1561.
14 Folger Xd.428 (84), Elizabeth St Loe, 20 October ?1561. This letter was previously assumed to be dated 1560, but this is not possible as Bess was at Chatsworth, awaiting her husband, on 20 October 1560. It is much more likely to be 1561.

15 Folger Xd.428 (69), and Hunter, *A History of Hallamshire*, pp.107–8. 'Sir George Pierrepoint to my lady Sentloo at London', 13 November 1561.

16 Folger Xd.428 (70), 'Sir George Pierrepoint to my lady Sentloo at London', 13 November 1561.

17 Durant, *Bess of Hardwick*, p.45.

18 Hunter, 'Biographical Memoir of Sir William St Loe' in *Retrospective Review*, vol. II, second series 1828, p.314 et seq. This agreement, witnessed by Sir Edward Rogers and Sir Edward Warner also appointed Sir John Mason, Sir Richard Sackville (a friend of both Sir William Cavendish and Sir William St Loe) and Sir Richard Southwell as Ann Cavendish's guardians, 'in the event of the death of her mother Lady Cavendish' [*sic*: she was Lady St Loe by this time].

19 Baynton private family papers, copies of which are in the author's collection.

20 HMC: Series 5: Frank Bacon Collection: 23–30 July 1563.

21 Strickland, *Queen Elizabeth I*, p.158.

22 CPR: vol. II, Elizabeth, 15 August 1563, pp.495–6.

23 Folger Xd.428 (108).

24 Ibid.

25 Folger Xd.428 (78), William St Loe, son of 'Uncle William' (see Chapter 7) to Bess, dated 22 October 1564.

26 Folger Xd.428 (16), F. Cobham, 21 October 1564.

27 Folger Xd.428 (48), Elizabeth Leche to E. St Loe, *c.* 29 January 1565 and Xd.428 (35), from James Hardwick to E. St Loe, same date.

28 PRO: C3/170/13, Lady St Loe's statement to Sir Nicholas Baron, Keeper of the Great Seal of England.

29 Ibid. NB: The precise date of the death is not stated, but Sir William's probate certificate gives the date of his death as 'February 1565'. See PRO: PROB 11/48 (244) Morrison.

30 John Stow, *A Survey of London* (originally published in 1603, reprinted (Thoms) 1876), vol. I, pp.172 and 208. In 1603 Stow referred to a monument at Great St Helen's Church for 'Sir William Sanctlo and Sir William Santclo [*sic*], father and son'. This monument has not survived.

31 CPR: 26 March 1565.

10: A VERY ELIGIBLE WIDOW

1 PRO: PROB 11/48 (244) Morrison, February 1565.

2 Markham, *Life of Sir John Harington*, p.ii, '. . . Mary St Loo, so cruelly robbed by her stepmother Bess of Hardwick . . .'.

3 PRO: C3/159/9/2.

4 Ibid.

5 PRO: C3/170/13 (2).

6 APC: 1566 (see item dated December 6th regarding victualling of 'the bands serving the Queen's Majesty under Edward St Loe in the

remote north places of the realm of Ireland . . .'

7 CHA: drawer 143 (6). I am indebted to the papers of David Durant at Nottingham University library for a transcription of this 8-page original inventory (which saved me days of work). The precise date of this inventory is not known but it is presumed to be 1565–6.

8 Levey, *An Elizabethan Inheritance – The Hardwick Hall Textiles*, p.13.

9 Folger Xd.428 (73), 10 August 1565.

10 HMC: Salisbury Papers, vol. I, p.325.

11 Wormwauld, *Mary, Queen of Scots*, p.182.

12 Gartrid (Gertrude), Countess of Shrewsbury née Manners, daughter of the Earl of Rutland. Buried 16 January 1567 at what is now Sheffield Cathedral.

13 Durant, *Bess of Hardwick*, p.54.

14 CSP: (Domestic), Elizabeth, 1567 (Addenda), p.39.

15 Ibid. The original is a one-page draft, damaged.

16 Wood, *A History of Oxford Colleges*, p.5. Also Folger Xd.428 (18), letter from Crompe to Lady St Loe which mentions Jackson. Also *Alumni Oxonienses*, p.794, 'Henry Jackson BA October 1558; MA January 1562'.

17 Hunter, *A History of Hallamshire*, p.89.

18 Strype, *Ecclesiastical Memorials*, vol. 1, p.130. Letter dated 27 February 1568 from Sir John Mason.

19 *Boyd's Marriage Index*, February 1567–68. NB: The date given uses the 'old style calendar' when the calendar years began on Lady Day, 25 March. The date of the marriages was actually February 1568.

20 Wood, *A History of Oxford Colleges*, p.139.

21 Frederick Wood, *Collections for a Parochial History of Chew Magna*, p.139. '567–68 Fines 10–11 Elizabeth; Edward Seyntlo and Margaret his wife sell to George, Earl of Shrewsbury and Elizabeth his wife the manor of Chew Stoke als Stoke Militis'. This transfer occurred between Christmas and Lady Day 1568, so the Shrewsbury marriage must have occurred shortly after that of the four children and before Lady Day, 25 March.

22 Folger Xd.428 (85).

23 Folger Xd.428 (129), Elizabeth Wingfield to Lady Shrewsbury 21 October 1568.

24 For more information on Queen Mary, Bothwell, and the Casket Letters see Antonia Fraser, *Mary Queen of Scots* (Phoenix Press, 2001), easily the best book on the subject, p.339 et seq.

25 Folger Xd.428 (86).

26 CSP: (Scottish), Elizabeth, 1568–9, p.609.

27 HMC: (Pepys), p.147, Elizabeth Shrewsbury to the Earl of Leicester, 'from Tutbury, 21 Jan 1569'.

28 CSP: (Scottish), Elizabeth, 1568–9, p.606
29 HMC: (Pepys), Henry Knowles [sic: Knollys] to Cecil, 21 January 1569.
30 Ibid., Shrewsbury and Knollys to Cecil, 5 February 1569.
31 Ibid., Shrewsbury to Cecil, 8 February 1569.
32 Haynes, *Collections of State Papers*, p.510. White to Cecil, 26 February 1568.
33 Ibid.
34 HMC: (Pepys), p.144, Lord Shrewsbury to Cecil.

11: A DIFFICULT GUEST

1 Strickland, *Letters of Mary Queen of Scots*, vol. II, p.161.
2 Longleat: *Calendar of Manuscripts of Marquis of Bath*, vol. V, p.20.
3 Folger Xd.428 (21), William Cavendish to Mrs Linnacre, 23 February 1569.
4 Ibid.
5 CSP: Elizabeth, 1569, p.629.
6 Labanoff: *Lettres de Marie Stuart*, vol. v, p.436. (This translation also quoted by Rawson, *Bess of Hardwick*, p.156.)
7 CSP: Elizabeth, 1569, p.633.
8 Ibid., p.635–6.
9 Ibid., p.639.
10 Ibid., p.642.
11 Ibid., p.645.
12 Ibid., p.642.
13 Ibid., p.649.
14 Ibid., p.656.
15 Ibid., p.655.
16 Ibid.
17 Ibid., p.654.
18 Ibid., p.654.
19 Ibid., p.526.
20 Folger Xd.428 (102).
21 Durant, *Bess of Hardwick*, p.66.
22 Strickland, *Letters of Mary Queen of Scots*, vol. III. p.93. Huntingdon was descended from the Plantaganets, though his claim to the Crown was never seriously put forward.
23 CSP: (Scottish), 1569, vol. 11, p.655.
24 CSP: (Domestic), Elizabeth, 1569, p.695 (30 October 1569).
25 Nichols, *A Progress of Queen Elizabeth*, Appendix, vol. I, p.47.
26 Folger Xd.428 (88).
27 Folger Xd.428 (9).
28 Hunter, *A History of Hallamshire*, p.87.
29 Lodge, *Original Letters*, vol. ii, p.50.
30 Fraser, *Mary Queen of Scots*, p.423.
31 HMC: (Salisbury), vol. XIII, p.99.

32 Strype, *Ecclesiastical Memorials*, vol. I, p.499.
33 HMC: Salisbury I, pp.548–551, Examination of Hersey Lassells.
34 CSP: (Scotland), vol. IV, p.16.
35 CSP: Elizabeth, 1570, p.601, 4 August 1570.
36 Strickland: *Letters of Mary Queen of Scots*, pp.116–17.
37 Trevor Brighton,'Chatsworth's Sixteenth-century Parks and Gardens', *Garden History Journal*, 23/1, Summer 1995, pp.45–6.
38 CSP: Elizabeth, 1570, p.606.
39 CHA: (sundry papers), George 6th Earl to his wife, 24 April *c*. 1571. Also Folger Xd.428 (92).
40 Hunter, *A History of Hallamshire*, p.110.
41 CST: (Lambeth), vol. O, p.327.
42 Folger Xd.428 (29).
43 Strype, *Annals of the Reformation*, vol. II, part 1, p.396.
44 Ibid.
45 Ibid., p.401.
46 Hunter, *A History of Hallamshire*, p.89.
47 Folger Xd.428 (49).
48 BL: Cotton Caligula CIII, f.216. Quoted in Williams: *Bess of Hardwick*, p.102.
49 Hunter, *A History of Hallamshire*, p.90.
50 Folger Xd.428 (91).
51 CHA: Indenture dated 22 April 1572, signed by Shrewsbury.
52 HMC: Salisbury, vol. 1, p.26.
53 CSP: (Domestic). Elizabeth, 1566–79, Addendum, 20 June 1572.
54 Nichols, *A Progress of Queen Elizabeth*, vol. 1, Appendix, p.47.
55 Folger Xd.428 (89).
56 Strype, *Annals of the Reformation*, p.318. The Queen was affected by this mystery illness for some months, suffering a series of fevers and fits.
57 Hunter, *A History of Hallamshire*, p.91.
58 Ibid.
59 Rawson, *Bess of Hardwick and her Circle,* p.97, quotes original letter.
60 CSP: (Domestic), Elizabeth, August 1573.

12: A DANGEROUS MATCH

1 Howard, *Collections of Letters from the Original,* pp.235–7.
2 Williams, *Bess of Hardwick*, pp.112–13.
3 Folger Xd.428 (93).
4 Howard, *Collections of Letters from the Original,* pp.235–7.
5 Gristwood, *Arbella – England's Lost Queen*, p.12.
6 Howard, *Collections of Letters from the Original,* pp.235–237.
7 PRO: State Papers, Supplement (compiled by John Maddocks) 46/30/333.
8 Howard, *Collections of Letters from the Original,* pp.235–7.

9 Lodge, *Illustrations of British History*, vol. II, pp.124–5.
10 PRO: Letters and Papers on microfilm: SP12/99, f.3 (not calendared).
11 Hardy, *Arbella Stuart*, p.125.
12 Ibid., pp.126–7.
13 Ibid.
14 CSP: (Scottish), 1575, p.139.
15 CSP: (Scottish), 1574–5, p.94.
16 Lodge, *Illustrations of British History*, vol. II, p.50
17 Hunter, *A History of Hallamshire*, p.113.
18 Folger Xd.428, Gilbert Talbot to Countess of Shrewsbury, 14 May 1575. 'This bearer Mr Tyndall was at Hackney and found them well. I trust shortly all dregs of their misconduct will be wiped away and that their abode after this sort will be altered . . .' Also CSP: (Scottish), July 1575.
19 Folger Xd.428 (127).
20 HMC: Talbot Papers, vol. O, p.329.
21 Folger Xd.428 (98).
22 Folger Xd.428 (99), undated 1575.
23 Folger Xd.428 (136).
24 HMC: Talbot Papers at Longleat, vol. V, p.21.
25 Sheffield City Archives, Ref. MD 6279.
26 Williams, *Bess of Hardwick*, p.115.
27 Lodge, *Illustrations of British History*, vol. II, pp.129–30.
28 CSP: (Scottish), June 1577, p.229.
29 Lodge: *Illustrations of British History*, vol. II, pp.130–2.
30 Folger Xd.428 (97).
31 Hunter, *Archaeologia*, vol. 32, p.81, states that Arbella was born at Chatsworth.

13: RAISING ARBELLA

1 Quoted in Hardy: *Arbella Stuart*, p.20.
2 Gristwood, *Arbella – England's Lost Queen*, p.27.
3 Lodge, *Illustrations of British History*, vol. II, p.73. (Original now at College of Arms.)
4 Nichols, *A Progress of Queen Elizabeth*, p.6.
5 HMC: Longleat, Talbot Papers, vol. II, p.98.
6 Ibid.
7 Nichols, *A Progress of Queen Elizabeth*, p.5.
8 Lodge, *Illustrations of British History*, vol. II, pp.167–8.
9 Bickley, *The Cavendish Family*, p.22.
10 HMC: Salisbury Papers, vol. II, p.154.
11 Folger Xd.428 (110), 30 June 1577.
12 Lodge, *Illustrations of British History*, vol. II, p.154.
13 CSP: (Scottish), Elizabeth, 1577, p.229.
14 Hunter, *A History of Hallamshire*, Topcliffe to Lady Shrewsbury, 9 July 1577.

15 Labanoff, *Lettres de Marie Stuart*, vol. iv, p.369.
16 Folger Xd.428 (111) *c.* late July 1577.
17 Ibid.
18 Dunn, *Elizabeth & Mary*, p.466.
19 Folger Xd.428 (112).
20 Strype, *Annals of the Reformation*, vol. II, pt. 2, pp. 136–7.
21 CSP: (Scottish), 1577, vol. V, p.236; and quoted in Williams, *Bess of Hardwick*, p.135.
22 HMC: Longleat, Talbot Papers vol. V, p.22.
23 Ibid., pp.22–3
24 HMC: Salisbury Papers, vol. II, p.174.
25 Gristwood, *Arbella – England's Lost Queen*, p.29.
26 CSP: (Scottish), September 1579, p.350.
27 CSP: (Scottish), vol. 5, p. 314, The Earl and Countess of Shrewsbury to Earl of Leicester.
28 Rawson, *Bess of Hardwick and her Circle*, p.25.

14: ENOUGH TO ALIENATE THE HEART

 1 HMC: Salisbury Papers, vol. II, p.213.
 2 HMC: Salisbury Papers, vol. II, p.223.
 3 Lodge, *Illustrations of British History*, vol. II, p.170.
 4 HMC: Salisbury Papers, vol. II, p.226.
 5 Lodge, *Illustrations of British History*, vol. II, p.289
 6 Folger Xd.428 (112) 'This day my Lord intendeth to go to Worksop'. Letter from Gilbert Talbot to Lady Shrewsbury dated 1 August 1577.
 7 Mark Girouard, 'Robert Smythson' (*Country Life*) (issue unknown) 1966, p.96. NB: Worksop was burned down in 1761 but the plans survive among Smythson's papers.
 8 HMC: Longleat, Talbot Papers, vol. V, p.32.
 9 Lodge, *Illustrations of British History*, vol. II, p.239.
10 Ibid., pp. 237–9.
11 Folger Xd.428 (104), Shrewsbury to Bess, 10 October 1580
12 Folger Xd.428 (3), Robert Booth to Thomas Kniveton.
13 Folger Xd.428 (111), July 1577
14 CSP: (Scottish), 23 March 1584, p.49, Frances Battell to Lady Paulet.
15 Lodge, *Illustrations of British History*, vol. II, p.287.
16 HMC: Longleat, Talbot Papers, vol. V, p.26–7.
17 Ibid.
18 Lodge, *Illustrations of British History*, vol. II, p.244.
19 Ibid., p.234–5.
20 HMC: Longleat, Talbot Papers, vol. V, p.28.
21 CST: Lambeth, vol. 1, p.150.
22 Lodge, *Illustrations of British History*, vol. II, pp.239–40
23 HMC: Salisbury Papers, vol. II, p.228.

24 HMC: Longleat, Talbot Papers, vol. V, p.29.
25 HMC: Salisbury Papers, vol. V, pp.32–3.
26 Lodge, *Illustrations of British History*, vol. II, pp.196–7.
27 HMC: Series 5, Frank Bacon Collection, 1585, p.3. The Earl sold some broken pieces of plate and some steel to raise £361.
28 BL: Addl CH/73965.
29 Ibid.
30 CST: vol. II, p.117.
31 Kettle, *Oldcotes*, p.12.
32 Girouard, *Hardwick Hall*, p.82.
33 CSP: (Scottish), 1581, vol. vi, pp. 89–91.
34 HMC: Longleat, Talbot Papers, vol. IX(2), pp.443 et seq.

15: DISCORD

1 CSP: (Scottish), January 1581–2, p.108.
2 CSP: (Scottish), 6 May 1582, p.119, f.111.
3 Ibid.
4 CST: Lambeth, vol. II, p.110.
5 CST: Lambeth, vol. II, pp.118–19.
6 CSP: (Foreign), 22 January 1582, p.460.
7 CST: Lambeth, vol. II, p.120.
8 Duchess of Devonshire, *The Estate*, pp.177–8.
9 HMC: Longleat, Talbot Papers, vol. II (2), p.122.
10 HMC: Longleat, Talbot Papers, vol. V, p.39.
11 CST: Lambeth, vol. II, p.154.
12 HMC: Longleat, Talbot Papers, vol. V, p.40.
13 Labanof, *Lettres de Marie Stuart*, vol. v, p.389. Also quoted in Williams, *Bess of Hardwick*, p.162.
14 CST: Lambeth, vol. II, p.125.
15 Gristwood, *Arbella – England's Lost Queen*, p.40; also Kettle, *Oldcotes*, p.12.
16 HMC: Longleat, Talbot Papers, vol. V, p.45.
17 HMC: Longleat, Talbot Papers, vol. V, p.47.
18 CST: Lambeth, vol. II, p.133, and HMC: Longleat, Talbot Papers, vol. V, pp.50–51
19 CST: Lambeth, vol. II, p.133.
20 Labanof, *Lettres de Marie Stuart*, vol. v, p.436.
21 HMC: Longleat, Talbot Papers, vol. V, p.45.
22 HMC: Longleat, Talbot Papers, vol. V, p.51.
23 CHA: Nathaniel Johnson, unpublished MS, 'A History of the Earls of Shrewsbury', vol. V, f.38.
24 Ibid., f.289.
25 CSP: 26 July 1584, vol. II. Also, HMC: Longleat, Talbot Papers, vol. VII, p.129.
26 CHA: Nathaniel Johnson, unpublished MS, 'A History of the Earls of Shrewsbury', vol. V, ff.288–9, Shrewsbury to Lord Leicester.

27 HMC: *Calendar of Talbot Papers at Arundel,* Frank Bacon collection, Appendix, pp.192–5.
28 Ibid., p.191.
29 CHA: Nathaniel Johnson, unpublished MS, 'A History of the Earls of Shrewsbury', vol. V, ff.288–9.
30 HMC: Longleat, Talbot Papers, vol. V, p.52, Shrewsbury to Leicester.
31 HMC: Longleat, Talbot Papers, vol. V, p.51.
32 CSP: (Scottish), vol. VII, p.296.
33 HMC: Calendar of Talbot Papers at Arundel, Frank Bacon collection, Appendix vol. II, p.19.
34 Brodhurst, 'Elizabeth Hardwycke, Countess of Shrewsbury,' DAJ, vol. XXX, p.244, Roger Manners to his brother John, 23 September 1584.
35 Strype, *Ecclesiastical Memorials,* vol. I, pp.241–2.
36 CST: Lambeth, vol. II, pp.125–6.
37 CSP: 1580, pp.561–2.
38 Labanof, *Lettres de Marie Stuart,* vol. v, p.389.
39 CSP: (Scottish), 1584, p.511, Queen Mary to M. de Mauvisière, December 1584.
40 Labanof, *Lettres de Marie Stuart,* vol. vi, pp.51–7; also Leader, *Mary, Queen of Scots in Captivity,* pp. 553–7.
41 Wright, *Queen Elizabeth and her Times,* vol. II, pp.240–2.
42 CSP: (Scottish), December 1584, p.514, f.481.
43 CSP: (Scottish), December 1584. Also Williams, *Bess of Hardwick,* p.170.
44 CSP: (Scottish), 12 January 1585, Nau to Fontenay.

16: NO WINNERS

1 Folger Xd.428 (7).
2 Folger Xd.428 (10).
3 Bickley, *The Cavendish Family,* p.36.
4 BL: MSS dept, papers of Revd J. Hunter: notes on Sir Charles Cavendish of Welbeck.
5 CSP: April 1586, p.341, Item 366.
6 Ibid.
7 Gristwood, *Arbella – England's Lost Queen,* p.43.
8 CST: Lambeth, vol. G/II, p.136, item 332.
9 HMC: Longleat, Talbot Papers, vol. V, p.54.
10 Ibid., p.55.
11 Ibid., pp.55–6.
12 Lodge, *Illustrations of British History,* pp.308–10.
13 CHA: Johnson, 'A History of the Earls of Shrewsbury', vol. VI, p.35.
14 HMC: Longleat, Talbot Papers, vol. V, pp.58–9.
15 Ibid., p.62.
16 Ibid.
17 Ibid.

18 CSP: (Domestic), 1585, p.290.
19 HMC: Longleat, Talbot Papers, vol. V, pp.69–70.
20 Ibid., p.70. A signed copy is housed in the Talbot Papers at Longleat; the original, signed by Queen Elizabeth, is at Chatsworth House.
21 Ibid., p.71.
22 HMC: Series 5, Calendar of Talbot Papers at Arundel, Frank Bacon collection, Appendix, vol. II, p.15.
23 HMC: Appendix to the Sixth Report, 1586, p.455. States that in July 1586 320 deaths 'of the common plague' occurred in London.
24 CHA: E. Shrewsbury to the Earl, 4 August 1585.
25 HMC: 9/3, p.163, Item 324.
26 Ibid., p.161.
27 Ibid., p.166.
28 Ibid., p.163.
29 Ibid., p.164–5.
30 Ibid.
31 CST: 9 June 1585, vol. II, p.135, f.331.

17: DEATH OF A QUEEN

1 Somerset, *Elizabeth I*, p.400.
2 Routh, *Who's Who in Tudor England*, pp.317–20.
3 CSP: (Scottish), 17 July 1586, Queen Mary to Thomas Morgan.
4 Dunn, *Elizabeth & Mary*, p.468.
5 CSP: (Scottish), 17 July 1586, Queen Mary to Thomas Morgan.
6 Dunn, *Elizabeth & Mary*, p.468.
7 Somerset, *Elizabeth I*, p.428.
8 HMC: Report 9/3, p.231, states: 'the Earl of Shrewsbury being but 6 miles off . . .'
9 Strickland, *Lives of the Queens of Scotland*, (Longmans, 1854), vol. VII, p.428.
10 HMC: Appendix to 4th Report, Bagot papers, p.340.
11 HMC: Longleat, Talbot Papers, vol. V, p.73. Burghley to Shrewsbury, 22 October 1586.
12 Ibid., p.75. Burghley to Shrewsbury, 26 October 1586.
13 HMC: 9/3, p.217, notes in Burghley's own hand for the Earl of Shrewsbury.
14 CSP: (Scottish), 8 February 1587, pp.273–4, 'Account of the Queen of Scots' Death'.
15 Weir, *Elizabeth the Queen*, p.382.
16 Williams, *Bess of Hardwick*, p.190.
17 Ibid.
18 CSP: (Domestic), 16 May 1587, p.411.
19 HMC: Longleat, Talbot Papers, vol. V, p.80, 23 May 1587.
20 Ibid., 23 June 1587.
21 Lodge, *Illustrations of British History*, vol. II, p.542.

22 CHA: letter marked 'Hardwick Drawer 143/10', Charles Cavendish to his mother Countess of Shrewsbury, *c*. August 1587.
23 Ibid.
24 Gristwood, *Arbella – England's Lost Queen*, p.63.
25 CHA: letter marked 'Hardwick Drawer 143/10', Charles Cavendish to his mother Countess of Shrewsbury, *c*. August 1587.
26 HMC: Longleat, Talbot Papers, vol. V, pp.87–8, March 1588.
27 Stone, *Crisis of the Aristocracy*, p.254.
28 HMC: Longleat, Talbot Papers, vol. V, p.86, 27 February 1588.
29 Ibid., p.89.
30 Ibid., p.91, 18 June 1588.
31 CSP: (Domestic), 9 August 1588 (p.527) from Sheffield Lodge.
32 CSP: (Domestic), 15 August from Tilbury.
33 Weir, *Elizabeth the Queen*, p.397.
34 CSP: (Venetian), vol. 9, f.541.
35 Steen, *Letters of Lady Arbella Stuart*, letter no. 16; also p.21.
36 Worsley, *Hardwick Old Hall*, p.7.
37 Hunter, *A History of Hallamshire*. See letter 5 November 1588. From Nicholas Kinnersley at Wingfield to Bess at Hardwick. p.106.
38 Ibid.
39 John Foxe died in 1587.
40 John Foxe's draft is among his papers in the Harleian Collection at the BL.
41 HMC: Catalogue of Arundel Castle MSS; Talbot Papers, Appendix, p.197, f.2/97.
42 Nottingham Record Office (Portland Papers): DDP/51, f.19, and DDP42, f.27–8.
43 Hunter, *A History of Hallamshire*, 1 July 1589, p.107.
44 CST: Lambeth, vol. I, p.197.
45 HMC: Catalogue of Arundel Castle MSS, Talbot Papers, vol. G, p.386.
46 Ibid., Appendix, p.198.
47 Hardy, *Arbella Stuart*, p.57.
48 CST: vol. I, p.202.
49 Costello, *Eminent Englishwomen*, p.127.
50 Durant, *Bess of Hardwick*, p.152.
51 Ibid.

18: THE DOWAGER COUNTESS

1 HMC: (Rutland), vol. 1, pp.285–6
2 TCA: vol. G, p.335.
3 TCA: vol. H, p.135.
4 BL: Harl. 6853 (Gilbert, Earl of Shrewsbury against Eleanor Britton).
5 Ibid.
6 Ibid.
7 *Surtees Society Journal*, (1912) vol. I, p.148.

 8 CHA: Nathaniel Johnson, unpublished MS, 'A History of the Earls of Shrewsbury', vol. V, p.105.
 9 Hunter; *A History of Hallamshire*, pp.97–8.
10 Ibid.
11 TCA, vol. I, p.204.
12 BL: Harl. 4864, f.325.
13 HMC: Longleat, Talbot Papers, vol. V, p.100, John Stanhope to Gilbert, Earl of Shrewsbury, 22 November 1590.
14 CSP: (Domestic), 1591, p.238.
15 House of Lords MSS: Supplementary, 1576–93, H/S:146, f.30; also CHA: H7/8/10.
16 BL: 24783, f.113, papers relating to Gloucestershire, Dowager Countess of Shrewsbury to Mr Wm Lacye.
17 CSP: (Domestic), Elizabeth, 1591, pp.239–40.
18 Williams, *Bess of Hardwick*, pp.200–201.
19 SAJ: Stallybrass, 'Bess of Hardwick's Buildings and Building Accounts', p.355.
20 Weir, *Elizabeth the Queen*, p.410.
21 Wood, *In Search of Shakepeare*, pp.139–40.
22 Gristwood, *Arbella – England's Lost Queen*, p.82.
23 CSP: (Scottish), 1691, p.605.
24 Harington: *Tract on the Succession of the Crown*, pp.44–5.
25 Now archived at Chatsworth.
26 DAJ: vol. XXX, Brodhurst, 'Elizabeth Hardwick, Countess of Shrewsbury', p.249.
27 Ibid.
28 CHA: account book, details of items in ES's jewellery coffer, 1593.
29 Gristwood, *Arbella – England's Lost Queen*, p.97.
30 Durant, *Bess of Hardwick*, p.176.
31 CSP: (Domestic), Elizabeth, 1597, vol. 81, p.557.

19: MORE WINDOW THAN WALL

 1 DAJ: vol. XXX, Brodhurst, 'Elizabeth Hardwick, Countess of Shrewsbury', p.251.
 2 TTS: (vol. XXVI) 1922, Harry Gill, 'Hardwick Hall', p.5.
 3 CHA: Hardwick building accounts, (MS7). Also, Durant and Riden, *The Building of Hardwick Hall*, vol. II, p.lxii.
 4 CHA: Hardwick building accounts, June 1599.
 5 Ibid., October 1600.
 6 Ibid., 14 November 1601.
 7 CSP: (Domestic), Elizabeth, 1591–4, p.259–60.
 8 Hardy, *Arbella Stuart*, pp.65–6.
 9 Ibid. Also, Bradley, *Life of Lady Arbella Stuart*.
10 Gristwood, *Arbella – England's Lost Queen*, p.85.
11 DAJ: vol. XXX, Brodhurst, 'Elizabeth Hardwick, Countess of Shrewsbury', p.248. Brodhurst states that two payments were made

by WIlliam Cavendish for these properties, one of £2050 and one of £1300.

12 Details of the contract, providing a good idea of Bess's businesslike approach, can be seen in Pamela Kettle's fascinating, detailed account of the building of Oldcotes. See her *Oldcotes*, pp.14–16.

13 TCA: vol. H, p.423.

14 Craik, *Romance of the Peerage*, vol. III, p.258.

15 HMC: Longleat, Talbot Papers, vol. V, pp.120–1.

16 CHA: Nathaniel Johnson, unpublished MS, 'A History of the Earls of Shrewsbury', vol. VI, p.217.

17 BL: Sloane 4161.

18 Handover, *Arbella Stuart*, cited by Gristwood, *Arbella – England's Lost Queen*, pp.102–3.

19 TCA: vol. H, p.425.

20 CST: Lambeth, vol. H, 1593, p.178.

21 TCA: vol. I, p.186.

22 Craik, *Romance of the Peerage*, vol. III, p.247.

23 PRO: STAC 7/6/1.

24 DAJ: vol. XXX, 1908, Brodhurst, vol. III, 'Elizabeth Hardwick, Countess of Shrewsbury', p.253.

25 TCA: vol. I, p.247.

26 Hardy, *Arbella Stuart*, pp.75–6.

27 Gristwood, *Arbella – England's Lost Queen*, p.114.

28 Williams, *Bess of Hardwick*, p.259. Note: The original document is at Chatsworth.

29 Durant, *Bess of Hardwick*, p.192.

30 HMC: Salisbury Papers, vol. 15, p.65.

31 Levey, *Of Household Stuff*, p.8.

32 Folger Xd.428 (22).

33 CHA: Household accounts for 19 October, 41 Elizabeth (1600).

34 SAJ: Basil Stallybrass, in 'Bess of Hardwick's Buildings and Building Accounts', suggests that drawing number 33 in Smythson's portfolio might have been the plan for Kirkby.

35 Weir, *Elizabeth the Queen*, p.436.

36 Collins, *Historical Collections of the Noble Families of Cavendish*, p.21.

20: 'IN PERFECT HEALTH AND GOOD MEMORY'

1 Folger Xd.428 (120).

2 Folger Xd. 428 (6), Charles Cavendish to his mother.

3 HMC: Cecil Papers, vol. X, p.172.

4 Weir, *Elizabeth the Queen*, pp.433–4.

5 Ibid., p.431.

6 Ibid., p.449.

7 Three copies of Bess's will exist. (1): PRO: PROB II/111, ff.188–92; (2): PROB 10/252; (3): in the Chatsworth archives.

8 Bess of Hardwick's will, extracts printed in Collins, *Historical Collections of the Noble Families of Cavendish*, pp.4–15.
9 Girouard, *Hardwick Hall*, p.35.
10 Rawson, *Bess of Hardwick and her Circle*, p.361.
11 Gristwood, *Arbella – England's Lost Queen*, p.133.
12 HMC: Cecil Papers, vol. XIV, p.258.

21: SHARPER THAN A SERPENT'S TOOTH

1 Gristwood, *Arbella – England's Lost Queen*, p.135.
2 Steen, *Letters of Lady Arbella Stuart*, pp.120 et seq.
3 Ibid.
4 Now in the V & A Museum, London.
5 Plowden, *Lady Jane Grey*, p.144.
6 The details of Arbella's plan and Sir Henry Brounker's visit to Hardwick are in the Cecil Papers.
7 HMC: Hatfield, Cecil Papers, p.135, f.146; and transcribed in Steen, *Letters of Lady Arbella Stuart*, p.122.
8 HMC: Salisbury Papers, vol. 12, pp. 529–36.
9 HMC: Hatfield, Cecil Papers, p.135; also, Steen, *Letters of Lady Arbella Stuart*, p.123.
10 HMC: Hatfield, Cecil Papers, p.135; also, Steen, *Letters of Lady Arbella Stuart*, pp.134–5.
11 Cited in Gristwood, *Arbella – England's Lost Queen*, p.161.
12 Cited in DAJ: vol. XXX, Brodhurst, 'Elizabeth Hardwick, Countess of Shrewsbury' p.256; also, Hardy, *Arbella Stuart*, pp.116–17.
13 Weir, *Elizabeth the Queen*, p.480.
14 Ibid.
15 HMC: Hatfield, Cecil Papers, p.135; also Steen, *Letters of Lady Arbella Stuart*, p.167.
16 The report of this incident, extracted from Bess's letter to the Council, is transcribed and cited in Hardy, *Arbella Stuart*, pp.132–3.
17 HMC: Hatfield, Cecil Papers, p.135.
18 DAJ: vol. XXX, Brodhurst, 'Elizabeth Hardwick, Countess of Shrewsbury', p.257.
19 HMC: Hatfield, Cecil Papers, p.135; also, Steen, *Letters of Lady Arbella Stuart*, p.176.
20 'Elizabeth', an exhibition at the National Maritime Museum, Greenwich, July 2002.
21 Folger Xd.428 (68).
22 CSP: (Venetian), vol. X, p.3.
23 HMC: Hatfield, Cecil Papers, vol. XV, p.65.
24 Cited in Gristwood, *Arbella – England's Lost Queen*, p.202; also, Steen, *Letters of Lady Arbella Stuart*, p.43; also, BL: Sloane MS718, f.39.

22: END OF AN ERA

1 Williams, *Bess of Hardwick*, p.261.
2 HMC: (series 5) Frank Bacon Collection, p.18.
3 Folger Xd.428 (116), 30 March 1603.
4 CST: vol. II, p.277, f.29.
5 CST: vol. II, p.267, f.169.
6 HMC: Cecil Papers, vol. XV, p.65.
7 CST: vol. II, p.264, f.120 (17 September 1603).
8 CST: vol. II, p.262, f.93.
9 Gristwood, *Arbella – England's Lost Queen*, p.211.
10 CST: vol. II, p.264. f.124.
11 Ibid., p.277, f.300.
12 Ibid., p,265, f.140.
13 Ibid., p.268, f.182.
14 HMC: Cecil Papers, vol. XV, p.44.
15 Hunter, *A History of Hallamshire*, p.121.
16 Folger Xd.428 (40).
17 Cited in Gristwood, *Arbella – England's Lost Queen*, p.240.
18 CST: vol. II, p.275, f.260.
19 Hardy, *Arbella Stuart*, p.175; also Steen, *Letters of Lady Arbella Stuart*, p.202.
20 HMC: Salisbury Papers, vol. XII, p.584.
21 CSP: (Domestic), James I, 1605, pp. 269–71.
22 Hunter, *A History of Hallamshire*, p.90.
23 CHA: account books of William Cavendish 1605.
24 CHA: Nathaniel Johnson, unpublished MS, 'A History of the Earls of Shrewsbury', vol. V, p.393; also, CST: vol. L, p.244, f.44.
25 CST: vol. II, p.281, f.349.
26 CST: vol. II, p.278, f. 310.
27 CST: vol. II, p.279, f.327.
28 HMC: Cecil Papers, vol. XVI, p.360.
29 CST: vol. II, p.245, f.61.
30 Folger Xd.428 (72).
31 Folger Xd.428 (118).
32 CST: vol. II, p.329, f.59.
33 HMC: Cecil Papers, vol. XX, p.117.
34 HMC: Salisbury Papers, vol. XX, p.379, 24 December 1607.
35 CST: vol. II, p.290, f.473.
36 Folger Xd.428 (119).
37 HMC: (series 5) Arundel Papers, Frank Bacon collection, p.7.
38 CST: vol. II, p.291, f.481.
39 Ibid., f.134; and, vol. II, p.291, f.482.
40 Cited in Rawson, *Bess of Hardwick and her Circle*, p.346, 4 January 1608 (1607 by the old calendar).
41 HMC: Longleat, Talbot Papers, vol. V, p.132.

42 CHA: A Memorandum of declarations made by the Countess of Shrewsbury, subsequent to her will (Old drawer no:143/17).
43 CHA: Nathaniel Johnson, unpublished MS, 'A History of the Earls of Shrewsbury', vol. V, p.406.
44 HMC: Longleat, Talbot Papers, vol. V, pp.132–3.
45 HMC: Cecil Papers vol. XX, pp.67, 96 and 118.

23: A LONG ARM . . .

1 CST: vol. II, p.251, f.141.
2 CST: vol. II, p.283, f.384.
3 HMC: Cecil Papers, vol. XX, p.96. Gilbert Talbot to Lord Salisbury.
4 HMC: Arundel (Frank Bacon Collection), Appendix, p.211, f.2/211.
5 CST: vol. II, p.148, f.112.
6 HMC: Cecil Papers, vol. XX, p118. Gilbert Talbot to Lord Salisbury.
7 CHA: H29; also, cited in Stone, *Crisis of the Aristocracy*, Appendix, p.xxv p.785).
8 Nichols, *Progresses, Processions and Magnificent Festivities of King James I of England*, vol. 2, p.194.
9 Ibid.
10 HMC: Longleat, Talbot Papers, vol. V, p.134.
11 Ibid.
12 Ibid.
13 CST: vol. II, p.170, f.205.
14 Durant, *Bess of Hardwick*, p.218.
15 Collins, *Historical Collections of the Noble Families of Cavendish*, p.21.

BIBLIOGRAPHY

(NB: unless otherwise stated all books cited are UK publications, published in London).

CALENDARS CONSULTED AND CITED

Letters & Papers, Foreign and Domestic, Henry VIII, vols 1–21 and Addenda.

Calendars of State Papers Domestic, Edward VI, Queen Mary I, Elizabeth I and James I, vols 1–12 and Addenda.

Calendar of State Papers relating to Scotland and Mary Queen of Scots, vols 1–13.

Calendar of State Papers – Venice, vols 6–10 (HMSO).

Calendar of Patent Rolls (Henry VII & VIII, Edward VI, Queen Mary I and Elizabeth I (Public Record Office).

Calendar of the MSS at Hatfield House (Marquis of Salisbury).

Bain, Joseph (ed.), *Calendar of State Papers relating to Scotland* (Henry VIII, Edward VI and Queens Mary and Elizabeth), vols 1–2.

Batho, G. R. (ed.), *A Calendar of the Shrewsbury and Talbot Papers in the Lambeth Palace Library and College of Arms* (HMSO, vols. 1–11, 1971).

Dasent, John Roche (ed.), *Acts of the Privy Council of England*, vols. 1–18 (HMSO).

Dyfnallt Owen, G. (ed.), *A Calendar of the Manuscripts of the Marquis of Bath at Longleat (vol.V) Talbot, Dudley and Devereux papers* (HMC 58, 1975).

Fitzalan-Howard, Bernard, and Rosamund Meredith, *Calendar of Talbot Papers, Frank Bacon Collection; appendix to Calendar of Arundel Castle MSS* (HMC).

Fry, Edward A. (ed.), *Calendar of Wills in the Archdeaconry of Taunton*, 1912.

Hamilton, Hans Claude (ed.), *Calendar of State Papers relating to Ireland*, 1860.

Hardy, W. J. (ed.), *A Calendar of Fleet Fines for London*.

Jamison, Catherine (ed.), *A Calendar of the Shrewsbury and Talbot Papers in the Lambeth Palace Library and College of Arms* (HMSO, vol. 1, 1966).

Knighton, J. S. (ed.), *Calendar of State Papers Domestic, Mary I.* and *Calendar of State Papers Domestic, Edward VI* (HMSO).

Lemon, Robert, of the PRO (ed.), *Calendar of State Papers, Domestic Series of the reigns of Edward VI, Mary and Elizabeth, (James) 1547–1580*, 12 vols.

Lemon, Robert, and Mary Everett Green (eds), *Calendars of State Papers Foreign, Edward VI, Mary I, Elizabeth*, vols 1–23.

Morton, Ann (ed.), *Calendar of the Patent Rolls preserved in the PRO, Elizabeth I*, vol. 9: 1580–1582 (HMSO. 1986).

Murdin, Wm. (ed.), *A Collection of State Papers in the Reign of Elizabeth I.*

Redington, Joseph (ed.), *Calendar of Treasury Papers 1556–7.*

Sharp, John (ed.), *Calendars of Inquisition Post Mortem* (Henry VII) – second series, vols 1–3.

Strong, S. Arthur (ed.), *A Catalogue of Letters and Documents . . . in the library at Welbeck [Abbey]*, 1903.

Visitations of Somerset; Wiltshire; Gloucestershire; Derbyshire and London (pub: The Harleian Society – various dates in 19th and 20th century). These are accounts of sixteenth-century County Visitations made by royal Heralds (the original MSS are at the College of Arms).

Woodward, G. H. (ed.), *Calendar of Somerset Chantry Grants*, 1982.

PUBLISHED BOOKS (AND PAMPHLETS)

Ascham, Roger, *The Whole Works of Roger Ascham* (ed., Dr J. A. Giles, 1865).

Bagwell, Richard, *Ireland under the Tudors* (Longmans, 1885).

Baker, E. A., *Uncommon Volumes of Somerset* (Weston-super-Mare, 1900).

Barlow, Sir Montague, *Barlow Family Records* (Privately printed, 1932).

Bayley, J. W., *The History and Antiquities of the Tower of London* (Jennings and Chaplin, 1821), 2 vols.

Bickley, Francis, *The Cavendish Family* (Constable, 1911).

Birch, T., *Memoirs of the Reign of Queen Elizabeth* (Millar, 1754).

—— *Life of Henry VIII* (Faulkner, 1760).

Bradley, E. T., *Life of Lady Arabella Stuart* (Bentley, 1889).

Brodhurst, Frederick, *Hardwick Hall* (Nottingham, 1903).

Bunting, J., *Earls and Dukes of Devonshire* (Derbyshire Heritage, 2001).

Burnett, J., *History of the Cost of Living* (Penguin Pelican, 1969).

Byrne, Muriel St Clare (ed.), *The Lisle Letters*, 6 vols (Chicago University Press, USA, 1983).

Camden, W., *History of the Annals of England* (Harper, 1615).

—— *History of Princess Elizabeth* (London, 1688).

Cavendish, George, *The Life of Cardinal Wolsey* (London, 1908).

Chamberlin, Frederick, *The Sayings of Queen Elizabeth* (Bodley Head, 1923).

Cockayne, George E., *Complete Peerage* (London, 1910).

Collier, Payne, *Trevelyan Papers* (Camden Society, 1857).

Collins, Arthur C., *Historical Collections of the Noble Families of Cavendish* (Withers, 1752).

—— *The Sydney Papers* (London, 1746).

Collinson, J., *History of Somerset* (Taunton, 1898).

Collinson, Patrick (ed.), *The Sixteenth Century* (Oxford University Press, 2002).

Cooper, Elizabeth, *Life of Lady Arabella Stuart* (Hurst & Blacket, 1866).

Copnall, H., *Nottingham County Records* (County Records Committee, 1916).

Costello, Louisa Stuart, *Memoirs of Eminent Englishwomen* (Bentley, 1844).

Craik, I., *Romance of the Peerage*, 4 vols (Chapman & Hall, 1869).

Cressey, David, *Birth, Marriage and Death* (Oxford University Press, 1999).

Devonshire, The Duchess of, *The House* (Papermac, 1982).

Devonshire, The Duchess of, *The Estate* (Papermac, 1990).

Devonshire, The Duke of, *Hardwick Hall* (Nottingham, 1903).

Doleman, R., *Conference about the succession to the Crown of England* (Menston, 1972). A facsimile of pamphlet dated 1594.

Doran, Susan (ed.), *Elizabeth – the Exhibition at the National Maritime Museum, Greenwich* (Chatto & Windus, 2003).

Dovey, Zillah, *An Elizabethan Progress* (Sutton, 1996).

Dugdale, Sir William, *Visitation of Derbyshire 1662* (Harleian Society, 1879).

Dunn, Jane, *Elizabeth & Mary* (HarperCollins, 2003).

Durant, David, *Bess of Hardwick* (Peter Owen, 1999).

Durant, David, and Philip Riden, *The Building of Hardwick Hall* (Derbyshire Record Society, 2 vols, 1984).

Eales, Jacqueline, *Women in Early Modern England* (UCL Press, 1998).

Eisenberg, Elizabeth, *This Costly Countess* (Derbyshire Heritage, 2001).

Ellis, Sir Henry, *Original Letters Illustrative of English History*, 11 vols (Dawsons of Pall Mall, 1969), vols 1, 2 and 3.

Emerson, Kathy Lynn, *Wives and Daughters*: *Women of the 16th Century* (Whitston Pub. Co., USA, 1984).

Erickson, Carolly, *Bloody Mary* (Robson, 2001).

Fletcher, Anthony J., and Diarmaid MacCulloch, *Tudor Rebellion* (Longmans, 1997).

Foxe, John, *Acts and Monuments of the Church* [aka *The Book of Martyrs*, 1563], 8 vols: edited by J. Pratt (London, 1877).

Fraser, Antonia, *Mary Queen of Scots* (Weidenfeld & Nicolson, 1969).

Furniture History Society, *Hardwick Hall Inventories of 1601*, 1971.

Girouard, Mark, *Robert Smythson* (Country Life Ltd, 1966).

—— *Hardwick Hall* (National Trust, 1989).

Goldsmid, Edmund, *Secret Correspondence of Robert Cecil with James VI* (Edinburgh, 1887).

Goodman, Godfrey, *The Court of King James I* (London, 1839).

Graves, Michael, *Burghley* (Longman, 1998).

Gristwood, Sarah, *Arbella – England's Lost Queen* (Bantam Press, 2003).

Hall Ford, George, *The History of Chesterfield* (Whittaker, 1839).

Handover, P. M., *Arbella Stuart* (Eyre & Spottiswoode, 1957).

Hardy, Blanche Christabel, *Arbella Stuart* (Constable, 1913).

Harington, Sir John, *Tract on the succession of the Crown* (Roxburghe, 1880).
—— (ed.) *Nugae Antiquae* (London, 1779).
Haynes, Samuel (ed.), *The State Papers of William Cecil, Lord Burghley*, (Bowyer, 1740).
Hembrey, Phyllis, *The Bishops of Bath and Wells 1540–1640* (University of London, 1967).
Hey, David, *Packmen, Carriers and Packhorse Roads* (Landmark, 2001).
Hogrefe, Pearl, *Women of Action in Tudor England* (Iowa State University Press, USA, 1977).
Holinshed, Raphael, *The Chronicles of England, Scotland and Ireland* (Denham, 1587); reprint edition (London 1807).
—— *England in the Sixteenth Century* (Blackie, 1906).
Howard, Leonard, *Collections of Letters from the Original* (Withers, 1753).
Hubbard, Kate, *A Material Girl* (Short Books, 2001).
Hughey, Ruth, *The Arundel Harington MS of Tudor Poetry* (Ohio State University Press, USA, 1960).
Hunter, Joseph, *A History of Hallamshire* (London, 1869).
Kennet, White, *Memoires of the Cavendish Family* (Hills, 1708).
Kettle, Pamela, *Oldcotes* (Merton Priory Press, 2000).
Kingsford, Charles L. (and Stow, John), *A Survey of London* (Clarendon Press, 1927).
Labanof, Prince A., *Letters of Mary Stuart* (London, 1845).
—— *Lettres de Marie Stuart* (ed. A. Teulet, London, 1859).
Lacey, Robert, *Henry VIII* (Weidenfeld & Nicolson, 1972).
Leader, J. D., *Mary, Queen of Scots in Captivity* (Sheffield, 1880).
Lees-Milne, James, *Tudor Renaissance* (Batsford, 1951).
Levey, Santina M., *An Elizabethan Inheritance: The Hardwick Hall Textiles* (National Trust, 1998).
—— *Of Household Stuff: the 1601 Inventories of Bess of Hardwick* (National Trust, 2001).
Loades, D. M., *The Reign of Mary Tudor* (Longman, 1991).
—— *Two Tudor Conspiracies* (Cambridge University Press, 1965).
Lodge, Edmund, *Illustrations of British History*, 3 vols (Nichols, 1791 and 1838).
—— *Portraits of Illustrious Persons*, 12 vols, (Harding & Lepard, 1835).
Lyte, Henry, *History of Eton College* (London, 1911).
MacCulloch, Diarmaid, *Edward VI* (Penguin, 1999).
Markham, Clement, *Life of Sir John Harington* (Roxburghe Club, 1880).
Montgomery-Massingberd, Hugh, *Great British Families* (Michael Joseph, 1988).
Munby, Lionel, *How Much Is that Worth?* (British Association for Local History, 1996).
National Trust, *Of Household Things* (2001).
Neale, John E., *The Elizabethan House of Commons* (reprint: Fontana 1967).

Nichols, J., *Progress of Queen Elizabeth* . . ., 3 vols (London, 1788–1805).
—— *Progresses, Processions and Magnificent Festivities of King James I of England* (Nicols, 1828).
—— (ed.) *Diary of Henry Machyn 1559–1563* (Camden Society, vol. XLII, 1848).
—— *Legend of Sir Nicholas Throckmorton* (London, 1874).
—— *The Chronicle of Queen Jane and Two Years of Queen Mary* (Camden Society, 1850).
—— *Catalogue of the works of the Camden Society* (Camden Society, 1862).
Osborne, Francis, and Sir Walter Scott, *Secret History of James I* (Edinburgh, 1811).
Parsons, Robert, *Treatise: the broken succession of the Crown* (London, 1655).
Pearson, John, *Stags and Serpents* (Macmillan, 1983).
Picard, Liza, *Elizabeth's London* (Weidenfeld & Nicolson, 2003).
Plowden, Alison (ed.), *Elizabethan England* (Readers' Digest, 1982).
—— *Lady Jane Grey* (Sutton, 2003).
Pritchard R. E., *Shakespeare's England* (Sutton, 2000).
Proctor, John, *The Historie of Wyates Rebellion* (Caly, 1555).
Rawson, Maud S., *Bess of Hardwick and her Circle* (Hutchinson, 1910).
Raymond, S. A., *Gloucester and Bristol – A Genealogical Record* (Birmingham, 1992).
Read, Conyers, *Lord Burghley and Queen Elizabeth* (Cape, 1960).
—— *Bibliography of British History* (Clarendon, 1933).
Richards, M., *Gloucestershire Family Histories* (Gloucester, 1979).
Richardson, Walter C., *History of the Court of Augmentations* (Louisiana State University Press, USA, 1961).
Ridley, Jasper, *A Brief History of the Tudor Age* (Robinson, 1998).
Routh, C. R. N., *Who's Who in Tudor England* (Shepheard Walwyn, 1990).
Rowse, A. L., *Eminent Elizabethans* (University of Georgia Press, USA, 1983).
Rudder, Samuel, *A New History of Gloucestershire* (Gloucester, 1779).
Saint-George, Henry, and Sampson Lennard, *Wiltshire Visitation Pedigrees* (Harleian Society, 1954).
Sim, Alison, *The Tudor Housewife* (Sutton, 1996).
Sitwell, Sacheverell, *British Architects and Craftsmen* (London, 1847).
Smith, Emily T., *Life of the Lady Arabella Stuart*, 2 vols (London, 1889).
Somerset, Anne, *Elizabeth I* (Weidenfeld & Nicolson, 1991).
Starkey, David, *Elizabeth* (Vintage, 2001).
—— *The English Court from the Wars of the Roses to the Civil War* (Longman, 1987).
Steen, Sarah Jane, *Letters of Lady Arbella Stuart 1575–1615* (Oxford University Press, 1994).
Stone, Lawrence, *The Crisis of the Aristocracy 1558–1641* (Oxford University Press, 1965).
Stow, John, *A Survey of London* (reprint, London, 1876).
Strickland, Agnes, *Life of Queen Elizabeth* (London, 1904).

——— *Letters of Mary Queen of Scots* (Colbourn, 1842).
——— *Queen Mary's Book* (London, 1907).
——— *Lives of the Tudor Princesses* (Longmans, 1868).
Strong, Sir Roy, *Gloriana: Portraits of Elizabeth I* (Pimlico, 2003).
Strype, John, *Annals of the Reformation*, 4 vols (Clarendon Press, 1824).
———*Ecclesiastical Memorials*, 3 vols (London, 1721).
Swabey, Ffiona, *Medieval Gentlewoman* (Sutton, 1999).
Thompson, Francis, *Chatsworth – A Short History* (Country Life Ltd, 1951).
Toynbee, P. J. (ed.), *Letters of Horace Walpole* (Oxford University Press, 1903).
Tytler, P. F., *England under the reigns of Edward VI and Mary*, 2 vols (Bentley, 1839).
——— *Life of King Henry VIII* (Edinburgh, 1837).
Warnicke, Retha M., *The Rise and Fall of Anne Boleyn* (Canto, 1989).
Weaver, Frederick William, *Visitation of Somerset 1531 and 1575* (Exeter, 1885).
Weir, Alison, *Elizabeth the Queen* (Cape, 1998).
——— *Children of England* (Cape, 1996).
——— *Henry VIII and his Court* (Cape, 2001).
White, Gillian, *A Very Goodly Prospect: Guide to Hardwick Hall* (National Trust, 1997).
Whitmore, J. B., and A. Hughes-Clarke; *London Visitation Pedigrees* (London, 1940).
Williams, Alan, and Anthony de Reuck, *The Royal Armoury at Greenwich* (Royal Armoury Museum, 1995).
Williams, E. C., *Bess of Hardwick* (Longman, 1959).
Williams, Neville, *Elizabeth I* (Weidenfeld & Nicolson, 1972).
Wilson, Derek, *Sweet Robin* (Allison & Busby, 1997).
Wilson, Viole, *Queen Elizabeth's Maids of Honour* (Bodley Head, 1922).
Winwood, Sir Ralph, *Memorials of Affairs of State* (Ward, 1725).
Wood, A. A., *History of Oxford Colleges* (Clarendon Press, 1776).
Wood, Frederick, *Collections for A Parochial History of the Ancient Parish of Chew Magna* (Bristol, 1903).
Wood, Michael, *In Search of Shakespeare* (BBC Publications, 2003).
Woolley, William, *Woolley's History of Derbyshire* (Chesterfield, 1981).
Wormwauld, Jenny, *Mary, Queen of Scots* (St Martin's Press, New York, 2001).
Worsley, Lucy, *Hardwick Old Hall* (English Heritage, 1998).
Wright, T., *Queen Elizabeth and her Times* (Colburn, 1838).

UNPUBLISHED MSS IN BOOK FORM

Johnson, Nathaniel, 'A History of the Lives of the Earls of Shrewsbury', 7 vols. At Chatsworth House, Derbyshire.

PERIODICAL PUBLICATIONS

Archaeologia, vols:
XII – 'Sir John St Loe at the funeral of Edward VI', p.389.
'Quarrel between the St Loe brothers', pp.98–9.
XIII – 'Bayley, on poison gloves', p.99.
XVI – 'Sir John St Loe', p.382.
XVIII – 'Sir Wm St Loe moved from the Tower to Fleet prison', p.179.
XX – 'Early use of carriages in England – Sir Wm St Loe', p.458.
'Queen Mary's fall from her horse en route to Buxton', p.459.
'Burial of Elizabeth, Countess of Lennox at Sheffield', pp.73–82.
XXII – 'Alleged residence of Mary Queen of Scots at Hardwick Hall', pp. 73–82.
XXXII – 'Cavendish Brothers', p.74.
XXXII – 'Bess of Hardwick', p.81.
XXXIV – 'The Earl of Shrewsbury obtains licence to alienate Goodrich Castle from Henry & Grace Cavendish', p.486.
XXXVII 'Sir Wm St Loe commissioned to find suitable site for new royal Armoury', p.484.
LXIV – 'Bess of Hardwick's Buildings and Building Accounts'.

Derbyshire Archaeological Society, vols:
XVI – Currey, John, 'Almshouses of Elizabeth Countess of Shrewsbury'.
XXVIII – Hawkesbury, Lord, 'Catalogue of pictures at Hardwick Hall'.
XXIX – Brodhurst, Revd Francis, 'Sir William Cavendish'.
XXX – Brodhurst, Revd Francis, 'Elizabeth Hardwycke, Countess of Shrewsbury'.
XXXIII – Kirke, Henry, 'Aristocratic Squabbles'.
XCIII – Batho, Gordon, 'Gilbert Talbot 7th Earl'.

Retrospective Review, second series vols:

I – (1827), 'Journal of Robert, Earl of Leicester', p.277.
'Biographical Memoir of Sir James Croft', pp.469–499.
II – (1828), 'Expenses of Two Brothers . . . at Eton', pp.149–55.
'Biographical Memoir of Sir William St Loe' by the Revd. Joseph Hunter, pp.314–325.

Thoroton Society, vols:

V – Brodhurst, Revd Francis, 'Was Mary Queen of Scots ever at Hardwick Hall?'
VIII Brodhurst, Revd Francis, 'Hardwick Old Hall'.
XXVI Gill, Harry, 'Hardwick Hall' p.1–17.

Notes taken from Unidentified Periodical:
Cox, J. C., 'Notes on Churches of Derbyshire' (1890, identified only as vol. I, p.246).

ACKNOWLEDGEMENTS

I would like to thank the following people for help during the research phase of this book:

Derek Adlam, *Curator, Portland Collection*; Andrew, the late Duke of Devonshire, Deborah, the Dowager Duchess of Devonshire; Jeremy Ashbee, *Asst Curator, Tower of London*; Stuart Band, *Archivist Devonshire Collection*; Marian Benton, *Hon. Sec., North Mymms Local History Society*; Jean Bray, *Archivist at Sudeley Castle*; Dr Andrea Clarke, *Curator 16th & 17th Century MSS at British Library*; John Coulson, *English Heritage*; Rachel Cox, *Archives Asst, Royal Archives;* Dr Peter Cunich, *History Dept, University of Hong Kong;* Martin Durrant, *V & A Museum*; David Edge, *Curator & Armourer at the Wallace Collection*; Dudley Fowkes, *Derbyshire Archaeological Society*; Dr Kate Harris, *Curator, Longleat Historic Collection*; Alan Hargreaves; Val Higgs, *local historian, Northaw, Herts*; Colin Johnstone, *Archivist, Bath & North East Somerset Record Office*; Caroline Kelly, *Asst Keeper MSS and Special Collections, Nottingham University*; Joanne Kenyon, *BBC*; Bill Killick, *North Mymms Historical Society*; Alistair Lang, *National Trust*; Christine Leighton, *Freelance expert – 16th-century MSS*; Ann-Marie Leonard, *English Heritage*; Fiona Leslie, *V & A Museum*; Helen Marchant, *Chatsworth House*; Simon Neal, *Latin translator*; Charles Noble, *Keeper of Devonshire Collection*; Terence Pennell, *former Chairman, North*

Mymms Local History Society; Rachel Pringle, *Archivist, Somerset Archive and Record Service*; Theresa Randall, *Archivist, Staffordshire and Stoke on Trent Archive Service*; Michael Scott, *Photographer, Folger Shakespeare Library*; Linda Shaw, *Asst Keeper, MSS and Special Collections, Nottingham University*; Sir Roy Strong; A. G. Thomas, *Building Manager, St Helen's Church, Bishopgate*; Laura Valentine, *Royal Academy of Arts*; Brian Warren, *Hon. Archivist, Potters Bar & District Historical Society*; Philippa Watts, *freelance researcher*; Hannah Westall, *Archivist, Somerset Archive and Record Service*; J. S. William, *Bristol City Archivist*; Heather Wolfe, *Archivist, Folger Shakespeare Library*; Dr Nigel Wright, *House & Collections Manager, Hardwick Hall*; Robert Yorke, *Archivist, College of Arms*.

I would like to add a special acknowledgement to David N. Durant, who laboured over Bess's building accounts, transcribing great tranches of them, for his book about the building of Hardwick Hall. This saved me weeks of research time, which I was able to spend on transcribing other original documents. Mr Durant's working notes are archived at Nottingham University library, where he has generously made them available to researchers and scholars. My own working notes will, in due course, find a similar home.

PICTURE CREDITS

SECTION 2:

Sir William St Loe in tilt armour (The Victoria and Albert Museum)

Detail of Sir William St Loe (College of Arms)

Sir William St Loe, coronation procession (British Library)

Lady Katherine Seymour (née Grey) (Bridgeman Art Library)

Needlework cushion of the sacrifice of Isaac (National Trust/ Hardwick Hall)

Bess at forty (National Trust/Hardwick Hall)

Tapestry with head of Zenobia (National Trust)

George, 6th Earl of Shrewsbury (Courtauld Institute of Art)

Margaret Douglas, Countess of Lennox (Leeds Museum and Art Galleries/Bridgeman Art Library)

Margaret Douglas, Countess of Lennox and family (The National Portrait Gallery of Scotland/Bridgeman Art Library)

Mary, Queen of Scots (Bonhams, London/Bridgeman Art Library)

Page of ciphers (National Archives)

Execution of Mary, Queen of Scots (Bridgeman Art Library)

Tutbury Castle (Private Collection/Bridgeman Art Library)

Bess, Countess of Hardwick c.1585 (National Portrait Gallery)

George, 6th Earl of Shrewsbury (Richard Philp, London/Bridgeman Art Library)

The 7th Earl and Countess of Shrewsbury (National Trust/Hardwick Hall)

The Lady Arbella Stuart (Mansell Collection)

Sir William Cavendish, 1st Earl of Devonshire (National Portrait Gallery)

Robert Cecil (Bonhams, London/Bridgeman Art Library)

Bess in old age (British Library)

The Long Gallery at Hardwick (National Trust/Andreas von Einsiede/ Hardwick Hall)

Bess's tomb (and detail) (Derby Cathedral)

INDEX